RESEARCH FROM THE MOWAT CENTRE EMPLOYMENT INSURANCE TASK FORCE

MAKING EI WORK

RESEARCH FROM THE MOWAT CENTRE EMPLOYMENT INSURANCE TASK FORCE

Edited by

Keith Banting and Jon Medow

Queen's Policy Studies Series
School of Policy Studies, Queen's University
McGill-Queen's University Press
Montreal & Kingston • London • Ithaca

Publications Unit
Robert Sutherland Hall
138 Union Street
Kingston, ON, Canada
K7L 3N6
www.queensu.ca/sps/

Library and Archives Canada Cataloguing in Publication

Making EI work : research from the Mowat Centre Employment Insurance Task Force / edited by Keith Banting and Jon Medow.

(Queen's policy studies series)
Includes bibliographical references.
Issued also in electronic formats.
ISBN 978-1-55339-323-8

1. Unemployment insurance--Canada. 2. Labor market--Canada. 3. Unemployed--Government policy--Canada. I. Banting, Keith G., 1947- II. Medow, Jon III. Queen's University (Kingston, Ont.). School of Policy Studies IV. Mowat Centre Employment Insurance Task Force V. Series: Queen's policy studies series

HD7096.C3M34 2012 368.4'400971 C2012-904105-X

Table of Contents

Section IV
Federalism and Governance Challenges

Acknowledgements

In Spring 2010, the Mowat Centre convened the Employment Insurance (EI) Task Force. The Task Force's mandate was to review the current EI system, consult about its relevance to contemporary realities, and make recommendations about improving Canada's support system for the unemployed. In Fall 2011, the Task Force released its final report, *Making it Work: Final Recommendations of the Mowat Centre Employment Insurance Task Force*. In that report, the Task Force proposed a blueprint for a strengthened national program to support the unemployed.

The papers in this volume were originally prepared as background research for the Mowat Centre EI Task Force. The work compiled in this volume contributed enormously to the evidence-base for the Task Force's final report and the authors represented here were generous with their time, comments and advice on their colleagues' work during the Task Force's deliberations.

Pulling together a project like the EI Task Force, including its research papers, usually requires a tremendous effort from all involved. For an organization like the Mowat Centre, that meant a handful of extremely bright, dedicated individuals doing the work of a much larger group. In the case of the EI Task Force, each team member exceeded my highest expectations. I could not be more proud of the work we have done together.

Although the Task Force was a team effort, I would like to highlight the exceptional contributions of: Jon Medow, project lead; Mary Davis, lead economist; Neville McGuire, design; and Josh Hjartarson, overall policy direction. The rest of the Mowat team, including Laura Rosen-Cohen, Val Sladojevic-Sola, James Pearce, Shaun Young, Melissa Molson, Jim Nicholson, and Reuven Shlozberg all played key roles at crucial times.

I would also like to thank all those who served as advisers to the Task Force project, including: Rahul Bhardwaj, Ken Boessenkool, Mel Cappe, Ian Clark, Don Drummond, Bill Fearn, Danny Graham, Diane Gray, Ron Jamieson, Frances Lakin, William MacKinnon, Roy McMurtry, Alain Noël, Susan Pigott, and Robbie Shaw. Despite political, ideological and regional differences, we were able to find a large consensus on many items and develop 18 recommendations for renewal of Canada's system of support for the unemployed.

It is unfortunate that, thus far, the federal government has only taken very tentative steps towards a strengthened national system and has addressed none of the system's structural and foundational problems. The Task Force's three principles to guide reform were: (1) a reformed system should be there when workers need it, (2) it should contribute to a dynamic labour force and enhance productivity, and (3) it should treat workers and employers equitably. As it stands, the federal government's key piece of social policy to support those who lose their job is coming up well short when measured against all three principles.

The Task Force benefited from exceptional advice from many others who were not part of the advisory committee. We would like to thank all those who provided generously of their time and counsel, in particular David Carter-Whitney, Peter Gusen, George Jackson, James Lahey, Richard Shillington, Arthur Sweetman, and Armine Yalnizyan, all those who participated in our public consultation processes, those who acted as reviewers, as well as Mark Howes at McGill-Queen's University Press.

A particularly warm thanks is due to our three lead advisers throughout the process: Ratna Omidvar and Roy Romanow, the co-chairs of the Task Force's advisory committee, and Keith Banting, the project's research director. Their wise leadership allowed us to sketch an architecture for an improved system of federal support for the unemployed—one that we hope the federal government will act upon one day soon.

Matthew Mendelsohn, Director, Mowat Centre

Editors and Contributors

Editors

Keith Banting, Professor at Queen's University Department of Political Studies and School of Public Policy, and holder of the Queen's Research Chair in Public Policy

Jon Medow, Policy Associate, Mowat Centre at the School of Public Policy & Governance at the University of Toronto

Contributors

Ken Battle, President, Caledon Institute of Social Policy

Robin Boadway, Professor of Economics at Queen's University, and holder of the David Chadwick Smith Chair in Economics

Allison Bramwell, Post-Doctoral Research Fellow at the Program on Globalization and Regional Innovation Systems at the University of Toronto's Munk School of Global Affairs

Sujit Choudhry, Professor of Law, New York University School of Law

Kathleen M. Day, Associate Professor at the University of Ottawa Department of Economics.

Ross Finnie, Associate Professor at the University of Ottawa Graduate School of Public Policy and International Affairs

Jean-Denis Garon, Ph.D. Candidate and Teaching Fellow at Queen's University Department of Economics

David Gray, Professor at the University of Ottawa Department of Economics

Morley Gunderson, Professor at the University of Toronto Centre for Industrial Relations and Human Resources, the Department of Economics and the School of Public Policy and Governance, and holder of the CIBC Chair in Youth Employment

Ian Irvine, Professor at Concordia University Department of Economics

Stephen Jones, Professor and Associate Chair at McMaster University Department of Economics

Thomas R. Klassen, Associate Professor in the Department of Political Science and School of Public Policy and Administration at York University

Michael Mendelson, Senior Scholar, Caledon Institute of Social Policy

Alain Noël, Professor of Political Science at the Université de Montréal

Michael Pal, lawyer and doctoral candidate at the University of Toronto Faculty of Law

W. Craig Riddell, Royal Bank Faculty Research Professor of Economics at the University of British Columbia

William Scarth, Professor of Economics at McMaster University

Luc Turgeon, Assistant Professor at the University of Ottawa School of Political Studies

Leah F. Vosko, Professor and Canada Research Chair in Feminist Political Economy at York University

Stanley L. Winer, Canada Research Chair in Public Policy at Carleton University's School of Public Policy and Administration and Department of Economics

Donna E. Wood, Post-Doctoral Fellow at the University of Victoria Department of Political Science

Yan Zhang, Economist/Statistician in Small Area and Administrative Data, Statistics Canada

Chapter 1

Introduction: Debating Employment Insurance

Keith Banting

Countries, like individuals, have successes and failures. In the domain of social policy, most observers agree that the Canadian pension system has been a comparative success, helping to reduce the level of poverty among the elderly from 29.0 per cent in 1969 to 5.2 per cent in 2009, a level matched only by Sweden among other OECD countries. In comparison, Employment Insurance is a policy failure. Commentators are almost universally critical in their views. Admittedly, their reasons differ. Those committed to a strong social safety net worry that Employment Insurance (EI) fails to provide adequate protection, with over half of unemployed Canadians not receiving unemployment benefits. Those more concerned about preserving efficient markets complain that EI distorts incentive structures for employers and employees alike, especially in seasonal industries and high unemployment regions. Those committed to the equal treatment of Canadians across the country as a whole condemn the inter-regional differences in EI as profoundly unfair. Those most concerned about the ties that bind this fragmented country together worry about the regional tensions generated by the program. EI fails on all these counts.

The recession that began in the fall of 2008 was a stress test which exposed the weaknesses in EI more clearly. As the number of unemployed Canadians rose, the problems of EI moved to the centre of Canadian politics. In the federal budget tabled in January 2009, the Conservative government introduced temporary extensions to parts of the program. The Opposition parties condemned the government's response as inadequate, and introduced a motion of non-confidence in the government on the issue. For a brief moment, it looked as if the country might face an election over unemployment benefits. But the moment passed. The government and the Liberal Opposition created a Conservative-Liberal working group to report on the issues, but the two sides could not agree and the group broke up without even bothering to issue a final report.

This strange moment in our politics highlights the two ways in which EI is a policy failure. At the programmatic level, virtually everyone agrees EI has serious problems. At the process level, the country has repeatedly proven itself incapable of making progress on this file. The problems in EI are hardly new, having been laid before the country by a succession of studies by royal commissions, think tanks, and independent analysts. But the problems persist, generating a degree of fatalism about Canada's capacity to correct policy failure. At the time of writing (June 2012), the federal government is proposing another reform effort, which is discussed more fully in the final section. But, as we shall see, the proposed changes are unlikely to resolve the underlying issues.

The Mowat Centre Employment Insurance Task Force was based on the premise that progress is possible even on this most difficult file. The Task Force's research program drew together leading analysts from across the country to distill what we know about the program and the reform alternatives, to fill gaps in our knowledge, and to generate proposals for change. This research effort represents one of the more thorough analyses of a government program conducted in this country in some time, and stands as a refreshing reminder of the importance of evidence-based policy debate.

This book consolidates the research effort, and this Introduction provides an integrated view of the major debates and conclusions that emerge in the chapters that follow. The research program adopted a broad approach to the issues, and our authors do not always agree on the nature of the problems or the directions for change. This Introduction does not try to settle the debates in the authoritative manner of a sports referee. Rather, the purpose here is to distill the nature of the key controversies, unpack the reasons for the disagreements, and highlight the issues at stake. The purpose is also to put today's controversies in a historical context. As we shall see, our contemporary debates have deep historical roots, and many of the issues which preoccupy us today preoccupied policy-makers when unemployment insurance was introduced in 1940. Since then, each generation has had to grapple with similar questions, and formulate responses consistent with the economic and political context of its time.

The first section of this Introduction sets the context, providing a short history of EI, tracing key changes in the economic, social and political context in which it operates, and comparing the program with unemployment benefits in other OECD countries. The second section summarizes the core normative dimensions of the debates about EI, highlighting the different assumptions about the basic purposes of the program and the criteria against which it should be evaluated. The third examines key policy design issues, examining the debates about the directions for reform. The fourth section concentrates on the governance of EI, focusing in particular on the complexities posed by the federal system for programs to support the unemployed. The final section pulls the threads of the discussion together, assesses proposals for change advanced by the federal government in the spring of 2012, and reflects on the future.

1 Employment Insurance in Canada: Evolution and Comparative Perspectives

A The Historical Evolution of EI

In comparative terms, Canada had a slow start in launching unemployment insurance, trailing not only European countries but also Australia, Britain and the United States. A number of factors contributed to this slow start.[1] During the early decades of the twentieth century, Canada was only beginning the transition from a predominantly agricultural economy, and national politics were dominated by conservative interests, parties and ideas. However, decentralized political institutions were also a constraint. Social provision was seen as a local matter, and municipalities were responsible for "relief" of the unemployed. This approach was completely swamped by the mass unemployment of the depression years. In the worst year, 1933, nearly one quarter of the country's labour force was unemployed, and an estimated 15 per cent of the population was on some form of relief. The burden overwhelmed local officials. However, the financial burden would have been distorted even if provincial governments had taken over completely from their municipalities, as regions with the highest levels of unemployment also had the fewest resources with which to respond. Essentially, the country lacked a mechanism for spreading risk across the country as a whole. In addition, interwar provincial leaders were worried that if their jurisdiction acted alone, they would become a magnet for the unemployed across the country and would drive investment elsewhere. Not surprisingly, therefore pressure for federal action grew steadily, and in 1935 the federal government passed an *Employment and Social Insurance Act*. This legislation was struck down by the courts in 1937 as intruding on provincial jurisdiction, but in 1940 all provinces agreed to a constitutional amendment giving the federal government full authority over unemployment insurance. The federal government adopted the *Unemployment Insurance Act* in the same year.

Unemployment Insurance (UI) was the first major social insurance program in Canada, financed at the time by contributions from employers and employees with additional funding from the federal government. Other social programs established during the early twentieth century, such as local relief and mothers' allowances, were funded through general tax revenues and provided means-tested benefits available only to the very poor. UI was the first program premised on the assumption that large portions of the population as a whole required protection from the risks inherent in a market economy, and was the first to establish benefits as a right, complete with appeals machinery for claimants who felt unfairly treated. The new plan was modest in design. While it covered most of the urban, industrial workforce, it excluded workers in agriculture, fishing and private domestic service, as well as public employees and higher-income earners. Moreover, the benefit replacement rate was only 50 per cent of wages, with a supplement of 15 per cent for married claimants.

From that base, UI evolved through a complicated history. During the first three decades, the emphasis was on expansion, culminating in a major restructuring in 1971 which expanded coverage to include all employees, eased qualifying conditions, and increased benefit levels. The 1971 changes altered the character of UI in important ways. The program moved from its beginnings as a fairly narrowly defined insurance system, in which coverage and benefits were based on something close to actuarial principles, to a broader social program, with considerable internal redistribution among groups of workers. Redistribution flowed from workers in relatively secure forms of employment, such as public administration, to workers in sectors facing higher risks of unemployment. Significant inter-regional redistribution flowed from regions of low unemployment to regions of high unemployment, a flow that was accentuated by the extension of coverage to seasonal workers and the provision for extended benefits in regions with high unemployment rates. The 1971 reforms also broadened the role of the UI program, adding maternity benefits for the first time. In later years, these special benefits were extended to include parental benefits for fathers, sickness and compassionate care.

The 1971 changes also marked a turning point in another sense. During the next 20 years, the program was subject to a long process of retrenchment and restructuring. These changes reflected the new context in which social programs generally operated, a context defined by a new world of work, a new politics of social policy, and a new federalism in Canada.

The chapter by Morley Gunderson focuses on the new world of work, tracing changes in both the demand for, and the supply of labour. Central to his analysis is the combination of technological change and trade liberalization which triggered an industrial restructuring, hollowed out the middle of the job distribution, enhanced demand for skilled workers, and weakened demand for unskilled labour. These changes progressively narrowed the effectiveness of traditional approaches to unemployment benefits. UI was originally designed to cushion workers from temporary disruptions in employment, but proved less effective in helping workers who were permanently displaced as a result of industrial restructuring. New entrants to the labour force, such as young people and immigrants, faced greater difficulty finding the secure employment needed to build entitlement to unemployment benefits. Moreover, the growth of non-standard forms of employment, such as self-employment, permanent part-time work, temporary help agencies and on-call work, reduced the portion of the workforce eligible to participate in UI.

The new world of work also triggered a seismic shift in thinking about the role of social policy and the sources of economic security in a global, knowledge-based economy, with a new "social investment paradigm" coming to dominate policy debates. This approach discouraged efforts to protect individuals from economic change through income transfers, and emphasized the development of human capital to provide citizens with the knowledge and skills required to prosper in the new economy (Huo 2009). For the UI system, this perspective implied a shift from passive income support to active labour market programs, such as employment readiness and training programs. At the international level, this approach was led by the OECD, especially through its Jobs Study (OECD 1994) and a stream of successor documents. The same themes increasingly pervaded Canadian policy discourse (Banting 2006; Jenson and Saint-Martin 2003 and 2006). In a typical declaration, the federal finance minister argued in 1999 that "providing security and opportunity for Canadians in the future means investing in their skills, in their knowledge and their capacity to learn. ... In a real sense, good skills are an essential part of the social safety net of the future" (Martin 1999).

The new economics of work was reinforced by a new politics of social policy. The broad political coalitions and ideologies which had sustained the expansion of social programs in the postwar years weakened.[2] Global economic pressures put organized labour on the defensive, and business associations became more critical of social programs and the associated taxes. Social movements and equality-seeking groups faded as governments reduced their funding. The political party system went through a series of realignments which created more scope for retrenchment in social programs. The bureaucratic politics of redistribution shifted, with finance departments increasingly dominating policy development in both federal and provincial governments. These shifts in organized politics were paralleled by ideological shifts, as the postwar faith in government as an instrument of social progress faded, and trust in politicians and government declined. Finally, the new politics of social policy was reinforced by a crisis in public finances. The ratio of public debt to GDP rose steadily from the late 1970s until the mid-1990s, by which time Canada rivalled Italy as the most indebted of G7 nations. At the worst point, approximately 35 per cent of all federal revenues was pre-empted by interest payments on its debt.

Finally, UI was reshaped by the new federalism in Canada. Powerful decentralizing pressures were bearing down on the social role of the federal government. The growth in *québécois* nationalism led the Quebec provincial government to demand a larger role in social policy, a pressure which peaked after the 1995 referendum on separation. Wider regional economic conflicts also deepened, with the energy crisis of the 1970s and free trade in the 1980s pitting region against region. In response to these pressures, the federal system became more decentralized, and Quebec carved out an increasingly distinctive or asymmetrical place in the federation.

These shifts in the tectonic plates underpinning Canada's social policy architecture triggered dramatic changes in UI. The new world of work and the new politics of social policy combined to trigger a long, grinding process of retrenchment and restructuring. The cuts proceeded slice by slice, beginning in 1977 and culminating in 1996 when the program was renamed Employment Insurance (EI). Over this period, the standard replacement rate was reduced from the peak of 66 per cent established in 1971 to 60 per cent in 1978, 57 per cent in 1993, and 55 per cent in 1994. Benefit duration was shortened, and the terms of eligibility were redefined, contributing to a dramatic drop in the proportion of the unemployed who actually receive unemployment benefits. Within the EI budget, there was a progressive reallocation from unemployment benefits to active labour market programs, especially employment readiness and training.

The new federalism also left an imprint on the evolution of EI. In most countries, retrenchment in unemployment benefits pits politicians primarily against organized labour. In Canada, the most politically powerful opponents of retrenchment are Members of Parliament and provincial governments from poorer regions, especially in Atlantic Canada. This political dynamic emerged under both Conservative and Liberal governments, cushioning the depth of change in poorer regions. For example, in 1996 the Liberals introduced an "intensity rule" which reduced benefits for repeat users and those who accessed the system extensively in the past (Gray 2004). However, the cuts in EI sparked political backlash in Atlantic Canada, and the Liberals experienced serious losses in the region in the 1997 election, including the defeat of the minister who had steered the cuts through the House of Commons. So the Liberals introduced legislation to abolish the intensity rule in the fall of 2000, just before the call of the next election.[3] In addition, a series of pilot projects and other adjustments in the early 2000s raised the generosity of benefits for part-year seasonal workers (Gray 2006). The unemployed in more affluent provinces, however, lacked the same political protection. The result was growing regional variations in both qualification requirements and benefit duration.

In addition, parts of the EI system were decentralized, with intergovernmental relations in the sector taking on an increasingly asymmetric pattern. In the aftermath of the 1995 referendum on Quebec separation, the active labour market component of EI was quickly transferred to provinces through a series of Labour Market Developments Agreements (LMDAs). In 2005, a separate bilateral agreement between the federal government and Quebec transferred parental benefits to the province, contributing to growing asymmetry in the federation and growing divergence in the content of social policy between Quebec and the rest of the country. As we shall see, these changes contributed to growing dualism in Canadian social policy, as the country increasingly accommodated "deux nations" in social programs.

B Comparative Perspectives

Comparing unemployment benefits across countries is difficult because they vary significantly along multiple dimensions, including eligibility, benefit rates and benefit duration. Nevertheless, most assessments conclude that Canada has one of the least generous systems among OECD countries (Van Audenrode et al. 2005; Osberg 2009; International Labour Office 2000). Overall, the Canadian system is most similar to other Anglo-Saxon countries, such as the United Kingdom and the United States, and there has been considerable convergence between the Canadian program and that in the United States in recent decades (Campeau 2005, 164-65). In contrast, the Canadian system is much more limited than those in continental Europe and Scandinavia. The same pattern prevails in terms of expenditures on active labour market programs (OECD 2010, Figure 5.18).

Within this overall pattern, Canada stands out in several ways. Canada has one of the shortest qualifying periods for entitlement, but benefit levels are lower and benefit duration is shorter than is the norm in most OECD countries (Van Audenrode et al. 2005, Figure 2). This structure privileges some groups of workers and hurts others. Frequent and seasonal claimants are treated more generously in Canada than in other countries, but workers with long employment histories receive lower benefits for shorter periods than their international counterparts. In addition, the two-week waiting period for benefits in Canada is long compared to most other countries. Many countries have no waiting period; among those that do, a one-week waiting period is the norm. The Canadian two-week requirement undoubtedly reduces the administrative costs of dealing with a large number of claims for short spells of unemployment. But it simply displaces some of those costs onto social assistance at the provincial level.

Canada is an outlier in one other dimension. It is virtually alone among developed democracies in the regional differentiation that characterizes access to, length of, and amount of benefits. The EI program divides the country into 58 "economic regions," with access to benefits varying with the unemployment rate in each region. A comparison of 17 other OECD countries, including all eight OECD federations, concludes that Canada is unusual in this approach. The only other country with a regionally varied program is the United States, where unemployment insurance is delivered by the state governments. Otherwise, the norm is that workers receive the same benefits regardless of where they live (Boadway this volume; Radmilovic 2011).[4] As we shall see, this is undoubtedly the most controversial element of EI in Canada.

2 Understanding the Debates: Objectives and Criteria

Policy failure fuels debate. Repeated changes in EI over two decades have not solved the problems, and the chapters in this volume discuss changes in virtually every aspect of the program. As we shall see, however, our analysts differ on most issues, pointing in different directions for the future. Sometimes, the diversity of opinions can be traced back to conflicting evidence and data, and certainly there is considerable scope for such disagreements here. But gaps in the available evidence also leave substantial room for disagreement. In comparison with the United States and increasingly with Europe, Canada lacks both the data sources and the sophisticated studies needed to assess fully the performance of EI, one of the largest spending programs in the country.

Nevertheless, the debates in this volume are not driven exclusively by disagreements about the basic facts of EI today. Rather, they are deeply rooted in normative considerations. Few of the arguments advanced here are really new, but can be traced back to the program's origins. Now, as then, the contours of our debates reflect normative disagreements, which emerge most clearly in different conceptions of the basic objectives of unemployment benefits and different views about the criteria that matter most in assessing outcomes.

A The Objectives: Insurance Versus Redistribution

Should EI be seen as an insurance system or a redistributive social program? Two answers to this question run through the history of the program and through the contributions to this volume. The different answers reflect different conceptions of the basic objectives of unemployment insurance and its appropriate design. Advocates of both conceptions start from the assumption that the main purpose of EI is to insure against unexpected and involuntary job loss and the loss in earnings that entails, and that the risk of unemployment is not restricted to the poor, as middle-income earners also need to protect their economic position during periods of unemployment. Thereafter, the two conceptions divide.

One conception advocates a strict insurance model, with funding based on contributions by employers and employees and benefit levels closely related to contributions. In this view, the rationale for public provision of unemployment insurance is to remedy a clear case of market failure. In the case of unemployment benefits, private insurance markets are subject to adverse selection; because workers with a low risk of unemployment would have an incentive to opt out, it is highly unlikely that privately provided insurance against unemployment would emerge or persist.[5] The task therefore falls to government, which has the authority to require mandatory coverage. But beyond that, in this perspective, unemployment insurance should reflect the actuarial logic of insurance principles, with an individual's benefits tied tightly to premiums he or she has paid. In this volume, the contributions from Gunderson and Craig Riddell come closest to this conception.

The second conception endorses a broader rationale for government provision. Advocates of this perspective certainly agree that mandatory coverage responds to the problem of market failure. But they argue that public or "social" insurance programs also can serve a wider set of purposes, responding to diverse social problems by redistributing income across groups of workers. Any insurance program redistributes income in each time period from those who do not experience a bad outcome to those who do. But advocates of a "social" conception argue that unemployment insurance should go further, adjusting contribution and benefit rules in order to redistribute income in a stronger sense, producing differences in long-run average payments across categories of workers. Most often, advocates of this conception favour redistribution towards low-wage workers and workers from other vulnerable groups. In this volume, the contribution from Leah Vosko reflects this logic.

Robin Boadway and Jean-Denis Garon go even further in arguing that EI should incorporate a significant redistributive element. Since unemployment insurance programs typically do not fully replace earnings, workers also need to self-insure through precautionary saving, borrowing, assistance from family members or adjustments to consumption patterns. Low-incomes earners are less able to protect themselves in these ways. Not only are they likely to experience greater volatility in employment; they also normally have fewer alternative resources on which to draw and less room to adjust their consumption. Unemployment insurance is especially important for such people, and there are good reasons for the net benefits of unemployment insurance to be proportionately higher for low-income unemployed workers. On some issues, this logic leads Boadway and Garon to recommend moving away from a contributory system altogether.

In the words of one historian, "this debate between the social and actuarial visions of unemployment insurance would haunt its entire development" (Campeau 2005, x). This history continues here. The analysts in this volume differ in their conception of the objectives of the EI program, some giving more weight to an actuarial conception of insurance and others giving greater priority to social redistribution.

B The Criteria: Equity, Markets and Democratic Governance

Analysts also differ in the weights they attach to different criteria when they assess the EI system. At the risk of over-simplifying complex debates, three clusters of criteria run through the chapters in this volume and through debates over EI in the country: a concern for equity, a concern for economic efficiency, and a concern for democratic governance.

A concern for equity tests the fairness of the EI program. This approach asks whether EI provides adequate support to workers in time of need. It also asks whether individual workers in similar circumstances are treated similarly, and whether rules which appear to be neutral actually discriminate in practice against certain categories of workers, such as women or immigrants.

A concern for economic efficiency focuses on the implications of EI for the functioning of the Canadian economy, especially the flexibility of labour markets, the incentives for individuals to participate in the labour market and develop their human capital, the maintenance of fiscal responsibility and responsiveness to economic conditions.

A concern for democratic governance asks whether the process of developing EI is open, providing opportunities for stakeholders to articulate their views. It asks whether the program is transparent, enabling workers to understand their rights and obligations under the program. In the context of Canadian federalism, it also asks whether the program strikes the right balance between a national framework and regional diversity, and whether it facilitates coordination of programs between the two levels of government.

These normative issues are inherent in the very nature of unemployment insurance in Canada, and have shaped debates since its introduction in 1940. As we shall see, different conceptions of the purposes of EI and different balances among evaluation criteria continue to create scope for debate. It is now time to turn to some of those issues and debates. The next section examines important design issues analyzed in this book. The following section turns to governance.

3 Designing EI: The Policy Parameters

The big parameters of the EI program which our authors focus on include the problems of coverage and access to benefits, the regionalized nature of the program, support for displaced long-tenure workers, the role of special benefits, and financing.

A Coverage and Access to Benefits

Battles over coverage have been a consistent thread in the history of UI and EI. One of the most striking trends in recent decades has been the precipitous decline in the proportion of the unemployed who receive EI benefits. In 1990, over 80 per cent of the unemployed were receiving unemployment benefits; by the mid-1990s, the ratio had fallen to less than half and has remained there. Intense debate surrounds what precipitated the decline and what, if anything, should be done about it. In part, the decline was driven by policy decisions which cut the program in 1990, 1993, 1994 and 1996. But the decline was also driven by changes in the labour market, such as the growth of part-time jobholders, multiple jobholders, the self-employed, recent immigrants, and those without recent job attachment, all of whom are less well protected by EI.

The chapters in this volume conduct an active debate over how to respond to the decline. Three distinct positions emerge, reflecting differences in both analysis and normative perspectives. The first position broadly supports the direction of change in the last two decades, and seeks to push further towards a model reflecting actuarial insurance principles. The second position argues that the status quo offers inadequate support to important groups of workers, and advocates reversing the direction of the last twenty years by expanding EI coverage and enriching benefits. The third position insists that EI, however revised, cannot reach most of the unemployed who are excluded, and recommends the introduction of a new income protection program to help them.

The chapter by Gunderson comes closest to the first position. He supports the major features of the current program, including the replacement rate and benefit duration; and he is sceptical of extending eligibility to the self-employed, noting the problems generated by the anomalous extension of coverage to self-employed fishers in the 1950s. He also emphasizes that workers can protect themselves from the risks of unemployment or volatile earnings through other mechanisms which can be "complements or possibly substitutes for EI." The rise of the multiple-earner family represents a form of self-insurance for many workers, and market-based mechanisms such as compensating wage premiums for the risk of job loss can help. In discussing reforms to EI, Gunderson argues the program should be shifted more firmly towards insurance principles, with a tighter connection between contributions and benefits and a reduced emphasis on general income support. In the longer-term, he is open to proposals such as personal unemployment insurance lifetime savings accounts. But in the immediate context, his agenda focuses on administrative adjustments to enhance work-sharing and to respond more effectively to temporary shocks.

The second position is articulated in the chapter by Vosko. She is concerned about the low levels of support offered by the program, and the cumulative disadvantage faced by particular groups of workers. In a detailed empirical analysis, she argues that the current provisions disadvantage particular groups of workers, particularly women, younger workers, older workers, rural workers, and service workers. To repair the damage, she advances four specific recommendations: extend eligibility to solo self-employed workers, create a lower entry requirement of 360 hours, extend the duration of benefits, and increase the level of benefits. In her words, "there is no principled reason for perpetuating differentiation and exclusion on the bases of gender, immigrant status, age, sector or size of place of residence—nor is there a rationale that form of employment ... should exacerbate the disadvantage.".

The third position is advanced in the chapter by Michael Mendelson and Ken Battle and the chapter by Boadway and Garon. Mendelson and Battle agree with Vosko that EI privileges "core" workers, who tend to be male, over marginal workers who tend to be young, immigrants, women and part-time workers. They are also concerned that the only public source of support for excluded workers is social assistance or "welfare," which they regard as a debilitating system and which has also been subject to dramatic retrenchment over the last two decades (Finnie et al 2004). However, they disagree with Vosko about the extent to which the problem can be solved by reforming EI itself. They argue the self-employed cannot be included in an insurance-based program because of the difficulty of defining when exactly a self-employed person is unemployed; and they conclude that reducing the hours of work required for eligibility, even to 360 hours, would not solve the problem of the exclusion of large numbers of workers. They therefore argue that a new program is needed to fill the gap between EI and welfare. Their proposal calls for an innovative form of temporary unemployment assistance which they call the Jobseeker's Loan. The maximum benefit from the loan would be available once every five years, and repayment would be contingent on income.

Boadway and Garon are also sceptical about the inclusion of the self-employed in EI. They argue that such workers are already partially insured through the tax system, since costs in a loss year can be carried forward to future fiscal years, and they recommend this protection be strengthened by greater loss refundabilty. However, they share the concern about the general erosion of coverage, and recommend that the federal government adopt a two-tier system alone the lines of some European countries.[6] Under this model, workers who lose their jobs would initially be eligible for EI based on their past contributions. Those who exhaust their benefits or who did not meet the eligibility criteria for EI would be eligible for the second tier of benefits, which would be based on family need rather than contributions.[7] They also suggest improving support for low-income people generally by converting non-refundable tax credits to refundable ones, increasing their generosity and conditioning them on income.

These strategies differ considerably in scope. The Jobseeker's Loan proposed by Mendelson and Battle, which is developed and costed in considerable detail, is a modest program which could be added to the existing architecture of income transfer programs with relatively little difficulty. While a valuable addition to the country's redistributive toolkit, the authors would be the first to assert it would not solve all the problems in the sector. In comparison, the proposals advanced by Boadway and Garon would provide much more widespread support but also represent a large restructuring of the tax-transfer system, with greater cost implications and a considerable need for federal-provincial collaboration.

Of course, even more comprehensive reforms of the tax-transfers system are possible. Over the years, considerable attention has been paid to the idea of a guaranteed annual income or negative income tax. Elsewhere, Thomas Courchene and John Allen (2009, 26) have proposed moving in this direction. They argue that child tax benefits and the Old Age Security/Guaranteed Income Supplement (OAS/GIS) system represent the base of a negative income tax for families with children and seniors. All that remains is to make the basic personal and spousal amounts (and perhaps others) under the income tax refundable and payable monthly to adults. Courchene and Allen advance this proposal as part of a shift of the EI system towards insurance principles and the elimination of regional benefits (discussed next), which they assume would only be viable if accompanied by a new income support system.

Opposition to this approach comes in the chapter by William Scarth, which compares an increase in the generosity of EI with the introduction of a guaranteed annual income. His simulations indicate that switching towards a guaranteed annual income would produce small net gains in efficiency. However, because the benefits flow to all low-skilled workers, the revenue costs would be much larger and would necessitate a more substantial increase in taxes. In an open economy, he concludes, the inefficiency generated by the increase in taxes would negate much of the other advantages. As a result, Scarth comes down on the side of reforming EI rather than launching programs in new directions.

The contributions to this volume thus represent a lively debate on how the issues of coverage and access to benefits should be addressed, reflecting different conceptions of the basic objectives of Employment Insurance and the priorities among evaluative criteria, especially between equity and efficiency. In contrast, there is much more consensus on the next issue, the tension between regional benefits and a nationally standardized program.

B Regional Benefits Versus a Nationally Standardized Program

The most controversial feature of EI is its regionalized nature. As noted earlier, the massive overhaul of the system in 1971 introduced a regional extended benefit: the program divides Canada into 58 regions, and the unemployment rate in each region influences entrance requirements, benefit levels and benefit durations. As a result, EI is especially generous to seasonal workers in high unemployment regions, for whom the program basically provides a yearly source of income. For a long period, the regional effects were also been accentuated by less visible ad hoc adjustments such as a seemingly permanent "pilot" project which raises the replacement rate for many workers in 25 regions, and transitional measures which relaxed qualifying requirements in regions of high unemployment (Van Audenrode et al. 2005, 18-19; Gray 2006). As a result, benefits vary significantly between workers with equivalent work histories. (Aspects of these provisions are currently being modified, as is discussed in the last section.)

The regional dimension of EI has been controversial for at least four decades. Defenders argue that it reflects the diverse and fragmented nature of the Canadian economy and compensates for the greater difficulty of finding work in high unemployment regions. In the words of Human Resources Development Canada, one of the few defenders of the current program, "regional differentiation in the operation of the EI program was originally introduced in 1971 in recognition of the fact that not all areas of the country have equal employment opportunities" (HRDC 1996). More recently, the department has also argued that the program proved responsive to changes in the regional incidence of unemployment during the recession that began in late 2008, making benefits more readily accessible in hard-hit parts of Ontario, British Columbia and Alberta. "The current EI program has built-in flexibility specifically designed to respond automatically to changes in local labour markets, with entrance requirements easing and the duration of benefits increasing as the unemployment rate rises" (HRSDC 2009).

Opposition to the regional dimension of EI has been articulated by a long series of analysts and advisory commissions (Courchene 1970; Boadway and Green 1981; Kesselman, 1983; Royal Commission, 1985; Riddell, 1985; Commission of Inquiry 1986; the Newfoundland Royal Commission 1986; Lee and Coulombe 1995). The contributors to this volume are also overwhelmingly opposed, and their objections span technical, economic and equity considerations. The technical objections challenge the proposition that the local unemployment rate is a reliable indicator of the difficulty of finding work. Analysts argue that other factors, such as direction of change in unemployment, the number of job vacancies, individuals' education and skills, and their ability and willingness to move or travel for work are more important (Bishop and Burleton 2009; Mendelson, Battle and Torjman 2009). Critics also object that the program's performance during the recession was less impressive in Ontario, British Columbia and Alberta than the federal government suggests (Mendelsohn and Medow 2011: 2). However, technical weaknesses are potentially amenable to technical fixes, and do not go to the heart of the debate.[8] The real objections are those rooted in economics and ethical considerations.

The chapter by Gunderson summarizes the long-standing economic objections to regional benefits. He argues that this dimension of EI increases unemployment and especially seasonal unemployment and encourages repeat reliance on benefits. It weakens the long-term development of poorer regions by lowering wage costs for seasonal industries, discouraging capital investment, and limiting incentives to invest in human capital through education and training. He also argues that regional benefits have likely reduced inter-regional mobility and fostered sustained regional unemployment differences. This basic critique is shared by other contributors to this volume, such as Boadway and Garon.

The last critique is not unanimous, however. The chapter by Kathleen Day and Stanley Winer challenges the common complaint that the program retards out-migration from low employment regions, thereby slowing economic development and contributing to the persistence of regional inequality in earned incomes. They critically review the past four decades of empirical research on the issue, and conclude there is no convincing empirical evidence that regional variation in the generosity of EI has significantly altered internal migration patterns in Canada. Where a statistically significant effect exists, it is too small to have much of an effect on provincial economies. Their bottom line is that, if regional variation in EI is to be challenged, the challenge cannot be based on its effects on interprovincial migration.

The third objection is rooted in considerations of equity. Is it fair for the federal government to treat Canadians differently if they live in different regions? In this respect, EI is a major anomaly among federal social programs. The Canada Pension Plan, Old Age Security, Guaranteed Income Supplement and child benefits treat beneficiaries in all regions in the same way.[9] Traditionally, this equality of treatment in federal programs has been seen as strengthening national integration—a sense of national unity—across the country as a whole. While economic and cultural policies tend to pit the interests of one region against the other, national social programs have been seen as creating spheres of shared experience among Canadians generally. Canadians contribute to, and share in, these benefits on a similar basis, irrespective of the language they speak, the culture they celebrate, or the region in which they live (Banting 1995).

Objections based on fairness lie at the heart of some of the criticisms expressed during the Mowat process. In the research program, for example, Boadway and Garon recommend eliminating regionally differentiated benefits and the selective eligibility of fishers in the name of equity: "This would eliminate a source of arbitrary difference in rules for particular claimants that results in unfairness to workers in like circumstances." The Mowat report also highlighted the perverse results within provinces: "Even workers who work together or live in close proximity to one another can be treated differently because some neighbouring EI regions have very different unemployment rates. Two workers with identical work histories who are laid off from the same business at the same time can face different EI entrance requirements. One can receive benefits while the other does not, even if her or his re-employment prospects are roughly identical" (Mowat Centre 2011, 29). This pattern is most common when urban centres and neighbouring areas fall in different EI economic regions, as they often do across the country. "It is not clear why those who commute into urban centres to work should be covered by a more robust safety net than those who work and live in these same urban centres" (ibid).

The chapter by Michael Pal and Sujit Choudhry deepens the analysis by asking whether the EI program disadvantages vulnerable groups of Canadians and might be vulnerable to legal challenge under the Canadian Charter of Rights and Freedoms. Their analysis is based on two basic realities. First, recent cohorts of immigrants are having greater difficulty integrating into the labour market. Second, racial- and linguistic-minority immigrants settle overwhelmingly in the largest urban areas of Ontario, Quebec, British Columbia, and Alberta, where workers generally must work more hours to qualify for EI. The obvious question is whether Charter-protected workers are disadvantaged by the regional determination of EI benefits, and whether the differential treatment is sufficiently marked to constitute indirect discrimination, contrary to section 15 of the Charter. Pal and Choudhry analyze the empirical data, and conclude that Charter-protected workers do have to work longer to qualify than other workers.

Over the decade between 2000 and 2010, the scale of the differential treatment varied with fluctuations in the unemployment rate. But, in the final analysis, Pal and Choudry conclude that the differential impact was relatively modest, averaging about 4 per cent over the decade, and that it would likely not be sufficient to support a successful section 15 claim. Nevertheless, they caution that the issue remains relevant. If the number of hours required by minority workers relative to other workers increases again in the future, the issue of the constitutionality of the EI program might well re-emerge.

Of course, consensus on the undesirability of regional benefits does not lead to agreement on how to get to a standardized national program. Different interpretations of the objectives of EI lead to different proposals. On one hand, Vosko seeks to eliminate the differences by extending the more generous terms available in high-unemployment regions to the country as a whole. She suggest a uniform entry requirement of 360 hours, lowering the thresholds for accessing benefits of maximum duration, extending the maximum duration and making it equivalent across regions. On the other hand, Gunderson argues for a standard national program which "would be done by removing the extended benefits rather than by extending benefits to all regions." Consistent with his preference for strict insurance principles, he recommends "experience rating," whereby frequent users would pay more into the program and/or receive less from it. Technically, experience rating is separate from the issue of regionalized benefits, and is discussed more fully below. But experience rating would certainly have a major impact on usage of EI in high unemployment regions.

An intermediate position between these poles suggests that movement to a standardized national program can be facilitated by the introduction of a supplementary income support program to assume the redistributive functions of the current program. In practice, EI has become an income-transfer program in high-unemployment regions, providing income on an annual basis to seasonal workers. However, it is poorly designed as a transfer program, not targeting benefits efficiently on the most needy. From this perspective, the introduction of a separate income transfer mechanism such as those discussed earlier would strengthen the effectiveness of Canada's social architecture and potentially ease some of the political resistance in poorer regions to a standardized national EI program (see for example, Royal Commission 1985). Although none of the contributors to this volume advocate a major new income transfer programs on these grounds, it has been a long-standing component of social policy debates in Canada.

The intense regional politics which surround this issue lead some to search for middle ground. For example, Bishop and Burleton (2009) suggest that if regional differentiation must apply, differences could be restricted to duration and not eligibility. The Mowat Report also treads cautiously. It advocates a standardized national support system for the unemployed, with a single national entrance requirement and a single national benefit duration range. However, it does not specify a specific formula for either the entrance requirement or benefit duration, costing three options in each case, and it also rejects experience rating (Mowat Centre 2011).

C Displaced Workers

The chapters by Craig Riddell and Stephen Jones focus on a specific group of unemployed workers, long-term displaced workers. As we have seen, EI is very generous by international standards to seasonal workers who rely on EI each year, but does not provide additional support at the other end of the spectrum, displaced long-tenure workers. These workers, who have paid into the EI system throughout their work-life, are often displaced from well-paid manufacturing jobs and can only find employment in low-paid service jobs. They typically face very large earnings losses, not simply from their period of unemployment, but from re-employment at wages substantially below their old level. Earnings typically drop precipitously—initially by an average of 50 per cent and by about 25–30 per cent even after many years of re-employment.[10] Not only does the drop in earnings stress workers and their families economically; displacement is associated with higher levels of mortality, suicide, alcohol abuse, mental health problems, divorce, and reduced educational outcomes for children in the family.

The problems facing such workers are compounded by the limited effectiveness of retraining programs for this group. Governments often respond with training initiatives. For example, as part of the 2009 Economic Action Plan, the federal government temporarily enhanced training programs for long-term displaced workers. However, the chapter by Steven Jones provides a sceptical counterpoint. He surveys the literature on the effectiveness of training programs, and concludes the results are not encouraging. Both experimental and non-experimental research shows that the returns to training for displaced workers are less than the returns to formal schooling. Jones' summary assessment is that the results of most training programs for the long-term earnings of displaced workers are modest to poor. Less is known about the short-term impact of retraining on the prospects of getting a new job quickly. But, in Jones' words, the level of investment in training required to bridge the gap in long-term earnings "would be huge."[11]

Should EI therefore provide additional income support to displaced workers? Once again, our contributors disagree. And once again, the issue turns fundamentally on whether EI is an insurance program or a redistributive program. In his chapter, Riddell starts from the presumption that EI is an insurance program and should reflect the magnitude of the loss due to unemployment: "in insurance markets such as those for automobile and property insurance, this characteristic is both familiar and evident. The insurance payment in the event of totaling one's car is much larger than that for a 'fender bender.'" The EI program, however, does not provide benefits that reflect the cost of job loss. Long-tenure displaced workers, who lose the most from permanent job loss, are not treated any differently than displaced workers who have been employed for brief periods of time. Enhanced EI benefits could take the form of higher benefit levels, longer benefit durations, or mobility assistance for contributors of long tenure. In addition, Riddell suggests that wage insurance, which would replace a portion of lost wages during the early years of re-employment, is an attractive proposal, and that a demonstration project should be launched to study its effects. This broad approach is supported by other contributors such as Gunderson who also sees EI as an insurance program.

In contrast, Boadway and Garon, who believe that the EI should have a more redistributive purpose, are sceptical. In their view, "the EI system is ill-suited to deal with permanent reductions in earning capability." Wage insurance proposals tend to be seen as transitional, with the proposed wage replacement occurring for a specified period of time only. In their view, the tax-transfer system is better placed to moderate permanent changes in earnings. In their words, "the income-transfer system has as one of its objectives the redistribution of income from those with higher earnings to those with lower earnings. ... Inequalities that arise partway through the lifetime pose similar challenges that the income tax system is designed to address." They suggest reinstituting general income averaging so that workers who suffer a permanent reduction in earnings can average their tax liabilities across periods in their working life when they face different tax rates. In this case, the debates seem to turn more fundamentally on more on considerations of equity rather than economic efficiency.

D Special Benefits

In contrast to the structure of regular benefits, the special benefits provided for maternity, paternity, sickness and compassionate care are less controversial, certainly among contributors to this volume. The chapter by Luc Turgeon explores the history and issues associated with these special benefits, which in 2008/09 represented 27.8 per cent of EI benefits. As in many OECD counties, these benefits were grafted to an EI program in a long series of steps. The large restructuring of 1971 introduced maternity and sickness benefits; in 1983, adoptive parents became eligible for maternity benefits; in 2001 parental benefits were extended; and in 2004 compassionate care benefits were added. In the area, Canada is among the OECD leaders; only a handful of countries provide more generous paid leave programs.

Unlike regular EI benefits, the special benefits operate as a standardized national program with a single set of standards applying across the country. (The one exception is that the parental benefits program was devolved to the province in Quebec in 2005, a development discussed in more detail below.) The largest problem has been how to include the self-employed in an effective way. In 2009 the government adopted legislation extending special benefits to self-employed Canadians on a voluntary basis.[12] Those who choose to join pay the employee's contribution only; they must opt into the EI program one year prior to claiming benefits; and once having taken benefits they must continue to pay premiums indefinitely. The benefits have been available to the self-employed on this basis since January 2011, but the take-up has been low, with about 1,600 beneficiaries in 2011.[13]

One issue is whether special benefits should be removed from EI to stand as a separate program funded through general revenues. Courchene and Allen advance this approach, arguing that such benefits should be citizenship-based and not employment-based (2009: 21). Such a change would extend benefits to parents who have not been able to build up sufficient hours of work to qualify for the insurance-based system. It would spread the cost across all Canadians, and allow for a reduction in payroll taxes which are often seen as an impediment to job creation. In addition, it would eliminate tensions between the logic of employment insurance and the logic of special benefits, exemplified by the application of the standard two-week waiting period to special benefits.

The contributors to this volume disagree, preferring to retain special benefits as part of the EI system. Vosko argues her new entrance requirements and eligibility rules would extend the reach of the benefits. Turgeon suggests a mixed strategy. He also prefers to preserve the integration of special benefits in the EI system, in part because countries that finance parental leave out of general revenue tend to provide less generous benefits. The insurance model also makes the connection between payments and benefits more transparent, and justifies benefits that are related to earnings. However, Turgeon does suggest partial funding of special benefits from general revenues, noting that in Sweden, 15 per cent of the costs of parental leaves are met that way.

In general, then, our contributors are broadly supportive of the current approach to special benefits, which they debate largely in terms of equity. The public seems to agree. The parental leave program is generally very popular among Canadians, especially since the changes introduced in 2001, and undoubtedly enhances the legitimacy of the EI program more generally.

E Financing

The debate over moving special benefits out of the EI system points to a more general issue about the ways in which EI is financed. Is the current premium basis for EI appropriate? Is it appropriate for all of the programs built on the EI platform? These questions run through the long history of unemployment insurance in Canada, and they reappear in this volume.

Once again, this issue turns fundamentally on whether EI is an insurance program or a redistributive transfer. Those who see EI as insurance tend to support contributory financing. At the time of the introduction of UI in 1940, advocates of premiums argued that, compared to unemployment relief in the 1920s and 1930s, premiums would strengthen workers' right to benefits, and justify benefits related to wages.[14] In the contemporary period, those who wish the program to adhere more faithfully to an insurance model tend to favour tightening the relationship between premiums and benefits. In this context, the most frequent recommendation is for the adoption of experience rating, under which the premiums paid for insurance would increase with the frequency of use of benefits. Experience rating can be applied to employers, employees, or both. Employers that lay off workers more frequently would pay more; employers that lay off workers less often would pay less. In the case of employees, experience rating would relate the premiums they pay or the size of the benefits they receive to the frequency of their use of benefits.[15] Finally, as we have seen, in Canada experience rating is often seen as a means of reducing inter-regional redistribution through EI.

Among contributors to this volume, the case is advanced most directly by Gunderson who sees the idea as "the potential reform to EI that likely merits the most attention" (see Kesselman 1983; Riddell 1985; Poschman and Robson 2001). In theory, experience rating for employers should increase their incentive to find alternatives to layoffs such as smoothing their production process over seasons and retraining their workers during a cyclical downturn. Empirical evidence from the US confirms the theoretical expectation that experience rating reduces layoffs and unemployment, and Canadian evidence suggest that the application of experience rating to employees through the "intensity rule" in 1996 did reduce repeat use before its elimination in 2000 (Gray 2004).

In contrast, Boadway and Garon's approach to financing reflects their desire to enhance the redistributive role of EI. They argue that the current EI system is basically incoherent, neither deploying insurance-based principles nor achieving effective redistribution. While contributions are related to the size of benefits, they are not related to the probability of unemployment or its expected duration. Redistribution in the EI system is limited as well. It is true that the upper bound on insurable earnings means that a higher proportion of earnings are replaced for lower-income workers, and an EI Family Supplement does increase benefits for low-income families with children. But the upper bound on contributions means that benefits are financed through a regressive form of taxation; and the low replacement rate bears heavily on low-income workers.[16] Overall, redistribution to low-income workers is limited.[17] To resolve this incoherence, Boadway and Garon recommend shifting the financing of the system as much as possible from payroll-based contributions to general revenue financing.[18] Partial financing from general revenues has a precedent in Canada, as the federal government contributed a meaningful percentage of total costs between 1941 and 1990 (Campeau 2005: Table 2). Such a mixed funding model is common in other countries as well.

Other analysts position themselves between these two poles, arguing that while the premium structure is appropriate for regular benefits, it is not an appropriate base for other elements of the system. As we have seen, Turgeon argues that special benefits should be paid in part through general taxes. Similar arguments have been made about work-sharing. In the words of an early critic, "why should some workers have the advantage of close-to-full remuneration along with the social benefits of work, while others are simply laid off?" (Pal 1983, 90). But the most long-standing objection has been to funding training in this way. Since 1977, successive federal governments have increasingly loaded the costs of training onto the unemployment insurance system, culminating with the formal establishment of Part I and Part II of the *EI Act* in 1996. This trend was steadfastly resisted by unions and employers, and the approach has been criticized by an illustrious list of advisory commissions, from the Gill Report in 1962 (Committee of Inquiry 1962) to the Forget report in 1986 (Commission of Inquiry 1986) to the Canadian Labour Force Development Board in 1992 (Campeau 2005). In recent years, the historic objection to funding training through a regressive tax has been reinforced by growing concern that EI-funded training is limited to EI-eligible workers, leaving a growing number of workers out in the cold. This issue is implicated in the question of the federal-provincial relationships in this sector, and is pursued in more detail in the next section.

4 Governance and Federalism

In many countries, unemployment insurance is governed through collaborative institutions integrating representatives of business and labour—the "social partners"—in the process. Despite experiments with such tripartite processes in the 1990s, such an approach has never taken root in Canada. As a result, controversies over governance tend to flow from the federal system. Canada developed its income security system in the context of a federal state, with strong governments at both the federal and provincial levels.[19] Not surprisingly, relations between levels of government have been a central component of the architecture of Canadian social policy. This has been true of EI even though the federal government's formal jurisdiction over the program is complete. The chapters in this volume explore three dimensions of the federal-provincial interface: the interaction between EI and provincial social assistance programs, the decentralization of training, and the asymmetrical position of Quebec in the sector.

A The EI-Welfare Nexus

The relationship between EI and social assistance at the provincial level has been a troubled story from the beginning. The 1940 Rowell-Sirois Commission had recommended that the federal government accept responsibility for all of the unemployed, including people who were not eligible for UI or had exhausted their UI benefits (Royal Commission 1940). Initially, Ottawa resisted this advice. When the federal government introduced UI in 1941, it actually terminated the grants it had given to provinces for local relief during the depression years. However, in 1945, the federal government's ambitious proposals embodied in its Green Books revived the idea of full federal responsibility, and a number of provincial governments continued to press Ottawa to honour its proposals. In the end, the federal government rejected direct federal responsibility and opted for a shared-cost program to support provincial social assistance programs, partly as a way, in the words of a cabinet document, to "bury the Green Book proposals once and for all" (quoted in Struthers 1987, 24). In introducing the 1956 *Unemployment Assistance Act,* precursor to the 1965 Canada Assistance Plan, Paul Martin Sr., the Minister of National Health and Welfare, proclaimed that it would "write *finis* to the deadlock which has existed in this country for a decade or more... (as) each jurisdiction has argued that responsibility belonged to another level of government" (quoted in Dyck 1973, 55). The minister was overly optimistic.

The chapter by Boadway and Garon surveys the contemporary interaction between EI and provincial social assistance, both of which serve the unemployed population. Not surprisingly, the two programs create opportunities for cost-shifting and associated intergovernmental acrimony. The federal government has long complained that provincial governments, especially in Atlantic Canada, "game" the system by developing programs to ensure that seasonal workers got enough work to qualify for EI. Similarly, the provincial governments saw federal retrenchment in EI during the 1990s as an attempt to shift the unemployed onto their welfare rolls, while simultaneously reducing its support for provincial social assistance. Federal retrenchment in EI was probably one of the pressures provoking provincial governments to tighten eligibility and reduce benefits in their social assistance programs during the 1990s and 2000s. In effect, each side was raising the barriers to the unemployed.

Considerable controversy focuses on the size of the flow from EI to welfare. This flow is undoubtedly smaller than in the past. In addition to the tightening of eligibility at both levels, the growth of dual-income families undoubtedly reduces recourse to welfare. The chapter by Ross Finnie and his colleagues surveys the empirical literature on the issue. While the field is characterized by widely different results, recent studies tend to find a limited flow from EI to social assistance. The authors also present new data tracking long-term workers who exhaust unemployment benefits from 1994 to 2008. Despite tightened EI eligibility conditions since the mid-1990s, they find no evidence of an increased degree of subsequent dependence on social assistance. On the contrary, the flow declined. Only 4 to 5 per cent of EI exhaustees in this group received social assistance in the years following the exhaustion of the EI spell. These results relate only to longer-term workers and do not represent the entire population of EI exhaustees. But they do caution against exaggerating the flows.

The lack of flow is not necessarily good news. It points to a growing black hole between EI and welfare. The proposals to extend EI coverage advanced discussed earlier would help reduce the size of the hole. As we saw earlier, Boadway and Garon return to the ideas of Rowell-Sirois in 1940 and the Green Books in 1945, recommending that the federal government extend its benefits by adopting a two-tier system, with workers who exhaust their benefits or who did not meet the eligibility criteria for EI being eligible for the second tier of benefits based on family need rather than contributions. Under this model, provincial social assistance would cater to the very long-term unemployed and those who had not yet had a job.

B Special Benefits

The chapter by Turgeon asks whether special benefits should be devolved to provinces, as has happened in the case of Quebec. He notes that the Canada-Quebec agreement was designed to forestall some concerns that might emerge. It includes provisions for interprovincial mobility and guarantees that benefits in Quebec will be at least equivalent to those provided by EI. In addition, the agreement can be terminated by either party with one year's notice, so that the federal government could regain control over the program if a province provided inadequate benefits. As it turns out, the Quebec is much stronger, overcoming many of the limitations in the federal program. Eligibility is much less restrictive; there is no waiting period for benefits; the replacement rate is higher; and parents have a choice of benefit packages. This more generous program does require higher premiums, with a worker earning $40,000 paying $66.80 more per year in 2011.

Contributors to this volume disagree on whether special benefits should be devolved to other provinces as well. Noël, whose chapter is discussed more fully below, argues that other provinces should consider the Quebec model. Turgeon, however, is less convinced. He notes that devolution requires the province to collect premiums to finance the program, with the federal government collecting smaller premiums than in other provinces. His concern is that the value of such tax space varies considerably between poorer and richer provinces, making it difficult for poorer provinces to offer the same level of benefits as wealthier ones. As we have seen, his inclination is to leave special benefits as part of EI and improve its terms.

C Training

As we have seen, policy analysts vigorously debate the effectiveness of training programs. As is often the case in Canada, however, the debate over the basic effectiveness of training programs has been overshadowed by controversy over which level of government should deliver training and how it should be funded.[20]

Since the mid-1990s, Canada has witnessed a sharp decentralization of responsibility for active labour market programs, including training. The chapter by Allison Bramwell tracks the complicated history through two distinct phases. The first phase was triggered by the narrowness of the defeat of the "yes" option in the 1995 Quebec referendum on sovereignty. The federal Liberal government responded by devolving responsibility for occupational training through a series of Labour Market Development Agreements (LMDA), negotiated on a bilateral basis with individual provinces. However, this first phase left a messy outcome. As we have seen, unemployed workers who were not eligible for EI could not receive EI-funded training, a major problem given the decline in EI coverage. In addition, the federal government retained its own programs for key groups, such as youth, people with disabilities, Aboriginal peoples, older workers, and recent immigrants. This complicated division of labour generated considerable frustration, and led to a second phase of devolution. The federal government supplemented the LMDAs with Labour Market Agreements (LMAs), which provide funding for non-EI eligible client groups and low-skilled individuals. While the federal government retains its own programs for youth, the disabled and Aboriginal peoples, responsibility for the delivery of active employment measures has largely been devolved to the provinces.

As in other policy sectors, devolution has prompted a debate about whether Canada needs a stronger national policy framework to guide active labour market programs.Bramwell's chapter starts from the premise that the prognosis for a coherent national policy vision for workforce development is inauspicious at best, at least for the foreseeable future. In her view, decentralization has transformed workforce development into a de facto area of provincial jurisdiction, and the constraints on federal influence have to be taken as the starting point. She suggests that the federal government permanently devolve responsibility for all adult training programs—including the remaining client groups except Aboriginal peoples—to provincial governments. In addition, LMDAs and LMAs should be consolidated as a single conditional federal transfer with a standardized accountability framework. This would essentially consolidate provincial jurisdiction in return for provincial reporting on a common basis, providing a platform for comparartive learning and national debates.

In their chapter, Donna Wood and Thomas Klassen go further. They accept that the decentralized model has important advantages, but argue it has created three major governance problems (also Haddow 1998). First, there is no over-arching, pan-Canadian organizing framework that binds the whole together. Second, decision-making at the national level takes place behind closed federal-provincial doors, giving little opportunity for stakeholders or citizens to participate in policy development. Third, and perhaps most revealingly, there is a lack of transparency, coordinated reporting and comparative research to facilitate mutual learning. For example, there are no pan-Canadian reports of any use. As a result, it is very difficult for Canadians to understand the evolution of active labour market programs in the country as a whole, or to determine the results achieved by the large federal transfers to provincial programs. Accordingly, Wood and Klassen recommend a stronger architecture of national institutions to coordinate active labour market programs. Their proposed infrastructure includes a Canadian Labour Market Information Agency, which would generate consolidated data on a pan-Canadian basis, and an expanded role for the intergovernmental Forum of Labour Market Minsters (FLMM), which would become responsible for the "collective determination of all aspects of employment and training policy in Canada." Given the current nature of federal-provincial relations, both of these proposals seem ambitious.[21]

D Asymmetry and Dualism

In the aftermath of the failure of Canada's long efforts to reform the constitution in formal terms, governments sought to accommodate Quebec's distinctiveness through administrative arrangements (Lazar 1998). As a result, intergovernmental relations are characterized by growing asymmetry. Historically, the classic federal-provincial social programs were defined by multilateral agreements in which the intergovernmental division of labour and financial arrangements were consistent across the country. In recent decades, the federal government has increasingly relied on bilateral negotiations with individual provinces, often resulting quite varied patterns of intergovernmental relationships. But the largest role of asymmetry has been to allow for growing dualism between Quebec and the rest of the country. As we have seen, Quebec alone has taken over responsibility for parental benefits, and was an early adopter of full devolution of active labour market programs. This policy space was combined with other areas to generate a distinctive policy model. In the late 1990s, when the rest of Canada was moving in a neoliberal direction, reducing the redistributive role of the state, Quebec moved in the opposite direction, building universal child care, larger child benefits, and a formal strategy against poverty and social exclusion. As a result, Quebec has resisted the drift towards higher levels of inequality that has characterized the rest of the country (Fortin 2010; Banting and Myles forthcoming).

The chapter by Alain Noël explores the ways that asymmetry in the EI system has helped create space for dualism. He celebrates the flexibility inherent in the new governance process. In his words, "The governance framework, if one can even speak of such an entity, was never neat and tidy; the results remained uneven, and the outcome was not an integrated pan-Canadian arrangement. In a federation that usually proved rigid and inimical to change, this was a more than modest achievement."[22] He is therefore sceptical of proposals, such as those by Wood and Klassen, to build a formal, multilateral governance structure. Noël suggests that other provinces consider the possibility of emulating the Quebec approach to parental benefits. But there seem to be few signs of this happening. The Quebec model reflects the distinctive politics of the province (Noël forthcoming), and is unlikely to be emulated. Noël seems to agree: "the best avenue is probably to accept, and indeed celebrate, the coexistence of different values and approaches, and to facilitate engagement and exchange across models."

5 Conclusions

The historic nature of our contemporary debates is striking. The battle between the insurance model and the redistributive model of unemployment benefits, the tension between equity and efficiency in assessing outcomes, and different views about federal and provincial roles are as old as unemployment insurance itself. The basic questions have not changed in over 70 years. The answers to the questions, however, do change over time. Each generation has to find its own answers to the central issues inherent in the design of an unemployment insurance program. Over the last generation, the new world of work, the new politics of social policy, and the new federalism have reshaped the contemporary answers to old questions. EI itself has shifted dramatically, as has the intergovernmental division of labour in this sector.

The answers embodied in current legislation have not stilled the debate. EI remains a policy failure for many of our contributors. In part, the debate reflects the uneven nature of change in recent decades. Some aspects of EI have changed dramatically; other aspects have proven deeply resistant to reform. But the intensity of debate in this volume also reflects the very different perspectives our contributors bring to bear on the program. Occasionally, the contending perspectives are driven by different interpretations of empirical reality, as in the case of the impact of EI on interregional mobility. But more often, the different assessments and recommendations flow from conflicting assumptions about the basic objectives of EI and differing weights placed on assessment criteria. The balance in the debate does differ across the specific issues. The problems of coverage, the regional/national interface and financing invoke the most complex choices. The tensions between insurance and redistribution as objectives and between equity and efficiency as criteria are strongest here. In contrast, the debates over displaced workers and special benefits seem less complex, with different conceptions of equity predominating in the discussion.

Governance debates continue to be framed largely in federal terms. Here, too, the sector has changed significantly in recent decades, and the level of intergovernmental tension appears to have declined. The regionalized nature of the program remains politically sensitive, but that is a regional battle more than a strictly intergovernmental one. In intergovernmental terms, the seemingly smaller flow between EI and social assistance, the substantial devolution of training, and the acceptance of asymmetry have reduced conflict. But once again, policy change has not stilled policy debate. The retreat of both levels of government from protecting the unemployed has left a black hole between EI and social assistance which troubles many of our contributors. The division of responsibility over special benefits continues to be debated, and those who believe in the importance of a common Canadian approach to labour market policy remain troubled by the weaknesses of our national frameworks, institutions and processes.

At the time of writing (June 2012), a new round of changes in EI is emerging. The federal budget announced that the "best 14 weeks" pilot project will conclude in April, 2013. This pilot project offers a more generous weekly benefit calculation method primarily in high-unemployment, rural and eastern Canadian regions. While canceling this pilot project, the federal government will remodel the standard, national weekly benefit calculation method, taking some cues from the best 14 weeks pilot project (Canada 2012, 148). Subsequently, the government announced changes in the rules governing the search for "suitable employment," which would require recipients to expand their job search and accept lower wages than in the past. The proposed regulations distinguished between categories of workers in complex ways. For example, long-tenure workers would be required to accept 80 per cent of their previous wages after 18 weeks of benefit; frequent claimants would be required to accept positions at 70 per cent of their previous wages after six weeks (HRSDC 2012).

Anticipating the possible consequences of such changes is difficult. It remains to be seen whether the proposals will be implemented in the precise form in which they were announced, and whether the government will stick with them if faced with a public backlash on the scale that emerged in Atlantic Canada in the 1990s. In addition, the complexity of the regulations would increase the scope for discretionary judgment, and their administration would be critical and might well vary across regions. Finally, there has been remarkably little research in the Canadian context on some of the strategies being adopted, such as the effects of variations in the definition of suitable employment. As a result, predicting the consequences is especially hazardous.

Nevertheless, given the concerns debated in this volume, it is worth asking several questions. First, would the changes likely alter the internationally distinctive structure of the Canadian program in offering comparatively generous support to frequent and seasonal claimants, and comparatively ungenerous protection to long-tenured workers? On the one hand, the proposed regulations are designed to place greater pressure on frequent claimants than long-term workers to actively search for work, broaden their job search and possibly accept lower-wage positions. On the other hand, the protection offered to long-term workers will still be less generous than that offered by the existing regulations; long-term workers would be given less time to find employment commensurate with their training and experience. So the gap between the two groups of workers would be narrowed somewhat, but at an overall lower level of income protection.

Second, would the proposed changes reduce the regionalized nature of the EI program? The rules would not represent an explicit change in the regional differentiation in qualifying periods or benefit durations. For example, while the "best 14 weeks" pilot program is being closed and the approach to benefits is to be extended across the country as a whole, benefit calculations will continue to depend on regional unemployment rates. But would the proposed regulations governing "suitable employment" have the indirect effect of narrowing regional variation in benefit duration? Uncertainty here is even greater. But the impact is unlikely to be dramatic in traditionally high-unemployment regions where there is relatively little alternative employment, even at lower wages.[23] The biggest impacts are likely in regions that combine substantial numbers of frequent claimants and substantial numbers of job openings at somewhat lower wages. Such regions may well turn out to be in central Canada more often than Atlantic Canada.[24]

What is clear is that the changes will not still debate. EI will remain controversial. As long as policy analysts and Canadians generally embrace different assumptions about the objectives of unemployment benefits and the criteria by which we should assess them, the conversation over the future of EI will remain vigorous. Governments do not need consensus to act, as the current initiatives demonstrate. But healthy democracies do need vigorous debate, and the contributors to this volume do add to the richness of the debate over how Canada should respond to the needs of the unemployed in an often turbulent global economy.

Endnotes

1 For a fuller discussion, see Struthers 1983; Banting 1987 and 2005.

2 This paragraph is based on Banting and Myles (forthcoming).

3 The legislation died on the order paper when the election was called but was reintroduced and passed after the election.

4 Some countries approximate the same effect through variations in eligibility by industry.

5 For a nice example, see the discussion of Career Guard, an insurance plan introduced in Canada during the 1982-83 recession to protect executives who might be fired, in Green and Riddell (1993, S98-S101). For discussion of failed attempts to introduce unemployment insurance in private insurance markets before the introduction of public unemployment insurance in the United States, see Moss (2002).

6 For a survey of countries that offer unemployment assistance for workers who have exhausted their insurance benefits, or who do not meet eligibility requirements, see Van Audenrode et al. (2005, Table 10).

7 In principle, the self-employed could be eligible for the second tier if their family income is low enough for long enough, just like they are eligible for welfare now. The meaning of self-employed becomes less distinctive when people are earning very low sums of money for extended periods of time.

8 As the Mowat Report on EI notes, one potential remedy to the technical problems would be a more complex set of indicators, in addition to the local employment rate (Mowat Centre 2011, 26).

9 The Canada Pension Plan (CPP) does not operate generally in Quebec. However, the Canada and Quebec Pension Plans are highly coordinated, with broadly similar contribution rates and benefits.

10 The chapter by Finnie et al. also notes that many displaced workers who had previously had stable attachment to the labour force tend to have difficulty re-establishing stable employment and experience repeated periods of reliance on EI.

11 Existing evaluations of training programs tend to concentrate on the impact on wages. It is possible that evaluations of the implications for the re-employment of displaced workers would find larger impacts.

12 The decision of the federal government complied with the judgment of the Canadian Human Rights Commission that excluding such workers constituted a potential violation of the principle of equality.

13 CANSIM 276-0001.

14 On the historical debate, see Campeau (2005, ch. 4) who is sceptical that premiums generate a "right" to benefits, noting that governments have altered eligibility rules and benefit levels on a regular basis (ibid, xi).

15 In other OECD countries, experience rating tends to be limited to the employers' contributions. The Canadian experiment with experience rating in the form of the intensity rule which existed between 1996 and 2001 was unusual (Van Audenrode et al. 2005, 40).

16 To provide an element of redistribution at the upper end, up to 30 per cent of EI regular benefits must be repaid if the recipient's annual income exceeds $54,000 (in 2010) and he/she has collected EI benefits at least one other time in the last ten years.

17 For an estimate of the actual redistributive impact, see Finnie and Irvine (2011).

18 It is worth noting that the emphasis on a shift towards general revenue financing does not preclude experience rating. Boadway and Garon recommend both.

19 Indeed, the distribution of legislative authority in the field is more decentralized than in other OECD federations (Obinger, Leibfried and Castles 2005, Table 1.6).

20 The report of the Mowat Centre Task Force reflects this pattern. While it makes recommendations concerning federal-provincial relations in the training sector, it notes that "The Task Force has not addressed the question of how to improve training programs." (Mowat Centre 2011, 60-61).

21 The Mowat Centre report recommends an enhanced role for the FLMM to "develop a pan-Canadian human capital strategy and encourage the development of a national labour market" through evaluation research and public reporting of outcomes (Mowat Centre 2011, 60-61). Nevertheless, the role is clearly advisory and does not go as far as "the collective determination" of policy.

22 As a long-standing Quebec student of Canada's constitutional struggles, Noël's surprise is worth noting. "To be honest, I was myself skeptical at the outset, assuming that little could come out of mere administrative arrangements. I stand corrected."

23 Having said that, the impact is unlikely to be zero. Indeed the policy was triggered—or at least justified politically—by the fact that in January 2012, there were 294 claims for EI from out-of-work fish plant workers in Prince Edward Island while 60 temporary foreign workers were approved to enter the province to work in the same occupation (HRSDC 2012).

24 I am indebted to conversations with Matthew Mendelsohn, Arthur Sweetman and Craig Riddell for advice on these issues.

References

Banting, K. 1995. "The Welfare State as Statescraft: Territorial Politics and Canadian Social Policy." In S. Liebfried and P. Pierson, eds., *European Social Policy: Between Fragmentation and Integration*, 269-300. Washington, DC: Brookings Institution.

——. 1987. *The Welfare State and Canadian Federalism*. Montreal: McGill-Queen's University Press, Second Edition.

——. 2005. "Canada: Nation-Building in a Federal Welfare State" In H. Obinger, S. Leibfried and F.G. Castles, eds., *Federalism and the Welfare State: New World and European Experiences*, 89-137. Cambridge: Cambridge University Press.

——. 2006. "Disembedding Liberalism: The New Social Policy Paradigm in Canada." In D. Green and J. Kesselman, eds., *Dimensions of Inequality in Canada*, 417-452. Vancouver: UBC Press..

Banting, K. and J. Myles, eds. Forthcoming. *The Fading of Redistributive Politics: Policy Change and Policy Drift in Canada*. Vancouver: UBC Press.

Bishop, G. and D. Burleton. 2009. "Is Canada's Employment Insurance Program Adequate? TD Economics Special Report. Toronto: TD Bank Financial Group, 30 April.

Boadway, R., and A.G. Green. 1981. "The Economic Implications of Migration to Newfoundland."

Discussion Paper No. 189. Ottawa: Economic Council of Canada.

Campeau, G. 2005. *From UI to EI: Waging War on the Welfare State*. Vancouver: University of British Columbia Press.

Canada 2012. *Jobs, Growth and Long-Term Prosperity: Economic Action Plan 2012*. Ottawa: Public Works and Government Services Canada.

Commission of Inquiry on Unemployment Insurance [Forget Commission].1986, *Report*. Ottawa: Supply and Services Canada.

Committee of Inquiry into the Unemployment Insurance Act [Gill Report]. 1962. *Report*. Ottawa: Queen's Printer.

Courchene, T.J. 1970. "Interprovincial Migration and Economic Adjustment." *Canadian Journal of Economics* 3.4: 550-76.

Courchene, T.J. and J. Allen. 2009. "A Short History of EI, and A Look at the Road Ahead." *Policy Options*, September.

Dyck, R. 1973. "Poverty and Policy-Making in the 1960s: the Canada Assistance Plan." Ph.D. Thesis, Queen's University, Kingston, Ontario 1973.

Finnie, R. and I. Irvine. 2011. "The Redistributional Impact of Canada's Employment Insurance Program." *Canadian Public Policy*, XXXVII(2): 201-218.

Finnie, R., I. Irvine and R. Sceviour. 2004. "Social Assistance Use in Canada: National and Provincial Trends in Incidence, Entry and Exit." *Canadian Journal of Regional Science*, XXVII (2): 207-222.

Fortin, P. 2010. "Quebec is fairer." *Inroads: a journal of opinion*, Issue 26, Winter/Spring: 58-65.

Fortin, P. and M. Van Audenrode. 2000. "The Impact of Workers' Experience Rating on Unemployed Workers." Ottawa: Human Resources Development Canada.

Gray, D. 2004. "Employment Insurance: What Reform Delivered." *C.D. Howe Institute Backgrounder 82*. Toronto: C.D. Howe Institute.

—. 2006. "Has EI Reform Unraveled? Canada's EI regime in the 2000s." *C.D. Howe Institute Backgrounder 98*. Toronto: C.D. Howe Institute.

Green, D. and C. Riddell. 1993. "The Economic Effects of Unemployment Insurance in Canada: an Empirical Analysis of UI Disentitlement." *Journal of Labor Economics,* 11(1, pt. 2): S96S147.

Haddow, R. 1998. "How Ottawa Shrivels; Ottawa's Declining Role in Active Labour Market Policy." In *How Ottawa Spends: 1998-1999,* ed. L.A. Pal, 99-126. Toronto: Oxford University Press.

Human Resources Development Canada. 1996. "Regulatory Impact Analysis Statement: Amendments to the Employment Insurance Regulations, SOR 96-332 (28 June 1996).

Human Resources and Skills Development Canada. 2009. "Fact Sheet—Variable Entrance Requirements and Extended Employment Insurance Benefits." At http://www.rhdcc-hrsdc.gc.ca/eng/corporate/budget/2009/vereeib.shtml (accessed 11 November 2011).

—. 2012. "Connecting Canadians with Available Jobs: Backgrounder." At http://news.gc.ca/ (accessed 2 June 2012).

Huo, J. 2009. *Third Way Reforms: Social Democracy after the Golden Age.* Cambridge: Cambridge University Press.

International Labour Office. 2000. *World Labour Report 2000: Income Security and Social Protection in a Changing World.* Geneva: ILO.

Jenson, J. and D. Saint-Martin. 2003. "New Routes to Social Cohesion? Citizenship and the Social Investment State." *Canadian Journal of Sociology*. vol. 28: 1, 77-99.

—. 2006. "Building blocks for a new social architecture: the LEGO™ paradigm of an active society." *Policy & Politics*, 34: 3, 429-51.

Kesselman, J. 1983. *Financing Canadian Unemployment Insurance.* Toronto: Canadian Tax Foundation.

Lazar, H. 1998. "Non-Constitutional Renewal: Towards a New Equilibrium in the Federation." In H. Lazar, ed., *Canada: The State of the Federation 1997: Non-Constitutional Renewal.* Montreal: McGill-Queen's University Press.

Lee, F. and S. Coulombe. 1995. "Regional Productivity: Convergence in Canada." *Canadian Journal of Regional Science* 18: 39-56.

Martin, P. (1999). "A Presentation to the House of Commons Standing Committee on Finance, 2 November 1999. At http://www.fin.gc.ca/update99/speeche.html.

Mendelson, M., K. Battle and S. Torjman. 2009. *Canada's Shrunken Safety Net: Employment Insurance in the Great Recession.* Ottawa: Caledon Institute of Social Policy.

Mendelsohn, M. and J. Medow. 2011. *Help Wanted: How Well did the EI Program Respond During Recent Recessions?* Toronto: Mowat Centre for Policy Innovation, University of Toronto.

Moss, D.A. 2002. *When All Else Fails: Government as Ultimate Risk Manager.* Cambridge. MA: Harvard University Press.

Mowat Centre for Policy Innovation. 2011. *Making It Work: The Final Recommendations of the Mowat Centre EI Task Force.* Toronto. The Centre, University of Toronto.

Newfoundland Royal Commission on Employment and Unemployment [House Report]. 1986. *Building on Our Strengths: Report of the Royal Commission on Employment and Unemployment.* St. Johns: Government of Newfoundland and Labrador.

Noël, A. Forthcoming. "Quebec's New Politics of Redistribution." In K. Banting and J. Myles, eds. *The Fading of Redistributive Politics: Policy Change and Policy Drift in Canada.* Vancouver: UBC Press.

Obinger, H., S. Leibfried and F.G. Castles, eds. 2005. *Federalism and the Welfare State: New World and European Experiences.* Cambridge: Cambridge University Press.

Organisation for Economic Co-operation and Development (OECD). 1994. *The OECD Jobs Study: Facts, Analysis, Strategies.* Paris: OECD.

——. 2010. *Employment Outlook.* Paris: OECD.

Osberg, L. 2009. *Canada's Declining Social Safety Net: The Case for EI Reform.* Ottawa: Canadian Centre for Policy Alternatives.

Pal, L. 1983. "The Fall, and Rise of Developmental Uses of UI Funds." *Canadian Public Policy,* 9 (1: 81-93.

——. 1988. *State, Class and Bureaucracy: Canadian Unemployment Insurance and Public Policy.* Montreal: McGill-Queen's University Press.

Poschmann, F. and W. Robson. 2001. "Reprogramming the EI Cash Machine: Matching Employment Insurance Premiums and Payouts." *Backgrounder.* Toronto. C.D. Howe Institute.

Radmilovic, V. 2011. "Postal Code Lottery: Canada's EI System Compared." *Note,* Mowat Centre for Policy Innovation, University of Toronto. At http://www.mowatcentre.ca/research-topic-mowat.php?mowatResearchID=35 (accessed 15 May 2012).

Riddell, C. 1985. "Work and Pay: The Canadian Labour Market: An Overview" in W.C. Riddell, ed., *Work and Pay: The Canadian Labour Market,* 1-76. Toronto: University of Toronto Press.

Royal Commission on Dominion-Provincial Relations [Rowell-Sirois Report]. *Report* (Ottawa: King's Printer, 1940).

Royal Commission on the Economic Union and Development Prospects for Canada [Macdonald Report]. 1985. *Report.* Volume II, ch. 19.

Statistics Canada, Employment Insurance Program (E.I.), income beneficiaries by province, type of benefit, sex and age. CANSIM 276-0001. Accessed 3 July 2012.

Struthers, J. 1983. *No Fault of their Own: Unemployment and the Canadian*

Welfare State 1914-1941. Toronto. University of Toronto Press.
——. 1987. "Shadows from the Thirties: The Federal Government and Unemployment Assistance, 1941-1956." In J. Ismael, ed., *The Canadian Welfare State: Evolution and Transition*. Edmonton: University of Alberta Press.
Van Audenrode, M., A-A. Fournier, N. Havet and J. Royer. 2005. "Employment Insurance in Canada and International Comparisons." Prepared for Human Resources and Skills Development Canada, Gatineau.

Section I

Challenges Facing Coverage and Access to Benefits

Chapter 2

Employment Insurance in the New World of Work

Morley Gunderson

The world of work is rapidly changing, raising the issue of whether labour policies developed and designed for the old world of work are still relevant for the new world of work. Over time in Canada, EI has evolved from a basic insurance scheme to a mixture of insurance and income maintenance as well as having elements of fostering social objectives. It may be poorly designed as an income maintenance program, however, for a number of reasons (Gunderson 2004a). For example, EI is generally based on the individual as the unit of account while income maintenance is generally based on the family (albeit there can be concern over whether all persons within a family have access to the resources). EI benefit payouts are based on earnings and not on family wealth or need. Since the payouts are for only a short period it does not assist those who may have paid into the system for a lifetime, lost their job late in their career, and have structural difficulty finding a new job. EI is also based on being unemployed as the only measure of need and hence does nothing to assist the working poor. By providing passive income support, EI may exacerbate poverty in the long run by discouraging the structural adjustment and the move out of declining and seasonal industries, regions and communities.

While there is obvious controversy, the evidence (summarized in Benjamin et al. 2007, 575-579 and discussed subsequently) suggests that EI:

- increases both the incidence and duration of unemployment;
- increases labour force participation to qualify for EI;
- increases seasonal employment, especially because of the regionally extended benefits;
- increases repeat use of EI;
- leads to "spikes" at the weeks of employment necessary to qualify for EI;
- reduces the need for employers to have to pay a compensating wage for such work;
- fosters community reliance on EI running the risk of an artificial economy geared to EI; and
- reduces inter-regional mobility since there is less incentive to move

from declining to expanding regions, although the effect is often regarded as small (Audas and McDonald 2003; Day and Winer 2001; Lee and Coulombe 1995).

- On the more positive side, EI can foster a better job match by enabling longer job search rather than having to take the first job that becomes available, and this can increase the length of subsequent employment spells (Belzile 2001).
- As well, it serves its important role of sustaining consumption over spells of unemployment (Gruber 1997).

1 Changing Nature of Work and Implications for EI

From the demand side, skill-biased technological change, especially associated with the computer revolution and the shift to a knowledge economy, as well as trade liberalization, has exposed firms and their workers to the forces of international competition, globalization and offshore outsourcing. In part, as a result of these forces, industrial restructuring has occurred mainly from manufacturing to services, with the services being at the polar ends of the occupational distribution—high-end services in business, finance, administration and the professions, and low-end consumer services. These have been enhanced by deregulation, privatization (often associated with re-inventing government) and contracting out—all of which are associated with enhancing competitive market pressures. Unanticipated one-off shocks have also occurred in such forms as SARS, mad-cow disease, and storms. Shocks have also occurred in such forms as the dot.com bust and the recent financial crisis.

These demand changes have a number of implications for EI. Many of the changes are permanent and structural rather than short-term or cyclical, and EI is designed to deal more with the latter rather than the former. Many claims involve job loss for older workers who have paid into the EI system over their lifetime and are now permanently displaced from their former lifetime job, and who may feel too young to retire but too old to retrain or relocate. To the extent that the middle of the job distribution has been "hollowed out" there are few jobs like their former ones. Workers often do not have the skills to move up the occupational ladder into the higher-paying "good jobs" and hence are displaced to lower-paying jobs, often in the service sector, with their supply influx also lowering those wages, so that if they do obtain a new job it often involves substantial wage reductions that are "uninsured." In many circumstances, plant closings have affected whole communities that are isolated with few alternative opportunities. Older workers can be affected not only by the job and wage losses but also by the loss of property values, industry-specific human capital, deferred compensation associated with seniority, and the risk of pension loss—all of which are "uninsured." In essence, while commercial insurance is intended to insure against catastrophic losses, EI is not designed to insure against many of the losses associated with these demand changes. Youths are also facing new challenges. To the extent that the middle-rungs of the job ladders are often missing, they often do not have the opportunity to start at the bottom and move up the career ladder. If they are dropouts or lack education, they can be permanently trapped in the "bad jobs" of the low-wage service economy, if they can even obtain a job. Not being able to obtain an initial job can also leave a permanent legacy or long-run scarring effect (Beaudry and Green 2000).

From the supply side of the labour market, the ageing workforce means that more workers are in the age bracket when the previously discussed structural adjustments are occurring. For older workers the trend toward earlier retirement has reversed itself and they are increasingly transitioning into and out of retirement (Schirle 2008). The dominance of the multiple-earner family does provide some diversification against the risk of one-earner being unemployed, and the same applies to the fact that youths are increasingly working while in school and are living at home. Middle-age workers are trying to find work-family balance raising the issue of whether reductions in hours worked would alleviate unemployment and the need for EI. Recent cohorts of immigrants are increasingly having difficulty assimilating into the labour market in spite of their high levels of skill and education (Ferrer and Riddell 2008 and references cited therein).

Most of these changes from the supply side of the labour market imply a continued role for EI to facilitate the various life-cycle transitions that are occurring and to possibly support job search that could lead to a more productive job match rather than having to take the first job that comes available.

Various institutional changes are also occurring that can have important implications for EI. The decline of unionization and union power implies a decline in supplementary unemployment benefits that unions have often provided. But the decline of union power could also lead to more wage flexibility that could mitigate unemployment.

The most important institutional change is the increased pressure that governments face to reduce regulations given the increased inter-jurisdictional competition for investment and the jobs associated with that investment (Gunderson 1998a). Businesses are increasingly mobile and able to relocate their plants and engage in offshore outsourcing. This can foster the harmonization of legislative and regulatory initiatives including EI toward the lowest common denominator. While there is considerable debate over the extent to which such downward movement occurred in general, there is evidence that reforms in Canada in the late 1980s and mid 1990s reduced the greater generosity of the Canadian system downwards toward the less generous US system (Boychuk and Banting 2003; Gomez and Gunderson 2005).

Partially due to the pressures emanating from the demand and the supply side of the labour market, there has been an increase in non-standard employment in various forms such as: permanent part-time work; seasonal work; casual, temporary work on limited-term contracts; self-employment; temporary-help agencies; on-call work; telecommuting and home working (OECD 2008; Vosko 2010). This has given rise to the concern that some of such employment is often not protected by labour laws and regulations, including EI.

Related to the increase in non-standard employment, is the concern that lifetime jobs and job stability have declined. The evidence on this is somewhat controversial but it tends to suggest that *average* job stability (perhaps surprisingly) has not declined, in part because the workforce is increasingly made up of older workers who tend to have long tenured jobs and women whose job tenure is increasing. The evidence is more in agreement, however, that youths can expect less job security over their working life (Farber 2008; Cazes and Tonin, 2009). This does suggest a continued role for EI to facilitate the transitions between jobs and to possibly support job search that could lead to a more productive job match rather than having to take the first job that comes available.

2 Other Mechanisms for Dealing with Risk of Unemployment

In examining the role of EI in the new world of work, it is important to recognize the role of other mechanisms besides government regulations through EI for dealing with the risk of unemployment. Such mechanisms can be complements or possibly substitutes for government regulation through EI; they can also respond to the changing incentives created by EI.

The external labour market, for example, provides compensating wage premiums for risk including the risk of job loss (Adams 1985; Li 1986; Murphy and Topel 1987), and Topel (1984) specifically documents that the compensating wage premium paid for the risk of unemployment is lower when the risk is reduced by employment insurance. Such compensating wage premiums, in turn, provide an incentive for employers to provide greater employment stability and to reduce seasonal employment. Conversely, unemployment insurance reduces the compensating wage premium employers pay and reduces their incentive to stabilize their employment including seasonal employment. Since layoffs are insured by EI while wage reductions are not insured, workers may be reluctant to accept wage concessions to reduce the risk of layoffs.

Market responses to the generosity of EI can also occur in the form of "forum shopping" or substitution across different programs as some become more generous and others become more stringent. If EI becomes less generous, for example, workers will substitute by accessing other programs like the Canada Pension Plan Disability program, Workers'

Compensation and Social Assistance (Bolduc et al. 2002; Campolieti and Krashinsky 2003; Fortin and Lanoie 2000; Fortin et al. 1996; for Canada see HRSDC 2001; for the US see Autor and Duggan 2003 and Black et al. 2002; for Europe see Rege et al. 2008). This highlights that any cost savings from reducing the generosity of EI will be offset in part, at least, by increased costs associated with accessing these other programs, and the same applies if the generosity of these other programs is altered. The issue is compounded by the fact that EI is a federal program while workers' compensation and social assistance are provincial programs, creating a potential for inter-jurisdictional cost shifting.

Cost shifting can also occur between workers and employers for the payroll taxes that are used to finance programs like EI. The empirical evidence for Canada indicates that the majority of the cost of such payroll taxes (around 80 per cent) is ultimately borne by workers in the form of compensating wage reductions for the benefits associated with such programs (Kesselman 2001 and references therein). This highlights that most of the cost increase of any reforms to EI that would increase the payroll taxes used to finance EI will ultimately be borne by workers, even if part of the payroll tax falls initially on employers. Conversely any cost saving from reforms will also ultimately go to workers. The ultimate burden of the tax is not necessarily where it is initially imposed. There is no such thing as a free lunch.

3 Implications for EI and Its Design Features

The previous analysis highlights a number of implications for the continued relevance of EI and for its various design features that are most relevant to the changing nature of work.

A Benefit Replacement Rate

A key policy parameter of the EI system is the benefit replacement rate. Currently the rate at 55 per cent is likely sufficiently low to preserve work incentives, at least compared to the previous benefit rate of around 67 per cent under the Unemployment Insurance Act of 1971 which was associated with adverse work incentive effects. Whether a 55 per cent replacement rate is sufficiently high to provide viable insurance against the earnings loss is a more open question. In commercial insurance terms this is the equivalent of a 45 per cent deductable which would generally be regarded as a high deductable and hence a high burden on the insured party. This is especially the case for older displaced workers who have paid into the system for most of their working life and are now experiencing a catastrophic permanent job loss—and commercial insurance should be about insuring against catastrophic events more than repeat events where the cost can be anticipated and absorbed by the insured party. As indicated, the rise of the multiple earner family does provide additional insurance and even if both parties are collecting unemployment insurance this amounts to more than the earnings in a single job. The rise of non-standard employment also means there is a wider array of jobs to access and while many are not "good jobs" they can provide some insurance against job loss.

The previous analysis also highlighted that the cost of raising the replacement rate is largely borne by workers; furthermore, if the cost is not borne by workers, then there is the risk that higher payroll taxes will deter investment and the jobs associated with that investment. Raising the replacement rate would also likely increase the need for more stringent monitoring of claims and stronger activation measures to pressure individuals to return to work or to take training as a condition for continued receipt of EI so as to contain costs. Clearly a delicate balance has to be found, and it is not obvious that changing the replacement rate improves that balance.

B Benefit Duration and Regionally Extended Benefits

Similar issues apply to the other basic policy parameter of EI—the benefit duration period. Again a delicate balancing act is required between providing insurance and providing the incentive to seek employment. There does not appear to be sufficient theoretical reasoning or empirical evidence, however, to delineate what would be an optimal benefit duration period. In the absence of such information, it is not obvious that any change is merited. An issue that merits consideration, however, is whether the current policy of "cliff" benefits is merited, where benefits fall abruptly to zero once the maximum duration period is reached.

While neither theory nor evidence provides guidance for changing the benefit duration period, this is not the case with respect to regionally extended benefits whereby qualification periods are reduced and benefit periods extended for unemployed persons in high unemployment regions. This design feature of EI appears to be unique to Canada, and as discussed previously, the theory and evidence suggests that it has increased unemployment and especially seasonal unemployment and the repeated use of EI. As well, it has increased community reliance on EI, running the risk of an artificial economy geared to EI rather than viable market-based job creation. It has also likely reduced inter-regional mobility from low-productivity to high-productivity regions and fostered sustained regional unemployment differences. To the extent that individuals increasingly live in high unemployment regions (where benefits are based on their residence) but commute to work in low unemployment ones, this can further undermine the rationale for regionally differentiated benefits.

In response to these perverse effects a number of researchers have recommended eliminating or altering the regionally extended benefits (Kesselman 1983; Lee and Coulombe 1995; Macdonald Commission 1985; and Riddell, 1985: 32; and others cited therein). Presumably this would be done by removing the extended benefits rather than by extending benefits to all regions. As strongly stated by Lee and Coulombe (1995, 7): "the key to reduce regional disparities in living standards in Canada is to reduce regional disparities in unemployment rates. ... We suggest the best way to do this is to facilitate adjustments in the labour market by eliminating regional distortions such as regionally extended unemployment benefits and the perverse subsidy to seasonal unemployment that comes out of the UI system."

Altering regionally extended benefits will likely imply that economics has to confront politics as such changes will be politically contested given the dependence that has been built around the regional benefits and the fact that they are obviously concentrated in particular regions and communities. The political concern is compounded by the fact that any out-migration that may be fostered by the reduction of regionally extended benefits can involve the exodus of youth—the very persons who may facilitate the future development of such regions. The concern is further enhanced by the possibility that the human capital development of such youths may have involved provincial subsidies for their education and training, and such subsidies will be lost if they leave.

C Coverage of Self-Employed Fish Harvesters and Regional Development Issues

Another area where politics has likely trumped economics is with respect to the coverage of self-employed fish harvesters. As indicated previously, in 1956 coverage was effectively extended to self-employed fish harvesters because they were allowed to treat their buyers as employers. This was a clear departure from commercial insurance principles and from the exclusion of other self-employed workers because of the moral hazard problem since they effectively could control the insurable event by "laying themselves off."

This certainly made the fishing industry an attractive industry in Newfoundland. This was accentuated by the fact that the weeks-worked requirement for eligibility for unemployment insurance was converted to $100 worth of catch as the equivalent of a week of work. In some circumstances it would be possible to qualify for a year of unemployment benefits based on less than one week of work and certainly less than the 10 week qualifying period that earlier prevailed (May and Hollett 1995, 65). This obviously fostered an expansion of the fishing industry—an expansion that was further fostered by government supported "make-work" projects that often involved the building of wharfs and fish plants (House 1986, 406; May and Hollett 1995, 48). Not surprisingly, this all contributed to overfishing and the collapse of the fishing industry (Cashin 1993).

There was particular concern within Newfoundland that, for youths especially, alternating between unemployment and short-term often artificial jobs was becoming a way of life (House 1986). The phrase "Lotto 10-42" was used to describe the system where an individual would work

10 weeks to then collect 42 weeks of unemployment insurance (10 from regular UI and 32 from regionally extended benefits). Workers who worked longer than 10 weeks were sometimes called "scabs" because they were taking the jobs that could be occupied by others to build eligibility for UI, and employers were under pressure to provide rotating 10 week jobs. As well, the underground economy was being fostered since such work could go on while collecting unemployment insurance.

Clearly the combination of the design features of allowing coverage for self-employed fish harvesters, providing regionally extended benefits, and supporting make-work projects to enable eligibility for UI, all interact to potentially foster an artificial economy that is not built on sustainable job creation (Gunderson 1998b). There is, however, a more optimistic portrayal to this apocalyptic picture. In a system that has demand constraints in that few jobs are available, that system could be thought of as a work-conditioned income maintenance system that did encourage at least some work to obtain eligibility for UI. It could also be considered as a form of work-sharing when jobs are scarce (May and Hollett 1995, 81). Such practices could also serve as (hopefully) temporary initiatives to bridge a transition until demand increases as more recently has occurred with the mobility to Alberta and with the expansion of offshore oil and gas developments in Newfoundland and Labrador.

Whatever perspective is taken, a reconsideration of the extension of coverage to self-employed fish harvesters seems merited. It is not obvious why someone should be covered by EI if they harvest the sea but not the land (i.e., self-employed farmers are not covered) or if they are self-employed in any other endeavour. The prosperity that is now occurring in Newfoundland and Labrador associated with oil and gas developments suggest that the timing is now right for reconsideration.

D Active Adjustment Assistance vs. Passive Income Maintenance

Active labour market adjustment policies (ALMAPs) are ones that facilitate the reallocation of labour in the direction of basic market forces, from contracting to expanding firms, industries, occupations, and regions. They generally involve human capital investments in forms such as education, training, labour market information, job search and mobility. In contrast, passive income maintenance programs like unemployment insurance may discourage such reallocation by providing income assistance to persons who stay in the declining sectors.

As indicated previously, the Employment Benefit and Support Measures (EBSMs) came under the umbrella of the EI system in the mid 1990s in Canada. This was part of the shift from passive income maintenance to active adjustment assistance programs that had been recommended by a series of OECD reports in the 1980s and 1990s (Gunderson and Riddell 2001).

A continued emphasis on active labour market adjustment policies likely makes sense for a variety of reasons. They enhance efficiency by facilitating the reallocation of labour from declining to expanding sectors and thereby "greasing the wheels" of market forces. In that vein, they reduce the negative consequences of both *downside* adjustments (plant closings, layoffs, unemployment, and underemployment) as well as the *upside* adjustments (skill shortages and bottlenecks, job vacancies, inflationary wage premiums). Active adjustment assistance policies deal with the underlying *cause* of the problem (the need for adjustment) and not the *symptom* (unemployment). They facilitate equity or distributional objectives to the extent that persons in declining sectors are likely to be disadvantaged in terms lower wages and subject to layoffs or plant closings. They enable recipients to earn their income rather than receive it in the form of a transfer and in that vein they foster self-sufficiency by providing a "hand up" rather than a "handout." Active adjustment assistance programs encourage constant *marginal* adjustments and this can avoid the more costly *inframarginal* adjustments in such forms as mass layoffs and plant closings that can occur if passive income maintenance programs simply postpone such adjustments. Active adjustment assistance is also better designed to deal with the structural unemployment and permanent job loss associated with the industrial restructuring that is occurring in the transformation from the old to the new world of work. In contrast, the passive income maintenance of conventional EI may have been suited to provide short-term insurance to cover the risk of cyclical unemployment until claimants returned to their former job. Now many of the former jobs may be gone permanently and active adjustment assistance may be necessary to equip and reallocate people to the new jobs. Active adjustment programs can also be a requirement for continued receipt of EI so as to facilitate the return to work. Such activation measures have been increasingly required in most OECD countries, especially to counteract the disincentive to return to work in countries where EI systems are fairly generous (Gunderson 2004b; Martin and Grubb 2001, 27, 28; Nickell 2003, 16).

Overall, active adjustment assistance is consistent with the emphasis on flexibility and adaptability to market forces that is increasingly important in the new world of work.

E Hours Worked Eligibility Requirements

The earlier reforms that changed the qualifying period from one based on weeks worked to one based on hours worked is also an appropriate change that should be continued. It accommodates the more flexible work-time arrangements that are increasingly common in the new world of work as opposed to the old nine-to-five, five days-per-week that was prominent in the old world of work. The hours-requirement will also deter employers shifting to part-time jobs under 15 hours per week because they were formerly ineligible for coverage.

F Experience Rating

The potential reform of EI that likely merits the most attention is that of experience-rating – the well-established commercial insurance principle whereby the rate paid by the insured party varies positively with their "accident rate" or receipt of insurance. In the EI area, experience rating can be applied to employers, employees or both.

Experience rating applied to employers (as exists in the US but not in Canada) would involve their payroll tax premium varying positively with the "accident rate" (unemployment) of firms or possibly industry groups. This is in contrast to the current system in Canada of a fixed rate for employers and employees.

In theory such experience rating on firms should reduce layoffs and unemployment by increasing the cost to them of such outcomes (De Raff et al. 2004). It increases the incentive for them to find alternatives to layoffs such as smoothing their production process over seasons and retraining their workers during a cyclical downturn. It also means that firms or industries with a good unemployment record are not cross-subsidizing firms with a bad unemployment record. Experience rating is also in accordance with sound commercial insurance principles, for example, when discounts are given for good driving records.

Empirical evidence from the US, where the premium paid by firms depends on the claims of their workers in the recent past, strongly confirms the theoretical expectation that experience rating reduces layoffs and unemployment (Anderson and Meyer 2000; Card and Levine 1994; Safer 1982; Topel 1984, 1990). Anderson and Meyer (2000, 103), for example, conclude: "our estimates imply that a country contemplating a move to experience rating might expect UI claims rates to fall between 10 and 33 per cent, and seasonality of this rate to fall 16–40 per cent. These results clearly suggest that experience rating reduces UI claims and stabilizes employment. Both of these changes mean lower unemployment and, thus, likely higher social welfare." Simulations for Canada also suggest such positive effects (Beauséjour et al. 1998).

Experiencing rating in other areas such as workers' compensation also indicates that it has positive incentive effects by reducing accident rates because employers now pay more for the social costs of their production that involves risk (Gunderson and Hyatt 2002). In part for this reason, it is being extended in that area.

Employer experience rating for EI in Canada has been recommended by Kesselman (1983), Poschman and Robson (2001), Riddell (1995) and by the Department of Finance Technical Committee on Business Taxation (Mintz 1998). Clearly, it merits more consideration based on both theory and evidence.

As indicated previously, experience rating has also been applied in Canada to *workers* not through increases in their premium but through the "intensity rule" instituted in 1996 whereby benefit payouts were reduced for repeat users and those who accessed the system extensively in the past (Gray 2004; Nakamura, 2000). In commercial insurance terms this would be the equivalent of reducing the amount of the insurance claim payout rather than increasing the premium for those with high accident rates. The empirical evidence indicated that the intensity rule did reduce repeat use, but individuals also behaved strategically by ending their claims just before the intensity rule would apply (Gray 2004; Fortin and van Audenrode 2000). The intensity rule was abolished in 2000, however, in large part because it had a disproportionate impact on Atlantic Canada (Gray 2004: 9).

G Extending Coverage to More Forms of Non-standard Employment

As indicated previously, non-standard employment has increased in various forms: permanent part-time work; seasonal work; casual, temporary work on limited-term contracts; self-employment; temporary-help agencies; on-call work; telecommuting and home working. Unemployment insurance, however, was instituted in the old world of work designed largely to provide insurance against job loss on the part of "breadwinners" who lost their lifetime job. If the new world of work is increasingly characterized by young persons and multiple-earner families *churning* through various forms of non-standard work—perhaps permanently, perhaps as steps to an ultimate career job—the issue becomes the role of EI in such a system.

A natural reaction is to extend eligibility or coverage to the forms of non-standard employment that are currently not covered. Doing so for some forms such as self-employment, limited-term contracts and temporary-help agencies, however, would lead to the conventional commercial insurance problems of adverse selection and moral hazard since the parties often have control over the insurable event of unemployment. As well, in some forms such as seasonal employment and limited-term contracts, the insurable event is generally predictable, while commercial insurance is designed to cover unpredictable events and especially those that involve catastrophic losses. The problems that have arisen in areas of covering regularized seasonal work and self-employed fish harvesters have already been illustrated.

Other design changes, such as the hours- rather than the weeks-worked requirement for eligibility, make sense since they effectively extend coverage to persons with non-standard hours. As well, the active adjustment assistance programs under the EBSMs of Part II can facilitate persons who are involuntarily employed in non-standard jobs to make the transition to standard jobs if that is what they prefer.

H Personal Unemployment Insurance Lifetime Savings Accounts

A design feature that merits additional attention is the possibility of personal unemployment insurance accounts as are being utilized in some countries in Latin America and that have been proposed in the US (Ferrer and Riddell 2009; Hartley et al. 2010). While the design features can differ, they essentially involve requiring workers (and perhaps their employers) to pay into a personal unemployment insurance account that the individual can draw on if unemployed. The intent is to reduce the moral hazard problem since individuals have an incentive not to use up their account. Issues still exist, however, since governments cannot pre-commit to not assisting persons who have exhausted their account and individuals still have an incentive to use up their account toward the end of their work-cycle if they are not allowed to access any unspent balances. Such individual accounts could be used to protect against the risk of income loss from any range of events such as disability, injury at work, sickness, child support, parental leave and loss of income at retirement, or even for wage loss (Bovenberg et al. 2008; Stiglitz and Yun 2005).

A variant of such individual accounts for unemployment insurance in the US is outlined in O'Leary and Eberts (2005). Individuals receiving UI benefits would first be profiled so as to predict those most likely to exhaust their benefits. They would then be given up to US$3,000 to be used for three items: (1) to use as a voucher to purchase re-employment services (the equivalent of our EBSMs) from approved providers who would compete in providing the services, (2) to keep as a re-employment bonus if they return to work early, and (3) to keep and use as extended income maintenance if they exhaust their regular UI benefits.

Individual lifetime accounts clearly have the appealing feature of enabling individuals to inter-temporally pool risks over their own lifetime and to possibly pool them across a variety of potential events that would otherwise reduce their income—in effect, they are a form of forced-savings to mitigate such risks. More information is needed, however, at both a theoretical and empirical level on the effect of such individual lifetime accounts as well as the strategic behavioural responses the parties will make to them.

I EI Modifications for Job Loss from One-Off, Temporary, Unanticipated Shocks

EI can be a potentially important mechanism for persons who directly or indirectly are unemployed because of one-off, temporary, unanticipated shocks such as SARS, mad-cow, terrorist attacks or natural disasters like fires and storms (Gunderson 2004a). Passive income maintenance is appropriate to ease the transition when such workers return to their normal job after the shock and to encourage reporting of the pandemics and to accept quarantines. Since they can expect to return to their former job they do not need active adjustment assistance for a new job.

Income maintenance over the temporary unemployment spell can easily and quickly be provided through minor modifications to the EI system. These have occurred in Canada in response to past shocks and include: immediate eligibility for immediate benefits with no waiting period; waiving of job search or training expectations since such workers are expected to return to their original job; adjusting the duration of benefits to correspond to the duration of the shock; and raising the replacement rate since the disincentive not to return to work from a high replacement rate is minimized by the fact that recipients are expected to return to work once the shock is over. Many of these design features that involve a more generous system may also foster the incentive for individuals to report the problem (as in SARS and mad-cow) rather than hide it for fear of job loss.

J Employment-Insurance Assisted Work-sharing

The work sharing component of EI is also well-suited to deal with the adjustment consequences of such shocks if they would otherwise lead to layoffs of a portion of the workforce of the organization. This is part of the generally desirable equity and efficiency properties of work-sharing (Gray 2000; Reid 1996). They are equitable because they share the unemployment over the organization's workforce in the form of *hour* reductions rather than having it concentrated in the hands of a few in the form of *layoffs*. Work-sharing can have efficiency properties in that they enable organizations to retain their workforce and its embodied human capital rather than risk losing such workers if they are laid off. Work-sharing can also facilitate work-family balance for those on reduced hours.

As with the regular work-sharing component of EI, work-sharing can be viable to deal with the adjustment consequences of temporary one-off shocks since the job losses are not expected to be permanent or structural. They are designed to facilitate the transition until the situation (hopefully) returns to "normal." Such reductions in hours worked have helped Germany weather the recent financial crisis without substantial increases in unemployment (Eichorst et al. 2010).

This does mean that administrative rulings are required to approve requests for work-sharing and this requires distinguishing situations where the adjustment is expected to be temporary (and work-sharing is appropriate) as opposed to permanent (where active adjustment assistance through programs like EBSMs are appropriate to facilitate the more permanent structural adjustment). But the need for such administrative rulings seems a small price to pay for the potential advantages of supporting work-sharing through EI.

K Wage Insurance

Income losses associated with negative employment shocks can occur not only through job losses but also through hour reductions and wage reductions. EI provides insurance only against job losses, although the work-sharing component can support hour reductions. But wage reductions are not insured, and as indicated previously this may be one reason for a reluctance to accept wage concessions (which are not insured) to avoid the risk of job loss (which is insured). Wage insurance could also reduce resistance to trade liberalization and other changes that can foster growth and efficiency, but that can lead to job displacement.

In the new world of work, displaced workers often experience substantial wage reductions even if they are fortunate enough to find a new job. This is especially the case for long-tenured older workers who have paid into the EI system throughout their working life, and who are often displaced from well-paid manufacturing jobs and can only find employment in the low-end service jobs to the extent that the middle of the job distribution has been hollowed out. Morisette et al. (2007), for example, find earnings losses for older long-tenured displaced workers to be around 20–35 per cent which is similar to that found in US studies.

In such circumstances, increased attention has been paid to the possibility of providing wage insurance as a complement to unemployment insurance (Kletzer 2004; Lalonde 2007). While the design features differ, they basically involve governments replacing a portion of lost wages for a specified period of time and with a limit on the magnitude of the payment. Given the risk of substantial wage loss for displaced long-tenured workers, more attention is merited on examining the pros and cons of such wage-loss insurance.

4 Policy Implications

Even though unemployment insurance was established under conditions of the old world of work, the *basic principle* of a government mandated unemployment insurance scheme continues to be relevant to the new world of work. The risk of unemployment remains a very real risk and in fact may be increasing if job stability declines. Furthermore, individual workers find it difficult to diversify against that risk. Not only their earnings but also their human capital, social capital, pension, health, perception of their self-worth, and even the value of their homes are often affected by the risk of being unemployed.

EI in Canada has evolved from an insurance scheme to contain elements of more general income support and regional development for which it is not properly designed. As such, it is likely best to keep the focus on EI as an insurance scheme rather than a more general income support and regional development program. Design and implementation features that generally adhere to such commercial insurance principles and that are consistent with the changes of the new world of work, and that should thereby be continued include:

- The modest income replacement rate.
- The normal duration of benefits.
- The emphasis on active adjustment assistance through the EBSMs.
- Eligibility based on hours rather than weeks worked.
- Activation requirements to engage in job search or training.
- The use of modified EI to deal with unemployment from one-off, unanticipated, temporary shocks.
- EI-assisted work-sharing to deal with such shocks as well as other temporary bouts of unemployment.

Adhering to basic commercial insurance principles and adjusting to the changes associated with the new world of work, however, suggested a number of reforms in the design and implementation features that merit consideration. The most important were:

- Eliminate or reduce regionally extended benefits.
- Apply experience rating to employers.
- Apply experience rating to workers through restoring the "intensity rule" on repeat users.

A number of potential reforms also merit more attention but more information is needed about them before being seriously considered. These include:

- Extending coverage to various forms of non-standard employment.
- Personal unemployment insurance lifetime savings accounts.
- Wage insurance.

The main suggested reforms of reducing regionally extended benefits and applying experience rating to both employers and employees, unfortunately, are ones that are likely to meet the most political resistance.

References

Adams, J. 1985. "Permanent Differences in Unemployment and Permanent Wage Differences." *Quarterly Journal of Economics* 100 (February): 29-56.

Anderson, P. and B. Meyer. 2000. "The Effects of Unemployment Insurance Payroll Tax on Wages, Employment Claims and Denials." *Journal of Public Economics* 78: 81-106.

Audas, R. and J. McDonald. 2003. "Employment Insurance and Geographic Mobility: Evidence from SLID." WP 03-03. Ottawa: Social Research and Demonstration Corporation.

Auer, P. and S. Cazes. 2000. "The Resilience of the Long-term Employment Relationship: Evidence from the Industrialized Countries." *International Labour Review* 139: 379-408.

Autor, D. and M. Duggan. 2000. "The Rise in Disability Roles and the Decline in Unemployment." *Quarterly Journal of Economics* 118: 157-205.

Beaudry, Paul and David Green. 2000. "Cohort Patterns in Canadian Earnings: Assessing the Role of Skill Premia in Inequality Trends." *Canadian Journal of Economics* 33 (November): 907-36.

Beauséjour, L., M. Sheikh and B. Williams. 1998. "Experience Rating Employment Insurance Contributions." *Canadian Public Policy* 24 (September): 388-93.

Benjamin, D., M. Gunderson, T. Lemieux and C. Riddell. 2002. *Labour Market Economics: Theory, Evidence and Policy in Canada*. 6th edition. Toronto: McGraw-Hill.

Black, D, K. Daniel and S. Sanders. 2002. "The Impact of Economic Conditions on Participation in Disability Programs: Evidence from the Coal Boom and Bust." *American Economic Review* 92: 27-50.

Bolduc, D., B. Fortin, F. Labrecque and P. Lanoie. 2002. "Workers' Compensation, Moral Hazard and the Composition of Workplace Injuries." *Journal of Human Resources* 37: 623-52.

Bovenberg, A.L., M.I. Hansen and P.B. Sorensen. 2008. "Individual Savings Accounts for Social Insurance: Rationale and Alternative Designs." *International Tax and Public Finance* 15: 67-86.

Boychuk, G., and K. Banting. 2003. "The Paradox of Convergence: National Versus Sub-National Patterns of Convergence in Canadian and U.S. Income Maintenance Policy." In *North American Linkages: Opportunities and Challenges for Canada*, ed. R.G. Harris. Calgary: University of Calgary Press.

Campolieti, M. and H. Krashinsky. 2003. "Substitution between Disability Support Programs in Canada." *Canadian Public Policy* 29: 417-29.

Card, D. and P. Levine. 1994. "Unemployment Insurance and the Cyclical and Seasonal Properties of Unemployment." *Journal of Public Economics* 53: 1-29.

Cashin, R. (Chair). 1993. *Charting a New Course: Towards the Fishery of the Future*. Report of the Task Force on Incomes and Adjustment in the Atlantic Fishery. Ottawa: Ministry of Supply and Services.

Cazes, S. and M. Tonin. 2009. "Employment Protection Legislation and Job Stability: An European Cross Country Analysis." University of Southampton School of Social Sciences Discussion Paper, February.

Day, K. and S. Winer. 2001. "Policy-induced Migration in Canada: An Empirical Study." Applied Research Branch, Strategic Policy Paper W-02-02. Ottawa: Human Resources Development Canada.

de Raaf, S., A. Motte and C. Vincent. 2004. "Experience Rating Employment Insurance in Canada: A Literature Review." Ottawa: Human Resources Skill Development Canada.

Eichorst, W., M. Feil and P. Marx. 2010 "Crises, What Crises: Patterns of Adaptation in European Labour Markets." IZA Discussion Paper 5045 (July).

Farber, H. 2008. "Employment Insecurity: The Decline in Worker-Firm Attachment in the United States." Princeton University Industrial Relations Section Working Paper.

Ferrer, A., and W.C. Riddell. 2008. "Education, Credentials and Immigrant Earnings." *Canadian Journal of Economics* 41: 186-216.

——. 2010. "Unemployment Insurance Savings Accounts in Latin America: Overview and Assessment." World Bank Discussion Paper No. 910.

Fortin, B. and P. Lanoie. 1992. "Substitution between Unemployment Insurance and Workers' Compensation: An Analysis Applied to the Risk of Workplace Accidents." *Journal of Public Economics* 49: 287-312.

Fortin, B., P. Lanoie and C. Laporte. 1996. "Is Workers' Compensation Disguised Unemployment Insurance?" mimeo.

Fortin, P. and M. Van Audenrode. 2000. "The Impact of Workers' Experience Rating on Unemployed Workers," Ottawa: Human Resources Development Canada.

Gomez, R. and M. Gunderson. 2005. "Does Economic Integration Lead to Social Policy Convergence? An Analysis of North American Linkages and Social Policy." In *Social and Labour Market Aspects of North American Linkages*, ed. R. Harris and T. Lemieux, 309-56. Calgary: University of Calgary Press.

Gray, D. 2000. "The Worksharing Program in Canada: A Feasible Alternative to Layoffs?" C.D. Howe Institute Commentary 146. Toronto: C.D. Howe Institute.

——. 2004. "Employment Insurance: What Reform Delivered." *C.D. Howe Institute Backgrounder* 82. Toronto: C.D. Howe Institute.

Gruber, J. 1997. "Consumption-Smoothing Effects of Unemployment Insurance." *American Economic Review* 87: 192-205.

Gunderson, M. 1998a. "Harmonization of Labour Policies Under Trade Liberalisation." *Relations industrielles/ Industrial Relations* 53.1: 1-14.

——. 1998b. "Income Transfers under Increased Economic Integration: The

Case of Newfoundland." In *Integrating Cities and Regions: North America Faces Globalization*, ed. J. Wilkie and C. Smith, 393-422. Los Angeles: UCLA Program on Mexico.

——. 2004a. "Employment Insurance and Labour Market Risk in the New World of Work." Ottawa: Human Resources Skill Development.

——. 2004b. *International Experiences with Labour Market Adjustment: Lessons for Canada*. Ottawa: Human Resources Skills Development.

Gunderson, M. and D. Hyatt. 2002. *Economic Incentives: Strategies for Engendering Healthy Workplaces*. Ottawa: Health and Welfare Canada.

Gunderson, M. and W.C. Riddell. 2001. "Unemployment Insurance: Lessons from Canada." In *Labour Market Policies in Canada and Latin America*, ed. Albert Berry, 69-96. Boston: Klywer Academic Publishers, 2001.

Hartley, G., J. van Ours and M. Vodopivec. 2010. "Incentive Effects of Unemployment Insurance Savings Accounts: Evidence from Chile." IZA Discussion Paper 4681, January.

House, D. (Chair). 1986. Building on Our Strengths. St. Johns: Report of the Royal Commission on Employment and Unemployment.

HRSDC. 2001. *Did the Social Assistance Take-up Rate Change After EI Reform for Job Separators?* Ottawa: Human Resources and Skills Development Canada.

Kesselman, J. 1983. *Financing Canadian Unemployment Insurance*. Toronto: Canadian Tax Foundation.

——. 2001. "Payroll Taxes and the Financing of Social Security." In *Labour Market Policies in Canada and Latin America: Challenges of the New Millennium*, ed. A. Berry, 135-158. Boston: Kluwer Academic Publishers.

Kletzer, L. 2004. "Trade Related Job Loss and Wage Insurance: A Synthetic Review." *Review of International Economics* 12: 724-48.

Kletzer, L. and R. Litan. 2001. "A Prescription to Relieve Worker Anxiety." Policy Brief 01-2. Washington: Peterson Institute for International Economics, March.

LaLonde, R. 2007. *The Case for Wage Insurance*. Washington: Council on Foreign Relations Press.

Lee, F. and S. Coulombe. 1995. "Regional Productivity: Convergence in Canada." *Canadian Journal of Regional Science* 18: 39-56.

Li, E.H. 1986. "Compensating Differentials for Cyclical and Noncyclical Unemployment: The Interaction Between Investors' and Employees' Risk Aversion." *Journal of Labor Economics* 4 (April): 277-300.

Macdonald, D. (Chair). 1985. *Report of the Royal Commission on the Economic Union and Development Prospects for Canada*. Ottawa: Minister of Supply and Services Canada.

Martin, J., and D. Grubb. 2001. *What Works and for Whom: A Review of OECD Countries' Experiences with Active Labour Market Policies*. Paris: Organization for Economic Co-operation and Development.

May, D. and A. Hollett. 1995. *The Rock as a Hard Place: Atlantic Canada and the UI Trap*. Toronto: C.D. Howe Institute.

Mintz, J. (Chair). 1998. *Technical Committee on Business Taxation: Report*. Ottawa: Department of Finance.

Morissette, R., X. Zhang and M. Frenette. 2007. "Earnings Losses of Displaced Workers: Canadian Evidence from a Large Administrative Database on Firm Closures and Mass Layoffs." *Analytical Studies Branch Research Paper* 297. Ottawa: Statistics Canada.

Murphy, K. and R. Topel. 1987. "Unemployment, Risk and Earnings." *In Unemployment and the Structure of Labor Markets*, ed. K. Lang and J. Leonard. Oxford: Basil Blackwell.

Nakamura, A. 2000. "Make EI Fairer: Don't Open the Coffers to Well-off Repeaters." *C.D. Howe Institute Backgrounder*. Toronto: C.D. Howe Institute.

Nickell, S. 2003. "A Picture of European Unemployment: Success and Failure." London School of Economics, Centre for Economic Performance Working Paper (July).

OECD. 2008. *Growing Unequal? Income Distribution and Poverty in OECD Countries*. Paris: Organization for Economic Co-operation and Development.

O'Leary, C. and R. Eberts. 2005 "Personal Reemployment Accounts: Simulations for Planning Implementation." In *Selected Research Papers on Personal Reemployment Accounts*. Washington, DC: U.S. Department of Labor, Employment and Training Administration.

Poschmann, F. and W. Robson. 2001. "Programming the EI Cash Machine: Matching Employment Insurance Premiums and Payouts." *C.D. Howe Institute Backgrounder*. Toronto: C.D. Howe Institute.

Rege, M., K. Telle and M. Votruba. 2009. "The Effect of Plant Downsizing on Disability Pension Utilization." *Journal of the European Economic Association* 7: 754-85.

Reid, F. 1996. "Combating Unemployment Through Work Time Reduction." *Canadian Public Policy* 12 (June): 275-85.

Riddell, C. 1985. "Work and Pay: The Canadian Labour Market: An Overview." In *Work and Pay: The Canadian Labour Market*, ed. W.C. Riddell, 1-76. Toronto: University of Toronto Press.

Riddell, W.C. 1995. "Human Capital Formation in Canada: Recent Developments and Policy Responses." In *Labour Market Polarization and Social Policy Reform*, ed. K. Banting and C. Beach, 125-72. Kingston: Queen's University School of Policy Studies.

Schirle, T. 2008. "Why Have the Labour Force Participation Rates of Older Men Increased Since the Mid 1990s." *Journal of Labor Economics* 26 (October): 549-94.

Stiglitz J.E.,and J. Yun. 2005. "Integration of Unemployment Insurance with Retirement Insurance." *Journal of Public Economics* 89: 2037-67.

Topel, R. 1984. "Experience Rating of Unemployment Insurance and the Incidence of Unemployment." *Journal of Law and Economics* 27 (April): 61-90.

——. 1990. "Financing Unemployment Insurance: History, Incentives and Reform." In *Unemployment Insurance*, ed. W.L. Hansen and J.F. Byers. Madison: University of Wisconsin Press.

Vosko, L. 2010. *Managing the Margins: Gender, Citizenship and the International Regulation of Precarious Employment*. New York: Oxford University Press.

Chapter 3

The Challenge of Expanding EI Coverage

Leah F. Vosko

Employment Insurance (EI) has a critical place in Canada's income security system.[1] Its role is undermined increasingly, however, by a mismatch with labour market realities. This mismatch has consequences for individual labour force participants as well as EI's effectiveness as an economic stabilizer for Canada as a whole.

In recent decades, women's labour force participation rates have risen dramatically, international migration for employment has increased, industrial restructuring has transformed Canada's regional labour market patterns, and school-to-work and work-to-retirement transitions have become more complex. These developments have, moreover, taken place alongside fundamental changes in the nature of employment, including the expansion of part-time and temporary forms of paid employment and solo self-employment, as well as the polarization of working hours.

EI policy has not kept pace with such shifts and their cumulative impact. Although the stated intention of the EI hours-system introduced in 1996 was to address the changing nature of employment (*Employment Insurance Act*, S.C. 1996, c. 23 ["*EI Act*"]; *Employment Insurance Regulations*, S.O.R./96-332 ["*Regulations*"]), research to date demonstrates that full EI coverage still hinges on the full-time job where the worker has one employer, expects to be employed indefinitely and works on the employer's premises under direct supervision—an employment model long dominant among mid-aged male Canadian-born workers following a life-course divided into discreet segments of education, work, and retirement and sustained outside the labour force by (largely unpaid) female care-giving (see, for example, McBride 1999; McIntosh and Boychuk 2000; Vosko 2009; Porter 2003; MacDonald 2009; Battle, Mendelson and Torjman 2005).

This study charts the gap between EI coverage and changing labour market realities using a combination of policy and statistical analysis and identifies remedies for closing this gap. Its focus is regular benefits, with some attention to two special benefits, EI maternity and parental benefits (outside of Quebec, which has a separate benefit system).

The analysis is divided into three parts.

Part I outlines the guiding conceptual framework, introducing the focus on *labour market membership,* a notion used here to refer to who is and is not assumed to be a member of the labour market meriting income replacement when a separation of employment occurs.

Part II reviews the central features of the post-1996 EI system and provides a descriptive statistical portrait of inclusions and exclusions from its four *modes of coverage*—eligibility, entry requirements, level and duration of benefits. It examines, in particular, coverage through the lenses of gender, immigration status, age, size of area of residence (metropolitan/ urban/ rural), and sector.

Finally, Part III advances select policy options for expanding EI coverage organized around its four modes. These options emanate, on the one hand, from an understanding of EI as a vital plank in Canada's income security system that assumes, in principle, that coverage should reflect labour market realities, and thus its modes of coverage require adaptation to a more inclusive approach to labour market membership. They are motivated, on the other hand, by the evidence of exclusions on the bases of gender, immigration status, age, size of place of residence (metropolitan/ urban/ rural), and sector presented in Part II.[2]

Before proceeding, one further framing comment is in order. A guiding premise of this study is that EI is an income security program that has legitimately fulfilled both insurance-*based and* redistributive functions historically (Osberg 1979; Pulkingham 1998), albeit not without tension (Pal 1986). Consequently, the options for inclusive policy redesign considered here contrast with other studies prepared for the Mowat Centre EI Task Force. Underpinned by competing interpretations of EI's origins and aims, some such studies suggest that the program should be redesigned to adhere to insurance-principles exclusively (e.g., Gunderson), and that reforms in this direction could be coupled with changes to social assistance addressing the situation of workers lacking sufficient contribution levels for full EI coverage (e.g., Mendelson and Battle; Stapleton). A related contention of this study is that calls for reprioritizing narrowly-construed insurance principles can reinforce the sorts of exclusions being examined here, especially in the absence of effective institutional arrangements for extending protections to address the changing nature of employment: for example, as Rubery et al (1999, 42-43) show in comparing system-types in Europe: "women tend to benefit less than men from insurance-based benefits as they are less able to fulfill the eligibility requirements and the tightening of eligibility rules are likely to increase these problems." As illustrated by Schmidt and Reissert (1996, 248), the same goes for age: "just as older people tend to be better protected under insurance-based systems, the young are less well protected. Insurance-based systems are, therefore, biased toward protecting core workers (mostly male and elderly) over marginal workers (mostly young, female and casual)." An exclusively insurance-based system is thus ill-equipped for dealing with new pressures created by social and economic changes in the labour market. Some flexibility in functions is necessary, and has been necessary historically in the case of EI, to address major socio-economic changes and related demographic shifts.

1 Conceptual Framework

The ensuing analysis takes as its central focus *labour market membership*—that is, participation norms surrounding who labour protections aim to serve by the design of formal laws as well as associated policies on their application and enforcement. It is concerned specifically with *who* is and is not assumed to belong to the community of workers in the labour force, and thus who is entitled to, and able to access without undue hardship, the full range of EI benefits.

An emphasis on membership permits a focused exploration of a number of *axes of differentiation* and exclusion from protection. This analysis focuses on five different axes pertinent to EI coverage and, where possible, their intersection: gender, age, immigration status, size of area of residence, and industry.

Broadly speaking, gender relations impinge on EI coverage because they affect divisions of paid and unpaid labour shaping men's and women's labour force status (e.g., employed, unemployed or discouraged) and, among the employed, scheduling and work arrangements (see Neis 1993; Vosko 1996, 2009; Porter 2003; Townson and Hayes 2007; Standing Committee on the Status of Women 2007, 2009; MacDonald 2009; on maternity and parental benefits, see also Marshall 2003; Pérusse 2003).

Immigration status mediates EI coverage through entry category and territorial presence. Citizens, permanent residents, temporary work permit holders, and non-status workers have differential rights and access to supports based on the form of immigration and the duration of their stay in Canada (see Phipps and MacPhail 2002; Sweetman 2001; Shields 2004; MacLaren and Lapointe 2009; Standing Committee on the Status of Women 2009; Nakache and Kinoshita 2010).

Age also informs EI policy given assumptions about labour force attachment during school-to-work and work-to-retirement transitions common in the early and latter phases of paid working life (see Ferrall 1997; McGregor 2003; Osberg 2005; Canadian Labour Congress 2007; Expert Panel on Older Workers 2008; Riddell 2009).

The same can be said for both sector of employment and the population size of workers' place of residence—for example, patterns of industrial concentration vary across Canada (see Bakvis 2002; Klassen 2000; Cheal 2003; MacDonald 2009; McBride and Stoyko 2000).

Employment status and form of employment are also intimately related to EI coverage. Distinctions between different types of work for remuneration (self or paid employment) and among forms of paid employment (part-time or full-time, temporary or permanent) operate to fully or partially exclude certain categories of workers. This exclusion can be by design, as is the case for many of the self-employed, or by implementation, as is the case with part-time and temporary employees unable to qualify for partial or full EI benefits due to insufficient hours of insurable employment (see Clement 1986; Vosko 1996, 2000; Fudge, Tucker and Vosko 2002; Battle, Mendelson and Torjman 2006). However, since neither employment status nor form of employment are facets of workers' ascribed characteristics, they are of a different order and, where possible, analyzed in a cross-cutting manner.[3]

2 The EI System: Charting Inclusions and Exclusions from Coverage

In 1996, the federal government introduced the *Employment Insurance Act* to replace the *Unemployment Insurance Act*. The *EI Act* included Part 1 Unemployment Benefits and Part 2 Employment Benefits. It adopted a new hours-system for Part 1 benefits, the central focus of which fundamentally altered entry requirements, and duration and levels of benefits.

According to a Federal government report (HRDC 1994, 49, *emphasis added*) prepared for the *Social Security Review* that lay the groundwork for the new legislation, a major impetus for the new system was the changing nature of employment:

> ...The UI program will need to consider the needs of workers in "nonstandard" employment, who have increased significantly over the last decade. This includes part-time, temporary, self-employed or multiple job holders. Most of these workers are women... Many of these nonstandard workers are not fully covered by unemployment insurance for all the hours worked, and some are excluded from coverage entirely... In addition, the current program does not cover self-employed workers at all, other than those in the fishing industry... *Despite the challenges in providing coverage for self-employment, part-time work and multiple jobs, these types of nonstandard work are growing in significance. The issue of providing improved insurance coverage needs to be reexamined.*

Contrary to these stated aims, a large body of literature shows that EI coverage or "recipiency rates" applies most extensively to full-time, permanent, long-tenure workers in traditionally dominant sectors of Canada's economy (e.g., manufacturing and primary industries). Workers least well-protected are clustered in part-time and temporary forms of paid employment and self-employment, and in sectors of the economy long viewed as ancillary but experiencing considerable growth in recent decades, such as sales and service, a central domain of employment for women, younger, older, and immigrant workers (see, on gendered patterns, Phipps, MacDonald and MacPhail 2001; Vosko 2002; Townson and Hayes 2007; Standing Committee on the Status of Women 2009; on immigration status, Sweetman 2001; Standing Committee on the Status of

Women 2009; MacLaren and Lapointe 2009; on age, McGregor 2003; and, on region, Sidhu 2009).

Most research on EI focuses on coverage writ large. Yet to understand the mismatch between patterns of labour force participation and EI policy, it is critical to explore how EI's different modes of coverage operate in practice. Two modes of coverage relate to "getting in": *eligibility*, that is, considering the labour force as a whole, which workers are required (or permitted) to contribute to EI; and *entry requirements*, or the criteria eligible workers must fulfill to qualify for benefits. Another two modes of concern correspond to "adequacy of coverage": namely, *duration* and *level of benefits* among the eligible and qualified unemployed. The analysis pursued henceforth examines these modes of coverage.

The statistics reported are for the year 2007 as there have been few significant EI policy changes since then and because 2007 represents a pre-recession year.[4] Throughout the analysis, the focus is the currently employed population given the dual concern with the workers that EI is designed to serve as an income security program and those it should take to be members of the labour market meriting income replacement in instances of unemployment. Adopting this methodological approach produces some findings distinct from those reported in government documents that chart trends among the unemployed population, as the character of these populations differ.

A Getting In

1. Eligibility

Employees, and their employers, as well as self-employed fishers, are required to contribute to EI via premiums.[5] When employees lose their employment, or take maternity or parental leave, they are eligible to receive EI regular benefits provided they meet certain requirements. Employees and self-employed workers opting into the program as of 31 January 2010 are also eligible for special benefits.

Regular Benefits

Eligibility for regular benefits rests principally on whether a person is an employee or self-employed; whereas the former and their employers are required to contribute to EI, the latter and their clients are not.[6] The rationale behind this distinction is that paid employees face relations of subordination; they are party typically to employment relationships in which they relinquish control over how work is performed in exchange for the security and durability of a wage and other employment-related benefits. In contrast, the self-employed are not deemed suitable for coverage as they are assumed to be entrepreneurs (i.e., risk-taking business people who own their own tools and have capital assets). Yet forms of self-employment resembling paid employment in terms of their character and quality are prevalent in Canada (see, for example, Clement 1986; Hughes 1999; Fudge, Tucker and Vosko 2002; du Plessis et al. 2002; Cranford et al. 2005). One such form is solo self-employment, where the self-employed person does not normally employ others, a diverse category including persons in occupations and industries where the nature of the activity requires a degree of autonomy but not necessarily genuine control and often, but not necessarily, working with multiple clients (e.g., fishers, truck drivers, home childcare providers/ caregivers, editors). Ten per cent of the currently employed hold this form of self-employment and it is particularly common among older workers and recent and non-recent immigrants ; compared to paid employment, solo self-employment is also more prevalent as a main job among the currently employed in rural areas.[7] As Table 1 illustrates further, persons aged 55 or more represent 26 per cent of the solo self-employed but only 12 per cent of paid employees,[8] and people living in rural areas represent 12 per cent of the solo self-employed but 9 per cent of paid employees (see also Appendix A, Table 1).

Defying the image of the high income-earning entrepreneur, many of the solo self-employed also earn relatively low incomes despite the fact that the majority of them are full time (67 per cent) (Appendix A, Table 10). To explore the prevalence of low income, Table 1 uses an annual employment income of $20,000 or lower as a measure,[9] reflecting half of the 2007 maximum insurable earnings (MIE) of $40,000, the trigger for the low income supplement under the former UI system.[10] Almost half of the solo self-employed (48 per cent) report an annual employment income below this threshold—in contrast to a third (34 per cent) of paid employees. Further, some types of workers are over-represented among the low-income solo self-employed. For example, among solo self-employed women, 56 per cent have low annual employment incomes and the same pattern holds for recent immigrants. Among solo self-employed workers aged 15-24, more than three-quarters (78 per cent) are in this situation. Solo self-employed workers living in rural areas[11] and solo self-employed workers in the service sector [12] are also significantly more likely to have annual employment incomes of $20,000 or less.

The exclusion of most of the self-employed from eligibility for regular EI benefits overlooks a sizeable subset of self-employment that resembles paid employment—solo self-employment, much of which delivers low income. On the surface, this legislative exclusion appears neutral to gender, age, immigration status, and size of place of residence. However, the poor quality of a considerable segment of this subset of work carries particular consequences for older workers and recent immigrants who are overrepresented among the solo self-employed as well as for the relatively high percentage of solo self-employed women and young people earning extremely low incomes.

TABLE 1 Eligibility: Demographic Distribution of Paid Employees, the Solo Self-Employed and Low-Income Solo-Self Employed, 2007

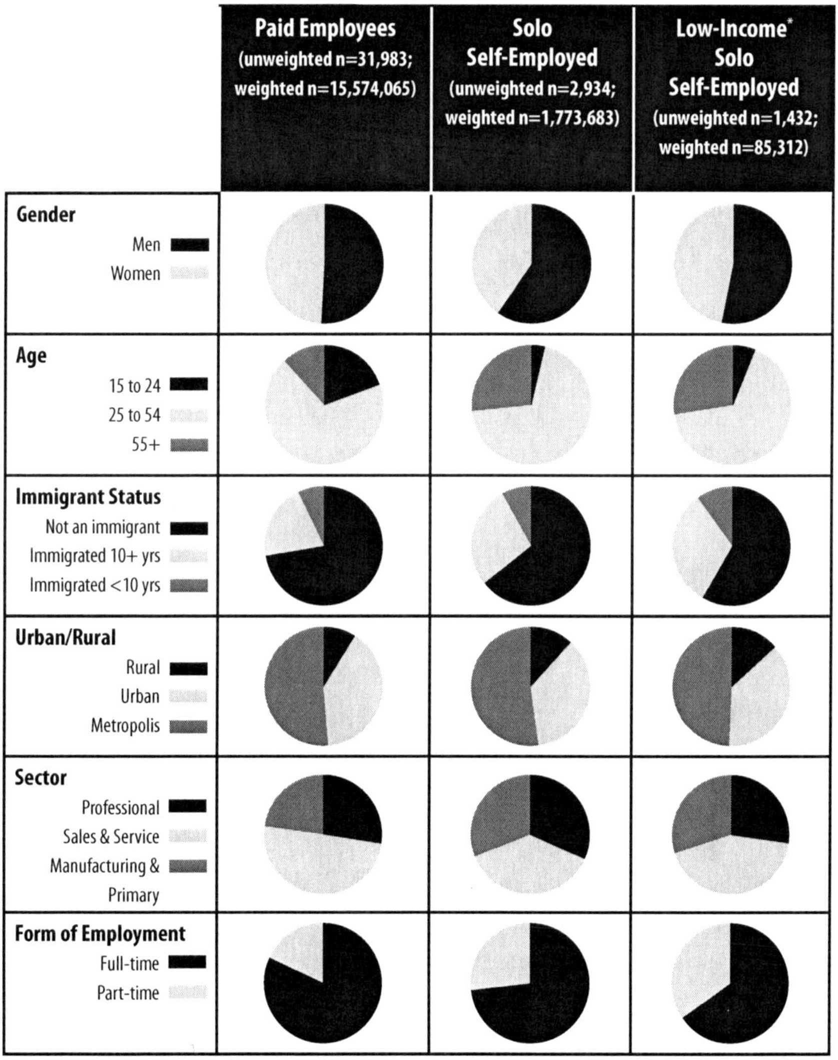

	Paid Employees (unweighted n=31,983; weighted n=15,574,065)	Solo Self-Employed (unweighted n=2,934; weighted n=1,773,683)	Low-Income* Solo Self-Employed (unweighted n=1,432; weighted n=85,312)
Gender Men Women			
Age 15 to 24 25 to 54 55+			
Immigrant Status Not an immigrant Immigrated 10+ yrs Immigrated <10 yrs			
Urban/Rural Rural Urban Metropolis			
Sector Professional Sales & Service Manufacturing & Primary			
Form of Employment Full-time Part-time			

* Low income refers to annual earnings of $20,000 or less [half of the 2007 maximum insurable earnings (MIE)].

2. Entry Requirements: Qualifying for Regular EI

Under EI's hours-system, workers making contributions can qualify for regular and special benefits if they have sufficient hours of insurable employment.[13] An eligible worker must accumulate the required number of hours of insurable employment in the qualifying period, defined as the shorter of the 52 week period preceding the start date of the claim or the period beginning with the start of a previous benefit period to the start date of the new benefit period. Normally, eligible workers need 420 to 700 hours to qualify for regular benefits, depending upon their regional rate of unemployment, the so-called Variable Entrance Requirement (VER) [*EI Act*, s.7 (2(b)): see Appendix B]. The exception is new and reentrants (NEREs) to the labour force who have accumulated fewer than 490 hours of insurable employment in the 52 weeks preceding the qualifying period, who need 910 hours regardless of the region in which they live [*EI Act*, s.7(4)]. For special benefits, workers can qualify with a flat 600 hours regardless of their NERE/non-NERE status.

Entry requirements are the mode of coverage where exclusions and partial exclusions from regular and special EI benefits among employees are most numerous. While the hours-system was introduced to enable more workers in "non-standard" forms of employment to gain access (HRDC 1994, 49), thresholds for entry are high—effectively higher than they were under UI's weekly system.[14] Furthermore, these thresholds still take the full-time permanent job with a single employer to be the norm even though its prevalence is waning, and less common among women compared to men, youth compared to mid-age and older, recent immigrant compared to non-recent immigrant and Canadian-born, rural compared to urban and metropolitan, and sales and service compared to manufacturing and primary workers (see Appendix A, Table 2).

Regular Benefits

Distinct patterns in the distribution of full- and part-time, as well as permanent and temporary, forms of employment between groups helps account for variation in the hours of insurable employment that eligible workers can accumulate in the 52 week qualifying period.[15]

Relating these trends to the hours required to qualify for regular EI benefits under the VER, Table 2 shows that, among all employees, 12 per cent of women (vs. 7 per cent of men) have fewer than 420 hours of insurable employment and fully 21 per cent of women (vs. 13 per cent of men) have fewer than 700 hours. Table 3 illustrates further that it would take the average female paid employee 12.9 weeks to qualify for benefits as opposed to 10.9 weeks for the average man and it reveals similar patterns in a region with a VER of 700. Considering entry requirements by form of employment also illustrates differences in the number of weeks of insurable employment required to qualify for benefits among sexes; for example, in a region with a VER of 420, it would take the average female full-time employee 11.1 weeks to qualify and the average female part-time worker 24.4 weeks. If they are NEREs, it would take these women fully 24.1 weeks and fully 52.9 weeks to qualify respectively (Table 3). Women's relatively high level of participation in part-time forms of employment vis-à-vis men's underscores the significance of these divergent entry requirements by form of employment.

TABLE 2 Entry: Proportion of All, Full-time and Part-time Eligible Employees Who Do Not Meet Minimum Hours Thresholds for Regular Benefits, by Demographics, 2007

	All Paid Employees (unweighted n=31,983; weighted n=15,574,065)			Full-time Employees (unweighted n=25,722; weighted n=12,439,742)			Part-time Employees (unweighted n=5,421; weighted n=2,718,821)		
	% who do not meet 420 hrs threshold	% who do not meet 700 hrs threshold	% who do not meet 910 hrs threshold	% who do not meet 420 hrs threshold	% who do not meet 700 hrs threshold	% who do not meet 910 hrs threshold	% who do not meet 420 hrs threshold	% who do not meet 700 hrs threshold	% who do not meet 910 hrs threshold
Overall	**9.7**	17.0	22.0	**4.2**	9.1	12.4	**35.3**	53.1	65.4
Gender									
Men	**7.3**	13.3	17.6	**3.5**	7.8	11.1	**38.8**	59.6	72.3
Women	**12.3***	21.0*	26.5*	**5.0***	10.8*	14.0*	**33.8***	50.4*	62.5*
Age									
15 to 24	**27.1**	46.7	56.9	**15.5**	33.6	41.6	**43.5**	65.8	78.8
25 to 54	**4.7**	8.9	12.2	**2.2**	5.1	7.5	**25.5**	39.8	51.3
55+	**10.1***	15.2*	20.1*	**3.0***	5.8*	8.9*	**37.2***	51.1*	63.3*
Immigrant Status									
Not an immigrant	**9.2**	16.1	20.9	**3.6**	8.1	11.5	**34.4**	52.1	62.9
Immigrated 10+ yrs	**7.6**	12.6	16.7	**3.1**	6.4	9.3	**34.6**	47.9	60.7
Immigrated <10 yrs	**15.3***	23.8*	27.2*	**6.5***	13.0*	15.4*	**49.6***	66.4*	72.9*

(continued on next page)

(TABLE 2 cont.)

	All Paid Employees (unweighted n=31,983; weighted n=15,574,065)			Full-time Employees (unweighted n=25,722; weighted n=12,439,742)			Part-time Employees (unweighted n=5,421; weighted n=2,718,821)		
	% who do not meet 420 hrs threshold	% who do not meet 700 hrs threshold	% who do not meet 910 hrs threshold	% who do not meet 420 hrs threshold	% who do not meet 700 hrs threshold	% who do not meet 910 hrs threshold	% who do not meet 420 hrs threshold	% who do not meet 700 hrs threshold	% who do not meet 910 hrs threshold
Overall	9.7	17.0	22.0	4.2	9.1	12.4	35.3	53.1	65.4
Urban/Rural									
Rural	10.8	18.9	24.4	6.2	12.0	15.6	33.9	53.2	67.2
Urban	10.0	18.1	23.2	4.3	9.9	13.0	35.0	53.7	67.4
Metropolis	9.3*	15.9*	20.5*	3.7*	8.1*	11.3*	35.7*	52.6*	63.4*
Sector									
Professional	4.7	9.6	12.7	2.2	5.5	7.6	27.5	45.8	57.0
Sales & Service	13.9	23.2	29.5	4.9	11.0	14.8	36.5	54.3	66.9
Manufacturing & Primary	6.6*	12.7*	16.7*	4.8*	10.1*	13.7*	36.9*	55.4*	66.0*
Certainty									
Permanent	5.9	11.1	15.2	2.4	5.5	8.0	26.9	44.7	57.8
Temporary	27.4*	44.5*	54.0*	16.4*	32.8*	41.3*	50.9*	70.1*	81.6*

* Indicates statisically significant differences between the groups at $p<0.05$

TABLE 3 Entry: Hours per Week and Numbers of Weeks Needed to Qualify for Regular Benefits, by Demographics, 2007**

	All Paid Employees (unweighted n=22,507; weighted n=110,738,653)				Full-time Employees (unweighted n=18,790; weighted n=8,912,159)				Part-time Employees (unweighted n=3,717; weighted n=1,826,495)			
	Avg. weekly hours	# of wks to work 420 hours	# of wks to work 700 hours	# of wks to work 910 hours	*Avg. weekly hours*	# of wks to work 420 hours	# of wks to work 700 hours	# of wks to work 910 hours	*Avg. weekly hours*	# of wks to work 420 hours	# of wks to work 700 hours	# of wks to work 910 hours
Overall	*35.5*	**11.8**	19.7	25.6	*39.3*	**10.7**	17.8	23.1	*17.0*	**24.7**	41.2	53.5
Gender												
Men	*38.4*	**10.9**	18.2	23.7	*40.7*	**10.3**	17.2	22.4	*16.3*	**25.8**	42.9	55.8
Women	*32.6**	**12.9**	21.5	27.9	*37.7**	**11.1**	18.6	24.1	*17.2**	**24.4**	40.7	52.9
Age												
15 to 24	*27.8*	**15.1**	25.2	32.7	*39.2*	**10.7**	17.9	23.2	*15.5*	**27.1**	45.2	58.7
25 to 54	*37.2*	**11.3**	18.8	24.5	*39.4*	**10.7**	17.8	23.1	*18.6*	**22.6**	37.6	48.9
55+	*34.1**	**12.3**	20.5	26.7	*38.9**	**10.8**	18.0	23.4	*16.1**	**26.1**	43.5	56.5
Immigrant Status												
Not an immigrant	*35.1*	**12.0**	19.9	25.9	*39.0*	**10.8**	17.9	23.3	*17.2*	**24.4**	40.7	52.9
Immigrated 10+ yrs	*36.7*	**11.4**	19.1	24.8	*39.2*	**10.7**	17.9	23.2	*17.4*	**24.1**	40.2	52.3
Immigrated <10 yrs	*33.7**	**12.5**	20.8	27.0	*39.0*	**10.8**	17.9	23.3	*15.0**	**28.0**	46.7	60.7

(continued on next page)

(TABLE 3 cont.)

	All Paid Employees (unweighted n=22,507; weighted n=110,738,653)				Full-time Employees (unweighted n=18,790; weighted n=8,912,159)				Part-time Employees (unweighted n=3,717; weighted n=1,826,495)			
	Avg. weekly hours	# of wks to work <u>420 hours</u>	# of wks to work <u>700 hours</u>	# of wks to work <u>910 hours</u>	*Avg. weekly hours*	# of wks to work <u>420 hours</u>	# of wks to work <u>700 hours</u>	# of wks to work <u>910 hours</u>	*Avg. weekly hours*	# of wks to work <u>420 hours</u>	# of wks to work <u>700 hours</u>	# of wks to work <u>910 hours</u>
Overall	*35.5*	**11.8**	19.7	25.6	*39.3*	**10.7**	17.8	23.1	*17.0*	**24.7**	41.2	53.5
Urban/Rural												
Rural	*36.1*	**11.6**	19.4	25.2	*40.2*	**10.4**	17.4	22.6	*16.9*	**24.9**	41.4	53.8
Urban	*35.7*	**11.8**	19.6	25.5	*39.6*	**10.6**	17.7	23.0	*16.9*	**24.9**	41.4	53.8
Metropolis	*35.4**	**11.9**	19.8	25.7	*39.0**	**10.8**	17.9	23.3	*17.1*	**24.6**	40.9	53.2
Sector												
Professional	*36.7*	**11.4**	19.1	24.8	*38.8*	**10.8**	18.0	23.5	*17.4*	**24.1**	40.2	52.3
Sales & Service	*32.4*	**13.0**	21.6	28.1	*38.1*	**11.0**	18.4	23.9	*17.0*	**24.7**	41.2	53.5
Manufacturing & Primary	*40.5**	**10.4**	17.3	22.5	*41.8**	**10.1**	16.7	21.8	*16.8*	**25.0**	41.7	54.2
Certainty												
Permanent	*36.4*	**11.5**	19.2	25.0	*39.4*	**10.7**	17.8	23.1	*18.1*	**23.2**	38.7	50.3
Temporary	*29.5**	**14.2**	23.7	30.8	*39.2*	**10.7**	17.9	23.2	*14.2**	**29.6**	49.3	64.1

** Based on average weekly hours worked in December, excluding those who reported working "irregular" work schedule (14%)
* Indicates statisically significant differences between the groups at $p<0.05$

Qualifying for benefits is particularly difficult for young workers, especially given their overrepresentation in part-time and temporary forms of paid employment (Phipps and MacPhail 2002). Twenty-seven per cent of all young workers (as opposed to 5 per cent and 10 per cent of workers aged 25–54 and 55 or more respectively) have fewer than 420 hours of insurable employment in the reference year (Table 2). In a region with a VER of 420, it would therefore take the average young person 15.1 weeks of insurable employment to qualify for benefits as opposed to 11.3 weeks for the average mid-age worker. Considering workers in part-time employment, in a region with a VER of 420, it would take the average young worker 27.1 weeks to qualify compared to 22.6 weeks for the average middle-aged worker; if these young workers are NEREs, it is unlikely that they would be eligible for EI benefits, as it would take them fully 58.7 weeks to qualify (Table 3). Young workers face unique barriers to entry as they have relatively high shares of part-time but temporary forms of employment and they represent the majority of those falling into the NERE category.[16]

Considering differences by immigration status, 15 per cent of recent immigrants (compared to 9 per cent of non-immigrants) have fewer than 420 hours of insurable employment. Such differences reflect recent immigrants' high levels of participation in part-time permanent employment. Entry requirements for NEREs are also a major hurdle for recent immigrants as they are subject to the 910 hour rule upon arrival to Canada. Consequently, considering all employees, 27 per cent of recent immigrants vs. 21 per cent of non-immigrants do not meet the 910 hours qualifying requirement commonly applied to the former. Similar patterns prevail among full-time employees and differences are even sharper among part-time employees (Table 2). Consequently, it would take the average recent immigrant in part-time employment fully 61 weeks to qualify for benefits under the 910 hour rule in comparison to the still onerous 53 weeks required of the average non-immigrant in the same employment situation (Table 3). Yet recent immigrants that qualify face other hurdles as well: for example, if they are on a closed work permit linking their presence in Canada to holding a particular job, they cannot collect regular EI benefits because they are required to leave the country if they become unemployed.

Finally, turning attention to sector, with the exception of those that are part-time, workers in sales and service are considerably more likely not to meet entry requirements than those in professional and primary industries due to their relatively lower average annual hours. It also takes sales and service workers a greater number of weeks to establish a claim than their counterparts in professional and manufacturing and primary sectors.

A notable overarching finding is that EI's entry requirements disfavour part-time workers. For instance, in urban areas and metropolises, where entry requirements tend to be highest, more than 50 per cent of workers in this group do not meet the 700-hour threshold (Table 2). Also attributable to the hours-system, it is much easier for permanent than for temporary employees to qualify for EI regardless of whether they are full-time or part-time, although the percentage of part-time temporary employees that do not meet the lowest potential entry threshold is exceedingly high at 51 per cent. Insensitivity of regular benefit requirements to the changing nature of employment in this formula contributes to disentitlement of workers falling outside the norm of the full-time permanent job in low-unemployment regions where workers in part-time and temporary forms of employment face high entry requirements.

Maternity and Parental Benefits

The distribution of hours also affects social groups' capacities to fulfill entry requirements for maternity and parental benefits—here, women are at a particular disadvantage.

As Table 4[17] shows, among all employees aged 20–39, 20 per cent of women as opposed to 9 per cent of men fail to meet the prescribed 600-hour threshold; correspondingly, it would take the average EI eligible woman and man 18 and 15 weeks of insurable employment respectively to meet this requirement. This difference is explained by women's large shares of part-time and temporary forms of employment; the average female part-time employee needs 36 weeks to qualify for these benefits and the average female part-time *temporary* employee needs 44 weeks.

Considering sub-groups of women, more than twice the percentage of all female employees aged 20–24 do not qualify for maternity/parental benefits compared to those aged 25–39. On account of their high levels of participation in part-time employment, recent immigrant women find themselves in a parallel situation to young women as a whole (Table 4).

For women in regions of high unemployment, qualifying for maternity/parental benefits can also be more arduous than for regular benefits, as the VER can reduce the hours-threshold for regular benefits to as low as 420 hours (Phipps 2006: 12). It can also be difficult for women who have their children close together, especially those employed on part-time and temporary bases (Townson and Hayes 2007, 31-32). Contributing to a cycle of disqualification, women who fail to meet the 600 hour entry requirement and are compelled to take unsupported leave[18] also often face a double penalty: they are neither entitled to receive EI maternity/parental benefits nor do they receive credit for the hours of insurable employment they accumulate before departing from the labour force. That is, if they take unpaid leaves from employment of a year, the equivalent of the combined duration of EI maternity/parental benefits, they are classified as re-entrants upon re-employment.

Furthermore, under EI's eligibility rules, even women who qualify for and take maternity/parental benefits (i.e., are not deemed NEREs) are required to meet the 420–700-hour entry requirements for regular benefits anew upon their return to the labour force.

TABLE 4 Entry: Proportion of All, Full-time and Part-time Eligible Female Employees Aged 20–39 Living Outside Quebec Who Do Not Meet Minimum Hours Thresholds for Maternity/Parental Benefits and the Average Hours Per Week and Number of Weeks they Need to Qualify, by Demographics, 2007**

				% of Those Who Do Not Meet 600 Hours Threshold			# of Weeks to Work 600 Hours		
	Average weekly hours (all)	*Average weekly hours (full-time)*	*Average weekly hours (part-time)*	% of all employees	% of full-time employees	% of part-time employees	All employees	Full-time employees	Part-time employees
Overall	33.4	38.5	16.6	19.5	10.9	47.4	18.0	15.6	36.1
(Among men)	(39.5)	41.4	17.5	(8.6)	(5.9)	(40.2)	(15.2)	(15.2)	(34.3)
Age									
20 to 24	29.2	38.8	16.1	32.6	21.7	51.2	20.5	20.5	37.3
25 to 39	34.5*	38.4	16.9	14.8*	7.9*	44.7*	17.4	17.4	35.5
Immigrant Status									
Not an immigrant	33.9	38.4	16.7	17.8	9.9	46.9	17.7	17.7	35.9
Immigrated 10+ yrs	35.1	39.4	18.0	19.2	11.0	37.9	17.1	17.1	33.3
Immigrated <10 yrs	30.0*	39.0	14.3*	27.3*	11.7	62.6*	20.0	20.0	42.0

(continued on next page)

(TABLE 4 cont.)

				% of Those Who Do Not Meet 600 Hours Threshold			# of Weeks to Work 600 Hours		
	Average weekly hours (all)	*Average weekly hours (full-time)*	*Average weekly hours (part-time)*	% of all employees	% of full-time employees	% of part-time employees	All employees	Full-time employees	Part-time employees
Overall	33.4	38.5	16.6	19.5	10.9	47.4	18.0	15.6	36.1
Urban/Rural									
Rural	32.7	38.3	17.5	19.6	11.3	45.6	18.3	18.3	34.3
Urban	33.3	38.3	16.7	19.9	11.5	47.6	18.0	18.0	35.9
Metropolis	33.6	38.7	16.5	19.2	10.3	47.5	17.9	17.9	36.4
Sector									
Professional	35.3	38.5	16.7	11.1	5.8	42.1	17.0	17.0	35.9
Sales & Service	31.9	38.1	16.6	23.5	12.8	48.6	18.8	18.8	36.1
Manufacturing & Primary	37.3	40.3*	16.1	19.9*	16.0*	51.6	16.1	16.1	37.3
Certainty									
Permanent	34.2	38.5	17.6	15.1	7.9	43.2	17.5	17.5	34.1
Temporary	28.6*	38.5	13.7*	38.4*	27.8*	62.5*	21.0	21.0	43.8

** Based on average weekly hours worked in December, excluding those who reported working an "irregular" work schedule (14%). Population includes employees only since the participation of the self-employed is voluntary and only became permissible in January 2010.
* Indicates statisically significant differences between the groups at $p<0.05$.

B Adequacy of Coverage

1. Benefits Duration

For regular EI, *duration of benefits*, the third mode of coverage, is set out in a schedule based on hours of insurable employment accumulated and the unemployment rate in the claimant's EI administrative region (Appendix C). The duration of maternity and parental benefits are, in contrast, fixed at 17 and 35 weeks respectively [*EI Act* s. 12(3) (a)-(b)].

Regular Benefits

For those fulfilling qualifying requirements for regular benefits, the means by which benefits duration is calculated resembles that used to determine entry. This aspect of coverage provides for longer benefits periods for the unemployed residing in high, rather than low, unemployment regions on the assumption that it takes the former longer to become re-employed. At the same time, even if eligible and qualified EI recipients reside in low unemployment regions, the duration formula also takes hours of insurable employment accumulated into consideration, providing those with 1,820 hours of insurable employment or more up to 36 weeks of benefits.

Exploring adequacy of coverage via benefits duration, Table 5 depicts the estimated number of weeks of benefits available to eligible employees in regions of less than 6 per cent, 7–8 per cent, and 13–14 per cent unemployment. These three regional types represent (1) comparatively low unemployment areas where the greatest number of hours are required to qualify and benefits of maximum duration are shortest, (2) recession prone areas, where a lower number of hours are required to qualify and longer benefits of maximum duration apply, and (3) very high unemployment areas, where the fewest hours are required to qualify and the longest benefits of maximum duration are available.[19]

Looking through this lens reveals differences in the average duration of entitlements (in weeks) to regular benefits among all eligible and qualified employees; predictably, given EI's aim of providing the most extensive support for the unemployed in high unemployment regions, for all employees the average duration of entitlement to benefits in low unemployment regions is approximately three-quarters that of those in very high unemployment regions (Table 5). Less predictably, in relatively low and recession prone unemployment regions, part-time employees as a whole are entitled to receive, on average, benefits for four months fewer than full-time employees. Permanent employees are also entitled to receive, on average, the maximum duration of benefits available within such regions whereas temporary employees, including those that are full-time, are entitled to receive, on average, benefits of considerably shorter duration. EI's duration formula thus provides for differential income protection to part-time (as opposed to full-time) and temporary (as opposed to permanent) employees.

TABLE 5 Duration: Average Number of Weeks of Entitlement to Benefits for Employees Eligible for Regular Benefits Who Meet Minimum Hours Thresholds in Relatively Low (<6%), Recession Prone (7–8%) and Very High (13–14%) Unemployment Regions, by Demographics, 2007

	All Employees That Meet Minimum Hours Entry Criteria			Full-time Employees That Meet Minimum Hours Entry Criteria			Part-time Employees That Meet Minimum Hours Entry Criteria		
	< 6% UE Average # of weeks (700+)	7–8% UE Average # of weeks (630+)	13–14% UE Average # of weeks (420+)	< 6% UE Average # of weeks (700+)	7–8% UE Average # of weeks (630+)	13–14% UE Average # of weeks (420+)	< 6% UE Average # of weeks (700+)	7–8% UE Average # of weeks (630+)	13–14% UE Average # of weeks (420+)
Overall	35.0	38	45	36	40	45	19	23	33
Gender									
Men	36	40	45	36	40	45	19	22	32
Women	32	35	44	35	38	45	19	23	33
Age									
15 to 24	24	27	37	29	31	39	18	22	31
25 to 54	36	40	45	36	40	45	20	23	36
55+	35	39	45	36	40	45	19	23	33
Immigrant Status									
Not an immigrant	34	38	45	36	40	45	19	23	33
Immigrated 10+ yrs	36	40	45	36	40	45	19	23	34
Immigrated <10 yrs	34	36	45	36	38	45	19	23	33

(continued on next page)

(TABLE 5 cont.)

	All Employees That Meet Minimum Hours Entry Criteria			Full-time Employees That Meet Minimum Hours Entry Criteria			Part-time Employees That Meet Minimum Hours Entry Criteria		
	< 6% UE Average # of weeks (700+)	7–8% UE Average # of weeks (630+)	13–14% UE Average # of weeks (420+)	< 6% UE Average # of weeks (700+)	7–8% UE Average # of weeks (630+)	13–14% UE Average # of weeks (420+)	< 6% UE Average # of weeks (700+)	7–8% UE Average # of weeks (630+)	13–14% UE Average # of weeks (420+)
Overall	35.0	38	45	36	40	45	19	23	33
Urban/Rural									
Rural	34	38	45	36	40	45	19	22	33
Urban	35	38	45	36	40	45	19	22	33
Metropolis	35	38	45	36	40	45	19	23	33
Sector									
Professional	36	40	45	36	40	45	20	23	34
Sales & Service	32	35	44	35	39	45	19	23	33
Manufacturing & Primary	36	40	45	36	40	45	19	23	33
Certainty									
Permanent	36	40	45	36	40	45	19	23	33
Temporary	26	29	38	29	32	39	18	22	31

There are also other noteworthy differences in the duration of entitlement to benefits among social groups *within* the three unemployment regions. For example, in relatively low unemployment regions, young qualified workers tend to have fewer weeks of entitlement to benefits than older qualified workers. Similarly, in recession prone areas, qualified female workers have, on average, a shorter period of entitlement when compared to men.[20]

Maternity and Parental Benefits

Even though the maximum duration of maternity and parental benefits is fixed at 17 and 35 weeks respectively, there remain differences in social groups' (especially women's) capacity to take full advantage of leave periods provided since the distribution of hours also influences benefit levels (see 2. Benefit Levels). Although it is impossible to estimate duration of maternity and parental benefits using the SLID, studies show that financial pressures increase women's probability to return to work early from maternity and/or parental leave (Phipps 2006, 25-26). According to Phipps (2006, 12-13, 25, 40), although benefit entitlements have increased in total for the new mother since 1971, when maternity benefits were introduced, weekly benefits have actually declined since the real value of maximum benefit has dropped along with the benefit rate (which declined from 66.7 per cent to 55 per cent over the years). MacDonald (2009, 260) emphasizes further that the consequences of this development for high-earning mothers should not be overlooked; these mothers' effective weekly replacement rate has also declined given the low level of the MIE.

A distinct gender issue linked to benefits duration relates to rules on combining regular and special benefits—namely, anti-stacking rules.[21] The *EI Act* stipulates that workers qualifying for maternity and parental benefits are entitled to a maximum of 50 weeks duration and a combined maximum of 65 weeks of regular and special benefits [*EI Act* s. 12(3)-(5)], effectively limiting the otherwise maximum duration of (both or either type of) benefits to women as the primary group who take these special benefits.[22] For example, a mother[23] who takes the maximum parental and maternity benefits allowable—50 weeks—and is laid off immediately upon or shortly after return to work [for variations on this theme, see *EI Act*, s. 12(3) (a)-(b)], will not be entitled to any EI benefits as she is required to accumulate 420 to 700 hours to re-qualify [*EI Act* s. 12(6), and Schedule I ("Table of Weeks of Benefit")]. Moreover, despite the increase to maximum combined special benefits from 50 to 65 weeks in 2002 (*EI Act* as amended by Bill C-49, *Budget Implementation Act* 2001), the underlying legislative intent was to "ensure full access to special benefits for *biological mothers who claim sickness benefits [linked to childbirth] prior to or following maternity or parental benefits*" [HRSDC 2009b (under "2002")]. Consequently, the order in which leaves are taken matters such that women (especially new parents) attempting to access sickness benefits not connected directly with maternity/parental leave will face greater hardship.

2. Benefit Levels

Benefit levels are derived based on the same formula for recipients of regular and special EI benefits. They are determined by dividing total claimant earnings in the last 26 weeks (the rate calculation period), ending with the last day of insurable employment, by the greater of the number of weeks worked in the last 26 weeks or what is known as the minimum divisor corresponding to the unemployment rate in the claimant's EI administrative region (see Appendix B). The result is then multiplied by 55 per cent to obtain the level of the weekly benefit [*EI Act* s.14(1)]. This system is, however, superceded in the 25 regions participating in the "Best 14 Weeks Pilot" in which average weekly earnings are based on the 14 weeks worked with the highest earnings.

For workers that qualify, the basic benefit rate is set at 55 per cent of the average insured earnings up to the MIE, an annual figure that remained fixed at $39,000 between 1996 and 2006 but increased to $40,000 in 2007, and stood at $43,200 in 2010. Depending on personal circumstances, a benefit rate could be higher or lower than 55 per cent but the MIE is fixed.[24] For example, low-income recipients with dependant children may be eligible for what is known as the family supplement (*Regulations*, s. 34). Replacing the pre-existing 60 per cent benefit rate for low-income individuals, this supplement provides additional benefits to low-income individuals with dependent children living in a low-income household by increasing the maximum benefit rate that a single individual in that household can receive from 55 per cent to a maximum of 80 per cent.[25]

Due to the minimum divisor and low across-the-board replacement rates, regular and special benefits levels reflect and perpetuate patterns of differentiation and exclusion apparent within other modes of coverage.

Regular Benefits

Among beneficiaries of regular EI, benefit levels reflect income segmentation on the bases of gender, age, immigrant status, size of place of residence, and sector as well as permanent or temporary employment status. As Table 6 shows, considering full-time employees, women's average[26] weekly benefit levels are 88 per cent of men's.[27] These percentages, moreover, hide gender differences in weekly earnings due to the MIE, which caps men's estimated average weekly benefit levels. Among part-time employees, women's estimated average weekly benefit levels are higher than men's, likely due to women's large shares of long-hours of part-time employment. In addition to reflecting the overall wage gap, gendered inequalities in full-time employees' average benefit levels flow from the divisor formula. This formula counts weeks not worked in its averaging process, and thus includes weeks with no or low weekly earnings. Women are further disadvantaged by this formula, given their large shares of not only part-time but certain types of temporary employment, such as casual employment, as well as their vulnerability to the general tendency among employers to provide fewer

TABLE 6 Benefit Levels: Estimated Average Weekly Benefits for Employees Eligible and Qualified* to Receive Regular EI Based on 55% Benefit Rate to a Maximum of $423 (MIE for 2007), by Demographics, 2007

	All Paid Employees (unweighted n=28,559; weighted n=13,810,848)		**Full-time Employees** (unweighted n=24,348; weighted n=11,739,321)		**Part-time Employees** (unweighted n=3,494; weighted n=1,718,251)	
	Median weekly wage ($)	Estimated weekly benefit ($)	*Median weekly wage ($)*	Estimated weekly benefit ($)	*Median weekly wage ($)*	Estimated weekly benefit ($)
Overall	*711.54*	391.35	*788.46*	423.00	*250.00*	137.50
Gender						
Men	*846.15*	423.00	*903.85*	423.00	*212.96*	117.13
Women	*576.92*	317.31	*673.08*	370.19	*269.23*	148.08
Age						
15 to 24	*293.03*	161.17	*384.62*	211.54	*185.71*	102.14
25 to 54	*807.69*	423.00	*846.15*	423.00	*355.77*	195.67
55+	*788.46*	423.00	*865.38*	423.00	*326.92*	179.81
Immigrant Status						
Not an immigrant	*769.23*	423.00	*846.15*	423.00	*260.63*	143.35
Immigrated 10+ yrs	*769.23*	423.00	*826.92*	423.00	*307.69*	169.23
Immigrated <10 yrs	*615.38*	338.46	*673.08*	370.19	*230.77*	126.92

(continued on next page)

(TABLE 6 cont.)

	All Paid Employees (unweighted n=28,559; weighted n=13,810,848)		Full-time Employees (unweighted n=24,348; weighted n=11,739,321)		Part-time Employees (unweighted n=3,494; weighted n=1,718,251)	
	Median weekly wage ($)	Estimated weekly benefit ($)	*Median weekly wage ($)*	Estimated weekly benefit ($)	*Median weekly wage ($)*	Estimated weekly benefit ($)
Overall	*711.54*	391.35	*788.46*	423.00	*250.00*	137.50
Urban/Rural						
Rural	*615.38*	338.46	*673.08*	370.19	*230.77*	126.92
Urban	*673.08*	370.19	*750.00*	412.50	*240.38*	132.21
Metropolis	*767.92*	422.35	*826.92*	423.00	*266.67*	146.67
Sector						
Professional	*1057.69*	423.00	*1105.77*	423.00	*476.66*	262.16
Sales & Service	*528.57*	290.71	*615.38*	338.46	*230.77*	126.92
Manufacturing & Primary	*769.23*	423.00	*788.46*	423.00	*230.77*	126.92
Certainty						
Permanent	*787.23*	423.00	*846.15*	423.00	*269.23*	148.08
Temporary	*402.78*	221.53	*486.87*	267.78	*231.17*	127.14

* Based on median wage and salary income of paid employees who worked 420 hours or more in the reference year.

hours to workers in weeks preceding a layoff (Townson and Hayes 2007, 29; Standing Committee on the Status of Women 2009, 7, 39).

Differences in benefit levels are also pronounced among workers of different ages (Table 6). Here again, considering full-time employees, the average weekly benefit level for mid-age and older workers is $423 (the maximum weekly benefit level) whereas it is $211.54 for those aged 15-24. Similarly, among part-time employees, the average benefit level for young workers is $102.14 compared to $195.67 for the mid-aged and $179.81 for older workers. Still, despite these otherwise higher benefit levels, unemployed workers in the 55 or more age group receive a smaller fraction of earnings accumulated over the years due to the existence of the MIE.

Correspondingly, recent immigrants' average benefit levels are lower than those of non-immigrants. Even among part-time employees, their estimated average weekly benefit levels are 89 per cent of their non-immigrant counterparts (Table 6), and patterns of differentiation persist by size of place of residence, sector, and certainty with regard to regular benefit levels. For all employees, as well as those that are full- and part-time, the estimated average weekly benefit levels of those from rural areas are lower than their urban counterparts, of those in sales and service are lower than or equal to those in professional and manufacturing and primary industries, and of those that are temporary are lower than those that are permanent (Table 6).

Furthermore, despite the intended levelling effect of the family supplement for the limited number of claimants receiving it (7.2 per cent in 2007/2008), differences still prevail among those accessing higher replacement rates through this mechanism (CEIC 2010). As Table 7 illustrates, even among employees in low income families, women's estimated average weekly EI benefits are still lower than men's. Similarly, the estimated average weekly EI benefits of young people living in low-income families are the lowest amongst all age groups, as are those of workers from rural areas in comparison to other places of residence, and sales and service workers when compared to those in other sectors. Only recent immigrants diverge significantly from this pattern. The extent to which the supplement delivers less divergent benefit levels to recipients with low-income is also muted by the fact that it is available to fewer female than male recipients, as well as fewer young, and older than mid-age, recipients since it is family-based. Among eligible and qualified employees, 44 per cent of women have incomes of less than $25,921, the maximum annual income that an eligible and qualified low-income individual's family can earn for this individual to receive the family supplement, but only 8 per cent of those in this situation qualify for the supplement (Table 8). Women form the largest claimant group for the family supplement (Townson and Hayes 2007, 40). But while *individuals* with low earnings in their previous jobs had an independent right to access supplemental benefits under UI, low-income individuals are denied supplemental benefits under EI if they do not support a dependent child and/or if they are not part of a low-income household (Vosko 2002).[28]

TABLE 7 Benefit Levels: Estimated Weekly Benefits for Employees Eligible and Qualified to Receive Regular EI and the Family Supplement Assuming a Maximum Supplement (80%), by Demographics, 2007*

	All Paid Employees (unweighted n=914; weighted n=401,156)		Full-time Employees (unweighted n=696; weighted n=306,578)		Part-time Employees (unweighted n=188; weighted n=79,724)	
	Median weekly wage ($)	Estimated weekly benefit ($)	*Median weekly wage ($)*	Estimated weekly benefit ($)	*Median weekly wage ($)*	Estimated weekly benefit ($)
Overall	*277.78*	222.22	*307.69*	246.15	*200.96*	160.77
Gender						
Men	*309.44*	247.55	*355.73*	284.59	*169.12*	135.30
Women	*259.79*	207.83	*289.06*	231.25	*211.54*	169.23
Age						
15 to 24	*205.26*	164.21	*247.29*	197.83	*159.43*	127.54
25 to 54	*300.50*	240.40	*317.31*	253.85	*231.97*	185.58
55+	*255.02*	204.02	*337.51*	270.01	*176.32*	141.06
Immigrant Status						
Not an immigrant	*288.46*	230.77	*317.37*	253.90	*211.89*	169.52
Immigrated 10+ yrs	*259.62*	207.69	*276.32*	221.05	*200.00*	160.00
Immigrated <10 yrs	*309.35*	247.48	*317.31*	253.85	*221.43*	177.14

(continued on next page)

(TABLE 7 cont.)

	All Paid Employees (unweighted n=914; weighted n=401,156)		**Full-time Employees** (unweighted n=696; weighted n=306,578)		**Part-time Employees** (unweighted n=188; weighted n=79,724)	
	Median weekly wage ($)	Estimated weekly benefit ($)	*Median weekly wage ($)*	Estimated weekly benefit ($)	*Median weekly wage ($)*	Estimated weekly benefit ($)
Overall	*277.78*	222.22	*307.69*	246.15	*200.96*	160.77
Urban/Rural						
Rural	*269.23*	215.38	*298.08*	238.46	*159.60*	127.68
Urban	*277.78*	222.22	*302.08*	241.66	*182.50*	146.00
Metropolis	*288.46*	230.77	*314.11*	251.29	*221.43*	177.14
Sector						
Professional	*326.75*	261.40	*365.38*	292.31	*226.39*	181.11
Sales & Service	*260.42*	208.33	*295.94*	236.75	*200.00*	160.00
Manufacturing & Primary	*316.58*	253.27	*330.36*	264.29	*236.11*	188.89
Certainty						
Permanent	*288.46*	230.77	*316.52*	253.21	*211.54*	169.23
Temporary	*277.78*	222.22	*314.89*	251.91	*201.92*	161.54

* Median wage and salary income of paid employees who worked 420 hours or more in the reference year and who meet the criteria for the family supplement (net family income of $25,921 or less, presence of a child under 18, and receive the CCTB).

The initial consequence of this shift was a dramatic decline in the percentage of female recipients, as well as older workers, receiving higher replacement rates.[29] MacDonald (2009, 258) shows further that while single mothers have benefited from the family supplement introduced under EI, mothers with higher-income spouses have lost eligibility due to this replacement for the low income supplement precursor. So too have older and younger workers without dependent children.[30] Not only does this design element penalize women as the majority of workers with low-income, it is also based on the problematic assumption that resources are shared in households.

Maternity and Parental Benefits

The same tendencies contributing to qualified women's low average weekly regular benefit levels vis-à-vis men's (Table 6) affect their low levels of maternity/parental benefits (i.e., women's lower average weekly earnings compared to men's). Table 9 profiles estimated maternity/ parental benefit levels for women by focusing on those of childbearing age and exploring patterns among women in this age group by immigrant status, size of place of residence, and sector. Among all female employees, estimated weekly benefit levels vary dramatically by age; those for women eligible and qualified for maternity benefits aged 20–24 and 25–39 are $179.81 and $359.62 respectively. Recent immigrant women are also worse off than non-immigrants and female service workers' estimated weekly maternity/ parental benefits are low compared to their professional counterparts.

Examining parental benefit levels among men illustrates further that the low estimated weekly maternity/parental benefit levels for many women aged 20–39 are more than a product of age. Bringing men into the picture reveals that, considering all employees in this age group, women's estimated average weekly maternity/parental benefit levels amount to just 70 per cent of men's, a gap that would be larger without the MIE (Table 10). Amplifying this difference, women are also far more likely to claim maternity/parental benefits than men; while 60 per cent of those who receive regular benefits are men, 94 per cent of those who receive maternity/parental benefits are women (Statistics Canada 2008b). Unlike among women, among men variations in estimated parental benefits based on immigrant status and size of place of residence are effectively flattened by the MIE.

3 Toward a More Inclusive Conception of Labour Market Membership: Alternatives for Expanding EI Coverage

The foregoing analysis has shown how inclusions and exclusions within EI's terms of eligibility, entry requirements, duration, and level of benefits take shape. In the process, it has demonstrated how each of EI's central modes of coverage contribute to a situation in which many women, younger, older, rural, and service workers are under-protected due to their participation norms.

TABLE 8 Benefit Levels: Proportion of Eligible Employees who Meet Minimum Entry Thresholds (420+) and are Low-Income and Proportion of these Low-Income Employees Entitled to the Family Supplement, by Demographics, 2007

	All Paid Employees (unweighted n=20,980; weighted n=14,058,581)		**Full-time Employees** (unweighted n=24,647; weighted n=11,923,169)		**Part-time Employees** (unweighted n=3574; weighted n=1,759,932)	
	% of employees who have low-income (≤ $25,921)	% of low-income employees eligible for Family Supp.	*% of employees who have low-income (≤ $25,921)*	% of low-income employees eligible for Family Supp.	*% of employees who have low-income (≤ $25,921)*	% of low-income employees eligible for Family Supp.
Overall	35.1	8.0	28.1	9.0	79.2	5.5
Gender						
Men	27.4	7.4	22.8	8.2	85.0	4.4
Women	43.5*	8.4*	34.8*	9.6*	76.9*	6.0
Age						
15 to 24	81.9	4.4	74.9	3.9	95.6	4.8
25 to 54	25.5	11.8	21.4	13.2	67.9	7.6
55+	30.4*	1.3*	22.9*	0.8*	70.3*	1.5*
Immigrant Status						
Not an immigrant	32.4	5.3	25.0	6.1	77.7	3.4
Immigrated 10+ yrs	26.4	8.0	20.9	9.2	69.1	4.5
Immigrated <10 yrs	41.3*	11.7*	35.2*	12.3*	73.7*	12.6*

(continued on next page)

(TABLE 8 cont.)

	All Paid Employees (unweighted n=20,980; weighted n=14,058,581)		Full-time Employees (unweighted n=24,647; weighted n=11,923,169)		Part-time Employees (unweighted n=3574; weighted n=1,759,932)	
	% of employees who have low-income (≤ $25,921)	% of low-income employees eligible for Family Supp.	*% of employees who have low-income (≤ $25,921)*	% of low-income employees eligible for Family Supp.	*% of employees who have low-income (≤ $25,921)*	% of low-income employees eligible for Family Supp.
Overall	35.1	8.0	28.1	9.0	79.2	5.5
Urban/Rural						
Rural	43.5	12.4	37.9	13.6	81.7	8.2
Urban	37.5	8.6	30.1	9.6	82.4	6.3
Metropolis	31.7*	6.3*	24.8*	7.2*	76.0*	4.2*
Sector						
Professional	17.4	6.7	14.0	7.9	51.2	4.1
Sales & Service	48.6	7.4	38.5	8.4	84.9	5.7
Manufacturing & Primary	30.4*	10.3*	28.0*	10.6*	88.5*	6.0
Certainty						
Permanent	29.2	8.5	23.0	9.7	77.0	5.9
Temporary	66.8*	8.1	61.6*	8.9	80.2*	5.9

* Indicates a statistically significant difference between the groups at $p<0.05$.

TABLE 9 Benefit Levels: Estimated Weekly Benefit Levels for Female Employees Outside Quebec Eligible and Qualified to Receive Maternity/Parental Benefits Based on 55% Benefit to a Maximum of $423 (MIE for 2007), by Demographics, 2007*

	All Paid Employees (unweighted n=4,681; weighted n=2,248,948)		Full-time Employees (unweighted n=3,835; weighted n=1,808,780)		Part-time Employees (unweighted n=739; weighted n=389,522)	
	Median weekly wage ($)	Estimated weekly benefit ($)	*Median weekly wage ($)*	Estimated weekly benefit ($)	*Median weekly wage ($)*	Estimated weekly benefit ($)
Overall	*538.46*	296.15	*622.06*	342.13	*259.62*	142.79
Age						
20 to 24	*326.92*	179.81	*403.85*	222.12	*228.82*	125.85
25 to 39	*653.85*	359.62	*692.31*	380.77	*346.15*	190.38
Immigrant Status						
Not an immigrant	*647.06*	355.88	*711.54*	391.35	*276.92*	152.31
Immigrated 10+ yrs	*583.33*	320.83	*692.31*	380.77	*259.62*	142.79
Immigrated <10 yrs	*500.00*	275.00	*520.83*	286.46	*230.77*	126.92
Urban/Rural						
Rural	*442.31*	243.27	*500.00*	275.00	*240.38*	132.21
Urban	*500.00*	275.00	*576.48*	317.06	*269.23*	148.08
Metropolis	*615.38*	338.46	*690.01*	379.51	*261.92*	144.06

(continued on next page)

(TABLE 9 cont.)

	All Paid Employees (unweighted n=4,681; weighted n=2,248,948)		Full-time Employees (unweighted n=3,835; weighted n=1,808,780)		Part-time Employees (unweighted n=739; weighted n=389,522)	
	Median weekly wage ($)	Estimated weekly benefit ($)	*Median weekly wage ($)*	Estimated weekly benefit ($)	*Median weekly wage ($)*	Estimated weekly benefit ($)
Overall	*538.46*	296.15	*622.06*	342.13	*259.62*	142.79
Sector						
Professional	*826.92*	423.00	*861.11*	423.00	*336.54*	185.10
Sales & Service	*461.54*	253.85	*538.46*	296.15	*225.10*	140.31
Manufacturing & Primary	*500.00*	275.00	*520.83*	286.46	*225.93*	124.26
Certainty						
Permanent	*612.24*	336.73	*673.08*	370.19	*288.46*	158.65
Temporary	*384.62*	211.54	*440.04*	242.02	*245.09*	134.80

* Women only

**Median wage and salary income of women aged 20–39 living outside Quebec who were paid employees and who worked 600 hours or more in the reference year.

TABLE 10 Benefit Levels: Estimated Weekly Benefit Levels for Male Employees Outside Quebec Eligible and Qualified to Receive Parental Benefits Based on 55 per cent Benefit to a Maximum of $423 (MIE for 2007), by Demographics, 2007

	All Paid Employees (unweighted n=9,703; weighted n=4,483,772)		Full-time Employees (unweighted n=8,474; weighted n=4,180,021)		Part-time Employees (unweighted n=981; weighted n=538,271)	
	Median weekly wage ($)	Estimated weekly benefit ($)	*Median weekly wage ($)*	Estimated weekly benefit ($)	*Median weekly wage ($)*	Estimated weekly benefit ($)
Overall	*769.23*	423.00	*807.69*	423.00	*230.77*	126.92
Age						
20 to 24	*403.85*	222.12	*451.99*	248.60	*199.76*	109.87
25 to 39	*891.30*	423.00	*903.85*	423.00	*280.30*	154.16
Immigrant Status						
Not an immigrant	*769.23*	423.00	*807.69*	423.00	*230.77*	126.92
Immigrated 10+ yrs	*826.92*	423.00	*846.15*	423.00	*240.38*	132.21
Immigrated <10 yrs	*888.89*	423.00	*903.85*	423.00	*376.02*	206.81
Urban/Rural						
Rural	*765.57*	421.06	*788.46*	423.00	*243.87*	134.13
Urban	*750.00*	412.50	*788.46*	423.00	*219.92*	120.96
Metropolis	*788.46*	423.00	*826.92*	423.00	*230.77*	126.92

(continued on next page)

(TABLE 10 cont.)

	All Paid Employees (unweighted n=9,703; weighted n=4,483,772)		Full-time Employees (unweighted n=8,474; weighted n=4,180,021)		Part-time Employees (unweighted n=981; weighted n=538,271)	
	Median weekly wage ($)	Estimated weekly benefit ($)	*Median weekly wage ($)*	Estimated weekly benefit ($)	*Median weekly wage ($)*	Estimated weekly benefit ($)
Overall	*769.23*	423.00	*807.69*	423.00	*230.77*	126.92
Sector						
Professional	*1029.41*	423.00	*1057.69*	423.00	*400.01*	220.01
Sales & Service	*557.69*	306.73	*634.62*	394.04	*221.15*	121.63
Manufacturing & Primary	*788.46*	423.00	*807.69*	423.00	*194.27*	106.85
Certainty						
Permanent	*848.48*	423.00	*884.62*	423.00	*25.00*	137.50
Temporary	*490.70*	269.89	*533.82*	239.60	*224.96*	123.73

*Median wage and salary income of men aged 20–39 living outside Quebec who were paid employees and who worked 600 hours or more in the reference year.

Such findings also reveal the cumulative effects of these modes of coverage on certain groups of workers, especially women, sales and service, and temporary workers as well as recent immigrants—that is, how exclusions from full EI coverage stemming from entry requirements are compounded by rules governing duration and level of benefits. Future research should explore more fully the extent to which EI's modes of coverage results in cumulative disadvantage. In the interim, a number of alternatives for policy redesign could address the mismatch between changing patterns of labour force participation and EI coverage, and thereby expand labour market membership in this domain. Given the realities of the labour market, particularly women's high labour force participation rates, the growth in international migration for employment, industrial restructuring in Canada's regional labour markets, and the complexity of school-to-work and work-to-retirement transitions, there is no principled reason for perpetuating differentiation and exclusion on the bases of gender, immigrant status, age, sector or size of place of residence—nor is there a rationale that form of employment, as it interacts with these axes, should exacerbate the disadvantage documented herein.

Several practical measures would contribute to a more inclusive conception of labour market membership to inform this income security program. Indeed, four policy options for the redesign of EI coverage directed at its different modes offer particular potential for limiting exclusions along these axes. By way of conclusion, the remainder of this discussion describes these alternatives, proceeding serially through the four modes of coverage.

A Getting In

1. Eligibility: (i) Extend eligibility for regular EI to solo self-employed workers and make contributions mandatory

There is a strong argument for extending eligibility to the solo self-employed given the extent to which many resemble eligible paid employees or are misclassified as independent contractors and earn low income, and lack genuine control over their work, especially women, recent immigrants, older and rural workers. The merit of mandatory coverage for the solo self-employed is that it maintains EI as a universal income security program characterized by cross-subsidization. In contrast, a voluntary approach in which a self-employed person can opt in and out of coverage risks undermining the stability of the system; for example, hypothetically, if a self-employed person eligible for special benefits as of 2010 opts in for a period sufficient to gain entry, then takes 50 weeks of parental benefits, and subsequently opts out of coverage, it will take the system decades to recover the loss of premiums. In this way, mandatory coverage responds considerably to critiques concerned with so-called moral hazard as it maintains insurance principles while simultaneously bolstering EI's redistributive function by extending eligibility to a group of workers for whom there is compelling evidence of a need for income security.

This option does not negate concerns about administrative challenges (e.g., defining the problem of unemployment among the self-employed). There are nevertheless models to follow in Canada, where the self-employed are covered under the CPP/QPP and required to make both the employee and employer-sponsored contributions as well as under Fishers' EI described above. There are also models outside of Canada: in Austria, for example, compulsory unemployment insurance coverage was extended in 2007 to freelance contractors on the basis that both of the contracting parties (i.e., the freelancer and the client) each contribute 3 per cent of the latter's gross income to the unemployment insurance fund, which grants the worker eligibility for unemployment benefits upon losing his/her job (Adam 2008; for other examples, see Boadway and Garon, prepared for the Mowat Centre EI Task Force).

Were eligibility extended to the solo self-employed, 10 per cent more of Canada's labour force would gain coverage at this level, for a total eligibility rate of 96 per cent. Considering the minimum and maximum hours' thresholds for entry (i.e., 420 and 700), 78 per cent and 71 per cent of the labour force currently qualify for EI respectively; extending eligibility to the solo self-employed would increase these figures to 86 per cent and 79 per cent.

2. Entry Requirements: (ii) Create a lower uniform entry requirement of 360 hours for regular and maternity and parental benefits, and ensure that usage for the latter does not affect access to full regular benefits

Numerous proposals pertinent to improving EI coverage involve modifications to the hours-system. However, the option of a uniform entry requirement of 360 hours is particularly salient to the preceding findings as it reflects the minimum level of labour force attachment that was required of an eligible employee before EI was introduced (12 weeks) multiplied by the average weekly hours of women and service sector workers (both 30 hours), two groups experiencing high levels of cumulative disadvantage.

Regular Benefits

With regard to regular benefits, the threshold envisioned seeks to eliminate disparities in access to benefits in very high and relatively low unemployment regions, as well as the high entry requirements to which part-time and temporary workers are subject in the latter.

A uniform entry requirement would remove the non-NERE/NERE distinction and its gendered and age-based effects. It would also flatten the VER.

Table 11a depicts the effects of changing the minimum hours-thresholds to 360. The light gray segment of each bar represents eligible employees working 420 or more hours who would qualify under the EI hours-system, the dark grey represents employees working between 360–

Table 11a Entry: Proportion of All Eligible Paid Employees Who Would Meet 360 hour Threshold for Regular Benefits, by Demographics, 2007

All Paid Employees

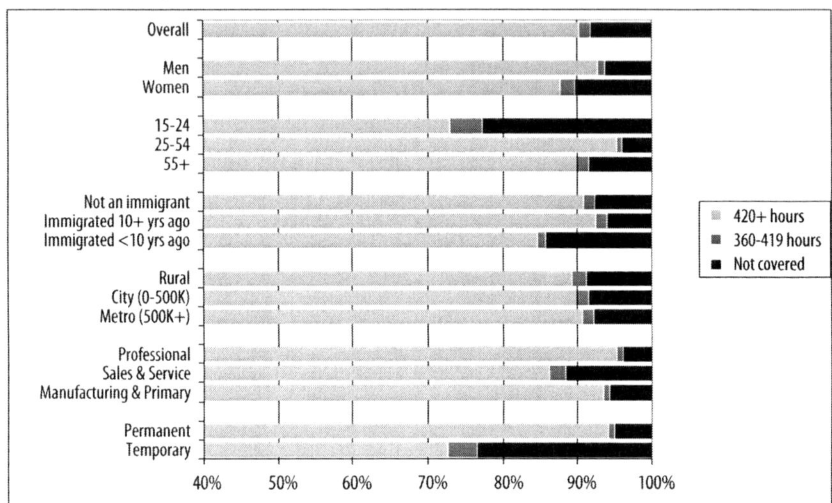

Part-time Employees

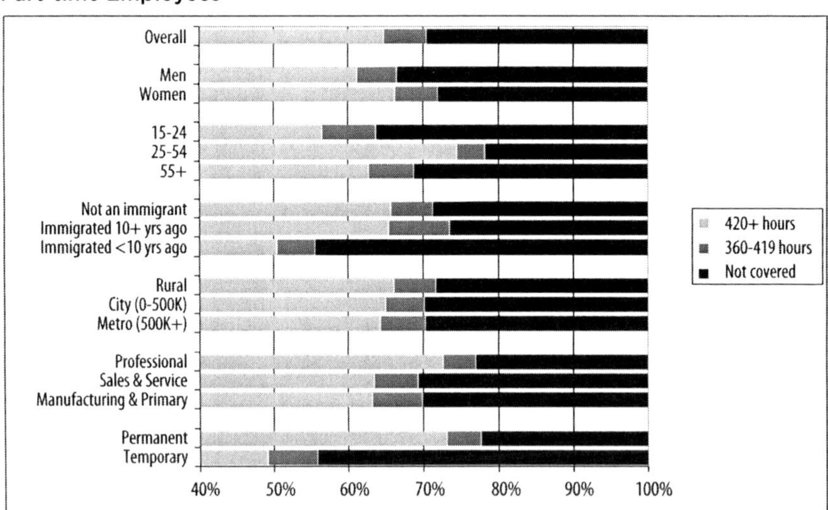

419 hours who would gain entry under a 360 hour threshold, and the black reflects eligible workers who would continue to lack access. Considering employees overall, almost 10 per cent do not meet the 420 hour threshold. This situation is acute among young people, more than a quarter of whom do not meet the current minimum qualifying requirement. With a 360 hour threshold, fully 92 per cent of employees would qualify. Among all employees, lowering the threshold makes the most difference for younger, temporary, sales and service, rural, and female workers respectively.

This policy option would bring the most significant improvements to part-time employees. Overall, only 64 per cent meet the 420 hour threshold—with those that are temporary, recent immigrants, and aged 15–24 least likely to qualify. With a 360 hour threshold, 71 per cent would meet the threshold.

Maternity and Parental Benefits

Modified entry requirements are also required for maternity and parental benefits. The current 600 hours required to secure access is significantly higher than both that required to receive regular benefits in high unemployment regions and the minimum requirements under the previous *UI Act* (the equivalent of 300 hours). It puts these benefits out of reach for those (many women) engaged in part-time and temporary forms of employment. It also limits qualification among women who have their children close together, young people gaining a foothold in the labour market, and recent immigrants with limited employment histories in Canada. A lower entry requirement for special benefits could remedy such inequities (see, for example, Phipps 2006; Cox 2007). Distinct entry requirements for regular and special benefits are also unprincipled: why should a pregnant worker, adoptive parent, or new parent be required to accumulate more hours of insurable employment than an unemployed worker?

Table 11b shows the effects of shifting to a minimum threshold of 360 hours for maternity and parental benefits, for eligible female workers aged 20–39 (outside Quebec). The light gray segment of each bar represents the percentage of eligible employees covered under the current 600 hour threshold, the dark grey represents those working between 360 and 599 hours who would gain entry, and the black segment represents those who would not be covered under this new threshold. Among all employees, lowering the threshold holds the greatest benefit for temporary employees and those who are younger, live in rural areas, or work in sales and service. A 360 hour entry requirement would also improve this mode of coverage markedly for part-time employees. Currently only 65 per cent of part-time employees meet the 600 hour threshold for maternity benefits; with a 360 hour threshold, 70 per cent would qualify.

EI anti-stacking rules mean that a worker who is laid off shortly after returning from maternity or parental leave may not have a sufficient number of new hours of insurable employment for a regular EI claim. The

Table 11b Entry: Proportion of All Eligible Female Employees Aged 20–39 Living Outside Quebec Who Would Meet 360 Hours Threshold for Maternity/Parental Benefits, by Demographics, 2007

All Paid Employees

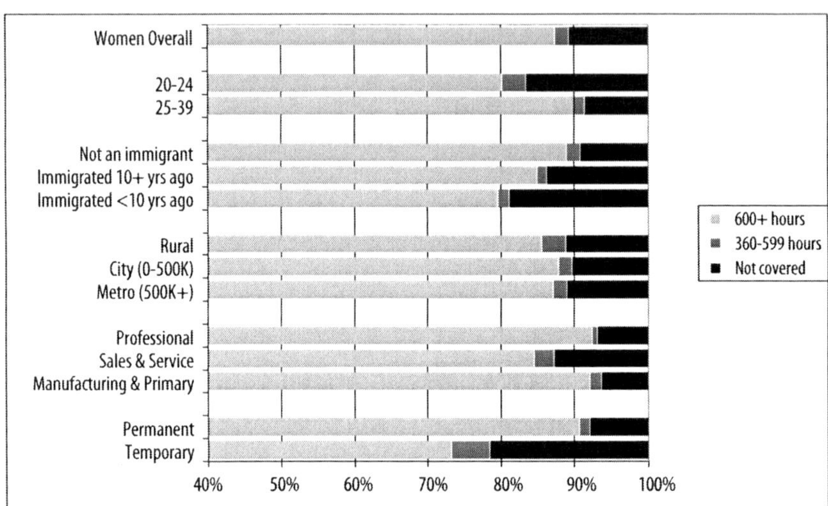

Part-time Employees

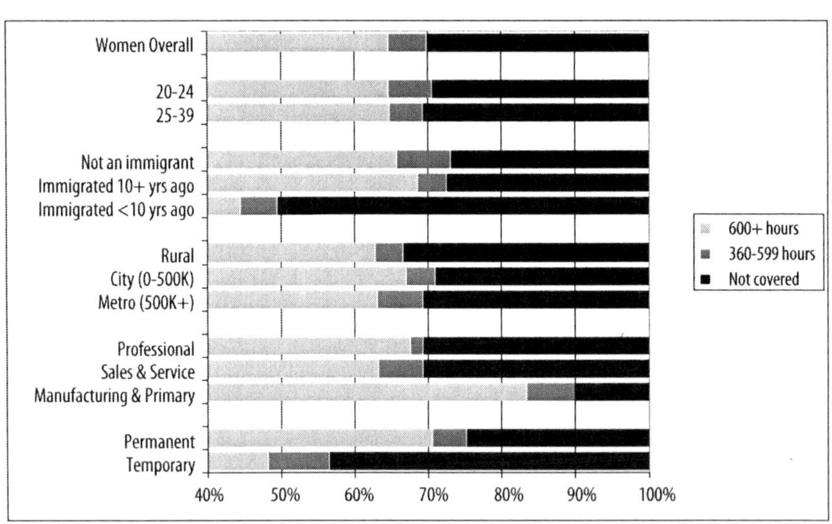

same problem arises in reverse if the layoff occurs just prior to a maternity leave. These rules effectively discriminate against those workers, primarily women, who exercise their legal right to maternity and parental leave. If, in such situations, the hours used to establish a claim for one type of benefit could be used for another type, as is the case with EI Work Sharing benefits, gender inequalities flowing from the current rules would cease.

B Adequacy of Coverage

1. Duration of Benefits: (iii) Weaken the link between the duration of regular EI benefits and regional unemployment rates

There is a need to weaken the link between the duration of benefits and regional unemployment rates by, first, instituting lower thresholds for accessing benefits of maximum duration, and second, by extending the maximum duration and making it equivalent across regions.

Building on the conclusions of the Expert Panel on Older Workers (2008, 60-61), the first aspect of this option responds to the high degree of disparity in maximum duration across the economic regions created by using the unemployment rate to calculate duration of benefits. Under the current EI system, this formula limits weeks of benefit entitlements for eligible and qualified unemployed people with low insurable hours of employment accumulated in relatively low unemployment regions. Flattening the duration schedule would ease this effect. One option entails lowering the threshold for access to benefits of maximum duration. Eligible and qualified employees in very high unemployment regions (13–14 per cent) require 1,575 hours of insurable employment to access benefits of maximum duration (45 weeks) whereas those in relatively low unemployment (less than 6 per cent) and recession prone regions (7–8 per cent) require 1,820 hours (36 and 40 weeks respectively). Were the same maximum weeks duration applicable to workers in very high unemployment regions available to those in relatively low and recession prone unemployment regions (i.e., 1,575 hours for 45 weeks), all eligible and qualified employees would benefit, although those that are younger would benefit most (Appendix A, Table 3; Appendix C).

The second aspect of this policy option emerges from the concern with making duration of benefits more equitable for workers. In response to structural changes in Canada's economy, a more generous weekly maximum of unemployment benefits should also apply regardless of the level of unemployment in the respective regions.

2. Benefit Levels: (iv) Reset the formula for determining benefit levels for all regular and maternity and parental benefits recipients by increasing the standard replacement rate to 67 per cent, raising the MIE, and introducing a flat rate top-up for all low-income earners regardless of family status.

Most proposals related to benefit levels address their inadequacy and the need for a more redistributive model to counterbalance strictly insurance-based principles. Many also call for raising the low-income supplement and making it individually based (e.g., Cox 2007). A promising option addressing these concerns, to apply to all qualified claimants, would raise the replacement rate to 67 per cent to reflect the highest rate applied to individuals starting in 1971 before benefit rates began to decline (Lin 1998, 44), and make it more consistent with replacement rates adopted elsewhere (Osberg 2009); raise the MIE to make the effective replacement rate of a greater number of claimants correspond to it; and provide for a flat-rate top-up to improve conditions of lower-earning beneficiaries (regardless of family status) both independently and vis-à-vis their higher-earning counterparts.

Table 12 depicts the results of this reset formula. It illustrates the option of a 67 per cent replacement rate, plus a flat-rate top-up for low-income earners, to a calculated maximum based on the midpoint of the second federal personal income tax bracket in a four income tax bracket system (to be adjusted annually). This mid-point captures the more than two-thirds of workers in Canada who make $52,767 or less per year.[31] Based on this sum, a weekly maximum insurable amount is calculated by dividing $52,767 by 52 ($1,015). Using this figure and the new replacement rate, the maximum weekly benefit becomes $680.

The flat-rate top-up selected for low-income claimants is $100. This notion is modelled on the top-up introduced in the United States in connection with the 2008/2009 recession, but is designed to be maintained post-recession in place of a separate low-income supplement and to be increased annually to reflect inflation (U.S. Department of Labor 2009). Consistent with the tenor of the family supplement, but raising its ceiling modestly (the current family supplement is capped at 80 per cent of weekly earnings), in no case would a low-income claimant's total weekly benefit exceed 85 per cent of his or her previous weekly earnings. Under the reset formula, claimants earning $626 or less per week (to be adjusted annually for inflation) are eligible for the flat-rate top-up. This threshold is calculated by adjusting the amount of the family supplement set in 1996 for inflation; $25,921 in 1996 is equivalent to $32,554 in 2007 dollars. Dividing this yearly amount by 52 weeks produces this $626 weekly figure.

This model provides support for low and lower waged claimants regardless of their family status, eliminating the need for a separate low-income benefit system. It also solves a fundamental problem produced by the current level of the MIE, specifically, that estimated weekly benefits of many full-time employees are capped by this amount ($423 in 2007), yielding effective replacement rates that are substantially lower than 55 per cent (Table 6). Under the proposed formula, professionals are the only group where the majority of workers would be in this situation (Table 12). Another benefit of the formula is that it helps reduce the extreme inequalities experienced by certain social groups; for example, the average recent immigrant would receive a weekly benefit of a level similar to those

TABLE 12 Benefit Levels: Estimated Average Weekly Benefits for Employees Eligible and Qualified to Receive Regular EI Based on 67% Replacement Rate Plus Top-up to a Maximum of $680, 2007*

	All Paid Employees (unweighted n=28,559; weighted n=13,810,848)			**Full-time Employees** (unweighted n=24,348; weighted n=11,739,321)			**Part-time Employees** (unweighted n=3,494; weighted n=1,718,251)		
	Median weekly wage ($)	Estimated weekly benefit ($)	Effective replacement rate	*Median weekly wage ($)*	Estimated weekly benefit ($)	Effective replacement rate	*Median weekly wage ($)*	Estimated weekly benefit ($)	Effective replacement rate
Overall	*711.54*	476.73	67.0	*788.46*	528.27	67.0	*250.00*	212.50	85.0
Gender									
Men	*846.15*	566.92	67.0	*903.85*	605.58	67.0	*212.96*	181.02	85.0
Women	*576.92*	486.54	84.3	*673.08*	450.96	67.0	*269.23*	228.85	85.0
Age									
15 to 24	*293.03*	249.08	85.0	*384.62*	326.93	85.0	*185.71*	157.85	85.0
25 to 54	*807.69*	541.15	67.0	*846.15*	566.92	67.0	*355.77*	302.40	85.0
55+	*788.46*	528.27	67.0	*865.38*	579.80	67.0	*326.92*	277.88	85.0
Immigrant Status									
Not an immigrant	*769.23*	515.38	67.0	*846.15*	566.92	67.0	*260.63*	221.54	85.0
Immigrated 10+ yrs	*769.23*	515.38	67.0	*826.92*	554.04	67.0	*307.69*	261.54	85.0
Immigrated <10 yrs	*615.38*	512.30	83.3	*673.08*	450.96	67.0	*230.77*	196.15	85.0

(continued on next page)

(TABLE 12 cont.)

	All Paid Employees (unweighted n=28,559; weighted n=13,810,848)			**Full-time Employees** (unweighted n=24,348; weighted n=11,739,321)			**Part-time Employees** (unweighted n=3,494; weighted n=1,718,251)		
	Median weekly wage ($)	Estimated weekly benefit ($)	Effective replacement rate	*Median weekly wage ($)*	Estimated weekly benefit ($)	Effective replacement rate	*Median weekly wage ($)*	Estimated weekly benefit ($)	Effective replacement rate
Overall	*711.54*	476.73	67.0	*788.46*	528.27	67.0	*250.00*	212.50	85.0
Urban/Rural									
Rural	*615.38*	512.30	83.3	*673.08*	450.96	67.0	*230.77*	196.15	85.0
Urban	*673.08*	450.96	67.0	*750.00*	502.50	67.0	*240.38*	204.32	85.0
Metropolis	*767.92*	514.51	67.0	*826.92*	554.04	67.0	*266.67*	226.67	85.0
Sector									
Professional	*1057.69*	680.00	64.3	*1105.77*	680.00	61.5	*476.66*	405.16	85.0
Sales & Service	*528.57*	449.28	85.0	*615.38*	523.07	85.0	*230.77*	196.15	85.0
Manufacturing & Primary	*769.23*	515.38	67.0	*788.46*	528.27	67.0	*230.77*	196.15	85.0
Certainty									
Permanent	*787.23*	527.44	67.0	*846.15*	566.92	67.0	*269.23*	228.85	85.0
Temporary	*402.78*	342.36	85.0	*486.87*	413.84	85.0	*231.17*	196.49	85.0

*Based on median weekly wage and salary income of paid employees who worked 420 hours or more in the reference year.

of his or her immigrant- and Canadian-born counterparts since his or her lower weekly earnings would result in being eligible for a top-up. Still, even though each of the components of this reset formula are principled (i.e., based on an inclusive conception of labour market membership), the formula cannot remedy all inequalities characterizing this mode of coverage since the MIE, as it is currently designed, reduces inequality in benefit levels due to its low level; hence, raising it generates greater inequality in some cases.[32] A final merit of the reset formula is that its top-up does not distinguish between full- and part-time employees, focusing instead on income as the criterion for receipt.[33]

To augment these merits, a best 14 weeks system could also be integrated into this model, meaning that the weekly wage figures in Table 12 would be derived using 14 rather than 52 weeks. This adaptation would address the situation of workers accumulating low weekly hours of insurable employment just prior to a layoff and those in highly variable forms of temporary employment (e.g., casual employment), and respond to how the divisor rule disadvantages workers in temporary or part-time employment just meeting the minimum hours-thresholds in relatively low unemployment regions (i.e., those who are faced with the highest divisor).

This policy option for determining benefit levels works to expand labour market membership by limiting inequalities in benefit levels through redistribution across social groups shown to be excluded from full EI coverage.

Appendix A

Background Statistical Tables

TABLE 1 Eligibility: Demographic Distribution of Paid Employees, the Solo Self-Employed, and the Low-Income Solo-Self Employed, 2007

	Paid Employees (unweighted n=31,983; weighted n=15,574,065)	Solo Self-Employed (unweighted n=2,934; weighted n=1,773,683)	Low-Income* Solo Self-Employed (unweighted n=1,432; weighted n=85,312)
Gender			
Men	51.1%	59.5%	53.2%
Women	48.9%	40.5%	46.8%
Age			
15 to 24	19.6%	3.8%	6.2%
25 to 54	68.4%	69.8%	66.4%
55+	11.9%	26.4%	27.4%
Immigrant Status			
Not an immigrant	72.3%	64.2%	58.4%
Immigrated 10+ yrs	20.5%	27.7%	31.6%
Immigrated <10 yrs	7.2%	8.0%	9.9%
Urban/Rural			
Rural	9.0%	11.8%	13.6%
Urban	39.8%	36.2%	37.0%
Metropolis	51.2%	51.9%	49.4%
Sector			
Professional	27.7%	31.9%	27.3%
Sales & Service	49.6%	37.1%	42.7%
Manufacturing & Primary	22.7%	31.1%	30.0%
Certainty			
Permanent	82.1%	73.1%	65.3%
Temporary	17.9%	26.9%	34.7%

* Low income refers to annual earnings of $20,000 or less (half of the 2007 maximum insurable earnings (MIE).

TABLE 2 Entry: Typology of Mutually Exclusive Employment Forms, by Demographic Groups, Canada, 2007*

		Regular EI Premium Payers					
	Total Labour Force**	Full-time Permanent Employees	Part-time Permanent Employees	Full-time Temporary Employees	Part-time Temporary Employees	Self-Employed Solo	Self-Employed Employers
Overall	15,183,707	60.6%	10.1%	10.3%	4.5%	9.4%	5.1%
Gender							
Men	7,993,749	63.1%	4.8%	11.1%	3.1%	10.7%	7.2%
Women	7,189,958	57.9%	15.6%	9.4%	6.0%	8.1%	3.0%
Age							
15 to 24	2,388,981	39.0%	23.7%	21.4%	13.2%	2.5%	0.3%
25 to 54	10,531,226	69.1%	6.6%	7.8%	2.0%	9.3%	5.2%
55+	2,263,500	50.4%	9.3%	8.5%	5.2%	16.8%	9.7%
Immigrant Status							
Not an immigrant	5,494,948	63.7%	10.3%	8.6%	4.7%	8.9%	3.8%
Immigrated 10+ yrs	1,591,196	63.0%	7.3%	5.3%	2.8%	13.7%	7.7%
Immigrated <10 yrs	516,143	56.9%	14.2%	8.4%	4.9%	11.6%	4.0%

(continued on next page)

(TABLE 2 cont.)

		Regular EI Premium Payers					
	Total Labour Force**	Full-time Permanent Employees	Part-time Permanent Employees	Full-time Temporary Employees	Part-time Temporary Employees	Self-Employed Solo	Self-Employed Employers
Overall	15,183,707	60.6%	10.1%	10.3%	4.5%	9.4%	5.1%
Urban/Rural							
Rural	1,487,440	51.1%	8.5%	15.9%	4.5%	12.9%	7.2%
Urban	6,093,979	62.1%	10.5%	9.7%	4.5%	8.3%	4.9%
Metropolis	7,602,288	63.3%	10.0%	8.0%	4.4%	9.8%	4.5%
Sector							
Professional	4,376,069	65.5%	4.6%	7.5%	3.4%	10.0%	9.0%
Sales & Service	6,810,386	58.0%	18.0%	8.2%	6.7%	7.2%	1.9%
Manufacturing & Primary	3,560,322	61.2%	2.5%	15.5%	1.6%	12.9%	6.2%

Applies to regular benefits
**Excludes unpaid family workers
These numbers are underestimates because figures omit missing data (i.e., people who did not report whether their job was full- or part-time).

TABLE 3 Duration: Average Annual Hours in Main Job for Eligible Employees Who Meet Minimum Hours Thresholds in Relatively Low (<6%), Recession Prone (7–8%) and Very High (13–14%) Unemployment Regions, by Demographics, 2007

	All Employees That Meet Minimum Hours Entry Criteria			Full-time Employees That Meet Minimum Hours Entry Criteria			Part-time Employees That Meet Minimum Hours Entry Criteria		
	< 6% UE Average # of weeks (700+)	7–8% UE Average # of weeks (630+)	13–14% UE Average # of weeks (420+)	< 6% UE Average # of weeks (700+)	7–8% UE Average # of weeks (630+)	13–14% UE Average # of weeks (420+)	< 6% UE Average # of weeks (700+)	7–8% UE Average # of weeks (630+)	13–14% UE Average # of weeks (420+)
Overall	1795	1773	1695	1879	1860	1811	1087	1065	939
Gender									
Men	1890	1871	1804	1937	1921	1875	1052	1020	882
Women	1685*	1661*	1574*	1804*	1782*	1728*	1099*	1080*	961*
Age									
15 to 24	1424	1368	1191	1592	1521	1372	1009	983	826
25 to 54	1855	1842	1799	1912	1901	1872	1133	1113	1023
55+	1805*	1794*	1734*	1907*	1860*	1868*	1097*	1081*	976*
Immigrant Status									
Not an immigrant	1784	1766	1690	1867	1852	1807	1101	1083	950
Immigrated 10+ yrs	1854	1831	1784	1923	1907	1877	1113	1087	1002
Immigrated <10 yrs	1751*	1713*	1634*	1821*	1783*	1735*	1078	1052	910*

(continued on next page)

(TABLE 3 cont.)

	All Employees That Meet Minimum Hours Entry Criteria			Full-time Employees That Meet Minimum Hours Entry Criteria			Part-time Employees That Meet Minimum Hours Entry Criteria		
	< 6% UE Average # of weeks (700+)	7–8% UE Average # of weeks (630+)	13–14% UE Average # of weeks (420+)	< 6% UE Average # of weeks (700+)	7–8% UE Average # of weeks (630+)	13–14% UE Average # of weeks (420+)	< 6% UE Average # of weeks (700+)	7–8% UE Average # of weeks (630+)	13–14% UE Average # of weeks (420+)
Overall	1795	1773	1695	1879	1860	1811	1087	1065	939
Urban/Rural									
Rural	1784	1758	1674	1868	1847	1788	1069	1039	920
Urban	1795	1771	1685	1884	1864	1807	1072	1049	923
Metropolis	1797	1777	1706*	1876	1859	1817*	1102*	1082*	956*
Sector									
Professional	1854	1839	1787	1905	1893	1860	1134	1107	988
Sales & Service	1686	1661	1564	1813	1792	1734	1076	1053	929
Manufacturing & Primary	1917*	1894*	1829*	1944*	1921*	1867*	1081*	1070*	921*
Certainty									
Permanent	1836	1820	1765	1911	1899	1869	1104	1084	969
Temporary	1494*	1438*	1274*	1601	1541	1398*	1020*	987*	836*

* Indicates statistically significant differences between the groups at $p<0.05$.

Appendix B

Variable Entrance Requirement

Unemployment Rate in EI Region	Required Number of Hours of Insurable Emploment in the Qualifying Period
6.0% and Under	700
Over 6.0% to 7.0%	665
Over 7.0% to 8.0%	630
Over 8.0% to 9.0%	595
Over 9.0% to 10.0%	560
Over 10.0% to 11.0%	525
Over 11.0% to 12.0%	490
Over 12.0% to 13.0%	455
Over 13.0%	420

Source: *EI Act* s. 7(2)

Appendix C Weeks Payable of Employment Insurance Regular Benefits

# of hours of insurable employment in qualifying period	6% and under	More than 6% but not more than 7%	More than 7% but not more than 8%	More than 8% but not more than 9%	More than 9% but not more than 10%	More than 10% but not more than 11%	More than 11% but not more than 12%	More than 12% but not more than 13%	More than 13% but not more than 14%	More than 14% but not more than 15%	More than 15% but not more than 16%	More than 16%
420–454									26	28	30	32
455–489								24	26	28	30	32
490–524							23	25	27	29	31	33
525–559						21	23	25	27	29	31	33
560–594					20	22	24	26	28	30	32	34
595–629				18	20	22	24	26	28	30	32	34
630–664			17	19	21	23	25	27	29	31	33	35
665–699		15	17	19	21	23	25	27	29	31	33	35
700-734	14	16	18	20	22	24	26	28	30	32	34	36
735–769	14	16	18	20	22	24	26	28	30	32	34	36
770–804	15	17	19	21	23	25	27	29	31	33	35	37
805–839	15	17	19	21	23	25	27	29	31	33	35	37
840–874	16	18	20	22	24	26	28	30	32	34	36	38
875–909	16	18	20	22	24	26	28	30	32	34	36	38
910–944	17	19	21	23	25	27	29	31	33	35	37	39
645–979	17	19	21	23	25	27	29	31	33	35	37	39
980–1014	18	20	22	24	26	28	30	32	34	36	38	40
1015–1049	18	20	22	24	26	28	30	32	34	36	38	40
1050–1084	19	21	23	25	27	29	31	33	35	37	39	41
1085–1119	19	21	23	25	27	29	31	33	35	37	39	41
1120–1154	20	22	24	26	28	30	32	34	36	38	40	42

(APPENDIX C cont.)

# of hours of insurable employment in qualifying period	6% and under	More than 6% but not more than 7%	More than 7% but not more than 8%	More than 8% but not more than 9%	More than 9% but not more than 10%	More than 10% but not more than 11%	More than 11% but not more than 12%	More than 12% but not more than 13%	More than 13% but not more than 14%	More than 14% but not more than 15%	More than 15% but not more than 16%	More than 16%
1155–1189	20	22	24	26	28	30	32	34	36	38	40	42
1190–1224	21	23	25	27	29	31	33	35	37	39	41	43
1225–1259	21	23	25	27	29	31	33	35	37	39	41	43
1260–1294	22	24	26	28	30	32	34	36	38	40	42	44
1295–1329	22	24	26	28	30	32	34	36	38	40	42	44
1330–1364	23	25	27	29	31	33	35	37	39	41	43	45
1365–1399	23	25	27	29	31	33	35	37	39	41	43	45
1400–1434	24	26	28	30	32	34	36	38	40	42	44	45
1435–1469	25	27	29	31	33	35	37	39	41	43	45	45
1470–1504	26	28	30	32	34	36	38	40	42	44	45	45
1505–1539	27	29	31	33	35	37	39	41	43	45	45	45
1540–1574	28	30	32	34	36	38	40	42	44	45	45	45
1575–1609	29	31	33	35	37	39	41	43	45	45	45	45
1610–1644	30	32	34	36	38	40	42	44	45	45	45	45
1645–1679	31	33	35	37	39	41	43	45	45	45	45	45
1680–1714	32	34	36	38	40	42	44	45	45	45	45	45
1715–1749	33	35	37	39	41	43	45	45	45	45	45	45
1750–1784	34	36	38	40	42	44	45	45	45	45	45	45
1785–1819	35	37	39	41	43	45	45	45	45	45	45	45
1820–	36	38	40	42	44	45	45	45	45	45	45	45

Source: *EI Act* SCHEDULE 1 [*Subsection 12(2)*]

Appendix D

Minimim Divisor Formula for Determining Regular Benefit Rates*

Unemployment Rate in EI Region	Required Number of Hours of Insurable Emploment in the Qualifying Period
6.0% and Under	22
Over 6.0% to 7.0%	21
Over 7.0% to 8.0%	20
Over 8.0% to 9.0%	19
Over 9.0% to 10.0%	18
Over 10.0% to 11.0%	17
Over 11.0% to 12.0%	16
Over 12.0% to 13.0%	15
Over 13.0%	14

*This formula also applies to self-employed fishers
Source: *EI Act s. 14[2(b)]*

Endnotes

1 Although its findings are the responsibility of the author, this study benefited from the expertise of Andrea Noack, who meticulously prepared the data tables required for the statistical portrait, comments from three policy practitioners, Keith Banting, and Barbara Cameron, the research assistance of Laurel Berkowitz, John Grundy, and Anastasia Mandziuk, and the financial support of the SSHRC under its standards grants program.

2 Although there may be financial implications for some options introduced to address this mismatch, which could be borne by a variety of actors and institutions (workers, employers, the federal government etc.), estimating their size is beyond the scope of this inquiry.

3 This is not to deny the lingering tendency to assume that workers holding certain employment statuses and/or forms of employment have particular personal characteristics.

4 Unless otherwise noted, the data source is Statistics Canada's Survey of Labour and Income Dynamics (SLID) and the reference point is respondents' main job in the year 2007 (Statistics Canada 2009). Representing the closest proxy to EI's 52 week qualifying period, this reference year is also used in policy Appendices C and D.

5 To ease regional industrial divisions, in 1957 the government began to collect EI premiums from self-employed fishers (excluding the wives of fishermen working on their boats until 1981), creating a distinct regime for access to income security among this group. Fishers' EI provides a maximum of 26 weeks of benefits, whose levels are determined based on earnings divided by a divisor varying with the regional unemployment rate (Appendix D).

6 The *EI Act* also makes certain clarifications to ensure that workers in potentially gray areas are eligible for EI, such as hairdressers who are not owner-operators of establishments and taxi drivers, commercial bus, school bus and other vehicle drivers. See Regulations s. 6 (d)-(e).

7 The SLID public use micro-data file allows for distinguishing between the experience of recent immigrants (immigrants residing in Canada for less than 10 years), non-recent immigrants (immigrants residing in Canada for 10 or more years), and non-immigrants. In it, however, immigrant status is suppressed for those living outside of major urban areas in order to protect confidentiality, and thus results for this axis can only be generalized to immigrants living in cities with 500,000 or more residents.

8 The prevalence of being solo self-employed also increases with age: 2 per cent of all workers 15–24 years of age were solo self-employed, compared to 7 per cent of those aged 25–34, 11 per cent of those aged 35–54, and fully 18 per cent of those aged 55 or more.

9 In this analysis, annual employment income is measured as the sum of wage/salary and self-employment income (not including those who reported a self-employment loss) in 2007. This combined measure is used because self-employed entrepreneurs can report their self-employment earnings as either wage or salary income or as self-employment income depending on the size and organization of their business.

10 The MIE is the highest level of earnings upon which eligible and qualified recipients can draw regular and special benefits even if their earnings exceed it. [Unemploment Insurance Act, S.C. 1971, c 48 ["*UI Act*"] s. 13 (1(b)(i)].

11 In this analysis, the size of workers' area of residence is used as a measure of the rural/urban distinction. This measure encompasses three groups: those living in metropolitan areas (with 500,000 or more residents), those living in urban areas (with less than 50,000 residents), and those living in rural areas.

12 This analysis of industry is based on grouping workers into three categories derived from the NOC 2006 classifications: professionals, sales and service, and manufacturing and primary industries. Roughly, professionals include those working in management, finance, natural and applied sciences, social sciences and government, and teachers and professors. Sales and service includes those working in clerical and technical positions, wholesale and real estate sales, retail sales, chefs and cooks, protective services, and child care and home support. Manufacturing and primary industries refer to those working in construction, trades, transportation, processing and manufacturing and other primary industry occupations.

13 Henceforth, the terms "workers" and "employees" are used interchangeably given that the empirical focus shifts to paid employees in analyzing entry requirements.

14 To qualify for regular benefits under UI, non-NERES needed the equivalent of 180 to 300 hours of insurable employment, depending on their regional rate of unemployment whereas NEREs need the equivalent of 300 hours (a minimum of 15 hours weekly for at least 20 weeks) *UI Act* s. 6(2)-(3).

15 In the SLID 2007, employees are asked how many hours they worked at their main job in the reference year. These hours are treated as an indicator of hours of insurable employment. Respondents are also asked how many hours they worked per week, on average, in December, and whether their schedule was regular. This analysis is thus based on the average weekly hours worked in December for paid employees with regular schedules.

16 Although this analysis groups together salaried and hourly workers because of data limitations, the vast majority of EI claimants are hourly workers whose average weekly hours are lower than their salaried counterparts. The inclusion of salaried workers may therefore skew weekly hours upwards.

17 Young people face additional obstacles if they sever an employment relationship to return to school as this reason makes otherwise qualified workers ineligible for benefits since s.29(c) of the *EI Act* does not include quitting a job to study as just cause for voluntary termination of employment.

18 In 2007, young workers made up 85 per cent of those who stopped working at their job in order to go to school (Statistics Canada 2008b).

19 Table 4 (as well as Tables 9 and 10) includes employees aged 20–39 living outside Quebec. This age group is selected since, in 2007, 3 per cent of live births were from mothers in this age group (Statistics Canada 2007). The self-employed are excluded since their participation in EI's maternity/parental program is voluntary. Workers from Quebec are excluded since Quebec operates its own maternity and parental benefits regime.

20 The *EI Act* deems that "just cause" for voluntarily leaving employment exists only where claimants have "no reasonable alternative to leaving" [s. 29(b)-(c)], a provision constructed narrowly by interpretation. For example, the Federal Court of Appeal has found that "personal reasons" do not establish just cause for leaving employment, and that "reasonableness" in leaving may constitute "good cause" but not "just cause" [Office of the Umpire 2009: (c) The meaning of "Just Cause", and (d) The test for just cause). More specifically, s. 29 (c(v)], Obligation to Care for a Child or a Member of the Immediate Family, provides just cause for leaving employment only under narrowly specified circumstances; s. 6.4.1 of the Digest of Entitlement Principles states that care must be "required", and alternative care-giving arrangements allowing for the retention of employment must be exhausted (Service Canada 2010).

21 These benefits durations are based on the average annual hours in the main jobs of eligible employees meeting the minimum hours-thresholds in the three regions (Appendix A, Table 3).

22 Consistent with these trends, administrative data from the Canada Employment Insurance Commission's (CEIC) Monitoring and Assessment Report 2009 (2010, 82) indicate that exhaustion rates are higher for women than for men across-the-board, "due to the fact that women, on average, are entitled to fewer weeks of regular benefits [than men]... since women generally have fewer hours of insurable employment."

23 This term is drawn from Townson (2009, 27), who labels these provisions as such since they determine the combined maximum duration for which benefits can be consecutively received (i.e., "stacked").

24 Before the extension of parental benefits to 35 weeks, the Canadian Human Rights Tribunal found that these rules (then amounting to a 30-week cap on combined maternity and parental benefits) had a discriminatory effect on women (McAllister-Windsor v. Canada 2001).

25 Between 2000 and 2001, when the federal government extended parental benefits to 35 weeks, the percentage of fathers claiming them rose from 3 per cent to 10 per cent. Shortly thereafter, there was also a significant rise in fathers claiming parental leave (to 15 per cent in 2005 and 20 per cent in 2006) (Marshall 2008, 8); however, this most recent trend flows from the introduction of the Quebec Parental Insurance Plan (QPIP), which offers more flexible and more generous leaves, as well as special incentives for fathers, than those applied under EI in the rest of Canada (e.g., 3–5 weeks of benefits are reserved exclusively for fathers).

26 In 2007, average weekly insurable earnings could not exceed $769.00.

27 To qualify, claimants must have at least one dependent child, have received the Child Tax Benefit for the month prior to the Sunday of the week in which they make a claim for benefits, and have a net family income of $25,921 or less. This last threshold has remained static since the introduction of EI. Consequently, "with the exception of 2002/03, the proportion of EI claimants receiving the Family Supplement top-up has been declining consistently since 1999/2000, reaching 5.9 per cent in 2008/09"(CEIC 2010, 81).

28 In calculating the measure of central tendency, the median is used instead of the arithmetic average. Because of some extreme income values (both high

and low), the average is not a valid measure of the centre of each distribution; specifically, the average skews the dollar amount upwards as it includes the small numbers of self-employed people and employees who report very high income and earnings respectively. For clarity's sake, therefore, the term "average" refers to the median.

29 In 2007/2008, the actual average weekly average benefit among all regular EI recipients was $345 (CEIC 2009). Although the time periods do not overlap perfectly (i.e., the reference year for the actual weekly average is the fiscal year and that for Table 6 is 2007), the reason for the discrepancy between this figure and the estimates in Table 6 is the higher number of previously low-wage workers in the unemployed population than the employed population surveyed through the SLID 2007.

30 Three-quarters of low-income paid employees who meet a 420 hour entry threshold living in low-income households are not eligible for the supplement because they do not have a dependent child and two-thirds of low-income paid employees who meet a 420 hours entry threshold are not eligible because they do not live in a low-income household.

31 In the transition from UI to EI between 1995/1996 and 1997/1998, the percentage of women receiving a low income supplement declined by 21 per cent and the percentage of older workers declined by 43 per cent (CEIC 2000, 21.4).

32 The higher percentage of low-income, female, part-time employees eligible for the family supplement depicted in Table 8 is attributable to the large percentage of young people, including many young men, without children employed on a part-time basis (Appendix A, Table 2).

33 For 82 per cent of Canadians, the major source of reported income is derived from wages and salaries.

34 For example, although women in the full-time category, on average, receive higher weekly benefits under this reset formula, it does not improve their standing vis-à-vis men (comparing Table 6 and Table 12). This problem is, however, a product of pay inequities (vertical and horizontal) that could be corrected by efforts to narrow the gender pay gap rather than the reset formula itself.

35 A further problem common to any system providing supplementary benefits based on a threshold is the potential for those with earnings just below the threshold to receive higher benefits than those with earnings just above it; in this instance, this problem is manifest in the situation of those in the rural versus urban category (Table 12).

36 However, in effect, part-time employees are to receive a higher replacement rate due to their relatively low income.

References

Adam, G. 2008. "Freelance Contractors to Get Social Security Cover." European Industrial Relations Observatory. At http://www.eurofound.europa.eu/eiro/2007/12/articles/at0712029i.htm (accessed 2 January 2011).

Bakvis, H. 2002. "Checkerboard Federalism? Labour Market Development Policy." In Canadian Federalism: Performance, Effectiveness and Legitimacy, ed. H. Bakvis and G. Skogstad, 159-203. Toronto: Oxford University Press.

Battle, K., M. Mendelson, and S. Torjman. 2005. "The Modernization Mantra: Toward a New Architecture for Canada's Adult Benefits." Canadian Public Policy 31.4: 431-38.

——. June 2006. "Towards a New Architecture for Canada's Adult Benefits." Ottawa: Caledon Institute of Social Policy.

Canada Employment Insurance Commission (CEIC). 2000. "Monitoring and Assessment Report 1999: Employment Insurance." Gatineau, Quebec: Publications Services, Human Resources Development Canada. At http://dsp-psd.pwgsc.gc.ca/Collection/MP43-192-1-2000E.pdf.

——. 2007 "Submission by the Canadian Labour Congress to Expert Panel on Older Workers on Employment Insurance and Displaced Older Workers." At http://www.canadianlabour.ca/news-room/editorial/submission-expert-panel-olderworkers-employment-insurance-and-displaced-older-w.

——. 2009. "Monitoring and Assessment Report 2008: Employment Insurance." Gatineau, Quebec: Publications Services, Human Resources and Skills Development. At http://www.rhdcc-hrsdc.gc.ca/eng/employment/ei/reports/eimar_2008/index.shtml (accessed 1 October 2010).

——. 2010. "Monitoring and Assessment Report 2009: Employment Insurance." Gatineau, Quebec: Publications Services, Human Resources and Skills Development Canada. At http://www.hrsdc.gc.ca/eng/employment/ei/reports/eimar_2009/PDF/EIMAR_2009.pdf (accessed 28 September).

Canadian Labour Congress. April 2007. "Submission by the Canadian Labour Congress to Expert Panel on Older Workers on Employment Insurance and Displaced Older Workers."

Cheal, D. 2003. "Finding a Niche: Age-related Differentiations within the Working-age Population." In Social Differentiation: Patterns and Processes, ed. D.L. Juteau, 81-116. Toronto: University of Toronto Press.

Clement, W. 1986. The Struggle to Organize: Resistance in Canada's Fishery. Toronto: McClelland and Stewart.

Cox, R. 2007. "Improving Maternity and Parental Benefits for Women Outside of Québec: Proposals for Law Reform." Report for the National Association of Women and the Law. At http://www.nawl.ca/ns/en/documents/200708_NAWL%20Proposals_MPB.pdf (accessed 1 October 2010).

Cranford, C.J., J. Fudge, E. Tucker, and L.F. Vosko, eds. 2005. Self-employed Workers Organize: Law, Policy, and Unions. Montreal and Kingston: McGill-Queen's University Press.

du Plessis, V., R. Beshiri, R.D. Bollman, and H. Clemenson. 2002. "Definitions of 'Rural.'" Research Paper for Statistics Canada, Agriculture Division. Agriculture and Rural Working Paper Series 61.

Employment Insurance Act, 1996 S.C., ch. 23.

Employment Insurance Regulations, S.O.R./96-332.

Expert Panel on Older Workers. 2008. "Supporting and Engaging Older Workers in the New Economy." Human Resources and Skills Development Canada. At http://www.hrsdc.gc.ca/eng/publications_resources/lmp/eow/2008/older_workers_2008.pdf (accessed 1 October 2010).

Fairness for the Self-Employed Act, 2009 S.C., ch. 33.

Ferrall, C. 1997. "Unemployment Insurance Eligibility and the School-to-Work Transition in Canada and the United States." Journal of Business & Economic Statistics 15.2: 115-29.

Fudge, J., E. Tucker, and L.F. Vosko. 2002. "The Legal Concept of Employment: Marginalizing Workers." Report for the Law Commission of Canada.

Government of Canada. 2010. "Canada's Economic Action Plan, Employment Insurance Special Benefits for the Self-Employed." At http://www.actionplan.gc.ca/initiatives/eng/index.asp?mode=2&initiativeID=74 (accessed 20 October 2010).

Human Resources and Skills Development Canada (HRSDC). 2009a. "Annual Reports on the EI Premium Rate and Maximum Insurable Earnings." At http://www.rhdcc-hrsdc.gc.ca/eng/employment/ei/premium_rate/index.shtml (accessed 28 September 2010).

——. 2009b. "The Government of Canada Delivers Employment Insurance Fairness for the Self-Employed." At http://news.gc.ca/web/article-eng.do?nid=493319 (accessed 24 October 2010).

——. 2009c. "Appendix VII: Review of Main Legislative and Regulatory Modifications to the Employment/Unemployment Program from 1930 to 2009." Last modified 16 October 2009. At http://www.hrsdc.gc.ca/eng/employment/ei/premium_rate/2010/appendix_7.shtml.

——. 2010. "Employment Insurance Pilot Projects Continue to Support Unemployed Canadians." At http://news.gc.ca/web/article-eng.do?nid=565529 (accessed 24 October 2010).

Human Resources Development Canada (HRDC). 1994. "Improving Social Security in Canada: A Discussion Paper." Ottawa: Minister of Supply and Services Canada.

Hughes, K.D. 1999. "Gender and Self-employment in Canada: Assessing Trends and Policy Implications." Ottawa: Canadian Policy Research Networks Study No. W/04.

Klassen, T. 2000. "The Federal-Provincial Labour Market Development Agreements: Brave New Model of Cooperation." In Federalism, Democracy and Labour Market Policy in Canada, ed. T. McIntosh, 159-203. Kingston: Institute of Intergovernmental Relations, Queen's University.

Leonard, J. 2009. "Time to Get Real On EI Reform." Policy Options (September). At http://www.irpp.org/po/archive/sep09/leonard.pdf.

Lin, Z. 1998. "Employment Insurance in Canada: Policy changes." Perspectives on Labour and Income 10.2: 42-47.

MacDonald, M. 2009. "Income Security for Women: What about Employment Insurance?" In Public Policy for Women: The State, Income Security and Labour Market Issues, ed. M. Griffin Cohen and J. Pulkingham, 251-70. Toronto: University of Toronto Press.

MacLaren, B., and L. Lapointe. 2009. "Making a Case for Reform: Non-Access to Social Security Measures for Migrant Workers." Canadian Foundation for the Americas. At http://www.focal.ca/pdf/Migrant%20Social%20Security%20Maclaren%202009.pdf.

Marshall, K. 2003. "Benefiting from Extended Parental Leave." Perspectives on Labour and Income 4.3: 4-11.

——. 2008. "Fathers' Use of Paid Parental Leave." Perspectives on Labour and Income 9.6: 5-14.

McAllister-Windsor v. Canada (Human Resources Development). 2001. 40 C.H.R.R.D/48.

McBride, S. 1999. "Towards Permanent Insecurity: The Social Impact of Unemployment." Journal of Canadian Studies 34.2: 13-30.

McBride, S. and P. Stoyko. 2000. "Youth and the Social Union: Intergovernmental Relations, Youth Unemployment and School-to-Work Transitions." In Federalism, Democracy and Labour Market Policy In Canada, ed. T. McIntosh, 205-68. Montreal: McGill-Queen's University Press.

McGregor, G. 2003. "Diminishing Returns: Age-Discriminatory Elements in the Employment Insurance Act." Journal of Law and Social Policy 18: 98-137.

McIntosh, T., and G.W. Boychuk. 2000. "Dis-Covered: EI, Social Assistance and the Growing Gap in Income Support for Unemployed Canadians." In Federalism, Democracy and Labour Market Policy in Canada, ed. T. McIntosh, 65-158. Montreal and Kingston: McGill-Queens University Press.

Nakache, D., and P.J. Kinoshita. 2010. "The Canadian Temporary Foreign Worker Program: Do Short-Term Economic Needs Prevail over Human Rights Concerns?" Institute for Research on Public Policy Study 5. At http://www.irpp.org/pubs/IRPPstudy/IRPP_Study_no5.pdf.

NAWL (National Association of Women and the Law). 2007. "Improving Maternity Parental Benefits for Women outside of Québec: Proposals for Law Reform." At http://www.nawl.ca/ns/en/documents/200708_NAWL%20Proposals_MPB.pdf (accessed 6 November 2010).

Neis, B. 1993. "'Shipped Girls' to 'Brides of the State': The Transition from Familial to Social Patriarchy in the Newfoundland Fishing Industry." Canadian Journal of Regional Science 16.2: 185-202.

Organisation for Economic Co-operation and Development (OECD). 2005. "OECD Employment Outlook." At http://www.oecd.org/document/1/0,3343 en_2649_33927_34855489_1_1_1_1,00.html (accessed 28 September 2010).

Osberg, L. 1979. "Unemployment Insurance in Canada: A Review of Recent Amendments." Canadian Public Policy 5.2: 223-35.

——. 2005. "Work and Well-Being in an Aging Society." Canadian Public Policy 31.4: 413-20.

——. June 2009. "Canada's Declining Social Safety Net: The Case for EI Reform." Ottawa: Canadian Centre for Policy Alternatives.

Pal, L.A. 1986. "Relative Autonomy Revisited: The Origins of Canadian Unemployment Insurance." Canadian Journal of Political Science 19.1: 71-92.

Pérusse, D. 2003. "New Maternity and Parental Benefits." Perspectives on Labour and Income 4.3: 12-15.

Phipps, S. 2001. "Unemployment Insurance—Employment Insurance Transition: An Evaluation of the Pre-2001 Maternity and Parental Benefits Program in Canada (Final Report)." Human Resources Development Canada, Strategic Policy, Evaluation and Data Development. At http://www.hrsdc.gc.ca/eng/cs/sp/hrsdc/edd/reports/2001-000616/uieit_e.pdf (accessed 28 September 2010).

——. 2006. "Working for Working Parents: The Evolution of Maternity and Parental Benefits in Canada." IRPP Choices 12.2. At www.irpp.org/choices/archive/vol12no2.pdf.

Phipps, S. and F. MacPhail. 2002. "The Impact of Employment Insurance on New-entrant and Re-entrant Workers." Final Report Prepared for the Strategic Evaluation and Monitoring Directorate, Human Resources Development Canada. At http://www.hrsdc.gc.ca/eng/cs/sp/hrsdc/edd/reports/2000000433/ieine.pdf.

Phipps, S., M. MacDonald and F. MacPhail. 2001. "Gender Equity within Families versus Better Targeting: An Assessment of the Family Income Supplement to Employment Insurance Benefits." Canadian Public Policy 27.4: 423-46.

Porter, A. 2003. Gendered States: Women, Unemployment Insurance, and the Political Economy of the Welfare State in Canada, 1945–1997. Toronto: University of Toronto Press.

Pulkingham, J. 1998. "Remaking the Social Divisions of Welfare: Gender, 'Dependency' and UI Reform." Studies in Political Economy 56: 7-48.

Riddell, C. 2009. "Older Workers in the New Economy: A Symposium on the Report of the Expert Panel on Older Workers." Canadian Public Policy 35.4: 469-71.

Rubery, J. M. Smith and C. Fagan. 1999. Women's Employment in Europe: Trends and Prospects. London: Routledge.

Schmid, G. and B. Reissert. 1996. "Unemployment Compensation and Labour Market Transitions." In International Handbook of Labour Market Policy and Evaluation, ed. G. Schmid, J. O'Reilly and K. Schömann, 235-76. London: Edward Elgar Publishing Limited.

Service Canada. 2009. The Extended Duration of Employment Insurance (EI) Regular Benefits. At http://www.servicecanada.gc.ca/eng/ei/information/extended_duration.shtml (accessed 24 October 2010).

——. 2010. "Employment Insurance—Digest of Benefit Entitlement Principles." Last modified June 11. At http://www.servicecanada.gc.ca/eng/ei/digest/table_of_contents.shtml.

Shields, J. 2004. "No Safe Haven: Markets, Welfare, and Migrants." Policy Matters (June). At http://ceris.metropolis.net/PolicyMatter%5C2004%5CPolicyMatters7.pdf (accessed 3 October 2010).

Sidhu, N. 2009. "UNINSURED: Why EI is Failing Working Ontarians." Report for Social Planning Toronto. At http://socialplanningtoronto.org/reports/uninsured-why-ei-is-failing-working-ontarians/ (accessed 28 September 2010).

Standing Committee on the Status of Women. 2007. Study: Elimination of Discrimination Against Women in the Employment Insurance Program. 39th Parliament, 1st Session. Ottawa: Public Works and Government Services.

——. 2009. Towards Improving Access to EI Benefits for Women in Canada: Report of the Standing Committee on the Status of Women. 40th Parliament, 2nd session. Ottawa: Public Works and Government Services.

Statistics Canada. 2007. "CANSIM—Results Table 102-4503: Live Births, Mean Age of Mother, Canada, Provinces and Territories, Annual (years)." At http://www4.hrsdc.gc.ca/.3ndic.1t.4r@-eng.jsp?iid=75.

——. 2008a. Educational Portrait of Canada, 2006 Census. Catalogue Number 97-560-X. At http://www12.statcan.gc.ca/english/census06/analysis/education/pdf/97-560 XIE2006001.pdf.

——. 2008b. "Employment Insurance Coverage Survey." At http://www.statcan.gc.ca/cgi-bin/imdb/p2SV.pl?Function=getSurvey&SurvId=4428&SurvVer=1&SDDS=4428&InstaId=16022&InstaVer=10&lang=en&db=imdb&adm=8&dis=2.

——. 2009. "Survey of Labour and Income Dynamics." At http://www.statcan.gc.ca/cgi-bin/imdb/p2SV.pl?Function=getSurvey&SurvId=3889&SurvVer=1&SDDS=3889&InstaId=15506&InstaVer=11&lang=en&db=imdb&adm=8&dis=2.

Sweetman, A. 2001. "Immigrants and Employment Insurance." In Essays on the Repeat Use of Unemployment Insurance, ed. S. Schwartz, and A. Aydemir, 123-54. Ottawa: Social Research Development Corporation.

Townson, M. 2009. "Women's Poverty and the Recession." Canadian Centre for Policy Alternatives. At http://www.policyalternatives.ca/sites/default/files/uploads/publications/National_OfficePubs/2009/Womens_Poverty_in_the_Recession.pdf (accessed 28 September 2010).

Townson, M. and K. Hayes. 2007. "Women and the Employment Insurance Program: The Gender Impact of Current Rules on Eligibility and Earnings Replacement." Canadian Centre for Policy Alternatives. At http://www.policyalternatives.ca/sites/default/files/uploads/publications/National_OfficePub/2007/Les_femmes_et_AE.pdf.

Unemployment Insurance Act, 1970-71-72 S.C., c. 48.

U.S. Department of Labour. 2009. "U.S. Department of Labor Announces Boost in Weekly Unemployment Benefit Amounts." At http://www.dol.gov/opa/media/press/eta/ETA20090196.htm (accessed 15 November 2010).

Vosko, L.F. 1996. "Irregular Workers, New Involuntary Social Exiles: Women and UI Reform." In Remaking Canadian Social Policy: Social Security in the Late 1990s ed. J. Pulkingham and G. Ternowetsky, 265-72. Toronto: Fernwood Press.

——. 2000. Temporary Work: The Gendered Rise of a Precarious Employment Relationship. Toronto: University of Toronto Press.

——. 2002. "Rethinking Feminization: Gendered Precariousness in the Canadian Labour Market and the Crisis in Social Reproduction." Prepared for the Annual Robarts Lecture, John P. Robarts Centre for Canadian Studies. At http://www.genderwork.ca/modules/precarious/papers/vosko.2002.rethinking.pdf.

——. 2009. "Precarious Employment and the Challenges for Employment Policy." In Public Policy for Women in Canada: The State, Income Security, and Labour Market Issues, ed. M. Cohen and J. Pulkingham, 374-95. Toronto: University of Toronto Press.

Chapter 4

The Design of Employment Insurance in a Federation

Robin Boadway and Jean-Denis Garon

This chapter explores the issues that arise in designing an unemployment insurance program in a federation. In keeping with Canadian usage, we use the term Employment Insurance (EI) when discussing the Canadian case and switch to the more general term "unemployment insurance" (UI) when discussing other countries. UI is the term used virtually everywhere else and better captures the event being insured. EI impinges on federalism in a number of ways, and it is useful at the outset to identify them to indicate the scope of our interest.

First and foremost, EI is by the Constitution an exclusive legislative responsibility of the federal government.[1] Although the meaning of EI is not defined by the Constitution, including whether it must be contributory in nature, its generally accepted purpose is to provide partial income replacement for workers who become involuntarily unemployed. In addition, it assists workers with finding suitable new employment. EI also provides special benefits for maternity and parental leave, compassionate leave, sickness leave and training.

Several structural elements of EI have provincial or regional consequences, even though the rules are defined without explicit reference to the provinces. Eligibility requirements (hours of insurable work) and duration of benefits both vary with the unemployment rate in designated regions spanning the country. This affects the generosity of EI among provinces, especially since regions do not cross provincial borders. Eligibility requirements are greater for new entrants (the so-called 910 rule), and that has a differential impact across provinces owing to differences in the demographic composition of provincial workforces and the nature of employment. The preferential treatment of fishers relative to other self-employed groups favours provinces that rely more on the fishing industry. Similarly, because of the uniform contribution and benefit rates across the country, some industries systematically benefit more from EI than others. Those with high rates of EI usage, such as seasonal industries or industries facing more volatile demands for their products, tend to draw on the system more than they contribute, while industries with relatively low layoff patterns pay more than they contribute. Provinces with persistently higher unemployment rates tend to benefit relative to others, and this is exacerbated by the regional differentiation mentioned above. Finally, there are special benefits for low-income families that naturally benefit low-income provinces more than others.

While regular EI benefits seem clearly to fall within the federal government's constitutional jurisdiction, that may not be so clear for extended benefits and training. Even though extended benefits for maternity, sickness and compassionate care involve leaving one's job, it is not so obvious that such policies should all be the sole domain of the federal government. Indeed, agreements with the provinces have effectively turned over to the provinces responsibility for training EI recipients. This raises the question as to whether training programs offered by the provinces should be conditioned on whether participants are EI recipients or not.

EI also assumes a federalism dimension to the extent that it is related to provincial programs. The effect of a program at one level of government may depend in part on the design of programs at the other. Moreover, there may be scope for coordination of program design. We have already mentioned training, where there may be obvious synergies between the training of EI recipients and of other unemployed workers. More generally, provincial social assistance and federal EI both serve segments of the unemployed population. Those who are ineligible for EI may be eligible for social assistance. To the extent that programs are coordinated, moving from one to the other can be facilitated, and sizeable gaps in coverage of those unable to find jobs can be avoided. As well, economies in monitoring and information exchange can be achieved by administrative cooperation and coordination.

EI can also affect provinces through its economic impact. Provinces benefit from the insurance provided by EI against regional economic shocks because of the ability to pool risks nationally. In that regard, it complements Equalization, which insures against volatility in provincial government revenues. As well, the EI system insures against aggregate or nationwide shocks more effectively than the provinces could. The advantage the federal government has in insuring against regional and national shocks is a main reason why it is a federal responsibility.

The EI system also has an effect on the development of regional economies. To the extent that some industries are favoured relative to others, such as those with more frequent and more predictable claims, activity in those sectors is encouraged. Over-reliance on such sectors, such as the fisheries or tourism, may influence the pattern of industrial development—and the provinces' strategies of economic development—in particular regions. As a consequence, migration may be affected by EI if potential migrants are employed in EI-favoured industries. On the other hand, to the extent that EI finances job search by the unemployed, which is one of its purposes, it might actually encourage mobility of workers among industries and regions.

Finally, it should be recognized that there are other elements of implicit insurance against the volatility of earnings, whether due to unemployment or not. The income tax system acts as a form of insurance to the extent that tax liabilities rise and fall with income. This is potentially important for the self-employed, although its efficacy depends on the extent to which tax losses are refundable when earnings become negative. For some workers, the family serves as an important form of insurance given that families can pool incomes. By the same token, one's social network and the voluntary sector can be sources of support for distressed workers.

The income tax-transfer system is also relevant for workers who have become permanently displaced from their jobs. When they are eventually re-employed, it is often at a lower wage. While EI is relevant for addressing the immediate needs of displaced workers when they become unemployed and for assisting them in finding jobs through training and employment services, its role is not to deal with persistent inequalities. The redistributive role of the tax system is meant to address market inequalities, whether they are due to differences in the earnings potential of workers throughout their lives or those that arise as a result of a sudden loss of earning power due to displacement.

In the remainder of this chapter, we consider the issues that arise in designing EI in a federal setting such as Canada's. This presupposes an understanding of the role of EI as a component of social policy. We begin with a discussion of the rationale for EI from a normative perspective. We argue that, in addition to insuring against involuntary unemployment, EI should play a redistributive role. It should especially target low-income workers for whom self-insurance is difficult and costly. This is followed by a recounting of the way in which EI is designed and delivered in other federations. Practices vary widely. EI can be contributory or tax-financed, or some combination. Varying degrees of responsibility of the federal and provincial/state levels of government can be found. EI may or may not be coordinated with welfare, and the two may be combined. And, eligibility and duration rules vary widely, but in all cases, monitoring for compliance is an important part of program design. The wide variety of practices elsewhere confirms that many options for reform are available. We then turn to a discussion of design issues and policy options. Our judgment is that a number of reforms should be considered, including:

- Reinforce the redistributive component of the program by moving to general-revenue financing and conditioning benefits on family income and responsibilities.
- Address better the needs of the longer-term unemployed by establishing a second tier of need-related benefits.
- Establish a common set of rules nationwide by eliminating regional differentiation of benefits and special treatment of self-employed fishers.
- Introduce some experience rating to the contribution rates of firms that are repeat users of EI via temporary layoffs.

- Disentangle training from EI so that eligibility for EI is not a criterion for training.
- Improve the ability of the tax-transfer system to insure the self-employed and displaced workers.
- Stress the importance of monitoring by EI administrators for continuing eligibility.

1 Normative Underpinnings of EI Policy

Although our main focus is on the design of EI in a federal setting, it is important first to understand the role played by EI as a component of government policy. This will have a bearing on federalism aspects of EI policy. Two dimensions of EI's role are particularly relevant, and will underpin the discussion in this section. One is that EI incorporates redistribution as well as insurance elements, or equivalently, equity versus efficiency elements. We return to the reason for that below. The other concerns the neglected importance of program administration for the integrity of the program, from the point of view of both redistribution and insurance. Put simply, EI programs that provide reasonable levels of social protection should be attractive enough to potential recipients that initial and continuing access must be fairly and effectively monitored for eligibility, and for encouraging the transition to employment. Similar issues arise in other social protection programs, particularly those delivered by the provinces.

The main purpose of EI is to insure against unexpected and involuntary job loss and the loss in earnings that entails. The important presumption is that at least some of those who are covered by EI are unable, or choose not, to insure against this particular form of earnings volatility through other means. Private insurance is presumably incapable of providing adequate insurance against involuntary unemployment or earnings volatility for well-known reasons of moral hazard and adverse selection. One feature of EI makes this problem particularly apparent. Reasonably full insurance would smooth income across employed and unemployed states, and this would almost certainly entail workers being better off when involuntarily unemployed than when employed, given that leisure accompanies unemployment. Given the difficulty of observing when workers are involuntarily unemployed, and choose to remain unemployed, this alone precludes private firms from providing full EI. This point is worth emphasizing because it highlights the importance of monitoring the unemployed for both initial and on-going EI eligibility.

The public sector has a distinct advantage in dealing with these information problems, and it is important to recognize that at the outset. The government can and does mandate participation in EI, which private insurance could not do. This may be justified as a response to both behavioural issues—workers choosing not to enrol if participation were voluntary—and adverse selection issues—markets not functioning because bad risks drive out goods ones. In addition to mandating participation, the government can exercise some coercion to obtain relevant information. It can screen applicants to determine eligibility, for example, to learn whether applicants were likely to have been laid off as opposed to having quit their job or been fired. It can monitor EI recipients to verify with varying degrees of accuracy that they are actively searching for jobs and accepting those offered, and can assist them in job search. Program administrators can also learn something about the personal circumstances of applicants, such as their family income, in the event that this affects the size and duration of their benefits. They can also oblige or offer financial inducement for recipients to engage in training programs. Administrative discretion is at the heart of the EI system, and is relevant for considering potential roles for federal and provincial governments.

The importance of the administration of EI reflects a relevant distinction between EI and other programs. Like social assistance, EI is a standalone program that differs in its form from the tax-transfer system, including the various refundable tax credits. The tax system—not just income taxes, but sales and excise taxes as well—is administered on a self-reporting basis, whereby liability for taxes or eligibility for refundable tax credits is reported in the first instance on a taxpayer's own tax return. Verification then relies on *ex post* random audits and penalties for misreporting. Given the low incidence of penalization and the limited size of the penalties for misreporting, paying taxes is to a large extent a voluntary exercise that, fortunately, most Canadian taxpayers seem to undertake honestly.[2]

In contrast, EI and social assistance eligibility are determined by *ex ante* gate-keeping methods and are monitored on a continuing basis *ex post*. Moreover, the implicit penalties for misrepresentation or violating the rules are large relative to incomes for those involved compared with the tax system. The advantage of this system is that, apart from possibly keeping errors to a minimum and presuming dishonest rather than honest behaviour, it allows the system to be flexible and responsive to changes in circumstance of recipients. This is an important feature of an insurance system, and allows the system to be based on a broader set of criteria than simply income.[3]

The need for responsive program administration applies regardless of the extent to which EI incorporates redistributive (relative to insurance) objectives. The case for EI including an insurance element is clear. Job loss entails an abrupt fall in earnings that, if uninsured, would translate into a sharp drop in consumption. To the extent that the risk of consumption volatility can be avoided, workers would be better off and would be willing to pay to avoid that risk. Under a pure insurance system, the risk of unexpected job loss and the expected length of unemployment would be reflected in each worker's EI premium. Setting those so-called fair insurance premiums is practically infeasible because of the difficulty of determining the true probability of involuntary unemployment and its expected duration, although as discussed below, some elements of job-loss risk could be imperfectly incorporated into premiums.

At the same time, there are arguments for EI incorporating a significant redistributive element alongside any insurance component. Given that full EI is not feasible, the fallback for workers is to self-insure against the contingencies of job loss, that is, to take actions to smooth their consumption in the event of job loss. Self-insurance can take various forms, including precautionary saving, adjustments to consumption patterns, and personal borrowing. The unemployed can also draw on financial or material assistance from family members or social and community networks. These same responses are required to deal with other sorts of inter-temporal smoothing requirements, such as retirement, changes in family circumstances and the need for lumpy expenditures. Persons who have low incomes, and especially those who do not have recourse to high-income family members, find it more difficult and costly to self-insure than others. They have less asset wealth to cushion themselves against adverse outcomes and less access to capital markets, and it is more costly for them to adjust their consumption patterns. Moreover, low-income persons may face relatively high volatility of employment and earnings, given their lower skills and attachment to employers, and might find re-employment more difficult. For such persons EI is most important. There are thus good reasons for the net benefits of EI to be proportionately higher for low-income persons, especially those from low-income families. This constitutes the redistributive role of EI.[4]

The argument that EI should assume a redistributive role in addition to providing insurance against job loss implies that there are important judgments to be made about program design, and these have a bearing on the relation between EI and other federal and provincial programs. To what extent should financing, eligibility and benefits reflect redistribution as opposed to insurance principles, given that the two will conflict? Although addressing this issue is beyond the scope of this chapter, it is worthwhile outlining some of the considerations that are relevant for judging how redistribution might be enhanced on the one hand and how the insurance properties might be improved on the other. This will inform our subsequent discussion of the design issues relevant in a federal setting.

The current system neither achieves effective redistribution nor deploys insurance-based contribution and benefit principles. Contributions are proportional to insurable earnings up to a maximum. While they are related to the size of benefits one is entitled to if unemployed, they are not related to the probability of unemployment or its expected duration as insurance principles would dictate. Some workers contribute with little chance of being eligible for benefits. The main features of EI that are meant to reflect insurance principles are the regional differentiation of eligibility and duration rules based on regional unemployment rates and the higher eligibility requirements for new entrants (the 910 rule). These are crude measures that are both imperfect and give rise to anomalies that could be considered unfair, as discussed in a later section.

The redistribution in the EI system is limited as well. The upper bound on insurable earnings is redistributive to the extent that a higher proportion of actual earnings are replaced for lower-income compared to higher-income workers. In addition, there are two explicit elements of redistribution. One is the EI Family Supplement, which increases the benefits paid if family income is less that $25,921 (in 2010), if there are children, and if either spouse receives the Canada Child Tax Benefit. Benefits can rise up to 80 per cent of insurable earnings depending on the number of children, and is clawed back as income increases. At the upper end, up to 30 per cent of EI regular benefits must be repaid if the recipient's annual income exceeds $54,000. These measures, though limited, at least accept the principle that progressivity can be built into the EI benefit structure. Otherwise, there is very limited targeting of net benefits to low-income workers. The benefit to low-income workers is itself compromised by the relatively low (55 per cent) replacement rate of insurable earnings. The upper bound on contributions implies that they are a regressive form of taxation. Benefits do not reflect the ability of workers to self-insure. For example, apart from the two measures just noted, they are generally not related to a worker's income, family income or assets. Eligibility requirements, especially for new entrants, are relatively more onerous for low-income workers given the greater difficulty they might have in securing permanent employment. Finally, EI recipients, like those on provincial welfare, are allowed to earn a limited amount of income. In the case of EI, the maximum allowed is $50 per week, although this was increased temporarily for 2009–2010 to $75 per week. Earnings above that are taxed back at a 100 per cent rate.

The consequence of the current design of the EI system is that, as opposed to being composed of a combination of insurance and redistribution, it mainly redistributes benefits among groups of workers regardless of their income. Those who face low risk of layoff contribute more than their expected claims, while those who are likely to be repeat claimants are net beneficiaries. This is exacerbated by regional differentials in eligibility and duration to the extent that there is persistence in regional unemployment differentials, and by stricter eligibility requirements for new entrants to the extent that those having trouble meeting the requirements pay into the system with little chance of drawing benefits. In addition, there are incentive effects that might further detract from the insurance properties of EI, such as the tendency for some firms to engage repeatedly in temporary layoffs because of the implicit EI subsidy,[5] or the incentive for employers, including provincial governments, to employ workers just long enough to meet eligibility requirements.[6]

There are measures that should be taken to improve both the insurance and redistribution properties of EI. Experience-rating should be used to reduce the ability of repeat users to benefit from the system. Financing should be made more progressive, as could the structure of benefits. We return to these issues when we consider priorities for reform.

2 The Federal and Provincial Interest in EI

EI is a federal government program, but it exists alongside other federal and provincial programs that address related objectives and serve some of the same citizens. In this section, we briefly outline the interests of the federal and provincial governments in the design and delivery of EI, and identify areas of potential conflict and commonality. In the next section, we review how other federations have designed programs to deal with the unemployed.

Section 91(2A) of the *Constitution Act 1982* succinctly confers exclusive legislative authority of the Parliament of Canada over "unemployment insurance," without elaborating on what unemployment insurance entails or its scope of application. There are sound economic reasons for EI being a federal responsibility. Involuntary unemployment is largely a consequence of shocks to the economy on either the demand or supply sides. They can be permanent shocks leading to structural unemployment, or transitory ones leading to temporary unemployment. These shocks can be mainly idiosyncratic shocks hitting different regions of the country unexpectedly, but with roughly equal chances. Or, they can be aggregate shocks that affect most regions of the economy simultaneously. In either case, the federal government is better placed to address the unemployment caused by the shocks. In the case of regional shocks, the federal government can pool the risks across the whole economy, insuring those regions particularly hard hit with unemployment from a national pool of revenues. The federal government alone can also address aggregate unemployment shocks that affect all regions of the economy.

More generally, the federal government can be taken to have a responsibility for achieving minimal national standards of redistributive equity or social citizenship. This is not an absolute objective, and depends on the extent of social consensus for nationwide solidarity. Depending on the extent of that consensus—which is a political matter—the provinces might also pursue varying degrees of provincial solidarity. The federal government addresses national standards of redistributive equity partly through its progressive income tax-transfer system whereby all persons of a given income level are treated comparably no matter where they reside. The equalization system is also a policy instrument intended to facilitate national social solidarity by making it possible for provinces to provide comparable levels of public services while at the same time allowing them to pursue their own provincial standards of equity. To the extent that EI is a redistributive program, it addresses similar objectives. A national unemployment insurance system achieves a common standard of redistributive equity for those whose income temporarily falls due to job loss, especially lower-income workers.

The federal government similarly assumes some responsibility for fostering efficiency in the Canadian economic union, which includes the unfettered mobility of workers from one region to another. This is particularly important for unemployed workers since migration from one province to another often involves some temporary unemployment. An EI system defined on a national basis can facilitate the inter-provincial mobility of labour, which is an important source of flexibility in an economy subject to regional and sectoral shocks.

The Constitution does not specify what is meant by unemployment insurance or what its scope should be, and there is no well-established international definition to serve as a guide. Must it be a contributory social insurance scheme whereby eligibility depends on one's contributions, or can it be a program financed out of general revenues and based on elements of need in addition to past earnings? To what extent must it be based on insurance principles whereby contributions and benefits are to some extent related to the risks associated with being unemployed? Must it be only for persons who are involuntarily unemployed, or can it include those who choose to leave their job temporarily for childbirth or care-giving? To what extent should it include measures to assist persons to find a job, such as through training or employment services? And, to what extent might its eligibility and benefit structure be based on characteristics unrelated to employment income, such as family income, asset wealth, and health? These are all key issues in designing EI, and it is not clear to what extent any of them are constrained by the Constitution.

Despite the fact that the Constitution makes EI an exclusive federal legislative responsibility, the provinces have an interest in how EI is designed and delivered, not only because their employed residents are mandated to participate in the program, but also because of the interface that exists between EI and provincial programs, especially social assistance. Moreover, by its very nature, EI has interprovincial redistribution implications, since it is not based on insurance principles.

At a very general level, the provinces have an interest in, or even a responsibility for, the well-being of all their residents, including especially those most in need. This is explicit in Section 36(1) of the *Constitution Act, 1982*, which expresses the joint commitment of the federal parliament and the provincial legislatures to pursuing equality of opportunity, economic development and the provision of basic public services to all citizens.[7] More generally, provinces may regard redistribution and social insurance as being among the more important objectives they should pursue. The bulk of provincial spending, including welfare, health and education, is essentially redistributive in nature.

More specifically, the provinces have an obvious interest in the design of EI, given its relation with provincial social assistance programs. Unemployed low-income persons who have exhausted their benefits for EI, or who have not satisfied the eligibility requirements, may become welfare recipients. This means that the eligibility and duration rules for EI have a direct bearing on provincial welfare obligations. From the perspective of the persons involved, a smooth transition from EI to welfare is important, so any coordinating arrangements that would facilitate that transition are relevant. One might argue that the federal government has an incentive to move the unemployed from EI to the provincial welfare system on this account. More generally, the federal government may not fully take account of changes in the EI program on provinces' financial situations. By the same token, provinces have an incentive to "game the system" by finding employment of a sufficient length of time for welfare recipients in order to make them eligible for EI and so move them from provincial welfare programs to the federal EI system. To the extent that training accompanies the EI system, the provinces' interest in transferring individuals from provincially-funded income security programs to federally-funded EI is further enhanced.

In practice, the transition from EI to welfare may be especially difficult for various reasons. Eligibility for welfare may include stringent asset requirements that oblige the unemployed to draw down their past savings before accepting welfare. For persons who have been employed for a long time before being laid off, this is a difficult requirement. Application for welfare itself might take some time and effort, and applicants might be deterred from applying, especially if there is some stigma associated with accepting welfare. The consequence is that a number of persons might be between EI and welfare with no means of support other than from family, from volunteer organization, and from limited federal and provincial refundable tax credits. Such persons may end up being a burden on the provinces if they fall into dire circumstances like homelessness, crime and indebtedness, including to unsavoury lenders.

The absence of insurance-based contribution rates in the EI system leads inevitably to inter-provincial redistribution. Sectors that are prone to higher expected rates of unemployment, such as seasonal industries or the fishery, will benefit at the expense of those with lower expected rates, such as those that depend more on service industries. Since different provinces' industrial structures will differ persistently, there will inevitably be implicit ongoing redistribution from low-unemployment to high-unemployment regions, putting the industries in the former at a relative disadvantage.

This inter-provincial redistribution is exacerbated by some further factors. One is the proportion of the unemployed who are eligible for EI. Different provinces might have different proportions of unemployed persons who have been part-time or self-employed workers, or new entrants who have not worked a sufficient number of hours. Not only are these persons not insured against volatile incomes, they may also be candidates for welfare. The system of regionally-differentiated benefits and eligibility works to the systematic disadvantage of some provinces to the extent that differences in regional unemployment rates are persistent and are due to predictable seasonality.[8] These differences might in fact contribute to the persistence of the high unemployment rates in certain regions. As we discuss further later, the regional unemployment rate might not be the most accurate way of estimating the difficulty of getting a job. Finally, low-payroll provinces have higher equalization entitlements, while the advantage they obtain from greater EI transfers is not taken into account.

Taking a fiscal federalism or subsidiarity perspective, standard arguments about the assignment of functions would favour some provincial role in EI, albeit more in its delivery than its design. The provinces are responsible for virtually all other targeted transfers and public services delivered to individuals on the basis of eligibility and monitoring. They have a natural advantage in administering such systems in terms of local knowledge, accountability, potential for innovation, fiscal and yardstick competition (the ability of citizens to judge their province's performance by observing the performance of neighbouring provinces), and overcoming information problems associated with management (so-called agency problems). Moreover, as mentioned, there is an advantage in coordinating the delivery of EI with social assistance since recipients may move from one program to the other. Provinces also have some advantage in administering other services that accompany EI, such as training and employment services. Indeed, these services may also be part of provincial welfare programs, since the provinces have an interest in getting employable persons back into the workforce, especially the long-term unemployed.

In considering how to exercise these provincial interests, either in cooperation with the federal government or alone, a fundamental question is how to make provincial participation consistent with the federal government's exclusive legislative responsibility for EI. We return to this issue later.

3 Experience and Reforms in Other Countries

The design of economic policy is influenced by institutional constraints, and this is especially true in countries with several levels of government. It is therefore not surprising that there are significant differences in unemployment insurance (UI) across federations.[9] Policies must agree with the constitution, which defines the specific responsibilities of each tier of government. In the special case of social insurance policies, historical concerns must also be taken into account. For example, the specific way in which UI schemes are implemented is strongly influenced by the past involvement of labour unions and social or religious agencies. Nonetheless, all federations face common challenges of equity, efficiency and program administration, and the option to centralize or decentralize always lies at the heart of policy discussions.

This section reviews the characteristics of UI programs in other OECD countries where multi-order governance is of particular importance.

We focus mainly on three aspects that are especially relevant to policy debates about the Canadian EI system. The first is the extent to which UI programs are centralized or decentralized. If decentralization occurs, it may only involve an element of payments to the unemployed, such as to the long-term unemployed. The second is to what extent UI programs are coordinated with some other components of social insurance, mainly social assistance and public pensions. In some cases, governments have developed integrated transfer programs for employable persons incorporating both UI and welfare for the long-term unemployed. In other cases, UI may be kept separate from welfare, but with some features that smooth the transition from one program to the other. Third, we inquire into whether and how UI benefits are linked to past contributions to a specific UI fund and, when it is not the case, how UI benefits are financed. Other basic elements of program design will be noted where relevant, such as rules about eligibility and duration, including the role of monitoring, and the extent of regional differentiation in benefits.

We focus on a sample of seven countries consisting of Germany, Australia, the United Kingdom (UK), Belgium, Spain, Switzerland and the United States (US). These encompass federations of varying degrees of centralization, a multi-tiered country (Spain) and a unitary state that is in the process of devolving some fiscal responsibilities (UK). These countries illustrate the diversity of practices that one observes, as well as some commonalities. Among other things, they indicate what reforms are possible. The sources for country information are listed in the References.

A Germany

The German UI system, as well as its system of welfare benefits, is fully managed by the federal government. Common rules apply across the country, even though unemployment rates differ significantly among regions. It has recently undergone a major reform aiming to provide different resources to the employable and unemployable individuals. Since 2005, UI and welfare have been merged and a single jobseekers' allowance for all workers who have been employed full time has been implemented. With this program, involuntarily unemployed workers can first claim contributory benefits for between 6 and 24 months depending on the length of their contribution period. (Contributions must have been for at least 12 months.) When contributory benefits are exhausted, they can turn to the so-called UI2 program. It provides them with needs-based benefits financed by general tax revenues which can last for an indefinite period of time if the individual is still unemployed and in need. The UI2 program is means-tested, and need is monitored by the federal government every six months. This also allows it to implement a harmonized training and educational policy according to which young persons (up to 25 years of age) who claim the jobseekers' allowance are immediately placed into jobs or training for a fixed term with qualification possibilities. A separate social assistance program still exists, but only for those unable to work.

B Australia

In Australia, the UI and welfare programs are also exclusive responsibilities of the federal (commonwealth) government. Both systems are fully integrated, to a much greater extent than in Germany. The system of income support consists of a single needs-based, means-tested unemployment assistance program. It is funded by general taxation revenue, so benefits and eligibility are not based on any type of earmarked contributions. Benefits can be claimed for an unlimited period of time but they come with strong monitoring requirements. Claimants must be unemployed, and must either be actively searching for a job or be involved in an activity that will improve their employment prospects, such as training or continuing education. They must also be available and willing to accept suitable work. As well as being fully centralized, the Australian program applies uniformly across the nation without regional differentiation.

C United Kingdom

The UK is a unitary state, though some responsibilities have been devolved to Northern Ireland, Scotland and Wales. It is the national government that provides the unemployed with financial support. For those who are able to work and are actively searching for work,[10] two distinct types of Jobseekers' Allowance (JSA) exist.[11] The first type is a system of contribution-based JSAs, which can be claimed by those who have paid enough National Insurance Contributions (NICs) during the past two years. NICs are earnings-based and are paid by all workers in order to finance the contribution-based JSA as well as other social insurance programs, including State Pensions, Bereavement Allowances, and Employment and Support Allowance. These contribution-based benefits can be claimed for up to 182 days. The level of weekly benefits is fixed and depends on the claimant's age (one level for 18–24-year-olds and another for the 25-plus) and on whether the claimant gets regular revenues from a private (occupational or not) pension plan or from a part-time job. No other source of income (such as savings, other financial assets or spouse's earnings) is taken into consideration. Those claimants who are still unemployed after having claimed 182 days of benefits, as well as those who do not qualify for the contribution-based JSA, turn to the second type of benefits.

The second benefit is the income-based JSA. It is available to all low-income persons who are unemployed and not eligible for a contribution-based JSA, including the self-employed. To claim this benefit, the claimant must meet with a program administrator who determines the levels of benefits on a case-by-case basis. The weekly benefits that can be claimed are constrained by a maximum that depends on whether one is single, and whether one is younger than 25. Because this is an income-tested program, the benefits one can claim are further reduced as a function of savings, part-time work earnings, pension revenues, and spousal revenue. Once all these sources have been taken into account, it is quite possible for an unemployed person to be left without the right to claim benefits. If he has the right to do so, he can claim them for an unlimited period of time, subject to satisfying various monitoring requirements.

Three other relevant elements of the UI program in the UK should be noted. First, although self-employed individuals can contribute to National Insurance, this does not give them the right to claim either contribution-based or income-based JSAs. Second, if an individual can claim any of these benefits, a waiting period of three days applies. Finally, although the eligibility for contribution-based JSAs depends on past NICs, these contributions are not earmarked to a specific social insurance program, and the level of benefits are in no way related to either past earnings or on the level of past contributions.

D Belgium

Belgium is a federation where two distinct support programs exist, one for the unemployed, whether short- or long-term, and the other for individuals who are unable to work. All workers and their employers must pay social security contributions. The self-employed also contribute to social security, though their eligibility for benefits is limited as discussed below. As in the UK, these contributions serve several purposes and are not earmarked. Payments to the social security system are collected by the National Office of Social Security which redistributes them to funds dedicated to Invalidity Insurance, National Pensions, Family Allowances, and the National Employment Office in support of their respective financial needs. The federal government then supplements these contributions with subsidies. This system keeps the contribution system simple but prevents UI benefits from being closely conditioned on one's past contributions.

The basic allowances an unemployed person can claimed is equivalent to 35 per cent of insured earnings, subject to a daily and a monthly maximum and minimum. These maxima and minima depend on whether one is living alone, and whether one has family responsibilities (children). Those involuntarily unemployed can claim benefits for an unlimited period of time, but the maximum benefit falls after six months and again after one year (called the first, second and third periods). Monitoring for job search and training also become more stringent after one year. Interestingly, the job placement of the unemployed is under the responsibility of four different agencies, one each for Brussels, Wallonia and Flanders and the German-speaking community.

Welfare payments can only be claimed by those unable to work. These are means-tested benefits (called "integration income benefits") and recipients must satisfy some strict conditions. More precisely, they must not be in a position to acquire means of support through their own effort or in some other manner (including household income), and must have exercised their entitlement to all other benefits. In contrast with the UI program, which is federal, integration income benefits are decentralized and provided by each commune through agencies called "Centres Publics d'Action Sociale" (CPAS). Their financing is shared between communes and the federal government, whose share is 50 per cent to 65 per cent depending on the number of claimants. This generates many public debates in Belgium.

One notable feature of the Belgian system is that UI contributions are mandatory for the self-employed, and there is some access to benefits in the case of loss of livelihood through what is called the Independent Workers Regime. To be eligible, one must be engaged in a professional activity (including farming) for which the worker is not tied with a labour contract. One has also access to the Regime if working for an independent worker without a labour contract (a "helper"). The level of contributions is set by a federal organization (the INASTI) but payments are collected by so-called social funds for independent workers which are established as not-for-profit organizations. The contributions depend on whether the independent activity is one's primary or secondary occupation and are paid on a quarterly basis based on declared profits of the previous year, subject to administrative revision. The program gives independent workers the right to a minimal revenue replacement in case of bankruptcy, public health insurance, invalidity insurance and access to public pensions, and gives some benefits if they have to take care of a parent who is in palliative care. However, no proper income replacement is provided in case of job loss, and some level of self-insurance is therefore required.

E Spain

In the countries studied so far, the UI and welfare programs are well-coordinated because (with the exception of Belgium) the federal or central government has the ultimate constitutional responsibility for both of them. The advantages of integration are substantial, particularly in terms of implementing monitoring and training policies efficiently and consistently, and ensuring seamless transition between UI and welfare. However, even if full integration is always not possible because sub-national tiers of government are responsible for last-resort financial help, coordination is still possible, especially to smooth the passage from EI to welfare.

Spain is one such country where social protection and security are the responsibility of the autonomous regions whereas UI is under the federal government, and some amount of coordination exists. The UI program consists of two tiers, both managed by the federal government. The first tier is a contributory UI system. Contribution is mandatory, benefits are based on past contributions, and eligibility is based on requirements such as the duration of the working period. A claimant must have contributed for a minimum of 12 months in the six years preceding the legal status of unemployment. The duration of benefits is limited to up to 540 days, depending on age, contributions and other criteria. When these benefits are exhausted, the unemployed can claim benefits from the second tier of the federal program. These are akin to welfare payments and are called "Minimum Income for Insertion," with eligibility being subject to an income test. The goal of this second tier is therefore not primarily consumption smoothing, but rather to provide the longer-term unemployed with minimal purchasing power. When these two tiers are exhausted, those remaining unemployed can claim welfare from the provinces, or autonomous regions.

This system is interesting for several reasons. The two-tier federal program eases the transition from one program (UI) to another (regional welfare payments). The unemployed are kept in the federal program for a longer period, and undergo the transition from contribution-based benefits to income-tested benefits there. This allows the federal government to monitor job search and training for a longer period, even after contributory benefits are exhausted. It is also likely to reduce the number of longer-term unemployed who, for different reasons, would not be likely to claim welfare benefits. Claiming means-tested welfare benefits can be a stigmatizing process relative to claiming UI, and making the transition within the UI program can reduce that stigmatization. Low uptake of welfare by eligible unemployed (so-called Type-I errors) can also occur because of limited information or high costs of application, and these can be reduced by having a means-tested tier in the UI system. Finally, the second-tier with income testing may induce some harmonization of welfare rates among provinces and subdue the race to the bottom. However, the extended length of UI requires the federal government to be willing to bear some of the costs of welfare.

F Switzerland

In some countries, the level of coordination between welfare and UI is more limited. This is the case in Switzerland, a notably highly decentralized federation. Surprisingly, the Swiss UI system is supervised by the federal government under the "Loi Fédérale sur l'assurance-chômage obligatoire et l'indemnité en cas d'insolvabilité." All workers are required to contribute to the program, except for the self-employed.[12] Contributions are made by both workers and employers in the case of regular employment. Just as in the UK and Belgium, the workers' payments are used to finance several social security programs (called the "pillars" of social security). In case of unemployment, benefits are equivalent to 80 per cent of insured earnings (or 70 per cent for individuals without children) and are not means-tested. As with virtually all other UI programs, claimants must be searching for employment. Benefits are calculated on a daily basis and the number of insured days of unemployment depends on age and on the duration of past contributions. More precisely, one can claim up to 400 days of benefits if one has contributed at least 12 months, or 520 days if one has contributed for 18 months and is at least 55 years of age or is on disability or accident insurance.[13] The Swiss program does not insure individuals during a waiting period of five days, starting on the first day of unemployment.

Although the Swiss program is regulated by a federal law, its administration is substantially decentralized to UI funds in the cantons that can be under the supervision of either the public sector or of trade unions. Granting authorities are managed in the cantons by the "commissions tripartites" that manage the application of labour laws. When UI benefits are exhausted, a Swiss worker can, if necessary, seek help from welfare systems that are decentralized and established by each canton. The eligibility rules as well as the generosity of these programs vary from one canton to the next, but most of them perform job search and training monitoring, and seek to reintegrate workers in the job market.

G United States

Social assistance and UI systems are also relatively uncoordinated in the US. In contrast with what we observe in most other developed federations, UI is the responsibility of the states, whereas welfare is a shared responsibility. Social assistance programs are means-tested, temporary, often in-kind, and implicitly targeted to help women with children. For example, the Supplemental Nutrition Assistance Program (the food stamp program), is under shared responsibility and aims to provide direct help to low- and no-income families. The federal government defines the broad rules and pays the benefits, whereas the program is administered by the states. Another program, the Temporary Assistance for Needy Families, is under state responsibility. It aims at providing income assistance to needy families with children, and one can benefit from it for at most 60 months in a lifetime.[14]

UI programs differ among states in several regards: earnings required for eligibility, contribution rates, levels of benefits (including the replacement rate, the maximum and the minimum benefits), and the potential duration of benefits. All states, however, require claimants to be potentially employable and to be willing to work. Workers are left on their own once they have exhausted their claim for contributory benefits, since no long-term unemployment assistance program exists. If workers are still unemployed, they must rely on their own resources unless they are eligible for state welfare programs.

Because of the decentralized nature of UI, benefits, contributions and eligibility parameters vary across states. One interesting aspect of this system is that each firm receives different treatment under state UI programs because employers' contributions are determined using experience rating. According to this approach, each firm's contributions depend on its risk of layoffs, which is calculated using past experience. As noted by the OECD, the formulas used to calculate contributions vary significantly across states (OECD 2004). However, the federal government (Department of Labor) determines the minimal contributions of employers, which is currently 5.4 per cent of insurable earnings. A second source of regional variation also comes from the federal government's special benefits that can be claimed by unemployed individuals in high-unemployment states (United States Department of Labor 2004). This measure, called "extended benefits," provides unemployed workers with 13 additional weeks of benefits when a state is experiencing high unemployment.[15]

H Lessons of International Comparison

Some general observations from our cross-country comparison can be noted. First, relating the amount and level of benefits to the size of past contributions is not the rule. When this is the case, it is done in a rather indirect way due to the fact that social security contributions tend to be linked to income. Earmarked financing of UI funds is not the rule either. Employed workers are eligible for UI, but not the self-employed except in a very restrictive sense in Belgium. Also, regional differentiation in the determination of benefits and contributions seems to be more an exception than a rule. Only the United States deploys some level of regional differentiation. This is due to the fact that UI is under states' responsibility, but also because the federal government implements a program of extended benefits for high-unemployment states. Most countries' waiting periods tend to be much shorter than Canada's, which lasts for two weeks. There is a tendency in European countries to fund jointly several parts of the social security systems. Some distinct features that are found in some programs include the possibility for UI recipients to earn some income, and the existence of two-tier systems consisting of a first tier of contributory benefits and a second tier of means-tested benefits, where the means-testing might include spousal income.

4 Design Issues in a Federation

The above discussion indicates that different countries adopt very different approaches to UI design, its relation to welfare, and the role of subnational governments. This breadth of experience suggests that various options are available for reforming the Canadian EI system depending on one's view of the rationale for EI and the existence and effectiveness of complementary social programs for dealing with employment volatility. There are also different ways of dividing responsibilities between governments and, where necessary, harmonizing programs. In this section, we review some options that could be considered for EI reform in Canada. We begin with some key design issues for EI in general. These will set the stage for considering issues specific to a federal system.

A Redistribution vs. Insurance

A prior question is the balance between redistribution and insurance in EI. The argument for enhancing the redistributive role comes from the rationale for a public EI system, which is to provide insurance for job loss for those unable to self-insure at a reasonable cost. A case can be made for EI providing higher net benefits for low-income workers on these grounds, especially since full insurance is not feasible.

The existing system is roughly self-financing in the aggregate. The proportional contribution rate combined with the uniform benefit structure implies that EI redistributes from low-expected-unemployment to high-expected-unemployment workers. It does not fulfill a needs-based redistributive role except to the extent that workers in jobs with high-expected unemployment are lower-income workers. While it provides some insurance against job loss to all eligible workers, it does so inefficiently by favouring industries with higher-than-average and perfectly predictable layoff rates. The relatively high number of hours of work required for eligibility makes some contributors ineligible, and the limited duration reduces insurance for workers with longer than expected spells of unemployment. At the same time, the program guarantees portability among employers and provinces.

To enhance the redistributive role, EI would have to be better targeted to those who need it most, i.e., the lowest-income workers. This could be achieved by reforms of both contributions and benefits. On the contribution side, financing of EI could rely more on general revenues and less on earmarked payroll taxes. Relying entirely on general revenues (as in Australia) would enhance considerably the redistributive properties while not detracting from efficiency or insurance. Given that contributions currently bear little relation to expected benefits, little of insurance value would be lost by moving to general-revenue financing. Moreover, current eligibility criteria could still be applied since hours of work could still be used.

General-revenue financing would notionally change the system from a social insurance system to a transfer system, and it might be argued that the constitutional assignment to the federal government for "unemployment insurance" might somehow be jeopardized. That argument has little substance from an economic point of view. Contributions now are effectively a tax since they are mandatory and bear little relation to expected benefits. Changing the financing to progressive taxation from the current regressive one, such as through general-revenue financing, can be done independently of the choice of the benefit structure, and there seems little reason not to do so. We are not in a position to judge the constitutionality of the issue.

General-revenue financing would have a further benefit. It would disentangle contributions from benefits and eliminate the requirement to keep the fund in balance. To the extent that fund balance is imposed on a yearly basis, EI is precluded from being an effective automatic stabilizer to help counter the economic cycle.

Redistribution could also be enhanced by reforms on the benefit side. The current system restricts benefits by a ceiling on insurable earnings combined with limits on duration. This limits earnings insurance for higher-income workers, but largely insures them on the same terms as low-income workers. The taxability of EI benefits adds an element of progressivity, as does the tax-back of benefits for those earning more than $54,000 of income in the year, but these are relatively limited. As well, the EI Family Supplement targets very low-income families with children, but this, too, is relatively limited, as is the paltry amount of part-time earnings allowed while on EI. The restriction on the duration of benefits might constrain low-income workers more to the extent that re-employment is more difficult for them, given that they have lower skills. Reduction of the two-week waiting period would also particularly benefit low-income workers.

An alternative approach, and one that has been proposed by Battle, Mendelson and Torjman (2006), is to create a second-tier of benefits based on duration, as in Spain and Germany. A uniform EI benefit could apply for a given period, presumably somewhat shorter than the current system. Those who exhaust this first tier would move on to a second tier that is means-tested, thereby targeting benefits better. The means-testing could take account of family income or assets, number of dependents, and perhaps even allow for more part-time work with a less punitive tax-back rate than the current 100 per cent one. Making second-tier benefits conditional on family income would address the anomaly whereby laid off secondary workers with high-income spouses can claim full EI despite their superior ability to self-insure.

The duration of the two tiers could be longer than that of the current single-tier system, entailing a longer period of federal EI, at least for those in need. It would be administered as part of the EI system. Once the two tiers of benefits have elapsed, those still unemployed could move to provincial welfare. Such a system smoothes the transition to welfare, reducing administrative and waiting time, and, perhaps more important, increasing take-up by reducing stigmatization and application costs. It would also serve to reduce the differential treatment that long-term unemployed workers obtain from different provincial systems as a result of fiscal competition. Of course, there may still be a drop in income to the extent that provincial welfare systems are less generous than EI. And, the unemployed may be deterred from applying for welfare because of asset restrictions in provincial welfare systems. Those problems would obviously be up to the provinces to address.

This implicit reallocation of some costs of supporting the long-term unemployed from the provinces to the federal government could entail some minor adjustments in the system of social transfers. It would also free up provincial social assistance funds for other needy groups, including the disabled and single parents with small children. More generally, the whole system of transfers to the poor could be rationalized. In particular, all income tax credits could be refundable, thereby turning the income tax system into a proper negative income tax system.[16] This would reduce some of the need for transfers under the proposed second tier of EI as well as provincial welfare systems.

The advantage of a two-tier system is that it would improve the targeting of EI to those who need it most. There are alternative measures that could be taken. Regular EI benefits could be conditioned on family income and circumstances. The earnings replacement rate, currently low by international standards, could be increased and perhaps made contingent on earnings. Even reducing the waiting period below two weeks, which is higher than the international norm, would help lower income workers for whom self-insurance is costly, particularly adjusting their consumption patterns.

At same time, insurance could be enhanced without compromising redistribution unduly by deploying some experience rating in the case of repeat users. Repeat use is already discouraged to some extent by the reasonably stringent eligibility rules during the qualifying period (the most recent 52 weeks), although this is compromised by the regional differentiation of eligibility, discussed further below. Repeat use is a particular concern in two contexts. One is in seasonal industries where layoffs are predictable, so there is no real insurance rationale for EI. In this case, EI ultimately serves to subsidize employment in these industries. The other is the use of EI to finance temporary layoffs in sectors facing a downturn in demand. There is less predictability of unemployment than in the case of seasonal industries, but the probability of layoffs is higher than in more stable industries. The absence of experience rating combined with the fact that to draw EI requires being laid off implies that the EI system subsidizes temporary layoffs when it might be more efficient for a firm to reduce hours of work per employee and build inventories. This could be mitigated by some combination of experience rating, whereby either contributions or benefits are related to past claims, allowing EI to be claimed for reduced hours, and allowing workers to claim EI while continuing to work part-time. Exploring details of such schemes are beyond the scope of this chapter.

B The EI-Welfare Nexus

The fact that EI is delivered by the federal government, while welfare is provincial leads to inevitable concerns about coordination, gaps in coverage and complexity. The clientele served by EI and welfare overlap. EI beneficiaries are mainly the short-term unemployed, whether involuntarily or for maternity, compassionate or sickness reasons. Some EI recipients are temporarily laid off and will be rehired by the same firm; others will have left employment in one firm and will be searching for comparable employment elsewhere (frictional unemployment); and others have been permanently displaced and are seeking employment that may require different skills than the one they left (structural unemployment). In all cases, EI is intended to provide support until they return to their original job or find a new one. Welfare applies to the longer-term involuntary unemployed, both those who have not succeeded in getting a new job after having been laid off and those who have yet to secure employment. Welfare also applies to the disabled and non-working parents with children, but our main focus here is on those able to work.

The main structural differences between EI and welfare concern the sequence and duration of need, the eligibility requirements, and the level of benefit. While EI is a contributory program whose eligibility and duration depend on recent employment history, welfare is not related to previous employment, given that recipients include those who have not yet been employed. Instead, it is needs-based and financed from provincial general revenues (with some indirect federal assistance via the Canada Social Transfer). Of particular importance are the stringent asset limitations that restrict welfare eligibility, and that undoubtedly constrain the ability to move to welfare when EI eligibility ends. Duration of welfare benefits are indefinite as long as need is verified. Both EI and welfare recipients are allowed to earn some income, but the amounts are relatively low. EI and welfare programs have as an objective finding employment for recipients, and they deploy employment services and training to that end.

Full EI rates are substantially more than those of welfare, although the differences vary across provinces. For example, maximum insurable earnings under EI are $43,100 per year. Given a benefit rate of 55 per cent, the maximum EI benefit is $23,760 per annum, or $457 per week (Service Canada 2010). In Ontario, the welfare rate for single employable persons is $6,877 per annum or $132 per week, which is less than one-third of maximum EI eligibility and well below the poverty line (National Council of Welfare 2010). To put the comparison differently, the Ontario welfare rate would be equivalent to the EI weekly benefit for a worker who has average insurable earnings of only $12,504. This would be below the minimum wage income for a full-time worker. If instead, the comparison is with the median welfare rate for single employable persons, it is slightly more favorable for welfare. The median welfare rate is $140, which is still less than one-third of maximum EI benefits. EI benefits would be $140 per week is average insurable earnings were $13,230.

Part of the problem lies with the relatively low welfare incomes paid to single employable persons compared with either the disabled or welfare recipients with children. But, the bigger problem concerns the stagnation of provincial welfare rates since the early 1990s, coinciding with a dramatic reduction in federal transfers to the provinces. Provincial social assistance rates have declined in real terms since then, as documented in the National

Council of Welfare (2010). Among other things, welfare rates are not indexed to inflation, so changes must be legislated. Given the competing demands for funding health and education, provinces find this difficult to do. There may as well be fiscal competition factors that discourage provinces from unilaterally raising welfare rates.

The administrative requirements of the two systems are similar. In both cases, monitoring must be done for initial and continuing eligibility. In the case of EI, monitoring is particularly focused on the labour market behaviour of beneficiaries: involuntary layoffs, job search and job acceptance. Welfare is less concerned with verifying the fact of involuntary unemployment, though job search activities remain relevant. In addition, welfare eligibility entails verification of assets, part-time earnings and family circumstances.

Given that they both address the needs of the involuntary unemployed, there are apparent advantages to harmonizing EI and welfare. Harmonization could be of various sorts. The formal provisions could be harmonized so that the rules determining eligibility are similar, although it is not clear that much can be gained here. The EI system focuses much more on temporary and involuntary unemployment, while welfare is more concerned with determining needs and includes persons who have not yet been employed. It is not clear that the rules specifying what constitutes involuntary layoff, or rules governing when job offers must be accepted, should be the same under EI and welfare. Any harmonization of rules would be difficult since it would involve all provinces and territories, whose rules are not harmonized.

Harmonization could instead entail a common administration, analogous to the administration of taxes through the Canada Revenue Agency. This might make it easier for clients who move from one system to another. They would have only one agency to deal with, and their records would be available in a single place. The principle of subsidiarity might suggest that the administration of EI and welfare would best be located at the provincial level. The provinces are closer to those being served; they are likely to be more accountable; they are better able to innovate to improve delivery; and, the number of layers of management would be reduced. However, given that the administrative focus of case-workers is likely to be very different in EI than in welfare, it is not apparent that real gains of administration are possible given the difference in clients being served. The only real advantage of joint administration of EI eligibility and benefits, and welfare eligibility and benefits involves the movement of the long-term unemployed from EI to welfare. As mentioned, this only includes a subset of welfare recipients, since many have not been EI recipients. There are better ways of smoothing that transition than by unifying the administration, which we return to below.

Where more scope for harmonization exists is in the provision of employment services and training. Both EI and welfare have as objectives the re-employment of those who are able to work but are involuntarily unemployed. Employment services are particularly important for those who suffer permanent layoffs, and similar services apply as long as the worker is involuntarily unemployed, whether on EI or welfare. It would seem to be efficient to have one-stop employment services that can be used by both types of recipients. Two main problems exist. One is that, on average, EI recipients might be expected to have better job skills and more experience than welfare recipients, and would be suited for different types of jobs. A common employment service might not serve well the interests of welfare recipients, for whom placement is more difficult and takes more time. More important, it is not obvious how employment services could be harmonized given the fact that EI is federal and welfare is provincial. One possibility is for bilateral federal-provincial agreements to be signed whereby the provinces provide employment services for both EI and welfare recipients. This seems to have worked well in the case of training.

Like employment services, training is an instrument for improving the prospects for the unemployed to obtain a job. This is obviously relevant whether a worker is on EI or welfare. The provincial interest in training, even to those on EI, is obvious on various dimensions. The sooner training takes place, the smaller is the chance that EI recipients will eventually end up on welfare. When the duration of one's unemployment spell is expected to be long, it will be in the joint interests of the unemployed and the government to initiate retraining. This is especially true for the structurally unemployed who cannot expect to be re-hired in their previous sector, and whose human capital is specific. Although training is currently part of the EI program, and as such is directed to those eligible for EI, there is no compelling reason in principle to differentiate training for EI recipients from that to others, including welfare recipients, many of whom have never had a job. The fact that the federal government is exclusively responsible for EI may have resulted in the training component of EI being restricted to EI recipients, but that is an artifice of that particular division of responsibilities. Constitutional limitations aside, it would make more sense on economic efficiency grounds for federal-provincial training agreements to apply to all able but unemployed persons. EI benefits are of fixed duration, whereas welfare lasts much longer and can be the last resort for the long-term unemployed. Moreover, because of the stigmatization and costs of applying for welfare, some needy unemployed may be reluctant to apply. Ensuring that the unemployed have the skills to facilitate their re-employment is important, and this requires identifying potential unemployed workers who could benefit from skill improvement as soon as possible, whether or not they are EI recipients.

Given their responsibility for education and training, the provinces seem to be better placed to provide training. However, it is in the joint interests of both orders of government to fund these services. Training agreements exist between all provinces and the federal government.

They are of two sorts (Human Resources and Skills Development Canada 2011). Labour Market Development Agreements provide federal funding for provincially delivered training programs for those eligible for EI. In addition, there are separate bilateral Labour Market Agreements in support of provincial training programs targeted at workers who are not eligible for training under EI. The case for coordination is even stronger when eligibility for EI and welfare benefits are both conditional, to some extent, on one's involvement in a training program. The principle of equal opportunity, along with standard efficiency arguments, would support some national harmonization of training standards across provinces so workers have comparable job market opportunities.

A more ambitious approach to coordinating EI and welfare, as mentioned, is to change the EI system into a two-tier one along the lines of some European countries, while retaining welfare as a last-resort income support system for the long-term unemployed. Under a two-tiered system, workers who lose their jobs would initially be eligible for EI based on their past contributions. Those who exhaust their benefits or who did not meet the eligibility criteria would be eligible for the second tier of benefits which would be based on need rather than contributions. This would exist alongside welfare, which would cater to the long-term unemployed and those who had not yet had a job. This three-stage support program for the involuntary unemployed would recognize the fact that there are three fairly distinct classes of involuntary unemployed workers: those whose unemployment is temporary, the long-term unemployed for whom re-employment is difficult because of loss of skills, and the unemployed who have yet to acquire an attachment to the labour force.

The requirements for these three categories are somewhat different. For the temporary unemployed, EI plays an important insurance or consumption-smoothing role, especially for low-income workers. For these workers, training is of limited importance, though employment services may be important unless they expect to be re-hired by their original employer. The requirement that job loss be involuntary and that job seeking be undertaken are important eligibility considerations. The duration of benefits in this first, contributory, tier could be less than in the current EI program.

For workers whose job loss is longer term, the role of insurance wanes, while redistribution becomes more relevant. Basing benefits on need rather than past earnings, especially including family income, emphasizes this redistribution role. These workers also benefit from training. Given that they have had work experience and have presumably built up some skills, training can build on these skills. Those who remain unemployed for an extended period could then transfer to welfare, and the transition would be made easier if they are already receiving needs-based transfers.

Those who are not yet attached to the labour force would constitute the bulk of the welfare recipients. Seeking to facilitate the entry of welfare recipients into the workforce is both important and difficult, probably more so than for those who have previously lost jobs. New entrants will have had limited experience, and their innate education and skills are likely relatively low. The sort of training for which they are suitable will differ from that suitable for those with work experience. Determining the level of income support for these persons is contentious. Basic equity principles might suggest that welfare incomes should be sufficient to exceed basic poverty levels, such as Statistics Canada's Low Income Cut-off, which would be significantly higher than existing welfare incomes for single employable persons (National Council of Welfare 2010). As with EI, conditions are attached to welfare that require recipients to search for work and accept suitable jobs. However, this may be difficult to enforce because welfare is the last-resort source of income. Low welfare rates may be seen as means of inducing recipients to find work, albeit a fairly drastic means.

The issue of adequacy of welfare incomes is beyond the scope of EI reform measures. At the same time, the fact that welfare rates are relatively low compared with EI has some implications for the design of EI. It adds impetus to the case for a two-tiered system of EI with relatively lengthy duration of the second tier, given the sizeable income drop in going from EI to welfare. Enforcing job search requirements is likely to be easier in the second tier of an EI system than it is in welfare where there is no further fall-back source of income. The fact of low provincial welfare rates also adds urgency to reforms of the tax system so that those at the bottom end of the income distribution do not rely primarily on welfare for support.

C Regional Differentiation of Eligibility and Benefits

For the most part, the EI system does not use insurance principles to determine contribution rates, eligibility, or the level and duration of benefits. Contribution rates are uniform despite the fact that the risks of layoff and the expected duration of unemployment vary across industries. As a result, EI redistributes systematically from sectors with low probabilities of layoff, such as the public sector and stable industries like financial and other services, to those with high probabilities, including seasonal industries and industries subject to cyclical demand. Employment is implicitly subsidized in the latter industries relative to the former, and regions that rely on seasonal or fluctuating industries benefit relative to other regions.

There are some exceptions to this absence of insurance principles. One is that the ability to qualify for EI is slightly more onerous for recent EI recipients. Another is the longer qualifying period required for new entrants and those who have been out of the labour force for two years (the so-called 910 rule). The more important one for our purposes is the differentiation in the eligibility requirements and duration of benefits among the 58 regions of the country. The number of hours of insurable employment in the past 52 weeks required to qualify for EI varies from

700 in regions with a 6 per cent unemployment rate to 420 in regions with a 13.1 per cent unemployment rate. The number of weeks of benefits for those who meet the minimum eligibility requirement vary from 14 in low-unemployment regions to 32 in high-unemployment regions, and the differences remain significant for those who have accumulated more than the minimum eligible hours.

The rationale for these regional differences in eligibility and duration is to recognize the greater chance of being laid off and the longer time it takes on average to find a new job in high-unemployment regions. At the same time, there are a number of anomalous features of these provisions.

- Some regions that have higher unemployment rates might also be those that already benefit from an absence of insurance-based contribution rates. Thus, if a region has a concentration of seasonal industries or industries susceptible to fluctuating demand, it may also have a higher than average unemployment rate.
- If some regions have persistently higher unemployment rates, regionally differentiated benefits might discourage the reallocation of labour to other regions where it might be more efficiently employed.
- The probability of being laid off may not be well approximated by the regional unemployment rate. For example, in economic downturns, layoffs often target short-tenure workers who are not eligible for EI (even though they may have contributed) rather than those who are eligible. Differential eligibility requirements effectively discriminate against short-tenure workers in low-unemployment regions.
- More generally, the unemployment rate is not a very precise indicator of the difficulty of getting a job. Better candidates might be the employment rate or the average duration of an unemployment spell in a region. Alternatively, since these measures reflect to some extent past conditions, changes in the rate of unemployment might be better. However, no measure will be perfect.
- The definition of regions is to some extent arbitrary. The presumption is that a region should reflect a relatively well-defined labour market with distinct employment prospects within the region. In practice, this is difficult to apply. There is bound to be some heterogeneity within regions, so that different rates of unemployment exist in different industries within the same region. In principle, it might make more sense to differentiate by industries rather than regions, but that would also be difficult to implement. The possibility that workers can migrate from one region to the next also makes regional differentiation arbitrary.
- These problems imply that regional differentiation will always give rise to workers in comparable situations facing different EI rules simply because they reside in different unemployment regions.

These considerations lead to the conclusion that regional differentiation is too problematic to be warranted, and it is not surprising that it is little used in other federations that have federal-level EI schemes. Although regional differentiation is observed in the United States, it seems to be mainly explained by constitutional and political constraints rather than by efficiency concerns.

In the absence of regional differentiation, what alternatives might be used to deal with the fact that different workers might have systematically different chances of layoff and re-employment? One answer to that is to deploy a uniform set of rules throughout Canada and rely on the administration of EI to ensure the integrity of the system. The rules state that eligibility for EI requires that workers have lost their job through no fault of their own, that they are willing to work, and that they are actively looking for work. As long as these criteria are being diligently enforced, it is not clear why differential eligibility and duration rules should apply.

If regional differentiation must apply, the current system could be improved. Differences could be restricted to duration and not eligibility, as suggested by Bishop and Burleton (2009). More accurate measures of local conditions could be applied. As mentioned, candidates include the local employment rate or the average duration of an unemployment spell, although neither of these is perfect. More generally, if there is a desire to institute some insurance principles into the system, experience-rating of frequent users would be a better place to start.

One other provision that is discriminatory and has regional implications is the eligibility of self-employed fishers for EI. While it is true that many of them have a regular pattern of employment because of regulated fishing seasons, it is nonetheless anomalous that this category of the self-employed are eligible to the exclusion of all others.

D Part-Time Workers

Part-time workers are to some extent covered given that eligibility is based on cumulated hours of work rather than full-time work weeks. However, the hours required are quite high, and apparently rule ineligible many workers, especially those with limited seniority for whom the need for insurance is great. This could be addressed by reducing the minimum hours required for eligibility, assuming that those laid off after such a short period can be verified to be truly involuntarily unemployed. Bishop and Burleton suggest 350 hours as a minimum (2009).

There are some concerns with shortening the eligibility period. One is that it is more tempting to game the system by arranging to take short-term employment with the prospect of a spell of EI benefits afterward. This sort of temptation has been a concern in high-unemployment provinces. It may be particularly a problem for secondary workers with limited attachment to the labour force, who may have primary workers as partners so self-insurance is not an issue. As well, the shorter the period of earnings, the less is the rationale for income smoothing, because there is less income to smooth.

Workers who suffer significant reductions in hours worked without being laid off are typically not eligible despite the fact that the reductions may be involuntary and the need for income insurance great. Some countries offer insurance to workers whose work schedule is involuntarily and significantly reduced without being laid off (e.g., Belgium). It has been allowed on a discretionary basis for work-sharing agreements in Canada. Extending the EI system to include those whose employment has been significantly reduced would insure against unexpected fluctuations in income, especially during a recession. It would also mitigate the incentive for firms to use temporary layoffs to take advantage of EI for their workers. However, successful insuring of part-time workers would require good administrative oversight to verify that reductions in work schedules were involuntary and substantial. An eligibility aid would be to require minimum weekly hours of work along with minimum cumulated hours. The ability to condition benefits on family income, as in the second tier of the proposed two-tier system, would also help.

E The Role of the Income Tax-Transfer System

The income tax-transfer system, which serves primarily as a revenue-raising device, also redistributes income and provides some implicit insurance against fluctuating earnings. It is worth considering the role of income taxes and transfers as a complement to the EI system. There are three cases in which the income tax system, rather than EI, assumes the primary role as a social insurance device: the self-employed, displaced workers and the long-term unemployed.

Self-employed workers are those who operate their own businesses as professionals, contractors or consultants, as well as farmers and fishermen. In 2009, around 2.7 million Canadians earned at least a part of their income from self-employment, two-third of them being men. The number of self-employed is constantly growing, especially in times of recession (Statistics Canada 2008).

F The Self-employed

It would seem natural to include self-employed workers in EI. They are subject to the same labour market risks as regular employees, particularly during economic downturns. Moreover, self-insurance may be costly, given their modest average income, which was $22,866 in 2005 when 79 per cent of them reported incomes less than $20,000, while only 3 per cent reported incomes higher than $100,000. On the other hand, many self-employed have other sources of income, some of them being potentially insurable through the regular EI scheme. In 2005, 46 per cent of the self-employed had employment earnings. Another difficulty is that becoming self-employed can itself be a self-insurance device, especially in times of recessions (La-Rochelle-Coté 2010). This makes it difficult to determine their ability to self-insure.

Agreeing on a proper definition of what being unemployed means for the self-employed is a substantial problem. Independent work is more prone to volatility and does not involve stable work schedules. If the self-insured were insurable, it is not clear how the EI program could provide them with timely help in case of unemployment, and what timely would mean.

Eligibility to the program depends on the number of hours worked, which for regular employees is obtained from employers. For the self-employed, eligibility would rely on voluntary reports from the potential claimants, which is liable to be unreliable. Determining the amount of the contributions would also be difficult. Self-employed individuals declare their incomes at most on a quarterly basis. Contributions would have to be determined as a function of quarterly income, when they have to pay provisional accounts.

It is important to recognize that the self-employed are already partially insured through the tax system. They derive their income from the profits and face the risk of a loss in any given year. In a loss year, they nonetheless incur current and capital costs. To some extent, these costs are insured by the tax system since they can be carried forward to fiscal years. However, this insurance against losses is imperfect. Not only are negative tax liabilities not immediately refundable, they will never be credited if future profits do not materialize due to bankruptcy or a longer-term economic downturn. Allowing for full refundability of losses would provide them with an effective form of insurance. It would also incidentally encourage risk-taking and entrepreneurship and assist with the cash flow of risky firms. Governments seem reluctant to offer full loss refundability, perhaps because of the potential for abuse.

Some countries include the self-employed in EI, though there are difficult problems of implementation. Sweden is a case in point. To receive benefits, claimants must cease all their business activities for some period of time, disposing of all business assets and deregister the business (Swedish Unemployment Insurance Board 2007, 6). Belgium also insures the self-employed by UI, but a complicated administrative process determines contributions. Initially, a provisional account is set up and can last up to 15 quarters until a proper amount can be established. In addition to being administratively costly, timeliness of help is compromised and self-employment discouraged. Relying on the tax system to insure the self-employed seems preferable.

Finally, note that the treatment of the self-employed may be affected by human rights requirements. The 2010 decision of the federal government allowing self-employed workers to opt into extended EI benefits complied with the judgment of the Canadian Human Rights Commission that excluding such workers constituted a potential violation of the principle of equality.

G Permanently Displaced Workers

Displaced workers include those who suffer structural unemployment when their industry of employment suffers a major shock. They represent a special case of the unemployed both because of the long-run nature of their unemployment and because of the loss of the value of their skills when they are laid off. While EI can mitigate the immediate consequences of their job loss, and training can help them find a new job, in the long run, because their skills have depreciated, they typically face a permanent reduction on their earning power.

The EI system is ill-suited to deal with permanent reductions in earning capability. The income-transfer system has, as one of its objectives, the redistribution of income from those with higher earnings to those with lower earnings. Typically, these differences in earnings potential are life-long: some persons are born with greater earnings ability than others, and one task of the income tax system is to address those inequalities. Inequalities that arise partway through the lifetime pose similar challenges that the income tax system is designed to address. Income tax is not expected to fully insure permanent earnings inequalities, whether they arise at birth or partway through the life cycle. One improvement in the income tax system that would be particularly helpful would be to reinstitute general income averaging so that workers who suffer a permanent reduction in earnings can average their tax liabilities across periods in their working life when they face different tax rates.

H The Long-term Unemployed

The long-term unemployed, including those who have never been eligible for EI, rely mostly on provincial welfare systems for income support. They do get limited help from the income tax system through refundable tax credits, such as the Goods and Services Tax Credit and the Canada Child Tax Benefit. These are relatively small in size, especially for single unemployed persons. As we have mentioned, welfare incomes are very modest relative to standard poverty levels, and there is no apparent prospect for the provinces to improve their generosity.

Here, too, the income tax-transfer system could play a complementary role to provincial welfare systems in meeting the needs of the long-term unemployed. Simply making all income tax credits refundable would be a start. Their generosity for the lowest-income persons could be enhanced in a revenue-neutral way by conditioning them on income as is done with existing refundable tax credits. Employment services and training, such as those available for EI recipients, are also important for the long-term unemployed.

5 Recommendations

To conclude, based on our consideration of the rationale for EI and the special issues that arise in a federal setting, we propose the following policy recommendations.

- Change the financing of the system as much as possible from payroll-based contributions to general revenue financing. This recognizes that the contributions are a form of taxation that serve no real insurance function and are regressive. General-revenue financing would make the system more progressive, would eliminate the requirement for an EI fund that is self-financing on an annual basis, and would not detract from the setting of eligibility and benefits based on insurable earnings.
- Complement the financing system by charges on firms that are repeat users as a means of experience rating.
- Make benefits more progressive. For one, benefits could be conditioned on family income and family responsibilities. More ambitiously, a two-tier EI system could be established. The first tier would be earnings-based, and could be of relatively short duration. The second tier would be needs-based, including by family income and responsibility. Overall, duration of the two tiers would be longer than the current system. A two-tier system would explicitly recognize the three distinct categories of unemployed—short-term unemployed, long-term employed and those never employed). Ideally both tiers could be financed from general revenues as proposed above, but if contributions are deemed necessary, they should apply only to the first tier.
- Eliminate regionally differentiated benefits and the selective eligibility of fishers. This would eliminate a source of arbitrary difference in rules for particular claimants that results in unfairness to workers in like circumstances.
- Separate training from EI so that distinct training programs do not apply that are restricted to those eligible for EI and those that are not.
- Improve the income tax system to deal with variability of earnings of the self-employed, displaced workers, and welfare recipients. This includes improved measures of loss refundability for the self-employed, general income averaging, and converting all nonrefundable tax credits to refundable ones while increasing their generosity and conditioning them on income.
- Stress the importance of administration of EI as necessary for maintaining the integrity and generosity of the system.
- Reform provincial welfare systems so that payments to the long-term unemployed closer to poverty levels are indexed.

Endnotes

1 Unemployment insurance became a federal responsibility as a result of a constitutional amendment in 1940. The federal government had passed an unemployment insurance bill in 1935 the midst of the Great Depression, but it was declared unconstitutional, being an exclusive provincial responsibility.

2 For a recent comprehensive discussion of administration of tax systems, see Shaw, Slemrod and Whiting (2010).

3 The role of monitoring and administration in transfer programs is outlined in Boadway, Cuff and Marceau (2008). Theoretical treatments may be found in Boadway and Cuff (1999) and Boone, Fredriksson, Holmlund, and van Ours (2007).

4 The redistributive role of social insurance is discussed in Chetty and Looney (2006) and Chetty and Saez (2010).

5 This was emphasized as one of the key incentive effects of unemployment insurance in the 1970s by Baily (1978) and Feldstein (1978).

6 However, the current EI program allows firms to sign work-sharing agreements to mitigate the incentive for temporary layoffs, although at some cost to the EI fund. Section 36(1) states: Without altering the legislative authority of Parliament or of the provincial legislatures, or the rights of any of them with respect to the exercise of their legislative authority, Parliament and the legislatures, together with the government of Canada and the provincial governments, are committed to: (a) promoting equal opportunities for the well-being of Canadians; (b) furthering economic development to reduce disparity in opportunities; and (c)providing essential public services of reasonable quality to all Canadians.

7 The implications of regionally extended benefits for Ontario are discussed in Jacobs (2010) and Bishop and Burleton (2009).

8 We follow the common practice elsewhere in the world of referring to programs to insure the involuntary unemployed as "unemployment insurance."

9 The administrative rules in the United Kingdom define an unemployed worker as an individual who is at least 18 years old and below public pension age, who works no more than 16 hours per week on average, and who satisfies the other conditions for regular unemployment, such as being actively searching for a new job. In extreme circumstances, i.e. being a single parent, this extends to 16- and 17-year-olds.

10 The UK government has announced that they will replace the existing means-tested benefits and tax credit programs, including the JSA, with a unified Universal Credit. Nonetheless, the features of the JSA are worth recounting since they reflect the kind of UI programs that have been used in the past.

11 It is interesting to note that the Swiss federal government emphasizes the fact that the self-employed have a special responsibility so as to guarantee their financial security and that of their family in case of unemployment (http://www.ch.ch/private/00054/00058/00585/00590/index.html?lang=fr).

12 Because the duration of benefits depends on the duration of contributions but not their size, one suspects that the dependence on past contributions is more

designed to avoid adverse selection than to be based on insurance principles.

13 The TANF program was called "Aid to Dependent Children" between 1936 and 1962, to become the "Aid to Families with Dependent Children" until 1996. Under the *Personal Responsibility and Work Opportunity Reconciliation Act* of 1996 it became the "TANF Emergency Fund," which also reimburses the states 80 per cent of their expenditure increases due to subsidized employment to low-income parents and youth, and some short-term non-recurrent benefits.

14 The federal government determines which states qualify for that so-called "tier-III" part of UI. As of 26 March 2010, eligible states had a three month average unemployment rate of at least 6 per cent.

15 A recent proponent of a guaranteed annual income is Senator Hugh Segal in an article in the *National Post* on 15 December 2009 entitled "A Real Fix for Poverty." The concept has frequently been recommended by advocacy reports, including the Royal Commission on the Economic Union and Development Prospects for Canada (1985).

References

Acemoglu, D. and R. Shimer. 1999. "Efficient Unemployment Insurance." *Journal of Political Economy* 107: 893-928.

Baily, M.N. 1978. "Some Aspects of Optimal Unemployment Insurance." *Journal of Public Economics* 10: 379-402.

Battle, K., M. Mendelson and S. Torjman. 2006. *Towards a New Architecture for Canada's Adult Benefits*. Caledon Institute, Ottawa.

Bishop, G. and D. Burleton. 2009. *Is Canada's Employment Insurance Program Adequate?* TD Economics, Toronto.

Boadway, R. and K. Cuff. 1999. "Monitoring Job Search as an Instrument for Targeting Transfers." *International Tax and Public Finance* 6: 317-37.

Boadway, R., K. Cuff and N. Marceau. 2008. "Design of Assistance Programs to Address Real Income Volatility." In *Income Volatility and Food Assistance in the United States*, ed. D. Jolliffe and J.P. Ziliak, 217-58. Kalamazoo, Michigan: W.E. Upjohn Institute for Employment Research.

Boadway, R. and A. Shah. 2009, *Fiscal Federalism: Principles and Practice of Multiorder Governance*. New York: Cambridge University Press.

Boone, J., P. Fredriksson, B. Holmlund, and J.C. van Ours. 2007. "Optimal Unemployment Insurance with Monitoring and Sanctions." *The Economic Journal* 117: 399-421.

Browning, M. and T.F. Crossley. 2009. "Shocks, Stocks and Socks: Smoothing Consumption over a Temporary Income Loss." *Journal of the European Economic Association* 7: 1169-92.

Buera, F.J. and Y. Shin. Forthcoming. "Self-insurance vs. Self-financing: A Welfare Analysis of the Persistence of Shocks." *Journal of Economic Theory*.

Canton de Genève. 2010. "Indemnités de Chômage." At http://www.ge.ch/emploi-recherche/indemnites_chomage.asp#4.

Chetty, R. 2008. "Moral hazard vs. liquidity and optimal unemployment insurance." Working paper, Harvard University.

Chetty, R. and A. Looney. 2006. "Consumption Smoothing and The Welfare Consequences Of Social Insurance In Developing Economies." *Journal of Public Economics* 90: 2351-56.

Chetty, R.and E. Saez. 2010. "Optimal Taxation and Social Insurance with Endogenous Private Insurance." *American Economic Journal: Economic Policy* 2: 85-114.

Cullen, J.B. and J. Gruber. 2000. "Spousal Labor Supply as Insurance: Does Unemployment Insurance Crowd Out the Added Worker Effect?" *Journal of Labor Economics* 18: 546-72.

Feldstein, M.S. 1978. "The Effect of Unemployment Insurance on Temporary Layoff Unemployment." *American Economic Review* 68: 834-46.

Hamilton, B.H. 2000. "Does Entrepreneurship Pay? An Empirical Analysis of the Returns to Self-employment." *Journal of Political Economy* 108: 604-31.

Hipple, S. 2004. "Self-employment in the United States: An Update," *Monthly Labor Review* (July 2004): 13-23.

Human Resources and Skills Development Canada. 2010. "Report of the Chief Actuary to the Employment Insurance Commission on the Break-Even Premium Rate and Maximum Insurable Earnings." At http://www.hrsdc.gc.ca/eng/employment/ei/premium_rate/2010/index.shtml

——. 2011. "Labour Market Development Agreements," last modified 22 February 2011. At http://www.hrsdc.gc.ca/eng/employment/partnerships/labour_market_development/index.shtml.

Jacobs, L. 2010. "Canada's System of Regionally Extended and Differentiated Employment Insurance Benefits: An Equal Employment Opportunities Approach." Prepared for the Mowat Centre EI Task Force.

La-Rochelle-Coté, S. 2010. "Self-employment in the downturn." *Perspectives*: 1-13. At http://www.statcan.gc.ca/pub/75-001-x/2010103/pdf/11138-eng.pdf.

Macdonald, D. (Chair). 1985. *Report of the Royal Commission on the Economic Union and Development Prospects for Canada*. Ottawa: Minister of Supply and Services Canada.

Mäder, U., C. Knöpfel and S. Kutzner. 2010. *Social-welfare in Switzerland: Integration and exclusion through segmentation of clients*. Swiss National Fundation.

McCall, B.P. 1996. "Unemployment Insurance Rules, Joblessness and Part-Time Work." *Econometrica* 64.3: 647-82.

National Council of Welfare. 2010. "Welfare Incomes 2009". At http://www.ncw.gc.ca/l.3bd.2t.1ils@-eng.jsp?lid=331.

Organisation for Economic Co-operation and Development (OECD). 2004. *Employment Outlook*. Paris: Organisation for Economic Co-operation and Development.

——. 2008. "Wages and Benefits." In *Countries Chapters for Australia, Belgium, Canada, Germany, Switzerland, United States*. Paris: Organisation for Economic Co-operation and Development.

——. 2010. "Spain: Health and Welfare." At http://countrystudies.us/spain/48.htm.

Perry, D.B. 1997. *Financing the Canadian Federation, 1867 to 1995: Setting the Stage for Change*, Canadian Tax Paper no. 102. Toronto: Canadian Tax Foundation.

Service Canada. 2010. *Employment Insurance Regular Benefits*. Service Canada: Ottawa.

Shaw, J., J. Slemrod and J. Whiting. 2010. "Administration and Compliance." In Dimensions of Tax Design: the Mirrlees Review, ed. Besley, Timothy and Blundell, Richard and Gammie, Malcolm and Poterba, James, 1100-62. Oxford: Oxford University Press.

Statistics Canada. 2008. "Earnings of employees and the self-employed." Last revised 25 November 2008. At http://www.statcan.gc.ca/pub/71-222-x/2008001/sectionj/j-earnings-gains-eng.htm.

Swedish Unemployment Insurance Board (IAF). 2007. "The Swedish Unemployment Insurance Scheme." At http://www.iaf.se/Global/English/The_swedish_unemployment_insurance_scheme%5B1%5D.pdf.

Thurik, A.R., M.A. Carree, A. van Stel, and D.B. Audretsch. 2008. "Does self-employment reduce unemployment?" *Journal of Business Venturing* 23: 673-86.

United States Department of Labor. 2004. "State Unemployment Insurance Benefits." Last modified 13 January 2010. At http://www.workforcesecurity.doleta.gov/unemploy/uifactsheet.asp.

Sources of Country Information

http://www.direct.gov.uk/en/MoneyTaxAndBenefits/BenefitsTaxCreditsAndOtherSupport/Employedorlookingforwork/DG_10018757

http://www.cleiss.fr/docs/regimes/regime_belgique_ns1.html

http://www.rva.be/frames/Frameset.aspx?Language=FR&Path=D_opdracht_VW/&Items=3

http://www.admin.ch/ch/f/rs/837_0/

http://www.hmrc.gov.uk/ni/intro/basics.htm

http://www.cleiss.fr/docs/cotisations/recouvrement_belgique.html

http://www.cleiss.fr/docs/regimes/regime_belgique_ns1.html

http://www.belgium.be/fr/economie/entreprise/creation/independants/

http://www.admin.ch/ch/f/rs/i8/0.831.109.268.1.fr.pdf

http://www.ch.ch/private/00054/00058/00585/00590/index.html?lang=fr

http://www.rsvz.be/fr/tools/publications/rights_obligations_fr.pdf

Chapter 5

Fixing the Hole in EI: Temporary Income Assistance for the Unemployed[1]

Michael Mendelson and Ken Battle

1 The Gap Between EI and Social Assistance

A Why Unemployment insurance?

We may define three archetypes for income security programs: universal, selective and social insurance. A universal program pays every person in a broad demographic group the same amount, regardless of their income or needs. A selective program pays a variable amount of benefit to eligible recipients according to some test of their level of income (known as an income-tested program) or their needs, assets and other resources (characterized as a needs-tested program). A social insurance program collects premiums from contributors and pays benefits more or less scaled to their contributions. Both universal and selective programs are usually financed through general revenue, while social insurance plans are typically funded primarily through premiums.

Of course, the real world is neither so simple nor clear cut. In reality, there are a thousand and one variations on these three archetypes, including many hybrids. Nevertheless, this typology provides a useful lens through which to understand the income security system and analyze the roles that different types of programs can and should play.

Canada established its national unemployment insurance program in the shadow of the 1930s depression. The new national program was set up in 1940 as a social insurance, and this was not a mere whimsy. The federal government encountered significant legal and jurisdictional barriers as a consequence of deciding on the social insurance model for its new unemployment assistance program.

The British Judicial Committee of the Privy Council, which then functioned as Canada's final court of appeal, ruled that social insurance was indeed a form of insurance, like private insurance, and thus was within provincial and not federal jurisdiction under the *British North America Act*. Consequently, an amendment to the *British North America Act* was deemed necessary to permit the national government to operate a contributory unemployment insurance program. (An amendment to the *British North America Act* is more or less equivalent to a Constitutional amendment today.) Although Quebec had originally objected to empowering the federal government to run a national unemployment insurance plan, a new Liberal government in Quebec granted its approval and the required amendment was duly passed in 1940 with the unanimous consent of the provinces.

In persevering to overcome these barriers, the governments of the day demonstrated their determination to deliver unemployment assistance as a social insurance. Ottawa and the provinces needed the new national program to be a social insurance because that type of income security program has several unique characteristics vital to meeting the objectives of unemployment assistance for most unemployed workers, and for the nation as a whole.

On the macro-level, a social insurance program can act as a counter-cyclical stabilizer by building up a fund when times are good and then drawing down the fund when times are bad. On the micro-level, a social insurance scheme creates a relationship between an individual's contributions and that person's potential benefits. Here we are interested in the micro-level features of unemployment insurance.

In a social insurance plan, it is generally possible to maintain an individual account of the amount contributed by or on behalf of each participant. Benefits may then in turn be paid out more or less proportionally to the total amount of premium paid by each participant, according to various formulae. This feature gives social insurance programs the capacity—unique among income security programs—explicitly to pay higher benefits to those who have higher incomes. (Tax deductions and exemptions also pay higher benefits in the form of income tax savings to those with higher incomes, but do so implicitly and without the widespread understanding of much of the public.) In addition, because social insurance benefits are financed mainly from premiums, there is likely less public resistance to higher levels of benefits than would be found in most income-tested or needs-related income security programs.

In contrast, a non-social insurance program will usually be funded from general revenue, making it impossible or at best hypothetical to maintain a record of individual contributions and to relate benefits directly to past contributions. In an income security program funded from general revenue, public acceptability typically demands that differences in benefits be based on criteria such as income or need wherein those with the least get the most. As well, these programs may encounter significant public resistance to higher benefit levels.

A social insurance type of program is therefore especially suitable when the objective is to provide continuity of living standards for those with modest or middle incomes, rather than the more limited objective of providing protection against deep poverty for those with the lowest incomes.

Historically, the reasons for adopting the social insurance model of unemployment insurance in 1940 were many and complex. But through the assorted legal barriers and political compromises, the provinces and the federal government arrived at a social insurance model that offered some financial protection from unemployment for the "average" worker, not just a safety net for the destitute. And the model has remained sufficiently robust to survive for 70 years.

It is our contention that the original decision was correct. If Canadians want an unemployment insurance plan that allows the unemployed to maintain their standard of living at least for a short to medium term period of unemployment—which tangibly means keeping up mortgage and car payments, paying taxes, buying groceries and the other ongoing unavoidable expenses of everyday life—then unemployment protection designed as a social insurance makes good sense.

Better financial protection for the unemployed individual also has implications for the whole community. From the perspective of the overall economy, it is preferable to enable the unemployed to spring back quickly to work as the economy recovers from a downturn. If unemployed households are forced to begin stripping assets, such as selling homes and vehicles, this will reduce asset prices for everyone and inhibit economic recovery. As we have seen in the recent waves of house foreclosures in the United States, a neighbour's problem can very soon become a neighbourhood's problem.

B What Unemployment Insurance Cannot Do

While the social insurance model has advantages in respect of important objectives, it also has limitations. If unemployment benefits require premiums to be paid, then workers with little or no premiums collect little or no unemployment assistance. Yet, in a dynamic modern economy with a flexible labour market, there are many different forms of employment, and much entry and re-entry into the labour market. Immigrants, young people newly entering the labour market, re-entrants into the labour market and others will likely not be included at all in a contributory social insurance scheme because they cannot meet the work eligibility requirements.

The self-employed must also be excluded from an insurance-based unemployment program because of the difficulty of defining when exactly a self-employed person is unemployed—for example, is a self-employed consultant temporarily unemployed if she does not get a contract for two or three months? Osberg et al. (1995) ask the same question prior to proceeding to a "hypothetical" simulation: "Even though, for example, a self-employed economic consultant might in fact be working for weeks or months on a particular consulting contract, their payment is typically on an infrequent basis. One does wonder how it would be possible to accurately record the weeks of self-employment work effort which would qualify such individuals for UI (Unemployment Insurance, as Employment Insurance was then called) benefits, if UI coverage were extended." Is a small business owner unemployed if she sells her business and is seeking other opportunities for investment or for employment? In addition, how can the "unemployed" self-employed be paid unemployment insurance benefits if contributors voluntarily leaving a job—who represented 17.9 per cent of unemployed contributors in 2008[2]—are denied eligibility?

The tendency for the social insurance model to provide less protection for some groups has long been observed, as noted in Vosko (2011). Vosko cites, for example, Schmid and Reissert (1996, 248): "just as older people tend to be better protected under insurance-based systems, the young are less well protected. Insurance-based systems are, therefore, biased towards protecting core workers (mostly male and elderly) over marginal workers (mostly young, female and casual)."

We concur fully with this observation regarding social insurance programs. The policy question is what to do about it. One strategy is to attempt to adjust the parameters of social insurance programs. An alternative or perhaps complementary strategy is to introduce non-social insurance programs that fill the gaps left by social insurance programs. The following sections argue that the former strategy has only limited capacity to reach those currently left out of the Employment Insurance program, or at least to do so without also undermining Employment Insurance. We then present an alternative strategy.

C Who is Ineligible for Employment Insurance?

Figure 1 shows the total number of unemployed in Canada and their eligibility status for regular[3] Employment Insurance benefits from 2003 through 2010. Unemployment was falling from 2003 to 2007, but with the economic downturn beginning in mid-2008 the unemployment rate rose and then increased substantially in 2009, decreasing only a little in 2010. In every year in this period, well over half a million unemployed Canadian workers were not eligible for Employment Insurance, with more than 600,000 ineligible in most years. In 2010, with higher unemployment levels for the last two years, 784,000 unemployed Canadians were not eligible for Employment Insurance.

FIGURE 1 Eligibility and Ineligibility for Employment Insurance, 2003–2010

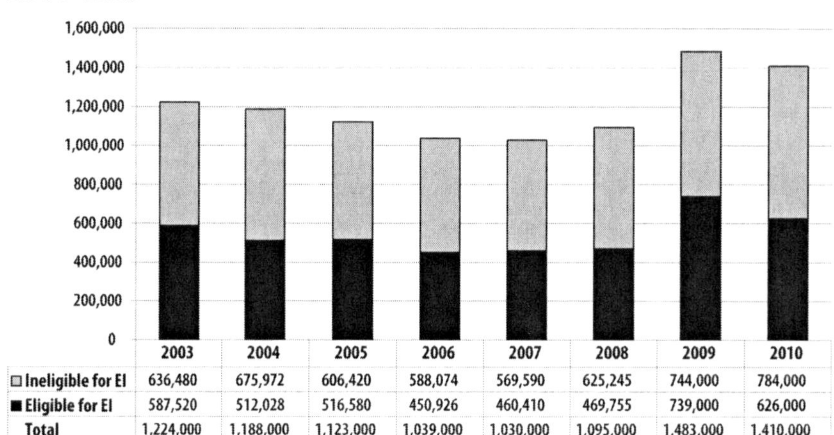

	2003	2004	2005	2006	2007	2008	2009	2010
□ Ineligible for EI	636,480	675,972	606,420	588,074	569,590	625,245	744,000	784,000
■ Eligible for EI	587,520	512,028	516,580	450,926	460,410	469,755	739,000	626,000
Total	1,224,000	1,188,000	1,123,000	1,039,000	1,030,000	1,095,000	1,483,000	1,410,000

Figure 2 shows the *percentage* of unemployed who were eligible[4] and ineligible for regular Employment Insurance benefits in each year in the seven year period 2003 through 2010. Figure 2 further displays ineligibility for Employment Insurance in two categories: those who were contributing participants in the Employment Insurance program (defined as having made at least one premium payment into Employment Insurance in the prior 12 months) but were in any case ineligible, and those who were non-contributors and consequently not eligible.

As can be seen in Figure 2, fewer than half of the unemployed have been eligible for regular Employment Insurance benefits since 2003. The share of the unemployed who are eligible for Employment Insurance declined from 48.0 per cent of the unemployed in 2003 to 42.9 per cent in 2008, but increased to 49.8 per cent in 2009, falling again to 44.4 per cent in 2010.

There were no legislative changes affecting the eligibility of the unemployed from 2003 to 2008, so the decline in eligibility over this period was not caused by policy changes. During this whole period up to 2008, unemployment rates were falling. Consequently, entry requirements were increasing in most regions (those whose unemployment rates fell sufficiently) and this may have reduced the proportion of the unemployed in aggregate eligible for benefits. However, unemployment rates also fell in 2005 (from 7.2 per cent in 2004 to 6.8 per cent in 2005) so the increase in eligibility in that year would be an anomaly.

FIGURE 2 Percentage of the Unemployed Contributing and Non-Contributing, Eligible and Ineligible for Employement Insurance, 2003–2010

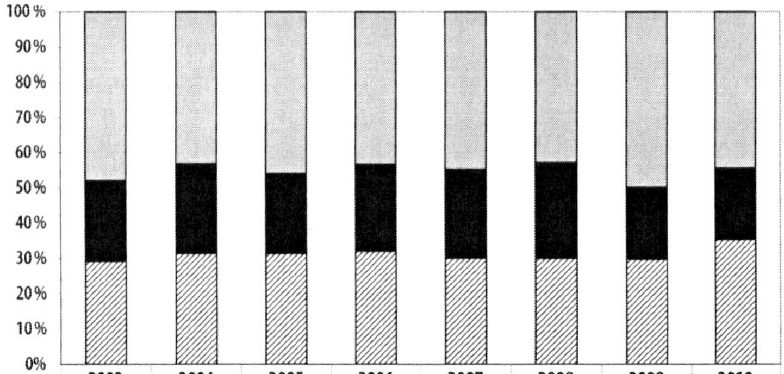

	2003	2004	2005	2006	2007	2008	2009	2010
Eligible Contributors	48.0%	3.1%	46.0%	43.4%	44.7%	42.9%	49.8%	44.4%
Ineligible Contributors	22.9%	25.5%	22.6%	24.6%	25.3%	27.2%	20.4%	20.3%
Non-Contributors	29.1%	31.4%	31.4%	32.0%	30.0%	29.9%	29.7%	35.3%

There were legislative changes in 2009 which temporarily lengthened the duration of benefits, but the rule changes in themselves did not reduce the number of hours required to be eligible for benefits or otherwise change entry requirements. Nevertheless, the automatic adjustment of entry requirements with higher rates of unemployment did result in a rapid reduction in the number of hours required for eligibility in most regions across Canada. Those changes, combined with the layoff of tens of thousands of full-time workers who had been steadily employed for many years, resulted in a large increase in the number of unemployed eligible for Employment Insurance benefits in 2009. Yet, despite this expansion of eligibility in 2009, eligible contributors remained only about half of the total unemployed.

By 2010, the increase in eligible contributors in 2009 had been entirely lost, accounted for by a substantial rise in the percentage of non-contributors among the unemployed. As we shall see below (Figure 4), this development is due to an increase in long-term unemployment as many more unemployed in 2010 were non-contributors due to being unemployed for the previous 12 months.

Ineligible unemployed may be further divided into those who are Employment Insurance contributors and those who are non-contributors. The former are ineligible because they do not meet the Employment Insurance qualifications for a regular benefit despite having contributed and being participants in the Employment Insurance scheme. The latter are not eligible because they were not participants in the first place.

Figure 2 shows that about 30 per cent of the unemployed were non-contributors from 2003 through 2009, with very little fluctuation. The percentage of unemployed who are non-contributors has been remarkably stable, even through widely varying labour markets. Despite a huge increase in unemployment in 2009, the portion of non-contributors remained a constant 30 per cent—the same as it was in 2006, with 400,000 fewer unemployed. Neither the rule changes in 2009 nor the automatic reductions in hours of work required for eligibility affected *non-contributors'* ability to participate in Employment Insurance and thereby become eligible for regular benefits. Since the percentage of non-contributors has remained constant through 2009 while the percentage of ineligible unemployed has been increasing, all of the change in the percentage of ineligible unemployed workers until 2010 was the result of variation in the share of eligible contributors—i.e., changes in the proportion of participants in the Employment Insurance program who are eligible upon becoming unemployed.

As noted above, in 2010 the number of non-contributors increased substantially for the first time. We will not know for a few years whether this augers a permanent change in the labour force, or whether the percentage of non-contributors will fall back to 30 per cent if and when unemployment decreases.

In sum: about 55 per cent of the unemployed in Canada are currently ineligible for Employment Insurance. This is a lower figure than in the previous few years excepting 2009, where ineligibility had been nudging upwards close to 60 per cent, possibly due to the effects of automatic adjustments in entry requirements as unemployment rates fell. Independent of any other long-term trend, until 2010 about 30 per cent of all the unemployed (i.e., about 60 per cent among the 50 per cent of unemployed ineligible for Employment Insurance in 2009) were ineligible because they were not participants in the Employment Insurance system, having not paid any premiums in the previous 12 months. Non-contributors remained a stable 30 per cent of the unemployed over the last several years until 2010, despite even the substantial changes in the labour market and consequently in Employment Insurance eligibility in 2009. We will not know for a few more years whether the percentage of ineligible among the unemployed will return to the 30 per cent long-term trend or remain at the elevated level of 35 per cent reached in 2010.

In the next sections we look more closely at each of the two categories of ineligible unemployed: those not participating in Employment Insurance and those who are participating but are still ineligible.

D Unemployed Workers Not Participating (Non-Contributors) in Employment Insurance

Figure 3 shows the percentage of unemployed workers in each province (except Prince Edward Island due to its inadequate sample size) who were non-contributors to Employment Insurance in 2009 and 2010. While the national average was 30 per cent in 2009 and 35 per cent in 2010, there are large differences among the provinces. Ontario, in particular, stands out with 36 per cent and 43 per cent of its unemployed being non-contributors to Employment Insurance in 2009 and 2010, respectively. In contrast, all of the Atlantic provinces had non-contributor rates in the low teens in 2010.

FIGURE 3 Percentage of Non-Contributors to Employment Insurance Among the Unemployed, by Province, 2009 and 2010

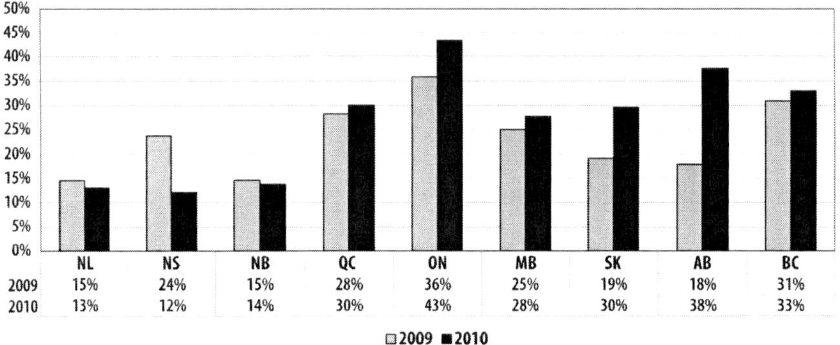

These are substantial differences among the provinces. Note that the regional variation in rules for Employment Insurance eligibility are not relevant to this group, as these are non-contributors and are not affected by variable entrance requirements or the number of weeks for which benefits are paid. Newfoundland's percentage might be lower due to seasonal benefits, but this does not explain Alberta's low rate in 2009—nor its sizable jump in 2010. Whatever the explanation for the provincial differences, the much greater prevalence of non-contributors among Ontario's unemployed must be one of the underlying explanations for relatively poor coverage of the unemployed by Employment Insurance in Ontario (Black and Shillington, 2005).

In 2009, 84 per cent of non-contributors reported having not worked for the previous 12 months (although actively engaged in the search for a job) and 16 per cent reported having had no insurable earnings. Put another way, up to, but not including 2010, of the approximately 30 per cent of unemployed who were non-contributors, about 25 per cent (370,000 in 2009) were non-contributors because they had not worked in the preceding year and 5 per cent (74,000 in 2009) did not have insurable earnings, despite reporting having worked in the previous year. The "25 + 5" per cent split remained quite stable over the 2003–2009 period, as can be seen on Figure 4. In 2010, the share of non-contributors went up to 35 per cent, and the share reporting not working in the previous year climbed to 32 per cent from the more or less stable 25 per cent of the previous seven years. It will be a few more years before we know whether this represents a permanent or temporary shift.

FIGURE 4 Percentage of Unemployed Not Contributing to Employment Insurance, by Reason for Non-Contributing, 2003–2010

	2003	2004	2005	2006	2007	2008	2009	2010
No Work in Previous Year	23.9%	25.7%	26.0%	26.3%	24.8%	25.5%	24.8%	32.3%
No Insurable Employment	5.1%	5.7%	5.4%	5.7%	5.2%	4.3%	4.9%	3.0%

As we have seen, over the period 2003 to 2009, the proportion of non-contributors among the unemployed appeared to be impervious to both fluctuations in the level of unemployment and easing the rules for eligibility among contributors—as seen in 2009, when automatic adjustments in the entry requirements had no effect on the proportion of non-contributors among the unemployed. In 2010, the percentage of non-contributors increased, rather than decreased, due to longer-term unemployment. Rule changes such as reducing entry requirements that are ordinarily contemplated to improve lack of coverage of Employment Insurance will therefore likely have no effect on improving coverage for non-contributors, who form the majority of those ineligible for Employment Insurance. To the extent that differential proportions of non-contributors explain differential Employment Insurance coverage among the provinces, loosening entry requirements and other rules will also have no impact on lessening these provincial variations.

Until 2009 (the year 2010 may be an anomaly due to the recession), roughly 5 per cent of the unemployed report having been employed the previous year but with no insurable earnings.

Presumably, bringing the self-employed into the Employment Insurance system would improve the coverage among this 5 per cent of the unemployed, if it were possible to do so. However, as discussed previously, there are significant administrative barriers to including the self-employed in Employment Insurance. In a social insurance program such as the Canada Pension Plan, it is possible to include the self-employed because a person either meets the program's age requirement or not. There are stringent eligibility tests for Canada Pension Plan disability benefits. But there are no means to identify objectively when a self-employed person really is "unemployed" in the same way as other workers. Indeed, there is no way to define "unemployment" for the self-employed.

Attempting to include a group whose employment status is so nebulous is an invitation to mismanagement, rapidly escalating costs and abuse of the Employment Insurance program. It would also necessitate doing away with the requirement that unemployment be involuntary on the part of the employee in order to qualify for Employment Insurance. It is our view, therefore, that there is no mechanism to include the self-employed in Employment Insurance without undermining the whole program.

The recent voluntary inclusion of the self-employed in Employment Insurance for purposes of "special benefits" is a case in point. Although the program does not make the self-employed eligible for regular benefits, it does allow them to opt into the program to become eligible for maternity, parental, sickness or compassionate care benefits. Of course, only those with a high likelihood of using the benefits will opt in (in insurance terms this is known as "adverse selection"), so the addition will undoubtedly be a net financial burden on Employment Insurance financing. But it will also be impossible to enforce rules. Will the Employment Insurance program police the parental leave program to ensure that the small business owner does not in fact go into work?

This extension of special benefits in the Employment Insurance program to the self-employed doubtless will have a very small impact on costs. Given the small size of special benefits for the self-employed, fraud and infractions will likely simply be ignored. But the extension of special benefits for the self-employed should not be taken as evidence that a much larger program for the self-employed of mandatory inclusion in Employment Insurance for regular benefits would be realistic.

Despite its support for the self-employed and its wish to create greater security for the self-employed, the Canadian Chamber of Commerce arrived at the same conclusion:

> Self-employed workers are not insurable under the Employment Insurance Act for one key reason—"moral hazard"—the problem that arises from the fact that self-employed workers can control whether they accept work or create the conditions necessary for unemployment. Extending Employment Insurance benefits to the self-employed appears to contradict the original intent of the Employment Insurance Program—to provide insurance coverage against temporary unemployment through no fault of the individual worker. Program administrators would face the challenge of distinguishing between involuntary and voluntary unemployment among self-employed workers. The moral hazard problem is considered to be less serious in the case of special benefits (like maternity and paternal) since the conditions triggering these benefits provide Program administrators with greater control over access to them. (The Canadian Chamber of Commerce 2009, 8)

E Unemployed Workers Participating in, but Not Eligible for, Employment Insurance

Figure 5 shows the percentage of unemployed workers who were participating in the Employment Insurance program (i.e., had made at least one premium payment in the previous 12 months), but were in any case ineligible. There are two categories of reasons for ineligibility: an invalid job separation (such as leaving voluntarily to return to school) and insufficient hours to qualify.

As can be seen, ineligible contributors were a gradually increasing proportion of the unemployed from 2005 to 2008 until the big increase in unemployment levels in 2009 and the consequent automatic loosening of entry requirements in Employment Insurance. In 2009, 20.5 per cent of the unemployed were ineligible contributors. However, by 2010 the percentage of ineligible contributors had resumed its upward trend, following the trend line established from 2005 through 2008, to reach 31.4 per cent in 2009. The 31.4 per cent of the unemployed who were ineligible contributors in 2010 were the sum of 18.3 per cent ineligible due to invalid job separation and 13.1 per cent ineligible due to insufficient hours.

There has been very little variation over the 2003–2009 period in the percentage of unemployed contributing workers who were ineligible for Employment Insurance due to insufficient hours. In 2005, the highest proportion was ineligible for Employment Insurance due to insufficient hours—10.5 per cent of the unemployed. In 2009, the lowest proportion was ineligible, but this was only a little changed at 8.0 per cent. The only big jump in those ineligible due to insufficient hours was in 2010 to 13.1 per cent. It will be a few years before we know whether this higher percentage of contributors who find themselves ineligible due to insufficient hours is a new trend, or a reflection of the second year of relatively high unemployment.

FIGURE 5 Percentage of Unemployed Contributing to Employment Insurance but Ineligible for Benefits, by Reason for Ineligibility, 2003–2010

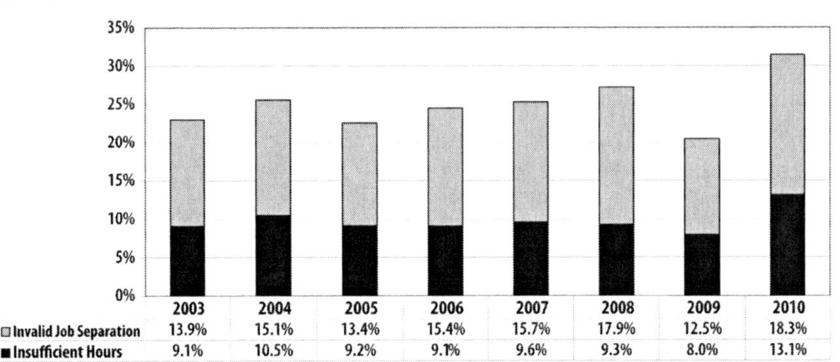

	2003	2004	2005	2006	2007	2008	2009	2010
☐ Invalid Job Separation	13.9%	15.1%	13.4%	15.4%	15.7%	17.9%	12.5%	18.3%
■ Insufficient Hours	9.1%	10.5%	9.2%	9.1%	9.6%	9.3%	8.0%	13.1%

Despite the surge in unemployment in 2009 and 2010 and the consequent less stringent entry requirements, the total range of change in eligibility due to insufficient hours amounted to only about five percentage points. This is evidence that reducing the hours of work required to qualify would not have a huge impact on eligibility, unless taken to extremes. Were the prior work requirements so diminished as to, say, reduce the number ruled ineligible by half, this would still increase eligibility only by about 6 to 7 per cent of the unemployed at most in 2010, and by only 4 or 5 per cent in most years. At the same time, such extreme lessening of work requirements would substantially alter the social insurance nature of the Employment Insurance program, effectively all but severing the connection between contributions and benefits.

The evidence overall suggests that there is little scope for improving Employment Insurance coverage through reducing hours of work required for eligibility. This conclusion accords with the views of Human Resources and Social Development Canada as reported in Black and Shillington (2005) and as reported orally to these authors as well. According to officials at Human Resources and Social Development Canada, their internal models showed at that time that there would be little significant increase in the coverage of unemployed in Toronto were the entrance requirements lowered even to the lowest levels of all regions in Canada.

F Social Assistance

Although Employment Insurance and social assistance (better known as welfare) are the two main income security programs for working age adults in Canada, there has been little empirical research (i.e., research on what actually happens to people in the interaction of the two programs) on the relationship between the two programs. With only a few exception, the empirical studies have looked exclusively at the extent to which workers who have been collecting Employment Insurance benefits but have now run out of benefits (so-called exhaustees) enrol on welfare (e.g., Finnie et al. 2011). However, this is only one piece and, as Finnie shows, a rather small piece of the inter-relationship between the two programs. As we have seen, many unemployed workers are not eligible for Employment Insurance to begin with, so the more fundamental question is where do these workers go if they are excluded from EI and in financial need?

The most detailed research not limited to the study of exhaustees was presented in two studies undertaken in the mid-1990s under the sponsorship of Human Resources Development Canada, following various reductions in what was then called Unemployment Insurance in 1993—principally the exclusion of so-called "voluntary quits."

The first study—*Studies of the Interaction of UI and Welfare Using the COEP Dataset*—focused on the effects of reductions in Employment Insurance on take-up rates for welfare. The results were straightforward:

a cut in Unemployment Insurance eligibility results in an increase in the number of welfare cases. The authors found:

> ...a substantial February to May decline in UI take-up among VQs [Voluntary Quits] with little re-employment success and a coincidental rise in welfare take-up among the same group that was at least of equal magnitude and probably larger. This result was robust to conditioning on cross cohort differences in the interval between separation and the first interview and in other personal and economic variables. This suggests that for this group the Canadian UI and welfare programs may act as close substitutes, that the incentive and income distribution effects of Bill C-113 may have been mitigated by the availability of a substitute program, and that the examination of UI in isolation from other social programs is highly problematic. (Browning et al. 1995, 7)

The second empirical study looked at the flow of clients between Employment Insurance and welfare. *The Interaction of Unemployment Insurance and Social Assistance* used administrative data from what was then called Unemployment Insurance and welfare in British Columbia, New Brunswick, Newfoundland, Prince Edward Island and Alberta over the period 1986–1992. In essence, the study found that many people used both Unemployment Insurance and welfare, with some drawing welfare benefits before going on Unemployment Insurance and others drawing welfare after being on Unemployment Insurance. Both the Unemployment Insurance population and the welfare population were found to have had workforce experience. Indeed, the study was not able to identify a statistically valid set of observable labour force characteristics differing between those using both Unemployment Insurance and welfare versus those using only one or the other program":

> We find that a large proportion of welfare recipients have some attachment to the workforce and that there is a large overlap in the clientele of UI and SA. There is also evidence of an upward trend over the 1986–92 period in the extent to which the programs serve a common group of participants. Welfare spell durations had a distinct bimodal distribution, with UI-SA interaction concentrated among short welfare spells. SA use was found to be associated with substantially longer UI spells in New Brunswick but not British Columbia. (Barrett et al. 1996, 7)

One further broad empirical study of the interaction of Unemployment Insurance and welfare, outside of the Human Resources Development-sponsored series, was undertaken with a sample of Quebec lone-parent households who had received welfare payments at least once over the period 1979–1993. The study found that reductions in Unemployment Insurance benefits resulted in increased use of welfare by lone-parents in Quebec (Fortin et al. 1999).

All of these studies were of programs and conditions quite different than today's. The study period of 1986–1992 coincided with the end of an economic boom accompanied by rising inflation (1986–1989) and the onset of a significant recession characterized by price stability and rapidly rising unemployment (1989–1992). In the latter period, both Unemployment Insurance and welfare rolls were rapidly increasing. Between 1988 and 1992, the percentage of the Ontario population relying on welfare doubled from 6 per cent to an astonishing 12 per cent. Many workers who might never have dreamed of needing public assistance found themselves relying on one (or both) of these programs. The major reductions in Unemployment Insurance, along with its Orwellian renaming as "Employment Insurance," were yet to occur. On the other side of the equation, welfare was relatively easier to get and somewhat more generous than it is at present, but the system of refundable tax credits—notably the Canada Child Tax Benefit, which provides substantial benefits to lower-income families—was not yet in place. Thus it may be that the findings from these studies are not fully representative of what would be found were similar research done with today's array of programs.

More up-to-date evidence that welfare is being used as a bulwark against unemployment can be found by analyzing the relationship between unemployment rates (i.e., percentage of unemployed among the labour force) and welfare caseloads. Figure 6[5] shows the proportion of the Ontario population on welfare and the provincial unemployment rate.

As is immediately evident from a look at Figure 6, unemployment rates and welfare caseloads have been highly correlated in Ontario over the last 20 years. A regression analysis of the data produces an R-squared of over 80 per cent, meaning that more than 80 per cent of the variation in the caseload data in Ontario is explained by changes in the unemployment rate. This correlation is particularly striking since this period encompasses a number of substantial policy shifts both towards making welfare more generous and less intrusive and later in exactly the opposite direction. This strong correlation can most readily be explained by the proposition that a substantial number of the unemployed have turned to welfare—at least in Ontario. (And the fact that unemployment remains an excellent explanatory variable for caseload changes suggests that welfare rules and benefit changes are a lot less important in determining welfare caseloads, including the notable post-1995 decline, than is ordinarily supposed.)

FIGURE 6 Percentage of Population on Social Assistance and Unemployment Rate in Ontario, 1988–2008

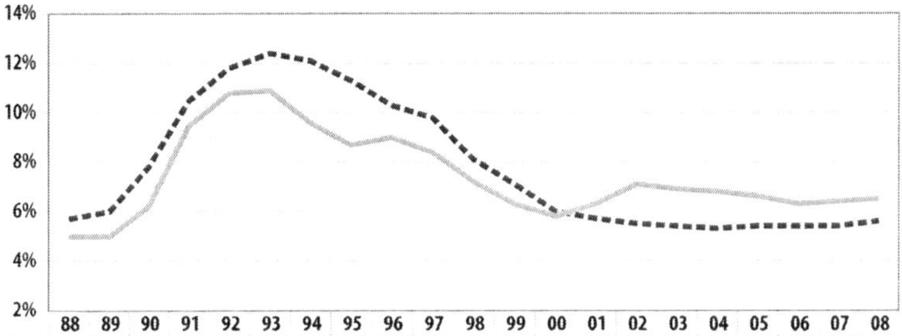

	88	89	90	91	92	93	94	95	96	97	98	99	00	01	02	03	04	05	06	07	08
Welfare %	5.7	6.0	7.8	10.5	11.8	12.4	12.1	11.3	10.3	9.8	8.1	7.1	6.0	5.7	5.5	5.4	5.3	5.4	5.4	5.4	5.6
Unemployment %	5.0	5.0	6.2	9.5	10.8	10.9	9.6	8.7	9.0	8.4	7.2	6.3	5.8	6.3	7.1	6.9	6.8	6.6	6.3	6.4	6.5

In the 1998 Employment Insurance Coverage Survey, unemployed respondents ineligible for Employment Insurance were asked about their source of income. The results of the survey are shown in Table 1. Some 23 per cent of unemployed persons ineligible for Employment Insurance stated that welfare was their source of income. A further 12 per cent said that they were using savings or were relying upon loans from friends or family. These latter sources are obviously limited in time, so that if alternatives are not found, we can anticipate up to 35 per cent of ineligible unemployed Canadians eventually turning to welfare.

Although the empirical evidence is outdated or indirect, all the data that exists confirms that welfare is indeed being used as an alternative source of income for some portion of those who are unemployed and ineligible for Employment Insurance. The possible numbers are difficult to quantify but, coincidentally, the number of ineligible unemployed in 1998 was almost identical to that in 2009—so, at a rough guess, if the proportions remained roughly similar, this would suggest that between 170,000 and 260,000 of the ineligible unemployed drew on welfare in 2009 and 2010.

While welfare is a necessary program of last resort for many Canadians, it imposes significant social and personal costs. Yet, as we saw in the earlier discussion of Employment Insurance coverage, it is difficult to see how Employment Insurance can be redesigned to expand coverage substantially while remaining a viable social insurance plan. So why not instead reform welfare to make it less invasive, eliminate asset stripping and raise benefit levels?

Countless attempts to liberalize welfare have been undertaken over the last forty years or so, and all have been rolled back or at best allowed to erode through the gradual effect of inflation, to the extent that welfare is today as ungenerous and onerous as it has ever been in the last few decades in almost every jurisdiction. The lesson of history is that reforming welfare is a dead end as long as welfare remains a program used by a significant

TABLE 1 Main Sources of Income of Unemployed People who are Not Eligible for Employment Insurance

Main Source of Income in Reference Month	Unemployed Persons Not Eligible for Employment Insurance	
	Number	%
Living at home and relying on parents	246,000	34
Social Assistance	171,000	23
Spouse or partner's earning	139,000	19
Savings	51,000	7
Loans and assistance from friends or family	35,000	5
Other government transfers	22,000	3
Pension of self or spouse	19,000	3
Own wage or salary	15,000	2
Other sources or no sources	36,000	5
Total	**734,000**	**100%**

Source: *Roller*, 1999.

portion of the population. Instead, advocates of reform have suggested strategies to establish broad-based alternative programs such as the Child Tax Benefit (The Ontario Social Assistance Review Advisory Council 2010). This is not to say that welfare can never be improved and we should just give up on it entirely: rather that the strategy for changing welfare is to transform it from a program serving 5 or 6 per cent of the population to a program serving 1 or 2 per cent of the population, by providing other forms of financial assistance for many of those in need.

In line with this strategy, we propose instead a new program "between" Employment Insurance and welfare, which will provide financial assistance to those among the unemployed who need it, while avoiding the potential long-term negative consequences of welfare and permitting welfare to get on with the task of better serving its core clientele. In Part 2 we describe the conditions under which adding a new program of this nature to Canada's income security system would be ethically and economically justified; set out a possible design for such a program; and discuss some of its implications.

2 Filling the Gap between EI and Social Assistance

A Should the Gap be Filled?

Being on welfare is an unpleasant, psychologically depressing and perhaps even devastating experience for the recipient (Herd et al. 2005). The amounts paid by welfare are extremely low, especially for single employable recipients. Individuals who would otherwise have to be on welfare would indisputably be better off were they able instead to obtain assistance from a much less invasive and demeaning program paying higher benefits. But the same could be said about any program paying higher benefits with fewer conditions. A program "between Employment Insurance and welfare" might be good for recipients. However, would Canada be better off? Are there broader social or economic arguments as to why society as a whole should be willing to pay for such a program?

We can ask these questions more generally: Why provide any income security programs at all? Why not just let market forces distribute income and let the chips fall where they may, as some would doubtless advocate?

There are two different types of responses to these questions. First, we might argue that an income program is needed for ethical or moral reasons. For example: "in a wealthy country it is wrong to allow families to live in abject poverty" or "it is unfair for unemployed workers to bear the full financial risk of unemployment" are two ethical claims for income security programs. Second, it might be argued that there is a net benefit to a particular social program so that we are as a whole better off as a result of paying for the program—whether economically better off in the sense of having a higher GDP or by using some other measuring stick. Employment Insurance acts as an economic and social stabilizer such that GDP is higher in the long run with the program than without it. The ethical aspect may be said to be about fairness; the analysis of net benefit may be said to be about utility.

With respect to the ethical dimension, in *A Theory of Justice* the philosopher John Rawls sets out a framework for understanding whether a social program (or any other social arrangement) should be part of a fair and just society (Rawls 1971). Rawls asks us to consider social policy from behind what he calls a "veil of ignorance." Behind the veil of ignorance the observer does not know "his place in society, his class position or social status, nor does he know his fortune in the distribution of natural assets and abilities, his intelligence and strength, and the like" (Rawls 1971, 137). Would a well-informed and intelligent observer from behind the veil of ignorance choose a society with or without the particular social program, on the assumption that he could find himself, figuratively speaking, cast into any position within that society with any possible natural endowment?

The Rawlsian theory of justice is not by any means universally accepted, but it is an especially useful framework for exploring the ethical dimensions of income security programs because it focuses us on the distributive fairness of a program, and not just on its utility. From behind the veil of ignorance, most of us would likely choose a society in which there were at least some less harsh alternative to welfare given the possibility that we might end up as one of the unlucky unemployed without eligibility for Employment Insurance. Whether through a Rawlsian lens or other framework, the ethical argument is that a more just society is one in which both opportunities and outcomes are more equally distributed, so that if less dehumanizing and more generous temporary assistance than welfare can be offered without huge cost to society, it should be done.

Turning from the ethical to the utilitarian perspective, one of the key purposes of a new temporary assistance program for the unemployed not eligible for Employment Insurance but who are in financial need would be to divert them from welfare. The assumption is that diverting unemployed people from welfare reduces the likelihood of their going on to welfare in the future. Diversion also insulates them from the negative experience of welfare which many believe makes employment much more difficult in the future, so that diversion increases the likelihood of their getting and keeping a good job. This is far from a new idea. Many provinces have considered various ways to divert clients from welfare for this reason. It is difficult to find information on diversion programs in Canada, but in the United States there are diversion programs of various kinds in all but three states. Thirty-five states offer a single lump-sum payment as an alternative to welfare for applicants who would otherwise be eligible (Rosenberg et al. 2008).

Unfortunately, as in many areas of social policy, there are no acceptable quantitative analyses of whether diversion programs actually decrease long-term costs to the state or increase the overall income of the recipients. Nevertheless, we know that some administrators in the field have been acting on this premise and that a utilitarian argument is possible.

A utilitarian argument for a temporary unemployment assistance program may also be made in respect of less tangible benefits for the whole community. As is evident in the current economic downturn, the liveability and vitality of a neighbourhood is affected for everyone by each household in the neighbourhood. Excluding the very wealthy who can live behind gated fences, most Canadians' well-being is affected in concrete ways by the well-being of their neighbours. If unemployed people in the neighbourhood cannot afford to keep up mortgage or rental payments, the value of everyone's property declines. If the appearance and orderliness of a neighbourhood declines, this affects everyone in the neighbourhood.

As Canadians increasingly live closely packed together in cities, it is more apparent that we are not isolated atoms unaffected by those around us. Rather, the quality of our life is at least partly dependent upon the quality of life of those around us. Again, it is difficult to quantify this phenomenon, but by helping to sustain material and psychological well-being for at least a little longer, giving the jobless time to search for a job, the potential benefits of a temporary unemployment assistance program extend not only to the recipient household but to all the other households in the community. This too is a utilitarian argument.

A third benefit of a new alternative to welfare is the effect on welfare itself. Welfare was intended by the founders of the Canadian income security system to provide a last-resort safety net for the relatively few people who have nowhere else to turn. It never was meant to become a major income source for so many people in need. The objective of temporary unemployment assistance would be to divert the most "job ready" needy from welfare and so leave the welfare rolls smaller. The expectation is that more of those who do have to resort to welfare will be hard to employ and require more intensive assistance to become employable. Clearing the caseload of those who are only temporarily in financial need would permit the welfare administration to be less of a warehousing operation and more of an opportunity planning organization.

Finally, we need to be concerned about the potential effects of a temporary unemployment assistance program on the labour market. As is discussed further below, such a program is likely to be taken up by relatively few workers, so that any effect likely would be minor. To the extent that there is an effect, any program which lessens the cost of unemployment and encourages people to report that they are actively seeking work, will necessarily increase the unemployment rate and participation rate. On the other hand, by reducing the cost of unemployment, a temporary assistance plan would also increase the length of job search, possibly resulting in a better match up of workers and jobs, which in the long run decreases unemployment and improves productivity.

Assessing the net effects on the labour market would require weighing the negative effects on unemployment and the positive effects on participation and job search, which can only be done with some experience of a program in real life. The extent of any such effects would also depend upon the specific parameters of the program: A smaller program with less generous payments will necessarily have less impact on the labour market. So, while this is likely a negative on the "utility" argument, it is probably a small negative.

Regretfully, the utilitarian arguments are not resolvable without better data. In the following sections, we set out the parameters for a specific temporary unemployment assistance plan, with a design new to Canada's income security system. This undertaking will allow us to estimate very roughly the scope and cost of this program and to discuss several critical administrative issues.

B Essential Characteristics of Temporary Financial Assistance for the Unemployed

An income-tested program providing temporary assistance for the unemployed in financial need—but without the asset stripping, myriad rules and stigma of welfare—could provide an option "between" social insurance and needs-tested social assistance. We would see a new program of this kind as a complement to a stronger Employment Insurance (strengthened in its social insurance characteristics) roughly analogous to the way that the income-tested Guaranteed Income Supplement complements retirement benefits in the Canada and Quebec Pension Plan.

There are several essential characteristics for an effective temporary unemployment assistance program. It should be minimally invasive and non-stigmatizing. It needs to be temporary, so that no one can remain on it for longer than some specified period (e.g., six months every five years). It should allow recipients to carry on with their job search and continue most essential aspects of their normal life. And it needs to give recipients the opportunity to get back on their feet without losing everything and having to restart their financial life from zero.

The fundamental purpose of this chapter is to open discussion of a new temporary unemployment assistance program between Employment Insurance and welfare. Once the need for a temporary assistance program is accepted, all the rest is "detail"—but without this detail, it is difficult to imagine what such a program would actually look like. In this second part of this chapter, then, we explore options and alternatives for these all-important details including the specific elements of program design. We do so mainly to stimulate discussion of a temporary income plan and not because we are wedded irrevocably to any of the design features discussed below. Our intent is to draw a clear picture of what such a program could be by offering a concrete example.

C Federal or Provincial? or Both?

Among the multitude of design issues for social policy reform in Canada is the question of which order of government should be responsible for the new program. The 1930s legal ruling preventing the federal government from delivering social insurance programs would not apply because the temporary assistance program would neither be contributory nor a social insurance program. Since the temporary assistance program would in essence constitute a payment of money to an individual, it would be constitutionally within the spending power of either order of government. Constitutionally, the temporary assistance program could therefore be financed and delivered by either the federal or provincial orders of government, or some combination of the two.

We argue in *Towards A New Architecture for Canada's Adult Benefits* (Battle et al. 2006) that the temporary income assistance program would be best if financed and delivered by the federal government. There are several reasons for this preference (discussed in more detail in *A New Architecture*). First, the federal government is the order of government primarily responsible for macro-economic policy, particularly the level of unemployment, so it makes sense that Ottawa would also be responsible for programs meant to ameliorate the effects of unemployment and which may also act as counter-cyclical measures. Second, since temporary assistance would be a closely complementary measure to Employment Insurance, the two programs need to be coordinated and the governing rules should be continuously harmonized as they evolve over time. Third, as a minimally invasive program requiring little detailed interaction with recipients, temporary assistance is the kind of program which the federal government is well-suited to deliver, leaving the provinces and territories with more capacity to provide the intensive case work and education and skills acquisition opportunities required by longer-term recipients of social assistance. Finally, a federal program could offer an opt-out provision for those provinces that wish to operate the new temporary program at the provincial level, whereas it is hard to see how a provincial program could have a federal opt-in provision, so a federal program is more flexible in this respect.

In the discussion below, we assume that the new program would be federal rather than provincial. But notwithstanding our preference for a federal program, the *social policy* goal of providing non-welfare assistance to the unemployed in financial need who are not eligible for Employment Insurance could also be met by a provincially financed and delivered program.

D Temporary Income Based on Retrospective Monthly Income Reporting

The simplest way to deliver a temporary unemployment assistance program would be via a monthly income test. Using this delivery mechanism, recipients would be required to submit a completed form every month stating their previous month's income and any other pertinent information required. The amount of the temporary income benefit would then be determined according to the previous month's income. This mechanism for administration is known as a "retrospective" test of the previous month's income.

This standard type of delivery mechanism based on retrospective monthly reporting of income is similar to welfare. But the temporary income program would differ from welfare in several important respects: It could have a single flat rate benefit; it could be calculated on the basis of individual income rather than household income (more on this below); it could contain no adjustment for factors such as presence of spouse and number of children, housing tenure or costs and the other many calculations of individual needs required in welfare. In short, the new temporary income program could be simplified with much less personal information and much less policing than is the case for welfare. In this crucial respect, the new temporary income program would be very different and far less complicated and intrusive than needs-tested social assistance.

Retrospective monthly income reporting is a viable administrative alternative for a temporary income program. Nevertheless, this delivery mechanism does have some downsides. It requires setting up a whole new administrative system with all its associated costs and inevitable growing pains.

Monthly reporting and payment based on the previous month's income was used for the Manitoba Mincome experiment, a large guaranteed annual income experiment in the 1970s. Despite the common assumption that a guaranteed income would be simple to administer, Mincome encountered many complicated administrative issues, as found in an unpublished study of Mincome administration done by Mendelson. For example, if there is an error or misreporting in one month, does this result in a deduction the next month? And would this end up with a benefit cheque which consists of dozens of adjustments carried forward in incomprehensible ways? The amount of processing and complexity of actual calculations turned out to be a challenge for the Mincome experiment. All of this added to administrative costs. Of course, information technology is immeasurably more powerful today than it was in the 1970s, but despite this, some of the Mincome administrative complexity would doubtless be encountered if our temporary assistance program used a monthly retrospective income text.

Without emergency funding available immediately as in the welfare system, the question of timing of payments may also present some challenges for a temporary assistance program based on retrospective income testing.

Using a retrospective test of the previous month's income, benefits could be paid about one month after submission of the monthly forms. This practice implies that the benefits paid would not be perfectly "timely" in that the amount would not reflect income exactly at the time of benefit payment, as the benefit calculation would be a maximum of about two months out of date at most. (For a discussion of "timeliness" and why it is important, see Mendelson et al. 2003.)

To understand this problem, imagine the following scenario: A recipient's own income consists of a single lump sum payment on 1 September with no other income for the remainder of the month; the temporary income program requires the recipient to submit a report on monthly income by 30 September; and the temporary income benefit is then paid on 31 October. This scenario is an example of the longest possible delay between the payment and the income which is used to calculate the payment—about two months. This approach assumes that it is administratively possible to process information and make payments within a month.

Two months may be too long to wait for someone with no other income, so in this instance welfare might be required as a stop gap measure, which more or less defeats the whole purpose of the reform. Of course, this is an example of the longest lag time possible. But some time lag is unavoidable in any program based on retrospective income, and any time lag is difficult for those with little or no income.

Although the retrospective temporary assistance program would be designed to provide only a short-term financial respite and to be non-invasive as described, it might be similar enough to welfare to be perceived socially as just another welfare program—with all its negative characteristics. It might be seen as a program only for "poor" people, which would stigmatize those who are unemployed, actively searching for work and in financial need. One of the objectives of the temporary income plan is to avoid stigmatizing recipients so as to give them the best possible platform from which to get back into employment. To the extent that there is stigma associated with the program, unfortunately, this objective would not be fully met.

In the next section of this paper we set out a different and, we believe, novel design for a temporary unemployment assistance plan which might avoid many of the problems with a program based on retrospective reporting of monthly income. We set out a number of detailed parameters for the alternative program. All of these parameters could also be applied to delivery based on a retrospective monthly income reporting system. The difference is in the delivery mechanism.

E The Jobseeker's Loan Model

In this design, temporary unemployment assistance would be provided in the form of a forgivable loan whose repayment is contingent upon income reported through the income tax system. The program would be unlike any existing income security program. We have called this the "Jobseeker's Loan" (borrowing the name "Jobseeker's" from the UK, though our program design is nothing like theirs.

Rather than paying benefits adjusted for the previous month's income, the Jobseeker's Loan would make a loan available to all unemployed adults actively seeking employment. The loan would be entirely forgiven if income in that year as reported through income tax was very low, but the loan would be partially or fully repaid if income were higher.

The loan would be advanced to the recipient in biweekly instalments, like a paycheque. A maximum amount of loan would be available only within a defined period of time, say five years, so that once the loan was taken up it would require another five years before the recipient once again became eligible for the full Jobseeker's Loan. There would be rules to prevent "doubling up" so that a loan would not be available to anyone collecting full Employment Insurance benefits, welfare benefits or other social program benefits (in particular those that are not taxable). However, a loan could top-up partial Employment Insurance or other benefits where the amount of those other program benefits is less than the maximum amount of the loan.

It is possible to describe a Jobseeker's Loan program with just eight parameters, as set out on the first half of Table 2 under "input parameters." We have also set specific values for each of these parameters. These values could, of course, be different in amount. They represent what we consider reasonable configurations for the Jobseeker's Loan, but are here used only to illustrate how an income-contingent forgivable Jobseeker's Loan would work. Should the Jobseeker's Loan be implemented, more detailed work will need to be devoted to the actual values to be used.

Given the values of the eight parameters used to define the loan program, the result is the program parameters (dependent variables) in the bottom five rows of Table 2: a Jobseeker's Loan which pays $692 bi-weekly for up to 13 pay periods (26 weeks). This amounts to a maximum loan of $8,996 in each five year period. Below the first federal income tax bracket, the loan would be forgiven; between the first and the second tax brackets, an amount equal to 50 per cent of the federal tax rate on income (i.e., 7.5 per cent, half of the bottom 15 per cent tax rate) would be repaid, and the rest of the loan forgiven; above the second income tax bracket, an amount equal to the existing federal tax rate (i.e., 22 per cent) up to the full amount of the loan would be repaid, with the rest of the loan, if there is any, forgiven .

In the following discussion we explain each of these variables and describe some examples of how the Jobseeker's Loan program might work.

1. Percentage of Provincial Minimum Wage

There are many different ways that the maximum amount of Jobseeker's Loan could be set. One mechanism would be to set the loan as some percentage of the Employment Insurance benefit. However, Employment Insurance benefits paid to each recipient reflect that recipient's prior earnings, since benefits are calculated as a percentage of insurable earnings up to a maximum. Consequently it is difficult for an Employment Insurance recipient to obtain benefits greater than previously earned income.

The amount of the Jobseeker's Loan would not reflect the amount of prior earnings—or any earnings at all. Thus it lacks the built-in assurance of Employment Insurance that the loan will not exceed prior earnings. If this problem is to be prevented, the maximum loan has to be determined with a view to ensuring it is not greater than earnings for most full-time workers.

Here we illustrate the maximum loan as a percentage of the prevailing provincial minimum wage for a week's work, defined in respect of a number of hours. Using the minimum wage in each province maintains

TABLE 2 Variables Required to Define the Jobseeker's Loan Program

Jobseeker's Loan Input Parameters	Values
Percentage of provincial minimum wage	90%
Hours per week minimum wage	37.5
Eligibility period in weeks	260
Weeks of loan entitlement acquired for each week in the eligibility period (%)	10%
Jobseeker's Loan repayment tax rate for income below first federal rate	0%
Jobseeker's Loan repayment percentage of tax rate for income above first federal rate	50%
Jobseeker's Loan repayment percentage of tax rate for income above the second federal rate	100%
Percentage restoration of weeks	50%
Weekly gross loan	$346
Maximum eligible weeks	26
Maximum loan per eligible period	$8,996
Taxable income at which Jobseeker's Loan begins to be paid back	$10,382
Taxable income at which Jobseeker's Loan is fully paid back	$71,426

a relationship with income obtainable from work, and also reflects the existing standards in that province. It also provides something of an incentive for provinces not to fall too far below the national norm in their minimum wage levels.

2. Hours Per Week Minimum Wage

Using the minimum wage to set the maximum Jobseeker's Loan benefit makes it necessary to assume a number of hours as the standard work week. Here we assume 37.5 hours per week as reflecting the prevailing standard in Canada. Where the maximum loan is set at 90 per cent of minimum wage, Table 2 shows the maximum loan in Ontario, where the minimum wage is currently $10.25 per hour. The result is a Jobseeker's Loan per week of 37.5 X 90 per cent X $10.25 = $346. While this is a modest amount relative to the average wage ($880 per week in Ontario as of 2010), it is much more than is paid to single adults in the welfare system ($132 weekly in 2009).

3. Eligibility Period in Weeks

The claimant can claim up to a maximum number of weeks, less any weeks of Jobseeker's Loan she or he has claimed within the most recent of a defined number of weeks, called the "eligibility period." In this example, we have set the eligibility period as five years—i.e., 260 weeks. Upon reaching minimum age, say 19, an applicant obtains eligibility for up to the maximum number of weeks of Jobseeker's Loan. Upon reaching the maximum age of eligibility, say 65, each person would be eligible for a lump sum loan equal to any outstanding Jobseeker's Loan payable. This practice would be of most value to those with the lowest incomes as much of the Loan would be taxed back for those with higher incomes (who then, presumably, would not take it). The retirement benefit under the Jobseeker's Loan could be viewed as a boost to the Guaranteed Income Supplement for the lowest-income seniors.

4. Eligibility Per Weeks in Period

The claimant accumulates additional weeks of Jobseeker's Loan eligibility as a percentage of the number of weeks within the eligibility period, such that the eligibility period times the percentage equals the maximum number of weeks of Jobseeker's Loan. Eligibility is *accumulated* whether or not a person is working or available for work.

In the values set out in Table 2 as an illustrative example, the percentage of Jobseeker's Loan weeks' eligibility accumulated is 10 per cent, as it takes 260 weeks to acquire 26 weeks of eligibility, which then becomes the maximum number of weeks of Jobseeker's Loan in any five year period. Jobseeker's Loan can be claimed at any time at the discretion of the applicant, with the requirement that the claimant be actively engaged in the search for employment. There is nothing to prevent a recipient working part time while in receipt of the loan, so long as the recipient is able to demonstrate that she or he is still engaged in actively seeking full-time employment, except that the amount that must be paid back at the end of the year will thereby be increased if that person earns more than the basic exemption (see below).

5. Repayment Though Income Tax System

Upon paying income tax at the end of the year, the Jobseeker's Loan must be partially or fully repaid as a percentage of income, except for those whose income is very low. This repayment mechanism would function as a kind of income tax surtax designed so that the amount of Jobseeker's Loan repaid would climb as income climbed. At middle incomes, all of the Jobseeker's Loan would be repaid.

In this case, we have modeled the Jobseeker's Loan repayment schedule as a progressive percentage of the prevailing 2010 federal tax rate in the recipient's income bracket, with the Basic Personal Amount here used as the income threshold for maximum benefits. Up to the basic exemption level of $10,382, there is no repayment required. From $10,382 up to $40,970 (the second income bracket), the repayment rate is half of the income tax rate of 15 per cent, or 7.5 per cent of income. Between $40,970 and $81,941, the repayment rate is equal to the income tax rate in that bracket (22 per cent). The repayment rate would also be 100 per cent of the prevailing tax rate for higher brackets, but this is not relevant since the Jobseeker's Loan in our model is fully taxed back within the second tax bracket—at $71,426.

Note that the tax rate is *not* a tax on the loan as income; rather, it is a repayment schedule as a percentage of income. For example, if a recipient has a Jobseeker's Loan of $2,000 and income of $15,382, she or he must repay 7.5 per cent of $5,000 or $375. The remaining $1,625 would be forgiven. The person would have to have had an income of $37,049 or more to be required to fully repay a $2,000 Jobseeker's Loan.

The added "marginal tax rate" on income is therefore nil up to $10,382, 7.5 per cent from $10,382 to $40,970 and 22 per cent from $40,970 to $71,426. However, as this constitutes a loan repayment rather than a tax, it is not clear that it should be seen as an addition to the marginal effective tax rate (e.g., is repayment of an income contingent student loan an addition to the marginal *tax* rate?). In any case, the increment to the average "tax rate" of each individual (i.e., total tax plus loan repayment as a percentage of total income) is, of course, much less than the marginal rate due to the Basic Personal Amount and the stepped nature of the marginal tax rate.

As illustrated in the example, the amount of loan which was not repaid in any year due to income being insufficient would be forgiven.

We have modeled here the Jobseeker's Loan repayment based on the assumption that it would reflect total income as reported in the tax system. This is the simplest course and may also be the most equitable. However, if this were not desirable, it would be possible to include other income not counted under the "regular" tax system, such as TFSA income and welfare income (while a person cannot collect a Jobseeker's Loan while on welfare, it is possible to have collected a loan and been on welfare during a single year).

Figure 7 illustrates the amount of loan repayable and the net amount of Jobseeker's Loan to a person claiming the maximum loan, at various income levels.

FIGURE 7 Net Jobseeker's Loan and Income Contingent Repayment

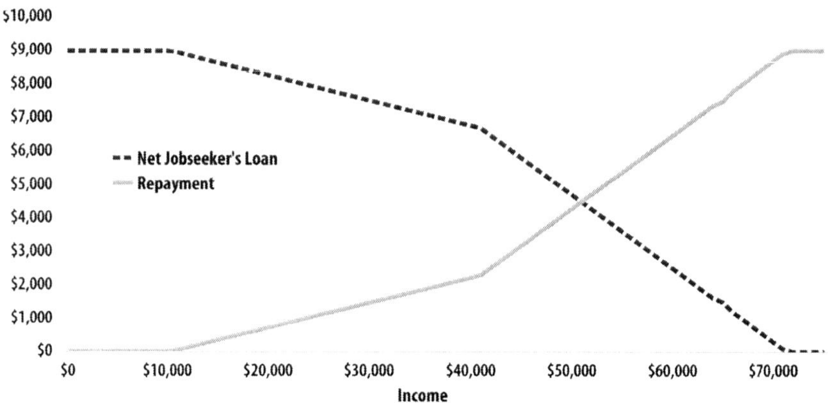

6. Percentage Restoration of Weeks

Recipients repaying the Jobseeker's Loan would be deemed to have recovered a portion of their eligibility for a new Jobseeker's Loan, as a percentage of the amount repaid. For example, if the weekly Jobseeker's Loan maximum is $346, and there is repayment of 2 × $346 = $692 of the Jobseeker's Loan, this would result in restoration of eligibility for one week of Jobseeker's Loan, assuming eligibility is restored at 50 per cent. Aside from making the overall program fairer, it also reduces the effective marginal tax rate on income as a result of the Jobseeker's Loan repayment by up to one-half (depending upon how one values the restoration of eligibility). Note that a full loan entitlement would still have to be regained over time, but the length of time needed to restore full eligibility would be reduced through loan repayment. Restoring half of eligibility is fair given that the loan is repaid. But restoring only partial eligibility will restrain frivolous claims for the Jobseeker's Loan.

7. Weekly Gross Loan

The weekly gross maximum loan is simply a function of the minimum wage and the percentage of the minimum wage reflected in the Jobseeker's Loan benefit level. Here, we are proposing a Jobseeker's Loan not adjusted for any personal budgetary factors. Costs such as home ownership or food expenses would also not be reflected, any more than they are for wages, and therefore would not have to be reported or accounted for in any way. Child benefits would continue to be provided through the federal Canada Child Tax Benefit and other federal and, in most cases, provincial and territorial child benefits (e.g., in Ontario the maximum combined payment from the Ontario Child Benefit and federal child benefits now is more than $5,000 per year).

We do not include here any deductions for payroll taxes such as

Canada/Quebec Pension Plan contributions or EI premiums, mainly for simplicity. These would be possible to include if thought desirable.

8. Maximum Eligible Weeks

As noted, the maximum eligible weeks—26 in this illustration—are a function of the eligibility period and the rate at which eligibility is accumulated.

9. Maximum Payable Per Eligible Period

The maximum loan in any eligibility period is simply the maximum number of weeks times the gross weekly benefit: 26 × $346 = $8,996.

10. Taxable Income at which a Jobseeker's Loan Begins to be Repaid

This is a function of the decision to use the federal Basic Personal Amount as the income threshold for maximum benefits for the purposes of this model—$10,382.

11. Taxable Income at which a Jobseeker's Loan is Fully Repaid

This amount—$71,426—is a function of the application of the federal tax system and the tax rate for calculating repayment required.

F Reporting Unit

In any income tax or transfer payment system, one of the critical variables is the reporting unit. In Canada, the personal income tax system is based primarily on individual income, not household income (unlike the United States). Canada's transfer payment system is mixed: Some programs—including refundable credits paid through the tax system—are based on household income, while other programs are based on individual income.

In this chapter, we propose that the Jobseeker's Loan be based on the individual reporting unit rather than the household. A couple, each of whom was receiving a Jobseeker's Loan, could get a maximum $692 a week (per couple), but of course only for a half of a year every five years.

It would be possible to adjust this amount so that the total received was some fraction of the sum of two individual benefits (in the Guaranteed Income Supplement, it is 81 per cent) when both members of a couple collected at one time, or otherwise define the reporting unit as a household or a couple. However, this approach would require the tax department to become even more intimately involved in personal lives to determine who is and who is not actually a "partner." This is no simple matter, as there are many forms of economic unit today. In contrast, with a forgivable loan based on individual income, the form of relationship is irrelevant. A married couple would be equally able to benefit from the forgivable loan as two sisters living together and sharing resources.

Another positive consequence of counting individual income rather than household income is to provide what is in essence a benefit to any at-home partner with no taxable income who returns to the labour market. This is especially important for the next few decades as the population ages and higher levels of participation in the work force are required to support pension and other benefits.

In the interests of least intrusiveness and in recognition of the increasing difficulty of defining what constitutes a couple expected to share economic resources, as well as to encourage workforce participation, we would view maintaining individual treatment as preferable, although this does add to costs. Note, however, that this is not a necessary feature of the Jobseeker's Loan: the program could as easily be organized to require repayment on a household basis.

G Costs of the Jobseeker's Loan

Obviously it is difficult to estimate the cost of the Jobseeker's Loan. How many people would actually take it up is hard to predict, as voluntary programs of this kind have typically been significantly undersubscribed. We will not in this paper attempt to provide a detailed estimate—only a rough ballpark estimate to show the scale of the program.

The size of the Jobseeker's Loan program in any year will be dependent on the unemployment rate. By using 2010 as an example of a high unemployment year, we can estimate an approximate upper limit on the potential size of the program. According to the most recent results from the Employment Insurance Coverage Survey, there were about 700,000 unemployed Canadians in 2010 ineligible for Employment Insurance (Statistics Canada 2011). This figure does not include about 84,000 students who left their employment to return to school, and so would not be eligible for the Jobseeker's Loan as they were not actively engaged in looking for work and available for employment—at least given the rules suggested in this chapter.

The 700,000 unemployed are eligible for a Jobseeker's Loan only once every five years, so we can assume about one-fifth or 140,000 might take up the loan in an average single year (there are some additional phase-in costs which we do not consider here). Assuming all of these took up the full loan, the gross federal cost would be about $1.26 billion. However, it is likely that at least some of the loans would have to be repaid, so assuming a modest average repayment of $2,000 each, the net cost to the federal government would be about $980 million.

Add to this the cost of the Jobseeker's Loan retirement benefit. There were about 15,000 new, partial, or full Guaranteed Income Supplement beneficiaries in each year over the last five years (Service Canada 2010). Here we assume 20,000 full or partial new Guaranteed Income Supplement recipients a year. These people represent the lowest-income seniors. Assuming all of them are entitled to the Jobseeker's Loan retirement benefit, it would cost about $180 million annually.

Adding the cost of the unemployed and the retirement benefit brings the net federal cost back up to about $1.16 billion. But the new federal program would also result in some savings to provincial governments.

In Part 1, we estimated that 170,000 to 260,000 unemployed were ineligible for Employment Insurance and were relying upon welfare in 2009. Assume the figure is roughly the same for 2010—say, for purposes of a rough ballpark calculation, 200,000 people. If one-fifth of these 200,000 unemployed were eligible for and received the maximum Jobseeker's Loan—assuming that costs to provinces for social assistance would have been about $3,000 per person for half a year, the length of the loan—the total welfare saving would be about $120 million.

So, factoring in the savings to provinces, the overall net cost of the proposed Jobseeker's Loan comes to a little more than a billion dollars a year. This amount does not take account of macro-economic effects which might be especially important when unemployment is high, resulting in slightly higher Gross Domestic Product as a result of the program and consequently higher tax revenues at both the provincial and federal levels, which would further reduce the net cost.

This is anything but a precise estimate yet, but it does give us some sense of the expense of the proposed Jobseeker's Loan program, which is likely in the vicinity of one billion and not five or six billion dollars. One billion is certainly a very large figure, but it is well within the range of new government initiatives recently taken or promised. For example, the Conservative party estimated the cost of its promised income tax splitting for couples with children at $2.3 billion annually. The cost of the pension income splitting tax break, which goes almost entirely to benefit wealthy seniors with non-working partners, is $920 million today and will grow rapidly in the future along with the number of pensioners. The list could go on. The point here is that the new Jobseeker's Loan program would not be prohibitively costly.

3 Conclusion

This chapter has shown that inadequate coverage of the unemployed through the Employment Insurance program is due to non-participation in the Employment Insurance program as well as ineligibility of many who do participate. Consequently, liberalizing the eligibility criteria for Employment Insurance is not going to correct this deficiency. Indeed, given that Employment Insurance is and should remain a social insurance program, it is unlikely ever to be able to cover self-employment or many contractual and other unorthodox employment arrangements that have been growing in our labour force.

At present, welfare is the only resort for the unemployed in financial need who are not eligible for Employment Insurance. But welfare is a highly stigmatizing and invasive program. We have therefore proposed the development of an income-tested program between welfare and

Employment Insurance which would provide limited and temporary financial assistance to those in need who are actively engaged in job search.

The second part of this paper addresses the design of the program to provide temporary income to the unemployed. This program could be designed in the usual way with monthly reporting and the amount of benefit calculated on the basis of the report. However, we explore in detail the possibility of a novel type of design which instead pays a forgivable income-contingent loan to persons searching for work, with the repayment administered through the income tax system. We have called this the Jobseeker's Loan to distinguish it as a non-welfare program that is intended to provide temporary assistance for those looking for work, but is repayable for those with the means to do so.

The proposed new income security program for the unemployed fits within a larger agenda for reform of Canada's income security system set out in *Towards a New Architecture for Canada's Adult Benefits* (Battle et al. 2006). We have not here spelled out in detail the complementary reforms which could be undertaken along with the introduction of the Jobseeker's Loan. However, among these measures could be a substantial improvement in provincial welfare to transform it into a program that really does provide recipients with the opportunity to gain skills and knowledge needed for employment. We also believe that the Jobseeker's Loan could make reform of Employment Insurance itself more palatable, such as raising benefits to provide better continuity of living standards, increasing work sharing programs such as were implemented in Germany during the recession, and reducing or eliminating the favoured treatment of some unemployment regions across Canada. Overall, we would see the Employment Insurance program run more rigorously as social insurance, including real stewardship by business and labour, rather than by government.

The Jobseeker's Loan proposed in this chapter would fill a large hole in Canada's income security system at a reasonable cost.

Endnotes

1 The proposal in this chapter fits within a larger critique and re-conceptualization of income security in Canada which we discuss in *Towards a New Architecture for Canada's Adult Benefits* (Battle et al., 2006). Readers interested in this larger context should refer to *A New Architecture* which is available on the Caledon Institute of Social Policy website.

2 This and all subsequent data except where otherwise stated is from the Employment Insurance Coverage Survey as reported in Statistics Canada (2009, 2010).

3 In this and the following discussion "Employment Insurance benefits" means regular benefits and does not include parental leave, fishers' benefits and other benefits, unless otherwise stated.

4 "Eligible for Employment Insurance" includes both those who collected benefits and the small number who were eligible for benefits but did not make a claim (about 3 to 4 per cent of the unemployed population).

5 Data from Human Resources and Skills Development Canada (n.d.) and Stapleton (2009).

References

Barrett, G.F., D.J. Doiron, D.A. Green and W.C. Riddell. 1996. "The Interaction of Unemployment Insurance and Social Assistance." *UI, Income Distribution and Living Standards Series*. Ottawa: Human Resources Development Canada.

Battle, K., M. Mendelson and S. Torjman. 2006. *Towards a New Architecture for Canada's Adult Benefits*. Ottawa: Caledon Institute of Social Policy.

Black, J. and R. Shillington. 2005. "Employment Insurance: Research Summary for the Task Force for Modernizing Income Security for Working Age Adults." At www.mowateitaskforce.ca/resources/non-governmental-reports.

Browning, M., S. Jones and P. Kuhn. 1995. "Studies of the Interaction of UI and Welfare Using the COEP Dataset." *UI, Income Distribution and Living Standards Series*. Ottawa: Human Resources Development Canada.

Canadian Chamber of Commerce, The. 2009. "Reforming Canada's Employment Insurance (EI) Program." July 2009. Toronto: The Canadian Chamber of Commerce. At http://www.chamber.ca/images/uploads/EI/Reforming_Canadas_Employment_System20-07-09.pdf.

Finnie, R., D. Gray, I. Irvine, and Y. Zhang. 2011. "The Income Sources for Long-Term Workers Who Exhaust Employment Insurance Benefits." Mowat Centre EI Task Force. Toronto: Mowat Centre for Policy Innovation.

Fortin, B., G. Lacroix and J-F. Thibault. 1999. "The Interaction of UI and Welfare, and the Dynamics of Welfare Participation of Single Parents." *Canadian Public Policy – Analyse de Politiques*, vol. xxv supplement/numéro special 1, 115-32.

Herd, D., A. Mitchell and E. Lightman. 2005. "Rituals of Degradation: Administration as Policy in the Ontario Works Programme." *Social Policy and Administration*, 39(1), February 2005: 65-79.

Human Resources Development Canada. 1998. "An Analysis of Employment Insurance Benefit Coverage." *Working Paper* W-98-35E. Ottawa: Applied Research Branch, Strategic Policy.

Human Resources and Skills Development Canada. n.d. "Indicators of Well-being in Canada." At http://www4.hrsdc.gc.ca/h.4m.2@-eng.jsp.

Mendelsohn, M. and J. Medow. 2010. "Help Wanted: How Well did the Employment Insurance Program Respond During Recent Recessions?" *Mowat Note*. Toronto: Mowat Centre for Policy Innovation.

Mendelson, M., J. Millar and P. Whiteford. 2003 "Timing it Right? Tax Credits and How to Respond to Income Changes." York, UK: JF Rowntree Foundation.

Ontario Social Assistance Review Advisory Council, The. 2010. "Recommendations for an Ontario Income Security Review." May 2010. At http://www.mcss.gov.on.ca/en/mcss/publications/social/sarac/toc_sarac.aspx.

Osberg, L., S. Phipps, and S. Erksoy. 1995. "UI Implications of Extending Unemployment Insurance Coverage to Self-Employment and Short Hours Work Week: A Micro-Simulation Approach." *UI, Income Distribution and Living Standards Series*. Ottawa: Human Resources Development Canada.

Rawls, J. 1971. *A Theory of Justice*. Cambridge, MA: Harvard University Press.

Roller, S. 1999. "Report on the Main Results of the Employment Insurance Coverage Survey, 1998." Statistics Canada Catalogue no. 73F0008XIE. Ottawa: Statistics Canada.

Rosenberg, L., M. Derr, L. Pavetti, S. Asheer, M. Hague Angus, S. Sattar and J. Max. 2008. *A Study of States' TANF Diversion Programs: Final Report*. Princeton, NJ: Mathematica Policy Research, Inc.

Schmid, G. and B. Reissert. 1996. "Unemployment Compensation and Labour Market Transitions." In *International Handbook of Labour Market Policy and Evaluation*, ed. G. Schmid, J. O'Reilly and K. Schömann, 235-76. London: Edward Elgar Publishing Limited.

Service Canada. 2010. "CPP and OAS Statistical Tables." At http://www.servicecanada.gc.ca/eng/isp/statistics/cppstatbook/statbook2010.shtml#t3.

Stapleton, J. 2009. "The Silence of the Lines: Poverty Reduction Strategies and the Crash of 2008." *Ontario Alternative Budget*, February 2009. Ottawa: Canadian Centre for Policy Alternatives.

Statistics Canada. 2009. "Employment Insurance Coverage Survey." *The Daily*. 23 July 2009.

——. 2010. "Employment Insurance Coverage Survey." *The Daily*. 21 June 2010.

——. 2011. "Employment Insurance Coverage Survey." *The Daily*. 27 June 2011.

Vosko, L.F. 2011. "The Challenge of Expanding EI Coverage: Charting Exclusions and Partial Exclusions on the Bases of Gender, Immigration Status, Age, and Place of Residence and Exploring Avenues for Inclusive Policy Redesign." Mowat Centre EI Task Force. Toronto: Mowat Centre for Policy Innovation.

Chapter 6

Reforming EI Special Benefits: Exploring Alternative Financing and Delivery Options

Luc Turgeon

1 Introduction

Canada's post-war welfare state was built on the foundation of the nuclear family and the male breadwinner model. While men were expected to earn a "family wage," women were expected to stay at home to take care of children and elderly relatives. This model has been in crisis for the past forty years. First, it has been challenged as undesirable not only by the women's movement, but also by policy-makers. After all, Canadian women now constitute a majority of university graduates and their participation in the labour market is essential if Canada is to remain economically competitive. Second, the male breadwinner model has become less of an option for increasingly cash-strapped families. As a result, OECD countries have experienced a "crisis of care" that has led to the adoption of new policies, such as child care programs and elderly care programs. Canada's Employment Insurance (EI) special benefits—maternity, parental, sickness and compassionate care benefits—are programs devised to respond to such "crisis of care" issues.

Across OECD countries, these special benefits (to use the Canadian terminology) have a number of more precise objectives (see Phipps 2005, 24-8, for the goals of the federal government's maternity and parental benefits program). First, they provide a certain level of income security for an individual (and his or her family) if he or she must interrupt work for a temporary period of time. Second, considering widespread evidence of the importance of the early years for a child's development, parental leave programs ensure the presence of a parent during this crucial period in a child's life. Third, parental leave and especially paternity leave programs can contribute to greater gender equity, leading men to take greater responsibility with regards to child rearing. Fourth, considering the increasing demands on contemporary families, both parental and compassionate care benefits contribute to a better work-family balance for Canadians. Finally, considering the limited availability of home care services in many countries like Canada, these benefits allow elderly men and women to live their last moments in dignity surrounded by their loved ones.

Throughout the OECD, these new programs have often been grafted to programs that had previously been adopted to tackle other social problems.

This is how, in the 1970s, Canada's parental and sick leave programs came to be attached to its Employment Insurance program. One might wonder whether this approach is still the best way to organize and to finance special benefits. Indeed, some Canadian analysts and organizations have argued that the logic of parental leave is fundamentally incompatible with EI, that the latter is governed by considerations of labour force attachment and the former by the goal of helping families in the wake of the birth of a child (see Pal 1985).

This chapter analyzes the delivery of "special benefits" in Canada and whether they should be removed from the current EI program. It does so by exploring potential alternative delivery options in light of past proposals and practices adopted by other countries. The chapter is divided into four parts. The first part presents the current system in place in Canada. The second part discusses the limits of Canada's special benefits system. The last two parts explore different reform options. After exploring options for reform, the chapter ultimately recommends that the federal government maintain its current role in the delivery of special benefits, but moderately enhance the generosity of these benefits in part based on lessons learned from the Quebec experience.[1]

2 EI and Special Benefits in Canada

As mentioned in the previous section, there are four types of special benefits associated with Canada's EI system: maternity, parental, sickness, and compassionate care. In 2008/09 special benefits corresponded to 27.8 per cent of all EI benefits, for a total of $3.9 billion (Human Resources and Skills Development Canada 2009).[2] Parental leave benefits accounted for 14.4 per cent, maternity for 6.2 per cent, sickness for 7.1 per cent, and compassionate care for 0.1 per cent of EI benefits. Women received 67.2 per cent of all special benefits paid during that period. In this section, I first present a short history of the adoption of special benefits and the current eligibility criteria. In the second subsection, I present a brief statistical portrait of EI special benefits in Canada.

A Special Benefits in Canada

The Unemployment Insurance (UI) program was adopted in 1940 following a constitutional amendment that gave the federal government jurisdiction over Unemployment Insurance. However, it was only in 1971, in the wake of the Royal Commission on the Status of Women and a White Paper on Unemployment Insurance, that maternity and sickness benefits were included as part of UI, allowing maternity benefits to become available for biological mothers. These benefits were viewed as an adjustment to the economic security system put in place in the post-war period. As stated in a report of the Standing Committee on Labour, Manpower and Immigration in 1970:

> These additional benefits represent an adjustment in the economic security system to recognize the contingencies generated by a world in which women are a large portion of the labour force and in which a major segment of the population has no protection against interruption of earnings due to sickness. (cited in *Reference re Employment Insurance Act*, para. 22)

Eligibility for these new programs was restricted to those with previous participation in the labour market. Those claiming benefits had to have 20 weeks of insurable employment, which was more than the requirement for regular benefits. In the case of maternity benefits, according to the "Magic 10 rule," women had to demonstrate that they were employed 10 weeks before conception in order to make sure that they would not take a job once they became pregnant in order to obtain the maternity benefit. Both the maternity and sickness benefits programs provided for 15 weeks of benefits, corresponding to two-thirds of past wages up to a ceiling. A two-week waiting period applied to those benefits, as was the case for regular EI benefits.

In 1983, adoptive parents became eligible for maternity benefits, and the Magic 10 rule was abolished. In 1990, a 10-week parental leave that could be taken by either the mother or the father was introduced. The replacement benefit rate for special benefits was adjusted to 60 per cent with a ceiling, but was later reduced to 57 per cent in 1993 and then 55 per cent in 1994 (although the replacement rate for low-income claimants was brought back to 60 per cent in 1994, and was then replaced in 1996 by a family supplement). In 1997, in the wake of the switch from UI to EI, eligibility conditions were changed from 20 weeks of work to 700 hours (reduced to 600 in 2001). It was in 2001 that Canada's parental benefits were significantly improved. Parental benefits were extended from 10 to 35 weeks, for a combined total of 50 weeks if the mother, as in most cases, took the parental leave.

Compassionate care benefits were introduced in 2004. The program was intended for individuals who must temporarily leave work to provide care or support to a gravely ill relative at risk of dying within 26 weeks. These individuals must demonstrate that their regular weekly earnings from work have decreased by more than 40 per cent, and successful claimants receive six weeks of benefits. Originally, the program was available to eligible workers who were absent from work to provide care to a child, parent, spouse, or common-law partner. In 2006, the eligibility was expanded to include in-laws, siblings (including stepbrothers and sisters), grandparents (and step grand-parents), grandchildren, aunts and uncles, nieces and nephews, foster parents, guardians, and wards. It also included the spouses of these individuals, as well as family members of a spouse or a common-law partner. The qualifying period, the waiting period, and the benefit rates are the same as for the other special benefits.

For most of the period following the introduction of the maternity leave and sickness benefits programs in 1971, self-employed workers were not eligible to receive special benefits, as EI was designed for workers in an employer-employee relationship and funded by contributions of both the employer and the employee. However, in 2009 the government adopted the *Fairness for the Self-Employed Act* that made special benefits available to self-employed Canadians on a voluntary basis, that is, as long as they opt into the EI program one year prior to claiming benefits. As a result, such benefits have been available to the self-employed since January 2011.

B Quebec's Parental Insurance Program

While the provision of special benefits is a federal responsibility, a de facto asymmetry has appeared since 2006, following the creation of Quebec's Parental Insurance Plan. As a result of this plan, maternity and parental benefits are delivered in Quebec by the provincial government.[3] The creation of the Quebec program followed a fight about the constitutionality of using Employment Insurance to finance a maternity and parental leave program, with the Supreme Court eventually siding with the federal government's position that such a program was constitutional. However, before the judgment of the Supreme Court, the federal government had already signed an agreement that allowed the Quebec provincial government to create its own parental program (the legal details of this devolution will be discussed in section 4.2 below).

As a result of this agreement, the Quebec government now collects premiums to finance its parental leave program, and the federal government collects smaller premiums in Quebec than in other provinces. The Quebec parental plan offers two options to Quebec's parents, with both options being financially more generous than the Canadian parental benefits plan. The basic plan guarantees a lower replacement rate but for a longer period, and the special plan higher replacement rates but for a shorter period. Table 1 presents a summary of the basic and special plans.

There are five other significant differences between the Quebec and federal programs. First, there is no waiting period to obtain benefits in Quebec. Second, the maximum insurable earnings is much higher in

TABLE 1 Quebec Parental Insurance Plan

	Basic Plan		Special Plan	
	Number of Weeks	Replacement Rate	Number of Weeks	Replacement Rate
Maternity	18	70%	15	75%
Paternal (can be shared by the two parents)	7 25 (32)	70% 55%	25	75%
Paternity	5	70%	3	75%

Quebec than in the rest of Canada ($64,000 versus $44,200 in 2011). Third, eligibility for benefits is much less restrictive in Quebec; whereas the work requirement to be eligible for special benefits under EI is 600 hours, the entrance requirement and minimum insurable earnings in Quebec is $2,000 of earned income in the past year, regardless of the number of hours worked. Fourth, in order to pay for this more generous program, the Quebec government must collect higher premiums. In 2011 a person in Quebec with an income of $20,000 pays (by the author's calculations) $33.40 more in combined premiums than a worker with the same earning does in the rest of Canada; a worker with an income of $40,000 pays $66.80 more, and a worker with an income of $60,000 pays $158.66 more. Fifth, self-employed workers must pay into the program, and do not have the option to opt in as in the federal program. Moreover, while in the rest of Canada the self-employed pay the same premiums that employees pay, in Quebec they pay more than employees but less than the combined employee and employer premiums.[4]

As such, the Quebec Parental Insurance Plan constitutes both a model against which the federal maternity and parental leave programs can be evaluated, as well as a potential future alternative, one that would see responsibility for special benefits devolved to the provinces.

3 An Evaluation of Canada's Current Approach to Special Benefits

As mentioned in the introduction, EI special benefits have historically had a number of purposes. When evaluating EI special benefits, one must first analyze whether these objectives have indeed been met. In the first part of this section, I evaluate the impact of EI special benefits on three important factors: labour force attachment, income support, and gender equality. In the second section, I explore the issue of policy coordination and whether the special benefits system is integrated more broadly in Canada's welfare architecture.

A Evaluating EI Special Benefits

Since the 1970s, a constantly growing proportion of pregnant women have been eligible for maternity benefits. In 2009, 76.2 per cent of all new mothers had insurable employment, and among these, 88.0 per cent were receiving maternity or parental benefits. The situation was relatively different in Quebec, where 81.5 per cent of new mothers had insurable employment, and 94.7 per cent of new mothers with insurable employment were receiving maternity or parental benefits (Statistics Canada 2010). In fact, of all the births registered in Quebec in 2008, 84.5 per cent led to the payment of parental benefits (in comparison to 67.1 per cent in the rest of Canada in 2009).[5] An estimated 20 per cent of workers receiving Employment Insurance/Quebec Parental Insurance Plan benefits also received an employer top-up (Marshall 2010). In 2009, almost all mothers took advantage of the full 15 weeks of the federal maternity leave program (the average is 14.6 weeks), and on average parents took 32.6 out of the 35 paid weeks available with the parental leave program (Human Resources and Social Development Canada 2009: chap. 2). In Quebec, families with two employed parents took advantage on average of 54.2 of the 55 available weeks under the basic plan, and 42.2 of the 43 available weeks under the special plan.

The ability of a majority of Canadians to obtain maternity and/or parental leave benefits has had a number of positive impacts. Michael Baker and Kevin Milligan (2008a, 2008b) have shown that extended maternity leave, such as the one introduced in Canada in 2000, increased the time women were at home with their children, the likelihood that mothers stayed with their pre-birth employer, and the percentage of mothers attaining public health breastfeeding benchmarks.

While the maternity and paternity leave programs have allowed a majority of Canadians to obtain benefits, it is far from perfect. A 2003 study, conducted before the introduction of Quebec's parental leave program increased the national average, estimated that around 35 per cent of new mothers did not claim benefits. Overall, 16 per cent of new mothers were not in the workforce in the prior two years of their child's birth, 10 per cent were in employment but were not able to meet the qualifying hours, and 9 per cent were in the "other" category, which included self-employed workers (Evans 2007, 122, in particular). In certain regions of the country, it is easier to qualify for "regular" (those for laid-off workers) than for "special" EI benefits such as maternity leave. It is the opposite in other regions of the country. While in high-unemployment regions workers must have worked 420 hours to qualify for benefits after being laid off, women in the same regions must have worked 600 hours to qualify for maternity benefits. As such, the actual number of qualifying hours constitutes an important impediment to a small, but nevertheless significant, number of women.

In 2008/9, the average weekly maternity benefit was $350. Similarly, the average parental benefit was $360 (with men receiving a higher level of benefits) (Human Resources and Social Development Canada 2009: chap. 2). The Quebec program is much more generous, as shown by the fact that for an employed female worker in Quebec who gave birth and adhered to the basic plan, the average weekly benefit was $470 in 2008. Both the Quebec and the Canadian plans make provisions for the payment of supplements to low-income parents. The Family Supplement allows low-income Canadians outside of Quebec to receive up to 80 per cent of their insured earnings up to the overall regular benefit weekly maximum. Similarly, in Quebec, low-income workers can receive up to 80 per cent of their insured earnings.

It must be stressed that, from a comparative perspective, the Canadian parental leave system is relatively generous. When using the full-time equivalent paid leave indicator, which is the wage replacement rate multiplied by the duration of leave, Canada is among the OECD leaders. The FTE Paid Parental Leave in Canada corresponds to 28 weeks. Only Germany, Greece, Quebec, Sweden, Finland and Norway provide more generous paid leave programs.[6] In comparison, the FTE Paid Leave in the United States and Australia is 0, 14 weeks in New Zealand, 20 weeks in Denmark and 21 weeks in Ireland (Ray et al. 2009).

Many analysts have questioned the generosity of the program for low-income workers. Evans (2007) found that a majority of women who were likely to return early to employment were indeed low-income women. Research also indicates that women with lower earnings are both less likely to, and may not be able to, stay at home for the full duration of their maternity/parental benefits. Kathleen Lahey (as cited in Standing Committee on the Status of Women 2009) found that around 25 per cent of women were not able to take their full maternity leave, and that those were, on average, women who had an annual income of $16,000 or less.

Most parental benefits continue to be claimed by women, although there is some evidence that men are now more likely to claim parental benefits than they once were as a result of the longer parental leave introduced in 2001. For biological parents, women were responsible for 86.5 per cent of all claims in 2008/9 (Human Resources and Skills Development Canada 2009: Annex 2.9). Whereas 61.9 per cent of parental biological claims established by men were shared with their partner, only 6.4 per cent of women who established biological parental claims shared them with their partner. As for men who shared the benefit with their partner, they took an average of 10.8 weeks of benefits. The average claim duration by parents who shared the parental benefit was 32.0 weeks, and 32.3 weeks for those who did not share (Human Resources and Social Development Canada 2009: chap. 2). In comparison to other OECD countries, Canada (with the exception of Quebec) does not have a separate paternal leave program. However, since the introduction of the parental leave program, the percentage of fathers filing for benefits has increased tremendously, especially since the extension of the leave in 2001. In Canada, the percentage of eligible fathers who received parental leave benefits has increased from 3 per cent in 2000 to 30.1 per cent in 2009. But, this growth was driven largely by change in Quebec; if Quebec (which now has a separate paternal leave program) is excluded from this national calculation, then the proportion of eligible fathers who took advantage of parental leave was only 12.8 per cent in 2009, compared to 79.1 per cent in Quebec (Statistics Canada 2010).

In 2009, sickness benefits were claimed on average for 9.4 weeks, with an average weekly benefit of $327. Of those claiming benefits, 31.4 per cent used all 15 weeks. As for compassionate care benefits, claimants used on average 4.7 weeks, while 57.5 per cent used all six weeks of entitlements (Human Resources and Social Development Canada 2009). As shown by recent policy proposals by political parties, there seems to be an increased belief that the number of weeks of coverage under the compassionate care program is insufficient and should be extended.[7]

B EI Special Benefits and Canada's Welfare Architecture

It is not only important to evaluate special benefits on their own, but also how they "fit" with Canada's broader welfare architecture. Some commentators have argued that despite the inclusion of special benefits in an employment insurance program, these benefits have evolved over time in a way that reflects both the transformation of Canadian society as well as the growing importance of family policies in Canada's welfare architecture. As argued by Michael Prince (2009, 16-17),

> Indeed, in today's world of work and families, these income benefits are not really "special" or add-ons to the EI system. With dual earners the primary form of families, and gender equality of opportunity a prominent social value, these benefits are central elements within federal jurisdiction in family policy, income security and labour market programming. These benefits address important risks centred in the economy, the worker and the family; they represent efforts at addressing some of the challenges and stresses of work-family life relation. Eligibility for these benefits falls squarely within EI's logic of paying premiums into the program and accumulating sufficient insurable hours of employment over the past year.

However, not all analysts share such a perspective. In a well-known criticism of the inclusion of maternity benefits in EI, Leslie Pal (1985, 552) has argued that "the government has made a mistake in grafting maternity benefits to UI in 1971; efforts to improve these benefits within the context of UI have led to bizarre and even absurd results." More specifically, Pal (1985) presented a number of problems that are still relevant today and are related to the inclusion of maternity leave (and now parental leave) in EI. Two are especially important from the point of view of family policy. First, only working women are eligible for benefits, when non-working women also need support when a child is born. Second, there is a two-week waiting period before an individual can receive benefits, which makes sense for regular benefits but not for special benefits (Ibid, 558). Another limit of the Canadian parental program is the fact that, contrary to the case of Scandinavian countries, the system is not especially flexible. In Sweden, for example, parental insurance benefits can be used until a child's eighth birthday. Moreover, the earning-related portion is highly flexible, allowing a parent to be both on leave and work partially on the same day. Such possibilities do not exist in Canada.[8] One could also point to another important problem in relation to the interaction of special benefits with the broader family policy agenda: the difficult coordination with provincial child care programs. Currently, the transition from parental leave to work is especially difficult in Canada due to the absence of child care services (with the exception of Quebec) once a parent returns to work. Another problematic element resulting from the integration of parental and maternity benefits in the same program as regular unemployment benefits is the impact on the income security of certain workers; currently, a person who has received maternity or parental benefits during the previous 50 weeks is not eligible for regular EI if she is laid off once she returns to work.

Other analysts (e.g., Mintz 2010) have argued that special benefits should be paid through general taxes, since an increase in premiums to pay for general social benefits, due to maximum contribution limits, represents a greater burden on workers with low and modest incomes. Moreover, payroll taxes used to finance a program such as EI impose a burden solely on the working population and employers, an argument made over time by both unions and employers. One might argue that programs such as parental leave and compassionate care benefits are valuable to the entire community, and as such should be paid for by the entire community. This issue has become more relevant since 1990, when the program went from being financed from employer/employee premiums *and* the federal government's general revenues, to being fully self-financed from employer/employee premiums. Some economists and groups representing employers (and workers) have argued that the higher payroll taxes used to finance those benefits were an impediment to job creation and higher wages. For example, the Canadian Chamber of Commerce has argued that:

> Because the EI program has been used to support government spending in a variety of areas completely unrelated to the original purpose of the EI program, EI premiums rates have been kept at unnecessary high levels. (...) The social-program aspects of EI should be placed within general program spending. Reducing EI premiums for both employers and employees would reduce real wage costs to employers making it more attractive to hire more workers, and increase real wages received by employees. It would put in place incentives to boost productivity. (2009)

Poschmann (2005) has also argued that Ottawa has historically "collected far more money than needed to run employment insurance as an insurance program, and uses surplus EI premium revenue to finance numerous federal expeditions in areas of provincial jurisdiction." The argument here is that the inclusion of special benefits in EI has led to federal-provincial bickering and an unclear division of responsibility between the two orders of government, reducing accountability to citizens.

An evaluation of the current program demonstrates that Canada's special benefits system is relatively generous. The main problem with the program itself currently seems to be a lack of flexibility, a replacement rate in Canada outside Quebec that is of limited generosity for parents who cannot count on a maternal leave top up from their employer, and eligibility requirements that make it difficult for certain women to qualify for maternity benefits. Other problems identified are related to the financing of special benefits in Canada and their coordination with provincial programs. While such criticisms are not uncommon, very few analysts have explored the potential benefits and drawback of alternatives to the delivery of special benefits in Canada (a notable exception being Phipps 2005).

4 Alternative Approaches to the Delivery of Special Benefits

In this section, I explore whether there might be more effective ways of providing special benefits in Canada. After all, Canada is one of the rare countries that pays for special benefits through an employment insurance program, whereas most countries fund special benefits through a general social insurance fund or through general revenues. I first explore the option of financing EI special benefits through general taxation. It must be stated, however, that many more models of financing special benefits could be examined, including direct employer financing, portable leave saving accounts, income contingent loans, and concessional business tax arrangements (for two interesting discussions of these different financing options see Productivity Commission 2009; Wilkinson and Briscoe 1996). Those options are not explored since they are not viable in the Canadian context or because they are unlikely to find any substantial support from either policy-makers or important stakeholders.

Changing the delivery of EI special benefits could also be done in Canada through a process of devolution that would lead provinces to take charge of special benefits as part of growing provincial policies concerned with the reconciliation of work and family life. I explore three different reform options that would involve greater participation of the provinces in the delivery of special benefits, but ultimately conclude that the federal government should maintain its role delivering special benefits and moderately enhance benefits in part based on lessons learned from the Quebec experience with QPIP.

Each of these reforms involves different conceptions of justice, equity, and efficiency, as well as different conceptions of the Canadian political community and the role of the federal government. As such, I evaluate these alternatives according to four main criteria: 1) efficient program design; 2) efficient program delivery; 3) fairness and equity between men and women, and between salaried employees and non-salaried employees; and 4) the harmonious working of Canada's federal system.

A A New Federal Approach: A Stand Alone Program Financed Through General Revenues

A recommendation that has often been proposed is to take special benefits out of EI and to finance them through general taxation, with continuing federal responsibility for those benefits. This recommendation has come both from employers (as demonstrated previously) as well as from unions, who have at times expressed their preference that parental leave be taken out of EI, albeit with the caveat that such a move should be taken only after the adoption of a law that would guarantee a right to maternity leave. In a brief submitted to the Commission on Unemployment Insurance Reform (1986, 120), for example, the *Syndicat des fonctionnaires provinciaux du Québec* made a case for ending the financing of maternity leave through UI premiums:

> The worker who quits her job because of pregnancy is not really unemployed, since she still has her job. The benefits paid out to these workers should, therefore, be provided by a program other than Unemployment Insurance—for example, through Family Allowances—and should entirely be financed by the government.

On the other hand, the Canadian women's movement (outside of Quebec) has long opposed taking special benefits out of the UI or EI program on the grounds that inclusion in the federal social insurance program protected the program from provincial constitutional challenge. As argued by the Canadian Advisory Council on the Status of Women in a brief to the 1986 Commission on Unemployment Insurance Reform:

> It is not clear that the federal government would retain jurisdiction if benefits were removed from the [UI/EI] program. Canadian women's rights to earnings replacement while on maternity leave might then depend on provinces developing their own programs. Thus, a national program, with national standards, available to all women regardless of where they live, might be jeopardized. (quoted in DiGiacomo 2007, 10)

It is uncertain though whether taking special benefits out of EI would necessarily lead to a successful constitutional challenge. First, the Supreme Court could always justify the creation of a new stand-alone program in an area of provincial jurisdiction by arguing that it is consistent with the federal government's spending power. Second, in the 2005 reference case on EI, the Court made important statements that could lead to the conclusion that it will remain deferential to the federal government and is unlikely to strike down a stand-alone program financed through general revenues. Indeed, in its judgement, the Supreme Court (*Reference re Employment Insurance Act* 2005, para. 44) rejects a narrow interpretation of the federal power over EI as a carve-out from the provincial power over property and civil rights, arguing that "the specific power cannot be evaluated in relation to the general power, because any evolution would then be regarded as an encroachment." Indeed, the Court concludes that while the provincial legislatures have jurisdiction over social programs, "Parliament also has the power to provide income replacement benefits to parents who must take time off to give birth or to care for children (Ibid., para. 77)." Such a broad definition of the purpose of maternity and parental leave program suggests that the Court could view such a stand-alone program simply as a normal evolution of the EI program, with the same objective of providing income replacement benefits.

A certain number of countries finance special benefits such as parental leave through general taxation. New Zealand introduced such a system in 2003 in a situation of budget surplus. The system, however, is not especially generous, as female employees are only entitled to 12 weeks of paid leave. In 2011, Australia will also introduce its first paid parental leave scheme, which like New Zealand, will also be financed through general taxation. It will pay 18 weeks of parental leave at the minimum wage for primary care givers that earn less than AU$150,000 annually. Furthermore, under this scheme employers will deliver the benefits and, in order to be eligible, parents will need to have worked continuously for at least 10 of the 13 months prior to the expected birth or adoption date. (For more on the Australian Plan see O'Neil 2010.)

There are a number of advantages to financing special benefits out of general taxation. First, it would spread the cost of such benefits across all Canadians. This is especially important, as previously mentioned, in light of the fact that all Canadians benefit from parental leave and compassionate care leaves. Second, it would decrease payroll taxes that can be an impediment to job creation. Third, it would eliminate the negative interaction between the logic of employment insurance and the logic of special benefits mentioned in the previous section, exemplified in the case of the two-week waiting period.

However there are important drawbacks to such an approach. First, countries that have historically financed parental leave out of general revenue have tended to provide less generous benefits.[9] Although there are no intrinsic obstacles to financing generous income replacement benefits out of general taxation, the fact that citizens contribute to an insurance system would seem to justify their receiving benefits that more closely reflect their earnings and contribution. Second, the parental leave program is generally very popular among Canadians, especially since the changes introduced in 2001. A survey (Human Resources and Skills Development Canada 2005) found that the average satisfaction scores after the introduction of the enhanced program were quite high (with an average score of 6.0 out of 7.0). Therefore, any attempt at creating a new, stand alone program, is likely to attract significant controversy.

B A Decentralized Approach: Provincial Parental Insurance Programs/Conditional or Unconditional Federal Transfers

A second ambitious reform proposal would be to follow the precedent of Quebec's parental insurance program to decentralize responsibility for all special benefits to the provinces. The legal framework is already in place for such a decentralization. Specifically, Section 64(5) of the Unemployment Insurance Act (1971) provided for the development of provincial sickness or maternity leave programs:

> Where under a provincial law any allowances, monies or other benefits are payable to insured person in respect of sickness or pregnancy that would have the effect of reducing or eliminating the benefits that are payable under this Act, to such insured person in respect unemployment caused by that illness or pregnancy, the premium payable under this Act shall be reduced or eliminated as prescribed but subject to paragraph (a) of section 65.

This opting out clause was maintained in 1996 when UI was replaced by EI. As stipulated in Section 69 (2) of the *Employment Insurance Act*:

> The Commission shall, with the approval of the Governor in Council, make regulations that provide a system for reducing the employer's and employee's premiums when the payment of any allowances, money or other benefits because of illness, injury, quarantine, pregnancy or child care under a provincial law to insured persons would have the effect of reducing or eliminating the special benefits payable to those insured persons.

Opponents of decentralization have argued that the process of devolution might lead to either a race to the bottom or a patchwork of very different benefits across the country. Shelley Phipps (2005, 29), for example, argues that "a potential danger of transferring responsibility for maternity/parental benefits to the provinces is that some provinces might choose to offer much less than is currently available, while others may only be able to afford the basic programs." Therefore, according to Phipps, "maintaining federal jurisdiction over maternity and parental benefits seems the safest way to ensure that benefits for parents are equal across the country" (Ibid., 43).

While it is undeniable that variations in generosity might appear in the different provincial programs, the Canada-Quebec Final Agreement on the Quebec Parental Insurance Plan demonstrates that a race to the bottom is unlikely if the federal government imposes conditions to the transfer of responsibility to the provinces. The Canada-Quebec agreement made provisions for interprovincial mobility (articles 1.2.2 and 5.1) and also guaranteed that any person residing in Quebec would receive a total amount of benefits substantially equivalent to what they would have been entitled to under the EI regime (article 5.4.2). Moreover, the agreement also included a clause stating that each party could terminate the agreement as long as it provided a one year notice (article 6.4.1). As such, if a province would significantly reduce benefits, the federal government could regain control over the provision of special benefits. Finally, even in the case of less constraining intergovernmental agreements, one has to take into consideration that the principle of universal maternity and parental benefits has largely become accepted in Canada, which constitutes an obstacle to a widespread retrenchment by the provinces in case of devolution.

There are two approaches to devolution that could be adopted. The first approach entails the creation of provincial parental insurance programs along the same lines as the Quebec program, with the federal government reducing EI premiums. A province could then decide to follow the Quebec model and adopt a parental insurance program, or could in fact decide to finance such a program through general taxation with the potential benefits and drawbacks discussed in the previous section.

There are three main advantages to the adoption of provincial parental insurance programs. First, such an approach would entail clearer lines of accountability, with provinces clearly in charge of family policies. Second, it would allow provincial governments to have parental insurance programs as generous as the provinces' voters desire. Third, it would allow provincial governments to experiment with new approaches that could allow a more seamless integration between the parental leave program and child care.

Besides a certain degree of policy variations between provinces, a main drawback of this approach, which entails the federal government in effect ceding tax space to the provinces, is that the value of such tax space varies considerably between poorer and richer provinces, making it difficult for poorer provinces to offer the same level of benefits as wealthier ones. While increase in equalization payments could be made to avoid such potential pitfalls, the reality is that the equalization payments as a share of the GDP have declined significantly over the last thirty years and the current political climate is not conducive to a more generous equalization program. Moreover, the creation of ten provincial parental insurance programs would undoubtedly result in increased administrative and delivery costs.

The second approach is an alternative to simple devolution, and would call for the federal government to create a new conditional transfer to the provinces, who would then be responsible to devise their own plans within parameters established by the federal government. Such an approach would obviously have the merit of ensuring the adherence of provinces to national standards. However, provinces might strongly oppose such an intrusion. Furthermore, a conditional transfer might lead to unclear lines of accountability, creating a process of blame avoidance between the two levels of government.

Another alternative, one the provinces would perhaps find less intrusive, would entail incorporating special benefits as part of the largely unconditional Canada Social Transfer. A clear benefit of such a program is that it would ensure a certain degree of inter-regional redistribution that would guarantee that poorer provinces could provide similar benefits to richer ones. The first obvious drawback to such an approach is that a lack of conditionality could lead to significant variations among provinces in the generosity of benefits, as provincial governments channel these resources to other priorities. Considering the ever-growing share of provincial budgets dedicated to health care, this is a real concern. Second, in light of the experience of the deep cuts to social transfers in 1995, this approach also has the drawback of limiting funding predictability and the potential of deep cuts that could force provinces to reduce benefits.

A more clear-cut process of devolution is, thus, perhaps more desirable than the adoption of a new transfer program or the inclusion of special benefits in the CST. However, one might question the willingness of the federal government to withdraw from the provision of all special benefits considering their popularity among the public and the likely backlash that could come with such a process of devolution. Perhaps more importantly, besides Quebec, no other provincial government has expressed any desire to take responsibility for parental and maternity benefits. The option of devolving responsibility to the provinces for special benefits is therefore unlikely to be pursued.

5 Reforming Special Benefits: Recommendations

As noted at the outset, Canada's special benefits compare well overall with international practices. Moreover, while many analysts have argued that the financing of special benefits through payroll taxes is currently inequitable, an important advantage of funding special benefits out of an insurance program is that it makes the connection between payments and benefits more transparent than funding out of general revenues. Programs financed through social insurance plans tend to be more generous and they allow debates about the appropriate generosity of benefits to be linked with Canadians' willingness to pay. Moreover, considering the inherent difficulty of reforming the EI program because of both public opinion and government inertia, it is important to propose reforms within the parameters of the existing system.

An obvious approach would be for the Canadian government to make maternity and parental benefits as accessible, flexible, and generous as the Quebec Parental Insurance Plan, in line with the recent recommendation of the House of Commons Standing Committee on the Status of Women (2009). Considering the higher premiums that might come as a result of the higher replacement rate, it is questionable whether such a reform would be acceptable to a majority of Canadians in the current economic climate. Improving accessibility ought to be the first objective of any reform of special benefits. A modest proposal in the short term would be to improve eligibility by decreasing the number of hours required to work to be eligible for benefits. At a minimum, the number of hours should be decreased to 420 hours in the short term to avoid, in certain regions, situations where workers must work more hours to qualify for special benefits than for EI regular benefits. In the longer term, the federal government's objective should be to reduce eligibility requirements so that they are more in line with those in place in Quebec.

Reforms should also be made to the design of the different special benefit programs. First, seeing as new mothers and sick workers are unable to look for a job, the two-week waiting period to receive special benefits should be eliminated as it clearly has no rationale; indeed, Quebec's parental insurance system does not impose any waiting period. Second, workers who have received special benefits should be entitled to regular benefits when they come back to work in order to avoid a situation in which they can be laid off and have no access to benefits at all. Third, the current pilot project that allows a recipient to combine benefit and paid work should be made permanent.

In the long term, the replacement rate for special benefits should stop being attached to the replacement rate of regular benefits. While there is a reason to keep regular benefits lower (in order to encourage people to rapidly find a job), such an approach does not apply to special benefits. While a case can be made in the long term to align the replacement rate of the Canadian parental leave program to the one in place in Quebec, in the short term, it is more pressing to reform the compassionate care program to help Canadians face the imminent crisis of care associated with the ageing of the population. The current system lacks both flexibility and generosity. Four reforms should be adopted. First, the length of the leave should be significantly extended from six weeks.[10] Second, the current requirement that a family member be at risk of dying within the next 26 weeks should be modified. The program should allow family members to take a leave for the care of persons that, while not at imminent risk of dying, have chronic conditions such as cancer. Third, family members should be able to share the compassionate care leave. Finally, the program should be more flexible, allowing the leave to be taken non-consecutively over a longer period of time, for example over a year.

As for the financing of special benefits, an alternative approach that could be explored would be to finance a part of their cost through general revenues. The financing of part of EI out of general revenues has a precedent in Canada. Indeed, until 1990, the federal government contributed to the EI fund. It is also in place in other countries. In Sweden, for example, 15 per cent of the costs of the parental leave program are paid out of general revenues. Such measures would contribute to spreading the costs of social programs to all Canadians, a legitimate measure considering that we can all benefit from programs such as parental leave and compassionate care. Moreover, such measures would lead to lower premiums for employees and employers, a measure that could encourage job creation.

6 Conclusion

With the reform introduced in 2001 to maternity and parental benefits, and the introduction in 2004 of the compassionate care program, EI special benefits are now relatively generous, providing important help to Canadians who must interrupt work to care for a newborn or sick relative. However, the system is far from perfect. Maternity and parental leaves are often not accessible for a significant number of Canadians, many of whom need them the most. Moreover, many aspects of the program make little logical sense, such as the two week waiting period and the difference in required work hours needed to collect special benefits compared to regular benefits for those living in high unemployment regions of the country. Finally, the financing of special benefits falls only on the shoulders of workers and employers, when all Canadians benefit directly or indirectly from those benefits.

A number of reform options have been explored. The first one would involve financing EI special benefits from general taxation. A second approach would involve devolution of responsibility for special benefits to the provinces. While Quebec has long preferred this option, it is unclear whether there is an appetite for such devolution in other provinces. Finally, a preferable scenario would be a more modest reform of current rules of eligibility to special benefits, an extension of the number of weeks of entitlement under the compassionate care benefits and the financing of a share of special benefits through general revenues.

Ultimately, it is up to Canadians and their representatives to decide which of these options is more likely to contribute to the prosperity of the country and to the challenge of responding to the ongoing crisis of care. However, it seems clear that despite the important gains made over the last decade, the task of reforming the provision of special benefits in Canada is not over.

Endnotes

1 I would like to thank Keith G. Banting, Josh Hjartarson, and an anonymous reviewer for their constructive suggestions. Special thanks to Mike Pal both for his suggestions and for a helpful email exchange on the 2005 Supreme Court reference case on the Employment Insurance Act. They are obviously not responsible for any errors present in this text.

2 Data exclude maternity and parental benefits in Quebec, as they are offered under the Quebec Parental Insurance Plan.

3 Sickness benefits and compassionate care benefits continue to be delivered by the federal government.

4 In 2011, the rates are 0.537 per cent of insurable earnings for wage salaried workers, 0.752 per cent for employers, and 0.955 per cent for self-employed workers.

5 Unless specified otherwise, data for Quebec presented in this section are from Conseil de gestion de l'assurance parentale, Rapport sur le portrait de la clientèle du Régime québécois d'assurance parentale, 2008. www.cgap.gouv.qc.ca/statistiques/portrait.asp

6 Some countries, such as France, provide for longer maternity leave, although the leave is not a paid one.

7 The Liberal Party of Canada proposed during the last election to extend to six months the compassionate care leave benefits.

8 A recipient of EI regular, parental and compassionate care and fishing benefits can earn $50 per week or 25 per cent of his or her weekly benefits, whichever is higher. Currently, a pilot project in place since 2005 in certain regions, and extended until 5 August 2011 in all regions, allow a recipient to earn the greater of $75 or 40 per cent of weekly benefits.

9 An exception would be the new, and generous, German parental leave program that is financed through general taxation. However, that program is too recent to draw any conclusions about its viability and desirability.

10 For example, the Liberal Party of Canada has proposed to replace the Compassionate Care Program by a Family Care Employment Insurance. The new program would provide up to six months of benefits. The Liberal Party estimates are that such a program would cost $250 million per year.

References

Baker, M. and K. Milligan. 2008a. "How Does Job-Protected Maternity Leave Affect Mothers' Employment." *Journal of Labor Economics* 26.4: 655-91.

——. 2008b. "'Maternal Employment, Breastfeeding, and Health,' Evidence from Maternity Leave Mandates." *Journal of Labor Economics* 27.4: 871-87.

Canadian Chamber of Commerce. 2009. *Reforming Canada's Employment Insurance System*. At http://www.chamber.ca/images/uploads/EI/Reforming_Canadas_Employment_System20-07-09.pdf.

Commission of Inquiry on Unemployment Insurance. 1986. Report. Ottawa: Minister of Supply and Services Canada.

Conseil de gestion de l'assurance parentale. 2008. *Rapport sur le portrait de la clientèle du Régime québécois d'assurance parentale*.

Evans, P.M. 2007. "Comparative Perspectives on Changes to Canada's Paid Parental Leave: Implications for Class and Gender." *International Journal of Social Welfare* 16: 119-28.

DiGiacomo, G. 2007. "The Government of Canada's Contradictory Approach to Federal-Provincial Relations." *Working Paper 3*. Kingston: Queen's University.

House of Commons Standing Committee on the Status of Women. 2009. Towards Improving Access to EI Benefits for Women in Canada. *Report of the Standing Committee on the Status of Women*. Ottawa: House of Commons. At http://www.parl.gc.ca/HousePublications/Publication.aspx?DocId=3912853&Language=&Mode=1&Parl=40&Ses=2.

Human Resources and Skills Development Canada. 2005. *Summative Evaluation of EI Parental Benefits*. At http://www.hrsdc.gc.ca/eng/publications_resources/evaluation/2007/sp_ah_674_01_05e/page00.shtml.

——. 2009. *EI Monitoring and Assessment Report*. At http://www.hrsdc.gc.ca/eng/employment/ei/reports/eimar_2009/index.shtml.

Mintz, J. 2010. "Reform EI Now." *Financial Post*. 10 August. At http://opinion.financialpost.com/2010/08/10/jack-mintz-reform-ei-now/.

Marshall, K. 2010. "Employer Top-Ups." *Perspective on Labour and Income* (February): 5-12.

Pal, L.A. 1985. "Maternity Benefits and Unemployment Insurance: A Question of Policy Design." *Canadian Public Policy* 11.3: 551-60.

Phipps, S. 2005. "Working for Working Parents: The Evolution of Maternity and Parental Benefits in Canada." IRPP *Choices* 12.2.

Poschmann, F. 2005. "The Federal Provincial Fiscal Balance: Teetering on the Edge of Incoherence." *CD Howe Institute*. 11 March. At http://www.cdhowe.org/pdf/verbatim_1.pdf.

Prince, M.J. 2009. *Supporting Working Canadian Families: the Role of Employment Insurance Benefits*. Ottawa: Caledon Institute of Social Policy.

Productivity Commission. 2009. *Paid Parental Leave: Support for Parents with Newborn Children*, Report 47. Canberra: Productivity Commission.

Ray, R., J.C. Gornick, and J. Schmitt. 2009. "Parental Leave Policies in 21 Countries: Assessing Generosity and Gender Equality," *Center for Economic and Policy Research*. At http://www.cepr.net/index.php/publications/reports/plp/.

Reference re Employment Insurance Act (Can.), ss. 22 and 23, 2005 SCC 56, [2005] 2 SCR 669

Standing Committee on the Status of Women. 2009. *Towards Improving Access to EI Benefits for Women in Canada*. Ottawa: Communication Canada.

Statistics Canada. 2010. "Employment Insurance Coverage Survey." *The Daily*. At http://www.statcan.gc.ca/daily-quotidien/100621/dq100621b-eng.htm (accessed 21 June).

O'Neil, S. 2010. *Paid Parental Leave*. Canberra: Parliament of Australia. At www.aph.gov.au/Library/pubs/BN/eco/PaidParentalLeave.pdf.

Wilkinson, H. and I. Briscoe. 1996. *Parental Leave: The Price of Family Values?* London: Demos.

Chapter 7

Employment Insurance: A Macroeconomic Comparison with Other Income-Support Initiatives

William Scarth

1 Introduction

There are three broad approaches to the provision of income support. EI makes support conditional on the individual *not* having a job. On the other hand, the Working Income Tax Benefit (WITB—Canada's version of an earned income tax credit) makes support conditional on the individual having a job. Between these approaches, a guaranteed annual income (otherwise known as basic income) is intended to make support independent of labour force status. Given this interpretation, and a focus on economic efficiency considerations, economists often prefer a WITB. First, since both EI and WITB are more targeted than basic income, these approaches involve the government relying less on distortionary taxation to finance them. Second, since standard analysis suggests that a lower level of unemployment emerges with the WITB, it gets the highest marks on efficiency grounds.

But it is almost certainly the case that policy decisions are based at least as much on equity considerations as on efficiency issues. Since a WITB focuses on the working poor, and not on those in most dire need of assistance, it is unlikely to receive top marks on equity grounds. At the intuitive level, EI and basic income would seem to have more appeal from this point of view. The macroeconomic analysis in this chapter attempts to provide a balanced assessment of these several alternatives for providing support for those on low incomes.

Nobel Laureate Edmund Phelps (1997) has long argued that there is a better approach than any of the three discussed in the previous paragraph. He argues for the provision of subsidies to the employers of low-income individuals. Like the WITB, this policy is aimed at the working poor. Unlike the WITB, the preference in this policy is for government to intervene on the demand side, not the supply side, of the labour market.

The preference for intervention on the demand side is based on the impacts that Phelps expects for those other than the working poor. Stimulating labour demand rather than supply puts upward, not downward, pressure on the general level of wages of the unskilled. Thus, the individuals who do not qualify for direct participation in the program (those who are a bit too well off)—on the one hand, and those who are less well-off, namely the unemployed, on the other hand—can both benefit. Since the benefit paid out to the unemployed under EI is a fraction of the market wage, the increase in wages that can be expected under Phelps' program would constitute an indirect increase in the generosity of EI. The additional benefit of this employer-based employment subsidy is that it can be expected to lower the unemployment rate, not raise unemployment, as a more traditional increase in the EI replacement rate does.

One purpose of this chapter is to compare Phelps' proposal with the other three more traditional policy initiatives. The approach taken is relatively abstract, since the analysis involves a highly simplified general-equilibrium macroeconomic model. One advantage of this approach is that it focuses on each policy's *indirect* effects—those aspects that tend to receive insufficient attention when a detailed analysis of any one initiative is undertaken. A second advantage of this broad comparative approach is that the several competing policies are evaluated within the same analytical framework. But there are disadvantages as well. In order to focus on the full-model feedbacks within a fairly transparent model that non-specialists can fully appreciate, it is necessary to simplify each policy and to examine a stylized version of each. Thus, despite calibration of the model with realistic parameter values, the numerical results have to be interpreted as illustrative, not definitive.

Of particular interest for building a model that is suitable for Canada is the globalization constraint—that both physical capital and highly skilled labour are quite mobile internationally, while unskilled labour is not. The importance of the globalization constraint is that it makes it very difficult for the government to raise the revenue that is needed to provide EI without those taxes ending up being imposed on the "captive" factor of production—unskilled labour. Even if taxes are nominally levied on capital income, the true incidence of the tax is fully shifted to labour when the supply of capital is perfectly elastic at the yield that is available net of tax in the rest of the world. Granted, foreign investors continue to have some country-specific perceptions of risk, so capital is not perfectly mobile yet. But it is becoming more so as each decade passes. Policy makers need to look forward, and be ready for the day when the globalization constraint becomes fully binding. It is to ensure this readiness that perfect capital mobility is assumed in this analysis.

The more general question raised by the globalization constraint, then, is: how can we finance *any* of the policy options that aim to better the lot of unskilled labour if that group ultimately has to pay for these initiatives? In the second section of this chapter—in material drawn from Scarth (2007: chap. 9)—I show how this challenge might be met. The key is that the policy needs to lower unemployment. But, even if the unemployment rate can be reduced and the unskilled *as a group* can be assisted, many policy initiatives involve a trade-off—helping *either* the working poor or the unemployed *at the expense* of the other subset of unskilled individuals.

After the basic nature of this trade-off is clarified, we pursue (in section 3 of the chapter) a more extensive analysis involving numerical calibration and several policy options: a change in the level of EI benefits, both employee and employer payroll tax cuts, and the introduction of both basic income and Phelps' employment-subsidy proposal. The WITB is not examined explicitly, but within this simplified framework, it is very similar to an employee payroll tax cut. Following the chapter's conclusions in section 4, the appendix explains the details of the model.

2 Equity and Efficiency: The Globalization Challenge

Many citizens expect their government to provide support for low-income individuals, but they fear that the government may no longer be able to do this. To address this question specifically, let us pull together skilled individuals (the owners of human capital) and the owners of physical capital into one group that I refer to as capitalists, or the "rich." I assume that these individuals have the ability to re-locate their capital costlessly to lower-tax jurisdictions. Further, let us use the term labour to refer to the unskilled "poor," and assume that these individuals cannot migrate to other countries. Can the government help the poor by raising the tax it imposes on the capitalists and using the revenue to finance a change in EI arrangements—for example, a cut in the employee payroll tax rate? Those who focus on the globalization constraint argue that the answer to this question is "obviously no." They expect capital to relocate to escape the higher tax, and the result will be less capital for the captive domestic labour force to work with. Labour's living standards may well decrease as a result.

The standard analysis can be reviewed by referring to Figure 1, which shows the initial demand and supply curves for capital. The demand curve is the diminishing marginal productivity relationship that is drawn for an assumed given level of labour employed. Firms are prepared to hire more capital only if the rent they have to pay for each unit is lower. The supply curve is perfectly elastic at the yield that owners of capital can receive on an after-tax basis in the rest of the world. If the return for foreign investors in our economy is above what is available in the rest of the world (the height of the supply line), they are prepared to supply what we regard (as a small entity in the whole world) as an infinite quantity. On the other hand, if that foreign return is higher than what is available here, they supply zero. Before the tax on capital is levied to finance the payroll tax cut, the economy is assumed to be observed at the intersection of these demand and supply relationships, and the nation's GDP is represented by the area under the demand curve up to point *A* (the sum of all the additions to output that were made possible by hiring all these units of capital). Capital receives the dark grey rectangle below the supply curve, while labour's income is the residual part of GDP (the light grey triangle above the supply line).

FIGURE 1 The Capital Market

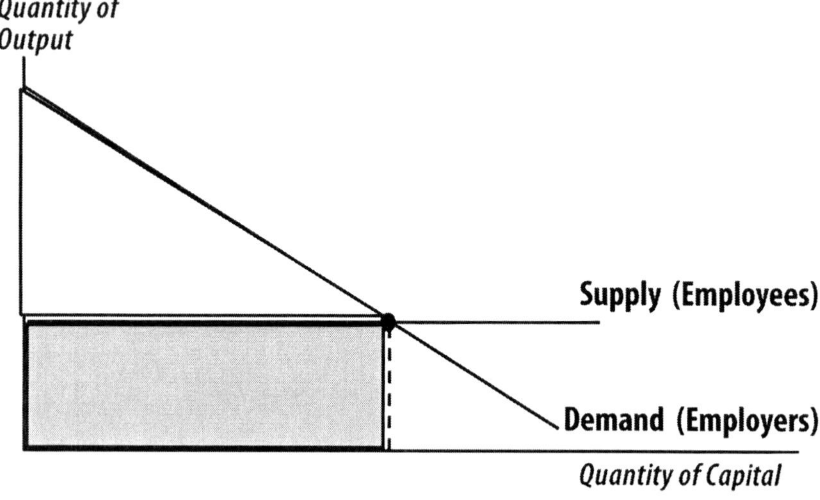

When the government raises the tax on capital, capitalists demand a higher pre-tax return, an increase that is just enough to keep the after-tax yield equal to what is still available elsewhere. Thus, the higher (dashed) supply curve in Figure 2 becomes relevant, and the outcome is now given by point B. Domestically produced output falls (by an amount equal to the black triangle plus the rectangle that is shaded medium grey), but capital owners do not suffer. Those that move their capital elsewhere earn the same income (the medium shaded grey rectangle) there, while those who keep their capital within this country, receive an increase in their pretax return (equal to the light grey rectangle) that is just sufficient to allow them to fully escape the burden of the tax. As usual in tax incidence analysis, a tax imposed on an item that is supplied perfectly elastically is fully passed on (in this case to labour). The capitalists still get the dark grey rectangle (after-tax), and the tax revenue that accrues to the government (the light grey triangle) comes completely from what used to be labour's income. But, abstracting from the inefficiency that is generated from the levying of the tax (discussed below), labour does not suffer. This is because the entire proceeds of the tax are given to labour. Let us suppose that this transfer takes the form of a guaranteed annual income. Since such a transfer has no incentive effects that could reduce some other pre-existing inefficiency in the economy (such as the level of unemployment), there will be nothing to compensate labour for the loss of the black triangle. This is the efficiency loss that is the analytical basis for the proposition that mobile capital is a bad thing to tax—it hurts labour.

FIGURE 2 A Tax on Capital with No Change in Unemployment

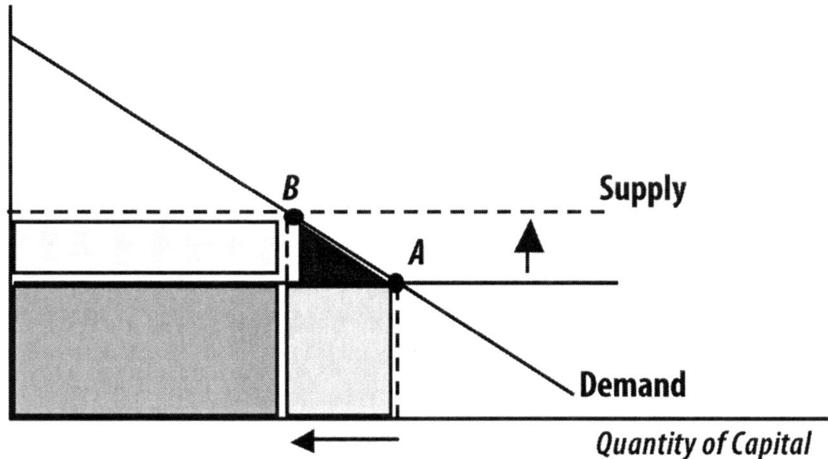

Now let us focus on a different use of the new tax revenue—a cut in the employee payroll tax rate. With this initiative, the unemployment rate can be expected to fall, so that each unit of capital is more productive since it has more labour to work with. This is shown in Figure 3 as a shift up in the position of the marginal product of the capital curve (shown by the higher dashed demand curve). The economy is observed at the intersection of the now-relevant supply and demand curves—the dashed ones that intersect at point *C*. Overall, by comparing the trapazoids formed by dropping the perpendiculars from points *A* and *C*, bounded from above by the relevant demand curve in each case, we can assess what has happened to the total income that is available to labour. It has been reduced by the shaded triangle (due to the introduction of the distorting tax on capital), but it has been increased by the shaded parallelogram (due to the reduction of the pre-existing distortion in the labour market—unemployment).

If the gain exceeds the loss, the tax on capital might be recommended after all. When the revenue is used to lower unemployment, it raises the total income of the poor (labour) and it does not reduce the income of the rich (the owners of capital). This approach to low-income support is not a zero-sum game, in the sense that labour is not helped at the expense of capitalists. As already noted, this is because the size of the overall economic "pie" has been increased by policy. Labour receives a bigger slice, while capitalists get the same slice as before (as imposed by the globalization constraint). This encouraging possibility is stressed by Moutos and Scarth

(2004), who use an asymmetric information model to defend the pre-existing distortion interpretation of the labour market, by Koskala and Schob (2002), who base the labour market distortion on the presence of unions, and by Domeij (2005), who relies on search frictions to defend this interpretation.

FIGURE 3 A Tax on Capital to Finance an Employee Payroll Tax Cut

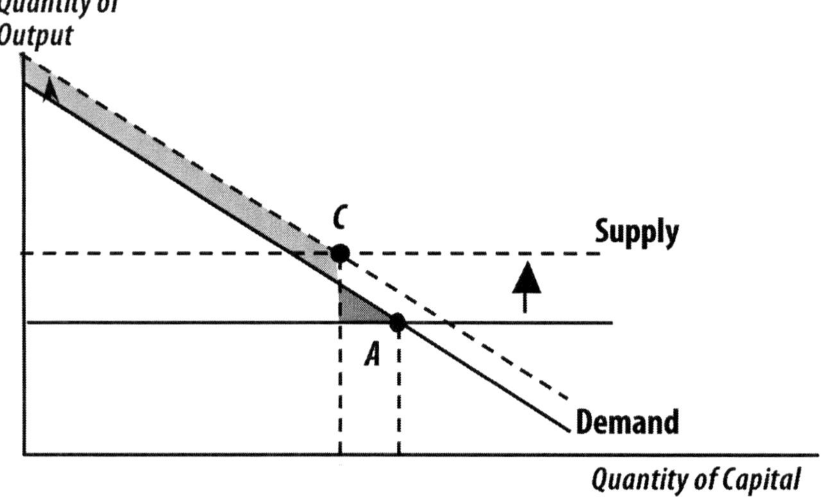

To complete this analysis, two questions must be pursued: First, is it reasonable to expect an employee payroll tax cut to lower unemployment? I summarize the standard analysis of this question in the appendix, and conclude that the answer is "yes." The second question concerns whether it is reasonable to argue that the gain can be bigger than the loss. I pursue this issue in the appendix as well (by specifying an algebraic version of the model summarized by Figure 1), and the answer is that—if there is no tax on capital in the first place—this revenue neutral cut in the payroll tax, financed by the introduction of a tax on capital, *must* be "good news" for labour. That is, this policy must raise the overall income that is available to unskilled labour—both the working and the non-working poor—taken together as a group. But there is one "bad news" development: the tax on capital drives some of this input out of the country. With fewer machines and skilled individuals to work with, unskilled labour is less productive, so the market wage falls. This hurts the working poor, but the payroll tax that these individuals pay falls enough to more than make up for the lower pre-tax wage, so these individuals turn out to be better off. But the unemployed poor do not fare so well. Since their EI receipts are tied to the going level of wages, there is an indirect and unintended cut in the generosity of EI. And since the unemployed do not pay payroll taxes, there is nothing to make up this loss. So the attempt to shift the financing of EI from the payroll tax to a tax that is intended to be on capital is good news in that it lowers unemployment, but it is bad news since it helps the working poor at the expense of the unemployed poor.

Second-best theory is the key to understanding the good news dimension of this outcome at an intuitive level. Recall an example introduced in the original paper on this topic (Lipsey and Lancaster 1956). In a two-good economy, standard analysis leads to the proposition that a selective sales tax is "bad." With a tax on the purchase of just one good, the ratio of market prices does not reflect the ratio of marginal costs, so decentralized markets cannot replicate what a perfect planner could accomplish—achieve the most efficient use of society's scarce resources. Society is producing and consuming "too little" of the taxed good, and "too much" of the untaxed good.

But this assumes that there is no *pre-existing* market distortion before the tax is levied. A different verdict emerges if it is assumed that there is an initial market failure. For example, if one good is produced by a monopolist who restricts output and raises price above marginal cost, a similar inefficiency is created (with society consuming "too little" of this good and "too much" of the competitively supplied good). One solution to this problem is to impose a selective excise tax on the sale of the *other* product. With this tax, *both* prices can be above their respective marginal costs by the same proportion, and society gets the efficient allocation of resources, even with the monopoly.

So the verdict concerning the desirability of a selective sales tax is completely reversed when we switch from a no-other-distortions situation to a with-other-distortions setting. The analysis in this section of the chapter shows that this same logic applies in a macroeconomic analysis of input markets. In this model, societal conventions involve the wage set at a value that fails to eliminate unemployment. Labour's price is "too high" so firms employ "too little" labour. By stimulating employment with the payroll tax cut, and by raising the revenue to finance this initiative by taxing the over-used input (capital), the government can increase overall efficiency (lower unemployment and raise GDP).

Despite the appeal of this intuition, we must remember that the size of the welfare loss that accompanies any distortion rises more than in proportion with the size of that distortion. By having no capital tax in the first instance, the analysis in this section of the chapter is biased in favour of finding that a small loss accompanies that tax. With the pre-existing distortion in the labour market involving significant unemployment, a large loss accompanies that distortion. The policy package introduces one distortion (in the capital market) to make possible the reduction of the other (in the labour market). It is, perhaps, not surprising that welfare improves overall when a small distortion partially replaces a larger one. I assess the significance of this bias in the next section, by reporting the simulation results that have been derived from an extended model—one that allows for plausible levels of several taxes before various policies are examined.

3 A More Complete Model

The more complete model involves the addition of an employer payroll tax, a personal income tax levied on wage incomes, a Phelps-style employment subsidy issued to firms, and a guaranteed annual income program. The model also involves allowing for two groups within the unemployed. One group has no chance of becoming employed (given the policies examined here), for example due to disability, lack of appropriate training, or being constrained to remain in regions where jobs cannot be had. The other group within the unemployed can and do respond to the economic incentives that are part of the government programs that are examined.

The effects of all policies on the unemployment rate are standard, and they follow from one basic feature: anything that raises the relative return of work lowers unemployment, while anything that raises the relative return from being idle raises unemployment. Thus, increases in the wage income tax, the payroll taxes, and the generosity of the EI and basic income programs raise the unemployment rate, while increases in the Phelps subsidy to employers for hiring unskilled workers lowers the unemployment rate.

Perhaps one aspect of this set of predictions warrants further comment. The employer payroll tax does not raise unemployment if there is no Phelps program in place. This prediction emerges from a number of labour-market analyses, such as Summers' (1988) model of asymmetric information and efficiency wages. It is a feature of any labour market analysis in which increases in productivity raise wages one-for-one in the long run. Summers has argued that a century of data is consistent with this prediction, so it is appealing that our model shares this feature.

The details of the model (the equations that define it and the numerical calibration) are given in the appendix. Here, I summarize the results. Table 1 reports two policy options. The first is an increase in the generosity of EI benefits, and the second is the introduction of a guaranteed annual income. Both policies are financed by an increase in the tax rate levied on domestically employed capital. The increase in the replacement rate within EI, from 30 per cent to 40 per cent, is large, but it is targeted to the unemployed, so even this increase in generosity of one third does not require a large rise in the tax on capital (just a rate increase from 20 per cent to 20.25 per cent). This is because, initially, capital (broadly defined to include both skilled labour and physical machines) earned 75 per cent of the GDP, while the unemployed received an amount equal to just 6 per cent of the remaining 25 per cent (that flowed to the unskilled). The guaranteed annual income, on the other hand, applies to all the unskilled, so the revenue implications are larger. Even limiting the level of basic income to 6.75 per cent of the unskilled wage rate means that the tax rate applied to capital must be increased by an amount that is eight times what is required to finance the more generous EI initiative (that tax rate must rise to 22 per cent).

TABLE 1

	Increase in EI Benefit by One-Third	Introduction of Basic Income: 6.75% of Wage
Effect on Unemployment Rate	up by 0.33 % points	no change
Effect on Total Income Available to Labour (Efficiency Index)	down by 0.82%	down by 4.0%
Effect on Income of Unemployed	up by 32.1%	up by 13.3%
Effect on Income of Working Poor	down by 0.94%	down by 0.94%

The unemployment rate rises with the increase in the generosity of EI benefits. The one-third increase in generosity leads to a one-third of one percentage point increase in the unemployment rate (from 6 per cent to 6.33 per cent). It is reassuring that this finding is broadly in line with the long history of empirical studies concerning earlier changes in Canadian EI legislation. Corak (1996) summarized that the doubling of EI generosity in previous decades raised the unemployment rate by between six-tenths and one full percentage point. Since both our initiative here and the simulated outcome are roughly one-third of this magnitude, our calibrated model can be said to pass this consistency with previous empirical studies test.

The unemployment rate is not appreciably affected by the introduction of basic income. But there is still a bigger loss in total income available to the unskilled (taken as a group), since much more capital is driven out of the country. Specifically, as reported in Table 1, the total income available to all labour (working or not) falls by 4 per cent with the introduction of the guaranteed annual income, and by only 0.82 of one per cent with the increase in EI benefits. Even though the unemployment rate is higher with the EI initiative, so the distortion in the labour market is bigger with this policy, the distortion in the capital market is much higher with the introduction of basic income.

Now let us turn to the effects on the material living standards of those in each group *within* the unskilled labour part of the population. For this discussion, I refer to capitalists as the rich, employed individuals as the working poor, and the unemployed individuals as the very poor. There are no entries in the tables referring to the outcomes for the rich. This is because perfect capital mobility implies that the rich are completely unaffected by all policies (recall that this analysis assumes perfect mobility at no cost—open borders—for both skilled labour and capital). But Table 1 does record the outcomes for each member of the working poor and each member of the unemployed for both policies.

The very poor are helped more by the increase in EI benefit generosity. This policy raises their material welfare by 32 per cent, while the introduction of basic income raises their living standards by just 13 per cent. The working poor are indifferent between these two initiatives since their material welfare falls by the same amount in each case—by just less than one per cent. It seems that the EI initiative dominates the introduction of basic income on both equity and efficiency grounds.

The results for three other initiatives are reported in Table 2: two-percentage-point cuts in both the employer and employee payroll tax rates and the introduction of an employment subsidy equal to 5 per cent of the going wage. All three policies involve essentially no change in the unemployment rate, and quite small reductions in the material welfare of the working poor. From these points of view (small costs involved), these initiatives might be appealing. However, they are not appealing overall, since the very poor (the unemployed) are made *worse off*. This is because capital leaves the country and this indirect effect dominates the forces that push the after-tax wage up (the direct effect of each policy).

The purpose in having a complete macro model is to make it possible for us to sort out just such competing effects for both segments of the labour group in a logically consistent fashion. It is interesting that some of the results of this modelling strategy bear so centrally on policies that have actually been undertaken in Canada recently. For example, since a WITB is very similar to an employee payroll tax cut, this result implies that—when financed by an increase in the capital tax rate—this initiative hurts the very group that it was most designed to help—the working poor.

From a political economy point of view, we would expect only the unemployed to vote for any of these initiatives. Capital owners would abstain, and the working poor would vote against each one. Economic advisers who focus on efficiency questions would vote against as well. This is because the overall income that is available to labour, including all those working and not working (see the second line in Tables 1 and 2), goes down in all cases.

But it would not take much altruism for the working poor to support a loss to themselves of just 0.94 per cent if the material welfare of those less well off, the unemployed, could increase by 32.1 per cent. Thus, if it has been decided that *some* initiative is to be adopted, the working poor can be expected to support the more generous EI benefit policy. Efficiency-

TABLE 2

	Cut in Employee Payroll Tax Rate of 2 % points	Cut in Employer Payroll Tax Rate of 2 % points	Introduction of Employment Subsidy: 5% of Wage
Effect on Unemployment Rate	no change	no change	down by 0.1 % points
Effect on Total Income Available to Labour (Efficiency Index)	down by 1.18%	down by 1.0%	down by 2.56%
Effect on Income of Unemployed	down by 2.4%	down by 0.1%	down by 0.34%
Effect on Income of Working Poor	down by 0.6%	down by 0.1%	down by 0.34%

oriented economists would agree, since the efficiency loss is the smallest in this case. When equity and efficiency goals involve a trade-off, it is appealing to choose the policy that delivers the biggest gain in equity along with the smallest loss in efficiency. However, it would be difficult to explain this policy choice to the group that is pushed from the working poor to the very poor, and the increased EI replacement rate policy involves a serious increase in unemployment. Nevertheless, if this dimension of the outcome is tolerated, the policy of increased generosity in the EI program appears to dominate the introduction of other new programs (an employment subsidy or basic income).

While not listed in the tables, I report one final policy option: an increase in EI generosity of the same amount (from a replacement rate of 30 per cent to 40 per cent) but in this case financed by an increase in the employer payroll tax rate, not by an increase in the tax rate that is legislated on domestically employed capital. This policy package involves the same increase in the unemployment rate (one-third of one percentage point) but no capital being driven out of the country. Thus, a smaller loss in overall efficiency emerges (a reduction of 0.38 per cent compared to 0.82 per cent when this initiative is financed by a higher tax on capital). There is also a smaller loss in material welfare for the working poor (a reduction of 0.90 per cent compared to the 0.94 per cent loss reported in Table 1). The pre-tax wage received by workers is now pushed down for a different reason than capital leaving the country. In this case, labour demand falls because employers must pay a higher employer payroll tax (a tax rate of 6.9 per cent instead of 5 per cent), and this results in the wage being very slightly lower than in the Table 1 experiments. Overall, then, the analysis appears to support continued reliance on EI over the introduction of the other broad approaches to tackling poverty, and to continue to rely on payroll taxes to finance EI.

4 Conclusions

This chapter has used a simplified general-equilibrium open-economy macroeconomic model to assess several income-support policies. The specification of each policy has been stylized, with no attempt being made to capture the details of caps on contributions, run-out dates on benefits, or claw-back arrangements that operate as an individual's income rises. The chapter is intended as a complement to analyses that are much more specific on these matters. Their advantage lies in focusing on details; the advantage of the present study is in pursuing indirect feedback effects that are difficult to evaluate unless a full-economy perspective is taken. I remind the reader of just three of the insights that have emerged, as examples of the payoff of this modeling strategy:

1. an employee payroll tax cut can hurt workers,
2. contrary to what Phelps has argued, wages fall with the introduction of an employment subsidy in a small open-economy setting, and
3. the globalization constraint does not preclude the government helping unskilled labour as a group, but it does mean that there is a trade-off between the welfare of workers and that of the unemployed poor.

It is hoped that these insights may inspire others to pursue sensitivity tests in related macro models, so that the debate on EI reform involves increased awareness of the indirect, sometimes unexpected, feedback effects that emerge (often outside the labour market), when the financing of any labour-market policy initiative is an integral part of the analysis.

In the meantime, we can summarize the central recommendation that has emerged from this inquiry—that EI not be replaced by other low-income support programs. Our analysis suggests that such a replacement would bring a desirable but fairly small increase in efficiency, but at the expense of a rather large loss in equity.

Appendix

The following equations define the model used to examine the effect of the payroll tax cut financed by an increase in the tax rate aimed at capital in section 2 of the chapter. The equations specify a production function, factor demand functions based on profit maximization, perfect capital mobility with the rest of the world, a fixed domestic labour force, a government budget identity, and a simple model of unemployment.

$y = Ak^{a}$	(1)
$aAk^{a-1} = r$	(2)
$(1 - a)Ak^{a} = w$	(3)
$r(1 - c) = r^{*}$	(4)
$u = b(1 - t) / (1 - t - f)$	(5)
$f\,wu = tw(1 - u) + crk(1 - u)$	(6)
$x = (y - r * k)(1 - u)$	(7)

The first equation is a Cobb-Douglas production function; output per employee, y, is a function of capital per worker, k. Capital is defined quite broadly to include both machines and human capital, so labour refers to the unskilled. Firms hire each factor up to the point that the marginal product equals the rental cost. The rental price of capital is r [equation (2)] and the rental price of labour is w [equation (3)].

Very different assumptions are involved for factor supplies. The supply of labour (the population of unskilled individuals) is completely inelastic (immobile internationally) and is set at unity. As a result, employment is one minus the unemployment rate, u. Capital is supplied completely elastically at the rate of return that this factor can earn in the rest of the world, r^*. This perfect capital mobility assumption is what imposes the globalization constraint—that capital can avoid paying any tax in this small open economy. This assumption is imposed in equation (4) which stipulates that the domestic yield, r, must be just high enough to generate an after-tax yield equal to what is available elsewhere. c is the tax rate levied on the earnings of capital employed domestically.

Equation (5) indicates how the unemployment rate is determined; it is based on Pissarides (1998). The wage at each firm-worker level is set with considerations of market power, outside opportunities, and fairness all playing a role. Formally, the parties to the wage determination process are assumed to behave as if they submitted their cases to an arbitrator. The arbitrator respects each side's objectives, the customary weight that is put on each side's objectives, and the reference points that are established by outside options such as welfare and EI. The parameter that embodies these market-power considerations in equation (5) is b. This relationship indicates that the unemployment rate rises with the generosity of EI (as parameter f (the fraction of wages individuals receive while unemployed) rises), and with the level of the employee payroll tax rate (as tax rate t rises).

Equation (6) defines a balanced government budget. The use of funds is listed on the left-hand side. As noted, parameter f is the "replacement rate" in the EI system—the fraction of market wages that an individual receives while out of work. For simplicity, we follow convention in the macro-theoretic literature [for example, Pissarides (1998) and Summers (1988)] and assume no waiting period or maximum period involved in EI coverage. Thus, the total of EI benefits distributed is equal to the payment made to each individual, fw, times the number of people unemployed, u. The sources of government funds that are used to finance EI appear on the right-hand side of equation (6). There is the employee payroll tax and it raises total revenue equal to the tax rate, t, times the total wage bill [wage rate, w, times total employment, $(1 - u)$]. The second revenue source is the tax on capital, equal to the tax rate, c, times the earnings of capital (the product of the pre-tax return, r, times the amount of capital per worker, k, times the number of workers, $1 - u$).

The equations determine y, k, r, w, u, x and one of the policy parameters (in this case, c). I assume that, initially, there is no tax on capital; then, I examine a cut in the contribution rate for EI (the employee payroll tax rate). The model determines what capital tax rate must be introduced to pay for this initiative, and I focus on three responses: in the unemployment rate, the wage rate, and the overall income available for all unskilled individuals [denoted by x in equation (7)].

To find these effects, I take the total differential of the equations, and then simplify the coefficients in the resulting relationships by imposing the no-capital-tax initial condition. Two results are definite: one is that $du/dt>0$ and the second is $(dx/x)/dt<0$. The third result is that holds as long as $(1 - t)^2>f$. The first result confirms standard beliefs; the cut in the employee EI contribution rate lowers the level of structural unemployment. The second result indicates that, in this model, what appeared to be just a possibility in the graphic analysis in the text of the chapter is an outcome that simply *must* occur. The payroll tax cut, financed by a tax aimed at perfectly mobile capital, is an initiative that *does* succeed in raising the material welfare of labour (when the employed and unemployed are lumped together in one group).

But the third result also indicates that it is dangerous to combine these two groups, since the income of the unemployed can be reduced by this initiative. The income of each unemployed equals fw, and since f is constant in this case, the verdict concerning the desirability of this payroll tax cut for the unemployed depends entirely on whether wages rise or fall. A sufficient, though not necessary, condition for wages to fall is that the EI replacement rate, f, be less than one half and that the employee payroll tax rate, t, be less than one quarter. Since these are conditions that are certainly met in the actual economy, the third result expression is surely positive. Unemployed individuals are not affected *directly* by the payroll tax cut, but there is an indirect effect. This initiative must be financed, and the imposition of the tax on capital drives some capital out of the country. With fewer machines and skilled individuals to work with, unskilled labour is less productive, so the market wage falls. Since the EI benefit payment is proportional to the general level of wages, the payroll tax cut ends up being an unintentional reduction in the generosity of EI, so the very poor subset within the labour group is made worse off. This is an example of the important feedback effects that occur within a full macroeconomic context.

The more complete model reported in section 3 of the chapter involves the addition of an employer payroll tax, rate e, a personal income tax levied on wage incomes, rate i, a Phelps-style employment subsidy issued to firms, equal to proportion h of the going wage, and a guaranteed annual income program, with each payment set at proportion p of the going wage. The personal income tax involves a fixed tax rate levied on wage incomes above a threshold. It is assumed that the EI and basic income benefits received by the unemployed are not sufficient to push an individual's income above this threshold.

The final change in the extended model involves allowing for two groups within the unemployed. The overall unemployment rate is defined as $u = u^* + v$, where u^* is the part that is independent of taxes and subsidies (the group of individuals that has no chance of becoming employed) and v is the part that is determined by the incentives-based model that is discussed below. EI benefits are available to all the unemployed.

Equations (1), (2), (4) and (7) are unaltered, and there is a very simple change in equation (3). The revised relationship in this case involves the payment made by firms for each worker to be higher because of the employer payroll tax, and lower because of the employment subsidy:

$(1 - a)Ak^a = w(1 + e - h)$	(3a)

The unemployment rate is affected by many of the additional policy parameters (as discussed in the text of the chapter). The model now involves:

$u = u^* + v$	(5a)
$v = b(1 + e - h)(1 - i - t)/((1 + e)(1 - i(1+p) - t - f))$	(5b)

The final equation that differs in the more complete setting is the government budget constraint. There are now four uses of funds and four sources of funds:

$G + pw + fwu + hw(1 - u) = i(1+p)w(1 - u) + tw(1 - u) + ew(1 - u) + crK$	(6a)

The most notable new items are G and K, the level of government spending on programs that have no direct effect on the labour market and the total capital stock: $K = k(1 - u)$. I assume that the ratio of this other spending to GDP, $g = G/Y$, stays constant throughout this analysis, so I replace G by $gY = y(1 - u)$ in the derivations. In addition to this other set of programs, the three uses of funds [in the order that they appear in (6a)] are basic income benefits, EI benefits, and employment subsidy expenditures. The four revenue sources are income tax revenue collected from the employed, payroll taxes (EI contributions collected from employees and employers), and income tax revenue collected from the owners of domestically employed capital.

The numerical calibration of the model is now explained. It is assumed that there is no basic income or employment subsidy program initially, so the starting values for p and h are zero. The replacement rate in the EI system (parameter f) starts at 30 per cent. The initial income tax rate for employed labour, i, is 10 per cent, and the initial payroll tax rates, e and t, are 5 per cent. The initial tax rate on the earnings of capital, c, is 20 per cent. These assumptions, along with the specifications for unemployment and capital intensity that are noted below make the initial value of the other-programs-to-GDP ratio, g, be 19.3 per cent.

The foreign interest rate, r^*, is set at 10 per cent. The tax on domestically employed capital then implies that the starting value for the pre-tax return on capital within this small open economy is 12.5 per cent. Since I have followed Mankiw, Romer and Weil (1992) in defining capital to include skilled labour, I must specify capital's share of GDP to be much higher than is usual. I set a = 75 per cent. Then, with initial GDP set at unity and the initial unemployment rate being 6 per cent, these specifications imply that the starting values for k, w and A must be 6.0, 0.238 and 0.26 respectively. Finally, with the overall unemployment rate at 6 per cent, and the exogenous part, u^*, set at 4.5 per cent, equations (5a) and (5b) imply that parameter b must be 0.0097. With this information, the knowledge that the income of each member of the working poor, and of the non-working poor, are $w[(1+p)(1-i)-t]$ and $w(f+p)$, and with software that solves nonlinear simultaneous equations, interested readers can verify the results reported in Tables 1 and 2.

The purpose of the remainder of the appendix is to provide more details concerning the unemployment rate equation in the model. This specification is from Pissarides (1998), who intended that his model apply to an economy composed of a large number of union-employer pairs. The wage is set through an arbitration process involving both parties, and then the firm chooses the level of employment independently once the wage has been set. In this second stage, firms equate the marginal product of labour with the (net of subsidy and inclusive of taxes) wage that the firm has to pay (as is customary, and as is assumed in our full system).

I think that Pissarides' model is applicable to settings without formal unions. The employer must still balance its own objective of maximum profits with the norms of society concerning a "fair" wage, and with the options that workers have if they leave their current employer. As a result, I assume that workers and their employers interact *as if* they consulted a formal arbitrator. Here is a summary of the specific details.

The arbitrator's objective function is the product of the employees' and the employer's objectives, each raised to a power indicating the bargaining power of each constituency: $I^jP(1 - j)$. I is the excess income the workers get if they stay with this employer (over what they receive if they take their chances on a job elsewhere) and P is the firm's profits (the excess of what the firm owners get over what would emerge if they did not operate). With L, Y, q and w^* denoting the number of workers at this firm, the output (sales) of this firm, the unemployment rate among the subset of people in the country that have a possibility of working, and the average wage prevailing in the rest of the economy (assumed to be independent of decisions taken within each employer-employee pair) respectively, the expressions for I and P are:

$P = Y - w(1 + e)L + (hw^*)L$	
$I = wL(1 - i - t) + (pw^*)L(1 - i) - [(1 - q)$ $[w^*L(1 - i - t) + (pw^*)L(1 - i)] + q[(f + p)$ w^*L	

q and $(1 - q)$ are the probabilities that a separated worker is either unemployed or re-employed elsewhere. Since the population is unity and u^* individuals are chronically unemployed, the number of unemployed here is $v = q(1 - u^*)$. After differentiating the arbitrator's objective function with respect to her choice variable, w, setting that expression equal to zero, then imposing the fact that a full economy-wide equilibrium involves $w = w^*$, simplifying by using the fact that labour's share of income is $(wL/Y = (1 - a)/(1 + e - h)$, and by defining b to stand for $aj(1 - u^*)/((1 - a)(1 - j))$, we have the expression for v that appears in equation (5b) above.

The definition of I indicates that every individual faces a chance of unemployment after a job separation, so a literal application of this micro-foundation would not justify my interpreting the macro model's results as if the working poor and the unemployed were different groups. If readers are uncomfortable on these grounds, they should focus exclusively on the results that are reported for all of labour (the measure referred to as the efficiency index in the tables that lumps both these groups together). The conclusions of the chapter are supported even when attention is focused in this way.

References

Corak, Miles (1996), "Unemployment Insurance and Canada-US Unemployment Rates," *Policy Options*, July-August.

Domeij, D. 2005. "Optimal Capital Taxation and Labour Market Search," *Review of Economic Dynamics*, 8.3: 623-50.

Koskela, E. and R. Schob. 2002. "Why Governments Should Tax Mobile Capital in the Presence of Unemployment," *Contributions to Economic Analysis and Policy*, 1.1: 1-20.

Lipsey, R.G. and K. Lancaster. 1956. "The General Theory of the Second Best," *Review of Economic Studies*, 24.1: 11-32.

Mankiw, N.G., D. Romer and D.N. Weil. 1992. "A Contribution to the Empirics of Economic Growth," *Quarterly Journal of Economics*, 107.2: 407-37.

Moutos, T. and W. Scarth. 2004. "Some Macroeconomic Consequences of Basic Income and Employment Subsidies," in *Labor Market Institutions and Public Regulation*, ed. J. Agell, M. Keen and A.J. Weichenrieder, 195-220. Cambridge, Mass.: MIT Press.

Phelps, E.S. 1997. *Rewarding Work: How to Restore Participation and Self-Support to Free Enterprise*. Boston: Harvard University Press.

Pissarides, C.A. 1998. "The Impact of Employment Tax Cuts on Unemployment and Wages; The Role of Unemployment Benefits and Tax Structure," *European Economic Review*, 42.1: 155-183.

Scarth, W. 2007. *Macroeconomics: An Introduction to Advanced Methods*, Third Edition. Hamilton: McMaster Innovation Press.

Summers, L.H. 1988. "Relative Wages, Efficiency Wages and Keynesian Unemployment," *American Economic Review Papers and Proceedings*, 78.2: 383-388.

Section II

Regional Benefits versus a National Program

Chapter 8

The Impact of Regionally Differentiated Entitlement to EI on Charter-Protected Canadians

Michael Pal and Sujit Choudhry

1 Introduction

Employment insurance programs are intended to support workers through temporary periods of unemployment. Internationally, Canada's Employment Insurance ("EI") program is one of the few to determine coverage for unemployment on the basis of region (Van Audenrode et al. 2005, 19). The federal government divides the country into economic regions for the purposes of EI. Whether a worker qualifies for EI and the duration of her benefits depend partially upon the unemployment rate in the region where she lives. Unemployed workers in EI regions with high unemployment rates qualify more easily for EI and receive more weeks of benefits than those in regions with low unemployment rates.

The consequences of a regionally differentiated employment insurance program have been well documented (Bishop and Burleton 2009, 6-10; Chamber of Commerce 2009, 4-7; Neil 2009, 4-5). Existing research has focused upon the impact of regionally differentiated benefits on particular regions, provinces, and cities. These studies demonstrate that in seeking to assist vulnerable unemployed workers in regions of high unemployment, the EI program has harmed vulnerable unemployed workers in other areas of the country by restricting their access to, and support from, EI.

The impact of regionally differentiated access to benefits on minority workers, however, has not been fully explored. This study investigates whether the EI program disadvantages Canadians protected by the Canadian Charter of Rights and Freedoms (1982) and considers the constitutional implications of the differential impact the regional EI system has on minorities. All Canadians are protected by the Charter of Rights and Freedoms (1982). We use the term "Charter-protected Canadians" in this chapter to refer to specific minority groups whose differential treatment by a government program and pre-existing disadvantage potentially engage the equality rights in section 15 of the Charter: visible minorities, recent immigrants, naturalized citizens, and those whose mother tongue is neither one of the two official languages. We analyze how the regional differentiation in the EI program affects the ability to qualify for EI of visible minorities, recent immigrants, naturalized citizens and those whose mother tongue is neither one of the two official languages.

We hypothesize that because racial and linguistic minority immigrants settle overwhelmingly in the largest urban areas of Alberta, British Columbia, Québec and Ontario, where more hours of work are generally required to qualify for EI (see Bishop and Burleton 2009, 6-10; Chamber of Commerce 2009, 4-7; Neil 2009, 4-5), minority workers' access to EI is restricted in comparison to others. If so, the EI program's regional differentiation of access to benefits may compound already-existing disadvantages that exist for minority workers in the labour market which make it more difficult for them to qualify for EI in the first place. We quantify the average number of hours for which a worker in each of these minority groups must have been employed in order to qualify for EI and compare those results to other workers.

The negative impact of regionally differentiated benefits upon Charter-protected Canadians potentially raises both political and legal issues. Recent immigrants, the vast majority of whom are visible minorities with a mother tongue other than English or French, fare worse in the labour market than other workers (Federation of Canadian Municipalities 2009: *iii*, 21-23; Mahon 2008, 356; Picot and Sweetman 2005, 6-14; Reitz and Banerjee 2007; Statistics Canada 2010). If EI fails to insure vulnerable workers in times of unemployment, the program may need to be redesigned to more effectively deliver insurance for workers. Further, if Charter-protected workers are disadvantaged by the regional determination of qualification for EI and benefits, then these workers may have a claim of indirect discrimination counter to section 15 of the Charter.

This chapter will proceed as follows. We first outline the relevant portions of the EI program. Second, we review the highlights of the EI literature on regionally differentiated benefits and immigrant workers. Third, we detail our research design and methodology in measuring the impact of regionally differentiated benefits on Charter-protected Canadians. Fourth, we present our empirical findings. Fifth, we explore the legal implications of these findings, particularly whether they give rise to a claim under section 15 of the Charter. Sixth, we consider the case of temporary foreign workers, a sub-set of workers that is disadvantaged by the current program. Seventh, we briefly consider some policy options for reforming the regional entrance requirements.

2 The EI Program

The relevant features of the EI program are largely set out in the *Employment Insurance Act* (1996) (the "Act") and regulations. Qualification for EI depends on a variety of factors, including having the proper type of job separation (i.e., termination without cause), type of work and number of hours of employment within the previous 52 weeks. The Act's Variable Entrance Requirements ("VERs") mean that the number of hours an individual is required to work to qualify for the program varies across EI regions, as does the level of benefits.

The VERs have two key components. First, for the purposes of EI, the country is divided into 58 economic regions, with qualification for EI benefits depending upon the regional unemployment rate. As the regional unemployment rate fluctuates, so too does the number of hours worked in the previous 52 weeks needed to qualify for EI, with a range of 420 to 700 hours (*EI Act*, 1996: s. 7). The boundaries of the economic regions are adjusted periodically. Section 54 (w) of the Act permits regulations to be made setting regional boundaries and regulation 18 obliges the federal government to review the boundaries every five years. The regional determination of benefits was brought into existence in 1977 (Lin 1998, 43-4). In 2000, the boundaries were reviewed and modified to the current 58, and were unchanged by the 2005 review. As of the time of writing, no results have been announced from the required 2010 review.

Second, the duration of benefits also varies significantly by region according to the regional unemployment rate. Those who qualify for EI in regions with a 6 per cent unemployment rate or lower (the bottom category) receive 14–36 weeks of benefits, while workers in regions with unemployment rates above 16 per cent (the highest category) are eligible for between 32 and 45 weeks. The temporary, 5-week extension by the *Budget Implementation Act* 2009 of the duration of benefits set out in the *EI Act* [Schedule 1, s. 12(2)] expired in September 2010. Regional variation in access and extent of benefits can have stark consequences for similarly situated unemployed workers in regions with different levels of unemployment.

3 The Failings of the Regional Entrance Requirements

Recent studies drawing out the implications of regionally differentiated benefits (Bishop and Burleton 2009; Chamber of Commerce 2009) have concluded that the number of hours an individual must work to qualify for EI varies widely by city and province, as do the weeks of benefits, and the ratio of EI beneficiaries to unemployed workers. Unemployed workers in regions with overall low unemployment rates are not well-served by the program, as they face more stringent requirements to qualify for EI and receive fewer weeks of benefits, even if there is no practical difference in their job prospects with unemployed workers in regions with high unemployment. Over 800,000 unemployed workers did not qualify for EI during the recession in May 2009 (Courchene and Allan 2009). Large urban areas in Canada often have lower unemployment rates than rural areas (Chamber of Commerce 2009, 5-6).

There are also fundamental problems with the VERs that have received less scrutiny. The process and substantive criteria used to determine EI regional boundaries by the federal government are flawed. The process by which the boundaries are reviewed is not transparent and has become highly politicized. This politicization has likely detracted from the program's ability to effectively deliver insurance for unemployed workers in a fair and equitable manner.

As there are no criteria for the drawing and review of regional boundaries listed in the Act or the regulations, judicial oversight of the process is difficult. The Act delegates the power to make regulations regarding boundaries [s. 54 (w)] to the Employment Insurance Commission, under the auspices of the federal government department responsible, i.e., Human Resources and Skills Development Canada. Information published by HRSDC indicates that the goal in creating regional boundaries is to "define geographic regions on which to base EI entitlement and duration of benefits (HRSDC 2000)." EI regions exist "in recognition of the fact that not all areas of Canada have equal employment opportunities (HRSDC 2000)."

HRSDC lists four criteria that it takes into account (HRSDC 2000). First, the "cornerstone" of the determination of regional boundaries is "the rural/urban split." The federal government assumes each Census Metropolitan Area ("CMA") is its own economic region. A CMA is a category created by Statistics Canada of at least 100,000 people that largely encompasses an urban core and its suburban areas, such as the Greater Toronto Area or Metro Vancouver. Rural areas outside of CMAs are combined to create other economic regions. Second, the drawing of boundaries must ensure "homogeneous labour markets" that experience similar rates of unemployment. The intent here appears to be to treat like regions alike. Third, regions must be contiguous, within the same province, and respect the boundaries used by Statistics Canada to aggregate Census data. Fourth, regions must have labour forces that are large enough to allow accurate monthly estimates of the regional unemployment rate. These last two criteria are intended to provide administrative ease.

Whether the four criteria are applied fairly in setting the boundaries, or are the criteria that should govern economic regional boundary determination for the purposes of EI at all, is hard to determine. The process of assigning regional boundaries lacks sufficient transparency, especially given the importance of the regional map to unemployed workers. HRSDC does not give detailed reasons for boundary adjustments that relate them to the criteria it has set out, apart from a brief analysis of regulatory changes. As a consequence, there are serious concerns that the federal government adjusts the boundaries of EI regions for political reasons unrelated to the stated goals of creating homogeneous labour markets and ensuring administrative ease both during and apart from the five-year reviews.

For example, recent enrichments of the program have enhanced benefits for those who already qualify, or those who face relatively low hurdles to do so, rather than aiding the unemployed with little prospect of being covered by EI. The expansion of the minimum and maximum weeks of coverage in the 2009 federal budget aided workers receiving benefits, rather than relaxing the coverage rules. The federal government often uses various so-called "transitional measures" that generally relax the already lower hurdles for qualifying for EI in regions of high unemployment (Busby 2008, 4 and fn 7; Van Audenrode et al. 2005, 18-19). These transitional enrichments are often difficult to phase out, for political reasons. Transitional measures introduced in 2000 for example in Eastern Quebec and Northern New Brunswick remain in place today (Busby 2008, 4 and fn 7; Van Audenrode et al. 2005, 18-19).

Even if regional boundaries were determined transparently and non-politically, access to EI is governed by the regional unemployment rate, which is a blunt measure for assessing the needs of unemployed workers. The EI program assumes the regional unemployment rate to be the sole relevant condition for ascertaining the need of the unemployed to access EI. In doing so, it fails to consider other relevant factors, such as labour market segmentation and stagnation. If there is no market for certain types of workers, or no movement in the overall labour market, low regional unemployment is a misleading proxy for need among unemployed workers. By tying not only access to, but also duration of, benefits to the regional unemployment rate, the program provides a "double whammy" (Mendelson et al. 2009, 2; see also the Expert Panel on Older Workers 2008, 60-61) for the unemployed in regions with low overall unemployment.

4 Regionally Differentiated Benefits and Charter-Protected Workers

Immigrants to Canada, the vast majority of whom are visible minorities with mother tongues other than English or French, fare worse overall in the labour market than non-immigrants. The Labour Force Survey found that while the unemployment rate for the Canadian-born aged 25 to 54 is 6.1 per cent, for recent immigrants (arriving within five years or less) of the same age group it is 14.7 per cent, with the difference decreasing the longer immigrants are in Canada (Statistics Canada 2010). Even immigrants who have been in the country for more than ten years, however, still have an unemployment rate higher than that of Canadian-born workers. The unemployment rates for recent immigrants from the key source regions of Africa (21.2 per cent), Asia (15.1 per cent) and Latin America (16.1 per cent) are much higher than for the Canadian-born (Statistics Canada 2010).

In a study of specific urban communities comprising large metropolitan areas and 85 per cent of the immigrant population, the Federation of Canadian Municipalities ("FCM") found reason to be concerned about poverty among urban immigrants. Immigrants in these urban areas received social assistance at twice the rate of immigrants in the rest of Canada (2009: *iii*). The study found that 43 per cent of all recent immigrant households had low incomes, nearly three times that of non-immigrant households (FCM 2009: *iv*). The unemployment rate among recent immigrants was 1.4 times higher than for non-immigrants across Canada, but 2.3 times higher in the urban areas included in the study. This data is part of a larger trend. Relating earnings to education, Aydemir and Skuterud (2005) found a significant drop in immigrant income since the 1960s, controlling for factors such as the economy at time of entry.

The operation of the labour market hinders the ability of minority workers to compete for jobs and to earn sufficient hours of work to qualify for EI, even beyond the difficulties caused by the period of adjustment necessarily confronted by immigrants (Reitz and Banerjee 2007). Minority workers are likely to face additional barriers compared to other workers, such as a lack of Canadian credentials, language barriers, and limited Canadian work experience. Advantages provided by high levels of education among immigrants are negated by their settlement in urban areas, where they must compete with highly educated native-born workers (Reitz 2003). Foreign experience (Aydemir and Skuterud 2005; Green and Worswick 2004) and credentials (Reitz 2001) are discounted in the labour market. These barriers hamper the ability of minority workers to accumulate enough hours of employment to qualify for EI.

EI potentially compounds these pre-existing disadvantages faced by minority workers through the VERs. Given worse employment and earning prospects among recent immigrants than the Canadian-born, the regional distribution of access to benefits is problematic if found to disproportionately hinder access to EI among Charter-protected workers. The concentration of immigrants in the largest urban areas of British Columbia, Alberta, Ontario and Québec (Statistics Canada 2007), which are also the regions that tend to face the highest hurdles in order to qualify for EI, suggests there may be a differential impact.

Existing research on minority workers has explored various aspects of EI, but not dealt directly with the impact of the variable regional requirements on their relative eligibility for benefits. Amendments to EI in 1996 that made it more difficult to quality for the program and reduced benefits have been harmful to vulnerable workers (Evans 2002, 87; Mahon 2008, 356; and Shields 2004), which includes minority workers. The 2004 Monitoring and Assessment Report of the EI program from HRSDC (under the auspices of the Employment Insurance Commission) suggested that the significant barriers new immigrants face in entering the labour market result in these workers being unable to work the requisite number of hours (HRSDC 2004). Recent immigrants are marginally less likely to qualify for EI than other Canadians with qualifying job separation (HRSDC 2009). De Silva (1997) investigated immigrant participation in Unemployment Insurance (UI) and found that there were significant differences in the probability of UI usage across ethnic groups. He also found that after 1975, certain groups of immigrants had a higher propensity to use UI than earlier immigrants. A more recent study by Sweetman (2001) concludes that immigrants have a lower participation rate than native-born Canadians. Siklos and Marr (1998) found that UI claims by immigrants varied by province of residence.

5 Research Design and Methodology

To quantify the impact of regionally differentiated benefits on Charter-protected workers, we measure the total number of hours Charter-protected workers must log on average in the previous 52 weeks to qualify for EI, and compare this to the number of hours required of other workers. We focus here on access to EI, rather than duration of benefits, because qualifying through the VERs is the prior and fundamental hurdle that faces most minority workers. Further research could be conducted on the duration of benefits to determine if the current rules disadvantage particular groups of workers.

We used custom Census data from Statistics Canada and EI data provided by HRSDC, and applied it to the boundaries that were in place from 2000–2010. From 2000–2005, we applied the 2001 Census data with the regional boundaries in place at the time. We then utilized the 2006 Census data from 2006 onwards with the regions current during that period. By matching Census data and regional boundaries in this fashion, we measure the impact of regionally distributing benefits with the most current demographic data available at the time. We broke down individual-level data in each EI region on the basis of visible minority status (using the definition in the *Employment Equity Act* 1995 and regulations), citizenship, immigration status, as well as by mother tongue. For the unemployment rate in each region, we used the yearly average derived from the Statistics Canada monthly unemployment numbers.

We created weighted averages for the number of hours of work required for the average individual in each group. Using Statistics Canada's standard definition of working age population (individuals aged 15–64) as the unit of analysis[1], we multiplied the total number of working age individuals in each region by the number of hours each individual in that region would have had to work to qualify for EI. We aggregated the total number of hours that would have had to be worked to qualify for EI for the working population as a whole. We then divided the aggregated number of hours by the working population to determine the average number of hours each individual must work. The same process was repeated for each sub-group by visible minority status, citizenship, immigration status, and mother tongue.

It is important to point out that our results do not incorporate the pre-existing disadvantages in the labour market that render it more difficult for minority workers to amass enough hours to qualify for EI, regardless of the VERs. Moreover, the data does not take into account the higher number of hours (910) required for New-Entrant and Re-Entrant workers (NEREs). This is 210 hours above the maximum 700 required for workers who are regular applicants for EI. To the extent that we can assume recent immigrants will account for a disproportionate share of new entrants to the labour force, the results are likely to understate the number of hours a minority worker must work to qualify for EI.

6 Results

A Census Metropolitan Areas

CMAs are one of the building blocks of the EI system. Each CMA forms its own EI region. In the boundary determination process, rural areas and urban areas with insufficient populations to qualify as CMAs are grouped into other regions. The immigrant population is concentrated in CMAs. Relevant measures of the potential differential impact of the VERs therefore include calculating their effects on minorities within CMAs and workers within CMAs compared to those outside of CMAs.

The data from 2000–2010 using working age population indicates that visible minorities in CMAs have consistently been required to work more hours in the previous 52 weeks to qualify for EI than non-visible minorities outside of CMAs, though the difference is modest. On average, visible minorities in the largest urban areas must work 10 per cent more hours than those who are not visible minorities and reside in regions outside of CMAs. The range is an 18.9 per cent gap in 2000, to a 4.4 per cent gap in 2010. The difference in the number of hours required to qualify has decreased over the course of the decade. As a large proportion of visible minority workers reside in CMAs, the results are attributable to the differential impact of the VERs on workers in CMAs as a whole. Comparing workers in CMAs to non-CMAs overall, working age individuals in CMAs from 2000–2010 have had to work 9.8 per cent longer to qualify for EI than those outside of CMAs.

As unemployment rates have varied, so has the number of hours of work required within and outside of CMAs. Unemployment rates have risen in urban areas in the recession years of 2009 and 2010 and the number of hours required to qualify for EI has therefore dropped. As unemployment increased in urban areas, resource economies in rural areas were comparatively better off, thereby narrowing the gap between CMA residents and those outside CMAs. This data indicates that while CMA residents and visible minorities living within them have been marginally disadvantaged by the regional EI system, the system has been flexible enough to alleviate some of these problems.

B Visible Minority Status

We also calculated the impact of visible minority status on the number of hours needed to qualify for EI, separate from the distinction between CMAs and non-CMAs. From 2000–2010, visible minorities had to work on average 645 hours to qualify, in comparison to 623 for the average individual and 620 for the average non-visible minority. As with the analysis for CMAs, the gap between visible minorities and non-visible minorities was greatest in 2000 and reached a low in 2010. The average differential from 2000–2010 was 4.0 per cent between visible minorities and non-visible minorities.

C Citizenship Status

Whether the Variable Entrance Requirements dependent on the regional unemployment rate have a differential impact by citizenship status is another potentially relevant category to investigate, as naturalized citizens and non-citizens are not evenly distributed across the country or EI regions. The main categories of comparison are citizens of Canada by birth and citizens by naturalization. On average, a citizen of Canada by birth was required to work 618 hours per year over the period 2000–2010, with a high of 647 in 2008 to a low of 588 in 2009. Naturalized Canadians needed to work on average 642 hours per year over the period, with a high of 678 in 2000 and a low of 594 in 2009. Naturalized Canadians were obliged to work 4.0 per cent more hours on average to meet the VERs. We also compared dual citizens of Canada and another country and workers who exclusively hold Canadian citizenship. Those holding exclusively Canadian citizenship were required to work 621 hours per year on average, with dual citizens needing 640 on average. As with visible minority status, there were only marginal differences between the Canadian-born and naturalized citizens, and dual and exclusively Canadian citizens.

D Immigration Status

Immigration status is also another potentially relevant variable. If recent immigrants settle in the urban areas and provinces where it is has been generally hardest to qualify for EI, then immigration status may be related to an increased number of hours of work needed to qualify for EI. From 2000–2010, immigrants to Canada had to work on average 642 hours to qualify, with 618 required for workers who are not immigrants. We also tracked those who had immigrated to Canada within 5, 10 or more than 10 years before the Census date. While there was a modest gap between immigrants and non-immigrants, there was almost no difference between those who immigrated earlier to Canada and those who immigrated more recently. This lack of variation between earlier and more recent arrivals is likely due to the fact that all of these categories of immigrants have disproportionately settled in the same, large urban areas (Statistics Canada 2003).

E Mother Tongue

Language is another variable through which to quantify the impact of the regional EI system as many new Canadians have mother tongues other than English or French, given the increasing importance of Asia, Africa and Latin America as sources of immigrants (Statistics Canada 2003). From 2000–2010, those with English as a mother tongue were required to work 630 hours on average, while those with French as a mother tongue needed 592 hours. Workers who had a mother tongue other than English or French had to work 638 hours on average. This is a marginal increase from English native speakers (638 to 630), but a larger one in comparison to French native speakers (636 to 592). The average gap from 2000–2010 between those whose mother tongue was not an Official Language and those with French mother tongue was 7.7 per cent. In every year but 2010, the number of hours required was higher for non-official language speakers than French native speakers. There was only a marginal difference between native English speakers and non-official language speakers over the same time period.

F Summary of the Results

Overall, there are consistent but only modest differences between visible minorities and non-visible minorities, naturalized citizens and the Canadian-born, dual citizens and citizens of Canada only, immigrants and non-immigrants, and workers with mother tongues other than the Official Languages and those who are native anglophones and francophones. The finding of only modest results is likely due to the reversal of the pattern from earlier in the decade of relatively low urban unemployment in comparison to higher rural unemployment levels. As the labour market worsened in the middle of the decade, and particularly in 2009 and 2010, urban unemployed rose, access to EI was eased in cities, and the ability of minority workers residing in cities to qualify for EI approached that of workers in rural areas. The EI program was flexible to some extent in its response so that the gap between minorities and the average worker lessened in the context of rising unemployment. Minority workers continue to have their credentials, skills, and experiences discounted in the labour market, however, and face stiff competition for jobs in urban areas, which affects their ability to qualify for EI. While our data indicates that Charter-protected workers face some additional barriers due to the regional entrance requirements, future research should deepen the analysis to incorporate differential labour market experiences within EI regions on the basis of Charter-protected status as well as the impact of the flat rate for new entrants.

7 Legal Implications

A EI and Equality Rights

While we have found modest results with regards to minority workers, distributing employment insurance on a regional basis remains a problematic policy. As discussed above, the VERs disadvantage specific cities and provinces (Bishop and Burleton 2009; Chamber of Commerce 2009), the determination of regional boundaries is not transparent, and the regional unemployment rate is a flawed measure by which to assess need. Further, our results likely understate the barriers faced by minority workers. Immigrants as new entrants to the labour market will face the

910-hour rate for NEREs wherever they live, thereby hindering their ability to qualify for EI even having worked the same number of hours as someone who is not a new entrant. The regional entrance requirements and the flat rate for NEREs combine to decrease access to EI for specific groups of workers without justification for doing so, which compound the disadvantages facing minority workers with foreign education and experience. For all of these reasons, reform of EI, including the VERs, should remain a priority.

Unfortunately, the political dynamics of the EI program hamper reform. It is politically unpalatable for the federal government to remove entitlements in place for specific regions, as well as potentially costly to ensure the unemployed in all regions of the country should have equal access to EI benefits. The prospect of reform of the EI program in a manner that will lead to greater equity and improved policy design through the political process is elusive. Constitutional litigation through the courts is therefore a potentially promising venue through which to pursue reform of the VERs. In this section, we provide a general, though not comprehensive, overview of the legal considerations that would likely arise in a future constitutional challenge to the EI program's VERs.

EI is a government program authorized by federal legislation and administered by the federal and provincial governments. It must therefore be compliant with the Canadian Charter of Rights and Freedoms (1982), including the equality rights guarantee in s. 15. Section 15 protects individuals from discrimination on the basis of personal characteristics, known as prohibited grounds, either specifically listed in section 15, such as race or sex, or covered by grounds analogous to those listed in the section (*Andrews v. Law Society of B.C.* 1989). Section 15 forbids both direct and adverse effects discrimination on these prohibited grounds. Direct discrimination is where government action, such as legislation, explicitly distinguishes between individuals on a prohibited ground. Adverse effects discrimination occurs where a facially neutral law or government action has a disparate and negative impact on an identifiable Charter-protected minority (*Eldridge v. B.C. 1997*: para. 62; *Vriend v. Alberta* 1998: para. 82-86 per J. Cory).

While the current data would likely not be sufficient to support a successful s. 15 claim for adverse effects discrimination, Charter-protected workers have faced varying levels of differential treatment as unemployment rates have fluctuated over the 2000–2010 period. In the future, the number of hours required by minority workers relative to other workers may again increase, so the issue of whether the EI regional benefits program could be considered unconstitutional adverse effects discrimination remains relevant. The Supreme Court of Canada (the "Court") has not directly considered this issue, but has subjected the legislation governing EI to s. 15 scrutiny [*Tétreault-Gadoury v. Canada (Employment and Immigration Commission)* 1991] and assessed its constitutionality on other grounds (see *CSN v. Canada* 2008 and *Reference re Employment Insurance Act* 2005). Future legal analysis could also focus on the potential for indirect discrimination caused by the 910-hour rule, which applies to immigrants as new entrants to the labour market.

B The Section 15 Test: Distinctions on Enumerated or Analogous Grounds

An analysis using section 15 is complicated by uncertainty regarding the legal test for rights violations. The standard test for section 15 was introduced in *Law v. Canada* (1999). *R. v. Kapp* amended the *Law* framework in 2008, but the analysis in *Kapp* on section 15 is abbreviated. *Kapp* does appear to have re-instituted the two-part test for section 15 from *Andrews v. Law Society of B.C.* (1989), with *Law* providing guidance on the application of the second part of the *Andrews* test, so we apply that approach here. Claimants previously had to establish differential treatment in comparison to another group similar but for the impugned personal characteristic such as race or gender, known as a mirror comparator group. The requirement of identifying the proper comparator group had hindered rights claimants. The recent decision of the Supreme Court of Canada in *Withler v. Canada (Attorney General)* (2011) de-emphasizes or perhaps even abandons the need for the claimant to establish a mirror comparator group.

For a s. 15 claim to be made, there must be a distinction drawn on an enumerated or analogous ground that discriminates against an individual by perpetuating a disadvantage based in prejudice or stereotyping (*R. v. Kapp* 2008: para. 17; *Withler* 2011: para. 30). The *EI Act* and regulations draw distinctions on the basis of region and place of residence, therefore the obvious way to challenge the Act would be for discrimination by place of residence. Yet place of residence is neither listed in section 15 nor considered an analogous ground and is therefore not protected by the Charter. (*R. v. Turpin* 1989: 1333 is somewhat ambiguous, but *Corbière v. Canada* (1999) is more definitive: paras. 15, 62, as is *Haig v. Canada* 1993.) As a consequence, challenging EI through section 15 for discrimination on the basis of place of residence is likely to be a losing proposition.

Workers could challenge the constitutionality of the Act, however, on the basis of other grounds of discrimination. Race, ethnicity, language and national origin are all enumerated grounds protected under section 15, while citizenship status has been found to be an analogous ground (*Andrews* 1989). The Act does not distinguish on its face between workers on the basis of race, ethnicity, language, citizenship, or immigration status, so there can be no claim for direct discrimination. A claim could still proceed under section 15 by asserting not direct discrimination, but adverse effects discrimination.

As the empirical analysis conducted above demonstrates, distributing benefits on a regional basis has a modest negative impact on several distinct groups that are protected from adverse effects discrimination under the Charter. These are distinctions drawn on enumerated grounds. The current effects on minority workers are an insufficient foundation upon which to base a constitutional challenge. If the negative impact were to increase as a result of prolonged lower unemployment rates in urban regions where immigrants settle relative to rural regions with few minority workers, a Charter challenge for adverse effects discrimination on the basis of race, ethnicity, citizenship, national origin or language would be a live issue before the courts.

C The Section 15 Test: Disadvantages Based on Prejudice or Stereotyping

For a s. 15 claim to succeed, the distinction drawn on enumerated or analogous grounds must have a discriminatory impact based on prejudice or stereotyping. How would a s. 15 claim proceed to try and make out adverse effects discrimination? First, a claimant must prove that the impugned law perpetuates prejudice and disadvantage on the basis of a prohibited ground. The typical case is where a law exacerbates the pre-existing disadvantages of a historically marginalized group (*Withler* 2011: para. 35). There are certainly pre-existing disadvantages and prejudice facing visible minorities, new immigrants, and those for whom neither English nor French is their mother tongue (Reitz and Banerjee 2007). Providing less access to EI, and fewer weeks of benefits if an individual eventually qualifies, may exacerbate pre-existing disadvantages.

The nature and scope of the interest affected must be also considered at this juncture. Generally, the more severe the impact, the more likely discrimination will be found to have occurred (*Law* 1999). The more important the interest at stake, the more likely it will be that the distinction causes disadvantage. Qualification for a government program that insures unemployed workers is arguably a core interest for minority workers.

A court must also consider whether there is the absence of a purpose or effect that ameliorates the conditions of a *more* disadvantaged group than the claimants. This portion of the test traditionally guards against allowing relatively advantaged groups to claim discrimination by government programs that aid relatively less advantaged groups. There is a risk a claim by minority workers in low unemployment areas could fail at this juncture. The EI scheme attempts to provide benefits at a satisfactory level to workers in areas of high unemployment. High unemployment is a chronic problem in some regions of the country. A claim that the VERs are unconstitutional could be viewed as relatively advantaged workers in lower unemployment areas attempting to limit an ameliorative program targeting more disadvantaged workers in high unemployment areas.

A claim by minority groups for fair treatment under EI, however, need not necessarily be seen as an attempt to reject the distribution of benefits to other unemployed workers in need. A constitutional challenge to EI could legitimately be framed as about ensuring that benefits are equally distributed to all vulnerable workers. The unemployed in regions of relatively low unemployment may be as disadvantaged as the unemployed in regions with higher unemployment rates. Virtually all increases in low-income populations in the most populous cities in Canada were among recent immigrants (Picot and Sweetman 2005, 14-5). There is an argument to be made that minority workers are collectively among the most vulnerable workers in Canada.

Second, a claim that government action results in substantive inequality must also prove that the disadvantage caused by the law is based in stereotyping that does not correspond to the actual needs and circumstances of the claimant. Unemployed minority workers whose access to EI is limited because of the VERs have had their actual needs and circumstances largely ignored. The VERs are responsive to need only if the overall unemployment in a region increases. The VERs do not adequately capture or respond to augmented need for EI benefits among groups that are disproportionately disadvantaged in a labour market where the overall unemployment rate is low.

The EI scheme assumes all workers in an economic region are uniformly affected by the regional unemployment rate. In fact, racial and linguistic minorities fare much worse (Aydemir and Skuterud 2005; Federation of Canadian Municipalities 2009; Picot and Sweetman 2005, 6-14; Reitz 2001; Reitz and Banerjee 2007; Statistics Canada 2010). Recent immigrants without Canadian credentials, less Canadian experience, and English (or French in Québec) as a second language are likely to be less competitive in the job market, thereby harming their ability to work sufficient hours to qualify for EI. The legal requirement under section 15 to take into account the actual needs and circumstances of workers means acknowledging that the regional unemployment rate is a crude measure of actual need.

The counter-argument is that the current EI program is responsive to the actual needs and circumstances of workers. As unemployment rates have increased in the last few years of the 2000–2010 period, the difference in the average number of hours required by minority workers and other workers has decreased. It is therefore arguable that the EI program has responded appropriately.

D "Reasonable Limits" Under Section 1 of the Charter

Even if the legislative scheme is found to violate section 15, it may be saved constitutionally by the operation of section 1 of the Charter. Section 1 permits rights to be curtailed by "such reasonable limits prescribed by law as can be demonstrably justified in a free and democratic society." For section 1 to save the rights violation, there must be 1) a pressing and substantial government objective, 2) a rational connection between the government action and the objective, 3) minimal impairment of the right, and 4) proportionality between the curtailment of the right and the value of the objective (*R v. Oakes* 1986). From our analysis, the EI program is potentially vulnerable at both the rational connection and minimal impairment branches of the section 1 test, so we focus on those two aspects.

The rational connection branch of *Oakes* requires that the evidence, or a common-sense understanding, shows a causal connection between the limitation of the right and the benefits the scheme purports to cause. [For two of the few instances where the usually easily hurdled rational connection test was not met, see *RJR-MacDonald v. Canada* (1995) and *Benner v. Canada* (1997).] On the surface regional differentiation appears to be reasonably linked to insuring the employed, on the presumption that unemployment is most insidious in regions of high unemployment. The government would argue that the EI regime limits the rights of the unemployed in low unemployment regions only so as to target those with fewer job opportunities for aid and to encourage participation in the labour force. On this view, the limits placed on workers in low unemployment regions would be rationally connected to the objectives of helping workers in regions of high unemployment who are the least likely to be able to find work, and of encouraging employment for those most likely to find work.

Yet on several levels the current program is not rational. By failing to take into account the conditions faced by minority workers in the labour market, such as lack of Canadian credentials or experience, the EI program does not adequately take into account the actual needs of minority workers, which goes to the lack of a rational connection between the scheme and the goal of insuring unemployed workers. Using the regional rate as the exclusive indicator of need ignores that the labour markets in a particular region may be stagnant, even if the regional unemployment rate is low. There may be no movement in the market and therefore no opportunity for the unemployed to find jobs. It also fails to account for the specific labour markets that exist for different types of jobs (Bishop and Burleton 2009, 9-10). Any claim of a rational connection between the scheme and the legislative goals is further undermined by the politicization of the boundary drawing process. There is a lack of substantive justification for adjusting boundaries or EI policies in light of the program's stated goal of insuring unemployed workers. The opaque process for determining regional boundaries and arriving at the criteria applied to define the boundaries would also work against the government's defence of the EI program in a s. 1 analysis.

The EI scheme could also be considered to be more than minimally impairing of the rights of Charter-protected minority workers. By splitting the country into 58 regions and requiring a different number of hours worked for each unemployment rate from 6 per cent to 16 per cent, the EI scheme creates multiple tiers of entitlement. A tiered benefit program creates more differentials in coverage than are necessary. There could be a requirement of a flat number of hours worked below 10 per cent and another amount required for unemployment rates above 10 per cent (see the recommendations of Bishop and Burleton 2009, 7-8 and the Chamber of Commerce 2009, 10). CMAs could also be combined with outlying areas for the purposes of designing EI regions where the CMA boundaries do not correspond to the boundaries of a "homogeneous labour market" because outlying areas contain workers that should be considered part of the same labour market. A legislative scheme does not have to be the *least* impairing imaginable to pass constitutional assessment under section 1 (*Harvey v. New Brunswick* 1996: para. 47; *R. v. Edwards Books and Art* 1986, 782), but it does need to be minimally impairing. The EI program as currently designed is open to a challenge that it impairs the rights of minority workers to a more than minimal extent. While in the abstract it is not clear on which side the s. 1 analysis would fall, a Charter challenge to the VERs appears to have some ammunition with which to fight a legal battle.

8 Temporary Foreign Workers

A distinct constitutional law issue involves temporary foreign workers (TFWs), a particularly vulnerable group (Fudge and MacPhail 2009). Canada increasingly relies upon low-skilled TFWs to fill short-term gaps in the labour market (Elgersma 2007). TFWs and their employers are obliged to pay into the EI system and TFWs are formally eligible to receive EI, but in practice TFWs are largely ineligible (Basok 2004, 54; Fudge and MacPhail 2009, 31; Hennebry and Preibisch 2010; Nakache and Kinoshita 2010, 20-21).

To qualify for EI, TFWs must have worked the required number of hours over the previous 52 weeks, which they are unlikely to have done as most have only been in Canada briefly. TFWs must also remain in Canada after their employment ends and be actively looking for work [*Employment Insurance Act* 1996 s.7(1)-(3)]. Many TFWs are legally in the country only on work permits that are "closed," i.e., tied to a specific employer. If they lose that job, they have no legal status to search for work with another employer. Though there is some confusion on this point in the case law, the jurisprudence generally holds that TFWs cannot meet the statutory requirement of actively looking for work if they are legally barred from finding work with an alternate employer (Nakache and Kinoshita 2010, 20-21).

TFWs on "open" permits may be able to qualify if they remain in Canada and have worked the requisite number of hours as their permits allow for work with other employers. It is generally high-skilled workers who have open permits, while more vulnerable low-skilled TFWs tend to have more restrictive ones (Nakache and Kinoshita 2010, 20) and are consequently less likely to be able to qualify for EI.

The formal eligibility, but informal exclusion of most TFWs, requires vulnerable workers to pay into EI without being insured against job loss.

The policy rationale appears to be that if TFWs and their employers did not have to pay into EI, employers would have an incentive to employ TFWs over Canadian workers. The underlying assumption of competition between Canadian and foreign workers is of dubious logic given the reluctance of Canadians to do the jobs most TFWs do. Even if the assumption were correct, a preferable solution would be to exempt TFWs, but not their employers, from paying into EI.

The current arrangement legally requiring contributions to EI by TFWs but in effect barring their access is potentially constitutionally suspect as adverse effects discrimination. Though legislation and regulations set by the federal government distinguishes TFWs from workers in Canada as a whole on the enumerated or analogous grounds of citizenship and national origin, the EI legislation and regulations treat TFWs identically to other workers. There is therefore no direct discrimination against TFWs through EI. However, the combined operation of the regulatory regime over the TFWs and the neutral EI rules arguably result in adverse effects discrimination against a vulnerable set of EI contributors. The policy rationale for mandating contributions by TFWs is unpersuasive, therefore making it difficult to justify under section 1. We do not engage in a full legal analysis of the situation of TFWs, but raise the issue as one that is potentially deserving of Charter scrutiny and further scholarship.

9 Policy Options

Numerous studies have recommended reforms to the Variable Entrance Requirements in order to alleviate the resulting inequities. There are two broad sets of potential options. First, regional entrance requirements could be eliminated entirely. A flat rate requirement for the number of hours worked in the previous 52 weeks could be set for all unemployed workers, as there is currently for NEREs. A uniform entrance requirement would undoubtedly involve a standard number of hours lower than that which prevails under the VERs today (Courchene and Allan 2009, 25). A standard entrance requirement would therefore increase the number of recipients and program costs, but would likely increase both equity and policy effectiveness by ensuring all workers are treated alike.

Second, the regional system could be kept in place but modified. The process of determining the boundaries should be reformed, given the centrality of regions in assigning eligibility and benefits. At the very least the determination of regional boundaries should be rendered transparent. The Act should be amended to list the criteria that must be considered in the boundary review. The criteria should be designed to minimize the opportunities for political interference that undermine both equity and policy effectiveness. The criteria should also be rationally connected to the goal of insuring unemployed workers. Using the regional unemployment rate to determine eligibility and duration of benefits has the advantage of being simple to administer, but the resulting inequities are too great. Labour market segmentation and stagnation should be considered as additional factors to determine regional eligibility.

10 Conclusion

Our study has provided further detail of the implications of designing EI as a regional program. While the discrepancy between the average number of hours of work required by minority workers in comparison to other workers is currently modest, the differential impact of the VERs remains a live issue as economic conditions evolve. If economic growth occurs in the largest urban areas where minority workers overwhelmingly reside relative to rural or resource driven regions, the differential impact will increase. Pre-existing disadvantages in the labour market are compounded by any operation of the EI program that harms minority workers. Minority workers may in the future have a claim for adverse effects discrimination pursuant to section 15 if the negative impact of the regional entrance requirements further exacerbates their existing position of relative disadvantage in the labour market.

This study was restricted to analyzing the impact of the regionally differentiated rules for EI entitlement on Charter-protected workers and the potential basis for a constitutional challenge to EI on this basis. Future research should measure the full impact of the regional rules by also analyzing the impact of the pre-existing disadvantages existing for minority workers in the labour market. Beyond regional differentiation in EI entitlement rules, there are other aspects of the EI program that may have a significant impact on Charter-protected Canadians. As noted above, the 910-hour rule that applies across Canada raises the entrance requirement for all workers new to the labour market, including recently arrived immigrants, far above the maximum entrance requirement of 700 hours applicable for all other Canadians.

The structure of EI and its role within the federal social safety net means that it serves as a source of yearly income for specific groups of low-income workers, rather than as protection against unexpected unemployment (Medow 2011). Rural seasonal workers receive more regular federal support than low-income, year-round workers with equivalently low yearly incomes. Favoured rural seasonal workers tend not to be racial minorities or immigrants, while low-income minority workers tend to live in cities. The federal social safety net therefore privileges one form of low-income worker above another. This situation of inequity in regular yearly income support, fueled by the regionally differential roles of EI, could also likely provide fruitful ground for future legal analysis and could form a basis for potential legal action.

Appendix

TABLE 1 CMA Results, 2000–2010

Working Age Population	% Difference	
Year	CMA Visible Minority vs. CMA Non-Visible Minority	CMA vs. Non-CMA
2010	4.4	6.6
2009	4.8	6.0
2008	7.8	7.4
2007	8.4	7.9
2006	8.5	7.5
2005	7.6	8.3
2004	13.1	13.6
2003	11.2	11.0
2002	9.5	10.2
2001	15.2	14.5
2000	18.9	16.2
Average % Difference	**10.0**	**9.9**

TABLE 2 Working Populations

2010			
Average Hours /Individual	**Total**	**Visible Minority**	**Non-Visible Minority**
CMA	609	595	614
Non-CMA	572	607	570
2009			
Average Hours /Individual	**Total**	**Visible Minority**	**Non-Visible Minority**
CMA	604	596	607
Non-CMA	571	617	569
2008			
Average Hours /Individual	**Total**	**Visible Minority**	**Non-Visible Minority**
CMA	671	672	671
Non-CMA	626	672	624
2007			
Average Hours /Individual	**Total**	**Visible Minority**	**Non-Visible Minority**
CMA	670	672	670
Non-CMA	622	671	620
2006			
Average Hours /Individual	**Total**	**Visible Minority**	**Non-Visible Minority**
CMA	664	668	663
Non-CMA	617	668	615
2005			
Average Hours /Individual	**Total**	**Visible Minority**	**Non-Visible Minority**
CMA	649	644	651
Non-CMA	600	646	598

TABLE 2 Working Populations (cont.)

2004			
Average Hours /Individual	Total	Visible Minority	Non-Visible Minority
CMA	648	643	649
Non-CMA	571	621	569

2003			
Average Hours /Individual	Total	Visible Minority	Non-Visible Minority
CMA	631	631	631
Non-CMA	569	611	567

2002			
Average Hours /Individual	Total	Visible Minority	Non-Visible Minority
CMA	638	633	640
Non-CMA	579	617	578

2001			
Average Hours /Individual	Total	Visible Minority	Non-Visible Minority
CMA	662	665	661
Non-CMA	579	634	577

2000			
Average Hours /Individual	Total	Visible Minority	Non-Visible Minority
CMA	676	689	672
Non-CMA	581	641	580

TABLE 3 Visible Minorities, 2000–2010

Working Age Population				
Year	Average Individual	Visible Minority	Non-Visible Minority	% Difference VM vs. NVM
2010	594	596	593	0.52
2009	590	598	589	1.5
2008	652	672	648	4.0
2007	650	672	646	3.7
2006	644	668	640	4.4
2005	628	644	626	2.9
2004	615	641	611	4.9
2003	604	629	601	4.7
2002	613	632	611	3.4
2001	627	662	621	6.6
2000	636	684	628	8.9
Average Hours	**623**	**645**	**620**	**4.0**
% Difference between visible and non-visible minorities: 4.2%				

TABLE 4 Citizenship Status, 2000–2010

Working Age Population					
Year	Citizen by Birth	Naturalized	Canadian Only	Dual Citizens	% Difference Naturalized vs. Citizen by Birth
2010	593	595	593	597	0.34
2009	588	594	590	594	1.0
2008	647	670	650	668	3.6
2007	645	669	648	667	3.7
2006	639	665	643	661	4.1
2005	624	643	627	640	3.0
2004	609	638	613	635	4.8
2003	599	627	603	622	4.7
2002	607	630	610	627	3.8
2001	619	657	624	654	6.1
2000	625	678	632	672	8.5
Average Hours	**618**	**642**	**621**	**640**	
% Difference naturalized vs. citizens by birth: 4.0%					

TABLE 5 Immigration, 2000–2010

Working Age Population					
Year	Non-Immigrants	Immigrants	10+ Years	Within 10 Years	Within 5 Years
2010	593	595	595	596	597
2009	589	594	594	595	595
2008	647	670	670	670	669
2007	645	669	668	670	669
2006	639	665	665	665	663
2005	624	643	644	643	643
2004	609	638	637	640	640
2003	599	627	626	627	627
2002	609	631	630	631	631
2001	619	657	655	661	661
2000	625	678	674	684	684
Average Hours	**618**	**643**	**642**	**644**	**644**
% Difference recent immigrants (2001–2006) vs. non-immigrants: 4.1%					

TABLE 6 Mother Tongue, 2000–2010

Working Age Population					
Year	Total	English	French	Non-Official Language	French vs. Non-Official
2010	594	593	595	593	-0.34
2009	590	593	581	592	1.9
2008	652	659	623	665	6.7
2007	650	658	615	664	8.0
2006	644	654	604	660	9.3
2005	628	639	592	640	8.1
2004	615	622	583	633	8.6
2003	604	617	559	622	11.3
2002	613	619	590	626	6.1
2001	627	634	589	652	10.7
2000	636	645	585	672	14.9
Average / Individual	**623**	**630**	**592**	**638**	
% Difference between French and non-official language: 7.7%					

Endnote

1 "Core" working age population (ages 15–54) is also at times used by Statistics Canada. We used the 15–64 age-range in order to capture older workers between the ages of 54 and 64.

References

Case Law

Andrews v. Law Society of British Columbia, [1989] 1 S.C.R. 143
Benner v. Canada, [1997] 1 S.C.R. 358
CorbiËre v. Canada, [1999] 2 S.C.R. 203
CSN v. Canada, [2008] 3 S.C.R. 511
Eldridge v. British Columbia, [1997] 3 S.C.R. 624
Haig v. Canada, [1993] 2 S.C.R. 995
Harvey v. New Brunswick, [1996] 2 S.C.R. 876
Law v. Canada, [1999] 1 S.C.R. 497
R. v. Edwards Books and Art, [1986] 2 S.C.R. 713
R. v. Kapp, 2008 SCC 41
R. v. Oakes, [1986] 1 S.C.R. 103
R. v. Turpin, [1989] 1 S.C.R. 1296
Reference re Employment Insurance Act, [2005] 2 S.C.R. 669
RJR MacDonald v. Canada, [1995] 3 S.C.R. 199
TÈtreault-Gadoury v. Canada (Employment and Immigration Commission), [1991] 2 S.C.R. 22
Vriend v. Alberta, [1998] 1 S.C.R. 493
Withler v. Canada (Attorney General), 2011 SCC 12

Legislation

Budget Implementation Act, 2009
Canadian Charter of Rights and Freedoms, 1982
Employment Equity Act, 1995
Employment Insurance Act and Regulations, 1996

Articles and Reports

Aydemir, A. and M. Skuterud. 2005. "Explaining the Deteriorating Entry Earnings of Canada's Immigrant Cohorts: 1966-2000." *Canadian Journal of Economics* 38.2: 641-72.

Basok, T. 2004. "Post National Citizenship, Social Exclusion and Migrants Rights: Mexican Seasonal Workers in Canada." *Citizenship Studies* 8.1: 47-64.

Bishop, G. and D. Burleton. 2009. "Is Canada's Employment Insurance Program Adequate?" *TD Economics Special Report*, April 30. Toronto: TD Economics.

Busby, C. 2008. "Fixing a Persistent Problem: Canada's Regional Pockets of Unemployment." *C.D. Howe e-brief*, October 23. Toronto: C.D. Howe Institute.

Canadian Chamber of Commerce. 2009. *Reforming Canada's Employment Insurance (EI) System*. Ottawa: The Canadian Chamber of Commerce.

Courchene, T.J. and J.R. Allan. September 2009. "A Short History of EI, and a Look at the Road Ahead." *Policy Options*, September, 18-28.

De Silva, A. 1997. "Immigrant Participation in the Unemployment Insurance System." *Canadian Public Policy* 23.4: 375-397.

Elgersma, S. 2007. *Temporary Foreign Workers*. PRB 07-11E. Ottawa: Library of Parliament.

Evans, P.M. 2002. "Downloading the Welfare State, Canadian Style," in *Diminishing Welfare: A Cross-National Study of Social Provision*, ed. G.S. Goldberg and M.G. Rosenthal, 75-102. Westport: Auburn House.

Expert Panel on Older Workers. 2008. "Supporting and Engaging Older Workers in the New Economy." Ottawa: Expert Panel on Older Workers. At http://www.hrsdc.gc.ca/eng/publications_resources/lmp/eow/2008/older_workers_2008.df.

Federation of Canadian Municipalities. 2009. *Immigration and Diversity in Canadian Cities and Communities*. Ottawa: Federation of Canadian Municipalities.

Fudge, J. and F. MacPhail. 2009. "The Temporary Foreign Worker Program in Canada: Low Skilled Workers an Extreme Form of Flexible Labor." *Comparative Labor Law and Policy Journal*, 31: 101-39.

Green, D. and C. Worswick. 2004. "Earnings of Immigrant Men in Canada: The Roles of Labour Market Entry Effects and Returns to Foreign Experience" in *Canadian Immigration: Economic Evidence for a Dynamic Policy Environment*, ed. T. McDonald, E. Ruddick, A. Sweetman, and C. Worswick, 77-110. Montreal and Kingston: McGill Queen's University Press, Queen's Policy Studies Series.

Hennebry, J.L. and K. Preibisch. 2010. "A Model for Managed Migration? Re-Examining Best Practices in Canada's Seasonal Agricultural Worker Program." *International Migration (early view)* no. doi:10.1111/j.1468 2435.2009.00598.x. At http://onlinelibrary.wiley.com/doi/10.1111/j.1468-2435.2009.00598.x/abstract.

Human Resources and Skills Development Canada (HRSDC). 2000. "Backgrounder: Employment Insurance Regional Boundaries." At http://www.rhdcc-hrsdc.gc.ca/eng/cs/comm/news/2000/000218_e.shtml.

——. 2004. "EI Monitoring and Assessment Report." Ottawa: HRSDC.

——. 2009. "EI Monitoring and Assessment Report." At http://www.hrsdc.gc.ca/eng/employment/ei/reports/eimar_2009/index.shtml.

Lin, Z. 1998. "Employment Insurance in Canada: Policy Changes." *Statistics Canada Perspectives*, Summer 1998: 42-47.

Mahon, R. 2008. "Varieties of Liberalism: Canadian Social Policy from the 'Golden Age' to the Present." *Social Policy and Administration* 42.4: 342-61.

Medow, J. 2011. *Hidden Regional Differentiation: EI and Unequal Federal*

Support for Low Income Workers. Toronto: Mowat Centre EI Task Force.

Mendelson, M., K. Battle and S. Torjman. 2009. "Canada's Shrunken Safety Net: Employment Insurance in the Great Recession." *Caledon Commentary*, April. Ottawa: Caledon Institute of Social Policy.

Nakache, D. and P.J. Kinoshita. 2010. "The Canadian Temporary Foreign Worker Program: Do Short-Term Economic Needs Prevail Over Human Rights Concerns?" *IRPP Study*, 5. Montreal: IRPP.

Neill, R.F. 2009. "Using a Wrench as a Hammer: Why EI is the Wrong Tool to Respond to Loss of Income in an Economic Downturn." *AIMS Commentary*, May. Halifax: Atlantic Institute for Market Studies.

Picot, G. and A. Sweetman. 2005. "The Deteriorating Economic Welfare of Immigrants and Possible Causes: Update 2005." *Analytical Studies Branch Research Paper Series*. Ottawa: Statistics Canada.

Reitz, J.D. 2001. "Immigrant Success in the Knowledge Economy: Institutional Change and the Immigrant Experience in Canada, 1970-1995." *Journal of Social Issues* 57.3: 577-611.

——. "Social Risks for Newcomers to Canada: Issues Respecting the Role of Government in Ontario." Research Paper No. 11, Panel on the Role of Government in Ontario. At http://www.law-lib.utoronto.ca/investing/research_papers.htm.

Reitz, J.D. and R. Banerjee. 2007. "Racial cohesion, social cohesion and policy issues in Canada." In *Belonging? Diversity, recognition and shared citizenship in Canada*, ed. T.J. Courchene, K. Banting, and L. Seidle, 489-545. Montreal: Institute for Research on Public Policy.

Shields, J. 2004. "No Safe Haven: Work, Welfare and the Growth of Immigrant Exclusion." In *Immigrants, Welfare Reform, and the Poverty of Policy*, ed. P. Kretsedemas and A. Aparicio, 35-60. Westport: Praeger.

Siklos, P. and W. Marr. 1998. "The Unemployment Insurance Compensation Usage of Canada' Immigrants in Selected Provinces, 1981-1988." *Journal of Population Economics* 11.1:127-47.

Statistics Canada. 2003. "Canada's Ethnocultural Portrait: The Changing Mosaic." Ottawa: Statistics Canada.

——. 2007. "Immigration in Canada: A Portrait of the Foreign-Born Population, 2006 Census." Ottawa: Statistics Canada.

——. 2010. "CANSIM Summary Tables." At http://www40.statcan.ca/l01/cst01/labor89a-eng.htm, and http://www40.statcan.ca/l01/cst01/LABOR92A-eng.htm. Ottawa: Statistics Canada.

Sweetman, A. 2001. "Immigrants and Employment Insurance." In *Essays on the Repeat Use of Unemployment Insurance*, eds. Saul Schwartz and Abdurrahman Aydemir, 123-54. Ottawa: Social Research and Development Corporation.

Van Audenrode, M., A-A. Fournier, N. Havet, and J. Royer. 2005. *Employment Insurance in Canada and International Comparison*. Montreal: Groupe d'analyse.

Chapter 9

The Regionalized Aspects of EI and Internal Migration in Canada

Kathleen M. Day and Stanley L. Winer

1 Introduction

Over the past four decades, empirical researchers have repeatedly tried to find evidence that regionalized aspects of public policy in Canada blunt the tendency for people to move from economically disadvantaged to relatively more advantaged places. The seminal academic impetus for these endeavours was Thomas Courchene's (1970) study, which suggested that public support of various kinds for more disadvantaged regions retards economic development and regional convergence by reducing the migration of labour out of the less prosperous provinces.

The regionalized nature of the generosity of the unemployment insurance system is one of the policies that is often pointed to in this respect, and it is easy to see why.[1] Consider, for example, the stylized facts presented in Table 1. Panel A of the table, for 1978–1996, shows how the generosity of the Unemployment Insurance (UI) program, as it was then called, varied regionally, as measured by minimum weeks required to qualify for insurance payments (MIN) and weeks of benefits to which a person with MIN weeks of employment would be entitled (MINWKS).[2] MIN tends to vary directly and MINWKS inversely (though not perfectly so in either case) with average weekly wages.

In 1996 some important adjustments were made to the unemployment insurance system, and its official name was changed to Employment Insurance (EI). As indicated in panel B of Table 1, since 1996 qualification for insurance benefits depends upon hours of work instead of weeks of work, a more stringent requirement for many part-time workers than the previous one. However, the table also shows that the pattern of regional variation observed in the post-1996 system remains similar to that of the earlier period, with qualifying requirements tending to be less stringent and weeks of benefits longer in the higher unemployment provinces. And so the same concern that regional variation in program generosity induces inefficiencies in the allocation of labour across the country applies to the reformed insurance system.

The purpose of this chapter is to review and critically assess empirical research on the relationship between internal migration and the

TABLE 1 Some Stylized Facts Concerning Earnings and Unemployment Insurance in the Canadian Federation

PANEL A: 1978–1996			
Province	Ave. Weekly Earnings (AWE)[1] (Current $)	MIN[2] (Weeks)	MINWKS[3] (weeks)
NL	418	10	39
PE	363	10	38
NS	391	11	35
NB	397	11	36
QC	429	11	34
ON	453	13	26
MB	401	14	25
SK	396	15	22
AB	446	14	25
BC	458	13	31
AVERAGE	415	12.2	31.1
CV[5]	0.07	0.15	0.20
CORR with AWE[6]		0.36	-0.35

PANEL B: 1997–2008				
Province	Ave. Weekly Earnings (AWE) (Current $)	MINH[4] (Hours)	MINH[4] (Weeks)	MINWKS[3] (weeks)
NL	640	420	11	32
PE	570	426	12	29
NS	613	475	13	24
NB	620	461	12	24
QC	659	496	13	23
ON	735	610	16	18
MB	631	621	17	17
SK	642	650	18	16
AB	733	624	17	17
BC	695	560	15	20
AVERAGE	654	534	14.4	21.8
CV[5]	0.08	0.17	0.17	0.25
CORR with AWE[6]			0.53	-0.58

1. Average weekly earnings data are rounded to the nearest integer.
2. MIN is minimum weeks required to qualify for benefits under Unemployment Insurance.
3. MINWKS is weeks of insurance benefits for a person with MIN or MINH weeks of employment.

(continued on next page)

4. MINH is minimum hours required to qualify for benefits under Employment Insurance (converted to its equivalent in weeks assuming a work week of 37 hours in the fourth column of the table).
5. CV is the coefficient of variation.
6. CORR is the coefficient of correlation.

TABLE 2 Changes to Regional Extended Benefit Provision

Date of Legislation	Regionally Extended Benefit Provision
***UI Act* of 1971**	Introduction of regional extended benefit as fifth phase of benefits. Individuals eligible to receive regional extended benefits if the regional unemployment rate was at least 4 per cent AND at least 1 percentage point higher than the national rate. Eligibility for these benefits was determined after all other benefits had been exhausted, and was continually re-evaluated from week to week. The maximum number of weeks or regional extended benefit was 18.
1977 Amendments	Number of benefit phases reduced to three. Two weeks of regional extended benefit for every half percentage point by which the regional unemployment rate exceeds 4.0 per cent, up to a maximum of 32 weeks.
1990 Amendments	Single benefit schedule. Table 2 of Schedule relates weeks of benefits to regional unemployment rate
1994 Amendments	Two weeks of regional extended benefit for every percentage point by which regional unemployment rate exceeds 4 per cent. Weeks of benefits range from 14 to 50 weeks.
***EI Act* of 1996**	Schedule I of Act relates weeks of benefits to hours of insurable employment and regional unemployment, with weeks of regular benefits ranging from 14 to 45 weeks
2009 Amendments	Across-the-board increase in benefits of five weeks between 1 March 2009 and 12 September 2010. Weeks or regular benefits range from 19 to 49 weeks.
2 September 2010	Return to 1996 schedule of benefits

regional variation that has long characterized the generosity of Canada's unemployment insurance system. Such an empirical relationship is a prerequisite for any claim that the insurance system is responsible for misallocation of labour resources across the country. The extent to which the insurance system "distorts" the regional allocation of labour is identified by the Mowat Centre EI Task Force (Mowat 2010, 5) as a key issue, along with associated questions about interregional equity in benefit generosity (p. 7).[3]

The chapter proceeds as follows. In the second section, we discuss from a theoretical perspective why we should expect regional variation in insurance generosity to alter interregional migration decisions and to reduce national economic wellbeing. In section three we introduce additional details concerning the regionalized nature of the insurance system in Canada. Section four discusses the way in which empirical researchers have tried to study the consequences for migration of the regional variation in program generosity that we document, and summarizes the key empirical findings of the Canadian literature. Then, in section five, we present our assessment of the "bottom line" of this work.

To anticipate our conclusion, we can say that on balance there is no evidence that regional variation in the unemployment insurance system has altered internal migration patterns in Canada in a substantial manner. Simulations based on empirical estimates suggest that even the complete elimination of the legislated regional variation in the system would not be a large enough shock to have an important effect on regional labour markets. This conclusion implies that if a change in the degree of regional variation in the Employment Insurance system is contemplated, justification for such a change is not to be found in the removal of incentives for people to remain where the generosity of the program is relatively great.

2 Why Might Regional Differences in EI Alter Internal Migration?

If individual migration decisions depended solely on earned incomes or labour productivities in any region or province, regional differences in the generosity of unemployment insurance benefits would have no direct effect on migration. People would tend to move to places where their earned incomes were greatest, a process that would lead towards equalization of real wages and labour productivities across regions and provinces. Wages will be bid up in places of net in-migration, and down where people are leaving, until real wages and thus marginal labour productivities are more or less the same (adjusted for migration costs). As a result, "free" migration, that is, migration that is unaffected by any government policy, would tend to maximize the contribution of labour services to national economic output and, at the same time, to equalize earned incomes across the country.

However, a more complete view of the migration process must allow for economic migration between regions that depends on interregional differences in *expected comprehensive incomes*, where *comprehensive income* in any place includes, in addition to earned income or wages related to productivity, personal taxes paid, transfers received and the imputed value of public services provided by any level of government.[4] Guesses about the probability of employment in each labour market will also enter into the calculation of expected income.

Differences across regions in comprehensive incomes may arise from an unemployment insurance system that is more generous in some places than in others, or from differences in tax burdens or in valued public services. Such differentials will lead people to migrate for reasons that are not directly related to real wages or labour productivity alone. Migration will then lead to the equalization of expected comprehensive incomes rather than of earned incomes, as wages adjust upwards or downwards with in- and out-migration to compensate for differences across the country in the relationship between individuals and the public sector. As a result, total and average output and income in the country as a whole will be reduced because the tendency of unrestricted migration to equalize real wages and marginal productivities across locations is short-circuited. And since earned incomes are not equalized, interregional disparity in earned incomes must also be increased.

In his seminal work on policy-induced migration, Courchene (1970, 1978) pointed to the regionalized structure of the unemployment insurance system, which provides greater support to people in more depressed places, and to federal grants like Equalization that go only to poorer provinces, as policies that create incentives to remain in poorer regions even though their earned income would be higher if people moved to a relatively more prosperous province like Ontario.[5] For this reason, he referred to the relationship between the public sector, migration and economic welfare outlined here as the *transfer dependency hypothesis*.

As an empirical statement, this hypothesis may be true. But it is worth pointing out that in principle at least, the same sort of reasoning that underlies Courchene's analysis can be used to argue that higher rather than lower earned incomes in the poorer provinces will result from government policies that favour them. Consider, for example, the case of people from the Atlantic Provinces who are attracted to Ontario because of the fiscal benefits they can enjoy there in the form of better schools accompanied by lower taxes, a situation made possible by the larger and richer Ontario population.[6] The resulting migration adds to the Ontario labour force and depresses the real wage and the marginal productivity of labour in Ontario. Workers will continue to migrate to Ontario even if the real wage is less than in the Atlantic region as long as they receive compensatory benefits in the form of better or cheaper public services. They will continue to migrate until the resulting decline in the real wage in Ontario just compensates for the advantages that in-migrants receive from the relatively richer Ontario public sector.

In the Atlantic Provinces, to continue this example, the outflow of people leads to a reduced supply of labour and thus an increase in the real wage and in the marginal product of labour. This increase in the real wage compensates those who stay for the disadvantages of the less generous fiscal treatment that they receive from Atlantic governments. The overall result of migration in this case is a situation in which the real wage and marginal productivity of labour are higher in the Atlantic region than in Ontario.

In this example, national output and average earned income in the country as a whole could be increased by moving workers out of Ontario and *back* into the Atlantic region. In such a situation, a federal unemployment insurance system that provided more generous benefits to residents of Atlantic Canada could help to offset the effects of the greater net fiscal benefits provided by Ontario's government.

It is important to keep in mind that regardless of which case appears to be the most applicable, the relevance to policy-making of both Courchene's original view and the one just outlined hinge on the actual strength of the relationship between the public components of expected comprehensive incomes and internal migration flows. Many factors besides public policy differentials will also be important for prospective migrants, not the least of which are the probabilities attached by migrants to various components of comprehensive income, some of which will vary with their labour market status and the state of regional economies. Migration costs are also important and, if substantial, such costs may make even large differentials in the pubic components of expected comprehensive incomes irrelevant. In the end, the matter *is* an empirical one.

In order to resolve the empirical issue of concern in this chapter, we need to look at the results of empirical studies dealing with the relationship between regional variation in the generosity of unemployment insurance and internal migration. Before we turn to that literature, it is worth considering what the relationship might look like if the provisions that governed access to insurance benefits and benefit periods were in fact uniform across the country. Could there still be any connection left between the insurance system and internal migration to be uncovered by empirical research?

The answer is that even in this special case there may still be a relationship between the unemployment insurance system and internal migration through the implicit subsidization of job search activities. The reporting requirements of the insurance system do not prevent claimants from travelling to look for work in other cities or provinces. This activity is costly and time consuming, and by offering financial support, the insurance system may make recipients more mobile than if they had received no support while unemployed.

The actual effect of insurance on job search will depend on what might be called the moral hazard effect of insurance payments on job search, versus the income effect. By the moral hazard effect we mean the tendency for an individual insurance recipient to look only in their present location while searching for a job, rather than moving somewhere else where job prospects are better. (Exiting the labour force is not permitted under the unemployment insurance rules.) Income is also higher with insurance payments, and on this account job search in other places is more affordable and for this reason may occur to a greater extent.[7]

The strength of the moral hazard effect relative to the income effect will depend on the value of "location" in individual preferences, just as will the effect on migration of regional differences in comprehensive incomes. Some people with a strong preference for a particular location may stay put no matter what, while others may be footloose. So this issue is also empirical. We should also note that both the job search effects of unemployment insurance on location and the effects of differentials in comprehensive income will be observed at the same time in the same data. To the best of our knowledge, no one has succeeded in separating out these effects from the overall migration response to the unemployment insurance system.

There may also be a general equilibrium effect of unemployment insurance that involves interregional migration even if the generosity of the system is uniform. Unemployment insurance has a vital role to play in maintaining aggregate demand in times of recession. There is no particular reason why such an effect will be felt uniformly across regions or provinces. The general effects of insurance payments on aggregate demand may precipitate internal migration flows by boosting demand in some regions more than in others along with the associated employment prospects. This effect will also be embedded in the observed response of migration to expected comprehensive income differentials. It is fair to say that distinguishing the general equilibrium effects from the other effects we have discussed is difficult and has not, to our knowledge, been attempted.

3 Regional Variation in Unemployment Insurance Benefits in Canada

Before moving on to a detailed review of the empirical research on the relationship of unemployment insurance and migration, it is helpful to look more carefully at the nature and evolution of regional variation in insurance benefits in Canada. When unemployment insurance was first introduced in Canada in 1941, only certain types of employment were covered and there was no explicit regional variation in the single type of benefit available. Today, virtually all Canadian employees may be eligible not only for regular benefits, but also for a variety of special benefits, including fishing benefits, sickness benefits, maternity leave, parental benefits and compassionate care benefits.

Although an unemployment insurance system with no explicit regional differentiation in its legislated provisions may have regional effects due to differences in regional economic structure—fishing benefits are a case in point—from the perspective of interprovincial migration the parameters of the system that explicitly vary across regions likely matter most.[8] In Canada, such variation exists only in the category of benefits known as "regular" benefits—that is, in benefits associated with a loss of employment. The massive overhaul of the system in 1971 introduced a regional extended benefit that directly linked benefits received to regional unemployment rates. Under this provision, regular benefits could be extended by up to 18 weeks, depending on the relationship between the regional and national rates of unemployment. Sixteen UI regions were defined by the 1971 Act, some of which corresponded to entire provinces.

Since regionally extended benefits were first introduced in 1971, they have been modified several times, as Table 2 below indicates. The requirement that regionally extended benefits be based on a comparison between national and regional unemployment rates was eliminated as early as 1977, to be replaced by a calculation based solely on the level of the regional unemployment rate. In late 1990, the calculation of weeks of benefits was further simplified by replacing the multi-phase benefit system that had been in place since 1971 with a single table that related weeks of benefits to qualifying weeks of employment and regional unemployment rates.

The *Employment Insurance Act* of 1996 constitutes one of the most important reforms of the Canadian unemployment insurance system since 1971, but it did not greatly change the nature of regional variation in benefits. Under EI there remains a single table of benefits that relates insurable employment, now measured in hours, and regional unemployment rates to weeks of benefits. According to this table, benefits range from 14 to 45 weeks. With the exception of the brief period from 1 March 2009 to 12 September 2010, this table has remained in effect since the passing of the 1996 Act.[9]

Entrance requirements as well as benefits once qualified also vary across the country. The "variable entrance requirement," or VER, was first introduced in 1977. The VER related weeks of insurable employment required to qualify for benefits to the regional unemployment rate. As shown in Table 3, under the initial incarnation of the VER the minimum weeks of work required to qualify for benefits could differ across unemployment insurance regions by up to four weeks, with fewer qualifying weeks required in high unemployment regions. In 1990 the maximum possible discrepancy between regions increased to ten weeks, only to be reduced to eight weeks in 1994.

A variable entrance requirement remains a feature of the EI system introduced in 1996, although the entrance requirements are now expressed in terms of hours rather than weeks of work. Consequently, it is difficult to directly compare the generosity of the VER under the old and the new systems. At most one can say that under the reformed system, it takes

TABLE 3 Variable Entrance Requirement, 1977–2010

Regional Unemployment Rate	Weeks of Insurable Employment Required to Qualify for Benefits
As of 4 December 1977[1]:	
6 % and under	14
over 6% to 7%	13
over 7% to 8%	12
over 8% to 9%	11
over 9%	10
As of 11February 1990:	
0% to 100%	14
As of 18 November 1990[2]:	
6 % and under	20
over 6% to 7%	19
over 7% to 8%	18
over 8% to 9%	17
over 9% to 10%	16
over 10% to 11%	15
over 11% to 12%	14
over 12% to 13%	13
over 13% to 14%	12
over 14% to 15%	11
over 15%	10
3 July 1994 to 31 December 1996:[3]	
6 % and under	20
over 6% to 7%	19
over 7% to 8%	18
over 8% to 9%	17
over 9% to 10%	16
over 10% to 11%	15
over 11% to 12%	14
over 12% to 13%	13
over 13%	12
As of 1 January 1997:[4]	***Hours* of insurable employment required to qualify for benefits**
6 % and under	700
over 6% to 7%	665
over 7% to 8%	630
over 8% to 9%	595
over 9% to 10%	560
over 10% to 11%	525
over 11% to 12%	490
over 12% to 13%	455
over 13%	420

(continued on next page)

(TABLE 3 cont.)

1. **Source:** Dingledine (1981), page 92
2. **Source:** Table 1 of Schedule, *Unemployment Insurance Act* 1971, revised 1990. See also McFarlane et el. (1992).
3. **Source:** Table 1 of Schedule, *Unemployment Insurance Act*, 1971, revised 1993–94. See also Rudner (1995).
4. **Source:** Section 7 of the *Employment Insurance Act* of 1996.

considerably longer for many part-time workers in all regions to qualify for benefits.

In order to provide a more concrete picture of the disincentive to migrate that is created by the insurance system, we compute what the minimum qualifying requirement, and weeks of benefits for minimal qualifiers, would have been for individuals in each province under the simplifying assumption that each entire province constitutes one unemployment insurance region.[10] So that we can compare qualifying requirements under UI and EI, we convert the hours required under EI to weeks assuming a work week of 37 hours, which is equal to the Canadian average value of hours of work per week over the 1987–2009 period.[11] Then we compare graphically the results of these calculations for a high unemployment province, Newfoundland and Labrador, to those for a province that has generally enjoyed low unemployment rates, Ontario.

As Figure 1 shows, until the introduction of the VER in 1977 there was no difference between the two provinces in the minimum qualifying requirement for benefits. Post-1977 there was very little variation in the minimal qualifying requirement in Newfoundland and Labrador, because the unemployment rate remained persistently high in that province.[12] In Ontario, generally lower provincial unemployment rates caused the minimal qualifying requirement to remain above that in Newfoundland and Labrador except during the recession of the early 1980s. After 1984 the gap between the two provinces tended to increase for much of the period, with the exception of a brief decline between 2000 and 2003. At its peak in 1998–1999, the gap in qualifying weeks between the two provinces amounted to approximately eight weeks (or 280 hours).

FIGURE 1 Minimal Qualifying Requirement for UI/EI 1966–2009

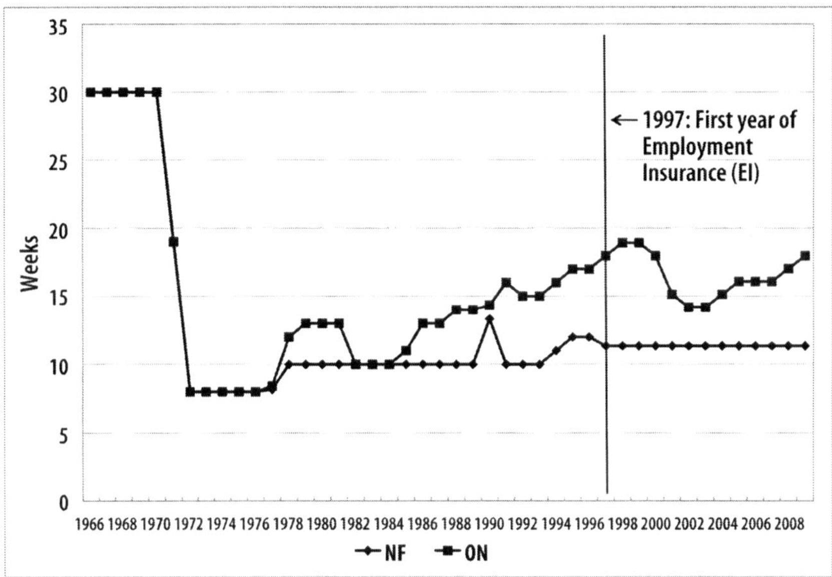

FIGURE 2 Maximum Weeks of Benefits for a Minimal UI/EI Qualifier 1966–2009

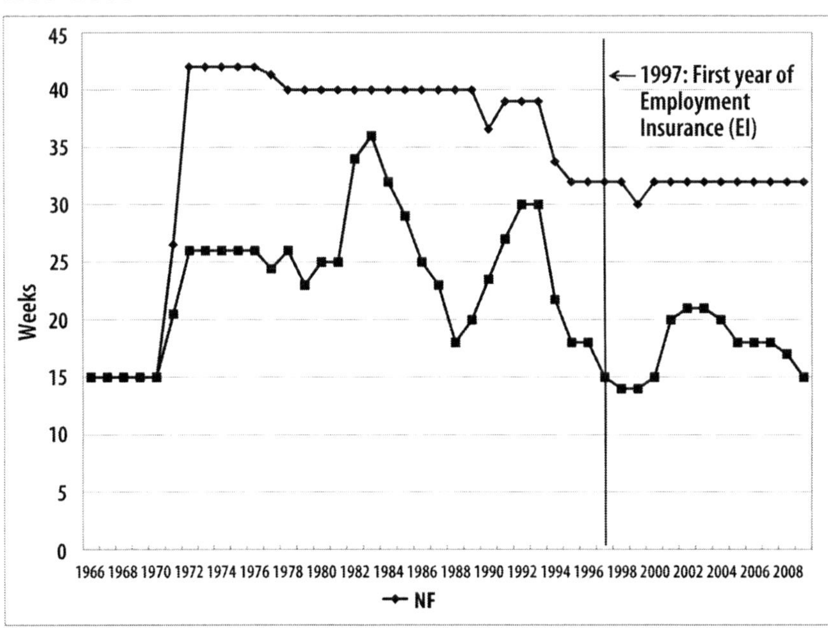

Figure 2 shows that not only was it easier for the typical Newfoundland worker than for the typical Ontario worker to qualify for benefits, a Newfoundlander who met the minimal qualifying requirement was also entitled to quite a few more weeks of benefits than his or her Ontario counterpart. In the initial years of regional extended benefits, from 1972–1981, the difference in weeks of benefit entitlement ranged from 14 to 17 weeks in favour of Newfoundland. Only during post-recessionary periods, such as 1982–1984 and 1992–1993, did the difference in weeks of benefits fall below ten weeks. In 2009 the difference in weeks of benefits for minimally-qualified workers was 17 weeks.

Note that neither figure shows any striking change in the gap between Ontario and Newfoundland as a result of the move from UI to EI in January of 1997. While this lack of any obvious impact may be the result of the assumption of a 37-hour standard work week, using province-specific values of average hours worked per week is unlikely to make much difference. In 1997, average hours per week were 37.2 in Ontario and 37.9 in Newfoundland. Since then, average hours worked per week have tended to increase slightly in Newfoundland and decrease slightly in Ontario.[13]

In describing regional variation in the unemployment insurance system, it is also important to point out that even a low unemployment province such as Ontario includes some high unemployment EI regions where individuals' minimal qualifying requirements and benefit entitlements are similar to those displayed for Newfoundland and Labrador. Furthermore, when it comes to migration decisions, the generosity of the unemployment insurance system is only one of many factors that individuals will take into account. Indeed, individuals who are already employed and have low expectations of being unemployed in the future may place little weight on unemployment insurance when deciding whether or not to move, and where to move to.

Finally, we should recognize that due to differences between regional economies, certain types of benefits—for example fishing benefits, which were first introduced in 1957—are unevenly distributed across the country and tend to be more heavily utilized in high-unemployment provinces. Fishing benefits remain a feature of the current EI system, and although there is no regional differentiation in EI provisions with respect to fishing benefits, they will as a matter of course be unevenly distributed across the country because the fishing industry is concentrated on the East and West coasts.

4 What has Empirical Research on Canada Found?

Studies of the effects of unemployment insurance on internal migration in Canada have mostly focussed on interprovincial migration, due to a lack of data on intra-provincial mobility. In all of these studies, some measure of migration appears on the left-hand side of the empirical model, while various factors believed to influence migration appear on the right-hand side of the model. There, however, the similarities end. Some studies use time-series data to study migration trends over long periods of time, while others use large microdata sets that generally span just a few years. Some studies estimate simple linear models of migration, while others estimate more complicated nonlinear ones. And different studies include differing sets of explanatory variables or different measures of unemployment insurance generosity. In this section of the chapter, we limit ourselves to outlining the important features of the relevant studies and their results. In the next section we evaluate their sometimes contradictory findings, and draw some general conclusions regarding the relationship between unemployment insurance and internal migration in Canada.[14]

Before looking at the individual studies themselves, a few general comments about data and statistical models are in order. First of all, only two of the existing Canadian studies employ data for the post-1996 period. In other words, most of the existing empirical evidence pertains to the old UI system, not to the current EI system. Nonetheless, as we have suggested above, since the changes to the system in terms of the migration incentives it creates are not substantial, we think that studies of UI are just as relevant to the current policy debate as studies of EI.

Second, both aggregate time-series data and microdata can provide important insights—albeit somewhat different ones—into the effect of unemployment insurance on migration flows. Since aggregate time series data generally cover a longer period, they can provide more insight into the effects of major changes in the insurance system. Moreover, the representation of fiscal structure in these studies is often more sophisticated. Microdata sets, on the other hand, allow researchers to control for a wider variety of individual characteristics that may also influence migration decisions.

Third, while no two migration studies include exactly the same set of explanatory variables on the right-hand side of the migration equation, there does exist a certain amount of agreement regarding the determinants of migration. For example, incomes and employment prospects in the sending and receiving regions, and moving costs (frequently proxied by distance), are generally considered relevant. Some studies also include measures of public goods and services available in different provinces, as well as taxes and transfer payments.[15]

Fourth, the choice of statistical model—linear or nonlinear—often depends on the nature of the data available. In linear models, the dependent variable is either a migration rate, or an actual gross or net migration flow. Such models can only be estimated using aggregate data (time series or census data), because migration rates and flows do not exist for individuals. Instead, researchers using microdata estimate nonlinear models such as logit and probit models, in which the dependent variable equals one if the individual moved and zero otherwise. Conditional logit models are multinomial versions of the logit model that are well-suited to migration modelling because they apply to situations where individuals face more than two options, such as a choice among the ten Canadian provinces. These models have a special property that allows them to be estimated relatively simply using aggregate time series data as well as individual data, and in comparison to simple linear models they ensure that the characteristics of all possible destination choices are taken into account. Table 4, which summarizes the important features of the studies we review, indicates which type of model is used by each study.[16]

Finally, when it comes to measuring the migration effects of unemployment insurance in Canada, all studies face the same major challenges: how to capture the relevant features of the system using a small number of explanatory variables, and how to distinguish the effect of regional differences in benefit provisions from the effect of differences in unemployment rates. Regional differences in unemployment rates lead to differences in benefit payments even in the absence of the variable entrance requirement and regionally extended benefits. In the following discussion, we shall pay particular attention to the methods researchers have used to deal with these two issues.

Since the focus of this chapter is on the impact of insurance benefits on internal migration, a useful way to classify the studies is in terms of the measure of insurance benefits included in the empirical model. In this respect, the twelve existing studies can be divided into four groups: (i) those that construct an index of unemployment insurance generosity, (ii) those that use a dummy variable to identify individuals who received benefits in the year prior to moving, (iii) those that adopt a structural approach to incorporating parameters of the unemployment insurance system, and (iv) those that employ more than one of the above approaches. Each of these groups of studies is examined in turn.

A Studies that Use Indices of Unemployment Insurance Generosity

The earliest studies of the effect of unemployment insurance generosity on interprovincial migration used relatively simple indices of generosity in their empirical models, whether linear or nonlinear. For example, Courchene (1970) uses the ratio of total unemployment insurance benefit payments to total earned income in each province in each year. The estimated coefficient of this variable supports his hypothesis that more generous unemployment insurance benefits tend to impede out-migration, holding unemployment rates in both the origin and destination provinces constant.

Boadway and Green (1981), Shaw (1985, 1986), and Winer and Gauthier (1982) follow Courchene's lead by defining measures of unemployment insurance generosity that reflect the actual rate at which benefits replace earnings. In these three studies, generosity is measured by dividing a measure of average weekly insurance benefits by average weekly earnings. All three

TABLE 4 Summary of Empirical Studies of the Effect of UI and EI on Interprovincial Migration in Canada[1]

Study	Data	Empirical Model	UI/EI Measure	Results
Courchene (1970)	Gross interprovincial migration rates of family allowance recipients, 1952–1967	Linear	Ratio of total UI benefits to earned income in the sending province (two equations only)	Higher UI benefits in origin have significant negative effect on out-migration
Boadway and Green (1981)	Net migration to Newfoundland, 1951–1978	Linear	Average weekly UI benefits per claim divided by average weekly earnings in Newfoundland	Increases in UI/EI measure significantly increase net migration to Newfoundland
Winer and Gauthier (1982)	Gross interprovincial migration rates of family allowance recipients, 1951–1978 Gross interprovincial migration rates of individuals in 10 per cent sample of income tax records, 1967–1977	Linear Conditional logit	Ratio of average weekly UI payments to average weekly wages in origin and destination Origin and destination values of index of UI generosity in (1)	More generous UI impedes out-migration and encourages in-migration in 10 of 18 equations Out-migration from Atlantic provinces negatively related to increases in generosity of UI in Atlantic region, positively related to increases in generosity of UI benefits elsewhere

(continued on next page)

(TABLE 4 cont.)

Study	Data	Empirical Model	UI/EI Measure	Results
Shaw (1985, 1986)	Gross migration rates between 17 census metropolitan areas, 1961, 1971, 1976, and 1981 censuses	Conditional logit	Average weekly payment of UI benefits in province divided by average weekly wage in CMA (generosity of UI), ratio of total weeks of UI benefits paid to total number of weeks of unemployment in province (probability of receiving UI)	Increased generosity of UI benefits in origin CMA significantly reduces out-migration In post-1971 sample, generosity of UI benefits in destination CMA also has positive and significant effect on out-migration
Liaw and Ledent (1987)	Gross interprovincial migration rates, 1961–1983	Nested logit	UI benefits per unemployed person in destination relative to unemployment benefits per employed person in origin	Relative unemployment benefits has no significant effect on out-migration from region; higher relative unemployment benefits in destination province is significant deterrent to in-migration
Day (1992)	Gross interprovincial migration rates, 1962–1981	Conditional logit	UI benefits constitute part of income in state of world in which individual is unemployed and covered by UI	UI benefits have significant impact through composite "price" variable: higher UI benefits in province encourage in-migration

(continued on next page)

(TABLE 4 cont.)

Study	Data	Empirical Model	UI/EI Measure	Results
Osberg, Gordon and Lin (1994)	Longitudinal sample of men residing in the Atlantic and Prairie provinces from the LMAS, 1986–1987	Bivariate probit	Indicator of receipt of UI benefits the year before moving	Receipt of UI does not significantly affect interregional migration.
Lin (1995)	Longitudinal data from the LMAS, 1988–1990	Conditional logit	Indicator of receipt of UI benefits the year before moving	UI benefits have significant positive impact on mobility only for adult women in 1990.
Audas and McDonald (2003)	Longitudinal sample from SLID, 1993–1999	Probit models of interprovincial migration and migration between EI regions; some models estimated using Instrumental Variables methods	Indicator of receipt of UI benefits the year before moving; region-specific UI benefit generosity (minimum weeks plus maximum weeks of UI benefit available); interaction between regional unemployment rate and indicator of post-1996 UI reform.	Receipt of UI/EI benefits inhibits migration of people who are moderately attached to labour market 1996 reforms increase mobility of those with low or no labour market

(continued on next page)

(TABLE 4 cont.)

Study	Data	Empirical Model	UI/EI Measure	Results
Finnie (2004)	LAD, 1982–1995	Panel logit	Indicator of receipt of UI benefits the year before moving	Receipt of UI associated with increase in out-migration of prime-aged men and women, and to a lesser extent younger men and women and new entrant women.
Day and Winer (2006, forthcoming)	Migration flows disaggregated by age, sex, and income class derived from income tax records, 1968–1996	Conditional logit	UI parameters enter "income" and "leisure" variables based on four states of the world, two of which involve receipt of UI benefits	UI significantly reduces out-migration through composite variables, but effects do not seem to be large in magnitude.
Ostrovsky, Hou and Picot (2008)	LAD combined with immigration records, 1996–2005	Multinomial logit (do not move, move to Alberta, move to another province)	Indicator of receipt of UI benefits the year before moving	Receipt of UI has significant positive impact on migration to Alberta of immigrants and long-time residents of Canada; no impact on moves elsewhere

studies find some evidence that increased unemployment insurance generosity, as measured in this fashion, in the origin province (or census metropolitan area in Shaw's study) reduces out-migration, while increased generosity in the destination increases in-migration. However, Winer and Gauthier (1982) find that their results are not consistent across all their Courchene-type equations; for example, for Ontario and the western provinces increased unemployment insurance generosity in the origin appears to *increase* out-migration rather than decrease it, while increased generosity elsewhere *reduces* out-migration instead of increasing it. For Newfoundland, though, the results are consistent with Courchene's hypothesis that more generous unemployment insurance benefits in a province will increase in-migration to and reduce out-migration from that province.

Both Shaw (1985, 1986) and Winer and Gauthier (1982) also extend Courchene's simple model, by including other measures of unemployment insurance. Shaw adds to his model a measure of the probability of receiving unemployment insurance benefits, defined for each province as total weeks of benefits paid divided by total weeks of unemployment. In addition, in an attempt to discern the effects of the 1971 reforms that introduced regional extended benefits, he divides his Census data into two subsamples, one covering the pre-1971 period and the other covering the post-1971 period. While his measure of the probability of receiving unemployment insurance benefits never has a statistically significant coefficient, his unemployment insurance generosity measure for the province of origin has a negative and significant coefficient that more than doubled in magnitude after 1971. Similarly, the coefficient of unemployment generosity in the destination is positive and significant only after 1971. These results suggest not only that more generous benefits in the province of origin inhibit out-migration, holding all else (including unemployment rates and job growth in the origin and destination provinces) constant, but also that the post-1971 increase in generosity of the system magnified this effect.

In their conditional logit models of interprovincial migration for the 1951-1978 period, Winer and Gauthier (1982) use a different index of unemployment insurance generosity designed to incorporate three aspects of the system: the variable entrance requirement, regional extended benefits, and the degree to which eligibility rules are enforced. For province *k*, the measure is defined as follows:

$$\mathrm{UIDEX}_K = \frac{\mathrm{MAX}_K}{\mathrm{MIN}_K} \bullet \frac{\mathrm{CA}_K}{\mathrm{CF}_K},$$

where MAX_k is the maximum number of weeks of benefits to which a person with minimum qualifying weeks is entitled, MIN_k is the minimum number of weeks required to qualify for benefits, CA_k is the number of claims accepted, and CF_k is the number of initial claims filed. Increases in the generosity of the system would lead to increases in the value of this index.

Winer and Gauthier present their results concerning this index in table 4-14 of their study, which indicates that the coefficients of $UIDEX_i$ (origin) and $UIDEX_j$ (destination) are statistically significant with the expected signs in only fourteen of 72 equations. However, in the eight equations explaining out-migration of low-income individuals from the Atlantic Provinces their coefficients are always statistically significant with the expected sign. They thus conclude that the unemployment insurance system did influence the migration decisions of at least this subset of the Canadian population. Their simulation results suggest that the 1971 reforms to the unemployment insurance system reduced out-migration of low-income individuals from Atlantic Canada, but increased migration between the four Atlantic Provinces.

The last study that falls into this category is that of Liaw and Ledent (1987). Although they use a more complex statistical model than the other studies, an extension of the conditional logit model known as the nested logit model, their index of unemployment insurance generosity—the ratio of unemployment insurance benefits per person in the destination to unemployment insurance benefits per person in the origin—is actually simpler than that of Winer and Gauthier. However, they interpret this variable as an indicator of the severity of unemployment in the destination relative to the origin, rather than a measure of unemployment insurance generosity. In their destination choice model they find that this variable has a negative and significant coefficient, implying that the higher the average unemployment insurance benefits in a province relative to those in the province of origin, the less likely it is that individuals will choose to move to that province. However, in their model of the decision to move, which includes the average benefit in the origin only, they find no evidence that the decision to move is affected by unemployment insurance benefits.

B Studies that Use Dummy Variable Indicators of Receipt of Benefits

Dummy variable indicators of receipt of benefits are found only in studies that use microdata. Because such data sets consist of observations on individuals, indices of unemployment insurance generosity that do not vary across individuals cannot be included in a model of migration to be estimated using such data if the number of time periods is short. The problem is that there is then insufficient time-series variation in the data set with which to identify the coefficient of the index variable. Information about the geographic location of the individual is often limited as well, so that geographic variation cannot be counted on to identify the coefficient of an unemployment insurance generosity index either.

However, in the microdata sets researchers have used to study migration, it is often possible to identify individuals who received income from UI or EI in the previous year. Thus all Canadian microdata studies that have examined the impact of these insurance schemes on interprovincial migration in Canada include a dummy variable that is equal to one if the individual received benefits in the year prior to migration, and zero otherwise. Because this variable is independent of the number of weeks of benefits it cannot tell us anything about the effect of regional extended benefits, but it will be affected by the variable entrance requirement since the VER affects the probability of receiving benefits.

The first two microdata studies of interprovincial migration and unemployment insurance in Canada were those of Osberg, Gordon and Lin (1994) and Lin (1995), both of which use data from the Labour Market Activity Survey (LMAS). The first of these studies examines the 1986–1987 period, while the second covers the period 1988–1990. For men, both studies reach the same conclusion: individuals who received unemployment insurance benefits the previous year are no more or less likely to make an interprovincial move than individuals who did not receive benefits. However, Lin found that in 1990 (but not 1989) women who had received benefits in the previous year *were* significantly more likely to move than those who had not received benefits.

Two other studies, by Finnie (2004) and Ostrovsky, Hou and Picot (2008), use panel data from the Longitudinal Administrative Database (LAD) maintained by Statistics Canada. This database is compiled from the tax returns filed by a sample of individual Canadians, and thus contains detailed information about income over a long period of time, but little information about personal characteristics such as level of education. Finnie's analysis covers the period 1982–1995, a relatively long period for a study that uses microdata, and he estimates separate models for men and women in each of four different age groups. His results indicate that after controlling for province of residence before the move, language, size of community, age, family status, earnings, provincial unemployment rate, and year, receipt of unemployment insurance benefits in the previous year has a positive and significant effect on the probability of making an interprovincial move for all groups examined except young men aged 20–24. The magnitude of these effects ranges from an 18 per cent increase in the probability of moving for 45–54 year-old women, to an increase of just 6 per cent for women aged 20–34.

In their study, Ostrovsky, Hou and Picot (2008) examine migration to Alberta from elsewhere in Canada, and focus on the differences between recent immigrants (those who have lived less than 15 years in Canada) and other Canadians over the 1996–2005 period. This study is of interest not just because it includes a variable related to unemployment insurance, but also because it is one of only two that deal with the period after the introduction of the Employment Insurance system. Their initial results for immigrants imply that those who received EI benefits in the year prior to moving were significantly less likely to move to Alberta. However, when they re-estimate their model for immigrants after supplementing the LAD data with information about the immigrant's region of origin and immigration class from Citizenship and Immigration Canada's immigration records, this result changes. After the addition of the new variables to the model, receipt of EI benefits significantly increases the probability that immigrants will move to Alberta. This finding is consistent with their results for the rest of the Canadian population.

C Studies that Adopt a Structural Approach

Two other studies, Day (1992) and Day and Winer (2006, forthcoming), use as their starting point somewhat more rigorous, theoretically consistent approaches to modelling migration in which labour market uncertainty is modelled using an expected utility framework. Both studies assume that individuals contemplating moves face uncertainty about labour market outcomes in each destination. This uncertainty takes the form of different possible states of the world, each of which has a probability attached to it. Individuals are then assumed to choose the destination where their expected utility—that is, the probability-weighted sum of utilities in the different states of the world—is maximized. This approach leads to the construction of explanatory variables that are complex nonlinear functions of incomes and leisure times in the different states of the world. Unemployment insurance enters these variables as a component of income or leisure time in one or more states of the world rather than appearing separately in the estimating equation.[17] Thus, in these models unemployment insurance is assumed to play a statistically significant role if the associated composite variable does.

In the first of these papers, both of which are estimated using time-series data, Day defines three states of the world, two of which involve unemployment. The two unemployment states differ in terms of whether or not the individual is covered by unemployment insurance. The probability of being unemployed in a particular province is measured by the unemployment rate, while the probability of being covered is simply the proportion of the population covered by UI. The question of whether or not one is covered by UI is relevant in this study because the sample period includes nine years prior to 1971, the year coverage was extended to virtually all employed Canadians. Unemployment insurance benefits in each province were also measured in a simple fashion as the average amount of regular benefits paid. Since the coefficient of the relevant composite variable (referred to as "Prices") has the expected positive sign in almost all equations, Day concludes that higher average UI benefits in a particular province will increase in-migration to (and decrease out-migration from) that province.

Day and Winer (2006, forthcoming) extend this approach and apply it to migration data similar to that used by Winer and Gauthier (1982), constructed from tax files for the period 1968–1996. First, they define four different states of the world that can be viewed as involving different degrees of labour market attachment, and hence different degrees of reliance on the unemployment insurance system. This approach allows them to incorporate more features of the UI system in the explanatory variables of their model. For example, unemployment insurance benefits in state 3 (weakly attached to the labour market) depend directly on MIN, the minimal number of weeks required to qualify for benefits, and MINWKS, the maximum weeks of benefits an individual with MIN qualifying weeks can receive. Benefits in state 2 of this model (working just enough to collect benefits for the remainder of the year) also depend on the regional variation in the unemployment insurance system.[18] Since the model assumes that individuals gain utility from leisure time—that is, time spent not working—as well as consumption, the parameters of the UI system enter the model through a composite leisure time variable as well as a composite income variable, both of which are probability-weighted sums.

Day and Winer estimate several specifications of their model for three different income classes, with most results pertaining to the 1974–1996 period. In most specifications and for most subsamples, the composite income variable does have the expected positive and significant coefficient, but the estimated coefficient of the other composite variable is sometimes insignificant or inconsistent with expectations. These inconsistencies are likely due to collinearity between the explanatory variables.

Due to the complex manner in which the UI parameters enter Day and Winer's model, it is not possible to infer their impact directly from the coefficient estimates. However, marginal effect calculations suggest that a decrease in generosity in the form of an increase in MIN in a particular province would reduce the net-in-migration of low- and middle-income individuals to that province.[19] This effect is largest in the Atlantic Provinces, and largest for the middle-income group. The marginal effects of changes in MINWKS are much smaller in magnitude and less clear-cut, in that the sign of the effect on net migration varies across provinces as well as models and income classes.

Day and Winer (2006, forthcoming) also simulate the effects on interprovincial migration of eliminating regional variation in the unemployment insurance *system*. They find that eliminating the variable entrance requirement alone would tend to move people out of the Atlantic region and Quebec, and into Ontario. Elimination of regional extended benefits alone has a similar effect, as does the elimination of all regional variation in the UI system, although the magnitude of the effect varies considerably from one model to another. But they also find that the overall volume of migration (i.e., the number of people who move) is not greatly affected, which means that even the complete elimination of regional variation in the unemployment insurance system is unlikely to have any important consequences for provincial unemployment rates.

D Studies that Use a Combination of Approaches

This final group of studies has just one member: Audas and McDonald (2003). This study uses microdata from the Survey of Labour and Income Dynamics (SLID), which allows Audas and McDonald to examine migration between official unemployment insurance regions, not just provinces. It is also one of only two studies that include the post-1996 period. Audas and McDonald's sample period of 1993–1999 allows them to examine the effects of the switch from UI to EI. Finally, this study goes beyond the dummy variable approach of other microdata studies by including an index of insurance generosity—in this case, the sum of maximum and minimum weeks of benefits in the insurance region[20]—and by using instrumental variables techniques in an attempt to control for the possibility that mobility decisions and past receipt of benefits may depend on the same unobservable factors. Failing to account for this possibility can lead to biased estimates of the coefficient of the receipt of benefits dummy variable.

Another problem addressed by Audas and McDonald, a problem that is encountered in other studies such as Day and Winer (2006, forthcoming) as well, is the correlation that exists between parameters of the insurance system and regional unemployment rates. The dependence of benefits and qualifying requirements on regional unemployment rates guarantees that such a correlation will exist. The existence of this correlation makes it difficult to distinguish statistically the effects on migration of unemployment rates from those of changes in program parameters.[21] Audas and McDonald use two methods of dealing with this problem: the first is to use employment rates and employment growth rates as explanatory variables instead of regional unemployment rates, while the second is to test for changes in the coefficients of unemployment insurance parameters after 1996. The first method will be effective if employment rates and employment growth rates are less highly correlated with unemployment benefits than are unemployment rates, while the second method focuses on the effect of a major change in the system.

Like other researchers, Audas and McDonald estimate different versions of their model for different subsets of their sample. They divide their sample according to the degree of labour market attachment of the individual, on the grounds that those who are strongly attached to the labour market may also face higher fixed costs of moving. Four levels of labour market attachment are defined, based on the number of weeks worked during the year.[22]

The results obtained by Audas and McDonald show that the degree of labour market attachment is indeed important when it comes to measuring the effects of unemployment insurance on migration between insurance regions. When the entire sample is pooled, neither receipt of benefits in the previous year, nor their insurance generosity index, appear to have a significant effect on mobility. However, when the sample is disaggregated, some evidence of insurance-related effects appears among those who are *not* strongly attached to the labour force—that is, among those who worked less than 50 weeks per year.[23] For those whose attachment to the labour market is deemed to be moderate, receipt of UI or EI benefits in the previous year seems to reduce mobility among both UI/EI regions and provinces, although the effect decreases in magnitude and/or significance when instrumental variables estimation is used. In addition, those with low or no labour market attachment appear to have changed their behaviour after the 1996 reforms, with the probability of moving increasing given the regional unemployment rate after the introduction of EI. Audas and McDonald suggest that this finding may reflect an increase in the difficulty of qualifying for benefits under the new system.

5 Our Evaluation: What is the "Bottom Line?"

If all the studies reviewed in the previous section had obtained similar results, it would be easy to draw a conclusion about the effect of unemployment insurance on interregional migration. However, they do not. Consequently, we need to look more critically at the various approaches to arrive at a judgement about the nature, strength and consequences of the evidence concerning the relationship between unemployment insurance and interregional migration.

First of all, consider the studies that use an index of some sort to represent the relevant characteristics of the unemployment insurance system. An obvious problem with this approach is that a single index may not adequately capture all the relevant aspects of the system. In particular, both the ease of qualifying for benefits and the generosity of benefits once an individual has qualified need to be taken into account. The simple ratio of benefits to earnings used in most of these studies may increase as it becomes easier to qualify for benefits and as the generosity of benefits increases, but it does not allow these two aspects of the generosity of the system to affect migration decisions independently. Only Shaw (1985, 1986) allows measures of both the generosity of benefits and the probability of receiving them to have separate effects on migration decisions (although the latter did not appear to have a statistically significant effect).

An additional problem with this approach as it was implemented by the various studies is that with only one exception, the index used does not distinguish between regular benefits, which since 1971 have been subject to regional variation, and other types of benefits, which are not.[24] This is a potential problem since in principle the unemployment insurance indices used could rise due to an increase in payments of, say, parental benefits or fishing benefits, in the absence of any changes in the degree of regional variation in regular benefits. Thus the inclusion of special benefits that do not vary across regions may to some extent contaminate the results, making it harder to determine the effects of the regional variation built into the system. Only the work of Courchene (1970), whose sample period pre-dates the introduction of explicit regional variation in benefits, is exempt from this criticism, although Winer and Gauthier (1982), in the second part of their study, employ an index that depends primarily on parameters of the system that vary across regions rather than on total benefits actually paid.

After 1990, the literature splits into two distinct strands: studies that use microdata, and studies that apply a more structural approach to time-series data. Studies that use microdata include a dummy variable for receipt of insurance benefits during the year prior to moving. But while these studies do provide many new insights into the determinants of migration, when it comes to investigating the effects of regional variation in the unemployment insurance system on internal migration they have some limitations.

First, all but one of these studies restrict their attention to the move-stay decision, ignoring the choice of destination. Even the one study that does consider destination choice—Ostrovsky, Hou and Picot (2008)—limits the destination choices to Alberta and any province other than Alberta. Consequently, unlike the time-series studies, these studies do not include both origin and destination characteristics as explanatory variables. In the presence of regional differences in unemployment insurance benefits, however, one might expect the identity of the province of origin to affect the nature of the relationship between receipt of benefits and the migration decision. When all origins are pooled, as is the case in these studies, it is impossible to capture such differences—only the average effect will be measured. Needless to say, this average effect may vary with the data set.

Second, a dummy variable indicator of receipt of benefits shares some of the same limitations as the benefit indices used in earlier studies. It does not reflect regional differences in weeks of benefits, because it will equal one for all benefit recipients regardless of the length of the period for which they received benefits. Only regional differences in the ease of qualifying for benefits will be captured by the dummy variable, since such differences should lead to more individuals with a value of one in high unemployment regions. Furthermore, these dummy variables do not appear to distinguish between receipt of regular benefits and other types of benefits that are not subject to regional differences in generosity.[25]

Finally, if some of the explanatory variables included in a model estimated using microdata are correlated with unobservable factors that also influence migration, the parameter estimates will be biased and cannot be interpreted as reflecting causal relationships between the explanatory variables. As Audas and McDonald (2003) point out, it is possible that such a correlation exists between the receipt of unemployment insurance benefits and unobservable factors that also influence migration decisions. Theirs is the only microdata study thus far that attempts to correct for this problem using an instrumental variables estimator, but it is not clear that their instrumental variables (industry dummy variables) are adequate.[26]

Indeed, the existence of such a correlation may partially explain the conflicting results emerging from microdata studies to date. It is notable that studies based on data sets such as the LMAS or the SLID that provide more information about personal characteristics such as education, industry, and occupation generate different results from those based on the LAD, which does not contain such information. In particular, the former studies (Osberg, Gordon and Lin 1994; Lin 1995; Audas and McDonald 2003) find little or no impact of receipt of unemployment insurance benefits on migration (even without using instrumental variables estimators), while the latter (Finnie 2004; Ostrovsky, Hou and Picot 2008) find that receipt of benefits has a positive impact on migration. This comparison suggests that the positive correlation observed in the LAD-based studies may simply be an artefact of the inability of the researchers to control for all important determinants of migration. If so, the microdata studies based on the LMAS and the SLID may provide a more accurate picture of the migration effects of receipt of unemployment benefits than to the LAD-based studies.

Of course, endogeneity problems that lead to correlations between the explanatory variables and the error terms of a migration model may also exist in studies that use time-series data. In fact, economic theory suggests that wages, unemployment rates and migration flows are all jointly determined. Flows of migrants between labour markets in response to wage and unemployment rate differentials should in principle lead to changes in those wage and unemployment rate differentials, leading to further changes in migration flows. But because annual rates of net in-migration to the Canadian provinces tend to be small, this endogeneity problem may be less serious than that facing microdata studies.[27] Furthermore, Day and Winer (2006, forthcoming) find that under favourable assumptions about the effect of migration on unemployment rates, even the complete elimination of regional variation in unemployment insurance would have a very small effect on those unemployment rates as a result of interprovincial migration.

Because it allows the researcher to include more policy parameters than other approaches, the structural approach adopted by Day (1992) and Day and Winer has the potential to provide more precise information about the migration effects of the design of unemployment insurance systems than do the other approaches. Day and Winer also focus directly on regular benefits, the category of benefits that does involve regional variation in both qualifying requirements and generosity of benefits. These models are also more firmly grounded in microeconomic theory, in that the estimating equation is linked to a specific functional form for individual utility functions. However, in practice these models suffer from a collinearity problem that makes it difficult to precisely estimate the effects of unemployment insurance parameters. This problem can be traced in part to the dependence of the insurance parameters on regional unemployment rates, which, as has already been noted, makes it difficult to empirically distinguish the effects of higher unemployment rates from the effects of a more generous unemployment system given the unemployment rate. All time-series studies likely suffer to some extent from this problem, although most don't report correlations between explanatory variables, making it impossible to determine the severity of the problem.[28] Day and Winer address this problem by carrying out simulations using more than one version of their model, rather than relying on just one set of estimates. This gives them two alternative estimates of the effect of any policy change, one of which is considerably larger than the other.

Thus no one approach or study can be said to clearly dominate all others, since all have their strengths and weaknesses. As one would expect, more recent studies have made use of advances in data, econometric methods and software that were not available to earlier researchers, but these advances have not succeeded in eliminating all the problems inherent in evaluating the effect of unemployment insurance on migration flows.

So what is the "bottom line" of this review? First of all, we know that theoretically, an unemployment insurance system can have two opposing effects on migration. The first is to finance job search, which would tend to increase migration, while the second is to influence the choice of destination by encouraging people to choose destinations with more generous benefits. The studies that use time-series data, together with Audas and McDonald (2003), suggest that if unemployment benefits have an effect on migration, it is the destination choice effect that is the stronger of the two. Secondly, although the results of Finnie (2004) and Ostrovsky, Hou and Picot (2008) suggest that it is the mobility-enhancing job-search effect that is stronger, there is reason to believe that this result simply reflects the dependence of both migration decisions and receipt of insurance benefits on the same unobservable factors, rather than a causal relationship between unemployment insurance benefits and migration decisions.

Thirdly, the work of Winer and Gauthier (1982), Audas and McDonald (2003), and Day and Winer (2006, forthcoming) suggests that only a subset of the population is influenced by unemployment insurance benefits when making migration decisions. This subset of the population consists of individuals who are more likely to make use of the unemployment insurance system because they are not strongly attached to the labour force in the sense that they are not likely to be employed for the full year. (Winer and Gauthier and Day and Winer divide their samples into income classes, but their low income class is likely to contain a high proportion of individuals who are not strongly attached to the labour force in the sense of Audas and McDonald.) Although neither Winer and Gauthier nor Day and Winer provide direct information on the proportion of tax filers that fall into their low income class, in Audas and McDonald's study moderately attached and weakly attached individuals account for only 12 per cent of household heads, while 78 per cent of household heads are strongly attached to the labour market. In light of the fact that such a small proportion of the labour force is likely to care much about unemployment benefits, it is not surprising that studies that aggregate across the entire population or sample do not always observe much of an effect.

Last but not least, the marginal effects and simulation results provided by some studies suggest that where a statistically significant effect exists, it is too small to have much of an effect on provincial economies. Even when they use the set of estimates that is most likely to yield large effects, Day and Winer (2006, forthcoming) find that a simulation in which both the variable entrance requirement and regional extended benefits are eliminated would only reduce Newfoundland's average unemployment rate over the 1978–1996 period to 16.5 per cent, as compared to an actual average unemployment rate over that period of approximately 16.8 per cent.[29] Thus, while there does exist empirical evidence that Courchene's (1970) argument about the direction of the effect of the regional variation in unemployment insurance generosity is correct, the magnitude of the effect appears to be too small to have serious consequences for the interregional allocation of labour services.

6 Conclusions

One of the difficulties of studying the relationship between the unemployment insurance system and internal migration decisions is that regional variation in unemployment insurance indicators such as the ratio of average benefits to average earnings arises from two different sources. The first is the explicit dependence of both qualifying requirements and benefit periods on regional unemployment rates, while the second is the existence of differences between regional economies. Most empirical studies of the migration effects of unemployment insurance do not clearly distinguish between these two sources of regional variation. A further source of difficulty is that there have not been any controlled experiments that can help us evaluate more accurately the migration effects of unemployment insurance in Canada.

Some studies do better than others in dealing with these and other issues that we have raised in the course of our review. If we look across all of the studies that have been produced so far, we can say that there is no evidence showing that regional variation in the generosity of regular benefits, either before or after 1996, has had an effect on the volume of interprovincial migration substantial enough to alter the provincial allocation of labour services. Simulations based on empirical estimates suggest that even the complete elimination of the explicit regional variation in the system would not be a large enough shock to have an important effect on regional labour markets.

This conclusion must be tempered with the observation that studies based on historical data can only evaluate the experiences that are reflected in that data. Since big shocks or radical policy changes rarely occur, simulations of the effect of such shocks based on estimates derived from historical data may produce inaccurate results. Day and Winer (2006, forthcoming) provide evidence that extraordinary events such as the closing of the Atlantic cod fishery after 1992 have large effects on internal migration flows, and one may ask whether the complete elimination of regional variation in the current EI system constitutes such a large shock. If so, the simulation results reported by Day and Winer might underestimate the effects of such a policy change.

On the other hand, Day and Winer find that the simulated effect of eliminating regional variation in the insurance system is even smaller when they repeat their simulation using estimates derived from a data set that covers the 1968–1996 period, a period that includes three years of data prior to the initial introduction of regional variation in unemployment insurance in 1971. This suggests that even the elimination of regional variation in the insurance system is not so large a shock that we need to be concerned that its effects have been grossly underestimated. Thus it appears safe to conclude that policy changes involving the degree of regional variation in the unemployment insurance system are unlikely to have serious consequences for the interprovincial allocation of labour services resulting from policy-induced migration. Furthermore, the few studies that consider migration at the sub-provincial level suggest that the effects of regional variation in the generosity of benefits are similar for both intra-provincial and interprovincial migration.

Perhaps the most important implication of our findings for the making of public policy is that if changes in the degree of regional variation in the insurance system are contemplated, justification for such changes is not to be found in the removal of incentives for people to remain where unemployment generosity is relatively high. These incentives exist, but there is no evidence that they have a large impact on interprovincial or interregional migration. There may be efficiency reasons for reducing the generosity of the system in higher unemployment regions, for example because this would alter work-leisure decisions in those regions in a socially beneficial manner. But the longstanding bias against regional variation in insurance generosity based on its consequences for the regional allocation of labour has not been substantiated.

Arguments for regional equity in access to, and in benefits from the insurance system of course remain valid. Such considerations may include concern with the individual inequities arising from regional differentiation in benefit generosity that were pointed to by the Mowat Centre EI Task Force in its 2010 discussion paper (Mowat 2010), and may also include long-standing arguments for greater interregional equity on a provincial basis. Like the effect of EI on labour-leisure choices in particular locations, these equity issues are not addressed by the literature we have reviewed.

What we can say here is that arguments for equity in the receipt of unemployment insurance cannot be bolstered by an appeal to the removal of inefficient interregional migration as a by-product of the pursuit of greater equity. They must stand on their own.

Endnotes

1 This is so despite the regional economic convergence that has occurred since 1945. On the nature of regional convergence in Canada, see for example Coulombe and Tremblay (2001).

2 A regional dimension was added to the conditions for qualifying for insurance benefits in 1978.

3 The efficiency issue and the issue of interregional equity in benefit generosity are linked because decisions about equity cannot be properly made without taking into account their possible consequences for the allocation of resources. Here the possibility arises that reducing the degree of variation in benefit generosity may at the same time enhance efficiency from a national perspective while also enhancing equity in access to the system and in benefits received.

4 Comprehensive income will also include, in principle, the expected discounted value of taxes required to service and retire any public debt.

5 In fact people have been leaving the poorer provinces like Newfoundland to go to central Canada for decades. But this net outflow, in Courchene's view, is not large enough.

6 In the same manner, one could also point to the more generous public sector in Alberta relative to Ontario made possible by oil revenues.

7 See Krueger and Mueller (2010) for a recent study of the relationship between job search and unemployment insurance in the United States.

8 Recently Mendelsohn and Medow (2010) have observed that provincial differences in access to EI during the 2008 recession were not as highly correlated with provincial unemployment rates as one might expect. They attribute this phenomenon to regional differences in the composition of the unemployed.

9 Benefits were increased by five weeks across the board between 1 March 2009 and 12 September 2010 as a temporary measure to compensate unemployed workers for the increased difficulty of finding employment during and immediately after the 2008–2009 recession. However, this absolute increase in weeks of benefits was independent of regional unemployment rates.

10 See Day and Winer (forthcoming) for a complete explanation of the calculations for the 1966–1996 period. The same methods were applied to EI for the period 1997–2009. Currently there are 58 different Employment Insurance regions in Canada.

11 Data on average actual hours worked for total employed, all industries and both sexes, were obtained from CANSIM Table 280022 (series V261492), retrieved 13 August 2010. During this period average weekly hours for Canada ranged from a high of 37.8 in 1989 to a low of 35.3 in 2009. Average weekly hours

also vary across provinces, but this variation is not taken into account in our calculations.

12 Note that the 1990 spike in the Newfoundland line is due to the temporary lapse of the VER in that year. The minimum qualifying requirements are not quite the same in the two provinces in that year because the 1990 value is actually a weighted average of the values for different months.

13 See CANSIM Table 2820022.

14 There exist many other studies of interprovincial migration in Canada that do not examine the role of unemployment insurance as a determinant of migration. See Grady and Macmillan (2007), Gomez and Gunderson (2007), and Day and Winer (forthcoming) for surveys of some aspects of this literature.

15 For example, see Winer and Gauthier (1982), Day (1992), and Day and Winer (2006).

16 See chapter three of Day and Winer (forthcoming) for further information on the properties of these models.

17 All time spent not working, including time spent receiving benefits, is treated as leisure time in these models.

18 In state 1 (employed all year) and state 4 (not attached to the labour market and receiving social assistance all year) individuals do not receive any unemployment insurance benefits.

19 The exact magnitude of the decrease is not clear as it varies considerably between models. For example, for Model 1 of Day and Winer (forthcoming), the marginal effect in Newfoundland of an increase in MIN is a decline in net in-migration of 96.5 middle-income people; for Model 2, the same marginal effect is only 7.4.

20 This index differs from that in equation (1) in that MIN in (1) is minimum qualifying weeks, not minimum weeks of benefits. Thus Audas and McDonald's index reflects only changes in the generosity of benefits at either end of the range of benefits, not changes in the ease of qualifying for benefits.

21 In principal, one can control for the effects of other variables such as unemployment rates by including them as explanatory variables in one's model. However, strong correlations between explanatory variables can result in large estimated standard errors for the coefficients of the correlated variables, leading to the conclusion that the estimated coefficients are not statistically significant.

22 Note that in Day and Winer (2006, forthcoming), the degree of labour market attachment is assumed to be unknown when the individual makes a migration decision. Audas and McDonald, on the other hand, rely on the information available to them about the ex post degree of labour market attachment.

23 Audas and McDonald define "strongly attached" differently than do Day and Winer (2006, forthcoming). "Moderate" attachment to the labour market in Audas and McDonald corresponds to state 2 (strongly attached) in Day and Winer, while "weak" attachment in Audas and McDonald corresponds to state 3 in Day and Winer. "Strong" attachment in Audas and McDonald corresponds to state 1 (employed all year) in Day and Winer.

24 These studies seem to use total unemployment insurance benefits rather than just regular benefits as the measure of benefits paid in the numerator of the index.

25 The variable definitions provided in the studies simply state that the dummy variable equals one if the individual received unemployment insurance benefits. The data files probably do not distinguish between regular and special benefits.

26 The quality of instrumental variables estimates depends heavily on the quality of the instrumental variables used. Audas and McDonald do not provide any information about the strength of their instruments, probably because tests for weak instruments were not widely used at the time they carried out their research.

27 Annual rates of net in-migration to the ten provinces ranged in absolute value from 0.01 per cent to 2.04 per cent during the 1971–2009 period. During the same period, rates of in-migration ranged from 0.26 per cent to 4.99 per cent, and rates of out-migration ranged from 0.33 per cent to 4.21 per cent. (Migration rates were calculated using data from CANSIM Tables 510001 and 510018, retrieved on 26 October 2010.)

28 Only Liaw and Ledent (1987), Day (1992), and Day and Winer (2006, forthcoming) report coefficients of correlation between at least some of their explanatory variables.

29 This hypothetical change in unemployment rates was calculated by assuming that all out-migrants from Newfoundland were unemployed, while all in-migrants were employed. Using their alternative model, the same simulation yielded no change in the average annual unemployment rate.

References

Audas, R., and J.T. McDonald. 2003. "Employment Insurance and Geographic Mobility: Evidence from the SLID." HRDC Working Paper Series 03-03. Ottawa: Human Resources Development Canada.

Boadway, R., and A.G. Green. 1981. "The Economic Implications of Migration to Newfoundland." Discussion Paper No. 189. Ottawa: Economic Council of Canada.

Coulombe, S., and J-F. Tremblay. 2001. "Human Capital and Regional Convergence in Canada," *Journal of Economic Studies* 28.3: 154-80.

Courchene, T.J. 1970. "Interprovincial Migration and Economic Adjustment." *Canadian Journal of Economics* 3.4: 550-76.

——. 1978. "The Transfer System and Regional Disparities: A Critique of the Status Quo." in *Canadian Federation at the Crossroads: The Search for a Federal-Provincial Balance*, ed. M. Walker, 145-86. Vancouver: The Fraser Institute.

Day, K.M. 1992. "Interprovincial Migration and Local Public Goods." *Canadian Journal of Economics* 25.1: 123-44.

Day, K.M. and S.L. Winer. 2006. "Policy-induced Migration in Canada: An Empirical Investigation of the Canadian Case." *International Tax and Public Finance* 13: 535-64.

——. 2006 (forthcoming). *Internal Migration and Public Policy in Canada: An Empirical Investigation*. McGill-Queen's University Press.

Dingledine, G. 1981. *A Chronology of Response: The Evolution of Unemployment Insurance from 1940 to 1980*. Prepared for Employment and Immigration Canada. Ottawa: Minister of Supply and Services Canada.

Dingledine, G., J. Hunter, and C. McKillop. 1995. *The History of Unemployment Insurance*. Ottawa: Human Resources Development Canada. At http://www.hrdc-drhc.gc.ca/insur/histui/hrdc.html.

Finnie, R. 2004. "Who Moves? A Logit Model Analysis of Inter-Provincial Migration in Canada." *Applied Economics* 36.16: 1759-79.

Gomez, R., and M. Gunderson. 2007. "Barriers to the Inter-Provincial Mobility of Labour." Industry Canada Working Paper 2007-09. Ottawa: Industry Canada.

Grady, P., and K. Macmillan. 2007. "Interprovincial Barriers to Labour Mobility in Canada: Policy, Knowledge Gaps and Research Issues." Industry Canada Working Paper 2007–10. Ottawa: Industry Canada. At http://mpra.ub.uni-muenchen.de/2988/1/MPRA_paper_2988.pdf.

Krueger, A.B. and A. Mueller. 2010. "Job Search and Unemployment Insurance: New Evidence from Time Use Data." *Journal of Public Economics*, 94.3-4: 298-307.

Liaw, K-L., and J. Ledent. 1987. "Nested Logit Model and Maximum Quasi-Likelihood Method." *Regional Science and Urban Economics* 17(1): 67-88.

Lin, Z. 1995. *Interprovincial Labour Mobility in Canada: The Role of Unem-*

ployment Insurance and Social Assistance. Ottawa: Human Resources Development Canada.

McFarlane, D.S., G.S. Pun, and A.D. Loparco. 1992. *The Annotated Unemployment Insurance Act 1993*. Toronto: Carswell.

Mendelsohn, M., and J. Medow. 2010. "Help Wanted: How Well Did the EI Program Respond During Recent Recessions?" *Mowat Note*. Toronto: Mowat Centre for Policy Innovation. At http://www.mowatcentre.ca/research-topic-mowat.php?mowatResearchID=22 (accessed 8 September 2010.)

Mowat Centre for Policy Innovation. 2010. "Making EI Work: Discussion Paper." Mowat Centre EI Task Force.

Osberg, L., D. Gordon, and Z. Lin. 1994. "Inter-regional Migration and Inter-industry Labour Mobility in Canada: A Simultaneous Approach." *Canadian Journal of Economics* 27.1: 58-80.

Ostrovsky, Y., F. Hou and G. Picot. 2008. "Internal Migration of Immigrants: Do Immigrants Respond to Regional Labour Demand Shocks?" Ottawa: Statistics Canada.

Rudner, K.L. 1995. *The 1996 Annotated Unemployment Insurance Act*. Toronto: Carswell.

Shaw, R.P. 1985. *Intermetropolitan Migration in Canada: Changing Determinants Over Three Decades*. Ottawa: Statistics Canada.

Shaw, R.P. 1986. "Fiscal versus Traditional Market Variables in Canadian Migration." *Journal of Political Economy* 94.3: 648-66.

Winer, S.L., and D. Gauthier. 1982. *Internal Migration and Fiscal Structure: An Econometric Study of the Determinants of Interprovincial Migration in Canada*. Ottawa: Economic Council of Canada.

Section III

Challenges Facing Long-Term and Displaced Workers

Chapter 10

The Income Sources for Long-Term Workers Who Exhaust Employment Insurance Benefits

Ross Finnie, David Gray, Ian Irvine and Yan Zhang

1 Introduction

This research is focused on the income sources of individuals in Canada who exhaust a spell of regular Employment Insurance (EI) benefits. It has two main goals, the first of which is to investigate the labour market outcomes and income sources of these "exhaustees" during their post-EI claim periods: Social Assistance (SA) or some other income support program, such as Canada/Quebec Pension Plan (CQPP), Canada/Quebec Pension Plan Disability (CQPPD) or Workers' Compensation (WC); a return to the labour market; a return to EI receipt; some combination of work and EI; or some other outcome. We track them in both the short and longer term. The short term corresponds roughly to the first year after the spell exhaustion, and the longer term, which we truncate at five years, could encompass multiple transitions across these various states. Consideration of such a longer time horizon is important not just for movements onto SA rolls, but also for individuals who might, for example, search for a job for a year and then decide to withdraw from the labour market.

The second main goal is to examine whether there has been any detectable change in these patterns over time: not only did EI become more difficult to access post 1994, but SA, too, has become increasingly less accessible as a result of major changes implemented in Alberta (1993), Ontario (1995) and British Columbia (2002), and a series of less dramatic changes in the operation of the programs in most provinces during the 1990s. Furthermore, labour market conditions have varied dramatically during this time frame.

To accomplish these goals, we follow a large sample of individuals who exhaust a spell of regular EI benefits over the period 1994–2002 in order to track their income-source patterns in the following years. The sample is drawn from a linked file based on the Longitudinal Administrative Database (LAD), derived from individual tax records, and EI administrative data. This merged database allows us to identify individuals who exhaust their regular benefits in a given year (as indicated on the EI file) and then track their income sources in the years following that benefit termination through the LAD. The favourable attributes of the LAD-EI database for carrying out this analysis are discussed in more detail below. In addition to identifying spell exhaustees, the EI file enables us to cross-verify the EI information contained in the LAD.

A prime motivation for the chapter is that EI presently benefits a smaller percentage of unemployed individuals than at any time in the program's recent history. Furthermore, SA entry involves stringent conditions, and leaves individuals who depend upon it far below the poverty line. There may thus exist a chasm in Canada's social safety network, in that many individuals who need social support may not be receiving it. These concerns were central to the Mowat Centre EI Task Force, and also to the report from the Expert Panel on Older Workers (2008).

The chapter is developed as follows. Section two initially presents some trend statistics for social insurance and social support programs in Canada; this is followed by a statement of concerns that surround the EI regime at the present time, a review of legislative changes, and a brief overview of some relevant literature. In section three we describe the database and sampling methods employed in the empirical section. Section four contains the main results, and section five offers some conclusions.

2 Background: Trends, Concerns, Program Reform, Existing Literature

A Employment Insurance and Social Insurance Usage Trends

The number of individuals claiming regular EI benefits has varied enormously in recent decades. In 1993, when the unemployment rate reached 12 per cent nationally (1993), 1.15 million individuals claimed regular benefits monthly under the program. Since 2000, in contrast, this number has been in the neighbourhood of half a million—prior to the recession that began in 2008. Figure 1 portrays the longer-term behaviour in annual frequency of the number of regular-benefit recipients.

FIGURE 1 Annual Regular EI Beneficiaries, 1980–2009

The decline since the early 1990s is attributable first to a substantial decline in the national unemployment rate. Second, several work-incentive-based reforms to EI were introduced in the 1990s that made benefits more difficult to collect and generally reduced the length of benefit-entitlement periods. Third, several active labour market policies and programs were introduced in 1996, under the title Employment Benefit Support Measures (EBSM), which were designed to facilitate job mobility, as opposed to providing passive income support.

At the onset of the 2008 recession, the number of beneficiaries climbed rapidly. However, while unemployment as of the start of 2011 continued to hover above 8 per cent nationally, the number of EI beneficiaries appeared to be declining. A partial explanation of that development is that a few waves of EI claimants had exhausted their benefit entitlements. November 2010 data indicated a decline in claimant numbers in the neighbourhood of 12 per cent relative to November 2009.

The number of SA beneficiaries peaked in 1994 at 3.1 million individuals and subsequently declined to about 1.7 million by 2004.[1] As a percentage of a growing population, the rate has declined by even more than these two figures indicate. The recovery from the 1990s recession also marked the first time in recent history that the number of SA beneficiaries actually declined in a significant way. Courchene (1994) emphasized that, prior to this episode, recessions had increased the number of SA recipients, but they remained remarkably resilient in the face of subsequent recoveries. This ratchet effect was broken, however, during the 1990s recovery. SA rates declined from the mid-1990s for similar reasons that EI declined—an improving aggregate economy, a tightening of access to benefits in combination with a reduction in benefits, and the work-incentive effects of the National Child Tax program.[2] These phenomena are revealed in Figure 2, which portrays the intertemporal patterns of SA and EI activity levels, and the unemployment rate for Ontario until 2010. Those provinces for which recent data are available indicate a similar pattern (Stapleton 2011).[3]

FIGURE 2 Annual Regular EI Beneficiaries, 1980–2009

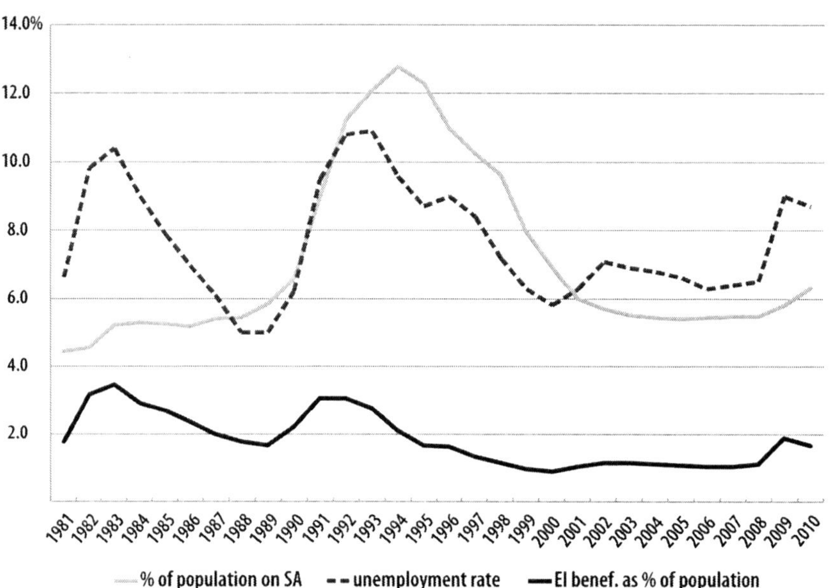

Retirement patterns have also undergone significant recent changes. Male participation rates in the 55–64 year age group had been declining since the mid 1970s, but this trend went into reverse in the late 1990s. Moreover, the Canadian patterns are mirrored in the US, the UK and several other European economies (Schirle 2008). How this phenomenon translates into changes in the flow of EI spell exhaustees to the CQPP regimes may emerge from our analysis.

We also examine the possibility that EI spell exhaustees may use WC to a greater or lesser degree. This issue of substitutability between WC and EI is addressed by Fortin and Lanoie (1999). The long term trend in Canada is for safer working environments (e.g., Workplace Safety and Insurance Board, 2009). We also consider the possibility that older EI claimants might substitute the disability provision of the Canada Pension Plan (CPPD) as a form of "non-employment" insurance—in effect a substitute for long-term EI benefits, which is addressed in Finnie and Gray (2009). More generally, where the funding responsibility for potentially competing social safety network programs lies partially with the federal government (e.g., EI,

CPPD) and partially with the provincial government (e.g., SA and WC), strategic uploading and downloading of clients is always possible if one level of government wishes to shift the cost to another level.[4]

The foregoing discussion indicates that there has been no detectable growth in the levels of dependence on the regimes of SA, CQPP or WC; in fact, the opposite is true. However, it reveals little regarding the use of these programs by EI spell exhaustees.

B EI Concerns in the New Millennium

Concerns about the structure and functioning of our employment and social insurance programs, particularly in the context of the current economic recession, have been expressed in numerous forums—most recently as part of the Mowat Centre EI Task Force:

1. Considerable holes characterize our knowledge in Canada regarding SA use in general, and in particular what happens to individuals whose EI payments are terminated without the claimant having found employment. Economy-wide data on SA appear to be available only up to 2006 at the time of writing, although some provinces do have more recent data. SA has become more difficult to access, and now supports single individuals predominantly—single parent recipients have declined dramatically as a percentage of all recipients.
2. Where EI exhaustees do succeed in accessing SA, the dollar support levels are low, and in addition SA may stigmatize the recipients.
3. While EI insures against job loss, the coverage from another unemployment-related risk, namely long-term, persistent wage loss, does not exist.
4. Retraining programs have limited success in seeing EI exhaustees find their way back to a job that pays a wage in the neighbourhood of their previous employment wage.
5. The role of EI upon the event of the loss of employment, however, may also be undergoing change in view of globalization/outsourcing and an increasing degree of self employment. The modern economy is characterized by an increased share of the labour force working in the service sector and a greater proportion of workers employed in non-standard arrangements, such as intermittent work and self-employment. This evolution of the structure of employment and the dynamics of the job market raises questions about the appropriate values of parameters in the program—the replacement ratio, the entry requirements, the length of the benefit durations, and the benefit calculation period (for the inclusion of the qualifying weeks of employment). Moreover, in this new economy what is the appropriate balance between active and passive policies?
6. The 1990s changes in EI regulations, which we describe below, combined with the dramatic decline in the number of claimants, raises the possibility that some individuals who might have qualified for EI benefits under the pre-reform rules but not during the post-reform period

may have found other ways to obtain public forms of income support. If claiming SA has become more difficult, it remains possible that individuals could still access SA with a lag (having run down their assets to the permissible level). Alternatively, individuals might take retirement earlier, make a claim under the disability provisions of the CQPP, or claim benefits from WC programs. In effect there are substitution possibilities among various social insurance and social support programs.

7. The appropriate division of government responsibilities in funding these various programs forms a tension between federal and provincial governments, and at the same time can give rise to moral hazard problems in program design and execution. For example, changes in the unemployment rate that result in greater numbers exhausting their EI benefits obviously promotes financial as well as humanitarian concerns at the provincial level. Consequently, any increased degree of understanding of the interactions between EI and these other social insurance and assistance programs should be of benefit to provincial governments as well as the federal authority that governs EI.[5]

C EI Reform in the 1990s

Since 1990, with the exception of the maternity and family supplement developments, virtually all additional reforms have made benefits more difficult to obtain.[6] Among the more important of the reforms adopted in the early 1990s were: (i) raising the quantity of insurable work required to be eligible for benefits in 1990 and again in 1994; (ii) substantially reducing the maximum number of benefit weeks in high unemployment regions in 1994; (iii) making workers who quit their jobs without good cause ineligible for benefits in 1993; (iv) reducing the replacement rate from 60 per cent to 57 per cent to 55 per cent in 1993 and 1994; (v) reducing the maximum weeks of benefit entitlement in 1994.[7]

Further changes of a more mixed nature followed in the mid- and late-1990s. We list those that are most pertinent to our study: (i) There was a change from a weeks-of-work basis to an hours-of-work basis as an EI qualification mechanism in January 1997, which especially affected part-time workers, multiple-job holders, and seasonal workers; (ii) the minimum hours of work required to qualify for benefits for new entrants and re-entrants into the labour market was increased in 1997; (iii) a "divisor" rule, which in essence required an additional two weeks of work in order to secure full benefits was introduced in 1996; (iv) the "clawback" rules, which were designed to reduce/reclaim the benefits going to those with higher "end-of-year" incomes went through several modifications; (v) there was a significant erosion in the real value of the maximum insurable earnings and a steady reduction in the contribution rates by both employers and employees from 1994/95 onwards. The *EI Act* of 1996 raised the degree of generosity for some groups of workers with specific employment patterns (notably seasonal workers working long weeks during the season), while having the opposite impact on others (notably full-year workers working short hours).

Employment Benefit Support Measures accompanied these developments in 1996. While these particular active labour market policy interventions were not new, the *EI Act* of 1996 set out a new administrative framework for them which culminated gradually in the adoption of Labour Market Development Agreements (LMDAs) with almost all provinces.

> The components were: Employment Assistance Services (EAS) through counselling, job search assistance, job placement and labour market information; Skills Development (SD) mainly in accredited training; Targeted Wage Subsidy (TWS) for employers who hired the unemployed; Targeted Earnings Supplements (TES) to supplement the earnings of the unemployed who accepted an otherwise low-wage job; Self-Employment Assistance (SEA) to assist in starting a business; and Job Creation Partnership (JCP) to assist clients in obtaining work experience. The intent of the EBSMs was to provide active adjustment assistance to encourage structural adjustment to new job opportunities rather than simply providing passive income support (as in conventional EI) that discouraged such moves. (Gunderson 2011)

From a fiscal balance viewpoint, one outcome of these myriad changes was that, even with contribution-rate reductions, the monetary value of combined contributions came to exceed the payments made to the unemployed as early as 1993/94—a time when Canada was still in a recession. Such excess revenues are perceived by employer groups as an employment tax, though such a perspective assumes that worker contributions are not significantly shifted back onto wages—an assumption based on an elastic supply of labour that is shared by few economists. Dahlby (1994) has also suggested that EI excess contributions may be an efficient, though regressive, way of generating tax revenue, since they act as a lump sum tax for those earning beyond the maximum insurable earnings threshold.

3 Literature Review on the Interface Between EI and SA

The interaction between Canada's EI and SA programs has been studied by numerous researchers, in particular, Fortin, Lacroix and Thibault (1999), Barrett et al. (1996), Grey (2002), HRDC (2001) and Finnie, Irvine and Sceviour (2004a, b). This literature presents quite different images of the interplay between these two significant income support programs. These differences appear to be largely attributable to the different periods of time the studies cover, as well as to other differences in terms of the groups focussed upon, methodological approaches, and so on.

In terms of the first point, Grey (2002) uses data from 1987 to 1997, at the end of which time the economy had resumed growth for a couple of years, whereas the Fortin, Lacroix and Thibault, and the Barrett et al. studies incorporate data only up to the early 1990s—a period dominated by the severe recession and subsequent growth in UI claimants and SA caseloads.[8] Finnie, Irvine and Sceviour (2004a) present trends on SA entry, exit and participation from 1992 through 2000, and find a radically different picture of welfare levels, welfare composition and welfare trends at the end of the period relative to the early 1990s.

Fortin, Lacroix and Thibault argue that a reduction in the generosity of EI benefits or a tightening of access conditions to them makes it less likely that those on SA at a given time will exit because the package of income support programs (EI and SA) on which such individuals may need to rely in the future becomes less certain and loses value. Thus the attraction of leaving SA for the labour market with its own uncertainties diminishes. In addition, the likelihood of re-entry onto SA should increase in this model for the reason that EI becomes less supportive and more difficult to access. Empirically, using a sample of single parents and including controls for demographic variables and economic conditions, they find support for both parts of these theoretical propositions based on data from 1979 to 1993.

Barrett et al. (1996) focus upon the question of whether there existed a significant clientele that relied upon both EI and SA, and arrive at an affirmative answer. Their data also span the late 1980s through the early 1990s, in their case for the provinces of British Columbia and New Brunswick. Grey (2002) arrives at a very different conclusion, finding that very few EI claimants who exhausted their claims went onto SA benefits shortly thereafter, and argue that the substantial lag in entering SA for those who did so was likely attributable to the fact that many individuals who exhaust EI possess assets, or are partnered with an individual who has an income stream, and therefore do not qualify for SA support at that point in time. Grey (2002) also emphasizes that once a person is on the SA rolls, he or she realises that obtaining this form of income support can be time-consuming and uncertain, and additionally so for auxiliary benefits such as a housing rental supplement or child supplements. Therefore, when attempting an exit from SA, individuals will weigh these costs against the likely benefits from holding a job. Furthermore, if EI benefits diminish, then the attraction of leaving SA diminishes correspondingly.

HRDC (2001) examines the EI-SA interface by investigating if there was a change in the pattern of SA receipt on the part of those who exhausted EI claims (as well as those who were unemployed but did not receive EI) from 1995 to 1997, thus covering the period which saw the enactment of some of the major reforms in EI described above. The study found no such change: Fewer job losers exhausted their subsequent EI claims, and the SA take-up rate declined after the EI reform of 1996 for EI claimants, regardless of whether or not they exhausted their entitlement.

The present study differs from earlier work in several ways. First, it employs a national-level database as opposed to selected provinces.

Second, we use more recent data spanning the interval 1994 to 2008. Third, we examine the pattern of transitions from EI to WC and CQPP as well as to SA. Fourth, we follow individuals for a longer period of time than has been done to this point.

4 The Data

A The LAD and the EI Link File

The LAD is a 20 per cent representative sample of Canadian tax filers, constructed from Canada Revenue Agency records, which follows individuals over time and matches them into family units on an annual basis. It thus provides individual-level and family-level information on incomes, taxes, and basic demographic characteristics in a longitudinal framework. Individuals are selected randomly into the LAD according to their social insurance numbers (SINs), and are followed over time by the same identifier. The LAD's coverage of the adult population is very broad, since the rate of tax filing in Canada is high. Middle-income and upper-income Canadians are legally required to file, while lower-income individuals have strong incentives to file in order to recover income tax and other payroll tax deductions made throughout the year, to receive various tax credits, and to apply for the National Child Benefit. Overall, the full set of annual files from which the LAD is constructed is estimated to cover 95–97 per cent of the adult population over these years, thus comparing very favourably with other databases (Finnie and Sweetman 2003). In terms of longitudinal tracking, there is very little attrition due to the administrative practice of linking individuals' records over time by means of their SIN.

The large number of observations in the LAD (approximately six million per year in recent periods) further allows us to identify sufficient numbers of EI exhaustees in order to conduct a robust and detailed analysis of these persons' subsequent income profiles. Finally, the income information on the LAD is detailed and deemed to be superior to what individuals provide in surveys.

While the LAD file is well-suited to the purposes of this study, it has some shortcomings. One is that it does not include some relevant individual-level attributes, such as education level. A second drawback is that it lacks more specific labour market information beyond the annual amount of earned income. For example, the LAD does not identify individuals who are unemployed unless they receive EI, nor does it contain any information on working time or job separations.

The EI administrative file—the "Link File" with which the LAD has been merged for this project—includes variables indicating the type of EI benefits a person received, and whether the person exhausted a spell of EI benefits. We are thus able to identify individuals who exhausted a spell of EI benefits in a particular year, and then follow them in subsequent years using the income information available in the LAD, since these include SA, CQPP, CQPPD, and WC benefits.

B The Samples

Since the focus of this study is on individuals who have a strong attachment to the labour market, we selected individuals who had no EI or SA benefits for two years preceding their EI claim. We also selected only individuals who filed a tax return for three consecutive years, excluding residents of the Territories and multiple jurisdictions, and non residents. The sample was also restricted to those between 21 and 64 years of age in the reference year—we stopped following them beyond the age of 65. Individuals were not selected if they were self-employed, farmers, or fishers, or received WC, Old Age Security, Federal supplements or CQPP in the preceding two years. We also excluded individuals whose reported earnings were below a threshold which deemed them to be just loosely attached to the labour force.

While the principal reason for limiting our sample in the above manner is to focus upon individuals who have a strong attachment to the labour market, the additional restrictions are necessitated by the fact that we do not know the order in which multiple sources of income in a given year might be received. For example, consider an individual who receives SA, then finds a job, becomes unemployed and finally receives EI. Consider another individual who might start the year with a job, become unemployed, receive EI and finally go onto SA. The LAD data do not enable us to distinguish between these two cases, but we are interested only in cases where EI receipt precedes SA receipt. Such uncertainty regarding the sequencing of income thus necessitates the restrictions that we impose on income source in the base year and the year prior to the base year—a claim initiated in that year (T-1) could continue to the base year (T0). We also excluded full-time students.

We next cross-checked to verify that these individuals, who are identified from the EI Link database, did indeed have EI benefits reported on their LAD file. This was true in approximately 95 per cent of all cases, and individuals with inconsistent EI records were then excluded. Our samples are also limited to those spells consisting of "regular" benefits—thus excluding, for example, those with maternity/paternity/adoption benefits. Finally, we selected all those individuals who exhausted a spell of EI benefits that commenced in a given year—T0, which becomes the reference year. Note that we do not pinpoint the exact timing of the exhaustion, which could occur in either year T0 or in the subsequent year, which we call T1. All individuals finally selected are then followed in the next five years (T1, T2, T3, T4, T5) to examine the transition of their income composition.

This set of restrictions left us with a sample of 90,845 individuals for the complete period, which includes all nine cohorts (labelled by a reference year) pooled together. These cohorts run from 1994 until 2002, and are identified by the year in which members commenced their EI benefits spell that was subsequently exhausted.[9] Some of these individuals disappeared from the data set subsequent to their observed EI exhaustion because they missed filing a tax form, or were otherwise censored because they no longer met our sample selection criteria based on age or student status. If this occurred, the record was censored at that point, even if the person re-appeared in the data or again met the selection criteria in a subsequent period, due to the uncertainty of their dynamics in the interlude. The number of such individuals is, however, relatively low, as will be seen in Table 1 below.

5 Empirical Results

A Incidence of Income Receipt from a Particular Source

The first post-exhaustion outcome that we investigate is the event of receiving income from a particular source. The data cover the entire period 1994–2002, for men and women together of all ages, living in all regions, subject to the sampling conditions described above. Our descriptive statistic is an incidence rate that is estimated as the proportion of the sample receiving income in a given year from: (i) SA on an individual level; (ii) SA at the family level—which includes "individuals;" (iii) EI, which represents a new spell by construction; (iv) WC; (v) labour market earnings[10]; and (vi) CQPP, including their respective disability regimes CQCPPD. The categories SA_I and SA_F denote individual and family based receipt of SA. An individual will always be a member of a family if he/she is the named recipient; but he/she may not be the named recipient and still be a member of a family where SA is received: SA is universally treated in "caseloads" where there is more than one member in a household.

The first set of our results is presented in Table 1. In the top panel, all of the cohorts, which are defined by the year in which they commenced an EI spell that was ultimately exhausted, are pooled together.[11] The values in the first column (T0) give the number of individuals receiving benefits from the sources described and who commenced an EI spell in that reference year that ended in exhaustion (in either T0 or the next year). The relative shares appear in the next column. By sample construction, their incidence rate for EI receipt in year T0 is 100 per cent. Most of these individuals (86.2 per cent) had earnings in year T0, though whether these earnings accrued before, after or during the EI spell we cannot tell, given the annual frequency of the data. The alternative program sources of income can, in contrast, be fairly safely assumed to have come after the exhaustion of the observed EI spell. This is not just because of the nature of the income (e.g., WC would make earnings less likely for individuals who needed earnings to qualify for EI). We have imposed the condition that the individual received no income from any of these social insurance sources in period

TABLE 1 Distribution of Income State in Years Since the Start of EI Exhaustion, Pure Incidence

Cohort	Income State	T0		T1		T2		T3		T4		T5	
		#	%	#	%	#	%	#	%	#	%	#	%
All	SA_1	1760	1.9	4940	5.8	4160	5.1	3410	4.3	3085	4	2800	3.7
	SA_F	2840	3.1	6270	7.4	5510	6.8	4725	5.9	4310	5.5	3995	5.3
	EI	90840	100	66950	78.6	14025	17.3	14220	17.9	13320	17.1	12105	16.1
	WC	1360	1.5	725	0.8	1200	1.5	1405	1.8	1445	1.9	1465	1.9
	Earnings	78310	86.2	52095	61.2	57635	70.9	57775	72.6	57005	73.4	55775	74
	CQPP	2870	3.2	7175	8.4	8605	10.6	9590	12.1	10370	13.3	10370	13.8
	Total Uncensored	90840	100	85170	93.8	79515	93.4	76810	94.5	75050	94.3	72850	93.8
	Non-Filer			4965	5.5	5055	5.9	4010	4.9	4100	5.2	4480	5.8
	Not Eligible (Student, Age, etc.)			705	0.8	605	0.7	455	0.6	405	0.5	365	0.5
	Total Censored			5670	6.2	5655	6.6	4470	5.5	4505	5.7	4845	6.2
1994	SA_1	325	3.6	835	9.9	715	9	585	7.6	495	6.6	420	5.8
	SA_F	495	5.5	1020	12.1	910	11.6	765	10	660	8.9	575	8
	EI	8915	100	7710	91.5	1195	15.1	1205	15.7	1170	15.7	1035	14.3
	WC	150	1.7	65	0.8	105	1.3	120	1.6	120	1.6	120	1.6
	Earnings	7335	82.2	4410	52.4	5140	65.1	5185	67.6	5230	70.1	5170	71.3
	CQPP	260	2.9	765	9.1	935	11.8	1000	13	1010	13.6	985	13.6
	Total Uncensored	8915	100	8420	94.4	7760	92.2	7410	93.9	7185	93.7	6985	93.8
	Non-Filer			440	4.9	610	7.2	450	5.7	445	5.8	420	5.6
	Not Eligible (Student, Age, etc.)			60	0.6	50	0.6	30	0.4	40	0.5	45	0.6
	Total Censored			500	5.6	660	7.8	480	6.1	485	6.3	465	6.2

(TABLE 1 cont.)

Cohort	Income State	T0		T1		T2		T3		T4		T5	
		#	%	#	%	#	%	#	%	#	%	#	%
1995	SA_I	250	2.6	725	7.9	620	7.1	465	5.5	395	4.7	340	4.2
	SA_F	420	4.2	880	9.6	795	9.1	625	7.4	535	6.4	470	5.9
	EI	9860	100	7575	82.4	1325	15.2	1485	17.6	1370	16.5	1195	14.9
	WC	175	1.8	75	0.8	125	1.4	155	1.8	140	1.7	180	2.2
	Earnings	8390	85.1	5210	56.6	5985	68.9	6045	71.6	6045	72.7	5940	74
	CQPP	320	3.3	835	9.1	985	11.3	1090	12.9	1155	13.9	1120	14
	Total Uncensored	9860	100	9200	93.3	8505	92.4	8145	93.7	7995	94.6	7750	93.1
	Non-Filer			570	5.8	635	6.9	495	5.7	410	4.8	520	6.3
	Not Eligible (Student, Age, etc.)			95	0.9	60	0.7	50	0.6	45	0.5	50	0.6
	Total Censored			660	6.7	695	7.6	545	6.3	455	5.4	570	6.9
1996	SA_I	200	2	670	7	565	6.3	415	4.7	375	4.3	325	3.8
	SA_F	335	3.3	835	8.8	720	8	585	6.6	510	5.9	470	5.6
	EI	10195	100	7620	79.8	1555	17.2	1465	16.6	1320	15.3	1360	16.1
	WC	135	1.3	70	0.7	150	1.7	160	1.8	180	2.1	170	2
	Earnings	8535	83.7	5705	59.8	6335	70.3	6365	72.3	6330	73.3	6240	73.9
	CQPP	355	3.5	860	9	990	11	1085	12.3	1190	13.8	1190	14.1
	Total Uncensored	10195	100	9540	93.6	8830	92.6	8495	94.2	8305	94.3	8130	94.2
	Non-Filer			585	5.8	640	6.7	475	5.3	460	5.2	470	5.4
	Not Eligible (Student, Age, etc.)			65	0.7	70	0.7	45	0.5	40	0.4	35	0.4
	Total Censored			655	6.4	710	7.4	520	5.8	500	5.7	505	5.8

(TABLE 1 cont.)

Cohort	Income State	T0		T1		T2		T3		T4		T5	
		#	%	#	%	#	%	#	%	#	%	#	%
1997	SA_I	160	1.6	505	5.2	410	4.5	330	3.7	305	3.5	265	3.1
	SA_F	270	2.6	645	6.7	545	5.9	455	5	435	4.9	395	4.7
	EI	10240	100	7960	82.7	1480	16.2	1290	14.4	1375	15.6	1275	15.1
	WC	160	1.6	80	0.8	115	1.3	165	1.8	140	1.6	125	1.5
	Earnings	8690	84.9	5150	53.5	5890	64.4	6025	67.1	5920	67.1	5710	67.5
	CQPP	405	4	975	10.1	1130	12.4	1305	14.5	1450	16.4	1485	17.6
	Total Uncensored	10240	100	9625	94	8975	93.3	8660	94.6	8510	94.8	8210	93.1
	Non-Filer			535	5.2	580	6	435	4.8	430	4.8	575	6.5
	Not Eligible (Student, Age, etc.)			80	0.8	70	0.7	55	0.6	35	0.4	35	0.4
	Total Censored			615	6	650	6.7	490	5.4	465	5.2	610	6.9
1998	SA_I	160	1.6	460	5	370	4.2	325	3.7	305	3.6	290	3.6
	SA_F	265	2.7	595	6.4	485	5.5	465	5.3	435	5.1	415	5.1
	EI	9820	100	7155	77.3	1375	15.5	1600	18.3	1425	16.8	1300	16
	WC	165	1.7	70	0.8	130	1.4	170	2	170	2	165	2
	Earnings	8180	83.3	5570	60.2	6115	69.2	6160	70.6	5965	70.4	5740	70.5
	CQPP	350	3.6	815	8.8	1010	11.4	1125	12.9	1250	14.8	1270	15.6
	Total Uncensored	9820	100	9250	94.2	8665	93.7	8415	95.2	8245	94.5	7910	93.4
	Non-Filer			495	5.1	520	5.6	365	4.1	445	5.1	505	6
	Not Eligible (Student, Age, etc.)			70	0.7	65	0.7	55	0.6	40	0.4	55	0.6
	Total Censored			570	5.8	585	6.3	420	4.8	485	5.5	560	6.6

(TABLE 1 cont.)

Cohort	Income State	T0		T1		T2		T3		T4		T5	
		#	%	#	%	#	%	#	%	#	%	#	%
1999	SA_I	155	1.7	405	4.7	355	4.3	320	3.9	290	3.6	285	3.6
	SA_F	250	2.7	520	6	500	6	450	5.5	410	5.1	395	5.1
	EI	9250	100	6500	75	1620	19.3	1615	19.9	1500	18.9	1340	17.3
	WC	130	1.4	85	1	140	1.7	160	2	170	2.1	195	2.5
	Earnings	8125	87.9	5665	65.4	6090	72.6	5955	73.1	5820	73.1	5690	73.4
	CQPP	290	3.1	710	8.2	870	10.4	995	12.2	1100	13.8	1105	14.2
	Total Uncensored	9250	100	8665	93.7	8155	94.1	7900	94.2	7685	94.3	7500	94.2
	Non-Filer			525	5.7	450	5.2	445	5.3	420	5.2	430	5.4
	Not Eligible (Student, Age, etc.)			60	0.6	60	0.7	40	0.5	40	0.5	30	0.4
	Total Censored			585	6.3	505	5.9	485	5.8	460	5.7	460	5.8
2000	SA_I	145	1.6	380	4.6	320	4	295	3.7	290	3.8	275	3.7
	SA_F	240	2.7	515	6.2	450	5.6	420	5.3	405	5.3	395	5.3
	EI	8900	100	6140	73.3	1515	18.9	1565	19.8	1495	19.5	1325	17.7
	WC	135	1.5	75	0.9	120	1.5	155	2	150	1.9	145	1.9
	Earnings	7890	88.7	5540	66.1	5850	73	5805	73.7	5705	74.5	5585	74.9
	CQPP	285	3.2	665	7.9	815	10.2	915	11.6	1005	13.1	990	13.3
	Total Uncensored	8900	100	8375	94.1	7855	93.8	7595	94.7	7420	94.2	7190	93.9
	Non-Filer			450	5	470	5.6	380	4.7	415	5.3	430	5.6
	Not Eligible (Student, Age, etc.)			75	0.8	50	0.6	40	0.5	40	0.5	35	0.5
	Total Censored			525	5.9	520	6.2	420	5.3	455	5.8	465	6.1

(TABLE 1 cont.)

Cohort	Income State	T0		T1		T2		T3		T4		T5	
		#	%	#	%	#	%	#	%	#	%	#	%
2001	SA_I	185	1.6	480	4.4	415	4	335	3.3	305	3.1	295	3.1
	SA_F	310	2.7	635	5.8	545	5.3	470	4.6	450	4.5	425	4.4
	EI	11580	100	8040	74.2	2035	19.6	2050	20.1	1835	18.5	1660	17.2
	WC	175	1.5	105	1	170	1.6	165	1.6	200	2	205	2.1
	Earnings	10520	90.9	7335	67.7	7940	76.3	7865	77.1	7740	77.8	7630	78.9
	CQPP	310	2.7	755	7	910	8.8	1025	10	1085	10.9	1095	11.3
	Total Uncensored	11580	100	10835	93.6	10165	93.8	9855	94.7	9620	94.4	9320	93.7
	Non-Filer			650	5.6	585	5.4	475	4.6	530	5.2	560	5.6
	Not Eligible (Student, Age, etc.)			95	0.8	85	0.8	70	0.7	45	0.5	65	0.7
	Total Censored			740	6.4	675	6.2	545	5.3	575	5.6	625	6.3
2002	SA_I	175	1.5	480	4.2	395	3.6	340	3.2	325	3.1	305	3
	SA_F	260	2.1	625	5.6	560	5.1	495	4.6	470	4.5	455	4.5
	EI	12085	100	8250	73.3	1935	17.7	1945	18.2	1820	17.5	1620	15.9
	WC	140	1.2	100	0.9	155	1.4	160	1.5	170	1.6	165	1.6
	Earnings	10640	88.1	7515	66.8	8290	76.1	8370	78.1	8255	79.1	8070	79
	CQPP	295	2.4	800	7.1	960	8.8	1055	9.9	1115	10.7	1130	11
	Total Uncensored	12085	100	11260	93.2	10600	94.2	10340	94.9	10085	94.1	9850	94.4
	Non-Filer			715	5.9	565	5	490	4.5	545	5.1	570	5.5
	Not Eligible (Student, Age, etc.)			110	0.9	95	0.8	65	0.6	85	0.8	15	0.1
	Total Censored			825	6.8	660	5.8	555	5.1	630	5.9	585	5.6

T-1, which ensures that any such income observed in year T0 could not be the continuation of such income. That said, we could still envisage some rare cases where these other income sources could be received prior to, rather than after, an exhausted EI spell in T0.

Individuals are followed for a five-year period following year T0 (labelled T1...T5). Since individuals may obtain income from more than a single source, these categories are obviously not mutually exclusive (and thus the proportions do not sum to unity). As noted above, T0 denotes the period in which the EI spell begins. This spell may end in either period T0 or in T1; the data do not permit us to distinguish. Hence the first year in which individuals definitively have no EI income from the reference spell is T2. This explains why there is a large decline between periods T1 and T2 in the incidence of receipt of EI income. This fact also explains why our presentation of the results concentrates on the receipt of these various income sources in periods T2 to T5 rather than from T0 or T1 to T5. While the absolute number of individuals tracked is given in the first column for each year (T0 through T5), we refer only to the percentages in the second column.

The first block in Table 1 presents the average incidence rates for all cohorts pooled together. Care should obviously be exercised in drawing inferences for policy purposes, because the observations span almost a decade. The incidence rate for receiving EI benefits in years T2 through T5 varies within a narrow band bounded by 16.1 per cent and 17.3 per cent. This set of results indicates a pattern of repeat use among EI spell exhaustees, and that the incidence of EI use does not vary a great deal as time elapses after the point of exhaustion.[12] This result was unexpected because we deleted from our sample individuals who received EI benefits in either year T1 or T2. During that pre-exhaustion interval, these particular subjects were not frequent users of EI.

The receipt of SA is rare relative to EI receipt. On an individual basis, the incidence rate varies between 3.7 per cent in T5 and 5.1 per cent in T2; on a family basis between 5.3 per cent and 7.4 per cent for the same time periods. The percentage drawing WC benefits varies little over the four years after year T1. Labour market earnings are reported by fewer than three quarters of the exhaustees in periods T2 to T5 (70.9 per cent to 74 per cent). This seems to be a fairly low number and suggests that some EI exhaustees are either having a difficult time finding subsequent employment, or alternatively are withdrawing from the labour market. The latter outcome could be associated with long-term unemployment. At this point, we cannot distinguish between these possibilities, as the Table 1 data contain "unconditional," univariate cross-tabulated data. The gradual, monotonic increase in the percentage claiming CQPP that we observe with the passage of time since exhaustion is to be expected, as more individuals attain the minimum age at which they become eligible for such benefits. At the same time, the 10.6 per cent number in period T2 is substantially above what one would expect given the age distribution of the population. A possible interpretation is that a disproportionately large percentage of the EI spell exhaustees in the greater than 60 years age bracket are making a retirement decision. This is clearly a question that warrants more detailed investigation.

The figures presented in the first block in Table 1 are plotted in Figure 3. All of the cohorts are pooled together. One of the conclusions we draw is that these incidence rates are remarkably stable over the period spanning years T2 through T5.

Figure 3 Incidence of Receipt of Income From Various Sources Over Time

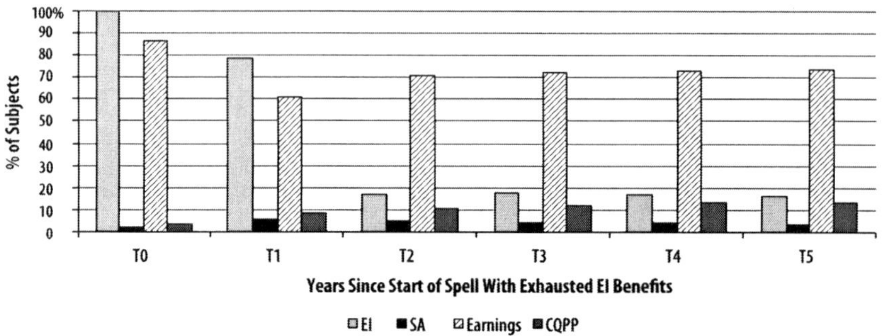

Turning now to the individual cohorts (below the first block in Table 1), there are substantial changes in the transition probabilities between the early and mid 1990s and the first years of the new millennium. In contrast to what one might have anticipated, the incidence of EI receipt in years T3 and T4 was lower for the early cohorts and higher for the cohorts of exhaustees between 1999 and 2001. The higher rate of EI use in the later years may reflect the weak labour market following the slowdown of 2001/02. Even though the unemployment rate rose to a considerably lower plateau post-2001, compared to the 1991–1995 recession, the incidence of EI use is higher in the later phase. Note that this pattern is not inconsistent with the aggregate unemployment trends at this time; rather it could reflect the presence of a significant number of repeat users. Because the repeat use of EI is associated with seasonal and part-year workers, its incidence is fairly impervious to the business cycle.

The incidence rate for SA receipt displays a marked pattern, whether the individual or the family is used as the accounting unit. The 1994 cohort sees transitions to SA_I that vary between 9.0 per cent and 5.8 per cent between years T2 and T5. These numbers decline to between 4.2 per cent and 3.6 per cent for the 1998 cohort and decline further by 2002 to between 3.6 per cent and 3.0 per cent. Transitions to SA_F follow identical patterns for the cohorts over time. These figures illustrate clearly that the more stringent EI program that prevailed at the turn of the millennium did not result in an overflow of individuals and households onto the nation's "welfare rolls." These empirical patterns are fully consistent with the data on aggregate SA activity that was mentioned above. In Figure 2 it can be seen that in Ontario SA dependency in 2010 is not much more than one half of the rate in 1994.

The apparent lack of substitution from the EI regime to the SA regime may be attributable at least in part to parallel developments in Canada's network of provincial SA programs. In addition to increased barriers to access described earlier, the real value of SA benefits fell during this period (National Council of Welfare 2003), and the National Child Benefit program, which de facto separated a child support payment from the adult support payment, likely had a favourable impact on labour-force participation. A second caveat is that in this chapter, we are looking only at transitions to SA from EI (regular benefits), and it is conceivable that individuals are going directly onto SA without passing through a spell of EI. However, Finnie, Irvine and Sceviour (2004b) provide evidence which suggests otherwise.

The third pattern to emerge from the cohort-specific analysis is that the pattern of retirements on the part of EI spell exhaustees evolved over the period. The percentage resorting to CQPP declines between the mid 1990s cohorts and the new millennium cohorts. The switch from a higher incidence rate of CQPP receipt to a lower incidence rate seems to occur in the late 1990s. The lower values observed in the later cohorts are consistent with what we know about aggregate retirement rates in the economy—more individuals are choosing to postpone the decision to retire.

Figure 4 displays averages of the values reported in Table 1 across the post-exhaustion years of T2 through T5. These averages are calculated in order to display trends (if any) across the cohorts from 1994 to 2002. Some of the patterns mentioned in the paragraph above are visible. For instance, the proportion of each cohort that is active in the labour market rises slightly during the boom year of 2000, followed by a relatively high value in 2001. The corresponding proportions for the receipt of EI show a similar pattern. The proportion of each cohort that receives SA benefits declines monotonically from 1994 until 1997, and tends to a low level of approximately 3 to 4 per cent thereafter.

The number of individuals in receipt of WC is never great, while those on CQPP rise in a steady fashion, as would be expected as the individuals in our samples age with the length of their respective post-EI periods. Nevertheless, these data show no obvious substitution toward the Canada and Quebec Pension plans as an alternative to the EI program for those who exhaust EI spells over the period in question, just as there has been no apparent switch to SA. These findings are consistent with those reported in Finnie and Gray (2009) for older displaced workers (who may or may not have exhausted their EI benefits).

B Typology Analysis of Receipt of Income

For this portion of our statistical analysis, the outcome of interest is not the event of receipt of income from a particular source, but rather the profile of the income sources for individuals within our sample. To this end we calculate the shares of individuals relying heavily on income from specific sources, or a configuration of sources, in the time periods following an EI spell's exhaustion. Individuals can fall into more than one of these categories. In particular, individuals who obtain SA in a subsequent year may simultaneously generate labour market earnings or obtain income from other sources such as EI. We develop a typology of categories, whereby the groups are defined with a view to understanding in particular what other major sources of income are generated by SA recipients, and on what alternative income sources do exhaustees tend to rely? By construction of a typology, these "types" are both mutually exclusive and exhaustive, and the shares must sum to unity. These types are defined as the follows: (i) SA receipt only; (ii) SA plus earnings, with SI receipt possible; (iii) SA plus SI receipt without earnings; (iv) SI plus earnings with no SA receipt; and (v) earnings only.[13] Note that the definition of these groups does not preclude the receipt of income from any number of other sources, such as investment income, but typically these amounts are small, and the sources named in the label are the critical ones. There are two broader categories at a higher level; the first three groups all involve SA receipt, while the second, fourth, and fifth all involve earnings. Since income sources are many, we have included a "residual" grouping to account for those individuals who do not fall into one of the five defined groups.[14]

TABLE 2 Distribution of Income State in Years Since the Start of EI Exhaustion, Typology Incidence

Cohort	Income State	T0		T1		T2		T3		T4		T5	
		#	%	#	%	#	%	#	%	#	%	#	%
All	SA only			515	0.6	2085	2.6	1770	2.2	1575	2	1535	2
	SA+Earnings, SI possible	2285	2.5	3145	3.7	2900	3.6	2370	3	2075	2.7	1810	2.4
	SA+SI, no Earnings	555	0.6	2615	3.1	525	0.6	585	0.7	655	0.8	650	0.9
	SI+Earnings, No SA	88005	96.9	63655	74.7	21465	26.4	22765	28.6	22630	29.1	21570	28.6
	Earnings only			10740	12.6	40095	49.3	40160	50.5	40260	51.8	40185	53.3
	Residual			4510	5.3	14215	17.5	11905	15	10495	13.5	9660	12.8
1994	SA only			45	0.5	430	5.4	335	4.4	275	3.7	255	3.5
	SA+Earnings, SI possible	420	4.7	410	4.9	415	5.3	350	4.6	295	4	250	3.4
	SA+SI, no Earnings	75	0.8	560	6.7	65	0.8	80	1.1	90	1.2	70	1
	SI+Earnings, No SA	8425	94.5	6840	81.2	1975	25	2070	27	2040	27.4	1900	26.2
	Earnings only			310	3.7	3495	44.3	3580	46.7	3705	49.7	3765	51.9
	Residual			250	3	1510	19.1	1255	16.3	1045	14	1010	13.9
1995	SA only			75	0.8	320	3.7	235	2.8	210	2.5	175	2.2
	SA+Earnings, SI possible	340	2.6	395	4.3	410	4.7	310	3.7	245	3	220	2.7
	SA+SI, no Earnings	80	0.7	415	4.5	65	0.8	75	0.9	75	0.9	75	0.9
	SI+Earnings, No SA	9445	96.7	7020	76.3	2165	24.9	2460	29.1	2405	28.9	2245	28
	Earnings only			865	9.4	4200	48.3	4135	48.9	4290	51.6	4300	53.6
	Residual			435	4.7	1530	17.6	1230	14.6	1090	13.1	1010	12.6

(continued on next page)

(TABLE 2 cont.)

Cohort	Income State	T0		T1		T2		T3		T4		T5	
		#	%	#	%	#	%	#	%	#	%	#	%
1996	SA only			65	0.7	265	2.9	225	2.5	180	2.1	175	2.1
	SA+Earnings, SI possible	270	2.6	430	4.5	385	4.3	300	3.4	260	3	215	2.5
	SA+SI, no Earnings	70	0.7	340	3.6	65	0.7	60	0.7	70	0.8	85	1
	SI+Earnings, No SA	9860	96.7	7120	74.6	2390	26.5	2445	27.8	2420	28	2420	28.7
	Earnings only			1125	11.8	4370	48.5	4490	51	4535	52.6	4515	53.4
	Residual			460	4.8	1535	17	1280	14.6	1170	13.5	1035	12.3
1997	SA only			45	0.5	190	2.1	160	1.8	145	1.6	140	1.7
	SA+Earnings, SI possible	205	2	315	3.3	295	3.2	220	2.5	220	2.5	170	2
	SA+SI, no Earnings	65	0.6	285	3	60	0.7	70	0.8	70	0.8	80	1
	SI+Earnings, No SA	9970	97.4	7635	79.3	2490	27.2	2510	28	2700	30.6	2655	31.4
	Earnings only			890	9.2	4050	44.3	4325	48.2	4160	47.1	4065	48.1
	Residual			455	4.7	2065	22.6	1690	18.8	1530	17.4	1345	15.9
1998	SA only			55	0.6	190	2.1	180	2.1	165	1.9	160	2
	SA+Earnings, SI possible	210	2.1	325	3.5	245	2.8	230	2.6	205	2.4	185	2.3
	SA+SI, no Earnings	55	0.6	215	2.3	50	0.5	55	0.6	65	0.8	70	0.9
	SI+Earnings, No SA	9555	97.3	6910	74.7	2290	25.9	2595	29.8	2585	30.5	2475	30.4
	Earnings only			1140	12.3	4380	49.5	4230	48.4	4185	49.4	4075	50
	Residual			605	6.6	1685	19.1	1440	16.5	1265	15	1180	14.5

(continued on next page)

(TABLE 2 cont.)

Cohort	Income State	T0		T1		T2		T3		T4		T5	
		#	%	#	%	#	%	#	%	#	%	#	%
1999	SA only			40	0.5	160	1.9	145	1.8	150	1.9	140	1.8
	SA+Earnings, SI possible	195	2.1	275	3.2	280	3.3	235	2.9	170	2.2	175	2.3
	SA+SI, no Earnings	50	0.6	205	2.3	60	0.7	75	0.9	85	1.1	75	1
	SI+Earnings, No SA	9000	97.3	6320	72.9	2350	28	2480	30.4	2480	31.2	2350	30.3
	Earnings only			1290	14.9	4150	49.5	4015	49.3	4010	50.4	4015	51.8
	Residual			535	6.2	1385	16.5	1200	14.7	1060	13.3	995	12.8
2000	SA only			60	0.7	160	2	160	2	140	1.8	145	1.9
	SA+Earnings, SI possible	190	2.1	265	3.2	240	3	205	2.6	205	2.7	185	2.5
	SA+SI, no Earnings	50	0.6	190	2.3	50	0.6	55	0.7	60	0.8	65	0.9
	SI+Earnings, No SA	8660	97.3	5970	71.3	2210	27.6	2385	30.3	2380	31.1	2195	29.5
	Earnings only			1395	16.7	4040	50.4	3940	50	3885	50.8	3930	52.7
	Residual			495	5.9	1320	16.4	1130	14.4	985	12.9	930	12.5

(continued on next page)

(TABLE 2 cont.)

Cohort	Income State	T0		T1		T2		T3		T4		T5	
		#	%	#	%	#	%	#	%	#	%	#	%
2001	SA only			50	0.4	185	1.8	165	1.6	150	1.5	160	1.7
	SA+Earnings, SI possible	265	2.3	380	3.5	305	3	245	2.4	230	2.3	205	2.1
	SA+SI, no Earnings	45	0.4	205	1.9	55	0.5	60	0.6	70	0.7	55	0.6
	SI+Earnings, No SA	11270	97.3	7810	72.1	2815	27.1	2930	28.7	2805	28.2	2680	27.7
	Earnings only			1755	16.2	5495	52.8	5460	53.6	5515	55.4	5530	57.2
	Residual			640	5.9	1545	14.9	1335	13.1	1175	11.8	1035	10.7
2002	SA only			80	0.7	185	1.7	165	1.5	160	1.5	185	1.8
	SA+Earnings, SI possible	195	1.6	345	3.1	320	3	280	2.6	240	2.3	205	2
	SA+SI, no Earnings	60	0.5	200	1.8	50	0.5	55	0.5	70	0.7	70	0.7
	SI+Earnings, No SA	11825	97.9	8035	71.4	2780	25.5	2885	26.9	2820	27	2645	25.9
	Earnings only			1965	17.5	5920	54.3	5985	55.9	5965	57.2	5990	58.7
	Residual			630	5.6	1640	15	1350	12.6	1180	11.3	1120	11

FIGURE 4 Incidence of Receipt of Income From a Given Source in Years T2-T5 (averaged) by Cohort

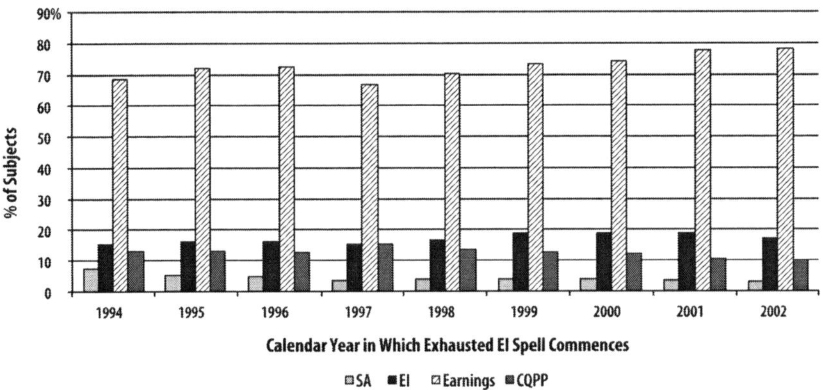

The first block of data in Table 2 defines income sources for all cohorts pooled together. It is clear that the percentage of spell exhaustees that depends only upon SA is small—slightly greater than 2 per cent for years T2 through T5 (row 1). Rows two and three indicate that the percentage of SA recipients that reports receipt of other sources of income coupled with SA, whether in the form of earnings or social insurance, is considerably greater. The percentage of spell exhaustees generating earnings, either alone or in conjunction with SA and SI is indicated in rows 2, 4 and 5. These entries indicate that in excess of 80 per cent of individuals fall into these three categories that involve earnings. While these numbers indicate a reasonable degree of success in re-integration into the labour market on the one hand, they also indicate a very high degree of continued recourse to the EI regime, as indicated by row 4. More than one quarter of exhaustees depend upon SI, which includes both EI and CQPP, in years T2 to T5. The corollary to the foregoing is that just about one half of spell exhaustees depend upon earnings alone in periods T2 to T5—see row 5. As mentioned above, it is important to bear in mind here that the spell exhaustees in our samples are not habitual users of EI by the selection criteria of our sample.

The figures discussed just above are plotted in Figure 5. It is apparent that these shares are pretty stable between years T2 and T5. Approximately half of the sample relies solely on earnings, and this share edges up only slightly over elapsed time since exhaustion. The share of those who rely partially or fully on SA benefits declines gently from 7.4 per cent in year T1 to 5.3 per cent in year T5. The share of the residual category is 17.5 per cent in year T2, and it declines slightly over time.

FIGURE 5 Principal Sources of Income Over Time

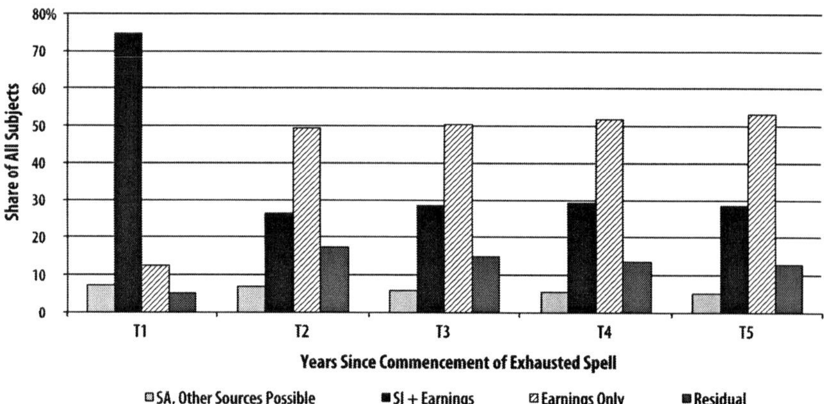

There is some degree of variation in these typology shares across the cohorts of our sample, which are listed below the first panel of Table 2. The first row of each cohort-specific block of information indicates that SA alone constituted a significant group early in the sample period (i.e., for the 1994 and 1995 cohorts) and a substantially smaller group by the end of the period. For the 1994 cohort, this group accounted for 5.4 per cent of the sample in T2 and 3.5 per cent in T5. These percentages declined quickly rather than slowly as the decade progressed, to the point where the 1996 cohort experienced values of 2.9 per cent and 2.1 per cent for the corresponding points in time. The further declines for later cohorts were gradual and small by comparison.

Complementary to this downward trend for SA receipt, the shares for those receiving earnings rise correspondingly in moving from earlier to later cohorts. Taking again the sum of rows 2, 4 and 5, approximately three quarters of the 1994 cohort generated earnings (with or without other income sources) by T2, and that figure rose to above 80 per cent by T5. These earnings groups accounted for an ever larger percentage of our sample in later cohorts, to the point that more than 80 per cent of the 2002 cohort generated earnings in T2 (irrespective of receipt from other sources), and almost 90 per cent generated earnings by T5. At the same time, it is to be noted that while the "earnings alone" category increased by about five percentage points, the group that received earnings plus SI continued to account for at least one quarter of the cohort in a period that saw a tightening of EI access criteria.

The figures contained in Table 2 pertaining to the specific cohorts are plotted in Figure 6. The share for those receiving earnings seems to rise slightly at times of favourable labour market conditions. The share of the group receiving social insurance income combined with earnings (but not SA receipt) rises slightly and progressively from 1994 to 2000, and then falls. The group that relies solely on SA benefits accounts for less than 2 per cent of the sample in most calendar years.

6 Analysis Broken Down by Region

The analysis presented to this point reflects the average behaviour of individuals from all regions of Canada. To determine if there exist regional differences in outcomes, we present a limited amount of the foregoing nationally-aggregated information in figures 7 and 8.[15] Figure 7 contains information on the incidence of receipt of a given source of income, and Figure 8 contains figures on income typology. We have aggregated the provinces of Canada into six regions: the Atlantic Provinces, Quebec, Ontario, Manitoba and Saskatchewan, Alberta, and British Columbia. To keep the analysis tractable while exploring regional differences, we aggregate along the dimension of elapsed time since the start of the reference spell (averaging values for the statistics in question from T2 to T5). Due in part to the generation of small data cells (which causes privacy considerations), we pool all of the cohorts between the years 1994 and 2002 together. The latter aggregation is equivalent to considering the "all cohorts" outcomes presented in tables 1 and 2. We are aware that both of these aggregations can potentially camouflage differing trends across years and cohorts, but they still permit us to expose time-invariant substantial differences between regions.

Consider first Figure 7. On the earnings front, there are marked differences between East and West. The Prairies, Alberta and British Columbia see a higher proportion of individuals returning to work than do the Atlantic Provinces, Quebec and even Ontario—whose manufacturing sector was hit hard in the recession of the early 1990s. Quebec and Ontario spell exhaustees relied more heavily on SA than did the western provinces. This was not the case for the Atlantic Provinces, where SI played a larger supporting role than anywhere else in the economy. This graphic does not indicate if the SI comes in the form of EI, WC or CQPP, but it is likely that EI accounts for much of that proportion.

FIGURE 6 Average Incidence of Receipt of Income From a Given Source by Region of Canada

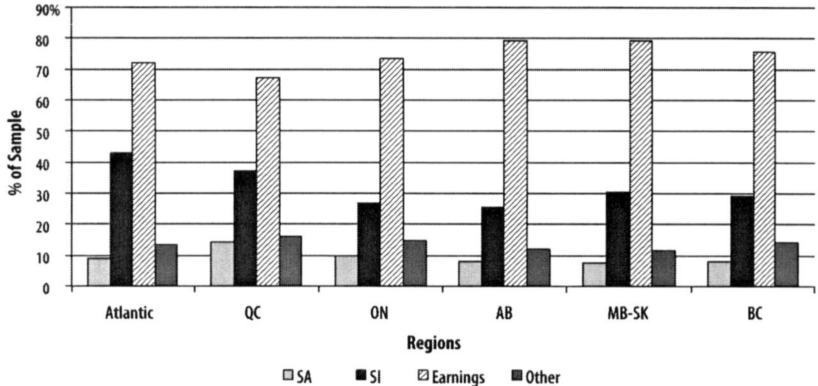

Turning now to the typology analysis listed in Figure 8, in contrast to the percentages in Figure 7, these categories are mutually exclusive, and therefore the values add to one hundred. Again the western regions experience a higher proportion of individuals who rely on earnings than is the case in the eastern regions, though the dividing line has shifted east of Ontario. The share of individuals relying on some form of SI is particularly high in the Atlantic region and Quebec, though the reason is slightly different: in the Atlantic Provinces, the higher value for the SI type is primarily due to a higher reliance upon EI than is the case in Quebec. In turn, both of these regions experience higher frequencies of CQPP receipt than the other four regions.

In summary, marked differences characterize the regions, and these differences are consistent with what we know about regional patterns in labour market behaviours in general. What distinguishes our findings is that they pertain to individuals who exhaust a spell of EI benefits. Nonetheless we are reluctant to draw inferences for policy purposes from these results. In particular, the higher incidence of eventual transitions to CQPP in specific regions possibly reflects the age characteristics of the underlying populations. This question may be worth pursuing in a future analysis.

FIGURE 7 Typology Analysis of Income Source by Region of Canada

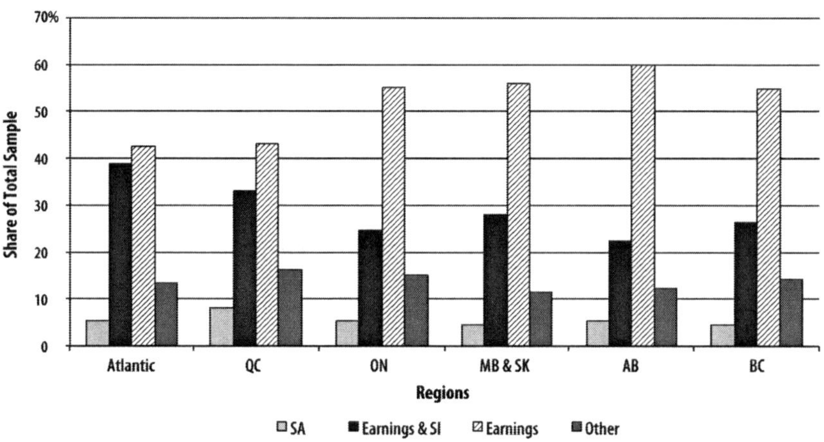

7 Conclusion

Our first objective for this paper is to study individuals' labour market outcomes after the exhaustion of a spell of regular EI benefits: their earnings, subsequent use of SA or one of Canada's other SI programs, and their continued use of EI. The second was to see if a shift occurred in these patterns between the 1994 and 2002 cohorts of spell exhaustees. The mid 1990s witnessed major changes in the EI system and the functioning of the labour market, a concurrent tightening of access to, and generosity of, SA, and the introduction of the work-focussed National Child Benefit program. Our use of the combined LAD-EI Link data base has allowed us to be among the first researchers to address these questions on a national basis and for such an extended period of time.

It is important that the results be interpreted both in the light of the changing economic circumstances and various policy changes of the time, and also in terms of the samples of individuals we have studied—those with a relatively strong historical attachment to the labour market. The methodological scope of this work remains primarily descriptive rather than causal. The rule changes to EI, SA and the NCB would have had their own effects on transitions from EI to other income sources. It should also be emphasized that transitions are analysed for those observed to exhaust a spell of regular EI benefits only, and the characteristics of this particular population of workers also likely changed over our estimation interval, especially as a result of the changes in EI that have affected entry into the program. All of our results are based on unconditional data—they are unadjusted incidence rates or shares of specified types of subjects. We have not estimated any behavioural or econometric models or explicitly taken into account the other factors that may have changed and affected the relevant dynamics. Nevertheless, by laying out these raw transition rates in a detailed fashion, the chapter provides a basis for further work of a more analytical nature.

Our principal findings are as follows:

- Despite more exigent EI eligibility conditions since the mid 1990s, there is no evidence of an increased degree of subsequent dependence on SA. On the contrary, the numbers and percentage of those exhausting EI spells and subsequently going onto SA has declined. These transition probabilities are not particularly high—in the range of 4 to 5 per cent of all EI exhaustees in the years following the exhaustion of the EI spell. Furthermore, just 2 per cent of EI spell exhaustees depend on SA alone within two years of the commencement of the exhausted spell.
- There appears to be a noticeable fall in the proportion of individuals moving onto government pension programs (CQPP) toward the end of our period of study. This transition decision is no doubt complex, and clearly depends upon the age structure of EI spell exhaustees. Yet the recent decline in this particular transition in our data is consistent with the economy-wide trend observed in Canada in this millennium for individuals to prolong their attachment to the labour market.
- Extended/repeat use of EI—even among these samples of individuals who have not had a history of EI income—is one of the strongest patterns to emerge from the data. Filing subsequent claims continues not just in the immediate period following the exhaustion of the reference spell, but for several more years at a comparable incidence rate. There has been no obvious tendency for this pattern of repeat use to decline during the period examined. While the number of individuals qualifying for EI support in general has dropped dramatically, the percentage of EI spell completers that rely on this form of income support in subsequent periods is striking and stable.
- A sizable percentage of individuals receive earnings within a year of completing their EI spell. This empirical pattern has been reinforced over our time interval. Between 80 and 90 per cent of individuals in the 2002 cohort generated earnings in the years following a spell completion, albeit many in conjunction with other forms of social insurance-source income.

These results point to a variety of possible further investigations. One would include modelling these incidence rates taking individual characteristics (age, place of residence, area size of residence, etc.) and current economic conditions (e.g., the unemployment rate) into account. Another area ripe for extension would be to attempt to incorporate into such a model the EI policy parameters (the entry requirements and the maximum length of the benefit period) that may affect these transitions. A third would be to incorporate policy changes in other programs (especially SA) into the analysis in like manner. And finally, a more complex model would include a mechanism for entry onto EI benefits to begin with, since this process determines the individuals who are (potentially) subsequently observed to exhaust EI benefits—the event that is the keystone for this study.

Endnotes

1 Social Assistance statistics are presented in official statistics both in caseload and individual units. A case may contain several individuals.

2 See Finnie, Irvine and Sceviour (2004a, b) regarding changes in the SA system, trends in SA participation, entry, exit, and re-entry rates, and an analysis of the factors underlying SA participation.

3 We are grateful to John Stapleton for providing us with this chart.

4 In the Canadian context, this issue is taken up in Gray (2003). It is also possible that a tightening of SA rules impacts the receipt of EI as a result of inducing a greater attachment to the labour force by marginal workers who might subsequently claim EI benefits. While we recognize that the interaction between EI and SA is a two-way street, we explore only the EI to SA route in this research.

5 It is also possible that a tightening of SA rules impacts the receipt of EI as a result of inducing a greater attachment to the labour force by marginal workers who might subsequently claim EI benefits. While we recognize that the interaction between EI and SA is a two-way street, we explore only the EI to SA route in this research.

6 As a caveat, Gray (2006) shows that a majority of the pilot projects that have been implemented within the regime since 1996 constituted an enrichment of benefits targeted primarily at seasonal workers.

7 A detailed description of the evolution of EI up to 1997 is given in Lin (1998) and Gray (2004).

8 UI claims began their descent in 1993, but SA caseloads began their decline only a year or two later, depending upon the province in question (see for example any of the annual reports on "Welfare Incomes" from the National Council of Welfare).

9 We began with the population of individuals aged 21–64 years in the cohort reference year and who have also filled in the preceding two years (about 2.7 million individuals). After excluding those individuals with non-trivial self-employment income during any of the three years in that window, approximately 2.5 million individuals remain. After excluding those individuals with low labour market incomes over that same window (and two other minor exclusions), about 1.6 million individuals remain. After excluding those with any positive social insurance income (of any type except EI) over that same window, 1.1 million individuals remain. After four more rounds of exclusion, including those who received special EI benefits, the precise sample size is 355,185 individuals. The final step is to select those who exhausted an EI spell that commenced in the reference year (N=90,845). Note that an individual selected early in the period could appear again as a new observation—but only if she/he had no EI or SA income for a minimum of two years, then filed

another EI claim, and then exhausted it.

10 Earnings include wages and salaries, net professional income, net self-employment, net joint partnership income (which could be negative), etc.

11 The event of exhaustion implies that the claimant has received all of the benefit weeks to which he/she was initially entitled. It does not include claimants who have reached the 52-week window (from the point of benefit period commencement) after which no more benefits can be received for that particular claim.

12 We note that because we have not counted the number of EI spells that each individual experienced over the period of years T2 through T5, we cannot identify any particular subject as a repeat user. The definition of a repeat user is typically an individual who has filed three or more claims during a five-year window. While we do discern a high incidence of EI use in each year during this interval, we do not determine the extent to which these figures reflect the same individuals claiming in consecutive years. It is therefore not certain that there is a pervasive pattern of repeat EI use by the same individuals. If many of those whom we observe receiving EI benefits in year T2 are also those whom we observe for the same event in years T3 or T4, that constitutes repeat use. If, on the other hand, the intersection of those groups is small, then there is only evidence of a fairly high recourse to EI use among our sample.

13 SI receipt means social insurance, which includes receipt of either EI, and/or WC, and/or CQPP benefits.

14 This residual group includes subjects with very heterogeneous income levels as well as configurations of income sources. These individuals are either not in the labour force or are on very long-term unemployment. In years T2 through T5, the mean value for their total incomes (including all taxable sources) was $7,600, while the median was only $1,925. The distribution of this variable for this type is thus very left-skewed, with a heavy concentration of individuals with very low incomes (the threshold for the lowest quartile is $315 annually), and very disperse, with a standard deviation of $15,875.

15 All of the figures that appear in this bar graph are drawn from tables that we have prepared, but there is a separate table for each region. Due to space constraints, we do not include them in this draft. They are available from the author.

References

Barrett, G., D. Doiron, D. Green and C. Riddell. 1996. "The Interaction of Unemployment Insurance and Social Assistance." Ottawa: Human Resources Development Canada.

Boadway, R., and D. Garon. 2011. "The Design of Employment Insurance in a Federation." Mowat Centre EI Task Force. Toronto: Mowat Centre for Policy Innovation.

Bolduc, D., B. Fortin, F. Labrecque and P. Lanoie. 2002. "Workers' Compensation, Moral Hazard and the Composition of Workplace Injuries." *Journal of Human Resources*, 37.3: 623-52.

Courchene, T.J. 1994. "Social Policy in the Millennium." Toronto: C. D. Howe Institute.

Dahlby, B. 1994. "The Distortionary Effect of Rising Taxes." In Deficit Reduction: What Pain; What Gain? Policy Study 23, ed. W.B.P. Robson and W.M. Scarth. Toronto: C.D. Howe Institute.

Expert Panel on Older Workers. 2008. "Supporting and Engaging Older Workers in the New Economy." Ottawa: Human Resources and Skills Development Canada.

Finnie, R. and D. Gray. 2009. "Displacement of older workers: re-employment, hastened retirement, disability, or other destinations?" Canadian Labour Market and Skills Research Network working paper No. 15.

——. 2011. "Labour-Force Participation of Older Displaced Workers in Canada: Should I Stay or Should I Go?" IRPP Study No. 15. Montreal: Institute for Research on Public Policy.

Finnie, R., I. Irvine and R. Sceviour. 2004a. "Social Assistance Use in Canada in the 1990s: Incidence, Entry and Exit." *Canadian Journal of Regional Science*, 27.2: 179-208.

——. 2004b. "Welfare Dynamics in Canada: The Role of Individual Attributes and Economic Policy Variables." Analytical Studies Branch Research Paper Series No. 231. Ottawa: Statistics Canada.

Finnie, R., and A. Sweetman, 2003. "Poverty Dynamics: Empirical Evidence for Canada." *Canadian Journal of Economics* 36.2: 291-325

Fortin, B., G. Lacroix and J.F. Thibault. 1999. "The Interaction of UI and Welfare, and the Dynamics of Welfare Participation of Single Parents." *Canadian Public Policy—Analyse de Politiques*, 25. supplement 1: 115-32.

Fortin, B. and P. Lanoie (1999) "Is Workers' Compensation a Substitute for Unemployment Insurance?" *Journal of Risk and Uncertainty* 18.2: 165-88.

Gray, D. 2003 "National Versus Regional Financing and Management of Unemployment and Related Benefits: The Case of Canada." OECD Social, Employment, and Migration Working Paper No. 14. Paris: OECD.

——. 2004. "Employment Insurance: What Reform Delivered?" C. D. Howe Institute Backgrounder. Toronto: C. D. Howe Institute.

——. 2006. "Has EI Reform Unravelled? Canada's EI regime in the 2000s." C. D. Howe Institute Backgrounder. Toronto: C. D. Howe Institute.

Grey, A. 2002. "Employment Insurance and Social Assistance: Evidence on Program Interaction," Applied Research Branch Working Paper SP-575-01-02E. Ottawa: Human Resources Development Canada.

Gunderson, M. 2011. "Employment Insurance in the New World of Work." Mowat Centre EI Task Force. Toronto: Mowat Centre for Policy Innovation.

Human Resources Development Canada. 2001. "Did the Social Assistance Take-up Rate Change after EI Reform for Job Separators?" Ottawa: HRDC.

——. 2002. "Did the Exhaustion of UI/EI Benefits and the Take-up of Social Assistance Change After EI Reform? (A Monitoring Study Prepared for the 2003 EI Monitoring and Assessment Report to Parliament)." Ottawa: HRSDC.

Jones, S. 2011. "The Effectiveness of Training for Displaced Workers with Long Prior Job Tenure." Mowat Centre EI Task Force. Toronto: Mowat Centre for Policy Innovation.

Lin, Z. 1998. "Employment Insurance in Canada: Recent Trends and Policy Changes." *Canadian Tax Journal*, vol. 46.1: 58-76.

Mendelson, M., and K. Battle. 2011. "Fixing the Hole in EI: Temporary Income Assistance for the Unemployed." Mowat Centre EI Task Force. Toronto: Mowat Centre for Policy Innovation.

National Council of Welfare. 2004. "Welfare Incomes 2003." Ottawa: National Council of Welfare.

Riddell, C. 2011. "Unemployment Compensation and Adjustment Assistance for Displaced Workers: Policy Options for Canada." Mowat Centre EI Task Force. Toronto: Mowat Centre for Policy Innovation.

Schirle, T. 2008. "Why Have the Labour Force Participation Rates of Older Men Increased Since the Mid-1990s?" *Journal of Labor Economics*. 26.4: 549-94.

Stapleton, J. 2011. "Trading Places: Single Adults Replace Lone Parents as the New Face of Social Assistance in Canada." Mowat Centre EI Task Force. Toronto: Mowat Centre for Policy Innovation.

Statistics Canada. 2010. "Low Income Cut Offs for 2008 and Low Income Measures for 2007." Income Research Paper Series. Ottawa: Statistics Canada.

Workplace Safety and Insurance Board of Ontario. 2009. *Annual Report*. Toronto: Workplace Safety and Insurance Board of Ontario. At http://www.wsib.on.ca/files/Content/staticfiles2009AnnualReport/2250A_wsibAR2009_ENG.pdf.

Chapter 11

The Effectiveness of Training for Displaced Workers with Long Prior Job Tenure

Stephen Jones

Displaced workers are individuals permanently laid off from a long-tenure job. Such workers pose a major policy challenge for three reasons. First, many face great difficulty finding a suitable new job and may experience a significant jobless spell. Second, when re-employed, many of the displaced take a substantial earnings drop, relative to the old job. Third, displaced workers' earnings losses appear very persistent in the months and years that follow. Aggregated over the period following a displacement, these earnings losses can dwarf the initial short-term income loss from unemployment and have hence become the central focus of the literature on training effectiveness.

Policy response naturally begins with the EI program, the centrepiece of Canadian adjustment programs. However, much support provided by EI—especially EI Part I—is passive support for a presumed temporary spell of short-term joblessness. While important for the job search of a displaced worker, and while other adjustment programs such as job search assistance may usefully supplement basic income support, EI does not address the larger problem posed by substantial long-lived earnings losses. Policy to tackle such earnings deficits is rather based on education, training, and skill development as means of bolstering the human capital of the displaced. A key issue is then the evaluation of the effectiveness of training. This forms the main focus of this chapter.

1 Magnitude of the Problem

A The Incidence of Displacement

Although there is considerable US evidence on displacement, based largely on the biannual Displaced Worker Survey (DWS),[1] Canadian evidence is relatively thin. Without a regular Canadian DWS, it is hard to track patterns and changes in the number of displaced workers and the nature of their experience.[2] The most comprehensive Canadian evidence comes from Morissette, Zhang and Frenette (2007) who use the Statistics Canada Longitudinal Worker File (LWF). These data integrate four administrative sources and cover 10 per cent of Canadian workers for 1983–2002, although this time frame means that most of the job separations they study are at least a decade old. The age of these data is obviously an important qualifier of the analysis's relevance to the current policy debate.

Definitions of displacement vary, with some being based on plant closures and others relying on mass layoffs to identify separations that are exogenous from the worker's point of view. Moreover, results vary depending on whether the prior job tenure of the group of displaced workers is limited. For prime age (25–49) displaced workers, Morissette, Zhang and Frenette find that the incidence of permanent layoffs lies in the range 6.6–9.1 per cent for men and 3.4–5.3 per cent for women. Of these, about 10 per cent were firm closures and about 20 per cent were layoffs linked to either firm closures or mass layoffs. On the broader layoff definition, these incidence rates mean that some 50,000 men were displaced in 2002, about one sixth of the 300,000 men laid off (for any reason) in that year. Analogous figures for women are about 23,000 displacements and 137,000 layoffs in 2002. An important point is the concentration of displacement within a relatively small group: most layoffs are not displacement.[3]

Seniority is important for the study of displacement since, as we shall see, losses rise sharply with prior job tenure. In terms of incidence, Morissette, Zhang and Frenette find that, on the firm closure layoff definition, about 10 per cent of all displacements had tenure of five years or more. Such long tenure workers represent less than one in one hundred of all annual layoffs.

B Unemployment Spells and Earnings Losses

Canada lacks clear evidence through time on the unemployment experience of displaced workers following their job separations. One would like to track the distribution of unemployment durations, compared with that for the non-displaced unemployed, and to see the evolution of such policy-relevant magnitudes as the proportion of EI eligibility used and the frequency of EI exhaustion among the displaced. Without regular DWSs, though, the available evidence is thin. Campolieti (2009) presents data on the experiences of job losers, but the analysis encompasses a much wider group than those typically viewed as displaced. Gray and Finnie (2009a, 2009b) use the Longitudinal Administrative Database, covering much the same time period as Morissette, Zhang and Frenette, and report that surprisingly few of the older displaced rely heavily on EI. And Bernard (2009) provides recent Canadian evidence on unemployment durations, although attention is not restricted to displaced workers.

Overall, in both Canada and the US, research on displaced workers has paid relatively little attention to short-term unemployment and non-employment following job separation, focusing rather on earnings losses in new employment. Nonetheless, some evidence suggests that Canadian displaced workers face longer unemployment spells than the average for the newly unemployed as a whole, reflecting their lack of familiarity with job search, potential mismatch of their skill sets with current labour market needs, and perhaps a reluctance to settle for lower wages. Both EI and job search assistance are likely of some help in cushioning this impact of displacement. But such transitory problems are secondary to the more enduring problem of lost earning potential.

Morissette, Zhang and Frenette assess earnings losses that displaced workers experience in new employment. There are many permutations of sample, definitions of displacement and estimation method, but the pattern of results is quite consistent. For the high seniority group, Morissette, Zhang and Frenette compare earnings in year five after job separation with those in year four prior to displacement, calculating the change as a proportion of the pre-displacement earnings.[4] The mean earnings drop is 25–35 per cent (men) and around 35 per cent (women) based on all displacements, and 25–34 per cent (men) and 35–37 per cent (women) based only on displacements owing to firm closure. For displaced workers at all seniority levels, and using all displacements, the earnings drops are 16–22 per cent (men) and 22–31 per cent (women).[5] Clearly, these are large losses five years after a displacement.

For older workers not covered by the Morissette, Zhang and Frenette sample aged 25–49, a complicating issue is the potential for self-selection out of the labour force and into (possibly early) retirement. Such selection would prevent potential earnings losses from being observed, although the resulting estimation bias could go in either direction.[6] The best evidence comes from Schirle (2007) who models this selection process carefully. She concludes it is not empirically critical: older workers face potential displacement earnings losses that are similar to those experienced by the prime-age displaced.

In summary, the balance of Canadian evidence is that many displaced workers cannot avoid an earnings loss. For workers with significant prior tenure, these losses are substantial. A ballpark figure from the best Canadian research would be around 25–30 per cent for those with at least five years' tenure, together with a figure of perhaps 20 per cent for displaced workers at all seniority levels. Such earnings losses are typically long-lived, with no sign in the data that they dissipate even five years after the displacement.

2 Causes of the Problem

A Potential for Skill Upgrading?

There is conclusive evidence that displaced workers typically suffer substantial and potentially permanent earnings losses. Does this mean that these earnings losses are the result of a skill deficit? And, as a distinct issue, would skill upgrading help displaced workers deal with these earnings losses?

The causes of displacement earnings losses are probably many and varied. Human capital that is *specific* to a job or firm may grow with tenure and be associated with substantial wage growth, and yet be non-transferable to a new job or firm following displacement. Key to assessing the importance of this cause is whether human capital is specific or general and, if specific, whether the specificity applies at the level of the firm, occupation or industry. A leading alternative is a long-term contracting framework wherein risk-neutral firms provide insurance against wage fluctuation to their risk-averse workers by making wages smoother than the corresponding path of productivity. Similarly, incentive pay schemes may use deferred compensation to overcome agency problems (related to work effort) within the firm. These agency models have low wages (under-compensation) at low tenure counterbalanced by high wages (and over-compensation) at high tenure levels, a pattern consistent with displaced earnings losses that are increasing in tenure. Finally, there are also theories of wage premia based on union wage effects, efficiency wages, and models of rent-sharing.

It is also important to note the considerable econometric literature that tries to disentangle the empirical wage-tenure relationship. In this work, the key is that wages and job tenure are *co-determined*, both resulting from workers' and firms' choices in equilibrium. Consequently, while a positive cross-section correlation between wages and tenure could arise from one or more of the above theories, it could also be *spurious*, driven by unobserved heterogeneity in worker, firm or worker-firm match type.[7]

This is obviously not the place to survey this econometric work extensively. Rather, I simply summarize this literature by suggesting that the simple least-squares estimate from cross-sectional data probably represents an upper bound on the true returns to tenure. If correct, this body of research would conclude that, while part of the displacement earnings loss could be attributed to a loss of a tenure-related wage premium, a substantial part of the loss would be for other reasons.

I now turn to the question of whether displaced workers need skills upgrading. If earnings reflect accumulated skills (with some firm or industry specificity) that are lost on displacement, then skill upgrading and replacement is a natural policy response. A thornier issue arises when lost specific human capital is *not* the main reason for earnings deficits. What if the earnings drop after displacement is due to long-term contracting reasons, such as deferred compensation, or industry-specific rents, or even a loss of a premium unionized job? Is there an argument that an upward-sloping wage profile for incentive reasons constitutes a "valid" cause of a pre-displacement wage premium, while a union rent does not? I have three comments.

First, it is hard to determine the cause of a pre-displacement earnings premium for any individual displaced worker. This parallels the practical, empirical difficulties many have encountered in attempting to identify the cause of displacement (trade, technical change, shifting final product demand).

Second, pragmatic policy might aim to compensate the losers from adjustment, regardless of the cause. Such compensation garners political support for policies that favour change, dynamism and economic growth, the argument being that, while the benefits of economic adjustment may be widespread, the costs of adjustment may narrowly be borne by a few. That said, a clear case where policy might economize on compensation costs is where pre-displacement earnings were unusually high for transitory reasons. Compensatory policy focused on long tenure displaced workers would naturally achieve this goal.

Third, does it then follow that the best mitigating policy should be to promote skills upgrading? There are comparatively few other policy levers that can raise post-displacement wages, although perhaps job search assistance can help secure better worker-firm matches without directly augmenting skills. But I think the answer to this question must be *contingent*, based on empirical evidence about effectiveness and efficiency of investments in skills. If the displaced were essentially unable to learn new skills to a level that paid off in terms of higher earnings, say, then perhaps some other form of compensation policy would be more suitable. But if there were a sufficient payoff to training and the acquisition of skills, then skills upgrading could help compensate the displaced. The effectiveness of training for this population is key.

3 Training

A Private and Social Returns

The private gain from training may exceed the social benefit, particularly in cases of *substitution*, whereby trainees benefit from jobs that they compete away from non-trainees. Trainees could displace non-trainees, and "displacement" is very much the *mot juste*. With many data sources, it may be hard to assess the importance of this effect without direct evidence on the labour market outcomes of non-trainees. General equilibrium effects could undo apparent training rewards but it might be hard for the analyst to discern.

Substitution may also be relevant for job search assistance. If their employment-related services genuinely improve match quality, then a worker's private gain might be mirrored by a social gain flowing from enhanced productivity. But if the private benefits of job search assistance derive mostly from outcompeting those without such assistance—without a concomitant increase in productivity—then the private benefits of job search assistance could mask little or no social return.[8]

B Barriers to Private Provision?

The case for *public* provision of training for long-tenure displaced workers also depends on an elaboration of the barriers to private provision. Credit constraints and other imperfections in capital markets, specifically the inability of individuals to borrow against future labour income, are often thought relevant to an explanation of the distribution of education achievements by income level. However, the evidence for credit constraints remains indirect and disputed, especially as higher family income can also improve the household environment conducive to the growth of cognitive and non-cognitive skills for education. Indeed, Carneiro and Heckman (2002) conclude that teenage ability far outweighs family income as a determinant of participation in post-secondary education. This opens up a voluminous literature of which a reasonable summary might be that the importance of credit constraints for human capital choices remains much disputed.[9]

With regard to displaced workers, *self-financed* training in particular may be subject to credit constraints and some aspects of public policy appear to be structured in light of this.[10] But again the evidence is mixed. Chapman et al. (2003) use the 1995 Canadian Out of Employment Panel (COEP) to examine self-financed training among job losers and suggest that liquidity does affect these choices. Yet they also note that credit constraints are not reported as the main reason why the COEP job losers do not undergo self-financed training. The extent that training is rationed owing to credit constraints remains an open issue.

Public intervention in training could also have a role even absent credit constraints, provided the private outcome involves equilibrium *under provision* of training. Such non-optimality can arise for several reasons. Wage compression (for institutional or legal reasons) may prevent workers from "paying for training" by accepting low initial wages: a minimum wage might thus discourage appropriate provision of training. Empirically, though, most evidence from the US and Canada suggests that this effect is small. Other types of wage compression, relative to marginal products, can also generate potential suboptimality of private training (Acemoglu and Pischke 1998, 1999, 2003). Examples would include imperfect labour markets, transaction costs, asymmetric information, contracting reasons relating to the eliciting of effort and diligence, and the interaction of general and specific skills. To give one example, "poaching" threats may make firms wary of too much investment in their workforce for fear of losing skilled workers to competitors. Asymmetric information may make it hard for workers credibly to signal that they have useful general skills to other employers, since the current employer may wish to keep such productivity information private, and this in turn produces suboptimal incentives for skill investments.

Two points on the optimality of private training bear emphasis. First, proponents of these non-competitive models of training with wage compression do not have specific recommendations to offer: "...we currently lack the type of detailed empirical information necessary to make precise policy recommendations" (Acemoglu and Pischke 1999, F128). Second, if inefficiencies in training arise for *non*-credit market reasons, the fix is probably not a program of loans. Indeed, attempts to solve non-credit problems by credit market subsidies could be counter-productive, perhaps generating overinvestment. Understanding the origins of suboptimal training investments is a prerequisite for knowing how to fix the problem.

4 Issues in the Evaluation of Training

A Methodologies

A large and developed literature exists on the economics and econometrics of active labour market programs, particularly training schemes, and research in this area can rightfully be regarded as at the forefront in the development of techniques for empirical program evaluation. Methodological issues fundamental to the assessment of causation, and to the separation of program *impacts* from program *outcomes*, are comprehensively assessed in Heckman, Lalonde and Smith (1999) and more recently in Imbens and Wooldridge (2009).

The fundamental problem in an assessment of causation is that, for a given individual, one can only observe the effect *with* treatment or the effect *without* treatment.[11] The counterfactual of what would have happened to a treated individual, had they not received the treatment, is unobserved. Comparison of the treated and the untreated may offer insight but is problematic if the treatment itself is endogenous: one group may *self-select* into treatment (training) and this self-selection may be associated with different characteristics than for the group that did not self-select. Individuals may also be selected into treatment by program administrators, perhaps in a well-meaning effort to help those in greatest need, or perhaps by selecting those most likely to succeed ("creaming"). If differences between the groups influence response to treatment, the untreated group may be a poor proxy for the true counterfactual. To tackle these problems using nonexperimental data, research methodologies have included instrumental variables, panel data estimates, selection-correction models and more recently matching and regression discontinuity estimators.

The major alternative in program evaluation is to use experimental data where assignment to treatment is random (independent of observed individual characteristics and potential outcomes). For some problems, experimentation can yield good estimates of the counterfactual and hence more reliable estimates of program impact. In the specific context of training, LaLonde's influential paper (1986) showed that a variety of econometric methods, applied to data drawn from a true experiment, were unable to match results from the randomized experiment itself.

Subsequent work has improved on these methods, however, and many have argued that randomized social experimentation may deliver answers only to very specific questions, such as the mean difference between two groups (Heckman 1991). When labour market interventions are multi-stage, the scope for clean experimental evaluation may be limited.[12] "Randomization bias" may contaminate experimental results: the behaviour of potential participants may be altered by the random assignment itself, perhaps by selection on risk aversion. Further, experiments are undoubtedly expensive and may pose significant practical, political, technological or ethical problems. Finally, experimental estimates usually reflect a partial equilibrium effect of an intervention. If treatment confers an advantage in employment prospects, say, a positive partial effect for the treated may or may not be at the expense of employment of the untreated control group, depending on the extent of displacement or substitution of non-trainees.[13]

Overall, I remain agnostic in the debate about experimental and nonexperimental methods and results. Although random assignment does not solve all problems, it has at times yielded more robust and credible estimates than were possible from nonexperimental data alone. Moreover, it has generated advances in statistical and econometric methods to deal with problems arising from such nonexperimental data.[14]

5 Effectiveness of Training Programs for Displaced Workers

Most of the voluminous literature on training program effectiveness, based on US evidence, has studied *disadvantaged populations* with few skills, checkered attachment to the labour market, and generally poor wage and employment prospects. Lessons from such a population do not apply directly to a population of Canadian displaced workers that exhibits past strong attachment to the labour market, evidenced particularly in long tenure and strong earnings on the old job. Accordingly, I will restrict my review of empirical results almost completely to research based on samples of displaced workers.[15] Moreover, I follow the training literature in a focus on long-term outcomes, specifically earnings replacement and recovery following displacement. This contrasts with attention to short-term re-employment outcomes, about which there has been less research. This longer-term focus reflects the greater overall importance of earnings changes over subsequent years and decades, relative to the transitory costs of initial joblessness.[16]

Important results on training effectiveness for the displaced fall into four groups. First, I review findings from (experimental) evaluations of displaced worker programs conducted in the US in the late 1980s, including demonstration projects in Buffalo, Texas and New Jersey (Leigh 1990, 1994). Second, there are credible nonexperimental studies of the effect of community college courses on displaced workers based on administrative records from Washington State (Jacobson, LaLonde and Sullivan 2005a, 2005b, 2005c). Third, I assess some preliminary results for the US *Workforce Investment Act* (WIA), legislation that replaced the *Job Training Partnership Act* in 1998 (Hollenbeck et al. 2005; Heinrich et al. 2009; and Decker 2009). Finally, I review the small amount of Canadian literature on the effectiveness of training in light of the international evidence.

A Dislocated Worker Demonstration Projects

The US Department of Labor's Dislocated Worker Demonstration Project began in October 1982 to study measures to aid the adjustment of workers displaced from manufacturing. It followed the Downriver program in Denver which had studied service delivery for the displaced following closing of an auto parts plant in August 1980. Although the Downriver program used treatment and comparison groups, workers were *not* randomly assigned on an individual basis; rather, *plants* were determined to be treatment or comparison plants, and workers were then selected at random from within these plants. The assignment by plant casts doubt on the positive results on earnings found in some Downriver programs (Leigh 1990).

Although there were seven sites involved in the Dislocated Worker Demonstration Project, the chief impact analysis was confined to Buffalo. The "target plant" sample in Buffalo was drawn from workers laid off from six steel and auto plants in the 12 months starting October 1982, the sample being male, white and married and with average prior job tenure of more than ten years: most had experienced a lengthy period of unemployment prior to the beginning of the project. A formal lottery generated random assignment to available program slots and resulted in 281 treated and 516 controls. The treatment consisted of job search assistance (JSA) with a possible follow-up of either classroom training (CT) or on-the-job training (OJT). Leigh notes (1990, 30) that the CT in Buffalo was typically very short-duration, while the OJT was chiefly a placement tool involving an employer wage subsidy. Some 55 per cent of participants received neither CT nor OJT.

The Buffalo Demonstration Project showed an impact on average weekly earnings of $134 from JSA alone for the target plant sample, an effect that is statistically significant (5 per cent level) and economically important (Leigh 1990, Table 3.3). With a mean prior wage of $10.78, this earnings impact was substantial, being about 28 per cent of pre-layoff earnings (based on a 40 hour week). However, there were *no significant effects* of supplementing this with either CT or OJT. Since Leigh reports that average costs per participant were $851 for JSA compared with $3,282 for CTplus JSA and $3,170 for OJT plus JSA, a conclusion from the Buffalo results is that the only potentially cost effective treatment was JSA.

An important limitation of the Buffalo Demonstration Project stems from the construction of the treatment and control groups. Specifically, individuals who were randomly assigned for treatment but chose not to participate were included as members of the comparison group. This creates a difficult self-selection problem that undermines random assignment. Moreover, the participation rate among recruited target-plant workers was only 16 per cent (Leigh 1990, 27), so this selection was quantitatively important. Although efforts were made to model individual participation decisions, including a selectivity variable in the final outcome specification (Corson, Long and Maynard 1985), difficulties with exclusion and other identification restrictions mean that such results lack the credibility of those from the initial random assignment design.

Results for a broader range of displaced workers were provided by the Texas Worker Adjustment Demonstration (WAD). The two main sites were Houston, where the displaced were mostly male petrochemical workers with relatively high prior earnings, and El Paso, where mostly female Hispanic workers had been displaced from low-paying jobs in light manufacturing. Under the WAD, individuals were randomly assigned to three groups: JSA (termed "Tier I" in the WAD evaluation), JSA plus training (termed "Tier I/II"), and no treatment (beyond other services available in the community). Unlike the Buffalo Demonstration Project, recruited nonparticipants were not included in the control group. Further, unlike Buffalo, the participation rate under the WAD was fairly high, with 71 per cent of those assigned to a treatment group choosing to participate (Leigh 1990, 32).

Results show some overall increase in annual earnings and weeks worked for the treated, with a substantial difference along gender/location lines. While men in both Houston and El Paso had short-term (annual) earnings impacts of $750 and $770, neither was statistically significantly different from zero. In contrast, the women in El Paso had a program-induced gain in earnings of $1,070, a large and statistically significant figure.[17] Analysis of the time-frame of earning gains, though, suggests that much of this female impact was very short-lived (Leigh 1990, Table 3.4).

The relative performance of JSA and training can be assessed using the WAD only for the Houston site, and only for men. Overall, the Tier I package of JSA yielded an earnings impact of $860, while the augmented Tier I/II combination of JSA plus training yielded an impact of $680 (Leigh 1990, Table 3.5). Thus, the net effect of the augmentation of JSA with training appears to be *negative*. Two interpretations were proposed first, that skill training takes time, so that serious job search may wait until training is completed, which could result in poor short-term earnings impacts; and second, that the training offered, mainly CT in skilled manual trades (e.g., air conditioning installation and maintenance), was poorly matched to the nature of the Houston target group, who were largely white-collar workers laid off from high paying petrochemical jobs. While both interpretations probably have some merit, the latter was judged critical by the authors of the initial evaluation and highlights the key role of the *match* of training to workers' characteristics and to labour market demand conditions. Whatever the reasons for the negative return to training beyond JSA, though, the results are in line with the Buffalo evidence. With average costs of $1,531 for Tier I (JSA) and $4,991 for Tier I/II, and with no apparent benefits from the more costly treatment, only JSA might be justified on a cost-benefit basis by these data. Whether training better matched to the clientele would yield greater benefits, and whether these benefits could cover the cost of such provision of training, are not questions that the WAD evaluation can answer.

The third major demonstration project conducted in the 1980s was the New Jersey Unemployment Insurance Reemployment Demonstration that ran in 1986–1987. Like the Texas WAD, it had the aim of evaluating an on-going system, rather than of assessing a one-time crisis intervention, but unlike the WAD, it also offered some advantage in the length of the follow-up period available for analysis. The intake group was targeted to be UI claimants with at least three years of prior job tenure and the NJ Demonstration used several screens after four weeks of benefit claim to filter out unemployed who did not qualify as displaced. Random assignment was implemented in week five of benefit claim following a (mandatory) job search workshop and a counselling/assessment session, and amounted to one of three treatments: JSA only, JSA plus CT/OJT (subject to some conditions on chosen training schemes), and JSA plus Reemployment Bonus. Training was here limited to upgrading existing skill sets, rather than learning an entirely new profession. The bonus treatment was a payment directly to the claimant of 50 per cent of the remaining UI entitlement if lasting full-time reemployment was achieved within two weeks of the bonus treatment offer, with a schedule that reduced the bonus by 10 per cent each week (and reaching zero 11 weeks after the offer).

Results from the New Jersey Demonstration imply an earnings impact in the quarter following the initial UI claim of $160 for the JSA plus bonus group, compared with $125 for JSA alone and $82 for the JSA plus training group, with the first two impacts being statistically significant (Leigh 1990, Table 3.7). All three figures rose in the second quarter but declined substantially by four quarters after the UI claim and were insignificantly different from zero. The effects of these initiatives seem to be quite transitory. Moreover, longer-term follow-up over the subsequent six years confirmed that those randomly assigned to the offer of retraining did no better than those assigned to receive only JSA (Corson and Haimson 1995). However, it should be noted that, among the group assigned to JSA plus training, only 15 per cent actually engaged in training, pointing out the role of *take-up* as well as the initial assignment.[18]

Overall, although random assignment and the demonstration project structure offered promise, firm conclusions from the various dislocated worker demonstration projects remain limited. Design issues, low take-up and the specificity of many of the sample populations have restricted the lessons that can be learned. The best summary is that these demonstrations found small positive effects of job search assistance, probably large enough to merit provision based on cost-benefit analysis. However, the demonstrations found uniformly small effects, sometimes negative, for training programs beyond basic job search assistance, and a robust conclusion is that these more expensive programs could not meet a simple cost-benefit test.

B Nonexperimental Studies of Displaced Worker Programs

There are evident limits to the questions that can be resolved directly from the demonstration evidence, at least without the addition of important additional statistical assumptions and econometric modeling. Moreover, with small and often distinctive (non-representative) samples, the external validity of the demonstration results is open to question. Finally, the follow-up period to study dynamics following an intervention is often very short. As a consequence, research has also used nonexperimental data to study the effects of existing training schemes and other policies for the displaced. Key issues in this research are how to control for differences between trainees and non-trainees, both along observed dimensions and also allowing appropriately for unobserved heterogeneity.

A leading example of such research is the analysis of administrative data on Community College training in Washington State conducted by Jacobson, LaLonde and Sullivan (2005a, 2005b, 2005c). Using a threshold of three years' prior tenure, the researchers study some 97,000 cases of displacement with separations between 1990 and 1994.[19] Of these, about 16 per cent had earned at least one community college credit by the end of 1996. Importantly, substantial federal funding for displaced worker retraining had not yet been implemented, so that most of the community college courses taken in the 1990–1994 Washington State sample were *self-financed*. Comparing trainees and others, Jacobson, LaLonde and Sullivan report that participants in community college were younger than other displaced workers, had somewhat lower job tenure (in line with the age difference), were more likely female and somewhat more likely to be rural. Interestingly, they also note that participants were substantially more likely than non-participants to have attended community college in the past.

Overall, these college participants complete an average of two-thirds of a year of schooling. To evaluate the effects, Jacobson, LaLonde and Sullivan employ two models, together with a hybrid combination of the two. The first model is a *binary program evaluation approach*, comparing adjusted post-program earnings of community college participants and non-participants. The adjustment amounts to a regression on observed characteristics, plus allowance for unobserved characteristics that are fixed or that change at a steady rate (based on individual earnings growth in the pre-displacement period). The second model estimates a *return* to community college that is assumed to be proportional to the credits earned. Given strong enough proportionality assumptions, one could estimate a return to community college credits using only participants, although there would be valuable further information in the earnings data from the non-participants.[20]

The hybrid approach used by Jacobson, LaLonde and Sullivan builds on the proportionality model but allows for a further discrete effect of *any* community college participation (as in the binary framework). Perhaps the benefits of community college are strongly non-proportional, based on networking contacts quickly acquired at college. Or perhaps the unobserved heterogeneity is not fully captured by the adjustment Jacobson, LaLonde and Sullivan are able to make based on past earnings. In some cases of this type, the hybrid model may correctly estimate the return to community college credits when either of the two preceding models would be biased.

Jacobson and his colleagues allow for a distinctive pattern of displacement effects on earnings through time, with a potential dip prior to displacement, a more substantial drop in the quarter after the separation, and a relatively rapid rise in the next few quarters, followed finally by slow to zero increase thereafter. Further, they allow for dynamic effects after community college training, with a potential transition period after college ends (a period when earnings often fall initially), followed by a period of potential growth in the year or more thereafter. In terms of the sample size, the quality and accuracy of the administrative data, and the resultant capacity for flexibility in the econometric modeling, the papers by Jacobson, LaLonde and Sullivan make an important contribution.

Estimation allowing for a transition period after community college yields a long-run positive effect of schooling of 9.3 per cent of post-displacement earnings for men and 7.6 per cent for women, both under the binary specification (2005c, Table 2, 285). When estimated assuming proportionality, analogous estimates of the impact on earnings are 11.7 per cent for men and 10.4 per cent for women. For both cases, estimated effects immediately after community college are negative, with the effects becoming positive several quarters after the end of the courses. Both sets of returns are substantial, perhaps slightly higher than generally accepted estimates of the return to formal schooling (in the 6–9 per cent range, as in, e.g., Card, 1999).[21] These figures represent the strongest set of non-experimental results for proponents of training for the displaced.

In the richer hybrid model, Jacobson, LaLonde and Sullivan find high estimates of the value of "just showing up" since this binary indicator appears to raise earnings by 6.8 per cent for men and 5.5 per cent for women. While this could be a networking-type effect, Jacobson and his colleagues' preferred interpretation is that its magnitude indicates residual selection into training. Observed controls may not be capturing all of the individual heterogeneity in factors such as motivation and dynamism, and remaining differences may be reflected in more motivated individuals being more likely to enroll for community college training.[22]

When earnings time trends are also included as controls, in addition to fixed effects, the pattern of results remain fairly consistent but the level of returns tends to rise (2005c, Table 3). In the most general specification, the return to a year of community college training represents an earnings gain (as a percentage of post-displacement earnings) of 9.4 per cent for men and 13.1 per cent for women. They interpret the rise in the estimated returns when worker-specific time trends are included as a form of compensation in the enrolment decisions of workers: those with relatively slower prior earnings growth tend to self-select into more courses as a means to compensate for their slower earnings path. Naturally, allowance for this type of selection raises the estimated effect of training.

A further important contribution of their study concerns *course content*. Specifically, they aggregate courses into two groups: "Group 1" comprises academic courses in mathematics and science, together with more vocational courses related to technical trades, technical professions and health; and "Group 2" comprises all other community college courses, notably academic courses in the humanities and social sciences, and vocational courses in less technical fields. Results (2005c, Table 5) from a variety of specifications show that the Group 1 courses have much larger impacts than those from Group 2. Indeed, in their preferred model, they estimate earnings gains from a year of Group 1 credits to be nearly 14 per cent (of post-displacement earnings) for men and a staggering 29 per cent for women. However, the analogous estimates for Group 2 credits are around 4 per cent but with standard errors large enough that they cannot reject the null hypothesis of no earnings effect whatsoever. These gains can be decomposed into about one third wage gains following Group 1 courses with the remainder being a consequence of increased work hours.

The age pattern of community college enrolment and returns is also worth noting. Older men and women are both much less likely to enroll or to complete at least one course than the younger displaced, and they also record a lower average number of credits completed. This is standard in models of age and schooling, since the older have fewer years remaining to reap the benefits of education, may have higher foregone earnings costs, and may find schooling harder after a longer period out of the classroom. However, the completion probability for at least one credit (conditional on community college enrolment) is not age-dependent, and the number of credits earned, given some completion, is also flat across the age distribution. It seems to be choices about enrolment, not success rates for enrollees, which govern the overall age difference in community college training completion.[23]

The evidence from Jacobson, LaLonde and Sullivan is probably the best available nonexperimental source on the effects of training for displaced workers and it does offer some promise of success, at least for the right type of course. That said, there are limitations and it is important to keep these in mind when evaluating results for policy purposes. First, Jacobson, LaLonde and Sullivan are rightly cautious about the size of the "just showing up" effect in their hybrid model, deeming such estimates as "implausibly large" (2005c, 298). Such returns to even *one* community college credit are probably a sign of self-selection into training that has not been fully accounted for in the model specification. Second, Jacobson, LaLonde and Sullivan follow Ashenfelter's (1978) analysis of the *Manpower Development and Training Act*, specifically his specification test based on "backcasting," which estimates whether training appears to have effects *before it actually occurs*. In a variety of specifications, Jacobson, LaLonde and Sullivan, (2005c, Table 7; and 2005b, Table 4), find that participation in community college schooling predicts earnings *prior* to enrolment, a clear flag suggesting model misspecification. It is hard to sign the bias likely indicated by this, however, since it depends on the potential persistence of the unobserved factors beyond the fixed effects and the worker-specific time trends. Participation in community college retraining tended to be high for workers with unusually large unexplained earnings drops between the pre- and post-displacement periods. If these drops were temporary—a phenomenon dubbed "Ashenfelter's Dip" in the literature (Ashenfelter 1978)—then estimated returns to community college are likely too large, while if they reflect permanent losses from displacement, the estimated returns to community college are probably an underestimate of the true value.

Finally, it bears emphasis that the Jacobson, LaLonde and Sullivan results are only directly applicable to the set of displaced workers studied who chose to participate in community college training, even if all of the other issues surrounding nonexperimental data are correctly handled. The results would not apply directly to displaced workers in Washington State at this time who chose not to participate. They would also not apply directly to the hypothetical set of workers who might be induced to participate if, say, public policy had offered enhanced subsidies to the cost of community college education. Since hours changes appear to drive a majority of the earnings gain impacts from the Group 1 courses, there may also be suspicions about substitution, with trainees potentially replacing other workers so that the partial equilibrium effects might exceed the general equilibrium outcome.[24] And of course the broader external validity of the estimated results must remain. We do not know how well the results would apply in other places and at other times.

C *Workforce Investment Act* (WIA) Results

The most recent US evaluation results on training effectiveness derive from the WIA of 1998. The goal of the WIA was to replace the piecemeal system of training programs under the *Job Training Partnership Act* (JTPA) with a unified and consolidated system that nonetheless gave local and state agencies flexibility in program design and promoted client choice. The WIA program currently serves over two million people, costs over $3 billion annually, and has three key elements: an adult program, a youth program, and a dislocated worker program. The first two of these elements are targeted largely at the disadvantaged, so it is the dislocated worker program that is our main focus. Decker (2009) provides a valuable overview of the first decade of the WIA.[25]

To date, no large scale experimental evaluations have been conducted on the effects of the WIA on dislocated workers. However, two substantial studies have assessed these effects using nonexperimental data and methods. Heinrich et al. (2009) use matching estimation methods to assess the effects of WIA services (as a package) and WIA training (as a specific component) for dislocated workers, finding very disappointing results. Initial effects on earnings are negative, which may not be surprising given the Jacobson, LaLonde and Sullivan results earlier, but there is only modest improvement even three or four years out (2009, Table VI.1). Indeed, they conclude that "it appears possible that *ultimate gains from participation are small or nonexistent*" (2009, 58, *emphasis added*). By demographics, they found somewhat worse performance for men than women but little other variation by race, age and veteran status, possibly because sample sizes were quite small for these sub-groups.

The other study of the WIA's effects on dislocated workers' earnings (Hollenbeck et al. 2005) seems contradictory, since it suggests positive impact estimates of $1,008 per quarter for men and $895 for women, with the largest effects occurring immediately. However, Decker (2009) notes that Hollenbeck and others' methodology uses the program exit point as the start of the observation period so that any earnings foregone during WIA program participation is essentially ignored in the calculation of a return. Once this methodological difference is amended, Decker suggests that the two papers are in fact fairly consistent. When direct and opportunity costs of WIA services are included, Decker argues that Hollenbeck and others' results on earnings impacts show a substantially negative return to WIA.[26]

In closing, I note that both sets of authors remain somewhat tentative about the nonexperimental results from the WIA, a viewpoint reinforced by Decker's (2009) overview. Until an evaluation with some random assignment is conducted, as with the US demonstration programs in the 1980s, doubts will remain that results reflect as much on the sensitivities of the methodology as on the nature of the underlying WIA-induced outcomes.

D Canadian Evidence on Adjustment Policies

Finally, I comment on assessments of Canadian adjustment policies. A valuable account of the various Federal Targeted Programs for this type of population is provided in the Expert Panel on Older Workers (2008, Table 1, 20).[27] Most such programs were short-lived and aimed at narrowly defined groups, particularly those affected by the restructuring of the fishing industry, and insofar as the programs were formally evaluated, the outcomes were quite discouraging.[28] Such programs were discontinued in 1998, in view of this perceived lack of success, although a number of alternative pilots have been tried. In October 2006, the Targeted Initiative for Older Workers (TIOW) was launched, and the TIOW is currently funded to March 2012, aiding the adjustment of workers aged 55–64. I know of no extant evaluation of the TIOW, nor whether one is planned.

There is some recent unpublished Canadian research that has looked at *self-financed* training and its effects. Frenette, Upward and Wright (2010) identify training by exploiting the tuition credits and education deductions present in the T1 tax files that comprise part of the LWF. Such credits indicate some self-financed training within the calendar year covered by the T1 form, including the count of months for which an education deduction is claimed, although for technical reasons they adopt a binary indicator of training uptake (rather than a proportion of the year). Note that this training must be limited to postsecondary education and that the tax data captures attendance rather than completion. Methodologically, Frenette, Upward and Wright model selection into the treatment (i.e., into postsecondary attendance) using a latent variable that depends on the distance between the individual's home and the closest postsecondary institution. This distance proxies for some of the costs of such education, building on work by Card (1995). The identifying assumption (exclusion restriction) is that this distance measure does not affect the returns to postsecondary education, given the selection process.

In preliminary results for those aged 25–44 in 1997, Frenette, Upward and Wright find evidence of positive selection into postsecondary education. Controlling for this selection, there remains substantial effects from postsecondary education on earnings. For men, on a base of approximately $30,000 in paid earnings in 1997 (all figures in 2007 dollars), estimated effects of formal training on earnings rise through time and peak nine years post-displacement at an earnings gain of $6,400. Analogous figures for women, on a $20,000 base, the peak effect comes with a $7,100 earnings gain after five years. There are obviously very large effects, relative to the literature, and warrant further investigation. That said, it is worth noting that Frenette, Upward and Wright find no significant effects for men aged 35–44 (the older part of their sample), so there are potentially interesting differences across demographic groups.

Finally, despite these apparent benefits, Frenette, Upward and Wright report that the take-up rate is very low for men, even among the younger group that appears to benefit more. Take-up following displacement is larger for women, both young and older. It remains puzzling why men appear so reluctant to pursue this nominally beneficial training. One possibility is that the geographic controls do not truly control for selection into formal training (i.e., the identifying assumption is not valid) and that the returns to training are overstated by results from the sample of displaced workers who choose to pursue postsecondary education. It will be interesting to see future work using these data and methods.

Another set of unpublished work concerns a variety of active labour market measures implemented by Emploi-Quebec (SOM 2003, 2006) using both federal funds from the Canada-Quebec Labour Market Development Agreement and provincial funds in supplement. Specifically, the focus was on training, wage subsidies and active counselling as means to facilitate transition back to employment and to enhance earnings on the new job. On some readings, this work has been interpreted as a counter-example to the broad sweep of conclusions from North American research on the efficacy of active labour market measures.

It is difficult to evaluate research that has not been subject to peer review and published in standard outlets, partly because documentation of the research design and assessment of the conclusions may be incomplete.

In the case of these Quebec studies, the voluminous unpublished reports do furnish some documentation, however, and highlight two key points.

First, the authors were aware of a number of selection-related biases in estimation (e.g., SOM 2003, 8-9). Nonetheless, the underlying design remained one where, relative to a treatment group whose members received active measures, the control group was composed of eligible individuals who did not participate in these programs. Clearly, individual choices to participate would therefore affect membership in the treatment/control group and a fundamental self-selection bias is unavoidable. As such, it is probably incorrect to term such a research design "quasi-experimental" (a term first used on page 246 of the 2003 report), since there was no plausibly exogenous variation that generated assignment into treatment and control groups.

Second, the report nonetheless attempted to address selection bias, both by using propensity score matching methods and by a version of Heckman selection-bias correction estimation. For both, predicted probabilities of participation in active measures are used to separate the treatment and control groups, so the estimation results hinge on the quality of these predictions. The report (SOM 2003, 9) documents that these predictions were based on personal demographics, job characteristics, and utilization patterns of EI in the pre-participation period. While it is hard to know what more could have been done, absent a truly experimental or quasi-experimental design, none of these proposed instruments seems unrelated to the likely outcomes of the active measures. Therefore, the exclusion restriction required of a valid instrument would fail and the estimates raise issues of credibility that haunt evaluations without random assignment.

6 Summary of Evidence on Training Effectiveness

Overall, my summary assessment is that most training programs have had results on earnings that are modest to poor. There has been less work on initial re-employment after displacement, probably because these costs are small relative to the long-term cost of earnings losses. Nonetheless, to the extent that short-term results are a key policy target, the long-term focus of the existing literature could constitute something of a mismatch of evaluative resources.

Since there are few experimental evaluations for displaced workers, results are necessarily thin, but based on these evaluations and available nonexperimental studies, conclusions on effectiveness are mixed and perhaps inconclusive, at best. It is not clear that past training for displaced workers has paid off as an investment. Moreover, even if returns to training were significantly positive—which is probably an over-optimistic assessment—on the order of the return to formal education, say, the investment in training necessary for the long-tenure displaced to cover their earnings shortfall is staggering, perhaps an order of magnitude higher than any such investments in the past. With any important role for self-selection into training based on returns,[29] and with the possibility of diminishing returns to training at an individual level, training may not solve the problem of displacement.

7 Concluding Remarks

The robust conclusion of this paper is that training of displaced workers is not a panacea. Job search assistance is the single adjustment mechanism that appears to pass clear cost-benefit tests in terms of earnings replacement across a range of studies, and even in this case, there are still doubts about general equilibrium effects if the assisted merely substitute for the unassisted. For training schemes beyond Jacobson, LaLonde and Sullivan, though, the broad sweep of results is much less sanguine. In limited cases and for particular displaced populations, training that was technically oriented has yielded returns on a par with those typically found in the literature on formal education, that is to say, returns in the high single digits. But given such returns, and the size and duration of earnings losses following displacement, the level of investment in training needed to bridge these gaps fully would be huge. Moreover, with allowance for selection into training, and if returns to training for any individual are diminishing, existing estimates of the marginal return to training may dramatically underestimate the required investment to meet the full displacement earnings shortfall. Although training might be a good investment even without complete compensation, existing calculations suggest that substantial foregone earnings might undercut such internal rate of return assessments for many displaced workers.

One general lesson from this review is the importance of building evaluation strategies into policy programs. Much earlier Canadian work did not have such assessments in place, and hence has yielded little in terms of robust conclusions. But the US experience is quite clear in showing the benefits of such evaluation and the problems that can arise in its absence.

A second conclusion is to raise the issue of the goal of training programs. Based on long-term calculations, where earnings losses in reemployment trump more transitory losses from periods of nonemployment, almost all of the evaluative literature in economics has addressed the extent of earnings replacement. If a major goal of policy is the short-run, however, then more attention needs to be paid to jobless durations following displacement and to the probability of reemployment, regardless of the salary and terms that such employment might offer.

Finally, these problems with training effectiveness prompt serious consideration of alternative means of compensating the losers from economic adjustment. Such steps might include modified or expanded EI coverage, even without any link to training expenditures. Current policies base eligibility only on recent work history, although displaced worker earnings often decline in the final year or two prior to displacement from the long-term employer. Obviously, a longer time frame for EI work histories might benefit such displaced workers. Moreover, the duration of EI may not be sufficient to assist the displaced following a separation. Indeed, if earnings losses are permanent, no temporary EI framework can really meet this need. It is for these types of reasons that many have proposed serious evaluation of a Wage Insurance (WI) program for the long-tenure displaced.[30] Such a program would raise new challenges, and perhaps some sort of pilot or demonstration of WI would be appropriate. Certainly, since evidence on training programs for displaced workers gives quite limited promise, it is important to search for other creative ways to ensure that the costs of economic restructuring do not fall disproportionately on a narrow group.

Endnotes

1 See, for example, the sequences of papers using the DWS by Farber (1993, 1998, 2004, 2005).

2 Canada had one DWS in 1986, covering separations in the period 1981–1985.

3 Morisette, Zhang and Frenette also supply figures for those aged 50–64, a group they omitted from their analysis for fear of confounding issues of non-participation. Nonetheless, this older sample yields similar results. Rates of layoff and displacement are close to those for the prime-aged group and the relative magnitude of layoffs, narrow definition displacement and broad definition displacement is also consistent for the 50–64 year olds (2007, Appendix Table 1).

4 Average earnings changes include individuals who experienced an earnings increase, as well as those who suffered a loss. Excluding those who gained, the average loss across just the set of losers would naturally be higher. This might be important for policies toward displacement that target only those that experience losses.

5 If displacements are restricted to firm closure, then a qualification from Morisette, Zhang and Frenette is that these types of earnings losses hold for the full sample (i.e., for all tenure levels) provided the model is estimated using only fixed-effects. However, when person-specific trends are also included, estimated earnings losses become insignificantly different from zero more than three years after displacement.

6 If older individuals with large potential earnings losses withdraw from the labour force, the exclusion of retirees would underestimate displacement earnings losses. But if long-tenured older workers have the best options for early retirement, they may leave the labour force even if potential earnings losses from displacement are small; this could lead to an overestimate of displacement earnings loss.

7 The heterogeneity would be unobserved to the researcher, but observed by the market participants. For example, firms could potentially retain unusually good workers, leading to long tenure positively correlated with high wages.

8 It is also possible that social benefits to training might exceed the private gains. The costs of displacement might be geographically concentrated in particular communities or regions, leading to multiplier-type effects that could compound individual displacement losses. Training could perhaps reduce reliance on EI and income assistance, and perhaps training can have wider effect in reducing illegal activity, increasing community participation and so on. On balance, though, I think the displacement or substitution effect is likely the most important quantitatively.

9 In addition to Carneiro and Heckman (2002), key papers that argue against an important role for borrowing constraints include Cameron and Heckman (2001), Keane and Wolpin (2002) and Cameron and Taber (2004). Contrary evidence in favour of borrowing constraints is presented by Kane (1996) and Ellwood and Kane (2000). More broadly on the issue of credit and liquidity constraints and their empirical importance, see Jappelli (1990) and Souleles (2000).

10 A recent Canadian example might be the "Learn$ave" experiment conducted by SRDC that subsidized saving for approved education or training (or for small business start-up costs). See Leckie et al. (2009).

11 More generally, when treatment is non-binary, one can only observe one level of treatment for a given individual.

12 For example, Heckman and Smith (2004) decompose participation in a social program into five stages: eligibility, awareness, application, acceptance and enrollment. At which stage(s) should we randomize?

13 Heckman, Hohmann and Smith (2000) provide a detailed empirical account of substitution and dropout bias, addressing the situation where control group members can find substitutes for the training program, and where treatment group members can drop out of the training program if they find a better alternative. Evidence suggests that classroom training was particularly vulnerable to these effects, while on-the-job training (with public subsidy) was less affected owing to a lack of ready substitutes.

14 A valuable account of this debate is provided by Glazerman, Levy and Myers (2003) who assess 12 studies of earnings impacts that sought to replicate experimental evaluation using nonexperimental methods.

15 Note, though, that the results from evaluations of training for disadvantaged populations are also quite pessimistic.

16 A valuable overview of the work on dislocated workers in the US is provided by the survey of Wandner (2010).

17 There were very few women in the Houston sample.

18 Perhaps this pattern of results highlights Heckman's general point that there is a limit to the questions that can be well answered by single randomization designs when the question of interest is multi-stage in nature.

19 Workers also had to be attached to the state labour force between 1987 and 1995 to qualify for this sample.

20 This is analogous to labour supply estimation, where one can estimate an hours-wages relationship using only participants with positive hours, but where efficiency can be gained by additionally using non-participant data.

21 Similarly, Heckman, Lochner and Todd (2007) suggest as a summary that an additional year of formal schooling might raise earnings by about 10 per cent. With adjustment for the full costs of education, this translates into an internal rate of return of the order of 7 per cent.

22 The high value of "just showing up" in Jacobson, Lalonde and Sullivan's results contrasts with evidence of credential or "sheepskin" effects in the literature on formal education, where returns to education are estimated to be large only if key phases are completed and a credential achieved (for Canadian evidence, see Ferrer and Riddell, 2002). If community college training is truly analogous to formal education, this apparent discrepancy probably reinforces the interpretation that the Jacobson, Lalonde and Sullivan "just showing up" effect is driven by misspecification.

23 Older workers may anticipate more difficulty in course completion and may hence choose not to enroll. That is, the success rate is based on the self-selection sample of those that did enroll.

24 This may also apply to earnings gains from higher wage rates if trainees crowd out non-trainees for a fixed set of higher wage jobs.

25 Interestingly, Decker (2009, 24) notes that the preliminary nonexperimental results from the WIA actually suggest somewhat better results for the adult program as a whole—with modestly increased earnings and employment for both men and women—than for the dislocated worker group.

26 Other nonexperimental work on the WIA include that of the US General Accounting Office, which noted that "Little is known on a national level about the outcomes of those being trained" (GAO 2005, 1), and Moore and Gorman (2009), which studied one California WIA program using regression methods and found very weak labour market benefits.

27 See also the descriptive accounts contained in the various reports by HRDC (1995, 1996a, 1996b and 1999).

28 Riddell, a member of the Expert Panel on Older Workers, recently commented that "Evaluation of these programs (which are generally of poor quality) are not encouraging: results range from disappointing to dismal" (2009, 14).

29 Kambourov, Manovskii and Plesca (2009, 2010) assess the importance of selection in a relative assessment of government and firm-sponsored training, arguing that occupation switchers tend to select into government-sponsored programs. Since switchers lose some specific human capital, assessment of the returns to public training must take this selection process into account.

30 Some of the issues relating to Wage Insurance are discussed in the Expert Panel on Older Workers (2008) and in Jones (2009).

Glossary of Acronyms

COEP Canadian Out of Employment Panel
CT Classroom Training
DWS Displaced Worker Survey
EI Employment Insurance
JSA Job Search Assistance
JTPA Job Training Partnership Act
LWF Longitudinal Worker File
OJT On the Job Training
TIOW Targeted Initiative For Older Workers
WAD Worker Adjustment Demonstration
WI Wage Insurance
WIA Workforce Investment Act

References

Acemoglu, D., and J-S. Pischke. 1998. "Why Do Firms Train? Theory and Evidence." *Quarterly Journal of Economics* 113: 79-119.

——. 1999. "The Structure of Wages and Investment in General Training." *Journal of Political Economy* 107: 539-72.

——. 2003. "Minimum Wages and On-the-Job Training." *Research in Labor Economics* 22: 159-202.

Ashenfelter, O. 1978. "Estimating the Effect of Training Programs on Earnings." *Review of Economics and Statistics* 60.1: 47-57.

Bernard, A. 2009. "Job Stability and Unemployment Duration in Manufacturing." *Perspectives on Labour and Income*. Statistics Canada, Cat. No. 75-001-X, November.

Cameron, S.V., and J. Heckman. 2001. "The Dynamics of Educational Attainment for Black, Hispanic and White Males." *Journal of Political Economy* 109: 455-99.

Cameron, S.V., and C. Taber. 2004. "Estimation of Educational Borrowing Constraints Using Returns to Schooling." *Journal of Political Economy* 112: 132-82.

Campolieti, M. 2009. "The Ins and Outs of Unemployment in Canada, 1976–2008." Unpublished paper, Department of Economics, University of Toronto.

Card, D. 1995. "Using Geographic Variation in College Proximity to Estimate the Return to Schooling." In *Aspects of Labour Market Behaviour: Essays in Honour of John Vanderkamp*, ed. L.N. Christofides, E.K. Grant and R. Swidinsky, 201-22. Toronto: University of Toronto Press.

——. 1999. "The Causal Effect of Education on Earnings." In *Handbook of Labor Economics Volume 3A*, ed. O. Ashenfelter and D. Card, 1801-1863. Elsevier.

Carneiro, P. and J. Heckman. 2002. "The Evidence on Credit Constraints in Post-Secondary Schooling." *Economic Journal* 112: 705-34.

Chapman, B., T.F. Crossley and T. Kim. 2003., "Credit Constraints and Training after Job Loss." CEPR Discussion Paper no. 466. Centre for Economic Policy Research, Research School of Economics, Australian National University.

Corson, W. and J. Haimson. 1995. "The New Jersey Unemployment Insurance Reemployment Demonstration Project, Six Year Follow-Up and Summary Report." U.S. Department of Labor, Employment and Training Administration occasional paper No. 95-2.

Corson, W., S. Long and R. Maynard. 1985. "An Impact Evaluation of the Buffalo Dislocated Worker Demonstration Project." Mathematica Policy Research, March 12.

Decker, P.T. 2009. "Ten Years of the Workforce Investment Act (WIA): Interpreting the Research on WIA and Related Programs." Mathematica Policy Research, October.

Ellwood, D. and T. Kane. 2000. "Who is Getting a College Education?" In *Securing the Future: Investing in Children from Birth to College*, ed. S. Danziger and J. Waldfogel, 283-324. New York: Russell Sage Foundation.

Expert Panel on Older Workers. 2008. *Supporting and Engaging Older Workers in the New Economy*, Ottawa.

Farber, H. 1993. "The Incidence and Costs of Job Loss: 1982–91." In *Brookings Papers on Economic Activity: Microeconomics* 1993: 1, ed. C. Winston and M.N. Baily, 73-132. Washington, DC: Brookings Institution Press.

——. 1998. "The Changing Face of Job Loss in the United States: 1981–95." Brookings Papers on Economic Activity: Microeconomics 1997, ed. C. Winston, M.N. Baily, and P.C. Reiss, 55-128. Washington, DC: Brookings Institution Press.

——. 2004. "Job Loss in the United States 1981–2001." *Research in Labor Economics* 23: 69-117.

——. 2005. "What Do We Know about Job Loss in the United States? Evidence from the Displaced Worker Survey, 1984–2004." *Economic Perspectives* 29.2: 13-28. Federal Reserve Bank of Chicago.

Ferrer, A.M., and W.C. Riddell. 2002. "The Role of Credentials in the Canadian Labour Market." *Canadian Journal of Economics* 35: 879-905.

Frenette, M., R. Upward and P.W. Wright. 2010. "The Long-Term Earnings Impact of Formal Training Following Job Displacement. Quasi-Experimental Evidence from Canada." Unpublished draft.

General Accounting Office (GAO). 2005. "Workforce Investment Act: Substantial Funds are Used for Training But Little is Known Nationally About Training Outcomes." GAO-05-650. Washington, DC: General Accounting Office.

Glazerman, S., D.M. Levy and D. Myers. 2003. "Nonexperimental versus Experimental Estimates of Earnings Impacts." *Annals of the American Academy of Political and Social Science* 589: 63-93.

Gray, D.M. and R. Finnie. 2009a. "Displacement of Older Workers: Re-employment, Hastened Retirement, Disability, or Other Destinations?" Canadian Labour Market and Skills Researcher Network (CLSRN), Working Paper No.15.

——. 2009b. "Does Work Pay After Displacement?" Paper prepared for HRSDC, Labour Market Policy Directorate.

Heckman, J.J. 1991. "Randomization and Social Policy Evaluation." NBER Technical Working Paper No 107.

Heckman, J.J., N. Hohmann and J. Smith. 2000. "Substitution and Dropout Bias: A Study of an Influential Social Experiment." *Quarterly Journal of Economics*: 651-93.

Heckman, J.J., R.J. LaLonde, and J. Smith. 1999. "The Economics and Econometrics of Active Labor Market Programs." In *Handbook of Labor Economics*, Vol. 3A, ed. O. Ashenfelter and D. Card, 1865-2097. Amsterdam: North Holland.

Heckman, J.J., L. Lochner, and P. Todd. 2007. "Earnings Functions, Rates of

Return and Treatment Effects: The Mincer Equation and Beyond." In *Handbook of the Economics of Education*, Volume I, ed. E.A. Hanushek and F. Welch, 307-458. Elsevier.

Heckman, J.J., and J.A. Smith. 2004. "The Determinants of Participation in a Social Program: Evidence from a Prototypical Job Training Program." *Journal of Labor Economics*, 22:2: 243-98.

Heinrich, C.J., P.R. Mueser, K.R. Troske, K-S. Jeon and D.C. Kahvecioglu. 2009. "New Estimates of Public Employment and Training Program Net Impacts: A Nonexperimental Evaluation of the Workforce Investment Act Program." IZA Discussion Paper No. 4569, November.

Hollenbeck, K., D. Schroeder, C.T. King and W-J. Huang. 2005. "Net Impact Estimates for Services Provided through the Workforce Investment Act." Prepared for Employment and Training Administration, U.S. Department of Labor.

Human Resources Development Canada (HRDC). 1995. "Evaluation of the Employability Improvement Program: Final Report." Evaluation and Data Development, Strategic Policy.

——. 1996a. "Evaluation of The Atlantic Groundfish Strategy." Evaluation and Data Development, Strategic Policy.

——. 1996b. "Program for Older Worker Adjustment: Evaluation Report." Evaluation and Data Development, Strategic Policy.

——. 1999. "Older Worker Adjustment Programs: Lessons Learned." Evaluation and Data Development, Strategic Policy.

Imbens, G.W., and J.M. Wooldridge. 2009. "Recent Developments in the Econometrics of Program Evaluation." *Journal of Economic Literature* 47.1: 5-86.

Jacobson, L., R.J. LaLonde, and D. Sullivan. 2005a. "Is Retraining Displaced Workers a Good Investment?" *Economic Perspectives* 29.2: 47-66.

——. 2005b. "The Impact of Community College Retraining on Older Displaced Workers: Should We Teach Old Dogs New Tricks?" *Industrial and Labor Relations Review*, 58: 398-415.

——. 2005c. "Estimating the Returns to Community College Schooling for Displaced Workers." *Journal of Econometrics* 125: 271-304.

Jappelli, T. 1990. "Who is Credit Constrained in the US Economy?" *Quarterly Journal of Economics* 105 (February): 219-34.

Jones, S.R.G. 2009. "Older Workers in the New Economy: The Role of Wage Insurance and the Rethinking of Employment Insurance." *Canadian Public Policy* 35: 499-511.

Kambourov, G., I. Manovskii and M. Plesca. 2009. "Returns to Government-Sponsored Training." http://www.econ.upenn.edu/~manovski/papers/gov_training.pdf

——. 2010. "Occupational Mobility and the Returns to Training." http://www.econ.upenn.edu/~manovski/papers/occ_mob_training.pdf

Kane, T. 1996. "College Cost, Borrowing Constraints and the Timing of College Entry." *Eastern Economic Journal* 22: 181-94.

Keane, M., and K. Wolpin. 2002. “The Effect of Parental Transfers and Borrowing Constraints on Educational Attainment.” *International Economic Review* 42: 1051-1103.

LaLonde, R.J. 1986. “Evaluating the Econometric Evaluations of Training Programs with Experimental Data.” *American Economic Review* 76.4: 604-20.

Leckie, N., T. S-W. Hui, D. Tattrie, and H. Cao. 2009. “Learning to Save, Saving to Learn: Intermediate Impacts of the Learn$ave Individual Development Accounts Project.” SRDC Report, Ottawa, March.

Leigh, D.E. 1990. *Does Training Work for Displaced Workers? A Survey of Existing Evidence.* Kalamazoo, Michigan: W. E. Upjohn Institute for Employment Research.

—— 1994. “Retraining Displaced Workers: The US Experience.” *Training Policy Study* 1. Geneva: International Labour Organization.

Moore, R.W. and P.C. Gorman. 2009. “The Impact of Training and Demographics in WIA Program Performance: A Statistical Analysis.” *Human Resource Development Quarterly* 20:4: 381-96.

Morissette, R., X. Zhang and M. Frenette. 2007. “Earnings Losses of Displaced Workers: Canadian Evidence from a Large Administrative Database on Firm Closures and Mass Layoffs.” Statistics Canada, Analytical Studies Branch Research Paper Series No. 291.

Riddell, W.. 2009. “Economic Change and Worker Displacement in Canada: Consequences and Policy Responses.” In *A Festschrift in Honour of David Dodge’s Contributions to Canadian Public Policy*, 223-35. Ottawa: Bank of Canada.

Schirle, T. 2007. “Earnings Losses of Displaced Older Workers: Accounting for the Retirement Option.” CLSRN Working Paper No. 22.

SOM Recherches et Sondages. 2003. “Étude des effets des mesures actives offertes aux individus par Emploi-Québec.” Rapport présenté à la Direction de l’évaluation, Quebec, Ministère de l’Emploi, de la Solidarité sociale et de la Famille.

——. 2006. “Étude sur le rendement de l’investissement relié à la participation aux mesures actives offertes aux individus par Emploi-Québec.” Rapport présenté à la Direction de l’évaluation, Direction générale adjointe de la recherche, de l’Èvaluation et de la statistique, Quebec, Ministère de l’Emploi et de la Solidarité sociale.

Souleles, N.S. 2000. “College Tuition and Household Savings and Consumption.” *Journal of Public Economics* 77: 185-207.

Wandner, S.A. 2010. *Solving the Reemployment Puzzle: From Research to Policy*. W.E. Upjohn Institute for Employment Research, Kalamazoo, Michigan.

Chapter 12

Unemployment Compensation and Adjustment Assistance for Displaced Workers: Policy Options for Canada

W. Craig Riddell

This chapter examines the role of Canada's Employment Insurance (EI) program in providing support and assistance to "displaced workers," those who permanently lose their jobs because of changing economic circumstances. Particular attention is paid to "long-tenure displaced workers," those who worked for their previous employer or in their previous industry or occupation for many years. Two specific roles of EI are examined: (i) income support during the spell of unemployment following job loss (i.e., EI Part 1) and (ii) adjustment assistance for those who may require job search assistance, counselling or retraining, as well as those who may need to relocate to areas with better employment opportunities (i.e., EI Part 2). Although these two roles are relevant in varying degrees for many unemployed job seekers, they may be especially important for displaced workers (DWs). One reason is that DWs (especially long-tenure DWs) may take longer to obtain re-employment than other unemployed individuals. Another reason is that DWs may be more likely to require some form of adjustment assistance.

Since the onset of the 2008–2009 recession the federal government has followed the recommendations of the Expert Panel on Older Workers (2008) and has introduced several initiatives that provide enhanced benefits for long-tenure displaced workers. In May 2009 the government announced the Career Transition Assistance program that provides additional support to long-tenure displaced workers. One initiative in this program extends the duration of EI benefits by up to two years for eligible long-tenure displaced workers who participate in longer-term training. Another allows earlier access to EI regular benefits for displaced workers investing in their own training using all or part of their severance package. Subsequently, the government also extended regular EI benefits for long-tenure displaced workers. Both of these new policies were introduced as temporary measures. One of the central questions to be addressed in this chapter is whether enhanced benefits for long-tenure DWs should become a permanent feature of the EI program.

The chapter is organized as follows. The first section examines the rationale for the public provision of income support during unemployment (EI Part 1) and adjustment assistance (EI Part 2). Section 2 provides evidence on the incidence of permanent job loss and summarizes what we know about earnings losses from displacement. Other consequences of job loss, such as those to the health of the job loser, as well as those for other family members, are also noted. The third section reviews policies that support displaced workers, with particular focus on policies that fall within the purview of the EI program, and what is known about their effectiveness. The final section assesses new policy initiatives that could facilitate re-employment and/or reduce the adjustment costs incurred by displaced workers and recommends future policy development in Canada.

1 The Case for Social Insurance and Labour Adjustment Policies

Change is an enduring feature of the economy and the labour market. Some firms expand their operations, while others contract or go out of business. New firms enter existing industries, and entirely new industries emerge. The dynamic nature of product markets results in continual flux in labour markets. About one-half of all new employer-employee matches end within the first year, and about one-fifth of all workers have been with their employer for less than one year (Farber 1999). In countries like Canada and the United States, roughly 10 per cent of all jobs are destroyed each year, and another one in ten existing jobs were created within the previous year (Baldwin, Dunne and Haltiwanger 1998; Davis and Haltiwanger, 1999).

Moreover, gross flows between labour force states (employment, unemployment and not-in-the labour force) are huge in comparison with net changes in stocks. For example, from one month to the next the number of unemployed workers changes little, but the flows into and out of unemployment are very large, as some workers lose or leave jobs and enter unemployment while some unemployed job seekers find jobs or exit from the labour force. In recent years, structural changes due to technological change, globalization, and the shifting world economic environment have received much attention. But there is nothing new about the importance of changing economic circumstances.

A Social Insurance

Because it is continually being bombarded by shocks, the labour market is a risky place. At each point in time, the employed face the risk of having their hours of work or wages reduced, being temporarily laid off, or permanently losing their job. Some of these outcomes impose more hardship than do others, but all imply some loss of income. Labour market risks are especially significant because labour earnings represent the major source of income for most workers and because risks to human capital wealth are very difficult to diversify (in contrast to financial wealth, for which the risk can be reduced by holding a diversified portfolio of assets).

The combination of substantial uncertainty about future employment and income prospects and the quantitative importance of labour market earnings to individual and family well being results in substantial demand for insurance against the risk of unemployment. However, comprehensive private insurance markets that would allow most workers to purchase insurance against the potential loss of income due to unemployment have generally failed to emerge or, if they emerged, to persist. The reasons for this private market failure—adverse selection and moral hazard—are well understood. Adverse selection refers to the tendency for individuals to self-select into voluntary insurance systems only if they are likely to benefit. High risk individuals are more likely to purchase insurance than low risk individuals. Unless sellers can charge higher prices to higher-risk buyers, there may not exist a price at which selling insurance is profitable, as raising the price simply selects higher-risk customers. Moral hazard refers to the propensity for individuals who are insured against risks to alter their behaviour in a manner that makes the bad outcome more likely, and thus raises the cost of providing insurance. Although adverse selection and moral hazard are present to some extent in all insurance markets, they are especially significant in the case of unemployment insurance.

The absence of comprehensive private insurance markets for the risk of unemployment provides the fundamental rationale for government provision of unemployment insurance (Green and Riddell 1993). However, public provision does not eliminate the presence of adverse selection and moral hazard. Adverse selection is substantially reduced by mandatory coverage, which prevents those who face low risk of unemployment from opting out. Moral hazard is more problematic. Most public unemployment insurance programs attempt to reduce moral hazard by requiring "active job search" during spells of unemployment, and by monitoring and enforcing the search requirement. Moral hazard is also reduced by various forms of co-insurance—such as Canada's two-week waiting period and a benefit replacement rate well below 100 per cent of prior wages. These features function like "deductibles" in other insurance markets. On the employer side, experience rating—which is used in most provincial workers' compensation programs—is another way to provide incentives to reduce the incidence of layoffs, but experience rating is not a feature of the EI system.

In this chapter I begin from the position that EI is, or should be, fundamentally a social insurance program. One important implication of that perspective is that EI benefits should reflect the magnitude of the loss due to unemployment. In insurance markets such as those for automobile and property insurance, this characteristic is both familiar and evident. The insurance payment in the event of destroying one's car is much larger than that for a "fender bender." And having one's house burn down generates a larger insurance settlement than a minor break-in. A central theme of this chapter is that this fundamental characteristic of insurance is to a considerable extent absent from Canada's EI program. Changes are proposed in order to reduce the importance of this flaw in our EI program.

B Adjustment Assistance Policies

Change creates new opportunities but destroys old ones. It is, in the words of Schumpeter (1942), a process of "creative destruction." The economic opportunities available to some individuals are enhanced, while those available to others are reduced. Adjustment to change can be painful for those adversely affected. Adjusting to change typically involves shifting labour and other resources from declining to expanding sectors, which thereby contributes to economic prosperity. There are costs and benefits associated with adjustment but, in general, the net benefits are positive, and often substantial in size. However, although the net benefits of adjusting to change are typically positive, a salient fact is that the costs and benefits are unevenly distributed in the population. Most technological and economic change results in a small number of losers, who each lose a great deal, and a large number of winners, who each enjoy modest benefits. This central feature of economic change makes labour market adjustment one of the most challenging problems that societies face. A variety of policies have been advocated or adopted to help meet this challenge.

Adjustment assistance policies can promote both economic efficiency and the pursuit of equity goals. Because adjustment involves shifting resources from less valued to more highly valued uses, it promotes economic efficiency and therefore higher living standards. Market mechanisms will encourage responding to change, but numerous factors may impede adjustment, resulting in slower responses than are socially optimal (Gunderson 1986). Well-designed adjustment assistance policies can reduce these obstacles and encourage responses that are closer to the social ideal.

Equity considerations also loom large in adjustment policy because economic change can cause considerable harm to some individuals and families. It is generally viewed as equitable to assist those adversely affected, particularly when the shocks have been unanticipated, when they result in significant declines in income or wealth, and when hedging against the shocks would have been difficult. A general theme resulting from economic analysis is that adjustment assistance should focus on workers rather than on firms or their shareholders (Riddell 1986).

Possibly the strongest rationale for adjustment assistance policies is that, in their absence, political pressures result in policies—such as subsidies to declining industries, bailouts of firms threatened with bankruptcy, and protectionist measures—that inhibit adjustment and harm society as a whole. The source of these pressures is easily identified. The benefits of adapting to change are widely distributed, whereas the costs are typically concentrated among a small number of employees and firms. Although the total benefits to society of adjusting to economic shocks often exceed the total costs, the individuals adversely affected form an effective lobby group and may exert considerable influence through the political process. Their influence arises in part because they are easy to organize (being concentrated in a specific sector and often a few regions), are threatened with substantial losses, and are willing to devote considerable resources to fighting the source of change. In contrast, those that stand to benefit are typically dispersed, difficult to organize, and not willing to devote significant time and money to fighting for the adjustment, given the modest gains to each individual. For these reasons, the types of policies adopted are often the opposite of those that would be recommended on the basis of social efficiency and equity considerations (Trebilcock 1986).

2 Job Displacement and Its Consequences

Because this chapter deals with job displacement it is useful to be more precise about terminology. I follow standard practice and define displaced workers as those who (i) have not been discharged for cause, (ii) have permanently separated from their previous employer, and (iii) had strong prior attachment to the industry of their previous employer. An implication of this definition is that displaced workers are a subset of those who lose or leave their previous employment during a specific period of time. Similarly, they are a subset of those who are unemployed at any point in time, which includes temporary layoffs (many of whom return to their previous employer), job leavers (quits), new entrants and re-entrants. An important implication of the "strong prior attachment" condition is that displaced workers may lose accumulated experience that is specific to the previous employer, industry and/or occupation.

From an international perspective, a great deal is now known about the incidence and consequences of job displacement. For more than twenty years the United States has carried out a regular Displaced Workers Survey (DWS) as a supplement to its Current Population Survey (the US equivalent of Canada's Labour Force Survey). The United States' DWS has been an important source of information about the extent and consequences of permanent job loss. In addition, administrative data from state unemployment insurance systems have been a key source of information used in several influential studies (discussed below). Many European countries also have excellent sources of administrative data that are valuable for analyzing job displacement. Unfortunately, Canada does not carry out a regular DWS, and does not make available to outside researchers the administrative data on the EI program, so the Canadian evidence is much more limited.[1] In Canada some analysis has been carried out with survey data and with administrative tax data.

A Incidence of Displacement

In the absence of a regular DWS, researchers at Statistics Canada have used administrative data based on tax records to provide information on the incidence of permanent job loss in Canada (Morrissette, Zhang and Frenette 2007; Picot, Lin and Pyper 1998). These data have advantages, but also disadvantages—one being that they do not provide timely information on job displacement. For example, the most recently available study (Morrissette, Zhang and Frenette 2007) covers the period 1983–2002, and displacements that occurred between 1983 and 1997.[2] Nonetheless, this study provides valuable (albeit not current) information on displacement in Canada.

In the administrative data, job separations are identified from the Record of Employment, which employers are required to issue when an employee working in EI insurable employment experiences an interruption in earnings. Morissette, Zhang and Frenette find that permanent layoff rates for men range from 6 per cent to 7 per cent in boom years, to 9 per cent in the recession of 1990–1992.[3] Comparable rates for females are much lower—3 per cent to 4 per cent in good times and 5 per cent to 6 per cent in downturns. Annual rates of displacement due to mass layoffs or firm closure range from 1.1 per cent to 2.4 per cent for males and 0.6 per cent to 1.1 per cent for female workers. These data indicate that permanent job loss affects a small proportion—about 5 per cent—of employees in any given year. Displacements due to firm closures and mass layoffs represent a much smaller fraction (about 1 per cent) of the workforce. However, because permanent job loss continues through both strong and weak economic conditions, the cumulative magnitude over longer periods is substantial.

In order to provide a more comprehensive and current picture of job displacement in Canada, I compiled data from the monthly Labour Force Survey (LFS) over the period 1976–2010. The LFS data have several advantages: (i) when appropriately weighted, LFS data are representative of the Canadian adult population; (ii) the LFS survey includes a question on job tenure with the current employer; (iii) LFS microdata files are released for public use in a timely fashion, and (iv) key variables such as unemployment, reasons for job separation, job tenure and province of residence are measured in a consistent manner over time. The key variable used—called "flows into unemployment"—characterizes the unemployed according to their activity immediately prior to looking for work. The principal categories are: temporary layoffs, permanent job losers, job leavers (quits), new entrants and re-entrants. These data thus allow us to examine the proportion of the unemployed that consists of permanent job losers, as well as how that proportion varies by such characteristics as gender, tenure in the previous job and region.

FIGURE 1

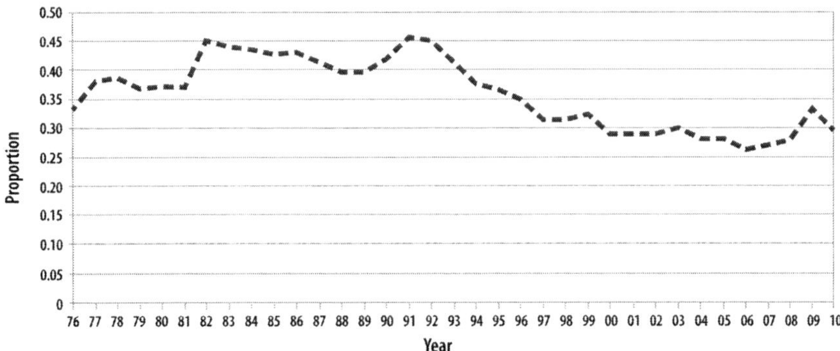

Figure 1 plots permanent job losers as a percentage of total unemployment over the period 1976–2010.[4] Several features stand out. In recent years, only 25–35 per cent of the unemployed became unemployed by permanently losing their job. The majority of the unemployed consists of new entrants and re-entrants (about 40 to 45 per cent). Job leavers constitute around 10 to 12 per cent and temporary layoffs approximately 7 per cent. The relative importance of permanent job losers has also been falling over time—from 35–45 per cent in the 1970s and 1980s to 25–35 per cent more recently. The fraction of permanent job losers in the unemployed pool rises sharply in recessions—such as 1981–1982, 1990–1992 and 2008–2009—and then gradually declines during the subsequent expansion—such as during the latter half of the 1980s, 1990s, and 2000 to 2007.

FIGURE 2

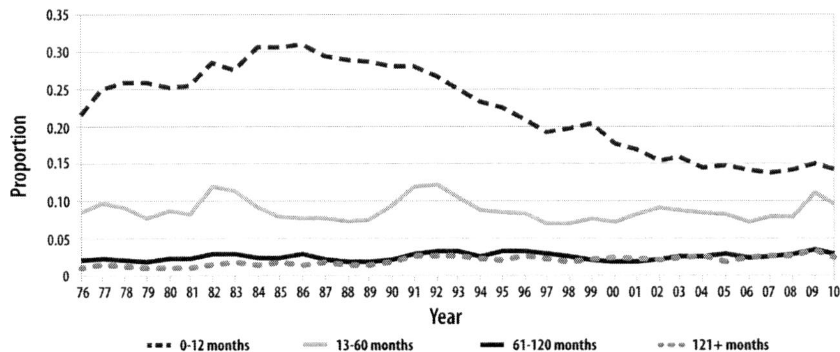

Figure 2 shows the proportion of unemployed who are permanent job losers by tenure in the pre-displacement job. The largest group consists of those who held their previous job for 12 months or less. In recent years this group constitutes about 15 per cent of total unemployment, though in the previous two decades it represented 20 to 30 per cent of unemployment. Note that these job losers would not be considered "displaced workers" as defined previously given their brief job tenure. The next largest group consists of those with one to five years of tenure in the previous job. In normal economic times these individuals represent about 8 per cent of unemployment, rising to 10–12 per cent in recessions. The final two groups are those with five to ten, and more than ten, years of previous job tenure. The times series behaviour of these two groups of "long-tenure displaced workers" is similar. Each represents about 2 to 4 per cent of total unemployment, their sum rarely exceeds 6 per cent of unemployment, and their importance relative to total unemployment has grown modestly over the period 1976–2010.

One additional feature of Figures 1 and 2 is noteworthy. Although the importance of permanent job losers relative to total unemployment has fallen over the past 35 years, this decline can be attributed to the reduction in the number of permanent job losers with job tenure of one year or less. The relative importance of permanent job losers who had held their jobs for at least one year has been relatively stable over the past three to four decades, though it has fluctuated cyclically.

FIGURE 3

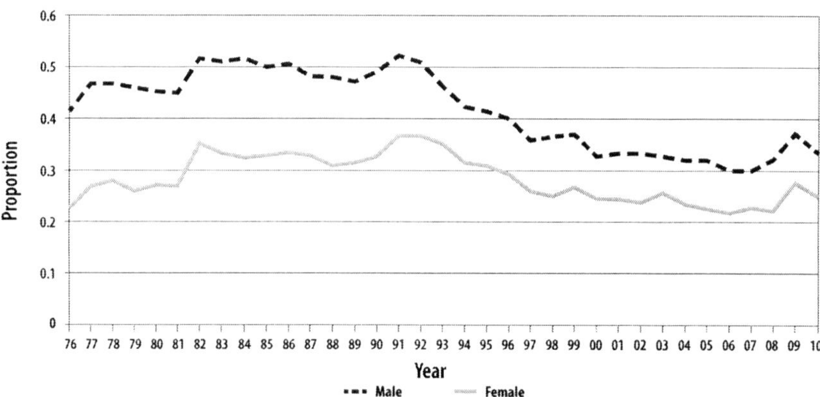

Figures 3 and 4 report the proportion of unemployed who are permanent job losers by gender and region. Male permanent job losers represent a larger fraction of unemployed men than is the case for female job losers, but the gender gap has narrowed over time. In recent years permanent job loss accounts for about 20 to 25 per cent of female unemployment and about 30 to 35 per cent of male unemployment. Throughout the 1976–2010 period, permanent job losers constitute the largest fraction of the unemployed in the Atlantic Provinces, followed by Quebec over most

FIGURE 4

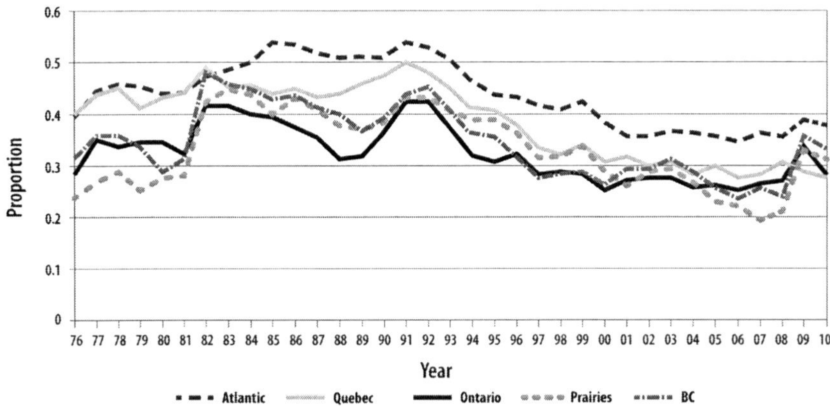

of the period. Ontario had the lowest proportion of permanent job losers among its unemployed during the 1980s and 1990s, but has been closer to the middle of the pack in the past decade. The Prairie Provinces display behaviour that is almost the mirror image of Ontario, having the lowest proportion of permanent job losers in the 1970s and in the past decade, but being in the middle of the distribution during the 1980s and 1990s.

This examination of LFS data on sources of unemployment yields several noteworthy conclusions. Despite the common perception that most unemployment arises because of layoffs and downsizing that is permanent in nature, "job losers" represent a minority of the unemployed. In recent years, permanent job losers constitute only about one-quarter to one-third of unemployment. In recessions the relative importance of permanent job losers approaches the upper end of this range, while in periods of strong economic activity it is closer to the lower end. In addition, the majority of permanent job losers had relatively little tenure (one year or less) in their previous job. Thus displaced workers—those who suffered permanent job loss and had substantial prior tenure with their previous employer—represent a small fraction of total unemployment. Even if we define "substantial prior tenure" as more than 12 months, this group constitutes less than 20 per cent of total unemployment.

Another noteworthy finding is that, although the relative importance of permanent job loss has declined over the past three to four decades, the contribution of permanent job loss by those with at least one year of prior tenure has remained stable. Indeed, the relative importance of permanent job losers with five or more years of tenure has increased modestly. Finally, it is important to note that permanent job loss by long-tenure displaced workers occurs in good times and bad. Even in periods of buoyant economic growth, long-term employees face the risk that they will be displaced.

B Consequences of Displacement: Earnings Loss

The magnitudes of earnings losses due to displacement have been extensively investigated. Key findings include: (i) average earnings losses can be substantial, (ii) losses are greatest for long-tenure employees, and (iii) losses persist for much longer than for other unemployed workers.

An influential study by Jacobson, LaLonde and Sullivan (1993) analyzed the consequences of displacement among workers in Pennsylvania. Their study has several key advantages: detailed administrative data linking workers and firms, several years of pre-displacement and post-displacement earnings and, of particular importance, a comparison group of non-displaced workers. Jacobson and his colleagues focus on workers with six or more years of tenure with the previous employer. Relative to the comparison group of non-displaced workers, earnings losses were very large: 24 per cent of expected earnings even six years after displacement.[5]

Moreover, the time pattern of earnings losses has some striking features. Not surprisingly, average earnings drop precipitously—by about 50 per cent—upon displacement. During the next two to three years, earnings recover to an important extent, prior to levelling off. A salient feature is that average earnings plateau at a level substantially below their pre-displacement level, and even further below the average earnings of the comparison group of non-displaced workers. There is little evidence in their data that earnings of displaced workers will ever return to their pre-displacement level or to the earnings levels experienced by their non-displaced counterparts. They also find that the earnings losses of displaced workers (relative to those who do not become displaced) began about three years prior to separation, suggesting that the events that lead to workers' separations cause their earnings to depart from their normal levels even prior to separation.

Farber (2005) analyzes US data from over twenty years of Displaced Worker Surveys covering the period 1981–2003. These surveys have the important advantage of being based on a representative sample of the adult population. In the most recent period, 35 per cent of displaced workers are not re-employed three years later, while about 13 per cent of full-time job losers are re-employed part time. Full-time job losers re-employed in full-time jobs earn 17 per cent less than their earnings before displacement. The average earnings loss increases dramatically with prior job tenure.

The more limited Canadian evidence yields results similar to those reported for the United States. Morissette, Zhang and Frenette (2007) focus on displaced workers aged 25–49 with at least five years of job tenure (high seniority displaced workers). However, they also present results for the broader group of all displaced workers, irrespective of prior job tenure. Their approach follows that of Jacobson, LaLonde and Sullivan (1993) and compares the earnings patterns of displaced workers to a comparison group of non-displaced workers. In their analysis of the consequences of permanent job loss they focus on job loss due to firm closures and mass layoffs.

Morissette, Zhang and Frenette (2007) find substantial and long-lasting earnings losses from such permanent job loss. As in the Jacobson, LaLonde and Sullivan (1993) Pennsylvania study, earnings start to decline before displacement. As expected, there is a sharp decline in earnings at displacement. A particularly noteworthy finding, similar to that observed in the Jacobson, LaLonde and Sullivan study, is the modest subsequent earnings recovery. Five years after displacement, earnings losses among high-seniority displaced workers are 25 to 34 per cent for men and 35 to 37 per cent for women. These are average losses, and include individuals who suffered larger as well as those who experienced smaller losses (perhaps even increases) in earnings. As was the case in the Jacobson, LaLonde and Sullivan (1993) study, the most striking aspects of these earnings losses are their large size and the fact that they persist for a long time.

Another noteworthy finding of the Morissette, Zhang and Frenette (2007) study is that earnings losses among the broader group of all displaced workers (i.e., irrespective of previous job tenure) are relatively modest and short-lived (approximately zero, on average, three years after displacement). Thus large and persistent earnings losses are characteristic of high seniority displaced workers, a group that constitutes a small minority (about 10 per cent) of the broader group of permanent job losers.

A useful complement to the Morissette, Zhang and Frenette (2007) study is a recent study by Schirle (2009). She uses data from the Survey of Labour and Income Dynamics (SLID) covering the period 1993–2004. In this study, displaced workers are defined as those who lost their job due to the company closing, the company moving, or being laid off due to business slowdown. This study focuses on earnings losses of displaced older workers, i.e., those who lose their job at ages between 50 and 69 years of age. However, comparisons to younger displaced workers are also provided. An important challenge in examining earnings losses among older displaced workers is that many may not become re-employed, but rather may retire from the workforce. For this group, re-employment earnings are not observed. The subset of those who do obtain re-employment may not be representative of the larger group of older displaced workers. Statistical techniques are used to take account of the self-selected nature of the sample of individuals who obtain a new job following displacement.

Schirle finds that, as with younger workers, older workers face large and persistent earnings losses after permanent job loss. Interestingly, once one statistically controls for job tenure, age plays only a modest role in the magnitudes of earnings losses. However, as also found in other studies, job tenure is a strong predictor of the magnitude of the loss in earnings. High seniority older men experience the largest earnings losses after displacement—over $22,000 in the year after job loss and longer term losses over $16,000 per year. In contrast, low tenure men experience average earnings losses of around $10,000 in the first year and longer term losses of $6,000 to $6,500. Shirle also finds that some earnings losses begin before displacement occurs, particularly among those workers who are laid off due to the company closing.

Although age and previous job tenure are related, age appears to play an independent role in the likelihood of becoming re-employed, but a more limited role in the magnitudes of earnings losses. In particular, older displaced workers are less likely to become re-employed within the time period covered by the data. For example, recent Canadian data indicate that the proportions of male displaced workers who are re-employed within five years of job loss are 83 per cent for men aged 25–44 but only 64 per cent for men aged 45–59 (Expert Panel on Older Workers 2008). However, Schirle concludes that, once one statistically controls for tenure, age has only a modest effect on the magnitudes of earnings losses.[6] In her study, earnings losses of younger men aged 25–34 are slightly smaller than those of older men but the differences are not statistically significant. Similarly, there are not large or statistically significant differences between the earnings losses of displaced workers aged 35–49 and those aged 50–69.

Schirle (2009) also finds differences in the consequences of permanent job loss by educational attainment and urban/rural status. The magnitudes of earnings losses of low-educated and high-educated workers are similar—around $13,000 in the first year—but this drop in earnings represents a larger percentage decline for workers with low education (about 40 per cent) compared to those with high education (about 23 per cent). Similarly, the earnings declines experienced by displaced workers living in urban and rural areas are similar in size, but relative to pre-displacement earnings are larger among workers residing in rural areas (about 40 per cent) compared to those urban areas (about 30 per cent).

These and other studies of displaced workers may understate earnings losses. One reason for possible understatement is that most studies compare earnings prior to displacement to earnings in the new job among those who obtain re-employment within the period covered by the data. However, not all displaced workers find a new job by the survey date. Those who remain without work at the survey date may do even worse than their counterparts who obtain a new job. In addition, most studies compare post-displacement to pre-displacement earnings. However, as noted in the Jacobson, LaLonde and Sullivan (1993), Morissette, Zhang and Frenette (2007) and Schirle (2009) studies, pre-displacement earnings may underestimate "normal earnings." In particular, the event that leads to displacement shows up in the form of declining earnings up to three years prior to displacement—perhaps because firms threatened with bankruptcy reduce employees' hours of work in an attempt to survive.

At the same time, earnings losses may be overstated if downsizing firms selectively lay off the least productive employees (Gibbons and Katz 1991). This type of "layoffs and lemons" behaviour does not, however, apply to plant shutdowns, and is unlikely to apply to mass layoffs. Both are important sources of displacement.

What explains the large earnings losses that persist for many years after permanent job loss? The leading explanation involves loss of human capital that is specific to the job, firm, industry or occupation, and thus not transferable to other settings. Evidence supporting this view includes studies by Jacobson, LaLonde and Sullivan (1993), Neal (1995) and Parent (2000) that find that workers who change industries after job loss suffer much greater losses. Additional evidence supporting the specific human capital view is provided by Poletaev and Robinson (2008) using measures of the skill content of jobs. They find that the earnings losses experienced by displaced workers are closely associated with the magnitude of the change in the skill portfolio between the pre-displacement and post-displacement jobs. Job losers who obtain new employment with skill content similar to that in their previous job are less likely to suffer earnings losses, even when doing so involves changing industry or occupation, while those unable to become re-employed in a job with similar skill content are likely to experience large declines in earnings.

Another explanation is the presence of internal labour markets and wage profiles that depend on seniority. For a variety of reasons, employers and employees may prefer wage structures such that workers earn less than their value to the firm early in their career and more than their value to the firm later in their career. This type of behaviour produces a wage profile that increases with tenure with the firm—indeed, one that increases with seniority more rapidly than does worker productivity. Employees with substantial tenure who permanently lose their jobs thus lose this "premium" (wages in excess of productivity) when they re-enter the job market and become re-employed at wages that more closely reflect their productivity. An additional factor is that some displaced workers may have been earning "economic rents"—wages in excess of productivity—and cannot be expected, on average, to be able to find new jobs that also pay wages in excess of worker productivity. For example, Kuhn and Sweetman (1998) find that earnings losses are larger for workers who lose jobs in the union sector and become re-employed in the non-union sector, compared with those who make a transition from the non-union to union sector or who remain in the union sector.

The pattern of earnings losses with prior job tenure accords well with explanations built on loss of employer-specific and/or industry-specific human capital, as well as those based on internal labour markets with seniority-based wage profiles. For example, a subsequent study by Jacobson, LaLonde and Sullivan (2005) analyzes the earnings of displaced workers in Washington State according to three categories of prior job tenure: 6 to 11 quarters, 12 to 23 quarters, and six or more years. Prior to displacement, the high-seniority category (six or more years) earned approximately double that of the low-seniority category, and about

50 per cent more than the middle-seniority group (12 to 23 quarters). After displacement, the average earnings of the three groups are almost identical. This common earnings pattern persists for four years after job loss, with the result that the group with most prior job tenure has suffered the largest earnings losses, and the group with the least prior job tenure the smallest earnings losses.

C Other Consequences of Displacement

Permanent job loss has additional negative consequences, which are only briefly noted here despite their economic and social significance. A recent US study by Sullivan and von Wachter (2009) concludes that displacement leads to a 15 per cent to 20 per cent increase in death rates, equivalent to a reduction in life expectancy of about 1.5 years for someone displaced at age 40. Eliason and Storrie (2009) examine the impact of job loss on overall and cause-specific mortality with Swedish data. They find a substantial rise in mortality among displaced Swedish men (over 40 per cent increase) during the first four years after job loss. For both men and women displacement results in an approximate doubling of mortality due to suicides and alcohol-related deaths. Mental health problems arising from job loss are reported in the study by Hamilton, Merrigan and Dufresne (1997).

There are also adverse consequences for the families of displaced workers. Charles and Stephens (2004) find that the incidence of divorce rises after a spouse's displacement, an effect that is not present for the onset of a disability. Lindo (2010) finds evidence that a husband's displacement reduces the wife's fertility. Parental job loss reduces the likelihood that teen-aged children will pursue post-secondary education (Coelli 2009). Inter-generational impacts appear to be long-lasting: children whose fathers were displaced have, as adults, lower annual earnings (about 9 per cent) and have higher incidence of employment insurance (EI) and social assistance receipt (Oreopoulos, Page and Stevens 2008).

D Summary and implications

In summary, the research on the consequences of displacement yields a number of salient and consistent findings:

- Earnings losses from permanent job loss are very large, especially for long-tenure workers.
- A major part of the earnings loss arises not from post-displacement unemployment, but from re-employment at wages substantially below their pre-displacement levels.
- These substantial losses appear to be long-lasting (perhaps permanent).
- One Canadian study finds that well-educated workers experience earnings losses that are similar in size to those experienced by workers with low education, but smaller as a percentage of previous earnings.
- The same Canadian study also concludes that displaced workers in ur-

ban areas experience earnings losses that are similar in size to those experienced by workers living in rural areas, but smaller as a percentage of previous earnings.

- Older displaced workers are less likely to become re-employed than their younger counterparts. However, age appears to play only a minor role in the magnitudes of annual earnings losses, once one statistically controls for worker seniority.
- Losses experienced by displaced workers with substantial job tenure are similar in magnitude and permanence to other catastrophic events, e.g., having one's house burn down (LaLonde 2007).
- In contrast, non-displaced unemployed workers become re-employed relatively quickly and do not suffer permanent earnings losses.
- The long tenure group that is most likely to experience large earnings losses is relatively small—about 5 per cent of unemployed workers and 15 to 20 per cent of permanent job losers.

These findings have important policy implications. Private insurance markets for losses associated with job displacement do not exist. In addition, publicly provided insurance (*Employment Insurance Act*, Part I) does not provide adequate insurance against the risk of permanent job loss. In particular, EI does not take into account the fact that earnings losses are much larger for long-tenure displaced workers. EI benefits depend only on employment in the twelve months prior to displacement, so the EI program treats job losers with long tenure and short tenure in an equivalent fashion. Furthermore, EI covers only a portion of the lost income during the unemployment period, whereas a substantial portion of the earnings loss suffered by long-tenure displaced workers is associated with permanently lower earnings in subsequent jobs. In many ways, the current EI program is similar to having automobile insurance that pays the same amount for "fender-benders" as for vehicles that are destroyed.

3 Policies to Deal with Displacement

A variety of policies to deal with displacement and its consequences have been proposed or implemented. These are briefly discussed here under two headings: (A) ex ante (preventive) policies and (B) ex post (adjustment assistance) policies.

A Ex Ante Policies

Policies that promote education and skill development may, in addition to their well-known benefits in other dimensions, also enhance the adaptability of the workforce to changing circumstances. A variety of evidence from case studies and more broadly based empirical research suggests that education improves the ability of individuals to adjust to changing circumstances (Schultz 1975). In the context of displacement, education is a strong predictor of the probability of re-employment after job loss. Displaced workers with more education have higher probabilities of re-employment and are more likely to be re-employed full-time (Farber 2005). Furthermore, this relationship appears to reflect underlying causal forces rather than simply being a correlation between education and re-employment rates: Riddell and Song (2007, 2011) conclude that education has a causal impact on re-employment. This recent evidence is consistent with the view that investment in skills can enhance adaptability.

Ex ante policies that focus more directly on workforce adjustments include restricting firms' ability to lay off workers or requiring advance notice of layoffs and/or severance pay. Such restrictions arise from both the common law and from employment standards legislation in the federal and provincial jurisdictions (Kuhn 2000). According to the common law, most labour contracts can be discontinued either by firing workers for cause or providing a reasonable amount of notice. All Canadian jurisdictions have minimum mandatory notice provisions for permanent layoffs in their employment standards laws. Most jurisdictions also require greater notice for mass terminations and plant shutdowns. Jurisdictions with mass layoff provisions also often require the employer to establish and finance a workforce adjustment committee, with employee representation, to develop an adjustment program for displaced workers and to help workers find new job opportunities. Severance pay is also required in some jurisdictions.

A limited amount of empirical evidence is available on the impacts of Canadian employment protection and advance notice provisions. Studies by Jones and Kuhn (1995) and Friesen (1997) conclude that advance warning of mass layoffs and plant shutdowns can have positive benefits. However, the impacts appear to accrue primarily for those who are capable of finding a new job quickly. For these workers, what would, in the absence of advance warning laws, be a short unemployment spell is instead replaced by an even briefer period of unemployment or an immediate job switch. For those who, in the absence of advance warning laws, are expected to have long unemployment durations, the presence of advance notice appears to have little effect (Jones and Kuhn 1995). The reason appears to be that, except in small amounts, pre-displacement job search is significantly less effective than post-displacement search in obtaining re-employment, a conclusion also reached in several US studies of displaced workers. There is also no Canadian evidence that advance warning reduces the earnings loss associated with lower wages in the post-displacement job compared to the previous job.

B Ex Post Policies

Ex post adjustment assistance policies include a variety of interventions designed to help displaced workers cope with the trauma of losing one's job and the associated reduced income and, importantly, to find suitable employment as rapidly as possible. These "active labour market policies" range from brief and inexpensive interventions like job search assistance to more intensive interventions such as retraining or assistance with relocating to regions with greater employment opportunities. There is a substantial body of international evidence on these policies.[7] The best evidence comes from the United States, which has a strong commitment to undertaking rigorous evaluations of labour market programs. In recent years there has been an explosion of new evidence on the impacts of these programs from the UK and continental Europe, reflecting advances in methodology and data quality and a growing commitment to serious evaluation of labour market programs. Unfortunately, credible Canadian evidence on the impacts of active labour market policies is seriously lacking. Thus this summary of "what works" is based principally on the US and European experiences.

A series of randomized UI experiments carried out in the US during the 1980s and 1990s provides credible evidence on the impacts of job search assistance. Meyer (1995) provides a useful survey of these studies. Job search assistance reduces the duration of unemployment by about 0.5 weeks. The impact is small but the intervention is brief and inexpensive, so has a favourable cost-benefit ratio. More recent evidence comes from evaluations of the UK New Deal for Youth that included mandatory job search assistance plus (if necessary) subsidized employment. Analysis shows positive impacts on re-employment among long term unemployed youth (see, for example, Blundell et al. 2004).

The literature on the impacts of government-sponsored training is voluminous. Results are also somewhat sobering: training often has little or no impact on earnings. Estimated impacts, even when positive, are generally modest in size. A brief summary of the extensive US evidence would include the following: (i) impacts of training on out-of-school youths are typically zero or negative; (ii) impacts on earnings of adult men are generally zero or positive but small in size, and (iii) impacts for adult women are generally positive and larger than those for adult men. However, in interpreting this evidence it is worth keeping in mind that US training programs are often targeted toward highly disadvantaged workers, who face multiple barriers to labour market success.

Training might be expected to be more beneficial for displaced workers who have strong prior labour force attachment, fewer barriers to employment and are often highly motivated. However, displaced workers may face a different set of obstacles. Older displaced workers often have low levels of education and may have literacy and numeracy deficiencies that need to be remedied prior to retraining. There is also the question of whether those who have been employed for many years can acquire new skills in a classroom setting as efficiently as younger individuals whose schooling experience is more recent. Thus it is not clear *a priori* that training will be more effective for displaced workers.

The empirical evidence on training impacts for permanent job losers is not as extensive as that for the disadvantaged, but it is similarly pessimistic about the potential for retraining.[8] Experimental studies, which provide the most credible evidence, suggest that training has little or no impact on the post-displacement earnings of job losers. Non-experimental studies face important econometric challenges relating to selection into training programs by the trainee or by program administrators on the basis of unobserved factors (such as motivation) that may be correlated with the impact of training. Nonetheless, non-experimental analyses can have advantages such as large sample sizes and a wider range of retraining interventions. Careful analysis by Jacobson, LaLonde and Sullivan (2005) provides evidence that community college programs for retraining displaced workers can have positive impacts. This study found that the equivalent of one year of community college coursework raised earnings of male displaced workers by 9 per cent and female displaced workers by 13 per cent. Jacobson, LaLonde, and Sullivan also concluded that the type of training matters: estimated impacts were larger for those taking more quantitative vocational and academic courses.

European programs focus more on speeding the return to work, especially among youths, than on raising earnings once re-employed. The difference in emphasis reflects the fact that European unemployed are typically less disadvantaged but experience longer spells of unemployment. A common finding of recent evaluations is that training results in substantial reductions in the duration of unemployment but has little impact on wages (Card, Kluve and Weber 2009; Kluve 2007).

My own assessment of the potential for training programs is similar to that articulated by LaLonde (1995) in an earlier review of the US evidence: you get (at best) what you pay for.[9] In thinking about the likely impact of training on earnings, the empirical evidence on the effects of other human capital investments provides useful guidance. In many countries, including Canada, an additional year of formal schooling raises earnings by approximately 8 to 10 per cent. Using these estimates as a benchmark, we could expect a 12-month training program to raise earnings by 8–10 per cent, and a 6-month program to raise earnings by 4–5 per cent. Impacts of this size may be large enough to justify investing in training on a cost-benefit basis.

However, except for very intensive and expensive training programs, these returns are not large enough to restore earnings losses experienced by long-tenure displaced workers. For example, using the estimates obtained by Jacobson, LaLonde and Sullivan for displaced workers in Washington State—which are at the upper end of estimated impacts of retraining—even two years of college level training would not come close to restoring the earnings losses experienced by long-tenure displaced workers.[10]

The final two policies I discuss are specifically directed towards long-tenure displaced workers. As noted previously, an important flaw in the current EI program is that it does not provide benefits that reflect the cost of job loss. Apart from some recent initiatives (discussed below), long-tenure displaced workers, who lose the most from permanent job loss, are not treated any differently than displaced workers who have been employed for brief periods of time. The report of the Expert Panel on Older Workers (2008) recommended enhanced benefits for displaced workers with substantial prior work experience and limited prior EI receipt. Enhanced EI benefits could take the form of higher benefit levels, longer benefit durations, or improved access to funds for training or mobility assistance. These would align benefits more closely with magnitude of loss, thus improving the social insurance dimension of Canada's EI program.

Design of this enhanced benefits feature requires careful assessment to ensure that the social benefits arising from improved insurance are maximized while the social costs resulting from any adverse side effects are minimized. Some lessons can be drawn from the European experience. Many European countries have unemployment insurance (UI) benefits and durations that depend on prior work experience (OECD 2007). In Austria, for example, those with less than three years of prior work experience (possibly with several employers) are entitled to 20 weeks of benefits, whereas those with three or more years of previous work experience are entitled to 30 weeks of benefits. In addition, employers that permanently lay off workers with three or more years of job tenure with that firm are required to make severance payments that equal approximately two months' salary.

By exploiting these sharp discontinuities at three years of previous work experience and three years of tenure with the employer, Card, Chetty and Weber (2007) provide convincing evidence that these features have small to modest effects on the duration of unemployment following displacement. In particular, entitlement to 30 weeks of benefits reduces the job finding rate by 5 per cent to 9 per cent, compared to workers displaced with less than three years of previous work experience. Similarly, the severance payment associated with reaching the three-year job tenure threshold reduces the job finding rate by 8 per cent to 12 per cent. Interestingly, they also find that longer unemployment spells do not result in improved matches in the subsequent job, using both wages and the duration of the re-employment job as measures of job-match quality. Thus, enhanced EI benefits for long-tenure displaced workers may have adverse side effects, and the social costs of any such effects need to be balanced against the social benefits from improved insurance against the risk of permanent job loss.[11]

Since the onset of the recent economic downturn the federal government has followed the recommendations of the Expert Panel on Older Workers and has introduced several initiatives that provide enhanced benefits for long-tenure displaced workers.[12] In May 2009 the government announced the Career Transition Assistance program that provides additional support to long-tenure displaced workers. One initiative extends the duration of EI benefits for eligible long-tenure displaced workers who participate in longer-term training by up to two years. Another allows earlier access to EI regular benefits for displaced workers investing in their own training using all or part of their severance package. Subsequently, the government extended regular EI benefits for long-tenure displaced workers. Both of these new initiatives are temporary in nature.

Enhanced EI benefits for long-tenure displaced workers should improve the insurance value of the EI program by reducing the income loss during the post-displacement unemployment spell. However, enhanced EI benefits do not help insure against the most significant income loss associated with job loss among long-tenure workers—the lower earnings in the post-displacement job compared to the pre-displacement job. As discussed previously, these reduced earnings continue for many years after permanent job loss, and are particularly pronounced for workers with substantial tenure in their previous job. To address this source of income loss, some US scholars (e.g., Kletzer and Rosen 2006; Kling 2006; LaLonde 2007) have recommended wage (loss) insurance. Such wage-loss insurance would supplement the employment income of the displaced worker in the post-displacement job. An example of wage-loss insurance would be an earnings supplement for up to three years in the post-displacement job, equal to 50 per cent of the difference in earnings between pre- and post-displacement jobs. This type of earnings supplement recognizes that, for long-tenure displaced workers, most of the income loss occurs after re-employment rather than during the post-displacement unemployment spell. In contrast, for other unemployed workers, the income loss occurs during the unemployment spell.

Wage insurance is an interesting policy proposal with attractive features. In addition to its key advantage of providing insurance against the risk of income loss due to displacement, wage insurance may also speed up the return to work. It deserves careful assessment. I support the recommendation of the Expert Panel on Older Workers that Canada undertake a rigorous demonstration project (preferably with random assignment to program and control groups) to assess the impacts of wage insurance.[13]

One response to this recommendation might be "been there, done that"—reflecting the fact that Canada did carry out a demonstration project (the Earnings Supplement Project, or ESP) that tested the impacts of an earning loss insurance program for displaced workers.[14] However, this view is mistaken. The ESP provided useful and policy-relevant information but it did not constitute a test of the impacts of wage loss insurance for dealing with the large losses experienced by a small subset of displaced workers. To understand this point we need to consider how one would design a demonstration project to test the effectiveness of wage insurance as a mechanism for improving the social insurance function of the EI program. Then we need to compare this hypothetical demonstration project to the ESP. When this is done it is apparent that the ESP, although it addressed the policy concerns at the time, did not test the effectiveness of a wage insurance program along the lines recommended by Kletzer and Rosen (2006), Kling (2006), LaLonde (2007) and the Expert Panel on Older Workers (2008).

To test the effectiveness of a wage loss insurance program we would first want to choose the experimental sample to be similar to the likely target group for the policy, in order to be most relevant to the policy that is subsequently implemented. In this case we would choose as an experimental sample those who lose a substantial amount from permanent job loss—i.e., long-tenure displaced workers. As a guide, we would probably draw the experimental sample from those with at least five years of previous job tenure, and with average tenure that is considerably longer (e.g., 10–12 years). Those randomly assigned to the treatment group would be offered an earnings supplement such as one based on the difference between the pre-displacement earnings and the post-displacement earnings in the new job. Second, we might require those in the treatment group to obtain a new job within a certain period of time in order to qualify for the earnings supplement, but if we did so, this time period would reflect the typical unemployment duration experience of long-tenure displaced workers. Third, the outcome measures on which the treatment and control groups would be compared would be those associated with the provision of insurance against adverse events. Thus we would compare the consumption of the treatment and control groups to see if an earnings supplement based on the difference between the pre-displacement earnings and the post-displacement earnings is effective in preventing a major decline in the family's standard of living. Similarly, we would also examine outcomes such as mental and physical health, as well as educational attainment among the children of the displaced worker.

Based on these considerations, it is clear that the ESP was not designed to test wage insurance in the form that the policy is currently advocated—that is, as a form of social insurance for those who suffer the most from permanent job loss. The ESP was designed at a time when the principal policy concern was that of speeding up the return to work of individuals receiving unemployment (EI) benefits. Indeed, the ESP arose as a consequence of UI bonus experiments carried out in several US states that provided rigorous tests of the hypothesis that a financial incentive to find work quickly could both speed up the return to work and reduce the costs to government of operating the UI program.

The ESP extended this idea of testing the effectiveness of a re-employment incentive to displaced workers (as well as to repeat users of EI). For the displaced worker component of ESP, the experimental sample was not confined to long-tenure displaced workers but rather to all permanent job losers. As a consequence, less than one-half of the experimental sample had job tenure in excess of five years and only 20 per cent had tenure of ten or more years (Bloom et al. 1997). We now know (although this was perhaps not well known at the time) that displaced workers with short previous tenure typically become re-employed at earnings levels similar to those in their pre-displacement jobs. These individuals are unlikely to benefit from an earnings supplement based on the difference between their pre-displacement and post-displacement earnings. Thus it is not surprising that the ESP take-up rate was low (around 20 per cent), as many of those in the treatment group would not benefit from the earnings supplement.

Furthermore, to qualify for the earnings supplement, those in the treatment group had to become re-employed within 26 weeks. For long-tenure displaced workers, who typically take longer to become re-employed than other permanent job losers, this time limit is too brief. Thus the parameters of the experiment were established such that most displaced workers in the treatment group would not benefit from an earnings supplement based on the gap between the pre-displacement and post-displacement earnings, and those that would potentially benefit were given an unrealistically short period of time in which to qualify for the supplement.

Perhaps the most important limitation of the ESP demonstration for assessing current policy interest in wage insurance arises from the fact that the outcome measures examined in the ESP are not the outcomes one would use to assess the social value of wage insurance. ESP was designed to examine whether providing a financial incentive to become re-employed quickly would speed up the return to work. From an insurance perspective this is a minor consideration. There is some policy interest in whether the offer of wage insurance would result in more rapid re-employment among long-tenure displaced workers. But the case for wage loss insurance doesn't depend on this factor. The case for wage insurance lies in its potential for providing insurance against a substantial decline in the standard of living of families in which a member with long employment tenure suffers permanent job loss. If we were assessing the adequacy of house insurance we would examine whether families whose house burned down had to subsequently live in substantially lower quality housing. In the case of permanent job loss we should be interested in assessing whether affected families suffer substantial declines in their standard of living, as well as other adverse effects such as marital difficulties, greater incidence of mental illness and increased mortality.

4 Conclusions and Recommendations

Canada's economy performed reasonably well in the postwar period, achieving high rates of employment growth and advances in living standards (Riddell 1999). A key contributor to this good performance has been a dynamic labour market that shifts workers into sectors where they are needed and out of declining sectors without lengthy intervening periods of unemployment. As a group, Canadians benefit from this process of adjusting to changing circumstances and opportunities. However, the costs of adjustment are unevenly distributed in the population.

A central finding of empirical research on displacement is that some workers suffer much more from losing their jobs than do others. On average, those who have held their jobs for an extended period of time experience substantial earnings losses, while those who have been employed for relatively brief periods of time experience small losses. Like other job losers, long-tenure displaced workers experience earnings losses due to reduced income during the period of unemployment following displacement. However, unlike other job losers, many long-tenure displaced workers become re-employed at significantly lower wages than they received in their pre-displacement jobs. Our existing social insurance programs, particularly Employment Insurance, do not take into account these salient features of the consequences of job loss.

A second key finding is that long-tenure displaced workers constitute a small minority of job losers. For example, our analysis of LFS data indicates that job losers with five or more years of tenure with their previous employer constitute about 5 per cent of unemployed workers and 15–20 per cent of permanent job losers.

I conclude with some recommendations. They are intended to address both the research and knowledge gaps relating to displacement and its consequences, as well as the policy gaps in addressing this important problem. To address the gaps in research and knowledge, Canada should follow the US and carry out a regular Displaced Worker Survey—for example, one undertaken every other year and covering permanent job loss that occurred during the previous three years. This survey could operate as an occasional supplement to the Labour Force Survey and therefore need not be expensive. The US experience with a regular DWS clearly indicates its value in providing timely information on the incidence of permanent job loss, the duration of unemployment following displacement, and the consequences for individuals and their families of such events. The US survey has also been an important source of data for research on the causes and consequences of permanent job loss. In a country like Canada, with significant exposure to external and internal economic shocks, the case for such a survey seems obvious.

There is also a strong case for enhanced EI benefits for long-tenure displaced workers and, more generally, for altering the parameters of the EI program to recognize that such workers suffer much more from job loss than do other unemployed workers. These changes should become a permanent feature of the EI program, but they should be introduced in a way that their effects can be rigorously evaluated.

I would not restrict the receipt or magnitude of these enhanced benefits to long-tenure displaced workers with little or no previous EI receipt, as was recommended by the Expert Panel on Older Workers. One reason why this condition may be too restrictive is that, as discussed previously, the economic forces that ultimately result in permanent job loss are often evident in the form of spells of unemployment and EI receipt in the period prior to displacement. Thus it might not be unusual for workers who ultimately experience mass layoffs or plant closures to have received EI in the period prior to dismissal. However, these enhanced benefits should be designed in a way to exclude seasonal workers, who are already richly rewarded by the EI program. These enhanced benefits should also be designed to minimize any adverse effects on the duration and intensity of job search.

For similar reasons, the benefits and support measures provided under EI Part II should focus more on long-tenure displaced workers—especially relatively intensive interventions such as retraining and mobility assistance. Thus I support the general nature of recent initiatives in this area, especially longer benefit durations and improved access to training for long-tenure displaced workers. Before adopting these features on a more permanent basis there should be a serious attempt to evaluate the consequences of these recent initiatives. However, until such evaluations are completed there is a good case for extending these new initiatives for a longer period of time. Furthermore, given the evidence on the effectiveness of retraining for displaced workers—which is, at best, mixed—greater emphasis should be placed on mobility assistance and less on training in EI Part II. In a country as regionally diverse as Canada, it is unfortunate that we respond to so-called "skills shortages" by temporary and permanent immigration rather than devoting resources to promoting internal migration.

Finally, since most loss from displacement occurs after re-employment, wage insurance seems the most promising approach for providing insurance to those who suffer most from economic and technological change. Canada should carefully assess the advantages and disadvantages of such a policy. The best way to do so would be to carry out a rigorous demonstration project, preferably using random assignment. An alternative would be to implement wage insurance as a pilot project with a sunset clause and a requirement for rigorous evaluation prior to renewal.

Acknowledgements

I thank Jacob Cosman for excellent research assistance, and Keith Banting, Stephen Jones, Bill Scarth, Arthur Sweetman, participants in the Mowat EI workshop, and anonymous referees for helpful comments.

Endnotes

1 Canada did carry out a DWS in 1986 that covered job loss experienced during the period 1981–85. However, this survey has not been repeated.

2 The authors examine post-displacement earnings during five years following displacement; thus the study covers displacements that occurred up to 1997, more than a decade ago.

3 Workers are classified as permanently laid off when they do not return to their former employer in the same year or in the following year following the layoff.

4 Data were extracted from the monthly public use LFS files and then aggregated to annual observations. All estimates use the survey weights so are representative of the Canadian adult population.

5 "Expected earnings" refers to the earnings that would have been experienced without displacement. These are estimated using the outcomes experienced by the comparison group of non-displaced workers.

6 Even if the magnitudes of annual earnings losses are independent of age, the present value of future losses will depend on age because younger displaced workers have more years remaining in the workforce.

7 See Card, Kluve and Weber (2009); Heckman, LaLonde and Smith (1999); Kluve (2007); and OECD (2006)for surveys of the international evidence.

8 See Jones (2011) for a careful review of the US and Canadian evidence.

9 It is also possible, as argued for example by Eberts (2005) and OECD (2006), that public training programs could be made more effective. Obtaining credible evidence on how to improve government-sponsored training would require a substantial commitment to evaluation research.

10 For example, consider a worker with pre-displacement earnings of $45,000 who obtains re-employment at $30,000 (i.e., experiences an earnings loss of 33 per cent). A one-year training program would be expected to increase earnings by at most 10 per cent, i.e., $3,000 and a two-year program by $6,000. This would still leave an earnings loss of $9,000, or about 20 per cent.

11 Although the Austrian evidence may not be directly applicable to Canada, it can be used to provide some guidance on the probable magnitude of adverse side effects. For example, increasing the maximum benefit duration from 20 to 30 weeks (an increase of 50 per cent) is estimated to reduce the job finding rate by about 7 per cent. In an equilibrium search model with a monthly job separation rate of .01 and an initial monthly job finding rate of 0.2, this 50 per cent increase in benefit durations would raise the equilibrium unemployment rate from 4.8 to 5.1 per cent. I thank Bill Scarth for suggesting these back-of-the-envelope calculations.

12 Note, however, that the federal government's definition of "long-tenure displaced worker" is too broad and would include many job losers that do not experience substantial wage losses.

13 See Jones (2009) for an assessment of the recommendations of the Expert Panel with respect to wage insurance.

14 See Bloom et al. (1999) for the Final Report on this demonstration project.

References

Baldwin, J., T. Dunne, and J. Haltiwanger. 1998. "A Comparison of Job Creation and Job Destruction in Canada and the United States." *Review of Economics and Statistics* 80.3: 347-56.

Bloom, H., B. Fink, S. Lui-Gurr, W. Bancroft and D. Tattrie. 1997. *Implementing the Earnings Supplement Project: A Test of a Re-employment Incentive.* Ottawa: Social Research and Demonstration Corporation.

Bloom, H., S. Schwartz, S. Lui-Gurr and S-W. Lee. 1999. *Testing a Re-employment Incentive for Displaced Workers: The earnings Supplement Project*. Ottawa: Social Research and Demonstration Corporation.

Blundell, R., M. Costa Dias, C. Meghir and J. Van Reenan. 2004. "Evaluating the Employment Impact of a Mandatory Job Search Program." *Journal of the European Economic Association* 2. 4: 569-606.

Card, D., R. Chetty and A. Weber. 2007. "Cash-on-Hand and Competing Models of Intertemporal Behavior: New Evidence from the Labor Market." *Quarterly Journal of Economics* 122.4: 1511-560.

Card, D., J. Kluve and A. Weber. 2009. "Active Labor Market Policy Evaluation: A Meta-Analysis." IZA DP No. 4002. Bonn: IZA.

Coelli, M.B. 2009. "Parental Job Loss, Income Shocks and the Education Enrolment of Youth." Department of Economics—Working Paper 1060. Melbourne: University of Melbourne.

Charles, K.C. and M. Stephens Jr. 2004. "Job Displacement, Disability and Divorce." *Journal of Labor Economics* 22. 2: 489-522.

Davis, S.J. and J. Haltiwanger. 1999. "Gross Job Flows." In *Handbook of Labor Economics*, ed. O. Ashenfelter and D. Card, 2711-805. Amsterdam: Elsevier.

Eberts, R.W. 2005. "After the Doors Close: Assisting Laid-Off Workers to Find Jobs." *Economic Perspectives* 29.2: 75-85.

Eliason, M. and D. Storrie. 2009. "Does Job Loss Shorten Life?" *Journal of Human Resources* 44.2: 277-302.

Expert Panel on Older Workers. 2008. "Supporting and Engaging Older Workers in the New Economy." Ottawa: Expert Panel on Older Workers. At http://www.hrsdc.gc.ca/eng/publications_resources/lmp/eow/2008/older_workers_2008.pdf.

Farber, H.S. 1999. "Mobility and Stability: The Dynamics of Job Change in Labor Markets." In *Handbook of Labor Economics*, ed. O. Ashenfelter and D. Card, 2439-84. Amsterdam: Elsevier.

Farber, H.S. 2005. "What Do We Know about Job Loss in the United States? Evidence from the Displaced Workers Survey, 1984–2004." *Economic Perspectives* 29.2: 13-28.

Friesen, J. 1997. "Mandatory Notice and the Jobless Durations of Displaced Workers." *Industrial and Labor Relations Review* 50.4: 652-66.

Gibbons, R. and L.F. Katz. 1991. "Layoffs and Lemons." *Journal of Labor Economics* 9.4: 351-80.

Green, D.A. and W.C. Riddell. 1993. "The Economic Effects of Unemployment Insurance in Canada: An Empirical Analysis of UI Disentitlement." *Journal of Labor Economics* 11.1: S96-S147.

Gunderson, M. 1986. "Alternative Mechanisms for Dealing with Permanent Layoffs, Dismissals and Plant Closings." In *Adapting to Change: Labour Market Adjustment in Canada*, ed. W. C. Riddell, 111-62. Toronto: Royal Commission on the Economic Union and Development Prospects for Canada and University of Toronto Press.

Hamilton, V.H., P. Merrigan and E. Dufresne. 1997. "Down and Out: Estimating the Relationship between Mental Health and Unemployment" *Health Economics* 6. 4: 397-406.

Heckman, J.J., R.J. LaLonde, and J.A. Smith. 1999. "The Economics and Econometrics of Active Labor Market Programs." In *Handbook of Labor Economics*, ed. D. Card and O. Ashenfelter, 1865-2097. Amsterdam: Elsevier.

Jacobson, L.S., R.J. LaLonde, and D.G. Sullivan. 1993. "Earnings Losses of Displaced Workers." *American Economic Review* 83.4: 685-709.

Jacobson, L.S., R.J. LaLonde, and D.G. Sullivan. 2005. "Is Retraining Displaced Workers a Good Investment?" *Economic Perspectives* 29.2: 47-66.

Jones, S.R.G. 2009. "Older Workers in the New Economy: The Role of Wage Insurance and the Rethinking of Employment Insurance" *Canadian Public Policy* 35.4: 499-511.

——. 2011. "The Effectiveness of Training for Displaced Workers with Long Prior Job Tenure" Mowat Centre EI Task Force.

Jones, S.R.G. and P. Kuhn. 1995. "Mandatory Notice and Unemployment." *Journal of Labor Economics* 13.4: 599-622.

Kletzer, L.G. and H.F. Rosen. 2006. "Reforming Unemployment Insurance for the Twenty-First Century Workforce." Brookings Institution Hamilton Project Discussion Paper No. 2006-06. Washington, DC: Brookings Institution.

Kling, J.R. 2006. "Fundamental Restructuring of Unemployment Insurance: Wage-Loss Insurance and Temporary Earnings Replacement Accounts." Brookings Institution Hamilton Project Discussion Paper No. 2006-05. Washington, DC: Brookings Institution.

Kluve, J. 2007. "The Effectiveness of European ALMP's." In *Active Labor Market Policies in Europe: Performance and Perspectives*, ed. J. Kluve,153-203. Berlin and Heidelberg: Springer.

Kuhn, P. 2000. "Canada and the OECD Hypothesis: Does Labour Market Inflexibility Explain Canada's High Level of Unemployment?" In *Adapting Public Policy to a Labour Market in Transition*, ed. W.C. Riddell and F. St-Hilaire, 177-210. Montreal: Institute for Research on Public Policy.

Kuhn, P. and A. Sweetman.1998. "Wage Loss Following Displacement: The Role of Union Coverage." *Industrial and Labor Relations Review* 51.3: 384-400.

LaLonde, R.J. 1995. "The Promise of Public Sector-Sponsored Training Programs." *Journal of Economic Perspectives* 9.2: 149-68.

——. 2007. *The Case for Wage Insurance*. Council on Foreign Relations, Council Special Report No. 30. New York: Council on Foreign Relations.

Lindo, J.M. 2010. "Are Children Really Inferior Goods? Evidence from Displacement-Driven Income Shocks." *Journal of Human Resources* 45.2: 301-327.

Meyer, B. 1995. "Lessons from the U.S. Unemployment Insurance Experiments." *Journal of Economic Literature* 33.1: 91-131.

Morissette, R., X. Zhang, and M. Frenette. 2007. "Earnings Losses of Displaced Workers: Canadian Evidence from a Large Administrative Database on Firm Closures and Mass Layoffs." Statistics Canada Analytical Studies Branch Research Paper No. 291. Ottawa: Statistics Canada.

Neal, D. 1995. "Industry-Specific Human Capital: Evidence from Displaced Workers." *Journal of Labor Economics* 13.4: 653-77.

Oreopoulos, P., M. Page, and A. Huff Stevens. 2008. "The Intergenerational Effects of Worker Displacement." *Journal of Labor Economics* 26.3: 455-83.

Organisation for Economic Co-operation and Development (OECD). 2006. "Boosting Jobs and Incomes." *OECD Employment Outlook*. Paris: OECD.

——. 2007. *Benefits and Wages 2007*. Paris: OECD.

Parent, D. 2000. "Industry-specific Capital and the Wage Profile." *Journal of Labor Economics* 18.2: 306-21.

Picot, G., Z. Lin and W. Pyper. 1998. "Permanent layoffs in Canada: overview and longitudinal analysis." *Canadian Journal of Economics* 31.5: 1154-78.

Poletaev, M. and C. Robinson. 2008. "Human Capital Specificity: Evidence from the Dictionary of Occupational Titles and Displaced Worker Surveys, 1984–2000." *Journal of Labor Economics* 26.3: 387-420.

Riddell, W.C. 1986. *Adapting to Change: Labour Market Adjustments in Canada*. Toronto: Royal Commission on the Economic Union and Development Prospects for Canada and University of Toronto Press.

——. 1999. "Canadian Labour Market Performance in International Perspective" *Canadian Journal of Economics* 32.5: 1097-134.

Riddell, W.C. and X. Song. 2007. "The Causal Effects of Education on Adaptability to Employment Shocks: Evidence from the Canadian Labour Market." CLSRN Working Paper No. 8.

——. 2011. "The impact of education on unemployment incidence and re-employment success: Evidence from the U.S. labour market" *Labour Economics* 18.4: 453-463.

Schirle, T. 2009. "Earnings Losses of Displaced Older Workers: Accounting for the Retirement Option" CLSRN Working Paper No 10.

Schultz, T. 1975. "The Value of the Ability to Deal with Disequilibria." *Journal of Economic Literature* 13.3: 827-46.

Schumpeter, J.A. 1942. *Capitalism, Socialism, and Democracy*. New York: Harper & Brothers.

Sullivan, D. and T. von Wachter. 2009. "Job Displacement and Mortaity: An Analysis Using Administrative Data." *Quarterly Journal of Economics* 124.3: 1265-1306.

Trebilcock, M.J. 1986. *The Political Economy of Economic Adjustment*. Toronto: Royal Commission on the Economic Union and Development Prospects for Canada and University of Toronto Press.

Section IV

Federalism and Governance Challenges

Chapter 13

Adult Training for the 21st Century: EI Reform, Decentralization and Workforce Development in Canada

Allison Bramwell

Unemployment is an urgent, complex and enduring policy challenge. Governments learned from the Great Depression that "too much poverty, inequality, economic insecurity ... can cripple economic efficiency" (Howell 2005, 8). Dramatic changes in the nature of employment driven by the combined pressures of global economic competition, technological change, and de-industrialization, and exacerbated by the recent global recession, underscore the increasing importance of active labour market policy in the 21st century. While many adult workers have successfully navigated these recent structural economic changes, many others have not. The permanent loss of stable, high-wage jobs in advanced manufacturing and resource-based sectors in many Western industrialized economies has been coupled with an increase in more precarious, non-standard forms of employment (Howell 2005; Vroman and Brusentsev 2005).[1] Rising inequality and income polarization suggest that Canada may not have the income support system to get us where we need to go (Banting 2006; Osberg 2006, 2009). Mounting concerns that those who find themselves on the margins of the labour market will fall further and further behind suggest that we may not have the adult training systems to get us where we need to go.

This paper frames current discussions about how training programs for unemployed adults, federally funded under the Employment Insurance (EI) program, should be designed, administered, and delivered. It is argued here that decentralization under Labour Market Development Agreements (LMDAs) and Labour Market Agreements (LMAs) has transformed active labour market policy into a de facto area of provincial jurisdiction. The federal government should permanently devolve responsibility for adult training programs for both EI and non-EI eligible unemployed adult workers to provincial governments under a single conditional federal transfer within a standardized accountability framework.[2] This would leave room for the federal government to renew its involvement in adult training through a combination of multilateral forums, fiscal federalism, and intergovernmental means without eroding recent gains in provincial autonomy that have created policy space for more far-reaching and innovative reform. These developments would be consistent with similar developments in other industrialized countries that integrate employment policies and programs on a regional basis to better match supply and demand in local labour markets. More robust, integrated, and regionally sensitive workforce development systems can improve employment prospects for the unemployed, but this discourse has been too easily dismissed in Canada and needs to find its way back on to provincial policy agendas.

The discussion proceeds in three parts. The first section provides a brief discussion of the recent trend toward decentralization in labour market policy across OECD countries, followed by a more detailed discussion of how federalism and intergovernmental relations have shaped the recent devolution of labour market policy in Canada which has long lacked a coherent and unified policy architecture for adult training. Strong federal structures that shape and fund national objectives are needed in order to address complex 21st century labour market challenges but policy flexibility is also needed to facilitate adaptation to changing economic circumstances that affect workers in different regions in different ways (Brown 2005; Boadway 2001). The second section of the paper discusses policy gaps in the provision of training for unemployed adults who are ineligible for Employment Insurance as well as recently negotiated funding agreements intended to address these gaps, with a particular focus on Ontario.[3] The final section outlines two proposals for reform that address concerns about national policy fragmentation and program coverage while encouraging the development of systems that match supply and demand in regional labour markets.

1 Decentralization, Asymmetrical Federalism and Workforce Development in Canada

Few policy areas straddle the divide between economic and social policy as neatly as labour market policy, which "stands at the crucial nexus of efficiency and equity" between "the associated imperatives to sustain growth and alleviate the maladies associated with market societies" (Haddow and Klassen 2006, 277). Active labour market programs are important policy tools that facilitate economic adjustment while helping redress income polarization. Upgrading the skills of unemployed workers and workers "trapped in low-skilled, low-paying, often insecure jobs" is "a central labour market policy challenge for the 21st century" (Nativel 2006, 34). Major changes in labour market policy in OECD countries since the 1990s include a shift in public spending from passive income supports to adult training programs, and a shift from short-term programs narrowly targeted to unemployed working age adults to longer-term approaches to workforce development. Workforce development refers to the integration of a range of employment-related policies and programs to deliver skills formation systems that address skills mismatches in labour markets and increase the ability of individuals to better adapt to economic change throughout their working lives (Hall and Lansbury 2006). In Canada, workforce development goes beyond labour market policy to incorporate a wider set of activities including immigrant integration, social security, labour, human capital formation, and economic development policy measures (Wood and Klassen 2009).

There has been a great deal of recent policy activism and experimentation with workforce development systems across OECD countries. Recent research indicates that in order to effectively facilitate the re-entry of unemployed workers into the labour market, training programs need to meet several important criteria. First, training must be of high quality and sufficient duration. Instead of haphazard, short-term programs, people need individual career counselling and access to longer-term training programs that provide career pathways to high quality, living wage jobs (Fitzgerald 2004). Second, training programs and the income supports to go with them must be accessible to a majority of the unemployed-but-employable labour force. Providing training to, or "creaming," workers who are able to re-enter the labour market most easily, or those who are eligible for income supports under existing programs like Employment Insurance, means that many others cannot access the training they need, putting them at higher risk for chronic unemployment (Vroman and Brusentsev 2005; Battle, Mendelson and Torjman 2006).[4] Finally, effective programs must match supply and demand sides of the labour market. Training programs require timely labour market information and regular collaboration among labour market stakeholders for planning purposes as well as for ensuring that qualified workers are matched with jobs in firms that require their skills (Crouch, Finegold and Sako 2001; OECD 2001, 2003, 2004, 2009).

A strong argument has been made in favour of decentralization to facilitate the implementation of workforce development systems, and many OECD countries, including Canada, have devolved responsibility for planning, implementation and administration of active labour market policies from national to regional levels over the past two decades (OECD 1999, 2001, 2003, 2004, 2009). Trends toward regional decentralization in labour market policy reflect "an increased perception of the territorial dimension of labour market policy" and "the need to facilitate greater cooperation with other [labour market] actors," as well as broader national shifts in the division of powers between national, regional and local governments (Mosley 2009, 75). While decentralization can lead to policy fragmentation, program duplication, and uneven program quality and administration, one of the more influential arguments in its favour is that it permits the development of flexible, regionally-sensitive policies and programs that are better adapted to local needs (Tiebout 1956 cited in Mosley 2009; OECD 2004, 2009; Gray 2003). Successful workforce development systems in other places indicate that integrated and collaborative approaches to workforce development systems are most effective when designed and implemented at regional and local levels (Giloth 2004).

To avoid the negative effects of decentralization, however, the development and delivery of regionally sensitive workforce development strategies typically occurs within a national policy framework. Most countries have confined devolution to active labour market policy and programs and retain national control over benefit systems such as EI, and even in countries with relatively decentralized delivery systems such as the US and Spain, "there is usually a strong effort to retain an overall common policy framework and accountability standards" (Mosley 2009, 76). Distinguishing between administrative and political decentralization, Mosley (2009, 79) finds that in the latter, lower levels of government play a central role in the implementation of labour market policies, especially in federal systems in which policy responsibility is devolved to state or provincial governments that are "politically, administratively and financially strongly independent actors" as in Canada, the US, Belgium, Denmark, Italy, Mexico and Spain. In these multi-level governance structures, the relationship between national and sub-national authorities is less hierarchical and more negotiated which implies the likelihood of more jurisdictional conflict in intergovernmental relations. The devolution of labour market policy in Canada is of particular interest because it represents one of the earliest examples of asymmetrical federalism in Canadian social policy.

A How We Ended Up with Asymmetrical Labour Market Development Agreements (LMDAs): A Brief History of Labour Market Policy and Recent Intergovernmental Relations in Canada

This section analyzes the impact of recent developments in active labour market policy on the prognosis for a national policy framework. The generally patchy and lackluster institutional performance in this policy area over the past twenty years has led many observers to express doubts about Canada's ability to come up with a coherent and comprehensive national skills development strategy (see, for example, Haddow 1995, 1998; Tuohy 1992; Bakvis 2002; Klassen 2000). Two policy changes in particular have radically re-oriented the pattern of federal-provincial relations in this area. First, the Labour Force Development Strategy (LFDS) announced by the Conservative government in 1989 was intended to address the long-standing perception that government-funded labour market programs were not assisting Canadian workers to obtain sufficient job-relevant skills, and that the training efforts of the private sector were similarly inadequate. Subsequently, the Ottawa-based bi-partite business-labour organization, the Canadian Labour Market and Productivity Centre (CLMPC) was established to oversee the implementation of the National Training Board (NTB) system, a formal, multi-level and multi-stakeholder, governance structure that was to be replicated at provincial and local levels with the intention of facilitating collaborative labour market planning and programming.[5]

Yet not too much later, in response to the narrow defeat of the "yes" option in the 1995 Quebec referendum, the federal Liberals under Jean Chrétien abruptly changed course and devolved responsibility for occupational training to provincial governments under the *Employment Insurance Act* of 1996, a move which transferred about $1.5 billion to the provinces to deliver training programs to EI clients and paved the way for decentralization and new forms of "collaborative federalism" (DiGiacomo 2001).[6] The federal government retained responsibility for the broad residual right to undertake pan-Canadian activities, for setting EI policy, managing the EI fund, delivering benefits, and determining eligibility, as well as the ability to develop and deliver active labour market measures for non-EI clients including youth, people with disabilities, Aboriginal peoples, older workers and recent immigrants (Simeon and Cameron 2002). While some provinces felt that they were not in a position to take up such an ambitious policy agenda, others were quite keen to take over complete control, and the result was two types of bilateral Labour Market Development Agreements (LMDAs)—co-management and full transfer—that were negotiated between each province and the federal government.[7] Ontario was the only outlier in the devolution process, and did not sign an LMDA until ten years later, in 2005.

Despite the apparently contradictory nature of these recent policy changes, however, the absence of formal constitutional provisions for labour market issues and worker training has historically resulted in much intergovernmental wrangling for control over active labour market policy (Haddow 1995; DiGiacomo 2001; Bakvis 2002).[8] In his analysis of pre-devolution federal-provincial relations surrounding the main training initiatives under Mulroney, Haddow (1995, 339) argues that intergovernmental conflict marked by "competing jurisdictional claims, policy-making capacities, and program goals have always plagued federal-provincial relations on training" and that, as a result, labour market policy has typically been subject to institutional tinkering without much substantive change (see also Tuohy 1992). Longstanding constitutional ambiguity drove patterns of intergovernmental conflict over labour market policy in Canada until the negotiation of the LMDAs when the federal government that had consistently sought to circumvent provincial influence over training since the early 1980s, suddenly demonstrated a clear willingness to cede authority to the provinces.[9]

Thus, while LMDAs may have solved a constitutional impasse in the short run, they have done little to lend coherence to larger national labour market strategies in the long run. In the wake of the federal devolution that resulted in LMDAs bilaterally negotiated with each province, subsequent federal-provincial relations have displayed the pattern of administrative asymmetry and differential outcomes that they had tried to avoid in constitutional negotiations (Haddow 1998).[10] The federal distancing from active approaches to training, culminating in the 1996 decision to permit the provinces to assume administrative control over federal training expenditures under EI, has had the essentially irreversible effect of barring future governments from undertaking ambitious and coherent national policy approaches to training (Haddow 1998; DiGiacomo 2001). As a result, Bakvis (2002, 215) predicted that "the development of national policies deemed necessary in an increasingly globalized economic environment now appears to be well-nigh impossible."

B Asymmetrical Federalism and Workforce Development in Canada

Many recent analyses of asymmetrical federalism suggest, however, that concerns about policy fragmentation and the erosion of national objectives resulting from decentralization, though legitimate, may be somewhat overblown because they underplay the shifting context in which labour market policy operates. Asymmetry is built into federalism which is, by definition "about the combination of unity and diversity" (Brown 2005, 2). Because constituent units—provinces in Canada—have powers of self-rule, "it is accepted that different units may employ that power in different ways and toward different ends" (Graefe 2005, 1). As Mosley (2009) observes, this dynamic is most evident in political forms of decentralization where sub-national orders of government have significant independent powers. When relationships between national and sub-national authorities are less hierarchical, intergovernmental agreements have to be negotiated, a process which is occurring more frequently in the Canadian federal system in the form of bilateral agreements in many policy areas, of which LMDAs are but one example. In order to address Canada's diverse geographic regionalism, economic disparity, urban concentration and religious diversity within a single national context, asymmetry is, in many ways, the only form of governance that makes sense. For example, labour market policies that work for the Toronto economy in the Great Lakes region are very different from what works for BC and Vancouver in the Pacific Rim region (Brown 2005). According to Brown (2005, 2-3) the "flashpoint" in Canada is not over asymmetry itself, but rather over the fact that "we do not have a strong political consensus [about] the best point on the spectrum between centralization and decentralization" and in the "continuing tug of war" between these two visions, "in a very uneasy compromise, has been asymmetrical federalism."

Asymmetry or "flexible devolution" is increasingly evident in public administration where centralized norms and procedures imposed on lower levels of government have been discredited as ineffective because they ignore variation in local and regional needs. While some critics dismiss this shift in policy design and delivery as another form of downloading, Brown (2005, 5) argues that "in reality it is a response that implicates the federal government significantly to ensure that national policy goals are articulated and that national policy coordination occurs, but allowing considerable flexibility in how those objectives are met." Under these new forms of governance, the federal government is "less concerned with ensuring that provinces adhere to strict conditions or broader national standards, but more interested in setting agendas and steering reform" (Graefe 2005, 1).[11] Periodic federal-provincial summit negotiations produce framework agreements that set out broad principles and policy priorities but leave a wide degree of flexibility for provinces to allocate resources and define program parameters, while also committing to transparency and nationally established performance and accountability measures (Graefe 2005). These types of bilateral agreements, of which LMDAs are one of the earliest examples, have become the preferred approach to managing intergovernmental relations in Canada, and are by nature asymmetrical.[12] Though LMDAs were administrative rather than constitutional, they represented an important re-ordering of federal-provincial responsibilities in the policy domain and resulted in a much greater degree of asymmetrical federalism than had previously existed (Klassen 2000; Bakvis 2002). These bilateral arrangements have also proved beneficial for the design and delivery of provincial workforce development policies and programs. Because they represent a wide range of types, from a unique agreement between the federal government and a single province, to similar agreements between Ottawa and each province, to agreements between two provinces, they provide the flexibility required to accommodate different provincial interests and circumstances.

The downside of these asymmetrical arrangements, however, is that this "softer form of federal control" puts the federal pan-Canadian project of "assuring some harmonization through national standards at risk" (Graefe 2005, 6). While it provides more room for provincial diversity, it can also result in "a more decentralized nation, with substantially different programming in different parts of the country, leading to public confusion and potentially undermining a sense of national purpose and common interest" (Wood and Klassen 2009, 254). In this context, some would argue that predictions from concerned observers that LMDAs would preclude further federal influence in labour market policy have come true. Workforce development in Canada lacks a coherent policy architecture because none of the bilateral agreements—LMDAs, LMPAs, or LMAs—were negotiated as part of a larger national vision or policy framework that was collaboratively developed between both orders of government with input from social partners (Wood and Klassen 2009). Because workforce development appears to have developed into a de facto area of provincial jurisdiction, there is little provincial interest in multi-lateral opportunities for collective dialogue and policy learning, let alone in developing pan-Canadian strategies to address labour market issues such as unemployment or skills and labour shortages. As Wood and Klassen (2009, 267) argue, it is not federalism itself that provides impediments to pan-Canadian approaches, but rather it is the series of "segmented, bilateral, executive dominated, federal-provincial agreements [that] ... are inadequate to achieve national workforce development goals and have the potential to ... undermine Canada's political union." While McIntosh and Boychuk (2000) propose the Forum of Labour Market Ministers (FLMM) as a possible multilateral forum for the discussion of national labour market issues, Wood and Klassen (2009, 266) argue that multilateral forums intended to discuss such pan-Canadian approaches are fragmented and lack policy influence, and that the FLMM "has not demonstrated a capacity to work towards common goals or coordinate workforce development policy on a pan-Canadian basis, or even provide significant focus for sharing experiences and policy learning."[13]

The governance challenge, therefore, is for federal and provincial policymakers and administrators responsible for workforce development to voluntarily find similar types of "innovative ties that bind" because "without a robust intergovernmental process to manage interaction between the two orders of government" Canada's ability to develop a highly skilled, educated, and inclusive workforce could be compromised (Wood and Klassen 2009, 267). These new forms of cooperative federalism continue to evolve and only time will tell whether or not collaborative arrangements developed in other policy areas like education can be replicated in the area of workforce development. Preoccupation with the tensions inherent in evolving forms of asymmetrical federalism, however, can obscure other equally pressing policy challenges. In the wake of the negotiation of LMDAs serious policy gaps remained that left too many unemployed workers without the support required for entry and re-entry into the labour market.

2 Policy Gaps and Partial Solutions: The Negotiation of Labour Market Agreements (LMAs)

The analysis now proceeds to an examination of how labour market policy in general, and training programs for unemployed adults in particular, has played out "on the ground" in Canada in recent years, with a particular focus on policy and program developments in Ontario. This analysis indicates that serious policy gaps remained after the negotiation of LMDAs (Lazar 2002). One of the more salient points to emerge from the preceding discussion of asymmetrical federalism and labour market policy is the fact that Canada has long lacked a coherent national policy approach to adult training for the unemployed. This policy ambiguity, coupled with the federal-provincial dynamics outlined above, left some provinces, notably Ontario, to operate in a virtual policy vacuum in this area for a decade.[14] Since the negotiation of the LMDA in 2005, Ontario has been playing catch-up to build a policy framework for adult training. This section provides a brief overview of changing labour markets and the rise of "precarious" non-standard forms of employment in which certain groups are over-represented, and a discussion of the disjuncture between EI and social assistance (SA) programs, historically one of the main impediments to federal-provincial harmonization of training programs for the non-EI eligible unemployed. It concludes with an analysis of how the negotiation of Labour Market Agreements (LMAs) has gone part of the way to addressing this policy gap in Ontario.

A The Downside of Hasty Devolution: Too Many Are Ineligible for EI-Funded Training

It is not the devolution of federal labour market policy responsibilities under the LMDAs per se that is to blame, but the ill-considered manner in which the devolution was carried out. The preceding analysis suggests that in its haste to divest itself of political and fiscal problems, the federal government gave up too much all at once and relinquished control over active labour market policy and programs without retaining binding mechanisms to encourage multi-lateral discussion and information-sharing, let alone to promote national labour market objectives. Even more problematic, however, has been the fact that the federal government retained responsibility for program areas that it has not been able to effectively fulfill. Under the LMDAs, the federal government devolved responsibility for active labour market programs, referred to as Employment Benefits and Support Measures (EBSMs), to the provinces and retained responsibility for setting EI policy, managing the EI fund, delivering benefits and determining eligibility.[15] Under the LMDAs, Employment Benefits serve only active and reachback EI-eligible clients, whereas Support Measures serve the unemployed regardless of EI status. Because so many of the unemployed are not eligible for EI, they are also ineligible to receive Employment Benefits, which are the interventions most likely to lead to re-employment. This differential access to training programs between EI eligible and non-EI eligible individuals, coupled with major contractions in eligibility discussed at length elsewhere, accounts for mounting concerns that too many Canadians do not qualify for the income and training supports they need to transition back into the labour market.

Many recent labour market analyses underscore the fact that certain groups have an above-average risk of unemployment including young Canadians, especially those who have only a high school education or less, women who leave the workforce to care for children or aging family members, displaced older workers with limited education and obsolete skills, Aboriginal people, visible minorities, low-wage workers and recent immigrants. These groups also tend to be most likely to remain trapped in non-standard work, or to be chronically unemployed.[16] According to the Caledon Institute (Battle, Mendelson and Torjman 2006), the proportion of "non-standard" work—often referred to as "precarious" or "marginal" jobs—has increased to approximately one-third of the labour force and includes the self-employed, multiple job holders, contract workers, and part-time workers (see also Osberg, Wien and Grude 1995). These types of jobs are typically associated with low wages, limited education and skills, lower job security, lack of pensions and benefits (such as health and disability), few opportunities for career advancement or improvement, lack of union membership, and little access to employer-sponsored or on-the-job training.[17] These labour market trends are exacerbated by rapid technological change in a global knowledge-based economy, which improves the employment prospects for highly skilled and educated workers and further reduces prospects for low-skilled and under-educated workers.

These labour market trends have important implications in terms of eligibility for income supports and training programs that help workers re-enter the labour market. The discontinuity between the federally funded Employment Insurance (EI) program and provincially funded social assistance (SA) programs is considered to be one of the primary barriers to a harmonized system of income and training supports for unemployed adult workers.[18] EI covers only those workers who have significant attachment to the workforce and excludes many workers who cannot accumulate enough insurable hours of work, often because they are employed in marginal or part-time jobs, cannot work full-time hours due to family commitments, or have disabilities that make it difficult to find and keep work. A Task Force on Modernizing Income Security for Working-Age Adults (MISWAA) examined the issue of income security for working age adults in Toronto and found that only 30 per cent of Ontario's labour force is eligible for the longer-term training available to active EI claimants under EI Part II (EBSM) training. Many of the 70 per cent who do not qualify can only access shorter-term support measures programs, but need more robust, long-term training programs as much, if not more, than those who are EI-eligible to help them find and keep a job. As a result, "unemployed Canadians who cannot meet EI's tougher eligibility rules have been denied the EI-linked skills and learning services that many so desperately require. Both for income benefits and skills and learning services, EI has favoured the unemployed who have standard jobs and effectively excluded those in nonstandard employment" (Battle, Mendelson and Torjman 2006, 21). This has resulted in a perverse situation where many workers have made mandatory contributions to the EI fund from which they are ineligible to benefit (Campeau 2005). Social assistance, or welfare as it is commonly known, is usually not an option for those who are not eligible for EI because it is a needs-tested, income support program of last resort. Most people who must temporarily rely on welfare subsist below the Low-Income Cut-Off (LICO) or poverty line and are only eligible for the most basic types of short-term "employability" training.

In an effort to address this gap, the federal government retained the responsibility to develop and deliver longer-term active labour market measures for populations of non-EI clients who tend to be under-represented in terms of access to Employment Benefits, including youth, people with disabilities, Aboriginal peoples, older workers, and recent immigrants, intending to serve these groups directly. The subsequent patchy and haphazard performance of these programs, that were subjected to numerous changes and tended to be out of sync with provincial programs, suggests however that the federal government has not been up to the task. Provincial governments wanting to fill this policy gap had to provide training for these client groups through their own provincially funded training or social assistance programs which tend to be of shorter duration, lower quality and "poorly targeted to those most in need," especially for women and the less educated (Task Force on Modernizing Income Security for Working-Age Adults 2006).[19] Furthermore, successive contractions in both the EI and social assistance programs in recent years have meant that even fewer people were eligible for what meagre training programs existed for the non-EI eligible. Concerns have mounted that if this policy gap widens, those who fall through the cracks will fall further and further behind (Battle, Mendelson and Torjman 2006; Jackson and Schetagne 2010; Osberg 2009). In addition, though this varies by province, there have historically been few provincial programs to address the training needs of those who are not eligible for either EI or SA benefits.[20]

B Filling the Policy Gap: Labour Market Agreements (LMAs)

Federal-provincial relations in the area of labour market policy leading up to the negotiation of LMDAS in the mid-1990s have been described as patchy and conflicted, with neither level of government having adequately responded to "the growing need for training and other employment services for all workers who need them," employed or not (Battle, Mendelson and Torjman 2006, 23). In contrast, the immediate post-LMDA labour market policy regime has been described as generally collaborative because LMDAs were negotiated with "a high degree of good will" and generated "little, if any, political tension between the two levels of government" (Klassen 2000, 190; see also Lazar 2002). Many provinces actively sought responsibility for labour market policy to demonstrate their capability to effectively design and implement programs, while the federal government initiated the transfer and did not want to be seen as "impeding the process it initiated" (Klassen 2000, 193). However, this cooperative environment began to attenuate in 2002 when "the limitations of the new regime became evident" and federal officials began to express regret over the permanent loss of federal influence over labour market policy while provinces had come to see workforce development as largely, if not entirely, under provincial jurisdiction (Wood and Klassen 2009, 256).

Perhaps most importantly, nearly 40 per cent of the population was not represented in Ontario. When Ontario finally signed an LMDA with the federal government in 2005, it was one of the few provinces along with Manitoba and Saskatchewan that also negotiated a Labour Market Partnership Agreement (LMPA) to address gaps in labour market programming for non-EI eligible adults. Federal funding under LMPAs was to cover six program areas: expansion of apprenticeship, integration of recent immigrants, literacy and basic skills, workplace skill development, assistance to Aboriginals, and employment supports for those facing barriers to re-entry such as older workers and persons with disabilities. The original agreement earmarked $1.368 billion over six years to Ontario, and the intention was to negotiate similar agreements with other provinces and territories. LMPAs were heralded at the time as a major breakthrough in the provision of training and employment programs for low-income adults who need them, and seen as evidence of government recognition of this major policy gap and its willingness to take concrete steps to address it (Task Force on Modernizing Income Security for Working-Age Adults 2006, 39; see also Battle, Mendelson and Torjman 2006). Though LMPAs never got off the ground, they paved the way for the substantively similar Labour Market Agreements that followed soon after.[21]

Subsequent intergovernmental relations under the Harper government have been referred to as a system of "open federalism." The 2007 Federal Budget outlined a new approach to labour market and training policy which saw the provinces as best placed to design and deliver these types of programs. Building on this federal policy approach, the trend has been toward the provision of fiscal transfers to provinces in the form of block grants accompanied by broadly defined accountability frameworks. Negotiations between federal and provincial governments resulted in the signing of LMAs in nine jurisdictions that provided funding arrangements to support skills development and training programs for various non-EI eligible client groups and low-skilled employed workers; with the exception of Aboriginal peoples, these groups corresponded roughly to the client groups outlined in the original LMPAs.

LMDAs and LMAs are, however, quite different types of agreements. LMDAs are essentially detailed service delivery agreements, administered under the *EI Act* to deliver former federal Employment Benefits and Support Measures (EBSM) training programs, and leave little scope for provincial policy development or innovation.[22] In contrast, LMAs outline high-level federal strategic objectives with accountability measures such as requiring provinces to report on a common set of performance indicators, while giving provincial governments the flexibility to design their own labour market programs. Each province receives an annual block grant, calculated on a per capita basis, which the federal government has committed to funding from 2008 to 2014 (Ministry of Training,

Colleges and Universities 2009). In addition, responding to the increased need for training of the unemployed resulting from the current recession, the Harper government provided $500 million over two years under the Strategic Training and Transition Fund to provide increased access to training that is not tied to EI eligibility (HRSDC 2010). In 2009–2010 Ontario received $193.7 million in core LMA funding, $62.5 million in unspent funds carried forward from 2008–2009, $103.2 million under the STTF, and an additional $1 billion to top up the LMDAs over the same two year period. Federal funds under the LMAs are intended to be used to provide increased opportunities for vulnerable groups in the labour market, and in particular to serve unemployed people who are not EI clients, or employed individuals who are low-skilled.[23]

C Getting Back on Track? LMA-funded Adult Training Programs in Ontario

As outlined in Part I of the Canada-Ontario LMA, Ontario programs were expanded to target unemployed non-EI clients from many of the same groups that were to be originally covered by federal programs after the implementation of the LMDAs, as well as several others including social assistance recipients, immigrants, persons with disabilities, older workers,[24] youths, Aboriginal peoples, new entrants and re-entrants into the labour market, unemployed individuals who were previously self-employed, as well as employed individuals who are low skilled—in short, nearly everyone who is not eligible for EI. Federal funds were combined with Ontario funds to support new and existing programs offered through the province's Skills to Jobs Action Plan, the Reaching Higher Plan for post-secondary education, and Employment Ontario investments in training for the unemployed, as well as labour market initiatives in affiliated ministries including Citizenship and Immigration, Community and Social Services, Health and Long-Term Care, Finance, and Government Services. Under the Government of Ontario's 2009–2010 Activity Plan, LMA funds were allocated to four cross-cutting priority areas, most of which involve more than a single ministry, including the Labour Market Integration of Immigrants, Foundation Skills Training and Supports, Labour Market Supports for Persons with Disabilities, and Technical Skills Training.

Perhaps because Ontario operated for so long without an LMDA and had independently recognized the need to implement labour market training and support programs, it already had a suite of pre-existing training programs in operation when the LMA was signed. Therefore, instead of creating new programs as several other provinces have done, Ontario used LMA funds to top up programs that were already working well. Existing programs were expanded so that more people, including unemployed non-EI clients and the employed low skilled, could access the training programs already on offer. The major provincial programs already in place included Job Connect, Literacy and Basic Skills, Apprenticeship programming, and Summer Jobs, all of which received additional LMA funds.[25] When the LMA was negotiated, not only could Ontario expand the amount of training offered to a broader range of clients, it also saw an opportunity to streamline federal and provincial programs. Though the streamlining process has gone more slowly than originally envisioned due to the recession, several existing Ontario programs have now been merged with the federal EBSMs delivered under the LMDA. The new Employment Services program has replaced numerous programs (Ontario's Job Connect, the former federal Employment Assistance Services, and Targeted Wage Subsidy programs) and the Ontario Skills Development program has been merged with Second Career. Both of these programs are available to both EI and non-EI clients, but each type of client must be administered separately according to the agreement under which they are funded.[26]

The LMA was seen as a big step toward being able to finally provide an integrated training system in Ontario. The LMA answered a number of important concerns outlined above about access to training for unemployed non-EI clients, and since the implementation of the LMA, employment and training services have been successfully expanded to serve more non-EI clients, including SA recipients. LMA funding mechanisms are considered to be much easier to administer and leave more room for provincial discretion in the design and delivery of regionally sensitive training programs, standing in stark contrast to the more complex administrative requirements of LMDAs that continue to operate on the basis of the anachronistic division between EI and non-EI eligibility. The LMA program is, however, still seen as being too administratively complex and cumbersome because training is funded from three different envelopes (provincial funds, LMDA funds, and LMA funds). Instead, Ontario envisions a single source of consolidated federal training funds that it can flexibly administer as it sees fit according to its particular labour market needs.

In short, the LMA has successfully helped Ontario to address the gaps in service provision left by LMDAs, and has given other provinces the flexibility to design regionally sensitive labour market policies. While the LMA expires in 2014, this does not appear to be a significant obstacle. Even more to the point, the provinces now already deliver almost all training programs for unemployed adults and, as was observed earlier, training has essentially become an area of exclusive provincial jurisdiction. Because it is already mostly done and working well, it is argued here that the responsibility for all adult training programs should be devolved to the provinces entirely, and the consolidation of federal funding should be made permanent.

3 Re-thinking Active Labour Market Policy in Canada: New Directions for EI Reform

The preceding discussion of the trend toward asymmetrical federalism and the negotiation of bilateral labour market agreements in Canada reveals significant change in the development and delivery of workforce development policy and programs over the past two decades. As Wood and Klassen (2009, 261) observe, there have been some major benefits to the devolution of labour market policy under LMDAs, which have provided provincial governments the "policy capacity, opportunity and motivation to develop integrated workforce development service-delivery arrangements" to people who need them most, and to leverage funding towards more strategic workforce development uses. At the same time, however, a paucity of data, including the lack of a consistent set of reporting requirements and performance indicators across jurisdictions, makes it difficult to determine whether asymmetrical bilateral arrangements have resulted in differences in program delivery across provinces and to assess the movement of individuals between EI and SA programs. Most worrisome, however, is the fact that adult training and workforce development programs in Canada lack a unified and coherent policy architecture. At this point, collaborative mechanisms appear to be insufficiently robust to promote multi-lateral dialogue and policy learning, let alone to develop pan-Canadian strategies to address labour market issues such as unemployment and skills and labour shortages. The governance challenge that remains, therefore, is for federal and provincial policy actors in the area of workforce development to re-commit to the intergovernmental processes needed to develop a highly skilled, educated, and inclusive workforce.

Workforce development is a complex policy field, and as Battle, Mendelson and Torjman (2006, 24) observe, "reforming adult benefits is a daunting task that has been attempted several times before, with little success." Regardless of what we might wish for, the prognosis for a coherent national policy vision for workforce development is inauspicious within the context of current federal-provincial relations in this policy domain, at least for the foreseeable future. It was suggested by observers at the time of the negotiations of the original LMDAs that future federal influence in this policy area would be unlikely (Haddow 1998; Bakvis 2002; DiGiacomo 2001; Klassen 2000), and subsequent analyses appear to have largely substantiated this prediction (Wood and Klassen 2009). Though the continued activity of the multi-lateral Forum of Labour Market Ministers suggests the possibility of federal-provincial collaboration, decentralization and the negotiation of bilateral agreements with all provinces and territories means that labour market policy and workforce development in Canada has largely developed into a de facto area of provincial jurisdiction. Future directions for the reform of adult training funded under the EI program need to be considered within the context of federal-provincial conflict that has resulted in weak performance in this policy area and to take current constraints on federal influence in national labour market policy as a starting point. New approaches to workforce development have to proceed within the context of new forms of asymmetrical arrangements, a situation that underscores the need for policy innovation in this area. Two possible directions for future reform are proposed here.

A Decouple Access to Training From EI Eligibility by Devolving Funds for Training Under LMAs to the Provinces

Brown (2002, 72) describes the current challenge for federalism not as one of how to increase federal policy influence across policy fields, but rather of how "to reach a new equilibrium between the competing pressures of equity and efficiency, and of decentralization and local initiative versus national objectives and control." As has been suggested throughout this analysis, the current tension in federalism and labour market policy is as much, if not more, about stability and flexibility as it is about negotiating national objectives and decentralization. Because there is so much variation in regional economies and the structure of regional labour markets, there is a strong argument in favour of decentralization to allow for the development of more effective approaches to adult training (Mosley 2009).

It is argued here that there is room for the federal government to renew its involvement in labour market policy through a combination of multilateral forums, fiscal federalism, and intergovernmental means without eroding the gains in provincial policymaking autonomy that have accrued in recent years. One reform of the EI program that would be comparatively easy to achieve while having far-reaching policy implications, would be to decouple access to training from EI by devolving responsibility for all adult training programs—and the funding to go with it—to provincial governments within a standardized accountability framework. This would essentially involve rolling funding for LMDAs and LMAs into a single *conditional* federal transfer. While unconditional block grants, which tend not to impose any conditions on receipt of federal funds and leave much room for provincial interpretation, are now the most commonly used form of fiscal transfer, they leave few levers for federal influence over provincial implementation strategies. In contrast, conditional block grants can be made for specific purposes such as encouraging social programs with similar entitlements across the country (Boadway 2001). While the vast majority of fiscal transfers tend to be unconditional, some ambiguity remains about whether or not fiscal transfers should be tied to central policy objectives.[27]

It has been argued here that the evolution of federal-provincial relations in the area of labour market policy means that the development of a coherent national policy framework for workforce development is unlikely. However, national objectives in labour market policy could be established and enforced through the use of conditional block grants that permanently fund adult training on condition that provincial governments commit to a set of federally determined accountability and transparency measures that apply equally to all jurisdictions, and include the collection and public reporting of data such as provincial labour market information, key performance indicators, and the results of regular program evaluations, to which provinces can add additional performance indicators as they see fit (Boadway 2001; Mosley 2009). There is some indication that many of these reporting mechanisms are already in place but further research would be required to examine the extent to which existing transparency and accountability measures meet national strategic objectives and are consistent across provinces.

This option builds upon existing intergovernmental relations, would not require politically untenable constitutional amendment, may (or may not) require only moderate increases in program spending, and makes use of existing policy levers under fiscal federalism. While this option would require amendments to EI, which could be politically difficult, it would create the policy space for more far-reaching and innovative changes. Removing anachronistic divisions between funding for EI and non-EI eligible unemployed workers would go a long way toward allowing provinces to develop more coherent approaches to workforce development for themselves. Labour market policy already operates under asymmetrical bilateral agreements that set out broad principles and policy priorities giving provinces a wide degree of flexibility in allocating resources and defining program parameters but that require a standard set of accountability measures beyond fiscal accountability.

As Wood and Klassen (2009) caution, however, there is a paucity of data to show how LMDAs and LMAs produce different outcomes across provinces. While fiscal federalism is "meant to be about flexibility" and is uniquely suited to asymmetrical applications, it is also about administrative accountability which requires asymmetrical approaches to be "transparent, coherent, and pragmatic" (Brown 2005, 7, 9). Furthermore, the policy space for innovation that would be created with this option may have another effect. The removal of administrative complexity, and improved service delivery that would result, could pave the way for developing more collaborative types of intergovernmental mechanisms, like those discussed above and below, that could lend coherence to provincial adult training policy frameworks.

B Toward a "Place-Based" Approach to Workforce Development

This proposed policy option builds on the previous one and advocates a broader re-thinking of active labour market policy and workforce development in Canada. The experiences of other countries that lack national strategies to ensure comprehensive skills development programs for the workforce as a whole suggest that Canada's reliance on supply-side active labour market policies that focus primarily on providing training for individuals without addressing the demand side of the labour market will become increasingly ineffective (Crouch, Finegold and Sako 2001). An over-reliance on supply-side training policies tends to result in fragmented skills formation systems that lead to "chronic [employer] underinvestment in skills, persistent but poorly understood skill shortages, and continuing strong growth in lower-skilled, lower-paid employment without clear career paths or development opportunities" and risks entrenching a "low-skills equilibrium" in national labour markets (Hall and Lansbury 2006, 579).

There has been increasing attention to the spatial dimension of labour market policy, as well as the need to establish collaboration between labour market actors for planning and program development while retaining a common national policy framework and accountability standards (OECD 2009; Mosley 2009). "Top down" federally-administered one-size-fits-all approaches that implement standardized policies and programs across a diverse array of local political economies typically "fail to provide a leg up the economic ladder for low-wage, low-skilled, frequently minority workers" because they lack regional sensitivity and flexibility. Experimentation with workforce development systems in other places indicates that collaborative and integrated workforce development systems designed and implemented at regional and local levels have the potential to meet local workforce development needs and to improve employment prospects for the unemployed by matching supply and demand sides of local labour markets (Giloth 2004; OECD 2009; Hall and Lansbury 2006).

The concept of local workforce development focuses on the ways in which firms, community-based organizations, and other labour market actors collaborate to develop intermediary mechanisms that source, recruit, develop and match skills in local labour markets. Rather than "work-first" approaches that place unemployed workers in low-skilled, contingent, and "precarious" jobs, local workforce development initiatives seek to provide individuals with access to career pathways which lead to high quality, stable, "family-sustaining" jobs in the local economy (Harrison and Weiss 1998; Fitzgerald 2004).[28] Successful workforce development initiatives are based on partnerships between labour market actors that form "an expanded network that links disadvantaged workers with job opportunities, educational opportunities, and support services" (Giloth 2004, 16). While local workforce development networks are community-driven, governments act as catalysts and facilitators that provide the policy context, resources, infrastructure and institutional frameworks for these networks (Hall and Lansbury 2006).

Building a local or "place-based" orientation to labour market planning and employment service delivery requires a policy framework to support local initiatives (Bradford 2007; Bramwell 2012). While most discussions of labour market policy and workforce development occur at national and provincial levels in Canada, because labour markets primarily operate on a regional basis, strategic initiatives are most productively implemented and delivered at that level. To better address the needs of unemployed adult workers for improved access to both training and employment opportunities, therefore, federal and provincial labour market policymakers need to integrate the local dimension of workforce development into active labour market planning and programming.

This idea is not as eccentric as it might at first appear in the Canadian context. Though Canada has had little experience with these mechanisms, there has been a great deal of experimentation with different models of local workforce development across industrialized countries, particularly in the United States but also in the United Kingdom, Australia, New Zealand, and Denmark, and policymakers by now have a very good idea of what works and what does not (Chapple 2005; OECD 2004, 2009; Hall and Lansbury 2006). Regional flexibility is built into federalism in the form of bilateral asymmetry in legislation, policy, and administrative procedure because of the general acceptance of the idea that national norms need to be sufficiently flexible to allow for adaptation to regional and local conditions (Brown 2005). Governance mechanisms already exist upon which local capacity could be built, and there is empirical evidence to indicate that many communities have a strong interest in developing locally sensitive workforce development strategies, but lack the policy support to get these efforts off the ground (Bramwell 2012).[29] This discourse has been too easily dismissed and needs to find its way back on to provincial policy agendas, particularly now that provinces largely have de facto jurisdiction over active labour market policy and programs for both EI and non-EI eligible unemployed adult workers.

4 Conclusions

There are mounting concerns that Canada does not have the income support system to get us where we need to go (Banting 2006; Jackson and Schetagne 2010; Osberg 2006, 2009). This paper has framed the discussion about whether or not we have the adult training system to take us where we need to go. A large proportion of unemployed adult workers have long been excluded from access to the training and employment supports they need to transition back into the labour market. Strong arguments in favour of the decentralization of policy and program responsibility for workforce development indicate that training and employment programs are most effective when delivered in a provincially—and increasingly locally—sensitive way. This analysis indicates that the decentralization of active labour market policy has been underway in Canada since the mid-1990s. The potential to develop an integrated national workforce development strategy attenuated with the negotiation of LMDAs, and taken together with the negotiation of LMAs to provide training funding for unemployed non-EI and employed but low-skilled clients, active labour market policy is now effectively a de facto provincial responsibility. In this context, two directions for reform of Canada's workforce development system for unemployed workers have been suggested here: permanently devolve policy responsibility and funding for training of unemployed non-EI clients and employed low-skilled workers to provincial governments under existing LMAs; and create a policy framework that integrates the local level for strategic policy, program delivery and planning purposes. The first effectively decouples access to training from EI-eligibility and the second facilitates the matching of supply and demand sides of the labour market on a regional basis.

Endnotes

1 While job growth in other industries was relatively strong from 2004 to 2008, manufacturing fared much worse than the rest of the economy, with the loss of nearly 322,000 or more than one in seven manufacturing jobs ... These losses resulted in the rapid erosion of the share of manufacturing jobs in the economy, from 14.9 per cent in 1998 to 14.4 per cent in 2004 before falling sharply to 11.5 per cent in 2008 (Bernard 2009). Employment in manufacturing tumbled again during the recent recession, with 177,000 fewer employed in the sector than the previous year, and accounted for only 10.4 per cent of employment by the end of 2009 (Usalcas 2010).

2 Except Aboriginal peoples.

3 Under the LMDAs, provinces were given the responsibility to deliver federal Employment Benefits and Support Measures (EBSM) programs. Employment Benefits are longer term, more direct forms of training such as returning to school to upgrade credentials, or receiving on-the-job training, that are most likely to lead to sustainable transitions to re-employment. Support Measures are short term, "softer" interventions such as resume writing workshops, career counselling, or information and referral to employment benefits, and are seen as less effective in facilitating sustainable re-entry into the labour market. Under the LMDAs, Employment Benefits serve EI-eligible clients (active claimants and reach back clients), whereas Support Measures serve the unemployed regardless of EI status, along with Labour Market Partnerships that support the employed at risk of losing their jobs.

4 There appears to be an important tension on this point between much of the literature on labour market training policy and the labour market economics literature. While most policy perspectives argue that access to training for all unemployed workers is a critical means to facilitate re-entry into the labour market, much econometric research on training programs finds a weak link between training programs for the unemployed and return to employment. For example, Jones (2011) argues that based on much experimental and non-experimental research, the returns to training, particularly for older workers with long job tenure tend to be low, because people who do successfully re-enter the labour market tend to find new jobs in less than a year, and with minimal training supports. These findings suggest that government expenditure on training for this group may not be the best use of resources. This does not, of course, address the question of what *types* of jobs displaced workers are able to find, and whether or not they are able to replace their former wage rates. It also does not address the social equity dimension of access to opportunities that support employment and re-employment, or the question of whether the returns to training would be higher if the quality of training was higher. Other research suggests that the returns to training vary by policy mix and type of labour market program, that outcomes vary by the method used to measure them, and that positive impacts on aggregate labour market outcomes can arise when appropriate strategies are adopted (Boone and van Ours 2004; Card, Kluve and Weber 2009; Martin and Grubb 2001).

5 The National Training Board was in turn intended to oversee the implementation of similarly designed Labour Force Development Boards (LFDBs) in each

province, and Local Training Boards to guide training initiatives at the local level. The LFDB structure was an important institutional innovation because it provided for non-governmental membership, led by labour and business, but also including representatives of various "equity groups" and educators who, taken together, would be given "an unprecedented degree of influence over national and provincial labour market initiatives" (Sharpe and Haddow 1997, 3).

6 The failure of the Charlottetown Accord coupled with the razor-thin defeat of the "yes" option in the sovereignty referendum seemed to galvanize labour market policy, and seeing an opportunity to appeal to Quebec and divest itself of responsibility at the same time, the federal government devolved substantial powers over training expenditures to the provinces.

7 Ultimately, four provinces and two territories, including British Columbia, Alberta, and Quebec opted for complete devolution, or full-transfer agreements, and five provinces and one territory opted for modified co-management agreements. For a more detailed discussion of the substance of these agreements see Bakvis 2002, 207-209.

8 While the rationale for federal involvement in training for the unemployed was that occupational training is essential to national economic adjustment, the provinces historically claimed legitimate jurisdiction on the basis of their exclusive control over education.

9 Haddow (1998) argues that the "substantially reduced" involvement in active labour market policy of the Chrétien Liberals between 1993 and 1997 had more to do with the fallout of failed constitutional politics, a fiscal policy anchored in deficit reduction and continued federal-provincial tensions than with labour market considerations themselves. Throughout the time that the federal government was attempting to build a national training strategy, federal officials were keenly aware of the larger underlying constitutional context of their efforts, knowing that any constitutional package that offered new powers to Quebec would have to be offered to all provinces, which would directly conflict with CLFDB attempts to build a national training strategy.

10 Stronger provinces that were able to resist federal policy, (primarily Quebec, Ontario, British Columbia and Alberta) negotiated full-transfer LMDAs that accommodated their authority, whereas smaller provinces tended to negotiate co-management LMDAs and remained more dependent on the federal government.

11 Graefe (2005) finds that these new forms of federal governance are evident in various social policy areas including health, disability, housing, child care, and workforce development.

12 There is some debate on whether or not the current federal-provincial labour market policy regime is asymmetrical or symmetrically bilateral. Wood and Klassen (2011) argue that the asymmetry in federal provincial labour market policy has attenuated because LMDAs and LMAs have now been negotiated with all provinces and territories. When overlaid with mechanisms for funding training for unemployed adults, however, important asymmetries remain. For example, one of the major controversies in the EI program is the allocation formula which has been criticized for its lack of transparency and for the unfair treatment of some provinces. Some provinces with predominantly rural and seasonal employment including Newfoundland and Labrador, Prince Edward

Island and New Brunswick, are allocated more EI benefits than they contribute to the system, whereas highly populated urban centres in British Columbia and Ontario like Vancouver and Toronto have much higher numbers of workers who do not qualify for EI, such as new Canadians, and therefore receive less than they pay into the system (Mendelsohn and Medow 2010; Campeau 2005; Battle, Mendelson and Torjman 2006; Hale 1998).

13 Pointing to several recent multilateral accomplishments in the area of labour market policy, others might be less pessimistic regarding the value of federal-provincial tables in generating a national consensus on policy issues, arguing that cooperative federalism can work when the needs of all partners are addressed. There are a number of examples: the ministers responsible for Labour have achieved consensus on important files related to safety and employment standards through the Canadian Association of Administrators of Labour Law (CALL); new forms of regionally focused federalism such as the establishment of the New West Partnership and the Council of Atlantic Premiers seek labour mobility in the western and maritime regions; and the Council of the Federation (COF) voted unanimously to adopt the labour mobility protocol of the Agreement on International Trade (AIT), ensuring labour market mobility within Canada.

14 For a more detailed discussion of why Ontario did not negotiate a LMDA in 1995, see Haddow and Klassen (2006).

15 Employment Benefits are longer-term, more direct forms of training such as returning to school to upgrade credentials or receiving on-the-job training, which are most likely to lead to re-employment. Support Measures, on the other hand are "softer," short term, interventions such as resume writing workshops, career counselling, or information and referral to employment benefits, which are seen as less effective in facilitating sustainable re-entry into the labour market.

16 There is also evidence to suggest that single males are facing increasing unemployment and having difficulty attaching to the labour market (Stapleton 2011).

17 Battle, Mendelson and Torjman (2006) observe that one in four workers in Canada are low-wage and earn less than two-thirds of the national median hourly wage (under $11 per hour), and that these workers tend to be women. In addition, the gender gap in EI coverage has recently widened, and tripled between 1996 and 2004, during which EI coverage for men fell from 49.3 per cent to 47.3 per cent, but for women fell from 47.3 per cent to 39.7 per cent during the same period.

18 Successive cuts in EI since the mid-1970s, accompanied by increasingly stringent provincial needs-tests so that only a small proportion of EI claimants are eligible for SA once their EI benefits expire, means that fewer Canadians are eligible for income supports and the training that accompanies them. Most importantly, the functional and perceived division of responsibility between EI and SA coupled with cuts to both programs means that there is a possibility that more and more people will fall through the cracks between the two programs. A lack of data and intergovernmental dialogue suggest that governments do not have a solid understanding of "who these people are, how and/or whether they are able to re-integrate into the labour market" and what will happen to them

in economic downturns (McIntosh and Boychuk 2000, 107). The potential for serious policy failures is clear and increasingly insistent calls for harmonization of EI and SA are understandable in this context (Duclos, 2007; Task Force on Modernizing Income Security for Working-Age Adults, 2006).

19 For example, almost 47 per cent of Ontario Works (the Ontario social assistance program, administered by the Ministry of Community and Social Services) have less than high school education as opposed to 33 per cent of the labour force; furthermore, 72 per cent of young adults and 55 per cent of lone parents who receive Ontario Works have less than a high school graduation diploma. Ontario did have several provincially funded training programs in place for under-represented groups that predate the LMAs, such as the Bridge Training Program for internationally-trained professionals.

20 Though it would require additional research that is beyond the scope of this chapter, Ontario and Quebec appear to be outliers in this regard. For example, because Ontario operated without an LMDA until 2005, it developed and funded its own suite of programs for this group including Job Connect, Literacy and Basic Skills, Apprenticeship programming, Summer Jobs Services, Bridge Training, and Language Training for Immigrants, to name a few. Quebec, as Noël (2011) points out, has long been interested in developing its own regionally-sensitive suite of training programs, and has devoted substantial additional provincial resources to achieve this.

21 This was due in part to the provinces actively resisting measures that they saw as attempts at federal incursion into provincial jurisdiction, and partly because the agreements had been negotiated with the Liberal government and were cancelled by the federal Conservatives in 2006.

22 There are provisions in the LMDA (section 3.3) that enable jurisdictions to make ongoing modifications to the design of benefits and measures as long as the modifications adhere to the requirement that similarity and consistency with the purpose and guidelines of Part II of the *EI Act* are maintained. Making these modifications is, however, an onerous process, which substantially limits the scope for provincial autonomy in this area.

23 Low-skilled refers to individuals who do not have a high school diploma or a recognized certification, or who have low levels of literacy and essential skills.

24 Most provinces, including Ontario, have recently signed temporary federal-provincial cost-shared agreements to administer the Targeted Initiative for Older Workers (TIOW) program which provides training to unemployed workers aged 55–64 in high unemployment regions.

25 It is also worth noting that, as mentioned above, MTCU was not the only ministry to receive funds under the LMA; the Ministry of Community and Social Services, the Ministry of Citizenship and Immigration, and the Ministry of Health and Long Term Care each also received extra funds to expand their training programs. In this way, employment services for Ontario Works (SA) recipients were also expanded.

26 While the LMDA transfer is the primary source of funding for the former federal ESBMs, Ontario also invests additional funding into these programs from its own resources.

27 Brown (2005) observes that Canada is unique among federations for the fact

that approximately 94 per cent of current intergovernmental transfers are largely unconditional.

28 For example, influential work on career ladders emphasizes the development of educational pathways that improve employability by providing individuals with credentials targeted at specific industry sectors (Fitzgerald 2004). Markusen (2004) argues that community economic development planners can target required occupations as well as local industries.

29 For example, local training boards, the last remaining vestiges of attempts to build a collaborative, multi-stakeholder, multi-level governance labour market policy framework under the Canadian Labour Force Development Board (CLFDB) in the early 1990s, still operate in Ontario.

References

Bakvis, H. 2002. "Checkerboard Federalism? Labour Market Development Policy in Canada." In *Canadian Federalism: Performance, Effectiveness, Legitimacy,* ed. H. Bakvis and G. Skogstad, 159-203. Toronto: Oxford University Press.

Banting, K.G. 2006. "Dis-Embedding Liberalism? The New Social Policy Paradigm in Canada." In *Dimensions of Inequality in Canada,* ed. D.A. Green and J.R. Kesselman, 417-52. Vancouver: University of British Columbia Press.

Battle, K., M. Mendelson, and S. Torjman. 2006. *Towards a New Architecture for Canada's Adult Benefits.* The Caledon Institute of Social Policy.

Bernard, A. 2009. "Trends in Manufacturing Employment." *Perspectives.* Statistics Canada, cat. No. 75-001-X.

Boadway, R.W. 2001. "Inter-Governmental Fiscal Relations: The Facilitator of Fiscal Decentralization." *Constitutional Political Economy* 12.2: 93-121.

Boone, J. and J. van Ours. 2004. "Effective Active Labor Market Policies." Discussion Paper No. 1335. Institute for the Study of Labor.

Bradford, N. 2007. *Whither the Federal Urban Agenda?* A New Deal in Transition. CPRN Research Report, F/65. Ottawa: Canadian Policy Research Networks.

Bramwell, A. 2012. "Networks Are Not Enough: Urban Governance and Workforce Development in Three Ontario Cities." *Urban Affairs Review* 48.3.

Brown, D.M. 2002. "Fiscal Federalism: The New Equilibrium Between Equity and Efficiency." In *Canadian Federalism: Performance, Effectiveness, Legitimacy,* ed. H. Bakvis and G. Skogstad, 59-86. Don Mills: Oxford University Press Canada.

Brown, D.M. 2005. "Who's Afraid of Asymmetrical Federalism? A Summary Discussion." *Asymmetry Series.* Institute for Intergovernmental Relations, School of Policy Studies, Queen's University.

Campeau, G. 2005. *From UI to EI : Waging War on the Welfare State.* Vancouver: University of British Columbia Press.

Card, D., J. Kluve, and A. Weber. 2009. "Active Labor Market Policy Evaluations: A Meta-Analysis." *CESifo Working Paper Series* No. 2570; Ruhr Economic Paper No. 86.

Chapple, K. 2005. "Building Institutions from the Region Up: Regional Workforce Development Collaboratives in California." *Working Paper*. Institute of Urban and Regional Development.

Clarke, S.E. and G.L. Gaile. 1998. *The Work of Cities*. Minneapolis: University of Minnesota Press.

Crouch, C., D. Finegold, and M. Sako. 2001. *Are Skills The Answer? The Political Economy of Skill Creation in Advanced Industrial Countries*. Oxford: Oxford University Press.

DiGiacomo, G. 2001. "Federal Occupational Training Policy: A Neo-Institutionalist Analysis." *Working Paper* 2.8. Kingston: Queen's University Institute for Intergovernmental Affairs.

Duclos, J-Y. 2007. "A Better Income Security System for All Canadians." In *A Canadian Priorities Agenda: Policy Choices to Improve Economic and Social Well-Being,* ed. J. Leonard, C. Ragan, and F. St-Hilaire, 233-66. Montreal: The Institute for Research on Public Policy.

Fitzgerald, J. 2004. "Moving the Workforce Intermediary Agenda Forward." Economic Development Quarterly 18.1: 3-9.

Giloth, R.P. 2004. "The 'Local' in Workforce Development Politics: An Introduction." In *Workforce Development Politics: Civic Capacity and Performance,* ed. R.P. Giloth, 1-29. Philadelphia: Temple University Press.

Graefe, P. 2005. "The Scope and Limits of Asymmetry in Recent Social Policy Agreements." *Asymmetry Series*. Institute for Intergovernmental Relations, Queen's University School of Policy Studies.

Gray, D.M. 2003. "National Versus Regional Financing and Management of Unemployment and Related Benefits: The Case of Canada." *OECD Social, Employment and Migration Working Papers* No. 14. OECD Publishing.

Haddow, R. 1995. "Federalism and Training Policy in Canada: Institutional Barriers to Economic Adjustment." In *New Trends in Canadian Federalism,* ed. F. Rocher and M. Smith, 338-368. Peterborough: Broadview Press.

Haddow, R. 1998. "How Ottawa Shrivels; Ottawa's Declining Role in Active Labour Market Policy." In *How Ottawa Spends: 1998-1999,* ed. L.A. Pal, 99-126. Toronto: Oxford University Press.

Haddow, R. and T. Klassen. 2006. *Partisanship, Globalization, and Canadian Labour Market Policy*. Toronto: University of Toronto Press.

Hale, G.E. 1998. "Reforming Employment Insurance: Transcending the Politics of the Status Quo." Canadian Public Policy 24.4: 429-51.

Hall, R. and R.D. Lansbury. 2006. "Skills in Australia: Towards Workforce Development and Sustainable Skill Ecosystems." *Journal of Industrial Relations,* 48.5: 575-92.

Harrison, B. and M. Weiss. 1998. *Workforce Development Networks:*

Community-Based Organizations and Regional Alliances. Thousand Oaks, California: SAGE Publications.

Howell, D.R., ed. 2005. *Fighting Unemployment: The Limits of Free Market Orthodoxy.* Oxford University Press.

Human Resources and Skills Development Canada. 2010. *Canada's Economic Action Plan: The Strategic Training and Investment Fund.* At www.hrsdc.gc.ca/eng/employment/partnerships/lma/index.shtml.

Jackson, A. and S. Schetagne. 2010. "Is EI Working for Canada's Unemployed? Analyzing the Great Recession." *Alternative Federal Budget Working Paper.* Canadian Centre for Policy Alternatives.

Jones, S.R.G. 2011. "Asymmetry at Work: Quebec's Distinct Implementation of Programs for the Unemployed." Mowat Centre EI Task Force.

Klassen, T. 2000. "Federal-Provincial Labour Market Development Agreements: Brave New Model of Collaboration?" In *Federalism, Democracy and Labour Market Policy in Canada,* ed. T. McIntosh. Kingston: Queen's University Institute for Intergovernmental Relations.

Lazar, H. 2002. *Shifting Roles: Active Labour Market Policy in Canada Under the Labour Market Development Agreements.* Canadian Policy Research Networks.

Markusen, A. 2004. "Targeting Occupations in Regional and Community Economic Development." Journal of the American Planning Association 70.3: 253-68.

Martin, J.P. and D.B. Grubb. 2001. "What works and for whom: A review of OECD countries' experiences with active labour market policies." Swedish Economic Policy Review 8: 9-56.

McIntosh, T., and G.W. Boychuk. 2000. "Dis-Covered: EI, Social Assistance and the Growing Gap in Income Support for Unemployed Canadians." In *Federalism, Democracy and Labour Market Policy in Canada* ed. T. McIntosh, 65-158. Montreal and Kingston: McGill-Queen's University Press.

Mendelsohn, M. and J. Medow. 2010. "Help Wanted: How Well did the EI Program Respond During the Recent Crisis?" Toronto: Mowat Centre for Policy Innovation.

Ministry of Training, Colleges and Universities. 2009. *Canada-Ontario Labour Market Agreement 2009-2010 Annual Plan.* At http://www.tcu.gov.on.ca/eng/training/labmark/LMA_Plan2009_10.html.

Mosley, H. 2009. "The Trade-Off Between Flexibility and Accountability in Labour Market Policy." In *Flexible Policy for More and Better Jobs,* ed. S. Giguère and F. Froy, 73-101. Paris: OECD.

Nativel, C. 2006. "From Welfare-to-Work to Welfare-in-Work: Concepts and Policies." In *Skills Upgrading, New Policy Perspectives,* 33-83. Paris: OECD.

Noël, A. 2011. "The Effectiveness of Training for Displaced Workers with Long Prior Job Tenure." Mowat Centre EI Task Force.

Organisation for Economic Co-operation and Development (OECD).

1999. Decentralising Employment Policy: New Trends and Challenges. OECD: Paris.

——. 2001. Local Partnerships for Better Governance. OECD: Paris.

——. 2003. Managing Decentralisation: A New Role for Labour Market Policy. OECD: Paris.

——. 2004. New Forms of Governance for Economic Development. OECD: Paris.

——. 2009. Designing Local Skills Strategies. Paris: OECD.

Osberg, L. 2006. "Pulling Apart: The Growing Gulfs in Canadian Society." *Policy Options* April-May.

——. 2009. *Canada's Declining Safety Net: The Case for EI Reform.* Canadian Centre for Policy Alternatives.

Osberg, L., F.Wien, and J. Grude. 1995. *Vanishing Jobs: Canada's Changing Workplaces.* Toronto: Lorimer.

Sharpe, A. and R. Haddow. 1997. *Social Partnerships for Training: Canada's Experiment with Labour Force Development Boards.* Caledon Institute of Social Policy and the Centre for the Study of Living Standards.

Simeon, R. and D. Cameron. 2002. "Intergovernmental Relations and Democracy: An Oxymoron if There Ever Was One?" In *Canadian Federalism: Performance, Effectiveness and Legitimacy*, ed. H. Bakvis and G. Skogstad, 278-95. Toronto: Oxford University Press.

Stapleton, J. 2011. "Trading Places: Single Adults Replace Lone Parents as the New Face of Social Assistance in Canada." Mowat Centre EI Task Force.

Task Force on Modernizing Income Security for Working-Age Adults (MISWAA). 2006. *Time for a Fair Deal.* Report of the Task Force on Modernizing Income Support for Working-Age Adults. At http://www.civicaction.ca/task-force-modernizing-income-security-working-age-adults.

Tiebout, C.M. 1956. "A Pure Theory of Local Expenditure." *Journal of Political Economy* 64: 416-24.

Tuohy, C.J. 1992. *Policy and Politics in Canada: Institutionalized Ambivalence.* Philadelphia: Temple University Press.

Usalcas, J. 2010. "Labour market review 2009." *Perspectives.* Statistics Canada cat. No 75-001-X.

Vroman, W. and V. Brusentsev. 2005. *Unemployment Compensation Throughout the World: A Comparative Analysis.* Kalamazoo: W.E. Upjohn Institute for Employment Research.

Wood, D.E. and T.R. Klassen. 2009. "Bilateral Federalism and Workforce Development Policy in Canada." *Canadian Public Administration* 52.2: 249-70.

——. 2011. "Improving the Governance of Employment and Training Policy in Canada." Mowat Centre EI Task Force.

Chapter 14

Asymmetry at Work: Quebec's Distinct Implementation of Programs for the Unemployed

Alain Noël

Canada's unemployment insurance program (UI) was born out of a 1940 constitutional amendment that granted exclusive competence over unemployment insurance to the federal government. Both the Supreme Court and the Judicial Committee of the Privy Council had declared an earlier unilateral federal attempt—the 1935 *Employment and Social Insurance Act*—unconstitutional, and confirmed that unemployment insurance stood entirely within provincial jurisdiction. Popular pressures in favour of a reform remained strong, however, and were reinforced, once the country entered into war, by the perception that programs were needed to prepare for the unemployment that would come with postwar demobilization. In the war context, the reluctance of some provincial governments to accept a constitutional amendment giving new powers to Ottawa appeared almost "unpatriotic" (Pal 1988, 148-50; Struthers 1983, 197-99). The compromise option of a concurrent jurisdiction, defended by the just-elected and rather accommodating Quebec Liberal government of Adélard Godbout, was rapidly discarded as well. The Mackenzie King government wanted and obtained full, exclusive jurisdiction. Even employment services, "an area hitherto sacred to the provinces," ended up "wholly under federal jurisdiction" (Campeau 2005, 60-67).

Not surprisingly, unemployment insurance came to be defined primarily by unilateral federal decisions and actions, with little input from the provinces (Pal 1988, 158-59). Until the late 1990s, reform proposals usually entailed more, not less, federal involvement in income security and social services. In the 1970s, for instance, a reformed UI stood as "the centrepiece of Trudeau's 'just society,'" and it thus constituted a jealously guarded federal prerogative (Campeau 2005, 83).

Many saw advantages to this federal dominance. In principle at least, a unique, integrated program facilitated labour and capital mobility and allowed the pooling of risks and redistribution across regions and provinces. At the same time, in a regionally segmented labour market, a strictly federal program often proved unresponsive to local or provincial circumstances and, when it did introduce regionally differentiated rules, ineffective in producing coherent and equitable outcomes (Mendelsohn and Medow 2010). From a governance standpoint, one could question as well the almost complete absence of inputs from provincial governments, even over regional dimensions of the program, except perhaps through the reactive politics of resistance to cutbacks (Banting 2005, 107, 119-20; Pal 1988, 161). At times, unemployment insurance was also used unilaterally to encroach upon provincial jurisdictions—with maternity leave benefits for instance—often resulting in less than optimal social protection (Banting 2005, 107).

One possible response to this pattern of unilateralism would be to reconsider the roles and responsibilities of the two orders of government in line with agreed upon principles, so as to design a more effective, efficient and accountable income security and labour market regime (Mendelsohn, Hjartarson and Pearce 2010). After all, other federations organize labour market policies differently and, in theory, a number of alternatives appear possible (Noël 2004). In the United States, for instance, a complex intergovernmental system governs unemployment insurance, which combines federal standards with important state variations (O'Leary and Straits 2004). The political obstacles to such a principled transformation, however, appear daunting. The Canadian federation—and this is undoubtedly an understatement—is not easy to change, and a redistributive program as political as EI is unlikely to be modified substantially through a purely technical exercise (a similar argument is made for equalization in Lecours and Béland 2010, 590).

Rather than addressing the issue from such a theoretical and normative perspective, this study uses a set of recent innovations to evaluate the potential of a different arrangement for the governance of programs for the unemployed. More specifically, the chapter considers four recent initiatives that, together, gave the Quebec government some leeway to fashion its own labour market and income support approach. Two of these developments pertain to the Employment Insurance program as such, and two to the broader federal income support system. They are:

- the 1998 Canada-Quebec Labour Market Development Agreement (LMDA) and the 2009 Canada-Quebec Labour Market Agreement (LMA), which devolved some active labour market measures to the Quebec government;
- the 2005 Canada-Quebec Final Agreement on the Quebec Parental Insurance Plan (QPIP);
- the 1996–1998 Quebec response to the National Child Benefit (NCB), which was not an agreement as such but nevertheless constituted a specific and accepted way of implementing a pan-Canadian approach aimed at low-income families; and
- the 2007–2010 adaptations of the federal Working Income Tax Benefit (WITB) to better complement Quebec's own income support programs.

Together, these four developments touched on the main dimensions of Employment Insurance (EI) and income security policy in Canada, namely training, parental leave and income support for individuals and families. More importantly, they represented governance innovations that enhanced the role of a provincial government and, potentially, made policies more coherent on a provincial scale. All were achieved by bilateral agreements or understandings between the federal and the Quebec government. In some cases, these agreements were conceived in a broader devolution context, in others they were not. Sometimes they involved formal, signed agreements, and sometimes not. Very often, they concerned Quebec only, thus introducing, albeit discreetly, some additional asymmetry in the Canadian federation.

Perhaps because they are still recent, or possibly because they concern relatively arcane issues that raise few political controversies, not much is known about these policy innovations, even though they constitute concrete instances of devolution and of asymmetric arrangements over key Employment Insurance and income security instruments.

The first aim of this chapter is thus to present these four initiatives and outline their purpose, institutional features, and achievements thus far. The second, more important, objective is to assess the contribution of these initiatives to the development of new and more flexible forms of governance, conducive to coordinated and coherent labour market and income support programs. To my knowledge, no study has considered these different initiatives as a whole, to evaluate what happens when the federal government gradually allows a provincial government to design its own version of the common Employment Insurance and income support framework. This chapter argues that, however limited, this experiment yielded positive outcomes, both from a policy and from a governance standpoint. It is not clear, however, whether it can be broadened or expanded.

The first part of the chapter reviews the cases and the literature and identifies core issues at stake in the federal governance of Employment Insurance and income security. The main theme of this section is that, in a federation like Canada, instrumental principles such as effectiveness, efficiency and accountability are not sufficient to guide policy decisions. Then, the policy and governance innovations under study in this chapter are examined, and their political significance is highlighted. All of them are by-products of the never-ending game of mutual adjustment between the federal and the Quebec governments. Finally, the significance of this discrete, incremental and unique experiment for the broader reform of Employment Insurance is assessed. It is doubtful that this case can serve as a model for broader reforms. At the very least, however, it points to the relevance and potential of flexibility in the management of the federation. When policy and governance innovations are allowed, the "laboratories of democracy" metaphor may remain a useful representation.

1 The Politics of Bilateral Agreements

A major theme in the recent literature on Canadian federalism is the increasing difficulty of reforming our institutions and practices. The problem starts with the constitution, which is for all practical purposes locked in, but it does not stop there. The country's electoral system and parliamentary institutions also appear almost impossible to transform. Recognition, self-government and land claims settlements with aboriginal peoples move at a geologic pace. The federal and provincial-territorial governments seem unable to agree on basic rules to govern the economic and social union. And the institutions and practices of fiscal federalism always appear to lag behind the evolution of economic and political reality.

These difficulties are obviously anchored in the country's enduring constitutional impasse, which prevents major institutional reforms and undermines trust among citizens and between governments. Other factors, however, also come into play. Indeed, even within provinces, major changes now seem difficult, whether they concern the electoral system, social programs, or economic development projects.

Whatever their cause, these difficulties tend to favour unilateralism in intergovernmental relations. Unable to obtain multilateral agreements, or even to trust each other, governments often prefer to act alone. The 1999 Social Union Framework Agreement, for instance, an attempt to establish new rules to govern intergovernmental relations, basically vanished out of existence, without ever having much of an impact on governance or on social policy (Noël, St-Hilaire and Fortin 2003). Negotiations with the provinces continued, but the process could hardly qualify as collaborative federalism.

Paradoxically, the main exceptions concerned areas of intervention where federal jurisdiction was relatively well established, without the need to evoke a putative federal spending power. This was the case, for instance, with multilateral or bilateral agreements on child benefits, disability policy, and job training (Noël 2003, 57). Perhaps because in such cases the need to affirm federal norms and controls appeared less necessary, collaboration seemed easier to achieve.

The four instances considered in this chapter belong to this set of exceptions. Chronologically, they are (i) the 1996–1998 National Child Benefits (NCB), a multilateral (without Quebec but with Quebec in mind) agreement on the reinvestment in family-related programs of provincial social assistance funds made available when the new federal child benefits for low-income families was introduced in 1998; (ii) the 1998 Canada-Quebec Labour Market Development Agreement (LMDA), complemented in 2009 by the Canada-Quebec Labour Market Agreement (LMA), which devolved active labour market programs and services to the Quebec government; (iii) the 2005 Canada-Quebec Final Agreement on the Quebec Parental Insurance Plan (QPIP), which allowed Quebec to create its own Parental Insurance Plan, outside the Employment Insurance program; and (iv) the 2007–2010 adaptations of the federal Working Income Tax Benefit (WITB), which adjusted the federal measure to better fit Quebec's own fiscal choices and priorities.

These four arrangements were born out of very different contexts. The National Child Benefit, for one, was an attempt to define in a more collaborative and multilateral fashion a new, pan-Canadian approach toward low-income families. Formally, the initiative was federal, but it concerned policies fully under provincial jurisdiction and sought to establish new pan-Canadian norms for these policies. The idea was to ensure that provincial governments reinvest, in compatible programs, the social assistance money freed up by higher federal transfers to low-income families. This is why the Quebec government refused from the start to participate in this initiative, which subordinated policy choices within its own areas of jurisdiction to federal priorities, even though in practice the conditions were not very stringent, and in no way incompatible with Quebec's own policy orientations (Boychuk 2002, 58-60; Noël 2002, 16-17). Asymmetry, in this case, was introduced by default, without any agreement.

With active labour market policies, the scenario was different. Formal, bilateral agreements were signed to devolve to provincial governments training programs and services that were financed through Employment Insurance and formally under federal jurisdiction, but were also close to provincial jurisdictions such as education and training. Initiated in the aftermath of the almost victorious 1995 Quebec referendum on sovereignty, this devolution was meant to show that Canadian federalism could be reformed so as to grant more autonomy to the Quebec government. To avoid any suggestion of "special deal" or asymmetry, however, bilateral agreements were signed with other provinces as well, starting with Alberta in 1996 and ending with British Columbia in 2008 (Wood and Klassen 2008, 337-38). As a result, all parties signed formal agreements, in a bilateral and relatively symmetric fashion.

By contrast, the 2005 Canada-Quebec Final Agreement on the Quebec Parental Insurance Plan was, and remained, unique. This agreement responded to a demand articulated by the Quebec government at least since the late 1980s, which became the object of a broad social mobilization in the 1990s. At the October 1996 Summit on the Economy and Employment, in particular, representatives from business, trade unions, and community organizations all agreed with the Quebec government on the creation of a distinct parental insurance provincial plan, to be financed by the recuperation of a portion of Quebeckers' unemployment insurance contributions. The federal government refused this idea from the outset, and the first negotiations in 1997 only confirmed the impasse. Despite broad agreement within Quebec society and the unanimous adoption by the National Assembly of a law creating the new regime in May 2001, a truce with Ottawa remained elusive. In March 2002 the Quebec government took the case to court, contesting the constitutionality of the federal use of EI to provide maternity leave benefits (Giroux 2008, 20-34). In January 2004, the Quebec Court of Appeal ruled that indeed this practice was ultra vires. The federal government immediately appealed and the Supreme Court reversed the decision in October 2005, on the basis of a "living tree," rather than "originalist," interpretation of the constitution (Calder 2006, 106-09).

Meanwhile, however, the political context had changed. First, in April 2003, the Quebec Liberal party of Jean Charest defeated the Parti Québécois government of Bernard Landry. Charest was not more committed to the project of a distinct Québécois parental insurance plan than his predecessor, but he obviously had a less antagonistic relationship with the federal government. Second, and more importantly, in December 2003 Prime Minister Jean Chrétien, who more than once had expressed his fervent opposition to any agreement on parental leave benefits, resigned and was replaced by Paul Martin. With a general election coming, and the need to counter in public opinion the damages of the sponsorship scandal, Martin appeared willing to consider changes that could improve his standing in Quebec. The January 2004 ruling of the Quebec Court of Appeal, even though it was contested, also reinforced Quebec's hand (Giroux 2008, 85-87). Negotiations resumed, and an agreement in principle was signed in May 2004, and confirmed by a final agreement on 1 March 2005 (Giroux 2008, 33-34).

The fourth initiative was, at least in principle, Canada-wide, and it could be seen as an expression of Stephen Harper's idea of open federalism. Indeed, it was introduced with the 2007 budget, deemed by Thomas Courchene as the best realized expression of this new vision of federalism (2007, 16). On this occasion, the Harper government emphasized the constitutional division of powers, improved and restructured the Canada Social Transfer, and established new and coherent rules for the equalization program. In the same spirit, albeit in a less spectacular, hardly noticed fashion, the federal government introduced a new and flexible Working Income Tax Benefit (WITB) to improve the earnings of employed low-income Canadians. The presentation of this new measure explicitly recognized the role of provincial and territorial income support programs and stated that the federal government was prepared "to consider province- or territory-specific changes to the design of the WITB to better harmonize it" with these programs, as long as these changes built on actions already taken by the provinces or territories to improve work incentives for low-income households, remained cost-neutral for the federal government, assured a minimum benefit level to all WITB recipients, and preserved the harmonization of the WITB with other federal programs (Department of Finance 2007, 80-81). In the following years, British Columbia, Nunavut, and Quebec took advantage of this flexibility to design their own version of the WITB, while other provinces maintained the standard federal version (Battle 2009). In Quebec, the main preoccupation in this case was to reach childless low-income workers, less favored by the programs put in place since the late 1990s, which primarily targeted families with children (Ministère des Finances 2010, 136).

The four initiatives considered here involved bilateral agreement. The LMDA and QPIP derived from formal, high-level contracts signed by ministers while the WITB followed a discreet arrangement reached by civil servants and the NCB expressed a tacit understanding to proceed as if there was an agreement, but they were all bilateral affairs. In all cases, though, the federal government defined a broad framework of principles and norms that, in theory, could apply to all provinces willing to avail themselves of an agreement. Even with the QPIP, a truly ad hoc arrangement that strictly responded to a Quebec demand, it is at least conceivable that another provincial government could ask for the same treatment.

This turn toward bilateralism has received mixed reviews in the literature on Canadian federalism. Scholars disagree both on the significance of the trend and on its normative implications. For some, mostly in Quebec, these bilateral agreements, however useful, appear too limited and marginal to speak of a genuine renewal, in a federation that remains inimical to decentralization and asymmetric arrangements (Caron and Laforest 2009; McRoberts 2009, 452, 460; Noël 2008, 34; Seymour 2009, 209). Without fully rejecting this pessimistic evaluation, Gérard Boismenu and Peter Graefe qualify it by noting that intergovernmental relations have changed in recent years, with the introduction of new policy instruments and an increased use of bilateral arrangements, which reflect a weaker federal stance in social policy negotiations (2004, 75, 86). It is precisely this perceived weakness of the federal government that worries many scholars outside Quebec, who fear the loss of national standards and accountability, once social policies become "subject to the political winds in provinces and territories" (Kershaw 2006, 199).

The recent assessment of workforce development policy prepared by Donna Wood and Thomas Klassen is a case in point. Acknowledging that they have not yet been able to establish the impact of existing bilateral agreements "on policy and programming outcomes" or to determine "whether there are significant differences between jurisdictions" (2009, 264), the authors nevertheless conclude that "a series of segmented, bilateral, executive dominated, federal-provincial agreements are likely inadequate to achieve national workforce development goals and have the potential to balkanize programs across the country, hollow out the centre, and undermine Canada's political union" (267). This is quite an impact for a set of bilateral labour market agreements that remains unknown to most Canadians. But there is more. Without a better integrated intergovernmental process, "Canada will almost certainly fall considerably short in its efforts to have the best educated, most skilled, and most flexible workforce in the world" (267).

Obviously, then, there is no consensus in the literature on the reality and significance of the turn toward bilateral agreements observed here. Some think the phenomenon remains marginal and insufficient to qualify as a genuine transformation; others consider it signals the beginning of an ominous trend. These judgments, of course, reflect the very different readings of Canadian federalism that prevail in Quebec and in English

Canada (Rocher 2009). If we take the case at face value, however, it seems safe to say that the observed evolution stands somewhere between marginal and ominous.

The developments presented here did not stem from a plan, and did not even form a sequence. They emerged more or less independently, through mutual adjustments and negotiations over different policy issues. In the end, they nevertheless formed a relatively consistent pattern, and brought a modicum of decentralization and asymmetry in a federation that does not change easily. Quebec scholars overlooked this evolution because it was circumscribed to a few policy issues and took place in a rather haphazard and disjointed fashion. They remained skeptical. In English Canada, some negative comments were expressed, but they concerned specific elements, such as the NCB or the LMDAs, more than the overall evolution, which was also left unnoticed. Most of these comments manifested a recurrent, but not always well documented, preoccupation with the "provincialization of social policy" (Boychuk forthcoming; Osberg 2000, 214).

Consider once again, as a starting point for a more temperate and constructive argument, the conclusions of Wood and Klassen, who stress the inadequacy of "segmented" and "executive dominated federal-provincial agreements ... to achieve national workforce development goals" (2009, 267). It is true that intergovernmental relations remain governed by political considerations and conflicts, and that they often produce less than coherent or optimal policies. Such a critique, however, may assume too much. First, even in a unitary state, labour market and income security policies are the product of bargaining and deliberation among a number of actors, and they naturally embody tensions and contradictions. Second, nobody knows for sure what it takes to obtain "the best educated, most skilled, and most flexible workforce in the world." As a matter of fact, the options at stake lie at the heart of the contemporary conflict between conservatives and social democrats, the former betting on market mechanisms, the latter on public investment (Boix 1998; Huo 2009). Third, in a federation, the diversity of social and political trajectories may be a good in itself. As Patrick Fafard, Rocher and Côté reaffirm in a recent article, a federation is not simply an institutional arrangement that can be judged by the efficiency and cohesion of its policies, but also a regime created to foster mutual trust between various entities sharing a common political space (2009, 560-61).

These three arguments add up. If labour market and income security policy is always an imperfect compromise between social actors, if a unique "best way" can never be established with certainty, and if the diversity favoured by a federal arrangement constitutes a good in itself, then the capacity to reach a definitive and integrated "national" approach may not be the best criteria to assess emerging forms of governance and policy instruments. When it is not possible to determine theoretically the best policy response to a problem, and when there are good reasons to think that different collective preferences and social contexts may call for distinct solutions, non-hierarchical, decentralized policy-making holds more promise than centralized or hierarchical responses. This is the logic behind the well-known metaphor of "laboratories of federalism" (Kerber and Eckhardt 2007). In such cases, there is no need to choose between efficiency and the normative principles associated with federalism: efficiency and social justice can be well served by a decentralized arrangement.

With these theoretical considerations in mind, this chapter probes the recent transformations in the governance of the Canadian Employment Insurance/income security regime from the bottom up, so to speak. Rather than focusing on general intergovernmental relations mechanisms or on putative pan-Canadian objectives, the analysis considers public policy from the standpoint of one province, Quebec, where devolution has been most important. Policies that may appear unsatisfying or incoherent from a pan-Canadian perspective may well look better once viewed in light of the labour market requirements, institutions, and choices of a single province. If this is the case, devolution may then emerge as a coherent and efficient strategy.

2 Asymmetry at Work

One of the reasons Quebec scholars did not pay much attention to the new politics of bilateral agreements was that, viewed from the province, these arrangements merely seemed to confirm that the Quebec government could pursue its own course of action in areas that belonged to its jurisdiction, possibly with some light but still debatable reporting requirements (Graefe 2008, 93-94).

The National Child Benefit was a case in point. The Quebec government was never involved in the intergovernmental negotiations that led to the 1998 announcement of the program. Only present as an observer, Quebec expressed repeatedly its general agreement with the common objectives but strong disapproval over issues of jurisdiction. The following note, taken from a 1998 federal/provincial/territorial document, was typical:

> Quebec agrees with the basic principles of the National Child Benefit, which aims to increase resources available for poor children and promote employment retention and the return to work. The family policy implemented by Quebec is consistent with this orientation. However the Government of Quebec has not taken part in the development of the National Child Benefit because it wishes to assume control of income support for the children of Quebec. Consequently, any reference to joint federal, provincial and territorial positions in this text does not include Quebec. (Quoted in Warriner and Peach 2007, 93)

When the different governments agreed on a framework that would ensure that provincial governments reinvest in family policy the social assistance money made available as a result of improved federal transfers to low-income households, they also accepted, implicitly, that Quebec would do as it wished. Two factors explained this unspoken compromise. First, Quebec was already pursuing policies compatible with the National Child Benefit. In fact, the province had moved earlier than any other government except British Columbia to introduce income-tested child benefits, and it went further than others in this respect (Boychuk 2002, 58). Quebec's non-participation, noted Ken Battle, one of the leading advocates of a pan-Canadian child benefit, would dash the hope of a pure "national standard" but the "benign result would be a higher combined federal-Quebec level of child benefits for Quebec's low-income families" (1999, 59). Second, the NCB agreement was not very demanding for participating provinces. Provincial governments were not asked to respect set norms or standards, to commit resources, or to modify programs (Battle 1999, 51, 58; Boychuk 2002, 59-60). In fact, given the number of programs accepted as compatible with the NCB and the fungible character of any public transfer, this agreement was largely symbolic.

In the circumstances, it is not easy, indeed not feasible, to assess what the Quebec government does with the resources made available by the NCB. In a recent study comparing the paths taken by Quebec and Ontario, Deena White acknowledges that the Quebec government does not account for its use of the funds made available by the introduction of the NCB, but nevertheless concludes that Quebec's new family policy is very much in tune with the program's priorities (2008, 181-82).

Overall, provincial governments invested NCB resources in the provision of day care services, the introduction of working income supplements, and the development of new programs for children at risk (White 2008, 177). In Ontario, the bulk of the effort went toward measures to make work pay, which combined some new financial incentives with a downward revision of social assistance standards. In Quebec, social assistance was also reformed to encourage work, but primarily with positive incentives. The most significant reforms took place in family policy, with the combined objectives of improving the earnings of low-income households, enhancing work-family conciliation, and contributing to early childhood development. New income supplements and children's allowances were created, a universal low-cost early day care and early childhood development program was introduced, and a renewed parental insurance program was put in place.

These innovations, as White notes, were announced in 1996, before the NCB agreement was reached, and they were implemented gradually between 1996 and 2006. There is no doubt that they would have taken place without the NCB. Indeed, the scale of the NCB simply does not match the scope of Quebec's family policy.

Consider the following figures. In 2007–2008, total provincial/territorial "reinvestments" associated with the NCB in participating provinces and territories were estimated at $586.4 million (National Child

Benefit 2010, 13). Based on the 2008 population of the provinces and territories other than Quebec, this total reinvestment amounted to $22.94 per person (population data drawn from Statistics Canada 2010). At that rate, if we assumed a uniform reinvestment per capita across provinces and territories—a rough but reasonable assumption—the total for Quebec in 2008 would have been about $178 million, if the province had been included in the NCB progress report. If instead we used as a benchmark the 2007–2008 reinvestments in the most committed province—British Columbia—the estimate for Quebec would go up to $407 million. Whatever the case, these sums would have represented very modest amounts compared to the overall cost of the province's family policy, which reached $5.1 billion that year (Ministère des Finances 2008, E16).

Alone, public expenditures on child care for children under five totalled $1.8 billion (2008, E8), roughly ten times the NCB reinvestment estimated for Quebec on a pan-Canadian basis. More to the point, this modest, notional federal contribution did not even match the fiscal loss Quebec citizens incurred because of their low-cost day care system. In 2008, economist Claude Laferrière calculated that the federal government saved at least $300 million through the reduction of child care tax deductions associated with Quebec's family policy (2008, 14; for an update, see Laferrière and Montreuil 2010). A simple correction for this tax effect, which penalizes the provincial choice of a low-cost public option, would have contributed more to Quebec's family policy than the estimated NCB reinvestments.

The NCB, of course, also included direct transfers to families, which were much more significant than the provincial "reinvestment" component. In 2008–2009, throughout Canada the federal government transferred $9.4 billion to low and middle income families with the Canada Child Tax Benefit (CCTB) and the National Child Benefit Supplement (National Child Benefit 2010, 5). If we add these transfers, the 2006 universal child care benefit, and the 2007 non-refundable tax credit for children, the federal government transferred $3.6 billion to Quebec families in 2009 (Ministère des Finances 2009, 1; on the 2006 and 2007 federal budget, which brought these two new federal benefits, see Hale 2008, 39).

The end result in Quebec was a significantly renewed and coherent policy framework, which very much improved the situation of low- and middle-income families. Family allowances and working income supplements combined with subsidized day care services and a generous parental insurance plan to fashion a new equilibrium in Quebec, favourable to early childhood development, labour market integration, women's employment, poverty reduction, and even population growth (Godbout and St-Cerny 2008; Ministère des Finances 2009). In an empirical, gradual fashion, the Quebec government followed a path of welfare state adaptation compatible with women's new roles in the family and in the labour market, and favorable to employment, equality, social development, and demographic renewal (Esping-Andersen 2009).

Once again, Quebec's accommodation to the NCB was only a small part of the story. Still, it could at least be said that the NCB did not prevent a major policy transformation that saw Quebec creating its own, distinct, family policy model. Put another way, it remained possible for Quebec, within the loose framework agreed upon by others, to pursue its national objectives, in areas within its own jurisdiction. This is hardly a superlative achievement for a federation, but it nevertheless constitutes a positive outcome, in an intergovernmental context more often marked by distrust, conflict, and stalemates.

During the same period, at the end of the 1990s, new bilateral Labour Market Development Agreements (LMDAs) were negotiated, with the aim of transferring to the provinces most of the Employment Insurance funds devoted to active labour market policies. Specifically, these funds concerned training programs, job creation measures, and wages and earnings subsidies. Devolution also involved counselling and placement services for EI recipients. Some provinces sought and obtained a full transfer of funds and responsibility, while others preferred to be involved in planning and management without taking charge of the actual implementation of programs and delivery of services. The bulk of the agreements were signed in a few months, between December 1996 and April 1997 (Klassen 2000, 174-76). In Quebec, not surprisingly, the April 1997 agreement involved a full transfer of funds and responsibility. Ottawa agreed to transfer 1,022 staff positions and $457 million (in 1997–1998; $594 million by 2000–2001), with the understanding that Quebec would respect federal Employment Insurance funding and eligibility rules and would ensure accountability and evaluation.

Quebec's main objective was to integrate all active labour market programs for the unemployed, whether they were EI clients, social assistance beneficiaries, or people without public income support. For this purpose a new autonomous agency, Emploi-Québec, was created, bringing together all the personnel and services involved in active labour market programs, whether they were associated previously with Human Resources Development Canada (HRDC), the Ministère de la Sécurité du revenu (social assistance), or the Société québécoise de développement de la main d'oeuvre (SQDM; the tripartite agency governing Quebec's own active labour market programs). The initial steps proved difficult, because employers and unions worried about the integration of social partners representing the community sector, and about the potential clash between the top-down, control-oriented management of social assistance and the more collaborative, market-oriented traditions of conventional labour market policies (Saint-Martin 2001). Early complaints and glitches transpired in the public sphere.

Soon, however, Emploi-Québec vanished from the news and went on designing and implementing labour market programs. In 2002–2003, the agency was spending $792 million on active labour market measures,

$591.5 million of which came from the Canada-Quebec Agreement, the rest coming from Quebec's own funds (Emploi-Québec 2002, 19). Over the years, Ottawa's contribution remained stable ($596.8 million in 2008–2009), but Quebec's share grew, especially after the 2008 Pacte pour l'emploi—a policy package designed to boost labour market participation—so that the total budget for active measures reached $953.5 million by 2008–2009 (Emploi-Québec 2008, 52).

In conformity with the Canada-Quebec agreement, funds that came from Employment Insurance were only spent on people who qualified given EI rules, which meant that the bulk of those who participated in measures belonged to this category. The funds added by Quebec nevertheless extended coverage. In 2008–2009, for instance, there were 180,967 participants covered under the Employment Insurance umbrella, 78,464 through social assistance, and 50,739 with no program affiliation, coming as people who did not receive public income support (Emploi-Québec 2010).

Among the provinces, Quebec was alone in using its own funds to extend coverage in such a way. It also was distinct in evaluating systematically the effects of such a strategy. Indeed, because it offered the same programs to EI eligible clients, social assistance beneficiaries, and people without public income support, Emploi-Québec was in a unique situation to evaluate the impact of active measures on these various groups. In December 2003, the Ministère de l'Emploi, de la Solidarité sociale et de la Famille released a thorough study assessing the gross and net effects of the different measures offered by Emploi-Québec (SOM 2003).

Five types of programs were considered: 1) collective employment preparation for the young or for long-term unemployed; 2) short-term individual counselling for job seekers; 3) full-time training and education (literacy development, language acquisition, skills-upgrading); 4) social insertion measures for those most distant from the labour market; and 5) wage subsidies, aimed at people who otherwise would not be easily employable. The study surveyed a large proportion of those who participated and completed their program in 2000 (experimental group), as well as a large number of otherwise similar non-participants (control group). Econometric techniques were used to match the two groups and correct, in particular, for selection biases. In the experimental group, 2,776 people responded to the survey and consented to have their personal information used to match their profile with non-participants; the control group counted 1,447 people. In the experimental group, respondents included EI-eligible clients, social assistance beneficiaries, and people without public income support, but the latter were not represented in the control group, since the relevant population could not easily be identified.

The results of this study were rich and detailed. The crux of the matter, however, was that a majority of respondents (76 per cent) had a job eighteen months after they completed their participation, most of them within at least six months. Respondents who qualified for EI programs and those without income support were more likely to be in employment than those who came from social assistance (SOM 2003, 12-13). These, however, were gross results. To assess the real impact of the different measures, the study considered as well the fate of non-participants, who also could end up with jobs, without the help of training or insertion programs. When this was done, net effects were calculated, to establish the true difference active labour market measures made.

With gross results, EI recipients appeared as the main beneficiaries of active measures. The story turned out to be very different when net effects were measured, because social assistance recipients were much less likely to find employment without active support. Net effects were positive across all categories, but not to the same extent. For people who received Employment Insurance when they started participating, the measure made a difference of six percentage points in the probability of holding a stable job eighteen months after completion (SOM 2003, 187). For those who did not receive Employment Insurance at the time but qualified for EI programs (because, for instance, they had received Employment Insurance in the previous three years; a good proportion of these people were social assistance beneficiaries), the same net effect rose to 19 percentage points (155). Finally, for participants coming from social assistance, there was a difference of up to 22 percentage points (113). Comparable net effects could not be established for people without public income support, for lack of a control group.

The results of this elaborate, quasi-experimental study ran counter to the largely pessimistic assessment of active labour market programs that long dominated the international literature (for example, Heckman, LaLonde and Smith 1999; Wunsch and Lechner 2008, 134). Recent studies and meta-analyses on this question, however, have been more favourable. These studies showed that positive effects could appear once specific programs were considered, job search assistance, private incentive schemes and training being more effective than subsidized public employment (Card, Kluve and Weber 2010; Kluve 2010). One should note, as well, that few studies ever compared social assistance and unemployment insurance recipients. American evaluations tend to focus on programs aimed at welfare recipients; European ones on unemployment insurance beneficiaries (Huber et al. 2009). It may well be that active measures make more difference for people more remote from the labour market (Heinesen, Husted and Rosholm 2011). In line with much of the recent literature, Emploi-Québec's assessment pointed to the positive impact on employment of training, counselling, and wage subsidies, an impact that existed for both men and women, and that proved particularly significant for older participants. The study documented as well other positive impacts, on incomes, personal motivation, and self-esteem for instance (SOM 2003, 245). Most importantly, it demonstrated that the Quebec government was right to use its own funds to offer active measures to people not eligible under the Canada-Quebec LMDA. Not only was the net effect more important for these people, but for many it also translated into a definitive exit from social assistance (244).

Building on this analysis, a further Emploi-Québec/SOM study published in 2006 estimated the relative costs and benefits of active labour market measures aimed at different categories of people, something that was hardly ever done in the literature (Card, Kluve and Weber 2010, F476). Taking into account the cost of a measure, its impact on individual employment and income, and the difference this impact made for public expenditures and revenues, this new study concluded that programs aimed at people on social assistance and at people who recently qualified for EI but were not currently receiving EI benefits, became, in just a few years, profitable for society, whereas measures targeted at current EI recipients were never justified from a strict cost-benefit perspective, because they did not produce a strong net effect and, in fact, contributed to lengthen a person's reliance on Employment Insurance (SOM 2006).

In February 2008, the Quebec government presented these results, which vindicated its encompassing approach to active labour market policies, at a federal-provincial-territorial workshop in Montreal (Serge Hamel, personal correspondence).[1] In the following months, the federal government signed new, complementary, bilateral agreements with all the provinces and territories. These additional agreements, called Labour Market Agreements (LMAs), provided new funds to extend active labour market measures to people on social assistance or without income support, and not eligible under EI rules. Across Canada, the federal government committed \$500 million per year to these LMAs, and it added another \$500 million for 2009–2010 and 2010–2011, for a two-year Strategic Training and Transition Fund that was introduced as part of the Economic Action Plan announced with the January 2009 budget (Human Resources and Skills Development Canada 2010).

For the Quebec government, this new bilateral agreement represented an extra \$116 million per year to invest in active labour market programs. For other provincial and territorial governments it appeared as an occasion to extend coverage and include people previously not reached by the LMDAs (Ministère de l'Emploi et de la Solidarité sociale 2010a, 35). With the additional commitments associated with Quebec's 2008 Pacte pour l'emploi, and the further amendments to the LMDAs and to the LMAs made necessary by the January 2009 Economic Action Plan, Quebec's total budget for active labour market rose to \$1,114 million in 2009–2010 (Emploi-Québec 2009, 37). This was a demonstration, noted a Quebec senior civil servant, that "asymmetry for Quebec may end up benefiting all provinces, and favour as well a greater coherence of action in employment measures."

Ottawa and Quebec probably could go further in supporting labour market integration and in coordinating their actions, but in the end the implementation and evolution of their bilateral labour market agreements appeared not as a negative case of deficient policy and inadequate governance but rather as one of successful devolution, conducive to innovation and the broader diffusion of best practices. As with family policy, it would be hard to make the case that Quebec's distinct policy orientations detracted from the objective of defining and implementing better active labour market policy in Canada. It would be difficult as well to maintain that a uniform, pan-Canadian standard would have guaranteed a better outcome. In fact, Quebec had to break the EI standard, with its own financial resources, to demonstrate that a better approach, one that was at the same time more inclusive and more profitable, was possible.

The pattern was similar with the Quebec Parental Insurance Plan, which replaced the EI funded maternity and parental leave on 1 January 2006. The federal measures offered 15 weeks of maternity leave and 35 weeks of parental leave, the latter to be shared as they wished by the parents. The program covered those who qualified for Employment Insurance, and replacement rates were set at 55 per cent of insured earnings, up to a maximum yearly insurable earnings of $43,200 in 2010 (leading to a maximum benefit of $457 per week), with a two-week unpaid waiting period (Service Canada 2010a). The Quebec Plan also included a maternity leave (15 or 18 weeks, depending on the plan chosen by the parents) and a parental leave shared by the parents (32 or 25 weeks), but offered as well a paternity leave (3 or 5 weeks). All of these options came with replacement rates that varied between 55 per cent and 75 per cent of past earnings, depending on the plan chosen (basic or special) and on the type of leave. The maximum insured earnings in 2010 was $62,500, and there was no unpaid waiting period (Ministère de l'Emploi et de la Solidarité sociale 2010b). Most importantly, because the Quebec Plan was not based on EI rules, eligibility was determined not by the number of hours worked, but rather by past earnings. This implied that self-employed workers could be covered as well, as long as they earned a minimum of $2,000 in the previous year (Conseil de gestion de l'assurance parentale 2009a, 4).

This new parental insurance plan moved Quebec closer to the most generous welfare states of continental Europe, with parental leaves and replacement rates not far behind those of Scandinavia, but with more generous provisions for self-employed workers (Conseil de gestion de l'assurance parentale 2009a). Not surprisingly, the program proved very popular, with very high approval rates in polls, among the general population as well as among the program's direct beneficiaries (Conseil de gestion de l'assurance parentale 2009b, 18). Take up rates became higher than expected, in part because the program, combined with other measures such as low-cost day care and new income support programs for families, contributed to a significant increase in births, and in part because fathers manifested more interest than expected in the paternity leave (Conseil de gestion de l'assurance parentale 2009b, 18).

One must be prudent in assessing the impact of such a recent program. A brief analysis by Claude A. Garcia of the Institut économique de Montréal nevertheless suggests significant effects. First, the number of births did increase, going from 76,300 in 2005 to 81,900 in 2006, 89,100 in 2009, and possibly 90,000 in 2010 (2010). Births also increased elsewhere in Canada during the same period, but not as rapidly. On this comparative basis, Garcia estimates that over half the increase in Quebec—about 6,600 births—can be attributed to the QPIP (ibid).

Making a similar comparison for the employment rate of women between 25 and 54 years of age, Garcia finds two jumps in the Quebec trend. The first one, an increase of more than two percentage points, occurred in 2002, presumably as a result of investments in day-care services that doubled between 1999 and 2002. The second, of a similar magnitude, came in 2007, following the introduction of the QPIP. The participation rate of women outside Quebec increased at a pace three times slower during the same period. By 2007, the employment rate of Quebec working-age women had surpassed that of their Canadian counterparts, even though the overall participation rate of Quebeckers remained slightly below that of Canadians. If the participation rate of Quebec women had grown at the Canadian rate during these years, notes Garcia, 92,000 Quebec women would have been out of employment in 2009, and the loss in work incomes for that year alone would have amounted to $3 billion (ibid).

Garcia also considers the paternity leave introduced by the Quebec Parental Insurance Plan, which turned out to be much more popular than expected when the program was designed. The author is less sanguine about this aspect of the program, which he sees as costly and ineffective in bringing fathers to share parenting responsibilities. He points to the fact that, even prior to 2006, in the context of the EI parental leave, Quebec fathers were more likely to take a leave than were fathers elsewhere in Canada, and concludes that the QPIP hardly modified an already existing trend (ibid). In this case, however, Garcia's comparison seems less convincing because he compares a shared parental leave, which still exists in the QPIP, with a specifically paternal leave. This paternity leave, argues Diane-Gabrielle Tremblay, is very different because it introduces a new right that fathers can claim in the workplace, along with replacement rates sufficiently generous to allow them to exercise this right. As is the case in Scandinavian countries, Quebec's paternity leave does contribute significantly to the involvement of fathers in parenting (Nicoud 2010; Tremblay 2010, 95).

The only downside of the QPIP is its rising cost, largely associated to its positive impact on couples' decisions to have children. Premiums have increased each year since the introduction of the program, and the program's administrators continuously struggle to maintain a balanced budget. The government argues that the growing cost of the program is justified by its impact on demographic growth and on labour force participation, but employers complain, suggesting that a somewhat less generous program could probably have the same effects (Presse canadienne 2010).

The Quebec plan may have had an impact on EI. Indeed, in the 2008 Speech from the Throne and in the 2009 budget, the Harper government made a commitment to amend the Employment Insurance program so as to provide special benefits (including maternity and parental leave) to self-employed workers. A *Fairness for the Self-Employed Act* was adopted in December 2009, which allowed self-employed workers to opt in and pay premiums that would qualify them, after twelve months, for EI maternity, parental, adoption, medical and compassionate-care benefits (Service Canada 2010b). It is not yet possible to assess the impact of a measure that only yielded its first benefits in January 2011, but it can at least be said that the new federal legislation is very different from the Quebec model. Indeed, because participation remains voluntary, the federal measure stands at a good distance from standard social insurance principles, and raises serious questions about the viability of an insurance that would only be subscribed by those most likely to make claims, namely young couples planning a family.

In a November 2009 submission to the House of Commons Standing Committee on Human Resources, Skills and Social Development and the Status of Persons with Disabilities regarding the *Fairness for the Self-Employed Act*, the Canadian Labour Congress (CLC) expressed its strong support for the Quebec Parental Insurance Plan, noting that in this case participation was mandatory for all self-employed workers, as it was for all employees. The CLC worried that a low participation rate in the new EI program for self-employed workers would lead to increased EI premiums for all, and eventually to declining public support for special benefits (Canadian Labour Congress 2009). Unlike Quebec, however, the federal government may not have had the option to create a new, distinct parental insurance plan, since this would probably have been unconstitutional. To make the program mandatory, the government would have had to impose regular EI premiums on self-employed workers, a solution that was probably not possible either. The best option, in this case, may well have been to resort once again to bilateral agreements, and allow willing provinces to introduce their own parental insurance plan. There was probably not, however, tangible provincial appetite for such an option.

The fourth program considered here, the Working Income Tax Benefit (WITB), was a federal initiative. In the 2007 budget, the Harper government introduced this new tax benefit to supplement the earnings of low-paid workers. Observers welcomed the initiative because low-income working-age adults have been largely forgotten in recent federal budgets, but they pointed as well to its limited character. At its maximum, the 2007 credit offered $500 to a single worker, and $1,000 to a family, as long as their net income ranged between $9,500 and $12,833 for individuals and between $14,500 and $21,167 for single parents or couples (Stapleton 2007). For all practical purposes, this meant that a person working full-time and all year at the minimum wage could not receive a benefit. The measure presumably targeted people leaving social assistance and working either part-time or for less than a full year (Battle 2009). The WITB was improved, however, with the 2009 budget, to provide a higher maximum benefit ($925 for single individuals, and $1,680 for single parents and couples for 2010) and cover workers with higher net incomes ($16,667 for individuals, and $25,700 for families for 2010), an income level that stood just above the level of a full-time, full-year minimum wage (Battle 2009).[2] Quebec's own version of the WITB, made possible by the flexible character of the federal measure, was designed to favour households without children, with maximum benefit that went up to $1,553 for individuals and to $2,401 for couples without children (Canada Revenue Agency 2010). Combined with the province's own work premiums, these benefits added up to more than $2,000 in income supplement for individuals, and more than $3,200 for couples without children (Ministère de l'Emploi et de la Solidarité sociale 2010c, 25).

In September 2009, the Ontario government-sponsored Institute for Competitiveness and Prosperity released a paper calling for a "Made in Ontario" WITB, on the ground that like Quebec, British Columbia and Nunavut, Ontario could obtain a better fit between its social assistance and income support policies than what was offered by the nominal, federal design (Milway, Chan and Stapleton 2009). Again, the idea that social policy innovations could come in different variants was making its way.

3 Laboratories of Democracy

The idea that justice and coherence are best served by centralized and uniform policies is a powerful one in social thought, and it is reinforced by national ambitions, when the central government is seen as a key nation-building instrument (Banting 2005; Simeon 2006). This idea underpinned, in Canada, the creation and development of unemployment insurance. If the country was to have a solid and socially legitimate economic union, it needed an integrated unemployment insurance that would pool the risks and treat all citizens fairly, if not equally. There was little room in this vision for the federal nature of the country, even though most of the associated social programs—notably in social assistance, education, and family policy—remained in the hands of provincial governments.

Almost by accident, through a series of loosely connected decisions, some decentralization and asymmetry was introduced in the income support/ Employment Insurance regime, starting in the late 1990s. Few observers noticed, and those who did were either skeptical that much had happened, or worried about the loss of policy integrity and the potential hollowing out of the centre. In fact, if we consider what happened with the National Child Benefit, the Labour Market Development Agreements, the Quebec Parental Insurance Plan, and the Working Income Tax Benefit, we find mostly progressive innovations, which produced coherent results, at least within Quebec, and promoted change through diffusion across Canada.

Quebec's family policy cannot be portrayed as an outcome of the pan-Canadian politics of child benefits. It emerged before the NCB was created and involved resources and ambitions that went much beyond the relatively modest scope of the federal program. If anything, Quebec's choices were constrained or contradicted by existing federal programs, as was clear with the childcare expenses deduction or with the Universal Child Care Benefit. Still, the development of this distinct policy framework remained possible within the existing constitutional and policy framework, and it demonstrated the potential for innovation in a decentralized, asymmetric, and to some extent bilateral context.

The evolution of labour market agreements was even more revealing because they involved specific, formal bilateral agreements, directly tied to the Employment Insurance regime. In this case as well the Quebec government went beyond the federal standard to offer active labour market measures to social assistance beneficiaries and to people without public income support. This experiment proved successful, more so in fact than the approach mandated by the LMDA, and by 2009 it was accepted and adopted by the other governments of the federation. The same cannot be said of the Quebec Parental Insurance Plan, but again a bilateral, asymmetric arrangement produced progressive policies that completed Quebec's general policy framework and were well received, and much used, by citizens.

The QPIP experiment created an opening in federal policy in favour of self-employed workers, but this opening appeared partial and not very coherent, probably because of the constraints created by the still awkward use of Employment Insurance to provide maternity and parental leave benefits. Finally, the more modest and discrete experiment with the federal Working Income Tax Benefit also pointed to the advantages of a decentralized, asymmetric approach.

This chapter started with three arguments. The first concerned the usual political foundations of social policies, and emphasized their imperfect, tentative character, as products of bargaining and deliberation among a number of actors. The second stressed the inherent uncertainty of policy innovations, which constituted imperfect responses to evolving challenges. And the third underlined the value of diversity in a federation, and the possibility that citizens might not always share the same policy preferences. Our findings about asymmetry at work were consistent with these arguments. Through a complex, multi-level process, social and labour market policies changed significantly in the late 1990s and 2000s and, at least in Quebec, it was for the better. The governance framework, if one can even speak of such an entity, was never neat and tidy, the results remained uneven, and the outcome was not an integrated pan-Canadian arrangement. But innovations were realized, progress was made, and ideas and models spread around. In a federation that usually proved rigid and resistant to change, this was a more than modest achievement. A more integrated, uniform arrangement might not have produced as much.

4 Conclusion

The Mowat Centre Employment Insurance Task Force is concerned by challenges facing coverage, by governance issues, and by the coordination of the country's different income support programs. This study does not address all these questions, but it casts some light on many issues associated with each set of challenges.

First, a close look at policy developments within Quebec allowed us to see that the story of the 1990s and 2000s was not solely one of declining coverage and social protection, even though such an evolution remained unmistakable (Banting 2006; Mendelsohn and Medow 2010, 3). New programs were also introduced to support families, facilitate labour market integration, help conciliate family life and work, and redistribute income, very much in the perspective advocated by promoters of a Third Way or of a new architecture for the welfare state (Esping-Andersen 2009; Huo 2009). These programs left many issues pending, but they nevertheless contributed to an increase in women's employment, to support for early childhood development, to the reduction of poverty and inequality, and to sustained demographic growth. Any attempt to review Employment Insurance and income support for Canadians should take these results into account.

Second, this study suggests that governance challenges need not be met by the introduction of strict principles and strongly codified working rules. Economists have long sought to establish rational rules for revenue and expenditure assignments in federations, but the empirical reality always defies their clean models. As Richard Bird noted, a country's institutions are forged through history, and not always in a neat and principled fashion (1986, 402). In a federation like Canada, where the division of powers stands as an explicit pact between nation and provinces, it does not seem well advised to proceed from such abstract, functionalist principles. More importantly, it may not be a good idea to seek a formal, multilateral governance structure. Belittled by many, the politics of bilateralism has not been ineffective. It has worked in various ways—with formal or implicit agreements, with parallel or unique arrangements, and with impetus both from above and from below—but overall it has allowed experimentation, change, learning, and diffusion. To be honest, I was myself skeptical at the outset, assuming that little could come out of mere administrative arrangements. I stand corrected. And so should those who fear the worst from agreements that, in a modest way, do bring the country closer to respecting the federal principle.

Third, this study indicates that many coordination challenges disappear once policy instruments are brought back to the provincial scale, where social protection instruments relevant for working-age adults tend to be concentrated. Centred on work integration, the family, and poverty reduction, the Quebec model of recent years has in fact been remarkably coordinated. Diane-Gabrielle Tremblay describes it as a "cumulative work-family balance" model to emphasize the cohesion of its different components, as well as its socially inclusive character. This model, Tremblay argues, is anchored in a strong and mobilized civil society that has long supported an active role for the state in family policy. By contrast, the Canadian model would be closer to the liberal, non-interventionist pole (Beaujot and Wang 2010; Tremblay 2010). If this is true, the search for a pan-Canadian approach to income support and Employment Insurance is unlikely to be successful. The best avenue is probably to accept, and indeed celebrate, the coexistence of different values and approaches, and to facilitate engagement and exchange across models. And for this, you need genuine decentralization and a willingness to live with asymmetry.

A Main Policy Lessons

1. Bilateralism and asymmetry in employment and income programs for working-age adults is not inimical to progressive innovation, policy coherence, good governance, and the diffusion of best practices. It is also consistent with the federal principle, and respectful of the diversity of labour market conditions and social preferences within the Canadian federation.
2. Integrating active labour market policies aimed at various categories of unemployed people is possible and productive, and granting priority to people receiving social assistance may be the best, most cost effective approach.
3. A generous family policy based on gender equality—including an inclusive parental leave program—is conducive to demographic growth and labour market participation.

B Recommendations

1. Any reform of the Employment Insurance program should be guided by the federal principle and respect, in particular, the constitutional division of powers. Bilateral arrangements and asymmetric solutions should remain possible.
2. Provincial governments should play a role, at least on a consultative basis, in the governance of the Employment Insurance program.
3. Active labour market measures should be integrated to better reach unemployed people not covered by the Employment Insurance program, and notably people receiving social assistance.
4. Provincial governments should consider the possibility of emulating the Quebec Parental Insurance Plan.

Endnotes

1 Serge Hamel, Direction générale adjointe de la recherche, de l'évaluation et de la statistique, Ministère de l'Emploi et de la Solidarité sociale, Correspondance with the author, 13 October 2010.

2 There is also a disability supplement (maximum of $462.50).

References

Banting, K. 2005. "Canada: Nation-Building in a Federal Welfare State." In *Federalism and the Welfare State: New World and European Experiences*, ed. H. Obinger, S. Leibfried, and F.G. Castles, 89-137. Cambridge: Cambridge University Press.

——. 2006. "Dis-embedding Liberalism? The New Social Policy Paradigm in Canada." In *Dimensions of Inequality in Canada*, ed. D.A. Green and J.R. Kesselman , 417-52. Vancouver: UBC Press.

Battle, K. 1999. "The National Child Benefit: Best Thing Since Medicare or New Poor Law?" In *Canada's National Child Benefit: Phoenix or Fizzle?*, ed. D. Durst, 38-60. Halifax: Fernwood Publishing.

——. 2009. "Beneath the Budget of 2009: Taxes and Benefits," Ottawa: Caledon Institute of Social Policy, February.

Beaujot, R. and J. Wang. 2010. "Low Fertility in Canada: The Nordic Model in Quebec and the U.S. Model in Alberta," *Canadian Studies in Population*, 37.3-4 (Fall/Winter): 411-43.

Bird, R.M. 1986. "On Measuring Fiscal Centralization and Fiscal Balance in Federal States," *Environment and Planning C: Government and Policy*, 4.4 (August): 389-404.

Boismenu, G. and P. Graefe. 2004. "The New Federal Tool Belt: Attempts to Rebuild Social Policy Leadership," *Canadian Public Policy*, 30.1 (March): 71-89.

Boix, C. 1998. *Political Parties, Growth and Equality: Conservative and Social Democratic Economic Strategies in the World Economy*, Cambridge: Cambridge University Press.

Boychuk, G.W. 2002. "Social Union, Social Assistance: An Early Assessment." In *Building the Social Union: Perspectives, Directions and Challenges*, ed. T. McIntosh, 51-67. Regina: Saskatchewan Institute of Public Policy.

Boychuk, G.W. Forthcoming. "The Federal and Territorial Dimensions of Income Maintenance and Redistribution in Canada: A New Politics?" In *The New Politics of Redistribution in Canada*, ed. K. Banting and J. Myles. Vancouver: UBC Press.

Calder, G. 2006. "A Pregnant Pause: Federalism, Equality and the Maternity and Parental Leave Debate in Canada," *Feminist Legal Studies*, 14: 99-118.

Campeau, G. 2005. *From UI to EI: Waging War on the Welfare State*, Vancouver: UBC Press.

Canada Revenue Agency. 2010. *WITB: Calculation and Advance Payments*, Ottawa, Canada Revenue Agency, 10 August. At www.cra-arc.gc.ca/bnfts/wtb/fq_pymnts-eng.html#q2.

Canadian Labour Congress. 2009. *Statement by the Canadian Labour Congress to the House of Commons Standing Committee on Human Resources, Skills and Social Development and the Status of Persons with Disabilities Regarding Bill C-56, Employment Insurance Special Benefits for Self-Employed Workers*, Ottawa, 24 November. At www.canadianlabour.ca/sites/default/files/Bill-C-56-Employment-Insurance-2009-11-24-EN_0.pdf.

Card, D., J. Kluve and A. Weber. 2010. "Active Labour Market Policy Evaluations: A Meta-Analysis," *Economic Journal*, 120 (November): F452-77.

Caron, J-F. and G. Laforest. 2009. "Canada and Multinational Federalism: From the Spirit of 1982 to Stephen Harper's Open Federalism," *Nationalism and Ethnic Politics*, 15: 27-55.

Conseil de gestion de l'assurance parentale. 2009a. *Dispositions des régimes d'assurance parentale dans certains pays d'Europe: comparaison avec le Québec*, Québec: Conseil de gestion de l'assurance parentale.

Conseil de gestion de l'assurance parentale. 2009b. *Plan stratégique* 2009-2012, Québec: Conseil de gestion de l'assurance parentale.

Courchene, T.J. 2007. "A Blueprint for Fiscal Federalism," *Policy Options*, 28.4 (April: 16-24).

Department of Finance. 2007. *The Budget Plan 2007: Aspire to a Stronger, Safer, Better Canada*, Ottawa: Department of Finance.

Emploi-Québec. 2002. *Plan d'action annuel*, 2002-2003, Québec: Emploi-Québec.

——. 2008. *Plan d'action annuel*, 2008-2009, Québec: Emploi-Québec.

——. 2009. *Plan d'action annuel*, 2009-2010, Québec: Emploi-Québec.

——. 2010. *Rapport final: Interventions des services publics d'emploi auprès des personnes sans emploi et travailleurs pour atténuer les effets du ralentissement Èconomique; Résultats cumulatifs finaux de 2009-2010*, Québec: Emploi-Québec.

Esping-Andersen, G. 2009. *The Incomplete Revolution: Adapting to Women's New Roles*, Cambridge: Polity Press.

Fafard, P., F. Rocher and C. Côté. 2009. "Clients, Citizens and Federalism: A Critical Appraisal of Integrated Service Delivery in Canada," *Canadian Public Administration*, 52.4 (December): 549-68.

Garcia, C.A. 2010. "Analyse du Régime québécois d'assurance parentale," *Textes d'opinion*, Montréal: Institut économique de Montréal, 23 September.

Giroux, M.. 2008. "La lutte pour un régime québécois d'assurance parentale," *Cahiers du CRISES*, Montréal: Centre de recherche sur les innovations sociales, Collection Mouvements sociaux, MS0803, January.

Godbout, L. and S. St-Cerny. 2008. *Le Québec, un paradis pour les familles? Regards sur la famille et la fiscalité*, Québec: Presses de l'Université Laval.

Graefe, P. 2008. "The Spending Power and Federal Social Policy Leadership: A Prospective View." In *Defining the Federal Government's Role in Social Policy: The Spending Power and Other Instruments*, ed. H. Telford, P. Graefe and K. Banting, 53-106. Policy Matters, Montreal: IRPP, 9, 3, September.

Hale, G. 2008. "International Capital and Domestic Politics: Balancing Political and Economic Management." In *How Ottawa Spends, 2008-2009: A More Orderly Federalism?* ed. A.M. Maslove, 33-58. Montreal and Kingston: McGill-Queen's University Press.

Heckman, JJ., RJ. LaLonde and JA. Smith. 1999. "The Economics and Econometrics of Active Labor Market Programs." In *Handbook of Labor Economics 3*, ed. O. Ashenfelter and D. Card, 1865-2097. Amsterdam: Elsevier.

Heinesen, E., L. Husted, and M. Rosholm. 2011. "The Effects of Active Labour Market Policies for Immigrants Receiving Social Assistance in Denmark," *IZA Discussion Paper*, No. 5632, Bonn: Institute for the Study of Labor, April.

Huber, M., M. Lechner, C. Wunsch and T. Walter. 2009. "Do German Welfare-to-Work Programmes Reduce Welfare and Increase Work?" *IZA Discussion Paper*, No. 4090, Bonn: Institute for the Study of Labor, March.

Human Resources and Skills Development Canada. 2010. *Labour Market Agreements*, Ottawa: Human Resources and Skills Development Canada. At www.hrsdc.gc.ca/eng/employment/partnerships/lma/index.shtml.

Huo, J. 2009. *Third Way Reforms: Social Democracy After the Golden Age*, Cambridge: Cambridge University Press.

Kerber, W. and M. Eckardt. 2007. "Policy Learning in Europe: The Open Method of Coordination and Laboratory Federalism," *Journal of European Public Policy*, 14.2 (March): 227-47.

Kershaw, P. 2006. "Weather-Vane Federalism: Reconsidering Federal Social Policy Leadership," *Canadian Public Administration*, 49, 2, Summer: 196-219.

Klassen, T.R. 2000. "The Federal-Provincial Labour Market Development Agreements: Brave New Model of Collaboration?" In *Federalism, Democracy and Labour Market Policy in Canada*, ed. T. McIntosh, 159-203. Montreal and Kingston: McGill-Queen's University Press.

Kluve, J. 2010. "The Effectiveness of European Active Labor Market Programs," *Labour Economics*, 17.6 (December): 904-18.

Laferrière, C. 2008. "Les garderies à sept dollars sont-elles une aubaine? Édition 2008." Montréal, UQAM, April. At www.er.uqam.ca/nobel/r14154/Doc_PDF/FGE2008/08-Qc-FGE-txt.pdf.

Laferrière, C. and F. Montreuil. 2010. “Les garderies à sept dollars sont-elles une aubaine? Édition 2010.” Montréal, UQAM, September. At www.er.uqam.ca/nobel/r14154/Doc_PDF/FGE2010/2010-txt-garde.pdf.

Lecours, A. and D. Béland. 2010. “Federalism and Fiscal Policy: The Politics of Equalization in Canada.” *Publius: The Journal of Federalism*, 40.4 (Fall): 569-96.

McRoberts, K. 2009. “Asymmetries in Canada and Spain.” In *Contemporary Canadian Federalism: Foundations, Traditions, Institutions*, ed. A.G. Gagnon, 441-68. Toronto: University of Toronto Press.

Mendelsohn, M., J. Hjartarson and J. Pearce. 2010. “Saving Dollars and Making Sense: An Agenda for a More Efficient, Effective and Accountable Federation.” *Mowat Note*, Mowat Centre for Policy Innovation, University of Toronto, October.

Mendelsohn, M. and J. Medow. 2010. “Help Wanted: How Well did the EI Program Respond During Recent Recessions?” *Mowat Note*, Mowat Centre for Policy Innovation, University of Toronto, September.

Milway, J., K. Chan, and J. Stapleton. 2009. “Time for a ‘Made in Ontario’ Working Income Tax Benefit.” Toronto: Institute for Competitiveness and Prosperity and Open Policy Ontario, September.

Ministère de l’Emploi et de la Solidarité sociale. 2010a. *Rapport annuel de gestion 2009-2010*, Québec: Ministère de l’Emploi et de la Solidarité sociale.

——. 2010b. *Québec Parental Insurance Plan*, Québec: Ministère de l’Emploi et de la Solidarité sociale. At www.rqap.gouv.qc.ca/a_propos_regime/information_generale/index_en.asp.

——. 2010c. *Québec’s Combat Against Poverty: Government Action Plan for Solidarity and Social Inclusion, 2010-2015*, Quebec: Ministère de l’Emploi et de la Solidarité sociale, June.

Ministère des Finances. 2008. *Budget Plan 2008-2009*, Québec: Ministère des Finances, March.

——. 2009. *Budget 2009-2010: Status Report on Québec’s Family Policy*, Québec: Ministère des Finances, March.

——. 2010. *Budget 2010-2011: Choices for the Future; Economic and Budgetary Action Plan*, Québec: Ministère des Finances.

National Child Benefit. 2010. *The National Child Benefit: Progress Report 2007*, Ottawa: National Child Benefit, May.

Nicoud, A. 2010. “Adieu boulot! Bonjour biberon!,” *La Presse*, June 19.

Noël, A. 2002. “Without Quebec: Collaborative Federalism with a Footnote?” In *Building the Social Union: Perspectives, Directions and Challenges*, ed. T. McIntosh, 13-30. Regina: Saskatchewan Institute of Public Policy.

——. 2003. “Power and Purpose in Intergovernmental Relations.” In *Forging a Canadian Social Union: SUFA and Beyond*, ed. S. Fortin, A. Noël and F. St-Hilaire, 47-68. Montreal and Kingston: McGill-Queen’s University Press.

——. 2004. "Introduction: Varieties of Capitalism, Varieties of Federalism." In *Federalism and Labour Market Policy: Comparing Different Governance and Employment Strategies*, ed. A. Noël, 1-23. Montreal and Kingston: McGill-Queen's University Press.

——. 2008. "Fédéralisme d'ouverture et pouvoir de dépenser au Canada," *Revista d'Estudis Autonòmics i Federals*, 7 (October): 10-36.

Noël, A., F. St-Hilaire and S. Fortin. 2003. "Learning from the SUFA Experience." In *Forging a Canadian Social Union: SUFA and Beyond*, ed. S. Fortin, A. Noël and F. St-Hilaire, 1-29. Montreal and Kingston: McGill-Queen's University Press.

O'Leary, C.J. and R.A. Straits. 2004. "Intergovernmental Relations in Employment Policy: The United States Experience." In *Federalism and Labour Market Policy: Comparing Different Governance and Employment Strategies*, ed. A. Noël, 25-82. Montreal and Kingston: McGill-Queen's University Press.

Osberg, L. 2000. "Poverty Trends and the Canadian 'Social Union.'" In *Canada: The State of the Federation 1999/2000—Toward a New Mission Statement for Canadian Fiscal Federalism*, ed. H. Lazar, 212-34. Montreal and Kingston: McGill-Queen's University Press.

Pal, L.A. 1988. *State, Class, and Bureaucracy: Canadian Unemployment Insurance and Public Policy*, Montreal and Kingston: McGill-Queen's University Press.

Presse canadienne. 2010. "L'assurance parentale coûtera plus cher aux Québécois," *Les affaires*, June 18.

Rocher, F.. 2009. "The Quebec-Canada Dynamic or the Negation of the Ideal of Federalism." In *Contemporary Canadian Federalism: Foundations, Traditions, Institutions*, ed. A.G. Gagnon, 81-131. Toronto: University of Toronto Press.

Saint-Martin, D. 2001. "Guichet unique et reconfiguration des réseaux de politiques publiques: le cas d'Emploi-Québec," *Politique et sociétés*, 20.2-3: 117-39.

Service Canada. 2010a. *Employment Insurance (EI) and Maternity, Parental and Sickness Benefits*, Ottawa, Service Canada, 25 October. At http://142.236.154.112/eng/ei/types/special.shtml#How.

——. 2010b. *Employment Insurance Special Benefits for Self-Employed People*, Ottawa, Service Canada, 22 October. At www.servicecanada.gc.ca/eng/sc/ei/sew/index.shtml.

Seymour, M.. 2009. "On Not Finding Our Way: The Illusory Reform of the Canadian Federation." In *Contemporary Canadian Federalism: Foundations, Traditions, Institutions*, ed. A.G. Gagnon, 187-212. Toronto: University of Toronto Press.

Simeon, R. 2006. "Social Justice: Does Federalism Make a Difference?" In *Dilemmas of Solidarity: Rethinking Redistribution in the Canadian Federation*, ed. S. Choudhry, J-F. Gaudreault-DeBiens, and L. Sossin, 31-44. Toronto: University of Toronto Press.

SOM Recherches et Sondages. 2003. *Étude des effets des mesures actives offertes aux individus par Emploi-Québec*, Rapport présenté à la Direction de l'Èvaluation, Quebec: Ministère de l'Emploi, de la Solidarité sociale et de la Famille, December.

——. 2006. *Étude sur le rendement de l'investissement relié à la participation aux mesures actives offertes aux individus par Emploi-Québec*, Rapport présenté à la Direction de l'Èvaluation, Direction générale adjointe de la recherche, de l'Èvaluation et de la statistique, Quebec: Ministère de l'Emploi et de la Solidarité sociale, November.

Stapleton, J. 2007. "Working Poor Get Little Relief from Flaherty," *Toronto Star*, 23 March.

Statistics Canada. 2010. *Annual Demographic Estimates: Canada, Provinces and Territories*, Ottawa: Statistics Canada, September (91-215-X).

Struthers, J. 1983. *No Fault of their Own: Unemployment and the Canadian Welfare State*, 1914-1941, Toronto: University of Toronto Press.

Tremblay, D-G. 2010. "Paid Parental Leave: An Employee Right or Still An Ideal? An Analysis of the Situation in Québec in Comparison with North America," *Employee Responsibilities and Rights Journal*, 22.1 (June): 83-100.

Warriner, WE. and I. Peach. 2007. *Canadian Social Policy Renewal, 1994-2000*, Halifax: Fernwood Publishing.

White, D. 2008. "La prestation nationale pour enfants au Canada: politique de la famille, de lutte contre la pauvreté ou d'insertion?" *Revue française des affaires sociales*, 4: 165-92.

Wood, D. and T.R. Klassen. 2008. "Intergovernmental Relations Post-devolution: Active Labour Market Policy in Canada and the United Kingdom, 1996-2006." *Regional and Federal Studies*, 18.4 (August): 331-51.

——. 2009. "Bilateral Federalism and Workforce Development Policy in Canada," *Canadian Public Administration*, 52.2 (June): 249-70.

Wunsch, C. and M. Lechner. 2008. "What Did All the Money Do? On the General Ineffectiveness of Recent West German Labour Market Programmes." *Kyklos*, 61.1 (February): 134-74.

Chapter 15

Improving the Governance of Employment and Training Policy in Canada

Donna E. Wood and Thomas R. Klassen

Since 1940 Canada's unemployment insurance program has provided the first line of defence for many workers who lose their jobs and require replacement income support. From the very beginning the program has included an active measures component, with the understanding that preparing the unemployed to return to work is an essential—if not the paramount—role of a short term income support scheme for working age adults.

In 1996, in conjunction with a major reform to the program—including a rebranding as Employment Insurance or EI—the Government of Canada offered to devolve responsibility for active measures for recipients of federal employment insurance benefits to interested provincial governments.[1] Although active measures could be provincially delivered, federal offices would continue to deliver passive income support. The federal offer was triggered by a desire to demonstrate "flexible federalism," particularly in response to Quebec's sovereignty demands. Decentralization and the enhanced local governance of employment and skills policy had also been promoted by the Organisation for Economic Co-operation and Development (OECD) as a key mechanism to boost economic growth and to create jobs (OECD 2003).

Devolution of active measures was realized through largely similar bilateral Labour Market Development Agreements (LMDAs) between the Government of Canada and each province. These agreements transferred federal staff, assets and funding to provincial governments in exchange for their commitment to design and deliver what are called in the federal EI legislation, "Employment Benefits and Support Measures" or EBSMs. It took a decade-and-a-half for all 13 jurisdictions to enter into individual bilateral agreements with the Government of Canada on devolved LMDAs.[2] The last agreement with the Yukon Territory was implemented in 2010. In addition to LMDAs, the Government of Canada has also negotiated different bilateral agreements with provincial governments to provide active measures for non-EI clients, disabled persons and older workers. As a result, there are now relatively symmetrical active measures programs for most client groups available across Canada, governed by 49 bilateral federal-provincial agreements using four different agreement templates.[3] Some of these programs are funded through employer and employee contributions to the Employment Insurance account, others through general tax revenues.

Increasing human capital and returning the unemployed (or underemployed) to the workplace is critical to the success of an economy and nation. Arguably, employment and training policy—rather than passive income support—is the cornerstone of the EI program. Driven by constitutional politics, over the past 15 years the Government of Canada and all provincial governments have agreed to a dramatic decentralization of active labour market measures. Yet pan-Canadian arrangements to ensure coordination, coherence and mutual learning between governments have remained completely static. Although each province may report to and engage with its own citizens, there is limited research, reporting and ways to assess overall program effectiveness.

Ensuring that governance of this policy area is improved and strengthened—whether programs are funded by the EI program or from other government sources—is essential if Canada is to have a workforce that is educated, skilled and flexible (Wood and Klassen 2009, 267). This chapter suggests improvements that could be made to the governance of employment and training policy. It does not examine governance arrangements for active measures within each province, nor does it address governance issues related to the income support part of the EI program (called EI Part 1).

We begin by outlining the current governance of active measures programming in Canada, how these arrangements have evolved over time and the problems that have been identified post-devolution. In order to shed light on alternative governance models and help us to better understand how the current system works, we take a comparative approach. First we look at how employment policy is governed in two very different political systems—the European Union (EU) and the United States (US). These were selected as, like Canada, both represent large, complex and mature multilevel governance systems. Then we consider how other policy sectors in Canada are governed, focusing specifically on the Canada Pension Plan and the pan-Canadian Public Health Network. These were chosen as both demonstrate promising practices in terms of non-government participation and federal-provincial cooperation. The five governance systems identified are compared, drawing out potential lessons for Canadian employment and training policy. The chapter concludes by proposing an alternative governance model for employment and training policy.

1 Background

There is no mention of labour market policy in the division of powers under the *British North America Act*. Provincial governments are responsible for education (including training) and social services (including last resort social assistance). Ottawa has responsibility for overall macro-economic policy, as well as, since a 1940 constitutional amendment, exclusive jurisdiction over a contributory unemployment insurance scheme.[4] In the 1950s and 1960s as the modern welfare state was established, the federal government also began to develop a broad range of active measures for individuals who were not eligible for unemployment insurance (UI), such as youth, aboriginal persons, older workers, recent immigrants and others. The federal spending power was also used to fund the expansion of provincial social services programming and purchase training for UI clients. In the 1970s many provinces also started to provide active measures using provincial funding, perceiving gaps in federal programming, or a need to strengthen provincial programs viewed as necessary for economic growth. They also entered into the policy domain due to concerns over rising social assistance caseloads and costs, which could be reduced with more programs to return social assistance recipients to the workforce.

As a result, a patchwork of programs arose, some federally funded (but often delivered by local agencies), others federally funded but provincially delivered, and yet others funded and delivered by provincial governments. The 1996 shift in governance that began with the LMDAs was an attempt to rationalize training policy and make it more responsive to provincial and local needs. This rationalization was initially sought as part of the Charlottetown and Meech Lake agreements, but with the failure of constitutional reform administrative re-alignment was used instead.

Active employment measures in Canada today are a combination of federal and provincial programs, some of which are charged to the EI account (funded solely by employer and employee contributions) and some of which are funded through federal general tax revenues, referred to as the Consolidated Revenue Fund (CRF). Table 1 provides an overview of active employment measures programming and the federal funding allocations in 2008/09 that are considered to be within the scope of this project.

As part of the 2009 Economic Action Plan, the Government of Canada also made new time-limited funding of approximately $900 million in 2009–201010 available for labour market adjustment until 2011 (an increase of 26 per cent of the base funding). This funding has now ended.

2 Problems with Current Governance Arrangements

The devolution of program design and delivery for active measures has led to positive outcomes in the governance of this policy domain. It has provided provincial governments with significantly greater flexibility to match programming to local conditions, thereby improving the effectiveness of labour market programming. Those involved with the sector believe that provincial governments (and their regional and local offices) have the necessary leadership and capacity to provide citizens and employers with the services they require (Wood 2010, 69). It has

TABLE 1 Active Employment Measures and Funding 2008/09

Program Name	Funding / Allocation Source	Control	Comments
Labour Market Development Agreements (LMDA)	$1,939.7 M (EI)	Federal-provincial	Provides labour market adjustment services for clients with an EI attachment. Designed and delivered by provincial governments. Indeterminate funding.
Pan-Canadian programming	$68.2 M (EI)	Federal	Provides funding for labour market partnerships and research and innovation. All programs are federally designed and delivered (Canada, 2010: 59).
Aboriginal Skills and Employment Training Strategy (ASETS)	$94.0 M (EI) $257.6 M (CRF)	Federal-aboriginal	Provides labour market adjustment interventions for Aboriginal Canadians. Delivery by 80 Aboriginal organizations across Canada.
Targeted Initiative for Older Workers (TIOW)	$35 M (CRF)	Federal-provincial	Provides labour market adjustment services for unemployed older workers. Designed and delivered (and partially funded) by provincial governments. Agreements expire 2012.
Labour Market Agreement for Persons with Disabilities (LMAPD)	$217 M (CRF)	Federal-provincial	Provides employment services and supports for disabled persons. Designed and delivered (and partially funded) by provincial governments. Ongoing funding.

(continued on next page)

(TABLE 1 cont.)

Program Name	Funding / Allocation Source	Control	Comments
Labour Market Agreements (LMA)	$500 M (CRF)	Federal-provincial	Provides labour market adjustment interventions for non-EI clients. Designed and delivered by provincial governments. Agreements expire 2014.
Aboriginal Skills and Employment Partnership	$30 M (CRF)	Federal-aboriginal	Provides labour market adjustment interventions for Aboriginal Canadians. Delivered in partnership with other organizations and provincial governments.
Youth Employment Strategy (YES)	$232 M (CRF)	Federal	Provides labour market adjustment interventions for youth. Designed and delivered by the federal government through contractual arrangements with private and not-for-profit service providers.
Opportunities Fund (OF)	$30 M (CRF)	Federal	Provides employment services for disabled Canadians. Designed and delivered by the federal government through contractual arrangements with private and not-for-profit service providers.

(continued on next page)

(TABLE 1 cont.)

Program Name	Funding / Allocation Source	Control	Comments
Total	$2,101.8 M (EI) $1,301.6 M (CRF) $3,403.4 M (total)		79 per cent of programs are under provincial design and delivery, 11 per cent are under aboriginal administration, and 10 per cent are under sole federal control. 62 per cent of programming is funded through the EI account, 38 per cent through CRF.

also restored harmony in federal-provincial relations in the sector, a very significant accomplishment. However, three major sets of governance problems remain. First is executive dominance along with weak federal-provincial coordination that results in limited opportunity for stakeholders or citizens to participate on a pan-Canadian basis. Second is a lack of transparency and reporting, as well as comparative research and processes to facilitate mutual learning. Third is a continued fragmentation and residual incoherence, making accountability and program management difficult. We analyze each of these problems below.

A Executive Dominance and Weak Federal-Provincial Coordination

The *Employment Insurance Act* of 1996 is the prime federal legislation that authorizes and controls the federal-provincial LMDAs and other active measures programs charged to the EI account. The non-EI funded programming in Table A is governed by federal policy parameters via the annual budget process. Federal executives in consultation with federal politicians decide how much money is to be made available, how it is to be distributed between provinces, overall strategic priorities and directions, the nature of the individual agreements, and outcome indicators for each agreement. There is no over-arching pan-Canadian organizing framework collectively agreed to that binds the whole together, nor a public process involving debate between federal and provincial legislators or the public at large.

Each bilateral funding agreement has been negotiated at the executive level between the federal government and each provincial government. Within the context of the accountability provisions contained in each agreement, each province then decides 1) how it will structure the federally funded programs and whether specific provincial legislation is required;

2) how the federal programs will relate to provincial programs; 3) to what degree and how non-government actors will be involved; and 4) how provincial citizens will be informed. Unlike other social policy programs (e.g., health and post-secondary education), the federal funding provided to provinces for active measures is largely conditional, in that provinces must adhere to the provisions of the applicable bilateral agreement; however, there are limited mechanisms for calling a province that does not conform to the terms of a particular agreement to account.

The Canada Employment Insurance Commission is the only means for stakeholders (specifically business and labour) to directly influence EI program policy. The commission has four members—the chairperson and vice-chairperson are senior Government of Canada officials, while the other two Commissioners represent the interests of workers and employers. These commissioners are appointed following informal and ad hoc consultation with their respective communities (unions and employers). That this consultation is informal and ad hoc means the commissioners are largely selected by the federal government. Furthermore, the commissioners are prohibited from holding any other office or employment, making them full-time civil servants. Consequently, these two stakeholder representatives, without staff or other resources, have to date played a marginal role in EI policy-making.

There are many pan-Canadian as well as provincial organizations that from time to time express an interest in employment and training issues (for example the Canadian Labour Congress, the Canadian Association of Manufacturers and Exporters, the Canadian Association of Small Business, the Canadian Association of Universities and Colleges, and national aboriginal organizations). Employer groups in particular often argue that using the EI account for active measures fragments the purpose of the EI program (Pal 1983). However, there is no ongoing or permanent institutional process or structure to bring these organizations together or mobilize them around specific concerns.

One explanation for the exclusion of many stakeholders is the dismal experience of the corporatist arrangements of the 1990s. When the Government of Canada was fully in charge of EI-funded active employment measures, in an effort to foster corporatism, it increased the involvement of business and industry by establishing the Canadian Labour Force Development Board in 1991 to allow business, labour and other social partners to develop policy. These corporatist boards, also established in most provinces, were largely abandoned a few years later as the lack of consolidated labour and business organizations in Canada (unlike in Europe, from where this model derived) made it impossible for the boards to reach consensus (Klassen 2000; Sharpe and Haddow 1997).[5] In part, due to the failure of the national board, the Government of Canada has established 37 national sector councils and related organizations for business, labour and professional groups to address human resource issues within their occupational sector; however, these have not forged formal linkages with provincial governments which now substantially control the Canadian workforce development system.

Notwithstanding devolution, the pan-Canadian institutional mechanisms that bring governments together on active measures have remained unaltered. The *Forum of Labour Market Ministers* (FLMM) was set up in 1983 and then formalized in 1993 to promote inter-jurisdictional cooperation on a wide variety of labour market issues. Three official working groups—labour market information, labour mobility and career development—are active and promising practices workshops have been held from time to time; however, post-devolution there have been fewer meetings of the broader forum, and limited ministerial engagement.[6] There is little, if any, structured involvement in the FLMM from legislators, aboriginal organizations, social partners, civil society or municipal governments. The FLMM is co-chaired by the federal government and a lead province where the lead rotates every two years on an east-to-west basis. A modest, provincially-managed, co-funded secretariat provides support, however the forum has no strategic policy capacity and in the past has not proven to be a locus of substantial federal-provincial negotiation. From time to time special commissions are put in place to examine labour market issues—for example, a special advisory panel of five members on labour market information was established in 2008 by federal-provincial labour market ministers and reported in 2009.[7] A key recommendation of the Advisory Panel on Labour Market Information was to adjust the FLMM governance structure, by including an enhanced secretariat and a renewed relationship with Statistics Canada and the Council of Ministers of Education Canada. To date there has been no government response to these recommendations.

B Lack of Transparency, Reporting and Comparative Research

In regard to labour market information, the Advisory Panel identified basic information gaps, parallel but separate and fragmented federal-provincial universes, a lack of public awareness about the importance of labour market information, and non-user friendly information. The only national report that is produced in Canada on employment policy is the annual *EI Monitoring and Assessment Report*, which provides little information on how services have changed under the LMDAs and cautions readers that interjurisdictional comparisons may be misleading due to differences in programming and labour market conditions. Dawkins concludes that this report is "vague to the point of being useless" (2009, 12).

The 49 bilateral federal-provincial agreements that govern active labour market policy have an array of differentiated accounting requirements. Reporting is problematic not only for provincial governments, who resist reporting to Ottawa in principle, segmented reporting also makes it gruelling for citizens and stakeholders to hold their governments collectively to account, as each province reports separately on each agreement, often at different times (Graefe and Levesque 2008). Although the federal government posts provincial LMA and LMAPD reports on their departmental website, many are missing or incomplete. There are no pan-Canadian reports. As a result, it is very difficult for Canadians to determine the results achieved for the almost $2.7 billion provided by the Government of Canada to provincial governments for employment and training programs.

With respect to research and information exchange for mutual learning, activities on a pan-Canadian basis are limited. Although the Labour Market Information Working Group and the Career Development Services Working Group under the FLMM maintain public websites related to the development and delivery of labour market information and career development services, they are not kept up to date.[8] Post-devolution "best practices" workshops have been held on occasion on selected aspects of labour market policy; however these workshops were only open to government officials. The federal government does undertake evaluations, posts results and facilitates the exchange of research among academics through the *Canadian Labour Market and Skills Researchers Network*; however, there is limited provincial engagement in this federally dominated process. Until 2010, Canada also funded a Work and Learning Knowledge Centre of the Canadian Council on Learning that brought together more than 90 organizations in a consortium to identify and capture existing knowledge on workplace learning. However, federal funding for this network was discontinued in 2009. Many provinces refused to participate, viewing federal involvement as intrusion on provincial jurisdiction over education.

C Fragmentation and Incoherence

As outlined in Table 1, of the $3.4 billion spent annually by the federal government on active labour market programming, 79 per cent of program expenditures are under provincial design and delivery, 11 per cent are under aboriginal administration, and 10 per cent are under sole federal control. Of current programming, 62 per cent is funded through the EI account, and 38 per cent through CRF. No consolidated information is available on the degree to which provincial revenues fund active measures, as this varies from one province to another. Wood estimated the federal contribution to support employment programming in Alberta as covering 50 per cent of the costs, whereas in New Brunswick it was 85 per cent (2010, 36, 50).

The $2.7 billion in federal money that is transferred to provincial governments each year flows through four separate agreements, each with its own client target group, accountability framework, and funding formula. This leads to a fragmented system that is very difficult to understand, let alone manage. For the LMDA, funding was initially allocated through a formula based on a standardized set of labour market objectives, adjusted in relation to the impact of the overall 1996 EI reforms.[9] LMA funding is distributed among provinces on a per capita basis. In neither of these agreements is a provincial contribution required; this contrasts with the TIOW and LMAPD agreements where provincial matching funds are required. The one-time funding that was made available between 2009 and 2011 in response to the economic downturn was distributed based on each jurisdiction's share of the unemployed.

The four agreements plus the additional funding made available in response to the economic downturn have different funding allocation formulas. Moreover, there is no multilateral federal-provincial negotiation process open for citizens to discern how much federal money is on offer or how these funds are distributed between provinces. Indeed, there is very little public information available on any part of this process. Determining how much money is being transferred to each province requires a detailed review of federal and provincial press releases that have been issued over various points in time. Since this is federal money, the Government of Canada determines the rules according to their priorities and available funds, both in the EI account and in the federal Consolidated Revenue Fund.

Despite devolution of federal programming to provinces that began in 1996, some incoherence remains. Although the 2007 federal budget outlined a new labour market training architecture that "clarified roles and responsibilities and recognized that provinces were best placed to design and deliver [labour market] programming" (Canada Department of Finance 2007, 212-15), the federal government continues to directly design and deliver its own programs for youth (through the Youth Employment Strategy) and disabled persons (through the Opportunities Fund). There is no formal process for federally-funded programs for aboriginal persons through the Aboriginal Skills and Employment Strategy program to be coordinated with provincial programming, drawing on the expertise of provincial governments which are now substantially responsible for the policy domain.

Although the 2007 budget offered to explore the feasibility of transferring federal youth, older worker and disability programming to the provinces, there has been no action to date nor, according to federal officials, are any plans underway (Wood 2010). In the same vein, provincial governments have been unwilling to discuss a greater federal role in non-devolved areas; for example, facilitating improved labour market information and research, and promoting consistency of programming across the country. While decentralization enhances many program outcomes, not everything needs to be decentralized. Mosely (2009) highlights potential negative effects of decentralization, such as problems in performance accountability due to the number of organizations involved, and difficulties in achieving standardization in labour market and performance data. Decentralization may also conflict with notions of equal citizenship and equal application of the law, especially within countries with a strong tradition of social rights. Despite devolution, in some matters federal and provincial actors, in effect, remain competitors (not collaborators) as they continue to seek jurisdictional supremacy, tax resources, and the approval of the public as it relates to employment and training policy.

In summary, the governance areas that need to be addressed are: (i) reducing executive (especially federal) dominance and providing a place for other actors to provide input; (ii) increasing transparency, research and opportunities for mutual learning; and (iii) reducing fragmentation and the remaining incoherence in the sector.

3 Alternative Governance Models

Governance is not synonymous with "government" and much recent scholarly attention—especially in the context of the deepening integration underway in the European Union—has been paid to examining different modes of governance; that is, different types or styles of coordination and control (Bahr and Treib 2007). An examination of governance calls attention to: (i) the actors involved, (ii) the rules governing the behaviour of actors, (iii) the processes in place to facilitate interactions between actors, and (iv) the mechanisms used to influence the policy making process (Zeitlin 2009). We will use these four components as an analytical framework to assess and compare the governance of employment and training policy in Canada with other political systems and policy areas. Specifically we examine how employment and training are governed in the European Union and the United States, and also how the Canada Pension Plan and public health are governed in Canada.

A European Union

From six founding members in the early 1950s to 27 member states today, the European Union (EU) has been slowly moving toward a fully federal system of governance. For governing such a large territory composed of different economic and social structures, creative governance solutions—beyond command and control from the centre—needed to be found. In 1993 an influential *White Paper on Growth, Competitiveness and Employment* stimulated political consensus around the structural nature of Europe's employment problem. This led to voluntary agreement among member states to coordinate their policy responses at the European level. The European Employment Strategy (EES) was officially launched in 1997 at the Amsterdam European Council, with its governance supported through a framework called the Open Method of Coordination (OMC). The EES and OMC are outlined in Articles 126 and 128 of the Treaty establishing the European Community.

OMC governance involves five stages, all of which impose deadlines, obligations, and common agendas that facilitate dialogue, progress and convergence among member states. First is the development of *Employment Guidelines and Indicators*, adopted by the Council (comprising employment ministers from each member state) based upon a proposal from the

European Commission (EC), the EU executive. Next, individual member states report on how they have integrated the guidelines into their national policies through the release of *National Reform Programmes*, allowing for cross-national comparisons and evaluation. On the basis of these plans, the Commission and Council issue a European-wide *joint employment report* that reviews progress made at both the member state and EU level in response to the employment guidelines. Fourth are *country-specific recommendations*, proposed by the Commission and adopted by the Council, suggesting policy initiatives to address country-specific problems. The publicizing of best as well as worst practices is intended to foster, with the support of public opinion, internal competition among the member states. The fifth component is a *mutual learning* process where member states, with the financial assistance of the EC, host peer review processes including study visits to member states focused on specific problem issues.

From the very beginning the EES called for the involvement of a variety of actors. Ministers from member states usually meet around four times a year, supported by the Employment Committee (EMCO), a group made up of two civil servants per member state as well as the European Commission. The European Parliament is expected to give an opinion and issue an annual progress report. There is also a structured process for the Council and the Commission to consult regularly with the Economic and Social Committee and the Committee of the Regions. The European social partners have a treaty-based mandate to be consulted on the EES, and meet with EMCO twice a year. In 1998 and again in 2001, the EES Employment Guidelines were amended to bring civil society actors as well as regional and local governments into the process.

There are mixed views on the effectiveness of both the European Employment Strategy and its OMC governance model. Certainly the involvement of non-state actors has increased significantly, as European social partners are formally consulted on the EES and meet regularly with Council and Commission officials. This has also stimulated increased participation at the national level, where most member states have established new processes to involve their social partners, civil society representatives, and local and regional governments in the preparation and implementation of their National Reform Programmes (Zeitlin 2005). OMC governance has pushed individual member states to upgrade their statistical monitoring and evaluation capabilities as they seek to provide comparable data for many key indicators, so that comparisons can be made and mutual learning take place (Kluve et al. 2007). New bodies and expert networks for monitoring and evaluation have been created, including the European Employment Observatory, which provides information, comparative research and evaluation on employment policies and labour market trends.[10] Transparency has improved significantly as ministers' and committee meeting opinions, reports and outcomes are now posted on public websites.[11] However, whether the OMC is just a "talking shop," or has delivered on fundamental change remains very much open to debate among academics (Hughes 2001; Moller 2010; Tommel 2010). On the other hand, policy-makers generally view the OMC as a success, and certainly better than 27 uncoordinated approaches (Begg, Erhel and Mortensen 2010).

B United States

Like Canada, the United States reformed the governance of many of its training programs in the late 1990s by decentralizing responsibility away from the federal level. This was partly due to the concern that there were inefficiencies and less than effective outcomes among many separate programs. The overall thrust of the reforms was to make employers, rather than unemployed workers, the primary customer of services (Troppe et al. 2007). This was possible because in the United States, unemployment insurance premiums are paid only by employers (that is, there is no worker contribution).

The reforms—specifically the *Workforce Investment Act* (WIA) of 1998—consolidated more than 60 Federal workforce-related programs into four grants to states and local workforce areas: Adult Employment and Training grants; Dislocated Worker Employment and Training grants; Disadvantaged Youth Employment and Training grants; and Adult Education and Literacy grants. These grant programs are administered by the federal Department of Labor, primarily through its Employment and Training Administration. Statutory formulas distribute funds to states based on measures of unemployment and poverty status for youth and adult allocations, and unemployment measures only for dislocated worker allocations. States in turn distribute funds to local workforce investment boards. WIA attempts to encourage productivity through a "high performance bonus," have been the subject of much criticism (Wiseman 2010).

A central aspect of the reform was to establish more than 600 local Workforce Investment Boards (WIBs). Each of these organizations is responsible for administering the programs in its jurisdiction and for contracting with local organizations to provide the services. The WIBs typically contract with local community colleges, secondary school districts, and private companies to provide the training. Private employers must comprise a majority of each Workforce Board and the chair must be elected from the private sector membership. Additionally, states themselves can enter into contracts with institutions of higher education, such as community colleges, or other eligible training providers to facilitate the training of a group of individuals.

Evaluations of the reforms have been generally positive, especially in pointing to the engagement of the private sector and the promotion of local flexibility (Social Policy Research Associates 2004). As well, cooperation between agencies has increased in many locations (Mason 2008). At the same time, results have not been consistent across the nation and criticisms have been raised about accountability measures that encourage meeting numerical targets rather than enhancing employability.

Although there has been decentralization, the federal level remains paramount in making decisions with the state governments playing little role beyond service delivery in accordance with federally mandated requirements. However, unlike Canada, federal legislators assume a much larger role (Congressional Research Service 2009).

C Canada Pension Plan

The Canada Pension Plan (CPP) created in 1966 is, like EI, funded entirely by contributions from workers and employers. Constitutional amendments in the 1950s and 1960s established pensions as a concurrent federal-provincial jurisdiction. As a result, provinces were entitled to reject the federal government's plan for a national pension scheme and establish their own contribution-based pension. However, only Quebec did so, creating the Quebec Pension Plan (QPP) at the same time, which is largely similar to the CPP. While primarily a retirement plan, the CPP also provides disability, death, survivor and children's benefits, and assists some disability beneficiaries' return to the workforce through vocational rehabilitation services and return-to-work supports.

The governance of the CPP requires that substantive amendments receive the agreement of two-thirds of the provinces that participate in the CPP as well as any with comparable plans. As such, Quebec participates in decision making regarding changes to the CPP legislation, even though it administers its own plan. This is critical to ensure the portability of QPP and CPP benefits. Reforms are supported by the analysis and advice of a small group of experts drawn from the academic and the financial services sectors who work closely with government bureaucrats. These experts, either individually or in small groups, are used a means to evaluate options and seek the perspectives of key stakeholders.

There is considerable public reporting for the CPP. Annual reports for both the CPP and the CPP Investment Board (which invests funds collected from workers and employers), detailing their activities, finances, and future objectives, must be submitted to Parliament and the public. Every three years, there is also an automatic review of the CPP and the Investment Board by the federal and provincial finance ministers. Commonly referred to as a Triennial Financial Review, this is an opportunity for policy shifts to be considered and approved. This review is partially based on the triennial reports of the Chief Actuary of the Office of the Superintendent of Financial Institutions which provides a detailed examination of the sustainability and other factors related to the CPP.

Significant reforms of the CPP in 1997 added two important governance elements in the CPP legislation. First, an incremental full funding requirement now requires any new increases to benefits to be fully funded. In other words, their costs must be paid as the benefit was earned and any costs associated with benefits that were paid but not earned would be amortized and paid for over a defined period of time. This reform was to avoid reforms that increase benefits without also at the same time ensuring that there were funds available to pay for these benefits. Second, a fail-safe mechanism was enshrined so that if Ottawa and the provinces cannot agree on reforms to keep the plan financially sustainable in the long-term, contribution rates will increase automatically to meet half of the anticipated deficiency (phased in over three years) and indexation of the CPP will be frozen for the next three years (Weaver 2004). Both of these reforms were designed so that if decision makers are unable to agree on reforms, the financial sustainability of the CPP is not jeopardized (Little 2008, 248-50).

However, the CPP has a decades-long history of little federal-provincial tension, as governments have generally agreed on required reforms and adjustments. The governance regime has been able to accommodate the desire of Quebec for a separate pension scheme, yet also maintain a system that provides workers with the same benefits regardless of province of employment. From an international perspective, the CPP and QPP are lauded as maintaining a high degree of policy coherence and stability when many other developed nations have seen significant reforms in their pension schemes (Béland and Myles 2005). This is particularly noteworthy since the CPP—unlike the other policy areas examined—is a specific program administered by the Government of Canada, rather than an intergovernmental agreement or framework that governs a program. A key feature of the CPP, which has been enhanced over the decades, is that data (on premiums, benefits, projections for the future, etc.) is available to all stakeholders.

D Pan-Canadian Public Health Network

Over the past decade, a number of new institutions and processes have been established to improve the governance of Canada's health system. Formed in 2004, the Public Health Agency of Canada (PHAC) is charged with developing national plans and systems for influenza pandemic and other infectious disease outbreaks in conjunction with provinces and territories. Federal/provincial/territorial (F/P/T) collaboration, as well as the development of new ways for government and experts to work together, is accomplished through the *Pan-Canadian Public Health Network*, established in 2005 by Canada's federal, provincial and territorial health ministers. Designed specifically to accommodate the principle of collaborative federalism, the mandate of the network is multi-faceted, ranging from facilitating information sharing among all jurisdictions in Canada, to working with and providing policy and technical advice to F/P/T deputy ministers of health on public health matters, to supporting the public health challenges jurisdictions may face during emergencies and/or crises. The development of collaborative public health strategies is another important area of focus for the network.[12]

The network is governed by a council, co-chaired by the chief public health officer of Canada (the federal co-chair) and a provincial co-chair. Each province or territory is represented on the council, usually by an assistant deputy minister of health or a chief (or associate) medical health officer. The council is accountable to the federal, provincial and territorial deputy ministers of health, and through them to the Council of Health Ministers. The network itself is composed of academics, scientists, public servants and members of non-governmental organizations who together form six expert groups on the following topics: communicable disease control, emergency preparedness and response, Canadian public health laboratories, surveillance and information, chronic disease and injury prevention and control, and health promotion. In each of their areas of expertise these groups coordinate activities, conduct research and facilitate the sharing of information. The expert groups are supported as needed by issue groups. Fierlbeck (2010) identified twenty-three permanent and five temporary issue groups. While there is a public website, there does not appear to be a permanent secretariat associated with the network or centralized contact information. Anyone seeking additional information is encouraged to contact their provincial representative on the council or the respective expert group.

Assessment of the effectiveness of the network is mixed. While Fierlbeck reports that "there is ... unanimous agreement that the Pan-Canadian Public Health Network is far superior to the system that existed previously," she also notes problems with the failure to facilitate and develop the main coordinating institution, the Public Health Agency of Canada (2010, 14). In her view there is little evidence of the political will and political leadership necessary to make the agency as effective as it could be using tools that are already present. In its 2008 review of PHAC, the Auditor General highlighted the difficulty PHAC experienced in securing provincial cooperation, noting that the agency must rely on the goodwill of the provinces and territories and did not necessarily receive accurate, timely and complete information.

McDougall (2009) also highlighted how the preservation of existing jurisdictional roles and responsibilities continues to trump policy effectiveness and respect for democratic principles. He is particularly scathing in his assessment of the work of the expert groups which, in his view, have achieved little substantive progress and "appear to be falling prey to much the same forces: the recurring pattern is that provincial and territorial ministers of health grow weary of such structures due to the lack of results, and gradually withdraw" (McDougall 2009, 27). He highlights problems of missed deadlines and the failure to reach F/P/T accords.

4 Analysis

We turn now to a comparison of the key features of the five governance models examined to extract elements that might be utilized in designing an improved governance model for employment and training policy in

Canada. Table 2 summarizes the key features of employment and training policy in Canada, as well as the other jurisdictions and domains studied in this chapter.

The table makes clear that governance structures and processes vary considerably across policy domains and jurisdictions. In terms of the actors involved, Canadian governance tends to be executive-centred, much more so than in the United States and Europe where employers and other stakeholders have defined formal roles. The rules for the Canada Pension Plan, Canadian active measures under EI, and workforce investment in the US are outlined in formal acts of the national legislatures, although in the case of CPP concurrent jurisdiction ensures that provincial governments are part of the decision-making process. This formal legislative approach contrasts with the rules that govern both the European Employment Strategy and the pan-Canadian Health Network. These are much softer, with greater ability to adapt and change.

In all the cases examined—except for employment and training policy in Canada—the institutional structures that facilitate interactions between actors or ensure transparency and public reporting are multilateral (not bilateral) in nature and include actors beyond just government executives.

The governance models examined in this chapter stress evidence-based policy making with considerable dissemination of information to the public and to stakeholders, a situation which does not exist with employment and training policy in Canada. Finally, it is only in the employment policy domain in Canada and the United States that the main causal mechanism to influence behaviour and action is money. Most of the European Union techniques such as benchmarking, policy diffusion, and formal mutual learning receive little consideration in employment and training policy in Canada. Unlike the United States, in Canada there are no defined processes for feeding evaluation results or employer views into active labour market programming, other than on a province-by-province basis.

5 Alternative Governance Model for Active Labour Market Programs in Canada

As identified above, in other countries as well as other policy areas in Canada, there are robust governance models that formally involve stakeholders beyond the executive, and also include greater transparency in accountability and reporting. The governance model we propose reflects the nature of the Canadian federation, the outcome of past reforms in employment and training policy, and the lessons learned from our examination of other political systems and policy fields.

Our objective below is not to design all the specific elements of a new governance regime, but rather to sketch the key reforms. These reforms to governance will lead to stronger policy that can sustain Canada's workforce development. Our governance model has four features:

TABLE 2 Comparison of Governance Models

Governance Element	Employment & Training Policy in Canada	Employment & Training Policy in the EU	Employment & Training Policy in the US	Canada Pension Plan	Pan-Canadian Public Health Network
Key Actors	Ministers & bureaucrats; no formal role for legislators or stakeholders (other than EI Commission).	Ministers & bureaucrats; formal role for EU parliament, EU institutions, social partners & civil society at EU and member state levels.	Congress and related agencies. State and sub-state agencies. Employers are given a privileged position at the delivery level.	Ministers and bureaucrats, with a separate role for Quebec. Active participation of experts.	Ministers & bureaucrats; formal involvement of academics, scientists, non-government organizations.
Rules	Constitutional division of powers; EI legislation; federal-provincial and federal-aboriginal conditional transfer agreements; federal contracting rules.	EU Treaties define roles. Supported by 5 stage formal OMC process. Limited financial transfers except through European Social Fund.	Congress remains paramount in allocating overall budgets and determining rules, but local agencies have flexibility in design and delivery.	Concurrent constitutional powers; CPP legislation provides overarching framework; understanding to keep the CPP similar to the QPP (and vice-versa). Program is delivered by Government of Canada.	Constitutional division of powers; rules set by Ministers of Health, not legislation. No formal agreements or transfer of funds.

(continued on next page)

(TABLE 2 cont.)

Governance Element	Employment & Training Policy in Canada	Employment & Training Policy in the EU	Employment & Training Policy in the US	Canada Pension Plan	Pan-Canadian Public Health Network
Interactions	FLMM involves executives only; otherwise interactions are primarily bilateral; limited reporting or transparency. No arm's length agents.	OMC process controlled by Ministers and EMCO. Extensive multilateral interaction. Transparency through websites, reporting and external agents.	Mostly focused on program delivery and ensuring greater coordination at the local level. High level of program evaluation.	Reliance on a small group of experts with Ministers of Finance given primary responsibility to manage this program.	Council reports through to Ministers of Health. Six expert groups plus issue groups undertake work. Public website provides some information.
Major Causal Mechanism(s)	Conditional federal grants; informal mutual learning.	External pressure using benchmarking; structured mutual learning; policy diffusion based on information exchange & comparison.	Conditional federal grants including performance bonuses; Congressional oversight and results from evaluations; feedback from employers.	Desire to ensure CPP and QPP are complementary. Long-term and largely predictable trends (fiscal sustainability, retirement patterns, etc.)	Mutual learning; pilot projects; policy diffusion based on information exchange.

A The creation of a national agency: The Canadian Labour Market Information Agency

This body would be charged with identifying, maintaining and disseminating labour market information; data gathering and analysis for comparative research across provinces/territories; monitoring and sharing best practices; assessing trends and policies across Canada and internationally; evaluating labour market program results (both Canadian and international) and comparative research. Its role would be to improve the quality, transparency and usefulness of labour market reporting and analysis. The agency would work with Statistics Canada, the Council of Ministers of Education Canada (CMEC), as well as federal departments, provincial governments and international bodies, such as the OECD.

To some extent, the role of this agency has historically been within Human Resources and Skills Development Canada (HRSDC) and continues today with federal officials in Ottawa as well as labour market analysts present in most regional Service Canada offices across the country. The agency would take on these functions, as well as providing overall direction and support to the national sector councils currently under the control of HRSDC. Now that most labour market programming has been devolved, it is imperative that relevant data and information—presented in a format that can be used by all (the federal government, provinces, business and labour groups, sector councils, etc.)—be made widely available. As such this agency, in part, could be created by transferring resources and staff that currently exist within HRSDC.[13] The agency would be supported by a core team of government officials from all jurisdictions, as well as a network of correspondents from key stakeholders, including business, labour, experts, ASETS holders, universities and colleges, private networks of employment service providers, etc. It would perform a similar function with regard to employment and training to that performed by the Canadian Institute of Health Information (CIHI) in the health sector and the Canadian Education Statistics Council in the education sector.

B A reformed and expanded FLMM with the mandate to act as a multilateral, pan-Canadian intergovernmental forum responsible for the collective determination of all aspects of employment and training policy in Canada

The forum, in its structure and modus operandi remains largely as it was in 1983 and now needs to reflect the significant shifts that have occurred over the course of several decades. The new FLMM's role would include the development of strategic directions and vision, how this vision would be assessed, and how it would be implemented through the transfer of federal funds to provinces and territories. The FLMM would be the governing body for the Canadian Labour Market Information Agency, and would also be charged with negotiating the new round of comprehensive labour market agreements. It would play a central role in the design of any stimulus packages to combat increasing unemployment, such as that announced in the 2009 budget. It would also act as the mechanism for provinces and territories to provide input into the EI income support program, and coordinate provincial social assistance programs with the federal EI program.

The reform proposed to the FLMM would require that the federal government agree to a loss of its priority-setting prerogative. However, given that the objective of the reform is to strengthen strategic (pan-Canadian) policy—which after all is the aim of the federal government—such a loss does not seem an insurmountable barrier.

Among reforms to the FLMM to meet this new mandate are the creation of a larger and permanent secretariat, the establishment of regular meetings of ministers and deputy ministers, and the enhancement of linkages with other intergovernmental forums, at a minimum the Council of Ministers of Education Canada and Immigration Ministers. The FLMM would be required to produce annual reports that address the accountability and transparency of labour market programs, as well as set in place a defined process to solicit the input of business, organized labour, aboriginal organizations responsible for ASETS programming, and other stakeholders involved in labour market policy in Canada. A key element of that discussion should include a process to discuss with employers in particular the present practice of funding active measures for EI claimants from the EI account.

The reformed FLMM would also be able to determine if there is a role for non-governmental stakeholders in the forum. The experience of the corporatist experiments of the 1990s suggests caution in this regard. However, there may be mechanisms that could ensure a more robust engagement of business and labour in policy formulation. The US and EU experiences might prove of utility in this regard.

C A consolidation of the many current bilateral federal-provincial agreements into one comprehensive agreement between the federal government and each province

In other words, each province would have only one labour market agreement with the federal government. The agreement would have a single funding formula (comprising EI and CRF components), and a common set of accountability and reporting requirements, regardless of client groups or program. The agreement should contain flexibility so that a province could re-allocate funds, say, from disabled to older workers should conditions dictate. This consolidation process would be a key responsibility of the reformed FLMM and would facilitate strategic policy.

We have not proposed a complete devolution of responsibility to the provinces, such as via a block funding arrangement. Although extracting the federal government altogether from the policy field, and allowing the provinces to proceed autonomously and independently might seem appealing in its simplicity, there is little evidence that it results in superior outcomes. The international experience suggests that both orders of government need to be engaged and involved in labour market policy. Labour market policy is complex and linked, has national as well as regional and local dimensions, and, as we have indicated, requires horizontal coordination with other policy fields from education to immigration. It is also unique in that the Government of Canada has constitutional jurisdiction for unemployment insurance and programs that assist the unemployed to get back to work, and collect the necessary funds to operate active employment programs. The degree of conditionality and the use of the different funding sources for a new consolidated agreement are key issues that would need to be considered by a revitalized FLMM with input from important stakeholders.

Such consolidation would not only reduce transaction costs, but more importantly, would ensure that employment and training policy are considered holistically and strategically. A consolidation also reflects the long-term trend of treating all labour force participants equitably, rather than in silos, be these people with disabilities, older workers or others. The loss of visibility that would occur in respect to specific client groups is minor and would be compensated by the greater attention given by labour market policy via the first recommendation.

D As part of the consolidation of agreements, and in keeping with greater multilateral decision making, federal and provincial governments would finish the work needed to consolidate, affirm and fully operationalize the devolution decision

This would include negotiating the transfer of responsibilities for programs for youth and persons with disabilities to provincial governments. With the exception of programs for Aboriginal persons, the federal government would no longer oversee direct services provided to the unemployed or employers.[14] It would also include negotiating an enhanced federal role in areas such as research, comparative benchmarking and pan-Canadian reporting, with full provincial support and participation. The reformed FLMM would be utilized to negotiate this final realignment, to occur in the context of the consolidated federal-provincial agreements.

6 Conclusion

Labour market policy, especially for active programs, presents particular challenges for policy makers. Decisions must reflect rapidly shifting economic and labour market conditions, often using limited and invariably incomplete data. Programs seek to intervene in the affairs of private actors—individuals and employers—whose behaviour is difficult to predict or influence.

Active labour market policy in Canada has been the locus of considerable reform in the past fifteen years, with the devolution of programming representing a dramatic change. The governance model we propose, which encompasses both programs funded by EI and those funded from consolidated revenues, seeks to strengthen the positive aspects of the devolution, while addressing its shortcomings, including those identified most recently by the Advisory Panel on Labour Market Information.

The Canadian Labour Market Information Agency which we propose recognizes that decision making is, and will need to become more, decentralized and therefore requires an information base that is available to all. The shift to greater multilateral decision making with the FLMM recognizes that some elements of labour market policy have pan-Canadian implications and that the current governance arrangements cannot adequately address these. The consolidation of existing agreements into a more comprehensive one is a general direction that governments have been pursuing although there is considerable work that remains. This consolidation needs to be undertaken in multilateral discussions. Lastly, as part of these discussions, the transfer of the remaining client groups (excluding programs for Aboriginal people) to the provinces is the logical conclusion to the devolution process. The governance reforms we propose are realistic and transformative ones that can be implemented in reasonably short order and will have immediate positive impacts on Canadian labour market policy.

Acknowledgements

We greatly appreciate the helpful advice and comments received from an anonymous reviewer, colleagues involved with The Mowat Centre EI Task Force, staff at the Mowat Centre and Keith Banting. We have also benefited from dialogue related to this chapter with colleagues at the OECD and other organizations.

Endnotes

1 When the term "provincial" is used in this chapter, it generally also includes territorial governments.

2 British Columbia, Nova Scotia, Prince Edward Island, Newfoundland & Labrador and the Yukon initially signed co-managed agreements where the federal government retained responsibility for program design and delivery.

3 This does not include Immigration Agreements which often contain a labour market component. In addition, the federal government has retained responsibility for aboriginal persons and youth, as well as pan-Canadian programming.

4 A recent Supreme Court ruling Confederation des syndicats nationaux vs. the Attorney General of Canada on 11 December 2008 confirmed that the federal unemployment insurance power must be interpreted generously, and its dual objectives are to remedy the poverty caused by unemployment, as well as maintain the ties between unemployed persons and the labour market. See http://lexisnexis.ca/documents/Arvida-en.pdf for more information.

5 Quebec, Saskatchewan and Newfoundland and Labrador have retained provincial boards, while Ontario has a system of local boards.

6 Between 1985 and 1995, FLMM deputy ministers met twenty-one times and ministers thirteen times. Post-devolution (between 1996 and 2008), federal-provincial deputy ministers met twelve times and ministers only seven, a significant decrease. There has been a seven year gap between ministers' meetings (2003–2010).

7 See http://www.imt-lmi.ca/eng/pdf/final_report_pdf-eng.pdf for details.

8 See http://www.flmm-lmi.org/english/View.asp?x=1103 and http://www.flmm-cds.ca/english/View.asp?x=1103.

9 Despite provisions for changes to the allocation formula available in the LMDA agreements, this formula has not changed nor has the funding been increased since 1996. The amount of funds that can be allocated to active measures from the EI account is governed by the EI legislation, which imposes a ceiling of 0.8 per cent of insurable earnings that can be dedicated to active measures.

10 See http://www.eu-employment-observatory.net/index.aspx for details.

11 See http://ec.europa.eu/social/main.jsp?catId=101&langId=en for details.

12 See http://www.phn-rsp.ca/About_e.html for details.

13 A model for such an agency is the European Employment Observatory (EEO). See http://www.eu-employment-observatory.net/index.aspx. The EU also has a separate Mutual Learning Programme; see http://www.mutual-learning-employment.net/contact-us/. The secretariat for both of these European Commission funded processes is provided by a private company, GHK Consulting.

14 Given federal constitutional responsibility for Indians and land reserved for Indians, we believe that oversight for aboriginal labour market programming should remain with the Government of Canada.

References

Bahr, H. and O. Treib, 2007. *Sectorialised Policy-Making in the EU: Modes of Governance in Social and Environmental Policy*. NewGov Policy Brief No. 07. Florence: European University Institute.

Bakvis, H. and P. Aucoin. 2000. *Negotiating Labour Market Development Agreements*. Research No. 22. Ottawa: Canadian Centre for Management Development.

Banting, K. 2005. "Canada—Nation Building in a Federal Welfare State." In *Federalism and the Welfare State: New World and European Experiences*, ed. H. Obinger, S. Leibfried and F.G. Castles, 89-137. Cambridge: Cambridge University Press.

Begg, I., C. Erhel and J. Mortensen. 2010. *Medium Term Employment Challenges*, Centre for European Policy Studies Special Report, January 2010. At http://ec.europa.eu/social/main.jsp?catId=101&langId=en (accessed 15 September 2010).

Béland, D. and J. Myles. 2005. "Stasis Amidst Change: Canadian Pension Reform in an Age of Retrenchment." In *Aging and Pension Reform Around the World*, ed. G. Bonoli and T. Shinkawa, 252-273. Cheltenham: Edward Elgar.

Campeau, G. 2005. *From UI to EI: Waging War on the Welfare State*, trans. R. Howard. Vancouver: UBC Press.

Canada. Department of Finance. 2007. *The Budget Plan 2007, Aspire to a Stronger, Better, Safer Canada*. At http://www.budget.gc.ca/2007/pdf/bp2007e.pdf, accessed 27 April 2011.

Canada Employment Insurance Commission. 2010. *Monitoring and Assessment Report 2009*. Publication Services, Human Resources and Skills Development Canada. At http://www.hrsdc.gc.ca/eng/employment/ei/reports/eimar_2009/index.shtml, accessed 30 July 2011.

Canada. Office of the Auditor General. 2008. *Report of the Auditor General of Canada. Chapter 5: Surveillance of Infectious Diseases—Public Health Agency of Canada*. Ottawa: Public Works and Government Services Canada. At http://www.oag-bvg.gc.ca/internet/docs/aud_ch_oag_200805_05_e.pdf.

Congressional Research Service (USA). 2009. The Workforce Investment Act (WIA): Program-by-Program Overview and Funding of Title I Training Programs. Washington, DC: Congressional Research Service.

Dawkins, I. 2009. *Insuring Prosperity: SME Perspectives on the Employment Insurance System*, Canadian Federation of Independent Business. At http://www.cfib-fcei.ca/cfib-documents/rr3089.pdf (accessed 3 February 2011).

Doern, B. 1969. "Vocational Training and Manpower Policy: a Case Study in Intergovernmental Liaison." *Canadian Public Administration*, 12.1: 63-71.

Dupré, J.S. 1973. Federalism and Policy Development: The Case of Adult

Occupational Training in Ontario. Toronto: University of Toronto Press.

European Commission. 2007. *Ten Years of the European Employment Strategy (EES),* Director-General for Employment, Social Affairs Opportunities. At http://europa.eu/rapid/pressReleasesAction.do?reference=IP/07/1455&format=HTML&aged=0&language=EN&guiLanguage=enhttp://europa.eu/rapid/pressReleasesAction.do?reference=IP/07/1455&format=HTML&aged=0&language=EN&guiLanguage=en (accessed 22 July 2010).

Fierlbeck, K. 2010. "Public Health and Collaborative Governance." *Canadian Public Administration,* 53.1:1-19.

Graefe and Levesque, 2008. Impediments to Innovation in the Canadian Social Union: the Case of the Labour Market Agreements for Persons with Disabilities, paper prepared for the 2008 meeting of the Canadian Political Science Association.

Haddow, R. 2003. "Canadian Federalism and Active Labour Market Policy." In *New Trends in Canadian Federalism: second edition,* ed. F. Rocher and M. Smith, 243-68. Peterborough, Ontario: Broadview Press.

Haddow, R. and T. Klassen. 2006. Partisanship, Globalization and Canadian Labour Market Policy: Four Provinces in Comparative Perspective. Toronto: University of Toronto Press.

Hughes, K. 2001. "The Open Method of Co-ordination: Innovation or Talking Shop?" *Centre for European Reform Bulletin,* December 2000/ January 2001. At http://www.cer.org.uk/articles/issue15_hughes.htmlhttp://www.cer.org.uk/articles/issue15_hughes.html (accessed 30 September 2008).

Hunter, J. 1993. The Employment Challenge, Federal Employment Policies and Programs 1900–1990. Ottawa: Public Affairs, Government of Canada.

Jacobsson, K. 2004. "Soft Regulation and the Subtle Transformation of States: the Case of EU Employment Policy." *Journal of European Social Policy* 14.4: 355-70.

Klassen, T.R. 2000. Precarious Values: Organizations, Politics and Labour Market Policy in Ontario. Kingston: McGill-Queen's University Press.

Klassen, T.R. and D.E. Wood. Forthcoming. "Evolving Federal-Provincial Accountability Regimes in Active Labour Market Policy." In *Understanding and Evaluating New Intergovernmental Accountability Regimes: Canada in Comparative Perspective,* ed. P. Graefe, J.M. Simmons, and L.A. White. Toronto: University of Toronto Press.

Kluve, J., D. Card, M. Fertig, M. Gora, L. Jobobi, P. Jensen, R. Leetmaa. 2007. *Active Labour Market Policies in Europe, Performance and Perspectives.* New York: Springer.

Little, B. 2008. Fixing the Future: How Canada's Usually Fractious Governments Worked Together to Rescue the Canada Pension Plan. Toronto: University of Toronto Press.

Mason, S.G. 2008. "Policy Design and Regional Cooperation under the Workforce Investment Act." *State & Local Government Review* 40.2:

101-114.

McDougall, C.W. 2009. "Still Waiting for a Comprehensive National Epidemic Surveillance System: A case Study of how Collaborative Federalism has become a Risk to Public Health." In *Special Series: the Role of Federalism in Protecting the Public's Health,* Institute of Intergovernmental Relations. At http://www.queensu.ca/iigr/working/PublicHealthSeries/McDougall_Still.pdf (accessed 24 July 2010).

Moller, K. 2010. "European Governmentality or Decentralised Network Governance? The Case of the European Employment Strategy." *RECON Online Working Paper*, 2010/08. At http://www.reconproject.eu/main.php/RECON_wp_1008.pdf?fileitem=5456398, accessed 24 July 2010.

Mosley, H. 2009. "The Trade-off between Flexibility and Accountability in Labour Market Policy." In *Flexible Policy for More and Better Jobs*, ed. Sylvain Giguère and F. Froy. Paris: OECD.

Organisation for Economic Co-operation and Development (OECD). 2003. Managing Decentralisation: a New Role for Labour Market Policy. Paris: OECD Publishing.

Pal, L.A. 1983. "The Fall and Rise of Developmental Uses of the UI Funds," *Canadian Public Policy* 14.1: 81-93.

Sharpe, A. and R. Haddow, eds. 1997. *Social Partnerships for Training Canada's Experiment with Labour Force Development Boards*. Kingston: School of Public Policy, Queen's University.

Social Policy Research Associates. 2004. The Workforce Investment Act after Five Years: Results From the National Evaluation of the Implementation of Workforce Investment Act. Oakland, CA. At www.doleta.gov/reports/searcheta/occ/.../SPR-WIA_Final_Report.pdf, accessed 30 July 2010.

Tholoniat, L. 2010. "The Career of the Open Method of Coordination." *West European Politics* 33.1: 93-117.

Tömmel, I. 2010. Civil society in the EU: A Strong Player or a Fig-Leaf for the Democratic Deficit?, Canada-Europe Transatlantic Dialogue: Seeking Transnational Solutions to 21st Century Problems. At http://www.carleton.ca/europecluster/publications/2010-03-IngeborgToemmel(CivilSocietyInTheEU).pdf (accessed 24 July 2010).

Tömmel, I. and A. Verdun. 2009. Innovative Governance in the European Union: The Politics of Multilevel Policymaking. Boulder: Lynne Rienner.

Troppe, M., M. Clagett, R. Holm and T. Barnicle. 2007. *Integrating Employment, Skills, and Economic Development: A Perspective from the United States* (Final Report to the Organisation for Economic Cooperation and Development). Washington, DC: National Center on Education and the Economy.

Weaver, R.K. 2004. "Pension Reform in Canada: Lessons for the United States." *Ohio State Law Journal*, 65.1: 45-74.

Wiseman, M. 2010. "American Experience with Workforce Investment

Grants: Food for Thought for European Social Fund Planners." Presentation made to Shaping the Future of the ESF ESF and Europe 2020, 23-24 June 2010 Brussels. At http://ec.europa.eu/social/main.jsp?catId=88&langId=en&eventsId=256, accessed 25 October 2010.

Wood, D.E. Forthcoming. "Balancing Accountability with Flexibility: Governing Active Labour Market Policy in Post-devolution Canada." In *Canada Country Report for the Organisation for Economic Development and Cooperation.*

Wood, D.E. and T.R. Klassen. 2009. "Bilateral Federalism and Workforce Development Policy in Canada." *Canadian Public Administration.* 52.2: 249-70.

Zeitlin, J. 2005. "Conclusion—the Open Method of Coordination in Action. Theoretical Promise, Empirical Realities and Reform Strategy." In *The Open Method of Coordination in Action—the European Employment and Social Inclusion Strategies*, ed. J. Zeitlin and P. Pochet, 447-503. Brussels: P.I.E. Peter Lang.

——. "The Open Method of Coordination and Reform of National Social and Employment Policies." In *Changing European Employment Regimes and Welfare Regimes*, ed. M. Heidenreich and J. Zeitlin, 214-245. London and New York: Routledge.

Queen's Policy Studies
Recent Publications

The Queen's Policy Studies Series is dedicated to the exploration of major public policy issues that confront governments and society in Canada and other nations.

Manuscript submission. We are pleased to consider new book proposals and manuscripts. Preliminary inquiries are welcome. A subvention is normally required for the publication of an academic book. Please direct questions or proposals to the Publications Unit by email at spspress@queensu.ca, or visit our website at: www.queensu.ca/sps/books, or contact us by phone at (613) 533-2192.

Our books are available from good bookstores everywhere, including the Queen's University bookstore (http://www.campusbookstore.com/). McGill-Queen's University Press is the exclusive world representative and distributor of books in the series. A full catalogue and ordering information may be found on their web site (http://mqup.mcgill.ca/).

School of Policy Studies

International Perspectives: Integration and Inclusion, James Frideres and John Biles (eds.) 2012. ISBN 978-1-55339-317-7

Dynamic Negotiations: Teacher Labour Relations in Canadian Elementary and Secondary Education, Sara Slinn and Arthur Sweetman (eds.) 2012. ISBN 978-1-55339-304-7

Where to from Here? Keeping Medicare Sustainable, Stephen Duckett 2012. ISBN 978-1-55339-318-4

International Migration in Uncertain Times, John Nieuwenhuysen, Howard Duncan, and Stine Neerup (eds.) 2012. ISBN 978-1-55339-308-5

Life After Forty: Official Languages Policy in Canada/Après quarante ans, les politiques de langue officielle au Canada, Jack Jedwab and Rodrigue Landry (eds.) 2011. ISBN 978-1-55339-279-8

From Innovation to Transformation: Moving up the Curve in Ontario Healthcare, Hon. Elinor Caplan, Dr. Tom Bigda-Peyton, Maia MacNiven, and Sandy Sheahan 2011. ISBN 978-1-55339-315-3

Academic Reform: Policy Options for Improving the Quality and Cost-Effectiveness of Undergraduate Education in Ontario, Ian D. Clark, David Trick, and Richard Van Loon 2011. ISBN 978-1-55339-310-8

Integration and Inclusion of Newcomers and Minorities across Canada, John Biles, Meyer Burstein, James Frideres, Erin Tolley, and Robert Vineberg (eds.) 2011. ISBN 978-1-55339-290-3

A New Synthesis of Public Administration: Serving in the 21st Century, Jocelyne Bourgon, 2011. Paper ISBN 978-1-55339-312-2 Cloth ISBN 978-1-55339-313-9

Recreating Canada: Essays in Honour of Paul Weiler, Randall Morck (ed.), 2011. ISBN 978-1-55339-273-6

Data Data Everywhere: Access and Accountability? Colleen M. Flood (ed.), 2011. ISBN 978-1-55339-236-1

Making the Case: Using Case Studies for Teaching and Knowledge Management in Public Administration, Andrew Graham, 2011. ISBN 978-1-55339-302-3

Canada's Isotope Crisis: What Next? Jatin Nathwani and Donald Wallace (eds.), 2010. Paper ISBN 978-1-55339-283-5 Cloth ISBN 978-1-55339-284-2

Pursuing Higher Education in Canada: Economic, Social, and Policy Dimensions, Ross Finnie, Marc Frenette, Richard E. Mueller, and Arthur Sweetman (eds.), 2010.

Paper ISBN 978-1-55339-277-4 Cloth ISBN 978-1-55339-278-1

Canadian Immigration: Economic Evidence for a Dynamic Policy Environment, Ted McDonald, Elizabeth Ruddick, Arthur Sweetman, and Christopher Worswick (eds.), 2010. Paper ISBN 978-1-55339-281-1 Cloth ISBN 978-1-55339-282-8

Taking Stock: Research on Teaching and Learning in Higher Education, Julia Christensen Hughes and Joy Mighty (eds.), 2010. Paper ISBN 978-1-55339-271-2 Cloth ISBN 978-1-55339-272-9

Centre for the Study of Democracy

Jimmy and Rosalynn Carter: A Canadian Tribute, Arthur Milnes (ed.), 2011. Paper ISBN 978-1-55339-300-9 Cloth ISBN 978-1-55339-301-6

Unrevised and Unrepented II: Debating Speeches and Others By the Right Honourable Arthur Meighen, Arthur Milnes (ed.), 2011. Paper ISBN 978-1-55339-296-5 Cloth ISBN 978-1-55339-297-2

Centre for International and Defence Policy

Afghanistan in the Balance: Counterinsurgency, Comprehensive Approach, and Political Order, Hans-Georg Ehrhart, Sven Bernhard Gareis, and Charles Pentland (eds.), 2012. ISBN 978-1-55339-353-5

Security Operations in the 21st Century: Canadian Perspectives on the Comprehensive Approach, Michael Rostek and Peter Gizewski (eds.), 2011. ISBN 978-1-55339-351-1

Europe Without Soldiers? Recruitment and Retention across the Armed Forces of Europe, Tibor Szvircsev Tresch and Christian Leuprecht (eds.), 2010. Paper ISBN 978-1-55339-246-0 Cloth ISBN 978-1-55339-247-7

Mission Critical: Smaller Democracies' Role in Global Stability Operations, Christian Leuprecht, Jodok Troy, and David Last (eds.), 2010. ISBN 978-1-55339-244-6

John Deutsch Institute for the Study of Economic Policy

The 2009 Federal Budget: Challenge, Response and Retrospect, Charles M. Beach, Bev Dahlby and Paul A.R. Hobson (eds.), 2010. Paper ISBN 978-1-55339-165-4 Cloth ISBN 978-1-55339-166-1

Discount Rates for the Evaluation of Public Private Partnerships, David F. Burgess and Glenn P. Jenkins (eds.), 2010. Paper ISBN 978-1-55339-163-0 Cloth ISBN 978-1-55339-164-7

Institute of Intergovernmental Relations

The Evolving Canadian Crown, Jennifer Smith and D. Michael Jackson (eds.), 2011. ISBN 978-1-55339-202-6

The Federal Idea: Essays in Honour of Ronald L. Watts, Thomas J. Courchene, John R. Allan, Christian Leuprecht, and Nadia Verrelli (eds.), 2011. Paper ISBN 978-1-55339-198-2 Cloth ISBN 978-1-55339-199-9

Canada: The State of the Federation 2009, vol. 22, *Carbon Pricing and Environmental Federalism*, Thomas J. Courchene and John R. Allan (eds.), 2010. Paper ISBN 978-1-55339-196-8 Cloth ISBN 978-1-55339-197-5

Our publications may be purchased at leading bookstores, including the Queen's University Bookstore (http://www.campusbookstore.com/) or can be ordered online from: McGill-Queen's University Press, at **http://mqup.mcgill.ca/ordering.php**

For more information about new and backlist titles from Queen's Policy Studies, visit http://www.queensu.ca/sps/books or visit the McGill-Queen's University Press web site at: **http://mqup.mcgill.ca/**